NIXON RECONSIDERED

NIXON RECONSIDERED

NIXON RECONSIDERED

JOAN HOFF

BASIC
BOOKS

A Member of the Perseus Books Group

Sections of chapter 4 previously appeared as "Outflanking the Liberals on Welfare," in *Richard M. Nixon: Politician, President, Administrator,* edited by Leon Friedman and William F. Levantrosser (Westport, Conn.: Greenwood Press, 1991). Reprinted with permission of Greenwood Publishing Group, Inc., Westport, Conn. Copyright © 1991 by Hofstra University.

Sections of chapter 6 previously appeared as "'Nixingerism,' NATO, and Détente," *Diplomatic History* 13, no. 4 (Fall 1989): 501–25. Reprinted with permission of *Diplomatic History.* These sections also appeared in *American Historians and the Atlantic Alliance,* edited by Lawrence S. Kaplan (Kent, Ohio: Kent State University Press, 1991), pp. 95–115. Reprinted with permission of The Kent State University Press.

Designed by John Chung

Library of Congress Cataloging-in-Publication Data

Hoff-Wilson, Joan, 1937–
    Nixon reconsidered / Joan Hoff.
        p.   cm.
    Includes bibliographical references and index.
    ISBN 0–465–05107–3 (cloth)
    ISBN 0–465–05105–7 (paper)
    1. Nixon, Richard M. (Richard Milhous). 1913–   .   2. United States—Politics and government—1969–1974.   I. Title.
E856.H64   1994
973.924'092—dc20   94–12598
                                                                                        CIP

98 ◆/RRD 9 8 7 6

To Robert H. Ferrell

and in memory of William Appleman Williams

for their very different views on Nixon

and invaluable advice over the years

CONTENTS

CONTENTS

PREFACE AND ACKNOWLEDGMENTS

I can still remember listening to National Public Radio on Election Day 1968 when the outcome of the presidential race was still in doubt. Then, sometime after midnight (on the West Coast, where I lived), Nixon's victory became clear, and the radio announcer played Bob Dylan's "Don't Think Twice, It's All Right." Although its subject was not political, the refrain somehow characterized the victory. In the words of *Ramparts* magazine, Nixon's election proved the United States "a first-class nation with third-rate people, and he was champion of the third-rate." According to this now-defunct publication, there was no "new Nixon," only an America that did not "care much anymore about excellence or justice or the rights of human beings."[1]

It was some time before I questioned that assessment or realized that dubious campaign tactics and presidential constitutional violations abounded long before Watergate, and were to continue long after it. Even as I entered Nixon's office in downtown Manhattan for our first interview, in 1983, I did not have a single positive personal memory of him. Instead, I carried with me to that interview a cartoonish mental picture of how he was going to appear: hunched, with heavy jowls, excessive bags under his eyes, and a deep, sinister cleft extending from his eyebrows to the tip of his nose. Instead, a slightly built and slightly ashen-complected (which helped account for his perpetual five-o'clock shadow on television) individual, whose facial skin was remarkably taut considering he had just turned seventy, walked across the room to shake my hand softly. His riveting dark eyes, which have usually been described as shifting or darting furtively, were the most commanding aspect of his appearance, as I assume they must have been when he was president. Nixon's eyes focused on me as an interviewer (just as they did on the camera in the most critical television appearances throughout his career) with an intensity that could be uncomfortable. He certainly did not shrink from looking directly at the person with whom he was speaking.

When I asked Nixon why many people maintain that he was shifty-eyed in face-to-face conversations, he told me bluntly, and I suspect with a good deal of accuracy, that those who made such comments "have not dealt with me one-on-one."[2] All the former White House aides I have interviewed confirmed that Nixon liked to talk and debate one-on-one for long periods of time—at least during his first term in office—and several of them told me that, anticipating this, they made sure to eat and go to the bathroom before meeting with him.

After my first interview with Nixon, which lasted almost five hours and ranged widely over both foreign and domestic topics, he gained a little weight and developed a greater declivity to his nose, and his jowls became a little heavier. Even just before his death, he never came anywhere near looking like the caricature that still prevails in the public's mind. Once he left office, Nixon became much more personable, at least publicly. His television interviews were more relaxed and congenial than those he gave as president. Nixon's body language, however, remained stiff and formal. In the course of our interviews, for example, he seldom gesticulated or drank the refreshments that were served. The part of his body with which he enunciated most of his thoughts and ideas was his dark, intense eyes.

In addition to two lengthy interviews with Nixon and conversations with other officials in his administration, this book is based primarily on extensive research into the Nixon White House papers and tapes released to date. There are 40 million pages of documents and 4,000 hours of secretly recorded conversations that make up the Nixon presidential collection, in addition to 5,312 microforms, 435,000 photographs, 2.2 million feet of film, and 2,200 pages of oral history. By the end of 1993, almost 5 million (4.8) of the 46 million pages (including 1.5 million of the most sensitive "abuse-of-power" documents) and 63 of the 4,000 hours of White House Tapes, accompanied by 2,700 pages of transcripts, had been made public. There are no transcripts for the remaining tapes—only a 27,000-page log to make selective listening easier for researchers and the general public.

When all of this material is finally open for research, the Nixon presidency will be the best-documented administration in U.S. history. It has been common practice since FDR's time for major portions of the *least* sensitive papers of modern presidents to be opened within a half-dozen years of their leaving office. In contrast, some of the least controversial materials from the Nixon years languished unprocessed, in part because of the complicated and litigious review procedures associated with making available the most sensitive and contentious paper documents. Of the 1.5 million most sensitive pages, approximately 30,000 documents (300,000 pages) have not yet been released by the National Archives, largely because of privacy or national security reasons. These closed paper records have been the subject of many legal battles, and the most recent ones are specifically directed at the remaining unreleased tapes.[3]

The sheer amount of material poses serious research problems for Nixon scholars—Nixon himself read and commented on only 250,000 of the 40 million pages of documents. As for the tapes, it would take one person eight hours a day for two years of just to *hear* all of them, before taking time to review or analyze them. Even with the 27,000-page log, poor sound quality and many legal delays will continue to plague researchers wanting to analyze and interpret *all* this unique documentary source material about the internal workings of the Nixon administration.

Only twelve and a half hours of the White House Tapes were used as evidence in the Watergate hearings and court proceedings. Sixty hours of these transcripts and tapes were not made public until June 4, 1991—seventeen years after Nixon's resignation. In May 1993, twenty-five more conversations were released, including those from the controversial months of May and June 1972—when the two Watergate break-ins, the arrests, and the cover-up took place. There were no transcripts for these tapes, and several different versions appeared immediately in newspapers—with no one being more authoritative than any other. This problem will repeat itself for all the remaining untranscribed taped conversations unless the National Archives undertakes the time-consuming task of providing authorized transcripts by trained personnel accustomed to the speech patterns of the scratchy-sounding voices on the tapes. On May 16, 1993, the National Archives announced that it would release four more hours, thirty-nine additional conversations, that August.[4]

From his resignation until the time of his death almost twenty years later, Nixon challenged the constitutionality of the 1974 Presidential Recordings and Materials Preservation Act passed by Congress. His attorneys sought a preliminary injunction to prevent any more conversations from being released. On August 9, 1993, federal judge Royce C. Lamberth ruled that the act prohibited the National Archives from releasing any more of Nixon's tapes until the "purely private material be returned for [Nixon's] sole custody and use."[5] It is estimated that 784,000 pages of the printed documents and untold portions of the tapes are "personal."

Internal disagreement within the National Archives over the processing and release of these tapes and how to determine what is "purely private material" has further complicated their release. In February 1979, a "negotiated agreement" between the National Archives and Nixon's attorneys called for the permanent removal of "any political document in the files that did not have a direct connection to the President's constitutional powers or statutory duties" and the return of these documents to Nixon, with the understanding that "he would donate them in the future to the National Archives." Subsequently the National Archives applied the standard of private-political association to all documents and tapes. For example, if a presidential aide wrote that a particular senator should be supported for reelection, that would be personal; if the suggestion was that the senator be supported because he favored the war in Vietnam, that would be a presidential document that should be opened and not returned to the former president. This standard has been questioned not only by Nixon's attorneys but also by Acting Archivist Trudy H. Peterson, who wrote a memorandum on May 18, 1993, that was leaked to one of Nixon's lawyers, R. Stan Mortenson. "We appear to be unilaterally abrogating the [1979] agreement [with the former president]," she said. With respect to the piecemeal release of short segments of conversations—some no longer than ten seconds—Peterson added that this "takes the conversation out of context of the rest of the activities going on at the time period. This is not fair to the researcher, who is left to puzzle out what else may have gone on in related conversations that month."[6]

Because the personal is constantly mixed with the public on these tapes, the archivists have already painstakingly reviewed the unreleased conversations using the standard of private-political association to release "abuse-of-power" references and other material. Now they are being given the impossible new task of redoing their work (on the tapes, at least) using a different standard.

Under the circumstances, Congress should amend the section of the 1974 act referring to the return of "purely private material" to the former president because it constitutes an impossible mandate drafted and passed in haste, as was true of so much post-Watergate legislation. Congress should also authorize funds for the transcription of the remaining tapes by trained archivists, to avoid endless controversy among competing versions when, and if, these secret conversations are opened to public scrutiny.

The numerous legal and processing battles over the Nixon papers and tapes underscore that it is in the best interests of the country to have its contemporary history written on the basis of as much nonprivileged information as possible. Americans deserve not only to be informed but also to know what sources are being used to inform them, as there is often a discrepancy between raw facts and interpretative conclusions, between news and historical evaluations. In the wake of Watergate, Edward Jay Epstein was one of the few investigative reporters to point out the obvious: unless sources are identified, no account of contemporary events "can be reviewed or corroborated by others with specialized knowledge of the subject."[7] This applies to the undocumented statements in Seymour M. Hersh's 1992 *New Yorker* article about the numerous ethnic slurs the tapes purportedly contain, as well as to the undocumented statements in Bob Woodward and Carl Bernstein's books about Watergate two decades ago and all the undocumented claims made about Nixon in between.[8]

Responsible contemporary history must be based on identifiable sources. This is why I did not badger archivists at the Nixon presidential facility to leak information to me, and why I refused all privileged access and did not accept any restrictions or "strings" on the interviews I conducted during the decade I researched and wrote this book. I have selectively included interviews conducted by others in the 1970s, before raw memories began to be replaced with self-embellished ones among those who participated in this controversial presidency. Interviewing Nixon and his better-known former aides rapidly became an exercise in futility because most of them seldom said anything they had not already uttered or written in the last twenty years.

Despite the media's glorification of exclusive interviews with the rich and famous, for historians such interviews serve primarily to give a sense or an impression of individuals who have influenced the course of history *as they respond to specific questions*. Such interviews cannot be relied on as hard evidence absent documentary proof of the statements or allegations. This is especially true when those interviewed are given carte blanche to edit, censor, and psychoanalyze what they say for the record. Historians who collaborate with their subjects, especially on controversial topics, often rationalize their efforts by saying that since memory is "a subjective process of active construction" (which it indeed is) and as long as the memory is "authentic" for the person, then this "social dimension" of memory outweighs the need to verify accuracy. Carried to its logical extreme with key figures involved in such an important event as Watergate, "collaboration" can end up fabricating history on a topic that is already replete with lies.[9]

While I believe that a collective biographical and quantitative analysis of those who served in prominent positions in Nixon's administration is long overdue (as is a study of their wives—the so-called women of Watergate), I think that historians must recognize rather than reinforce the limitations of interviews with individuals about events that took place a quarter of a century ago, especially those whose motives are ambiguous and whose reputations are still at risk or who are in the process of rehabilitation by telling researchers or reporters what they want to hear.[10]

Consequently, I requested documents for verification of oral statements made in the interviews I conducted, and I looked for such verification in primary sources for my own interviews and those I consulted that had been conducted by others. While not all the people I interviewed provided written documentation (including Nixon), a number did, and these are indicated in the endnotes. Robert Finch, for example, gave me permission to make photocopies from his papers before they were officially processed and catalogued at Occidental College. John Ehrlichman permitted me to photocopy several boxes of his personal papers, including his own selection of the most important handwritten notes he took at meetings with Nixon, before these were released by the National Archives. The widow of Fred J. Buzhardt, Jr., a counsel to the president in 1973 and 1974, also permitted me to photocopy some of her late husband's handwritten documents relating to the Watergate tapes. These were particularly informative because not all of the tapes Buzhardt reviewed were subpoenaed and subsequently released. His notes provide tantalizing, if erratic, tidbits of information not available elsewhere.

In addition, John Roy Price, counsel for the Urban Affairs Council, gave me access to some of his White House files; the late H. R. Haldeman sent me several documents from his personal papers; and Vee Burke gave me transcripts of internal White House memoranda and interviews her late husband conducted with leading participants in Nixon's attempt to reform the welfare system. I also read all the transcripts of the interviews Fawn Brodie conducted while researching her 1981 biography of Nixon that are deposited in the Marriott Library at the University of Utah, Salt Lake City. Curiously, the only tape and transcript missing from this invaluable collection of fresh memories about Nixon are Henry Kissinger's.[11]

As the senior editor for the University Publications of America microform edition of Nixon's presidential papers, I have an unusually broad familiarity with this vast, controversial collection of papers and tapes. I have come to an understanding of this presidency that is not based primarily on either Nixon's personality or his political ethics. In part, this is because Nixon's handwritten comments on the memoranda and news summaries he received clearly indicate how well he followed and understood the major foreign and domestic problems of his time. I am also the only historian to have subjected to computer analysis the sixty hours of tapes and 2,700 pages of transcripts released to date. Realizing that these transcripts contain a number of errors, I nonetheless believe that this computer search helps to determine what Nixon and his aides most likely said to one another on these tapes, as opposed to what we thought they said when we first heard about them in 1973. Important as they are for studying the Nixon presidency, the inaccuracies in the existing transcripts and the difficulty of faithfully transcribing the unreleased ones mean that, well into the next century, the White House tapes will continue to pose more questions for the conscientious researcher than they answer (as noted in chapter 10).

All the notes and transcripts of the interviews I conducted and those in my possession conducted by others, and declassified information I have obtained through the Freedom of Information Act or the Mandatory Review Provisions of the Executive Order 12356 as it applies to the Presidential Libraries of the National Archives, will be deposited at Indiana University and will be accessible to others for verification. Neither process for obtaining the declassification of classified documents proved satisfactory for those chapters in this work that deal with foreign policy because, as with all recent administrations, the bulk of the documents remain restricted for national security reasons. Part II highlights those controversial aspects of the Nixonian diplomacy for which the greatest amount of declassified information is available. Part I, on Nixon's domestic policy, is based largely on primary sources from the Nixon

Presidential Papers, including a number of documents declassified for me or other scholars through the Mandatory Review.

This work could not have been written without the help provided by librarians and archivists at the Special Collections Department of the Marriott Library at the University of Utah (Fawn Brodie Papers); the Library at Occidental College (Robert Finch Papers); the Archives of Artists of New Mexico and the Southwest, Fenn Gallery, Santa Fe, New Mexico (John D. Ehrlichman Materials); the National Security Archive in Washington, D.C.; and especially those at the Hoover, Truman, Johnson, and Ford Presidential Libraries and the staff for the Nixon Presidential Materials in Alexandria, Virginia. Since I have worked most closely with those archivists who processed the Nixon papers from 1979 until 1986, when they began to open, I would like to thank them individually for all their patience and help over the years.

In a much-appreciated, evenhanded manner, James J. Hastings, director of the Nixon Presidential Materials Project from 1979 to 1988, facilitated my research (and that of many others) in every way possible during the difficult times of processing and opening the first Nixon papers. Clarence R. Lyons, Jr., Hastings's successor as deputy director of what is now the Nixon Presidential Materials Staff, referred to in this book as simply the Nixon Presidential Materials (NPM), offered valuable information about the legal status and projected openings of the Nixon papers and tapes. Anita O. Happoldt handled my many Mandatory Review requests with efficiency, while Raymond H. Geselbracht helped me research specific collections that he had processed much more quickly than otherwise would have been possible, as did Bonnie C. Baldwin. My research also benefited from several very important Oral History Interviews with members of the Nixon administration conducted by Geselbracht and Frederick J. Graboske.

I owe a special debt of thanks to two archivists in particular at the Nixon facility: Bryon (Scott) Parham and Joan Howard. Parham has always responded to numerous queries from me by phone and looked up material for me with good humor and endless expertise when I conducted research in person at the Alexandria facility. The same was also true of Howard before she left the Nixon project as a result of the controversy over release of the remaining tapes. Howard more than anyone else taught me how to take advantage of the numerous research aids and explained the various systems by which the Nixon Presidential Papers are organized. Most important, she advised me to examine the Staff Secretary's Courier Files (SS-CF), which contain all of the material that was sent to President Nixon when he was away from the White House. Because they almost always contained many action memoranda to be signed, these proved an unexpectedly rich and invaluable source of information in several instances for figuring out how and when a particular decision was reached on important issues. Howard has remained a major source of information for me about the collection, even though she is not working on the Nixon papers. In the face of considerable criticism and pressure, she stood strongly by the standards employed by the archivists who initiated the processing of these important and controversial papers and tapes. Scholars using the Nixon collection owe a good deal to Joan Howard, as I do.

The staff of the Organization of American Historians in Bloomington, Indiana, endured the years during which my administrative duties overlapped with researching and writing this book in the 1980s. In particular, I am indebted to Mary Belding, Sharon Caughill, Jeanette Chafin, Ginger Foutz, Kara Hamm, Howard McMains, Michael Regoli, and Sheri Sherrill. Two Indiana University graduate students, Liann Tsoukas and especially Gayle V. Fischer, conducted bibliographical research in checking and correcting many of the citations. William Hamm oversaw the manuscript through several different computer versions with his usual patience and constructive criticism. Dee Scriven also organized research materials and edited an early draft.

Finally, two old friends and colleagues read this long-overdue manuscript in its later stages. The late William Appleman Williams offered both serious and whimsical comments—all of which benefited me in several rewritings. Most important, Robert Ferrell, emeritus professor at Indiana University, took the time to offer stylistic and substantive comments that have made the final version a better product than it otherwise would have been. Numerous colleagues, in conversations and in writing, have commented negatively on segments of the work over the years—largely because it de-emphasized Watergate. Nonetheless, they provided a necessary liberal paradigm against which I always had to measure the data and my own revisionist interpretations, as I tried to place into historical perspective the ingredients of what I am calling the "Nixon phenomenon" and its relationship to the modern presidency and electoral system in the United States.

The final irony of Nixon's long, controversial career came when his death on April 22, 1994, prompted an outpouring of praise from friends and foes alike. Almost all touted his foreign policy and commented on his "dark" side that led to Watergate. Few mentioned his domestic achievements; none thought that the contradiction of his personality and presidency could be explained; and none pointed out the ephemeral nature of his foreign policy, however brilliant it was at the time. This book attempts to do all these things. What follows is not a chronological narrative of Nixon's administration, but an analysis of its major policies, procedures, and personnel in an attempt finally to place Nixon and his administration in historical, rather than histrionic, perspective.

NIXON RECONSIDERED

NIXON RECONSIDERED

INTRODUCTION: NIXON IS MORE THAN WATERGATE

You can see why I believe so deeply in the American dream. . . . The American dream has come true [for me].

—Nixon, acceptance speech for presidential nomination, August 9, 1968

Some years ago, when I was considering writing this book, a friend said that the notion of Nixon without Watergate was impossible, and went on to describe that well-known contemporary cartoon showing Nixon emerging from a sewer, just barely lifting his head above the manhole. The caption read: "There he comes now." Yet I became more and more fascinated by the possibility of writing this almost a full generation after Nixon's resignation, when the dust has settled and tempers have cooled somewhat, when the principal of this story was in his eighties and appeared in the *New York Times* surrounded by five grandchildren, three of whom bear the name Eisenhower. It is time to look coldly at the five and a half years of Nixon's administration, to determine how they might have been written about if Watergate had not dominated our interpretation of the man since 1974, and to suggest how he will be interpreted in the textbooks of the next century.

In the 1990s there is much to be said in favor of some of the actions of the thirty-seventh president that is long overdue. It is even possible at this late date to understand the almost cataclysmic forces that bore in

1

upon him during his long political career—indeed, from its very inception—and made him not only the president he was but also a phenomenon in his own time.

What is it about Nixon that has made him a national "problem" for almost half a century? Nixon is more than Watergate because, despite Watergate, his name continues to dominate public awareness as few presidents in this century have. It is possible that historians in the next century will refer to the Age of Nixon as they now do the Age of Jackson. What is this Nixon phenomenon? First, there is his longevity. There is no more successful rule to operate by than to outlive your enemies, as proved by prominent men as different as John D. Rockefeller, Herbert Hoover, Armand Hammer, and even Alf Landon. Second, Nixon's long public career and truncated presidency represent both the best and the worst of the post–World War II political system in the United States—nothing more and nothing less. This is something that "Nixon-haters" have always simply refused to accept. Moreover, Nixon appeared on the American political scene at a critical, transitional time in the history of the modern presidency and the traditional two-party system. Unless he is placed in the historical context of the tumultuous time when he assumed office, his importance apart from Watergate cannot be understood. Finally, Nixon's presence on the political scene became a perennial obsession of a small group of intellectuals and liberal politicians from both major parties who began voting in the 1950s, rather than the general public. Gallup polls prior to Watergate always ranked Nixon among the "most admired." Even in the wake of Watergate, he ranked eleventh in a poll of "greatest presidents," and by 1985 that ranking had risen to eighth in a poll taken across the country.[1] This considerable popularity continued until his death in 1994, but throughout his long and tumultuous career it remained more partisan than personal.

THE MAN WE LOVED TO HATE

The intense dislike of Nixon by an elite group of politicians, journalists, and scholars initially arose largely in reaction to his aggressive campaign tactics and vindictiveness when dealing with those he perceived as enemies. From the beginning of his political career, there was a nastiness about Nixon that served both as a public stimulus for his support and as a private motivation for his determination to succeed against all odds. Even if he did not win, the race was worth the effort. The seemingly defiant nature of this personality trait annoyed many Americans, to say the least. Yet if Nixon had been a beloved political figure, like Washington, Eisenhower, or Reagan, he probably would not have become president of the United States and given his critics the satisfaction of the Watergate scandal. He thrived on the hate of his enemies, not the love of his friends. Finally, Nixon's substantive programs and management style as president further angered those who already disliked his public persona for a variety of political and personal reasons. For example, his critics charged Nixon with being "imperial" because of the structural changes he made in the executive branch, most of which came from a presidential commission established during his first term as president. Yet even the most mild of these changes confirmed his enemies' worst fantasies about the brand of New Federalism on which he based his reorganizational policies and what I am calling his aprincipled nature.

Dislike of Nixon cannot be completely explained by any summary of the highlights of his career before he became president. If it could, such rancor would mean that his enemies' attitude was based exclusively on reason and facts, when it is not. Instead, it seemed rooted in an often irrational reaction to the basic aprincipledness of Richard Nixon, which did not fully reveal itself in his public actions until he became president. I am not saying, as many others have, that Richard Nixon was unprincipled. Assorted presidents have been unprincipled, that is, lacking in positive moral scruples as defined by society at the time. The difference with Nixon, and it is this difference that I suspect accounts for the "profound rage" he generated in so many, is that he was aprincipled.

An *unprincipled* person is one who consciously lacks moral scruples and is presumably aware that standards are being violated. In contrast, the *aprincipled* person, seldom reforms his behavior or expresses remorse for transgressions against societal norms because there is no conscious admission of wrongdoing—no apparent awareness of conventional moral or ethical standards. It is this description I have in mind when I refer to Nixon as being aprincipled. However, I also believe that ever-changing postures and positions, not principled convictions, so characteristic of the aprincipled person, describe more politicians in the United States during the last fifty years than is usually acknowledged.

Even when Americans vehemently disagree with politicians' policies or actions, they usually assume that their elected and appointed leaders believe in what they are doing. This is why such nostalgic, nineteenth century–sounding principles as those exhibited by Ronald Reagan, and the more extreme and racist ones once displayed by George Wallace (who, incidentally, was allowed by the people of Alabama to change his mind on integration), are better than no principles. The secret White House tapes represent yet another example of just how far Nixon was prepared to carry his aprincipled pragmatism. He apparently intended to use these tapes not only to write his memoirs but to repudiate false statements about what he and others had said in private.

For years Nixon-watchers thought that they hated the principles he stood for, only to be even more enraged to find out that he had none or— worse yet—had coopted some of theirs. For example, many mistook his early anticommunism for ideological rigidity. When his foreign policy as president did not adhere to this leftist stereotype of him, his detractors criticized him for adopting policies they would have supported under another president. The same proved true of his progressive domestic initiatives. When it became painfully evident during Watergate that Nixon ultimately was not able to tell right from wrong, dirty tricks from criminal acts, or national security from obstruction of justice, it was the last straw—especially for liberal intellectuals, who had never given him the benefit of the doubt on lesser matters earlier in his career.

UNDERSTANDING NIXON WITHOUT WATERGATE

To come to terms with the Nixon phenomenon, his political fallibility and truncated presidency must be viewed other than through the scrim of Watergate. This is necessary because Nixon not only lived up to our worst expectations as president but he also achieved more than most of us would like to admit, making his presidency more than simply a chronicle of Watergate. Surprisingly, most of his lasting achievements are in domestic, rather than foreign, affairs, as this study documents—though few held this view at the time he resigned or twenty years later during the outpouring of statements about him following his death.

Of the hundreds of commentators who wrote or spoke about Nixon's resignation on the day it happened, only one—Rod MacLeish, the CBS news commentator, in a long forgotten political obituary of Richard Nixon—anticipated that future interpretations of Nixon would not remain mired in Watergate:

> [Nixon] postulated a return to that wider definition of wisdom and action
> which held that progress and justice were to be found in many parts of the

national body—in state and local government, in private industry, in the households of ordinary Americans. As President, Mr. Nixon made serious policy efforts to disperse responsibility as well as money for the alleviation of our domestic problems. Philosophically, that effort *may be his milestone,* his principal remembrance in the history of government rather than his crucial efforts in foreign policy which were an extension of what had gone before him.

Whether Mr. Nixon was right in his vision of the sources of our domestic cures, whether he succeeded in breaking the hold of the liberal idea upon the American way of looking at things will—like the resolution of his final controversy—await the judgment of history.[2]

Why has it taken twenty years to reconsider all of Richard Nixon's presidential record, rather than simply the worst segments of it? In part it is because of the standard Watergate view of him as nothing more than an evil aberration on the political landscape. But that is not the entire reason. As important is the fact that he became president of the United States at a critical juncture in American history, which gave him an unusual opportunity to take the initiative in domestic as well as foreign policy. Neither the positive nor the negative aspects of these initiatives have ever been completely understood in terms of what the cold war had done to the modern presidency and what modern industrialized capitalism had done to the American electoral system. Nixon did not create the "megastate," discussed later in this introduction, but his troubling presence on the national political scene for almost half a century belies any interpretation of him that does not recognize that Watergate mirrored the impact of the cold war on politics and society in the United States.

Over a decade of painstaking research into his presidential papers and tapes has convinced me that a confluence of conditions in the country in the late 1960s and advice from his closest aides contributed as much, if not more, to the successes and failures of Nixon's presidency as his individual psyche. These factors often determined the substantive agenda he pursued in domestic and foreign policy. Even in the best of times, but particularly in times of turmoil like the late 1960s and early 1970s, presidential policies seldom reflect exclusively the ideas or personality of any given president. They are, instead, the collective product of his aides and various divisions of the executive branch and his own personal administrative mode of operation. Under a caretaker manager such as Reagan, for example, advisers had an even stronger impact on policy than when

Nixon was in office. There is no indication that presidential dependence on advisers will diminish in the 1990s. It is only a matter of degree how much "hands-on" control presidents exert and which issues they choose to give priority.

I have divided those who advised Nixon on major issues into two camps: the "freethinking" outsiders, who brainstormed with the president about new ideas and comprehensive programs; and the "political-broker" insiders, who worked to draft and implement his legislative and administrative priorities. Their positive and negative contributions to his domestic and foreign policies are discussed in parts II and III. Naturally, there is some overlap with respect to those who advised him on major issues *and* on political dirty tricks or criminal activities.

Nixon once told me that he thought the "mark of a leader is whether he gives history a nudge."[3] There is no doubt that he nudged history as president—sometimes in ways he did not anticipate. Whether relying on freethinking outsiders or political-broker insiders, he essentially took the initiative and made many of his own decisions, particularly in foreign affairs. While it was to be expected that during his lifetime he and his closest advisers disagreed on who influenced whom the most, Richard Nixon came to the Oval Office with innovative diplomatic ideas that could not be "Kissingerized" even by Kissinger. And to the dismay of many liberals and conservatives in Congress, Nixon also moved rapidly into domestic reform, often on the advice of young, liberal Republicans, but without the fanfare that accompanied most of his foreign policy initiatives. Given the fact that until 1988, Nixon remained the only twentieth-century president to be elected with his party in control of neither house of Congress, his positive historical "nudges" in both foreign and domestic matters are truly impressive in retrospect. But so are the negative ones.

A MAN FOR HIS TIME

Following World War II there was general agreement between popular and elite opinion on two things: the effectiveness of most New Deal domestic policies and the necessity of most cold war foreign policies. During the 1960s, however, these two crucial postwar consensual constructs began to break down; and the war in Indochina, with its disruptive impact on the nation's political economy, simply hastened the disintegration of this consensus. By 1968 the traditional bipartisan, cold war approach to the conduct of foreign affairs had been seriously undermined. Similarly, the "bigger and better" New Deal approach to the modern welfare state had reached a point of diminishing returns, even among liberals.[4]

In 1968, when Nixon finally captured the highest office in the land, he inherited from Lyndon Johnson not only the Vietnam War but the plan for the Great Society. This transfer of power occurred at the very moment when both endeavors had lost substantial support among the people at large and, most important, among a significant number of the elite group of decision makers and leaders of opinion across the country—including Nixon, who, as early as 1966, had begun to sense "serious flaws" in the social programs of the Great Society.[5] On previous occasions, when such a breakdown occurred within policy- and opinion-making circles—before the Civil War and the Spanish-American War and in the early years of the Great Depression—domestic or foreign upheavals had followed. The end of the cold war, combined with a structural as well as a cyclical downturn in the U.S. economy, has precipitated yet another such period of disorientation in American foreign and domestic policies.

All the presidents who served during previous periods of transition have been rated either "average" or "failures" by scholars. Those traditionally deemed absolute failures by historians are John Tyler, Zachary Taylor, Millard Fillmore, Franklin Pierce, James Buchanan, Andrew Johnson, Ulysses S. Grant, Warren G. Harding, and Calvin Coolidge. Until 1982, when Nixon and Carter were added to this list, all the "failed" presidencies could be found clustered between the 1840s and 1870s (the notable exception being Lincoln) and in the 1920s, between World War I and the Great Depression. Beginning in the 1960s the country saw a similar series of failed presidents in Johnson, Nixon, Ford, and Carter. The end of the cold war has exacerbated the negative ratings of George Bush and even had a retroactively negative impact on the heretofore unblemished popularity of Ronald Reagan.

To varying degrees, most of the presidents in these past and present transitional periods failed as crisis managers because they refused to take risks. Nixon, in contrast, "[couldn't] understand people who won't take risks."[6] A breakdown in either the foreign or domestic policy consensus offers both opportunity and danger to any incumbent president. Nixon had more opportunity for taking risks at home and abroad during his first administration than he would have had if elected in 1960 because the disruptive impact of war and internal problems during the intervening eight years broke down any remaining national consensus on foreign and domestic policies.[7] Also, he inherited a wartime presidency, which in the

7

past had always enhanced the extralegal powers of the man in the White House for legitimate, as well as illegitimate, risk taking, especially in times of transition.

Periods of war and reform have usually alternated in the United States,[8] but in the 1960s they burgeoned simultaneously, hastening the breakdown of consensus that was so evident by the time of the 1968 election. This unusual situation transformed Nixon's largely unexamined and rather commonplace management views into more comprehensive and controversial ones. It also reinforced his natural predilection to take risks and to bring about change through executive fiat. Thus, the transitional period in which Nixon found himself offered a unique opportunity for domestic and foreign policy innovations. It also encouraged him and his advisers to find innovative ways to violate the civil rights of those in opposition to their policies.

The 2,027 days Nixon spent in office have been remembered most for Watergate, next for foreign policy, and least for domestic reform. I think this order should be reversed. Yet most scholars, journalists, and quite a few prolific ex-felons continue to skew this already deficient collective memory by attributing too much of Nixon's foreign policy to Kissinger; by concentrating on Nixon's personal style or lack of integrity rather than his national policies; by almost entirely ignoring his constructive domestic achievements; and by refusing to recognize the downhill course in American politics that Watergate exacerbated, but neither originated nor ended. The "system worked" during Watergate in that it held Nixon and his aides accountable, but it has not held any other aprincipled politician or policy maker constitutionally accountable since.

Nixon is more than Watergate because his five and a half years in the White House marked an important milestone in the history of the modern presidency based on an electoral system increasingly plagued by both a personality and an issues vacuum. Nixon did not originate these self-destructive aspects of U.S. politics. As the quintessential American politician since World War II, he inherited and learned to operate effectively within an aprincipled system that was disintegrating by 1968 into mindless media messages and talking heads without passion, personality, or substance. In the 1968 presidential campaign Nixon and Hubert Humphrey represented not only the last time two relatively ugly men ran against each other but the last time a broad spectrum of economic and foreign policy issues (as opposed to narrow single issues) still mattered to the American electorate.

For all these reasons, Nixon was a transitional president who faced the forces of the past and the requirements of the future in an exceptionally difficult period in U.S. history. The times, as they say, were out of joint. They were not the best of times, not perhaps the worst, but times of great transformation, difficult to comprehend then and now. Most transitional presidents cannot stand against such times, and Nixon proved no exception. But the way he chose to deal with his particular time of crisis remains unique. Sometime in the course of the 1960s Nixon recognized the abyss on which the U.S. presidency and the political system teetered and tried as consciously as any transitional president ever had to fill the void with new policies and a new political coalition. Before Watergate ended his presidency under a carcinogenic cloud of political gloom and cynicism, Nixon had succeeded to a greater degree than was recognized at the time. But in the process he also laid the groundwork that led to violations of civil rights and finally obstruction of justice.

It is this schizoid nature of the Nixon presidency that constitutes the real tragedy of Watergate—not that it destroyed Nixon's political career without affecting his international reputation, or that it produced ineffective and superficial attempts to ensure presidential accountability, or even that it failed to reform the financing of presidential campaigns or to return morality to a political system already paralyzed by Washington gridlock and media and financial excesses. The real tragedy of Watergate, when stripped of its distracting melodrama, is that all the national soul searching over Watergate obfuscated Nixon's place in history as the best and the worst of the modern presidents.

THE MODERN PRESIDENCY AND "BASTARD FEUDALISM"

There have been only three types of presidencies since George Washington: premodern, from George Washington through Calvin Coolidge; modern, including the transitional administration of Herbert Hoover, through Ronald Reagan; and the transition to postmodern, beginning with George Bush and seeming to emerge in full force with the ever-changing policies and contradictory personality of Bill Clinton.[9] Of the forty-one presidents the United States has had, only eleven of them have held office since 1933: FDR, Truman, Eisenhower, JFK, LBJ, Nixon, Ford, Carter, Reagan, Bush, and Clinton. Compared to traditional or premodern presidencies in which "Congress was the main engine of national policy-making," modern presidents have exhibited four new characteristics: (1) increased unilateral policy-making capacity at home and abroad; (2) centrality in national agenda setting; (3) increased media visibility, which often means increased influence over media content; and (4) increased reliance on a growing number of White House advisers, sometimes called the president's personal bureaucracy.[10]

Despite their increased authority to wage undeclared wars, modern presidents have exhibited widely erratic degrees of power and powerlessness. This is because three of the four characteristics of the modern presidency—those having to do with greater formal and informal power, agenda setting, and visibility—are directly related to these two types of volatility in popularity and succession. Consequently, the office of the modern presidency is one in which, in order to *exercise* power, presidents increasingly must resort to personal public appeals to perpetuate their own, but not necessarily their party's, popularity and the *appearance* of power. This "mediatizing" of American politics has been a two-way street, prompted as much by presidents as by the press. The hard lesson that has yet to be learned from this dangerous tactic is that "Ronald Reagan is the only modern president who has not left office symbolically slain by the people."[11]

The modern presidency comes with not only its own institutionalized bureaucracy in addition to that of the rest of the federal government but with one staffed by extremely technocratically oriented bureaucrats. While the numbers of these faceless, nameless, nonelected bureaucrats around the president boggle the mind, even more important since Kennedy has been the kind of individual they often represent: the know-it-all, arrogant, technocrat that so characterized the "best and brightest" around JFK, with their passionless, computerized solutions to all problems. This presidential bureaucracy now includes numbers of communication, polling, and media specialists who become not buffers but barriers between the president and the public, whose combined expertise has succeeded in ever-lowering voter turnout since 1960. The packaged, passionless presidency now served up to the American people every four years by these media consultants in soupy, sentimental, nostalgic statements about the good old days, or in nasty, negative, fifteen-second sound bites, reached new heights in the 1988 and 1992 presidential campaigns. However, this packaging of the modern presidency by communication, polling, and media specialists using computerized mass mailings and phone banks is designed not only to avoid the issues and dehumanize politics but also to hide the aprincipledness of the technocrats surrounding the president.

The men and women who attach themselves to potential presidential candidates, whose glib TV images increasingly take precedence over substance—campaign managers, pollsters, advertising professionals, and speechwriters—often exhibit the same rootless, nonideological brand of loyalty that is frequently as ephemeral as that of the public at large. They make a living selling information and advice to the highest bidder. While some of these experts, such as H. R. Haldeman and John Ehrlichman, did not desert when their candidate experienced setbacks (as Nixon had in the early 1960s), most do, forming the ranks of what the medievalist K. B. McFarlane has called *bastard feudalism*. McFarlane used this term to describe the manner in which lords and barons of fifteenth-century England lived in a state of "voluntary interdependence" with talented, younger men who competed for their favors and in whom there existed an "absence of any separate fund of political principles"—save temporary loyalty to the particular lord or baron. Thus, bastard feudalism was a "partnership to their mutual benefit, a contract from which both sides expect to benefit . . . [and] lordship lasted only so long as it was found to be good lordship or until it was ousted by a better."[12]

Unfortunately, joining and leaving the retinues of potentially great men in medieval England has its counterpart in contemporary American politics, and offers a quick road to success when a candidate wins at the polls. Success in this case often results in further employment by the state or national political figure or in competition for such services by other aspiring political lords. Examples of prominent shifts in the ranks of twentieth-century feudal bastards abound in any presidential year. Take 1968.

Daniel Patrick Moynihan, having already deserted what was left of the decimated male members of Joseph Kennedy's family, and disillusioned by his fall from grace in the Johnson administration over a controversial 1965 report on the black family, decided to become the leading liberal-in-resident during Nixon's first administration. After years of attaching his star to the political and financial fortunes of Nelson Rockefeller, Henry Kissinger also ended up in the Nixon camp at the end of 1968. Spiro Agnew similarly pledged feudal allegiance to Rockefeller, until the latter withdrew from the primary race without bothering to tell him in advance. Angered and embarrassed, Agnew quickly threw his support to Nixon, and much to everyone's surprise, including his own, became vice president. The cumulative impact of this modern-day version of bastard feudalism has resulted in a coterie of unelected "temporary adherents" around all presidents, whose lack of direct responsibility to the voters fosters more aprincipled and antidemocratic behavior within the White House than most Americans cared to think about before or after the debacle of Watergate.

GANGSTERISM, DEMOCRACY, AND THE MEGASTATE

This turning away from democratic procedures and values that are rooted in constituents' beliefs on the part of presidents and their aides did not take place exclusively during the administration of Richard Nixon; nor did it end when he resigned, as the Iran-contra travesty and Iraqgate have so clearly demonstrated. There is "'something' about the office" of the presidency, Paul Johnson has argued, that "seems to be forcing all [modern] Presidents into similar willful behavior patterns." As traditional moral and religious standards broke down in the twentieth century, political leaders all over the world have used the state to enforce "ethical" standards that are relative to time and place and that violate both human rights and human life itself. This has produced what Johnson calls "gangster statesmen" not only in developing nations but also in industrially advanced and democratically mature countries. In the latter, citizens have been gradually conditioned to prefer material comfort of the welfare state and unspeakable diplomatic actions, in the ubiquitous name of national security, to civil rights and liberties or humane foreign policies.[13] In unanticipated ways this modern industrialized state has created problems for democracy because it contains "repressive" as well as "welfare" functions—both of which have contributed to the formation of the aprincipled megastate.

The megastate and media politics constitute a form of pseudodemocracy in which citizen participation in the form of discussion and voting has become obsolete, because democracy stands in the way of modern centralized and monopolized power. In the megastate, democratic values are severed from democratic structures, making such values simply hollow representations, artificial constructions that must be endlessly decoded to be understood, according to poststructural theory. This means that government officials can "promote a 'democratic value' such as respect for human dignity, by secretly and illegally selling arms to secure the release of hostages, that is, by circumventing the established political processes of consultation and public deliberation and by violating the political sensibilities nurtured by the political culture (e.g., making arms available to governments that support terrorism and stifle dissent at home)."[14]

With the confluence of the megastate, media politics, and bastard feudalism, the potential for aprincipled behavior by purely ambition-driven politicians in the postmodern era is an ever-present danger in the United States.[15] The tendency among modern leaders to ignore constitutional or legislative restrictions when it suits their personal convictions on particular issues and to take secret actions, especially on foreign policy matters, is a serious problem for all mature Western democratic nations.

It is often said that in a democracy people get the presidents they deserve. If this is true, we seem to have allowed the creation of a type of postmodern presidency beyond citizenry control. Why? There are three basic reasons. First, at certain levels, the American political system inherited from the days of Andrew Jackson in the nineteenth century is working in less democratic ways than ever before. Second, for a variety of reasons, since World War II a romanticized version of the modern president has been shaped largely by historians and political scientists, and they and the journalists in agreement with them continue to imprint this skewed image on the public mind. Third, media politics, largely driven by the Oval Office, lends itself to ahistorical presentations of domestic, but especially foreign, policy issues, which has led to less discussion of both, particularly during the height of the cold war.

All these factors, in turn, have led to the unsatisfying technocratic and bureaucratic aspects of the modern presidency. It is a false assumption that the presidency brings out the best in the person elected, no matter how unqualified or mediocre or devious he may be perceived when running for the office. In fact, the pressures of campaigning and holding the office of the modern presidency tend to bring out the worst characteristics of its occupants. So we should really be looking for the worst, not the best, in presidential candidates in the primaries and debates, especially if the number of professionally ambitious, self-selected men running for office continues to increase, as it has in the last thirty years, and bureaucratic structures continue to dominate the decision-making process. No better case study of the strengths and weaknesses of the modern presidency exists than the administration of Richard Nixon.

PART I

REEVALUATING NIXON'S DOMESTIC POLICIES

REEVALUATING
NIXON'S DOMESTIC POLICIES

1

BEYOND THE NEW DEAL
AND THE GREAT SOCIETY

The way I look at most of our domestic programs is that we have done an excellent job of conceiving them and a poor job of selling them. . . . Great ideas that are conceived and not sold are like babies that are stillborn.

—Nixon, memorandum to Ehrlichman, August 1972

When Nixon was first elected president, numerous journalists, scholars, and politicians predicted that he would be a cautious, if not a "do-nothing, caretaker," president. Few listened when he said in 1969 that he intended "to begin a decade of government reform such as this nation has not witnessed in half a century." And most of us scoffed when in 1971 his speechwriters came up with the grandiose phrase "the New American Revolution" to describe his domestic programs.[1] Yet during his first term in office, Nixon acted as an agent for change in five areas of domestic reform: welfare, civil rights, economic policy, environmental policy, and reorganization of the federal bureaucracy.[2]

From the moment Nixon assumed office, the liberal and radical press, many individual Democrats, and a few liberal Republicans interested in domestic reform concentrated their attention on his personality and political ethics—not because Nixon's persona during his first years as president offended them any more than that of previous presidents but, in part, because his early substantive programs and specific domestic priorities

17

threatened to co-opt their own positions on a number of issues. They might have endorsed or accepted some of these plans and ideas from a president they liked and trusted, regardless of party, but not from someone they enjoyed calling Tricky Dick.

In some instances, Nixon's long-standing opponents blatantly ignored legislative and administrative innovations that would normally have appealed to them. According to Daniel Patrick Moynihan, these liberal critics, in particular, were a "natural constituency" for most of his domestic policies. If Nixon's domestic reforms were often opposed, as the political scientist Paul J. Halpern has noted, by those who "never even bothered to get the facts straight,"[3] it may well have been because many of his critics simply could not believe that Nixon would ever do the right thing except for the wrong reason. Thus, they (and I include myself in this group) seldom took the time to try to determine whether any of his efforts to make the 1970s a decade of reform were legitimate, however politically motivated. Consequently, far from accepting him in the role of catalyst for domestic reform, they claimed that Nixon never developed a coherent domestic program.[4]

Because of the inevitable comparison to FDR that first-term presidents face, Nixon naturally worried about reaching his first hundred days in office without conveying to the public a coordinated domestic program. Typically, however, Nixon's concern stemmed from a more fundamental worry that failing to get his domestic plans across would hurt the image of the United States abroad and thus negatively reflect on his major interest—foreign policy.[5]

In anticipation of strong partisan opposition to his first legislation on domestic reform, Nixon began to cajole his staff in March and April 1969 to set shorter deadlines for suggestions about domestic programs, about ways to incorporate constructive congressional ideas into such programs, and, most important, about coordinating publicity on domestic issues. To this end an informal team, known as the Five O'Clock Group, began meeting daily in the office of H. R. (Harry Robbins) Haldeman, Nixon's chief of staff, to discuss the next day's publicity opportunities and public relations problems in general. Their suggestions ranged from persuading cabinet members to be more "passionate" about administrative policies to writing letters and making complaint calls about unfavorable comments by columnists, television commentators, and even satirical television celebrities like the Smothers Brothers. The Five O'Clock Group consisted of Haldeman (or his representative), the speechwriter Raymond Price, appointments secretary Dwight Chapin, and various personnel from both the press and legislative divisions within the White House.[6]

Such attention to public relations has led some to conclude that Nixon was more concerned than any other modern president with public relations. I think this is an exaggeration: it is difficult to believe that Kennedy and Johnson were not equally, or more, concerned with their public images and press coverage, since neither came close at the beginning of his administration to enjoying the second-highest positive reporting in this century during his six-month honeymoon periods that Nixon did. The release of Nixon's handwritten and typed comments complaining about his treatment by the media, especially coverage of his domestic programs, and suggesting ways to improve it simply constitutes better-documented proof of his concern than has yet been reported for JFK and LBJ. Although the vast majority of periodicals and daily newspapers supported him all three times he ran for president, Nixon knew that four powerful newspapers, two national newsmagazines, and many TV anchormen would never come around. In this light, *not* to have attempted to counter such influential hostility would have been unusual.[7]

During his first year in office, all of Nixon's closest advisers and speechwriters agreed that there needed to be more coordination of the administration's domestic reforms if they were to be promoted effectively. One result was the concept of New Federalism. Designed to end the "pile on, political approach to domestic legislation," it never received the serious attention from the media that the administration hoped for. As a result, reform did not become the "watchword of this administration," but it was not for lack of coherent domestic programs or a clear legislative agenda, as some scholars continue to assert.[8]

In talking about his domestic initiatives with me, Nixon insisted that all of them reflected his own background and association with the progressive wing of the Republican party.[9] Aside from the improbability of such an assertion, his domestic reforms were far from conservative by Republican or Democratic standards. When I asked him what he considered his most important achievements in domestic policy, he singled out his success in desegregating southern schools and his Supreme Court appointments—Warren E. Burger, Harry Blackmun, Lewis Powell, and William H. Rehnquist—still insisting that Clement F. Haynsworth, Jr., would have been his best choice had he been approved by the Senate (neglecting to mention that this nomination demonstrated his handling of relations with Congress at its worst). Nixon also included on his list of significant firsts his initiatives on the environment and space and his declared (and well-financed) wars against cancer, illegal drugs, crime, and hunger.[10]

Ignoring his Supreme Court nominees, Nixon's closest aides usually place revenue sharing and environmental and land-use policies higher on the list of his domestic achievements than the former president does himself. According to John Ehrlichman, his counsel and domestic adviser, this continuing difference of opinion arose from the fact that Nixon paid more personal attention during his first term to domestic issues with "political juice," such as cancer research, labor legislation, drugs, crime, taxes, desegregation, and welfare, than he did to economic matters involving revenue sharing, housing, hunger, transportation, and consumer protection, or environmental and general health concerns. On those "gut" issues that Nixon considered "potent political medicine," he became actively involved in policy formulation; the rest—even the controversial subjects of campus unrest and antiwar demonstrations—he largely delegated to others, especially Ehrlichman.[11]

As for his domestic mistakes, Nixon cited wage and price controls, which he now says he supported at the time only because it looked as though Congress would take this initiative to control inflation if the White House did not, and the automatic cost-of-living adjustments (COLAs) for Social Security recipients. He thought that COLAs made sense at the time but not in light of the runaway inflation after he left office.[12] Of course, many have logically claimed that the secret White House taping system, the creation of the "Plumbers" unit within the White House to plug information leaks and ultimately conduct break-ins, the harassment of individuals on an "enemies" list, and the serious consideration Nixon gave to the Huston Plan for institutionalizing systematic federal surveillance of suspect groups and individuals were all domestic mistakes.[13]

Although Nixon and both his insider and outsider advisers realized that the odds were stacked against the administration's domestic programs' receiving serious attention by a Congress controlled by the Democrats and certain influential segments of the media, at the end of his first term as president he had taken strong action in several major domestic reform areas, especially with respect to welfare and environmental legislation and even in the area of civil rights. It has taken two decades for historians to begin to transcend Watergate with respect to Nixon's domestic accomplishments, which went beyond, and in some instances significantly tried to redirect, New Deal programs relating to welfare and reorganization of the government and economy and Great Society efforts to implement civil rights and environmental legislation, Native American policy, and spending for social services.

BEYOND CONSERVATION: ENVIRONMENTAL ADVANCES

Environmental legislation was not high on Nixon's personal list of federal priorities, despite polls showing its growing importance as a national issue. Gallup and other pollsters did not even think the environment important enough to include in their questionnaires until 1965. Between then and 1970, from a little over one-third to almost two-thirds of the public had become concerned about water pollution, but Nixon's record on the environment was "nonexistent" before he became president and before his staff convinced him it was a domestic "crisis."[14]

Often using poll data, Ehrlichman—with his assistant, Egil ("Bud") Krogh; John Whitaker, who served first as Nixon's cabinet secretary and later as undersecretary of the Interior Department; and Whitaker's assistant, Christopher DeMuth—substantially influenced both Nixon's ideas and the content of his environmental legislation by making it into a crisis issue. In fact, Ehrlichman, who had specialized in land-use law in Seattle, has been described by one forest conservation specialist as "the most effective environmentalist since Gifford Pinchot,"[15] referring to the controversial chief of the U.S. Forest Service under Presidents Theodore Roosevelt and William Howard Taft. He and Whitaker put Nixon out in front of Congress on environmental issues, especially with respect to the use of the permit authority in the Refuse Act of 1899 to begin to clean up water supplies before Congress passed any "comprehensive water pollution enforcement plan."[16] Curiously, Ehrlichman did not dwell on his own contribution to environmental reform in his 1982 book, *Witness to Power*, preferring to denigrate Secretary of the Interior Walter Hickel, whose anti- and then pro-conservation and pollution views he constantly had to counter. Hickel was finally fired in November 1970, when he refused to resign after angering Nixon over a combination of independent environmental and antiwar positions that he had taken.[17]

White House Central Files now clearly reveal how instrumental Ehrlichman, rather than Hickel, was in shaping the president's views on environmental matters, with the exception of national parks, which Nixon had long favored. All other environmental concerns were filtered through him (or Whitaker) to Nixon, who proved amenable to several different reform measures, including restructuring existing government departments. An interview I conducted with Raymond Price confirmed that, except for the parks issue, the "environment was not an emotional issue for Nixon." But he added, because the "press was in bed with the environmental extremists . . . the President got a bad press" on environmental questions when in fact he "was ten years ahead of his time."[18] This bad press also stemmed from his appointment of Hickel, an Alaskan, whose anti-environmental positions were well known before he underwent several dramatic and erratic conversions on the issues of oil spills, conservation, and use of pesticides on public lands.

Nixon's first move was to appoint a cabinet committee called the Environmental Quality Council (EQC). When its meetings proved filled with "too much scientific jargon . . . [and] no overall strategy," he put Ehrlichman in charge of a White House environmental task force composed of representatives from various executive departments and agencies. Their report of November 25, 1969, convinced Nixon that responsibility for environmental issues was hopelessly fragmented, and from that point he supported several different integrative remedies, including the creation of a new Department of Environment and Natural Resources (DENR), which would have eclipsed the Department of Interior by moving all antipollution programs out of it, and taken the Forest Service away from the Department of Agriculture and the Corps of (Civil) Engineers away from the Department of Defense. In the spring and summer of 1970, Nixon settled for a less comprehensive restructuring of all government environmental functions by recommending the creation of a Department of Natural Resources (DNS) and the Environmental Protection Agency (EPA). He obtained congressional approval for the latter at the end of 1970, appointing William Ruckelshaus to head it. His administration broke the jurisdictional deadlock in Congress over the National Environmental Policy Act (NEPA) by siding with Henry M. "Scoop" Jackson (Dem.-Wash.) over Ed Muskie (Dem.-Maine)—an alliance that cleared the way for subsequent environmental legislation, including EPA.[19]

In the meantime the president had accepted from Congress the creation of a cabinet level Council on Environmental Quality and appointed the well-known conservationist Russell Train to head it. Train succeeded Ruckelshaus as head of the EPA. From Nixon until Bush, these two men "were considered the strongest leaders the EPA had." Nixon remained personally convinced, however, that supporters of environmental legislation could be divided into two groups, depending on whether they were opposed to private enterprise. When it came down to "a flat choice between smoke and jobs," Nixon privately and publicly made no bones about favoring jobs and a strong economy. As a result, Nixon always insisted that the Office of Management and Budget's (OMB) cost-benefit analysis be brought to bear on the EPA's decisions as well as on those of other executive branch agencies—a practice environmental activists still hold against him. He continued to believe that the unusually detailed recommendations he made in his first State of the Union address in January 1970 represented a "moderate" position designed to appeal to the pro-capitalists among the environmentalists. In this message he called for $10 billion to clean the country's water supplies and to help pass stricter air pollution regulations. Subsequently Nixon made thirty-six environmental proposals and proclaimed the first Earth Week, in April 1971.[20] Nixon's personal beliefs kept him from participating in White House discussions on the environment to the degree he did on other domestic reform issues, such as welfare. "Just keep me out of trouble on environmental issues," Nixon reportedly told Ehrlichman. According to Whitaker, when he was assistant director of the Domestic Council, Nixon wanted "environmental cleanup, but not at such a cost-benefit ratio that [it would] hurt the economy. Don't try to 'out-clean' Mr. Muskie; there's no way you can do it." This remained his position even after he realized the political potential of environmental legislation in the 1972 presidential election against probable Democratic candidates like Muskie.[21]

By the summer of 1971, even one of Nixon's most consistent critics, the *New York Times*, was praising the president for having evolved into an environmentalist. Indeed, the Clean Air Act of 1970, which the administration supported, remains the "most controversial and far reaching effort to control air pollution." Other environmental legislation supported by the administration (as a result of Ehrlichman's and Whitaker's inside cajoling) included federal regulation of oil spill cleanup, pesticides into the ocean, noise pollution, and state coastal zone management. There were only two flaws in Nixon's pro-environmental stance, and both still tend to be remembered, while his positive record, which "has yet to be improved upon by any president," must be resurrected from Watergate-dimmed memories. In particular, Democratic environmental activists from the 1970s such as Barry Commoner still refuse to give Nixon any credit for demonstrating leadership on air and water cleanup, despite his record to the contrary.[22]

The first major area in which Nixon did not appear to support EPA actions concerned obtaining compliance from the big four automobile companies for emission control standards. In November 1969 and again in March 1973, his handwritten comments indicate that he wanted to give Detroit manufacturers the benefit of the doubt on this issue, although his first Health, Education and Welfare (HEW) secretary, Robert Finch, and his Air Quality Advisory Board did not. Throughout his administration he supported amendments to the Clean Air Act. As late as March 1974 the president and his advisers were still devising tactics over amendments to the Clean Air Act in order to walk a fine line between what they perceived to be pro- and antibusiness environmentalists in Congress. In this instance they agreed to allow Train, then head of the EPA, to oppose two of the administration's amendments in order to obtain a "legislative debate on the merits of the amendments," rather than silence him and turn the discussion into a partisan issue.[23]

Most damning, however, remains the widely quoted transcription of the taped White House conversation with Henry Ford II and Lee Iacocca, when the latter was still a CEO with the Ford Motor Company. In the course of that thirty-five-minute discussion over emission controls, Nixon referred to environmental and consumer protection advocates as "enemies of the system" who "aren't one really damn bit interested in safety or clean air." He continued: "What they're interested in is *destroying the system . . . I am for the system.*" To his way of thinking, extreme environmental or consumer protection would mean going "back and liv[ing] like a bunch of damned animals . . . like when the Indians were here. You know how the Indians lived? Dirty, filthy, horrible."[24] (This statement would later be used to discredit Nixon's positive record on Native Americans, showing how dangerous it is to conflate Nixon's private statements with his public actions.)

The second flaw usually cited in Nixon's environmental record is his veto of the Federal Water Pollution Control Act Amendments of 1972 and his attempt to impound funds appropriated by Congress under this legislation. Details abound about how hard Nixon's staff worked to keep water pollution legislation within the spending ceilings they had set. In fact, Nixon supported Secretary Hickel's initial water pollution proposal despite its inflationary financing components because "we either do this or fail to stop a *massive* budget-busting spree by Congress in this field." (Nixon also did not intend for this particular environmental legislation to become a precedent for uncontrolled spending on other environmental matters, because he thought water pollution measures took precedent over others.) It proved impossible for the administration to control spending on this issue because Congress ignored Nixon's recommended ceilings and overrode his veto in 1972. Whitaker told Ehrlichman on October 5, 1971, that "the political fallout if the President ever vetoes a Water Bill will be disastrous for him." A year later, on October 9, 1972, Whitaker recommended to Nixon that he sign the bill from Congress, even though he and Ehrlichman had tried so hard to defeat it. They believed that, given the state of antipollution technology, the additional $18 billion it contained would improve water quality only marginally. Whitaker's files indicate that Nixon had decided as early as July 24, 1972, to veto the legislation if it violated his spending ceiling, knowing that his veto would not be sustained.[25]

Ehrlichman and Whitaker agreed then, and still do, that the water pollution legislation enacted by Congress was budget-busting and designed to embarrass the president on a popular issue in an election year. Statistics later showed that the money appropriated in this legislation could not be spent fast enough to achieve its stated goals. Instead, the actual annual expenditures in the first years after passage approximated those originally proposed by Nixon's staff. The fact remains that Congress turned down more of the president's environmental legislation than it passed.[26]

When Congress overrode his veto, Nixon refused to appropriate all of the additional amount Congress had authorized, "impounding" half of the $18 billion. Nixon's papers indicate that his legal advisers had researched whether he could constitutionally spend only 50 percent of the money appropriated by Congress for clean water, telling him at the end of 1972 that

> the water bill as passed by Congress over the President's veto authorized Federal expenditures for the next three fiscal years of $5, $6 and $7 billion. As to the legal question, we think it is clear from the language of the legislation and the statutory history that the Executive Branch was granted discretion to make allotments to the States at levels below those maximum numbers, as long as the maximums were not exceeded. The money allotted to the States by the bill is available for expenditure by contract authority, and is thus not subject to Congressional review through the appropriations process during the three-year life of that legislation. By announcing allotment of $2 billion for the remainder of fiscal

1973 and $3 billion for fiscal year 1974, Bill Ruckelshaus of EPA was, in our view, operating within his statutorily delegated discretion. I note that two law suits have already been filed on this question, and we expect that our legal position will be vindicated in the courts. . . . To summarize, the President has increased the Federal spending priorities addressed to the clean water problem by 1,000 percent, he is following a course of construction of treatment plants which will allow us to achieve our clean water goals within a decade, and he is accomplishing this goal without fueling inflation and in the context of a fiscally responsible budget.

[All of the foregoing is totally consistent with the public positions of Ruckelshaus and other Administration spokesmen. One interesting sidebar: OMB reports that the sewage treatment plant construction program has now established EPA as the largest public works agency in the Federal Government.][27]

In 1975 the Supreme Court finally ruled that the executive branch could not curtail use of these funds by reducing authorized allotments to individual states. This ruling was the result of suits brought against the EPA administrator Russell Train, who agreed with Nixon and his staff that the additional spending would not improve overall water quality in the United States. In the interim Congress had passed the Budget and Impoundment Control Act of 1974, regulating presidential impoundments and, most important, creating the Congressional Budget Office, whose data-gathering powers allowed Congress from that point forward to submit its own draft budgets to control spending ceilings. Even though presidential impoundments dated back to Jefferson, over the years such actions had involved spending for foreign, not domestic, affairs. When Johnson refused to spend money for certain domestic programs, the Justice Department agreed with him that he was within his constitutional powers. Congress went so far as to legitimize Johnson's unilateral action by granting Nixon discretionary power in 1969 to impound up to $6 billion from approved domestic authorizations. Without congressional approval Nixon withheld twice that amount in 1970–71, and by the spring of 1973 had withheld $18 million. Consequently, partisan congressional opposition to impoundment began to develop among Democrats in Congress even before Watergate, but disagreement between the executive and legislative branches over environmental appropriations reached such hysterical heights by 1974 that the House Judiciary Committee considered making Nixon's impoundments part of the impeachment charges against him. The committee's own staff lawyers essentially agreed with what the president's legal advisers had been telling him since 1972: he had the constitutional and statutory right to impound funds.[28]

When he signed the 1974 budget reform bill into law on July 12, Nixon praised (and even took partial credit for) all but the impoundment sections, because he thought it would "impose sufficient discipline on ... Congressional [budgetary] procedures [to prevent] costly programs from being enacted without adequate consideration of their additional burden to the taxpayer." Like so much Watergate-influenced legislation, this one proved woefully inadequate, especially when it came to controlling impoundment actions by Presidents Ford, Carter, and Reagan. Finally, in 1985 the Supreme Court declared the impoundment control provisions of the 1974 act unconstitutional because they constituted a "legislative veto" in violation of the separation of powers, by granting one house of Congress the power to block proposed presidential withholding of allocated money. This decision represented widespread economic opinion by the middle of the 1980s, as all presidents since Johnson had argued, that one legitimate way of controlling inflation and more federal deficits caused by runaway spending by Congress was through what amounted to the Nixonian practice of impoundment, now euphemistically called "deferrals of money." Not only had Nixon been "right" on the environment, but the Supreme Court and economists ultimately agreed that presidents had the right and the implied duty to impound domestic funding allocations in the interests of the national economy. This supported Nixon's 1974 prediction that the impoundment control provisions "may well limit the ability of the Federal Government to respond promptly and effectively to rapid changes in economic conditions."[29]

BEYOND TERMINATION: NATIVE AMERICAN POLICY

Under considerably less pressure than environmentalists brought to bear on him, Nixon endorsed an enlightened self-determination policy for Native Americans that went beyond New Deal and Great Society programs. Until his administration, national policy had followed primarily an integrationist approach aimed at terminating tribal ties. After appointing Louis R. Bruce, a Mohawk in favor of self-determination, as commissioner of the Bureau of Indian Affairs (BIA), Nixon moved to change federal Indian policy "180 degrees from the past" by declaring in a special message to Congress on July 8, 1970, that the federal government would assist Indians in pursuing "[s]elf-determination . . . without the threat of eventual termination." In this address the president assured "the Indian that he [could] assume control over his own life without being separated involuntarily from the tribal group."[30]

From the end of World War II to the 1960s, national policy reversed New Dual reforms aimed at giving more recognition to tribal government and culture, substituting instead an integrationist approach aimed at terminating tribal life and assimilating Native Americans as individuals into mainstream society. This meant severing special government ties with tribes and making Native Americans subject to the same laws as other citizens. Despite Eisenhower's ambivalence, in keeping with this approach Congress passed in 1953 House Concurrent Resolution No. 180, Public Law 280, relegating to states the authority for maintaining law and order in areas where Native Americans resided. In 1968 Johnson delivered a message to Congress criticizing termination, making a few new recommendations. But Nixon's 1970 address went much further. His determination to strengthen the Native Americans' sense of autonomy without threatening their sense of community became evident when he asked Congress to repeal the 1953 House Resolution. Ironically, this congressional action dated from the time Nixon had been vice president. As president, he tried to end all remnants of federal policy forcing termination of tribal status and turned over more decisions about Native American policies to the elected tribal governments. During his first term, Nixon appeared to live up to praise from Bruce Willkie, the executive director of the National Congress of American Indians (NCAI), who said in the fall of 1970 that Nixon was "the first U.S. President since George Washington to pledge that the government will honor obligations to the Indian tribes." Around the same time Navajo tribal head Peter MacDonald, one of the few Native American Republicans, declared that Nixon should "be viewed as the Abraham Lincoln of the Indian people."[31]

Nixon's support for self-determination enjoyed a favorable press among Native Americans,[32] thus giving him an extended honeymoon in which to build a diverse and competent White House team for dealing with the "Indian problem"—a luxury he did not enjoy with African-Americans or women. It included the special assistant to the president, Leonard Garment, who was ever present on minority questions, Ehrlichman, Bobbie Greene Kilberg, Bradley H. Patterson, Jr., Frank Carlucci, Donald Rumsfeld, director of the Office of Economic Opportunity, and surprisingly, Vice President Spiro Agnew—who took a personal "interest in Indian affairs" after Nixon appointed him chair of the National Council on Indian Opportunity. Even the publicist and politico Murray Chotiner expressed similar sentiments. Curiously, the Urban Affairs Council (UAC) did not become involved despite the urgings of one of Moynihan's aides, Checker Finn. In some instances these presidential advisers had little in common except their concern for Indian affairs. Although a few of them thought that BIA Commissioner Bruce was "only moderately competent and need[ed] much help," they all ultimately pulled together on Indian matters.[33]

Agnew, for example, officially proposed the establishment of an Indian Revenue Sharing Program to Nixon in October 1971, with the support of Garment and the Department of the Interior. Native Americans experienced a "very significant deficiency with respect to the General Revenue Sharing Program," Agnew told the president; "this proposal would provide a major breakthrough in implementing a program of self-determination, the very basis of your Indian policy." Agnew also offered some of the calmest advice to Nixon after a small group of disgruntled Native Americans trashed the offices of the Bureau of Indian Affairs in 1972: "It is important that we not allow all of the progressive policies of your administration with regard to Indian matters to be submerged by the unlawful activities of a few urban militants who are not representative of the Indian community." While Agnew went on to express concern in this letter about the "softness" of the administration's response to "the recent criminal actions at the Bureau of Indian Affairs," fearing "we will look McGovernish," his position was enough in keeping with Garment's and Carlucci's for his suggestion that he be "placed in direct charge" of a special task force on Indian affairs to be accepted by the president.[34]

The influence of Nixon's more liberal Anglo advisers on domestic policy privately prevailed on this minority issue, despite the fact that the administration was being attacked by liberals and conservatives in Congress and most radical Native American activists for not doing enough to improve living and health conditions of Native Americans. The siege at Wounded Knee in 1973 that ensued after militants took over this reservation settlement in South Dakota simply exacerbated such criticism. That Nixon had "nothing to lose" by being liberal on Native American issues does not diminish his reform record in this area or the restrained patience his administration exercised in dealing with potentially explosive situations.[35]

Between the occupation of Alcatraz Island in 1969 and Nixon's resignation in August 1974, there were forty-five occupations of territory and/or buildings by Indians across the country. Instead of reacting punitively to increased Indian militancy on the part of young Red Power activists who occupied Alcatraz and later Wounded Knee, and in the interim caused $1.5 million in damage and untold bureaucratic chaos at BIA national headquarters, Nixon increased the BIA budget by 214 percent and requested a total, all-agency budget of $1.2 billion for Indian affairs in fiscal year 1973—an increase of $300 million in two years. His last budget, in 1974, called for overall federal Indian funding of $1.6 billion. Administration-sponsored appropriations for the BIA alone rose from $249 million in 1969 to $635 million in 1974. Funds for improving the health of American Indians doubled during Nixon's first term in office. In addition to intervening on behalf of Native Americans in land disputes, the president initiated, and Congress passed, legislation strengthening existing tribal governments, restoring previously terminated tribal status, and financing tribal commercial development. For example, his administration established the first special office of Indian Water Rights; signed a bill authorizing the secretary of agriculture to make direct and insured loans to Indian tribes though the Farmers Home Administration; fostered tribal commercial development through the Indian Financing Act of 1974; made special arrangements for presenting to any federal court the Trust Council's position defending Indian natural resources rights; filed a landmark Supreme Court suit to protect Indian rights in Pyramid Lake; and pledged that all available BIA funds would be funneled to priorities set by tribal governments themselves. Moreover, more than any previous administration, Nixon's, according to the American Indian Press Association, "increased the number of Indians holding high-level positions across the federal bureaucracy." Thus, appointments of tribal members as BIA commissioners, area directors, and superintendents "became the hallmark of the Nixon years."[36]

Nixon's official reversal of federal Native American policy also led to the enactment of a number of bills that strengthened tribal land claims. Most prominent among the administration's actions in this area were the return in 1970 of the sacred Blue Lake to the people of Taos Pueblo in New Mexico; the settlement in 1971 of the Alaska Native Claims issue; the negotiation of the 1971 federal agreement with the Florida Miccosukee tribe, one of the least assimilated groups in the United States, acknowledging its right to control its own affairs; and the restoration of the previously terminated Menominee Tribe to federally recognized status through the Menominee Restoration Act of December 22, 1973.[37]

Blue Lake and Alaska Native Claims

One of the most publicized of these land claims occurred over Blue Lake in New Mexico. It also most clearly indicates Nixon's interest in Native American issues and the influence of liberal insider advisers on policy, especially Bradley H. Patterson, Jr., Garment's executive assistant, and Bobbie Greene Kilberg. Patterson had been assistant cabinet secretary under Eisenhower from 1954 to 1961, and Kilberg served as a staff assistant to both Ehrlichman and Garment before going to work for Secretary of Labor Shultz. In this instance Kilberg, "the resident authority on Native American Affairs," deserves most of the credit for bringing the issue of leasing more grazing rights to white ranchers in New Mexico over the protests of the Taos Pueblo, who, since 1906, had claimed the land around Blue Lake in New Mexico as sacred.[38]

Ehrlichman, using the authority delegated to him by Nixon on Native American matters, had legislation drafted to prevent any more such leases and to return all sacred land, only to find that Scoop Jackson, chair of the Senate Interior Committee, and Democratic Senator Clinton P. Anderson from New Mexico both opposed it. Up to this point, even though the House had passed the bill, according to Ehrlichman, Nixon did not know anything about Blue Lake, the Taos Pueblo, or the leasing rights controversy. After Ehrlichman informed the president that his administration was publicly committed to the pro-tribe legislation, Nixon did not hesitate to fight these two powerful Democratic senators whose support he needed on foreign policy issues.[39]

This explanation is probably too self-serving on Ehrlichman's part. As early as April 1970, Garment had informed Nixon, in a memorandum containing extensive attachments, that the vice president supported the Blue Lake land transfer and that the issue could act as the "starting point" for launching a new Indian policy. Regardless of how little Nixon may have know about the initial details connected with the Blue Lake legislation, he quickly came to understand that supporting it might cost him votes on the Anti-Ballistic Missile (ABM) and support on other military matters in the Senate. (This is a good example of how easily Nixon's foreign policy goals became inadvertently intertwined with his domestic policies.) Nonetheless, on December 15, 1970, the Blue Lake bill became the first of the president's Indian proposals to become law.[40]

As he had with Nixon on the land dispute with the Taos Pueblos over Blue Lake, Ehrlichman later claimed that Secretary of the Interior Rogers C. B. Morton did not understand what was at stake in the Alaska Eskimo, Aleut, and Indian claims to millions of acres of land in Alaska. After Kilberg alerted him to the problem, Ehrlichman claimed that he had simply informed Morton that the president "wanted" the legislation compensating Alaska Natives in land and money. Only then did he "hastily obtain Nixon's actual approval" before the secretary "could discover the truth." It appears that Patterson, an aide to Garment, had more to do with negotiating the details of the Alaska Native Lands legislation than either Ehrlichman or Kilberg. By his own admission, Patterson handled 90 percent of Garment's Native American duties. Even though he "didn't know very much at the beginning," Patterson later claimed to have become a "resident overseer on Indian matters . . . in the White House."[41]

Although Nixon's special message on Indians in July 1970 had not included the long-standing controversy over Alaska Native Claims (which conflicted with the interests of those promoting the Alaska pipeline), in September the president wrote Representative Howard W. Pollack that "an early and just settlement of the Native Claims issue has my complete and personal backing." Not until February 1971, however, after much criticism from Alaska Natives of Secretary Morton's testimony in behalf of the 1969 legislation presented by the administration, did Nixon decide to open the issue up for reevaluation. Patterson had been working with the Department of the Interior, the BIA, and staffers from the vice president's office to rewrite the Alaska Native Claims Bill in consultation with the Alaska Federation of Natives (AFN)—only to find that career personnel in the Office of Management and Budget opposed any fair settlement. After Morton's testimony, Patterson realized that only presidential intervention could settle the contradiction between the 1969 legislation and the president's new policy.[42]

Rewriting the 1969 legislation that the administration had originally endorsed in a fit of absentmindedness (among other things, it contained a termination clause contradicting the administration's self-determination policy) proved such a major overhaul that the president's specific approval had to be sought through Ehrlichman. But it was not, according to Patterson, a question of using White House clout via Ehrlichman to hoodwink Secretary Morton as much as it was using it to overcome obstructionism from low-level personnel within OMB and even the Department of the Interior. Once it became known that the president backed the Alaska Natives, these pockets of executive-branch resistance melted away. In April Nixon met with the head of the AFN, Donald R. Wright, and Morton sent Congress the new Alaska Native Claims Bill transferring forty million acres and a billion dollars to aboriginal Alaskans.[43]

The relationship with Native Americans inside the contiguous territory of the United States began to turn sour shortly after Nixon appointed Morton, his floor manager during the 1968 Republican convention, as secretary of the interior in 1971, replacing the controversial Walter Hickel over conservation and antiwar issues. Morton began making personnel and jurisdictional changes that seemed to threaten the authority of Commissioner Bruce and the BIA. Although Morton almost immediately rescinded his orders diluting Bruce's power, he kept his controversial new advisers and so the public relations damage remained. Native American leaders continued to resent the secretary's appointment of Wilma Victor as a close adviser on Native Americans, William Rogers as an assistant secretary in charge of Indian Affairs, and John O. Crow as BIA deputy commissioner. Even Bruce was not fully accepted by some older tribal leaders, who feared that he had appointed too many urban (off-reservation) Indians under forty years old to the BIA, who would ultimately neglect the problems on the reservations. As it turned out, this generationally and geographically based fear proved unfounded because the Nixon administration spent less than $10 million on meeting the needs of urban Indians. (The president had originally intended to use the Office of Economic Opportunity as the "lead agency" to service the approximately 500,000 Native Americans living in cities. Early in his first term, however, Nixon decided to dismantle the OEO for reasons unrelated to this issue.)[44]

In the fall of 1971, tribal leaders began demanding that the BIA be removed from the Department of the Interior and placed in "receivership" at the White House, "to enable Native Americans to gain justice and protection of their land and resources." They argued that Nixon's reforms, especially his favorable disposition toward land claims by native peoples, were being "subverted" within the BIA by old-line bureaucrats, Morton's new appointments, and some members of Congress. Uncharacteristically, Nixon did not take advantage of this request by these moderate leaders to increase White House power over the bureaucracy (by transferring the BIA out of the Department of the Interior or by doing away with it entirely), as Ehrlichman, John Whitaker, and some of the more militant urban Indian activists would have preferred. (As early as September 1969, the Urban Affairs Council had been informed that Hickel was "eventually [going] to do away with the BIA and transfer its responsibilities to people-oriented agencies.") Obviously nothing had come of this before Morton took over as secretary of the interior. While Nixon personally intervened in the controversy over the BIA in the fall of 1971, all he did was tell Morton that "we should take a look at the whole bureaucracy with regard to the handling of Indian affairs and shake it up, shake it up good."[45]

The reasons behind the president's hesitancy in ordering structural changes that would either have eliminated the BIA or transferred it out of the Department of the Interior are not entirely clear from recently released documents. Part of his reasoning may have been political. Senator George McGovern, as chair of the Senate Interior Subcommittee on Indian Affairs, had been criticizing the administration for not unilaterally waiving tribal contract law in order to make it easier for tribes to take over services previously provided by the BIA, and for not immediately extending all BIA services to urban Indians. Congress had delayed almost two full years on some of the specific proposals in Nixon's 1970 address that would have resolved most of McGovern's complaints. So the president asserted that it was the responsibility of Congress "to liberalize contracting for Indian organizations," as he had requested. Since the president did not shrink from acting unilaterally on other matters of domestic importance, his hesitancy over what to do with the BIA could have partially resulted from the complexity of dealing effectively with BIA functions in relation to ending termination. After a group of militants attempted in September 1971 to place a citizens' arrest on a BIA deputy commissioner "on charges that he was reversing an enlightened Nixon policy," and then occupied and ransacked BIA headquarters in November 1972, doing away with the BIA or even freeing it from the control of the Department of the Interior would have appeared to be capitulating to the most extreme Indian faction. The president had delayed taking decisive action on the BIA for political reasons until 1972, but violence by extremists in the nation's capitol prevented him from acting at all against an agency he viewed with disdain. Thus, by March 1973, Nixon was still privately complaining about the corruption and mismanagement within the BIA and asking Ehrlichman: "When are we going to get action on this mess?"[46]

Alcatraz Island

The Nixon administration's new Native American policy faced its first openly confrontational test on November 9, 1969, when fourteen Native Americans took over Alcatraz Island. By June 1970 as many as seventy-five (almost half of them women and children) occupied the old prison site in San Francisco Bay. Several unrelated incidents apparently triggered the takeover: one was the burning down of a San Francisco Indian Center and the other (at least according to Robert Robertson, one of the major negotiators in the affair who worked for Vice President Agnew) was a statement by Secretary of the Interior Hickel in October 1969 that Alcatraz might make a nice "park near the people," and his suggestion that the Bureau of Outdoor Recreation should pursue this idea. Under attack from urban Indian militants at the time, Hickel may have said this in a futile effort to placate them. If that was his intent, it failed when the occupiers of Alcatraz said that they opposed the federal government's attempt to turn the island into a national park. "From the beginning . . . this has been a situation well suited to confrontational politics," Garment wrote in retrospect. "It has all the elements: an ostensibly good cause; a sympathetic public; an irresponsible, but PR-conscious group with a feeling of having 'nothing to lose'; a visible piece of real estate in a big urban setting and considerable ballyhoo."[47]

Both the individuals on the island and their demands changed several times, and a number of emergencies arose requiring Coast Guard rescue missions. Additionally, the lighthouse was so badly damaged by fire that it had to be temporarily closed, much to the consternation of ships' crews and dockworkers. Once federal employees operating the lighthouse were withdrawn, the government shut off all electrical and water supplies. Immediately, however, popular public support encouraged by coverage in the *San Francisco Chronicle* supplied money, food, and materials (even a generator for the lighthouse). By July, however, such support began to wane. Although some of Nixon's cabinet officers and other advisers favored stronger action than was ultimately taken, his more liberal White House staffers on Native American affairs won out. While there is no clear indication that the president himself became involved in the details over the occupation of the island, those conducting the day-to-day tactics and overall strategy assumed that "he must have sympathized with our approach."[48]

In the end, Washington's strategy was "to let the controversy go out without a whimper, if that." Among Nixon's most liberal domestic advisers, Alcatraz became a "symbol inside the White House for the lack of attention to meet the unmet needs of the Indians of America." Consequently, the administration's response became "one of restraint and willingness to remedy this lack of attention and to look at these unmet needs," and the situation dragged on into 1971, trying the patience of both sides. On December 10, 1970, Ethel Kennedy somewhat belatedly threatened over the telephone in a conversation with Garment to "take the Indians' case to the public" unless the government resupplied power and water to the island. By that time there were only twenty remaining Indians (including children) on the island, and the situation "finally disintegrated into just a matter of petty crimes and squalor." Even the publisher of the *San Francisco Chronicle*, who had supplied the generator for the lighthouse, told Thomas E. Hannon, the regional director of the General Services Administration, that "the whole Alcatraz situation had soured [and] that the [remaining occupiers] were a filty [*sic*], drunken lot," who now refused to return the generator he had given them.[49]

Thus, the Nixon administration took no precipitous action against the takeover, preferring to outwait the occupiers of Alcatraz for a year and a half. At every phase of this potentially explosive situation, both the public and private language and recommendations of White House advisers remained so conciliatory and cautious that no use of force to evacuate the small group of Native Americans was ever seriously considered. According to Patterson, both sides knew that Alcatraz "was purely a PR thing. It wasn't territory, it wasn't land. . . . We both knew we were dealing with symbolism, and . . . very skillfully managed PR. The tourist boat would go out, and the Indians would shoot an arrow at the tourist boat. It was all expertly managed symbolism and the press went wild about it." The very valuable lesson Nixon's aides learned from this incident was that "to handle Indian militancy, you recognize it is symbolism from beginning to end, some reality but mostly symbolism, . . . and you handle it with a great deal of care."[50] The next major confrontation between Native American militants and the government would change the language but not the conciliatory approach of Nixon's advisers.

Wounded Knee

By far the most inflammatory Native American incident that the Nixon administration had to face occurred with the bloody confrontation at Wounded Knee, a small Indian settlement on the remote Pine Ridge Sioux Reservation in South Dakota—the site of a mass grave resulting from a military confrontation between the Sioux and the U.S. Army in 1890. For seventy-three days beginning on February 27, 1973, approximately two hundred Native Americans under the leadership of the militant American Indian Movement (AIM) looted and then burned down the trading post, destroyed the seven Indian homes in Wounded Knee by either torching them or using them for slaughterhouses and toilets, desecrated its two churches with political slogans and obscenities, destroyed a museum, took eleven elderly hostages, and then barricaded themselves against assault from both federal marshals and the Oglala Sioux, who considered the takeover a criminal act. The situation took on surrealist overtones when Richard Wilson, tribal head of the Oglala Sioux, planned an invasion of Wounded Knee, and AIM leaders announced the formation of an Independent Sioux Nation with Wounded Knee as its capital. Only a blockade of the roads leading to Wounded Knee by U.S. marshals prevented these two Native American groups from attacking one another.

About the only thing the two groups had in common at that time was the desire to see their 1868 treaty rights fulfilled. In fact, after a tentative agreement was reached in May, the Oglala Traditionalist Council "demanded" that three of the six AIM leaders, who had been arrested, be put on temporary probation so that they could attend a meeting with Washington representatives to discuss the treaty. This one area of agreement notwithstanding, AIM and the Oglala Sioux tribe represented diametrically opposed aspects of Native American life and culture: AIM leaders were largely urban, not reservation, Indians; their tactics and antics defied even the minimal democratic processes observed by the reservation Sioux and the elected tribal leaders on the Pine Ridge Sioux Reservation whom they wanted to replace with force. (One of the government's unstated problems at Wounded Knee was to preserve the fragile democratic steps already taken by the Oglala Sioux on the reservation toward self-determination against the violently anachronistic and undemocratic methods of the AIM.)[51]

The Nixon administration had learned well at Alcatraz the lesson of restraint when dealing with Native American militancy. Wounded Knee was a much more violent version of Indian guerrilla warfare, but no less vulnerable to the time-consuming democratic process of negotiation and compromise. At the same time, the administration was aware that the BIA tradition of dealing only with elected tribal leaders was "unrealistic" if for no other reason than that many tribal leaders were "not popularly elected in any sense." So it realized from the beginning that AIM would have to figure into the negotiation equation, despite its lack of commitment to democratic procedures. For example, between June 1971 and the attack on Wounded Knee, the Offices of Economic Opportunity (OEO) and other federal agencies allotted over $200,000 to AIM in grants and collected another $200,000 from private church and civil rights groups and individuals.[52]

Except for an October 1973 FBI report and some of Bradley Patterson's untranscribed shorthand notes, most of the Nixon records about Wounded Knee are now open. These documents verify the central role played by Patterson in guiding policy through Garment to Ehrlichman and ultimately to the president. Most important, they indicate that the White House, not the Department of the Interior or the Justice Department, controlled policy during the most confrontational situation to develop with Native Americans during the Nixon presidency. Although the White House kept a low profile in the matter, Nixon's aides were in charge of the evolving policy. On poorly typed half-sheet notepaper, Patterson kept his Washington superiors informed about the details of his negotiations and those of others with representatives of AIM and the Oglala Sioux.

From the beginning of the occupation of Wounded Knee, the public and private language of the administration insisted that AIM members were "fundamentally publicity-seekers—tough, experienced, charismatic—but essentially nihilistic in that they have no 'cause' except the column inch." Unlike the benefit of the doubt accorded the shifting demands of the Alcatraz Indians, such AIM leaders as Russell Means, Clyde Belecourt, Leonard Crow Dog, Carter Camp, Denis Banks, and Pedro Bissonette were not accorded any legitimate status. This was partly because the "illegal antics" of the group had been responsible for ransacking the BIA offices in Washington, D.C., in November 1972, but mainly because in taking hostages they had committed the much more serious felony of kidnapping. They were always described publicly as a "small irresponsible group . . . of lawbreakers totally unrepresentative of the American Indian people," unlike "responsible tribal Councils and Chairmen." Privately, White House aides referred to them in even stronger language as "incendiary extremists," "trigger-happy nuts," and "the 'we will die today' types" who "in a perverse way, want a massacre."[53]

Initially the demands of AIM focused on the issue of "the Trail of Broken Treaties," in particular the April 29, 1868, treaty with the Dakota Nation signed at Fort Laramie, then Wyoming Territory. This had been the title of a twenty-point AIM position paper presented during the November 1972 march on Washington. The administration had issued a lengthy reply to it in January after agreeing to set up a task force cochaired by Garment and Carlucci to investigate the charges of bad faith. However, since the November occupation of BIA headquarters, the task force had refused to meet with AIM representatives because of the criminal charges they faced. The same position had been taken at the beginning of the Wounded Knee incident: no negotiations until the hostages were released and criminal charges of kidnapping dropped. AIM leaders, however, insisted that Senator James Abourezk (Dem.-S.D.), chair of the Senate Interior Subcommittee on Indian Affairs, meet with them; that Senator Ted Kennedy (Dem.-Mass.), chair of the Senate Subcommittee on Administrative Practices and Procedures, personally examine their "problems"; that Senator William Fulbright, chair of the Senate Foreign Relations Committee, investigate the "broken treaties"; and that Ehrlichman (and possibly even Kissinger) negotiate directly and immediately with them.[54]

While the administration worried about the implications of being forced either to comply with or to renegotiate the 1868 treaty with the Sioux, after the armed confrontation at Pine Ridge its key concerns became "how to get that bunch of armed headline hunters out of Wounded Knee without loss of life" and how to keep Nixon's legislative program for Native Americans from being "side-tracked"—all without calling attention to the fact that the White House was calling the shots during this crisis. Early in the armed conflict Garment and Patterson acknowledged to Kenneth Cole, deputy assistant to the president on domestic affairs, and to Vice President Agnew that Wounded Knee was "wrappedup [sic] in the larger question of how well we've followed up on the effectiveness of our Indian program—and that something like this is important as an alternative to a military-like option which has almost unthinkable consequences." But Cole vetoed a suggestion for a press conference briefing, blaming Congress by implication "for the lack of progress on our legislation," because it would direct too much publicity on the White House. As a result, Garment realized that the administration risked appearing "to be over-conciliatory," without gaining any political advantage for the passage of Nixon's Indian legislation. He seemed to take comfort in the fact that conciliation was in part "only appearance; we are going to put the ringleaders on trial."[55]

At first, Patterson offered AIM militants free passage through the roadblocks to the occupiers "without fear of arrest," but by March 7, when only women and children who were residents of Wounded Knee before the takeover had left, the offer was rescinded. A grand jury convened on March 12 to hear evidence about the violations of federal law that had taken place on the reservation.[56] Around that same time a Native American leader, Hank Adams, offered to mediate with AIM because of the "need to reduce the possibilities of violence, injury, or loss of life." Adams was not an AIM member, had not participated in the Wounded Knee occupation, and had the confidence of some of the Oglala residents. Adams's March 13 letter to Nixon became the basis for a ten-point proposal to the government on March 19, but it was rejected out of hand by Washington because of the continued occupation. Adams met with Garment and an arrangement was worked out whereby, in return "for all White House involvement . . . remain[ing] confidential," it would pressure the departments of Justice and the Interior to minimize their internecine disputes and withdraw all their previous competitive proposals for ending the strife with the understanding that they would begin to negotiate on the basis of the ten points. In this manner "the White House would make no unwarranted interventions in the matter, although it was . . . willing to help construct the mechanics for negotiating a settlement."[57]

Inevitably, as relatively unproductive meetings between Nixon's representatives and both groups of Native Americans dragged on in the spring of 1973, there was talk within the administration about setting firm deadlines and ultimatums, raising the specter of removing AIM's militant activists from Wounded Knee by force. "We made some contingency plans for heavy occupation and invasion, but they were not used," Patterson later recalled. "They would have involved tremendous amounts of force. . . . We looked that contingency in the face and said, 'No.'" Such action was never officially recommended by White House personnel, "since moving in with adequate force would mean a large loss of life," but it came from other sources, including chief of the U.S. marshals in Pine Ridge and from Caspar W. Weinberger as head of HEW. Weinberger sent Garment a memorandum on March 14 that contained a report about how much more firmly the occupation of a Public Health Service Indian Hospital in Gallup, New Mexico, had been handled in January. The administration, he wrote, could not "let these Indian things go too far"; it was being "rapidly pushed into a kind of ridiculous position particularly with the media jumping up and down with excitement every night." Weinberger wanted the White House to take advantage of the violence by completely isolating Wounded Knee and thereby bringing the situation to an end as rapidly as possible, thereby thwarting a "series [of such incidents] all over the country." Despite such advice, from the beginning White House staffers had been against the use of "massive federal force," even if it was "necessary to hold the status quo for a while ... neither attack[ing] nor retreat[ing]" so as to avoid "an Indian-White Man, or Indian/Government confrontation."[58]

Nonetheless, neither Garment nor Patterson completely believed that his advice against use of force would be followed. In April, Patterson informed Garment that "our friend in Defense" had assured him no military action was being contemplated "*without written, signed authorization from the White House,*" and that this decision had "apparently shut off the pressure from Justice, until further notice." Over a year later, in September 1974, Patterson put a confidential "note for the record" in his files saying that (as he had suspected) Fred Buzhardt, general counsel to the Defense Department, had told him upon "informal" questioning that during the crisis there had indeed been a discussion about having the president declare a "civil disturbance" at Wounded Knee, requiring Department of Defense forces. "Fred remembered," according to Patterson's confidential note to himself, "that Ehrlichman raised it with the President at the time and the President was 'amenable,' as was [the] Justice [Department], but that Richardson and Haig were strongly against it [Haig being deputy chief of staff at the time] and it was not considered an issue ... which the President wanted to override Richardson and Haig on—so he didn't." Buzhardt also told Patterson, however, that "*no one he knew ever actually drafted a proposed Presidential order*" for the use of U.S. troops during the confrontation at Wounded Knee.[59]

An agreement was finally reached with AIM to end its occupation of Wounded Knee on May 9, 1973, seventy-three days after it started, making it "the longest sustained armed confrontation fought on western soil in American history." In the course of the controversy the administration concluded that continued "cosmetic and public relations type activities or the announcement of new directions, the implementation of which is not well thought out," had reached a point of diminishing returns. Criticism of the administration by the press finally began to diminish as reporters realized that they were "being used" by masters of Indian guerrilla theater, and articles such as "Bamboozle Me Not at Wounded Knee" appeared in print. Subsequently, publications by both Indians and Anglos admitted that the administration's "policy of restraint . . . prevailed . . . thereby avoiding massive bloodshed."[60]

Most important, Wounded Knee forced branches of the executive office outside the White House to face up to the multifaceted nature of the "Indian problem." It prompted the Department of the Interior finally to take steps to improve relations with Native Americans, including the formation of a National Indian Advisory Council; the creation of an Independent Agency for Indian Affairs in the Executive Office of the president; the formation of a Presidential Commission on Indian Land and Services Eligibility; support for the restoration of Menominee tribal status; the creation of a Cabinet Committee on Indian Affairs, with Weinberger as chair; the reorganization and reorientation of the BIA, giving it more law-enforcement capability but with more authority concentrated in tribal governments and tribal superintendents and less in Washington and area offices; and, finally, presidential support for a constitutional amendment making it impossible for the U.S. government unilaterally to "terminate" tribal status. According to this Interior memorandum, such an amendment was needed to "set aside the fear of termination." If it were supported by the president, Native Americans, in turn, would "without hesitation" back his legislative package.[61]

By August 1973 the Nixon administration had established four interagency groups to deal with Native American matters—none of which had "any clear mandate or extensive experience with Indian problems," according to White House staffer Geoffrey C. Shepard. Recognizing that the government had a special relationship to American Indians because of federal treaties, but that the "BIA alone, for one reason or another, was incapable of fulfilling that special relationship," the Nixon administration added to the bureaucratic maze in this instance rather than streamlining the structure along corporate lines. Even the National Tribal Council Association (NTCA) finally passed a resolution complaining about the confusion in Congress and the White House and the resultant delay in reorganizing the BIA.[62]

The final attempt by the Nixon administration to improve its relations with Native Americans occurred in August 1973 through an OMB task force that took responsibility for Native American rights and recommended a permanent federal structure outside the executive office to handle them. Such a structure did not materialize before Nixon left office, and the question of implementing or renegotiating treaties with the Sioux was also left hanging, although some progress was made to better meet the housing and educational needs of American Indians.[63] With Ehrlichman gone and Garment busy with Watergate-related duties, Nixon's Native American initiatives began to drift in 1974.

Civil rights—not the cause of dispute between Native Americans and the federal government when Nixon came to office—constituted another major spinoff and unintended consequence of Wounded Knee. In March 1973, a civil rights team began looking into possible violation of rights on the Pine Ridge Reservation itself, and in August the Civil Rights Division of the Department of Justice created an Office of Indian Rights. Although the Treaty of 1868 remained a major issue for traditional headmen and chiefs, more mainstream concerns with civil rights began surfacing among urban Native Americans, complicating ongoing negotiations because lingering tensions at Pine Ridge increasingly became civil rights ones as the BIA police attempted to enforce federal law in a tribal setting. When Vine Deloria, a distinguished Native American author, entered the picture at the beginning of 1974 as an intermediary over Sioux treaty rights, Patterson told him that the executive branch of government had done all it could under President Nixon on Native American matters, especially treaty rights. American Indians must finally realize, Patterson wrote to Garment, "that it is Congress which has been the party which has violated the [1868] treaty." As the trials of Russell Means and other AIM leaders dragged on into 1974, Patterson dutifully, but rather unenthusiastically, followed their progress (fearing "another Chicago 7 Spectacular") and began monitoring the "new" issue of Native American civil rights just as Nixon became consumed by Watergate in the spring and summer of 1974.[64]

Even though the Indian Self-Determination and Educational Assistance Act was passed in 1975, after Nixon had resigned as president, it stands as testimony to what he had set in motion. Many Native Americans viewed the 1975 act—which finally provided for direct negotiation between the tribes and the federal government to administer former BIA programs—as the most significant piece of legislation since the

New Deal's Indian Reorganization Act of 1934 for assimilating Native Americans using tribal culture as a springboard. In a retrospective following Nixon's resignation, the American Indian Press Association News Service concluded that "the Nixon administration . . . has been in the eyes even of the most critical observers one of the most active in Indian affairs since that of . . . Roosevelt in the 1930s and 1940s."[65] While no president before or after Nixon has completely resolved the complex issue of ending termination through tribal self-sufficiency, Nixon's record continues to compare favorably with that of all other occupants of the Oval Office since World War II, despite the numerous confrontational incidents he faced that they did not.

BEYOND NORMAL RELATIONS: NIXON AND THE SUPREME COURT

Since World War II, the Supreme Court has become a "major domestic policy maker" in the United States. As a result, no president's relationship to that judicial body can be ignored, especially if he is interested, as Nixon was, in serving as an agent for domestic change. The unique importance of Nixon's impact on the Court and its impact on him remains a largely unexamined topic. According to conventional wisdom, Nixon's contact with the Court was all negative—consisting of one prepresidential case he argued and lost in 1967, two decisions his administration lost (publication of the Pentagon Papers in 1971 and executive privilege in 1974),[66] and his two unsuccessful nominees, Clement F. Haynsworth, Jr., and G. Harrold Carswell. His postpresidential battles with the Supreme Court make Nixon one of the most litigious of modern presidents.

Before Nixon became president, the Supreme Court had initiated at least five major domestic policies, independent of Congress or the executive branch, in the areas of school desegregation, reapportionment, privacy rights, criminal justice reform, and obscenity law. Under Nixon the Court initiated another major domestic policy by legalizing first-trimester abortions (further extending privacy rights). During the Nixon administration, however, more unanticipated precedents in case law took place under the Burger Court—to which Nixon had appointed four members, including Chief Justice Warren E. Burger himself. "In many ways," the constitutional specialist Martin Shapiro has written, "the transition from the Warren [to the Burger] Court is like that from the Marshall to the Taney Court,"[67] meaning that court-watchers mistakenly assumed that the "interventionist" courts under John Marshall from 1801 to 1835 and Earl Warren from 1953 to 1969 would be followed by relatively passive ones under Roger B. Taney and Warren E. Burger.

Of Nixon's successful appointments to the Supreme Court, Justice Harry A. Blackmun played the most crucial, if unexpected, role in changing the legal status of women because of his consistent support of abortion rights since writing the majority opinion in *Roe v. Wade* (1973). This is not to say that the Burger Court was as "interventionist" in the area of sex discrimination as the Warren Court had been on racial issues, because the Warren Court logically built on Reconstruction legislation from the last century. In contrast, when it began to expand equal rights for women in the 1970s, the Burger Court could draw only on case-law precedents set in race discrimination cases from the 1950s and 1960s.[68] Moreover, one of Nixon's appointments, future Chief Justice William H. Rehnquist, proved no friend of women's rights. While Nixon did not always agree with the expansion of rights by the Burger Court to African-Americans, women, and other minorities beyond what they had been under the New Deal and Great Society, he ultimately complied, in keeping with a note he once scribbled on a news summary. He might criticize individual decisions of the Supreme Court, it said, but he always defended it as an institution.[69]

Nixon inherited a complicated situation with respect to Supreme Court appointments. In 1968 Johnson unsuccessfully nominated his close friend and adviser, Associate Justice Abe Fortas, to replace Earl Warren as chief justice. Warren stayed on as a lame duck, but Nixon wanted to replace him as soon as possible. While the president was considering such possibilities as Thomas Dewey, Associate Justices Potter Stewart and John Harlan, and his own attorney general, John Mitchell, Fortas became involved in a scandal that forced him to resign from the Court: he had been accepting $20,000 a year from a man under investigation by the Securities and Exchange Commission. This delighted Nixon because it gave him two vacancies to fill with what he hoped would be law-and-order conservatives. Haldeman's handwritten notes also indicate that the Fortas affair demonstrated Nixon's early interest in using his staff to investigate possible financial wrongdoing by those he disliked.[70]

Investigations aside, his first two attempts to nominate southern conservative associate justices to the Supreme Court showed him and some of his advisers operating so ineffectively that few expected any innovative precedents to be set by a "Nixon" Court under Burger. It is generally true that the nominations of both Haynsworth and Carswell represented attempts by Nixon to implement a "southern strategy," but other elements of that short-lived approach exhibited more political astuteness. There is no doubt that Chief Justice Burger's reputation as a constitutional conservative pleased powerful southern Senators and state leaders, encouraging the administration to continue this practice of "stick[ing] it to the liberal, Ivy League clique who thought the Court was their own private playground." Even granting the fact that Harry Dent, Nixon's chief southern strategist, may not have been operating up to speed on these attempted appointments, the president's other advisers did not perform much better.[71]

In particular, John Mitchell, Nixon's most trusted adviser on judicial appointments, proved unusually remiss in providing the president with equally qualified potential candidates after the successful Burger nomination early in the summer of 1969. Like the attempts by other modern presidents to "pack" the Supreme Court, the Carswell nomination deservedly failed. Nixon admitted to me what others had long suspected: he had nominated Carswell out of anger and stubbornness following Haynsworth's defeat, which he always believed was unwarranted.[72]

Nixon and his staff went on to make much more careful selections after Carswell. But why were the Haynsworth and Carswell nominations so badly handled? In retrospect, it appears to have been a combination of presidential arrogance and surprising indifference after the success of the low-keyed, dignified approach in appointing Burger to replace Earl Warren as chief justice.[73] (Although the administration made the announcement of Warren's replacement a major public relations coup, the nomination was carefully concealed and handled with the precision of a military campaign.) Its efficient effort was aided by the fact that Burger promoted his own candidacy most skillfully. With Haynsworth and Carswell, inferior public relations and congressional liaison work prevailed. Inexplicably, for example, Nixon personally disengaged himself from the nominating process in these two unsuccessful nominations, and his closest liberal advisers on domestic policy did not become personally involved in either the selection process or its promotion. Instead, the president relied too much on Mitchell alone and on much more conservative, secondary-level aides such as Bryce Harlow and Harry Dent, whose crude pressure tactics all failed, although Ehrlichman was technically overseeing their actions (a fact that Ehrlichman carefully ignored in his memoirs when criticizing Mitchell's handling of the Haynsworth nomination.)[74]

The president and his aides did not appear to perceive either of these nominations as crises that required the urgency and total concentration they demonstrated on the environment and Native American policy. Perhaps Nixon should have tried harder to find a woman conservative enough to appoint, to offset liberal opposition to conservative male nominees. Here again, he made only a halfhearted effort when searching for his last two appointments to the Court. He told me he could never find a conservative enough woman qualified for the Supreme Court.[75]

Nixon might also have fared better with his nominations had he followed Pat Buchanan's advice to appoint an Italian-American after Fortas resigned in May 1969 over disclosure of questionable financial associations, in order to offset "criticism of ending the Jewish seat on the court." Instead, sectionalism and ideology, not ethnicity, were the determining factors for the White House. Moreover, Jews on the White House staff adamantly opposed making this a public issue in the appointment process.[76]

Moreover, the calm, logical legalese of the memoranda written by Clark R. Mollenhoff, deputy counsel to the president, did not help counter the emotional association being made between the questionable private financial dealings (and possible conflict-of-interest decisions) of Fortas and Haynsworth. Specifically, Haynsworth's negative decisions in cases involving labor unions led to a charge of conflict of interest in one of them during the confirmation process. While the issue had been subject to several investigations, all absolved Haynsworth. But certain senators refused to drop the issue.[77]

Once Senator Birch Bayh (Dem.-Ind.) made these unsubstantiated allegations, liberals opposed to Haynsworth for ideological reasons could hide their opposition behind these charges. Nixon's decision to make his letter of support for Carswell to Senator William B. Saxbe public reflected a similar reliance on legal logic rather than on the candidate's qualifications, which in Carswell's case were negligible. In this letter Nixon claimed that rejection of another of his nominees would constitute an attack on his constitutional authority to make such appointments. It is now clear that a confluence of ideology, timing, and presidential management is crucial for any successful nomination. No such convergence occurred on these two ill-fated nominations.[78]

With the exception of Harlow, perhaps inexperience (Dent did not always keep Harlow informed of his ill-advised attempts to use major corporations to pressure recalcitrant senators) and overwork (many of

Nixon's liberal advisers became occupied with the Alcatraz crisis in November 1969) can account partially for the unsatisfactory staff work. Since he did not place himself above the fray on other domestic (or foreign) issues, the president's personal reluctance to engage in arm-twisting tactics with individual senators on these two nominations remains a mystery. Consequently, his protestations about standing by Haynsworth and Carswell to the very end ring hollow, and his threats not to meet with individual senators who opposed them juvenile for such a seasoned politician.[79] Nixon only belatedly tried to come to Haynsworth's rescue in October and by that time it was too late for strongarm tactics, especially when they were ineptly carried out by his aides. Despite the president's public address on Haynsworth, the Senate rejected his nomination.[80]

Nixon's personal efforts were even more halfhearted and those of his staff even worse with respect to Carswell, a mediocre nominee if there ever was one. Carswell's history of making racist remarks immediately surfaced, along with his high reversal record as an associate judge on the Fifth Circuit Court of Appeals. Nixon told his staff to stop the fight for the nomination almost a month before the final vote on the Senate floor, blaming modern Republicans whom he swore never to invite to the White House. In an order that was never carried out, but which presaged similar ones in the future, he told Ehrlichman that he wanted all the senators voting against Carswell to be given the "Haynsworth Test," meaning a rigorous financial check and determination of whether they belonged to private clubs that discriminated on the basis of race or had signed mortgages with racially restrictive covenants.[81] This after-the-fact invective, however, does not explain Nixon's rather detached approach to appointing two conservative southerners to the Supreme Court. It was a mistake that he did not repeat—either tactically or ideologically.

The question remains: Did Richard Nixon place the Supreme Court above the partisan ferocity with which he usually conducted political activity? Not when it came to trying to go beyond the "court-packing" efforts of both FDR and LBJ with sons of the Old South—only when it came to fighting for their confirmations. He had no compunction, for example, about having Mitchell begin to gather information about Justice William O. Douglas's "nonjudicial sources of income," given Fortas's sudden resignation over similar revelations. When Nixon also asked Mitchell to write "a confidential report on how many [other] justices of the Supreme Court owned stock in corporations," the attorney general demurred. Such information, he said, could be obtained only through the "rather devious means" of tax returns, which, if it ever came to light, "would present real trouble for the president."[82]

Nixon's relations as president with the Supreme Court began with two debacles over unsuccessful nominations and then ran the gamut from executive privilege to freedom of the press to desegregation to impoundment to abortion rights (all discussed in subsequent chapters). Despite his four appointments—Burger, Blackmun, Powell, and Rehnquist—Nixon found, as so many presidents before and after him, that the Court could not be relied on to deliver the opinions he wanted, especially on issues he deemed critical. Nonetheless, the intensity of his political and intellectual interaction with the Supreme Court before, during, and after his presidency outstripped that of FDR and LBJ.

These examples of Nixon's policies on domestic issues such as the environment, Native Americans, and relations with the Supreme Court indicate that he could go beyond the New Deal and the Great Society plans as an agent for change only when his more liberal advisers were strongly engaged in the process. As the following chapters document, Nixon also exceeded the accomplishments of the New Deal and the Great Society in the areas of civil rights, social welfare spending, domestic and international economic restructuring, urban parks, government reorganization, land-use initiatives, revenue sharing, draft reform, pension reform, and spending for the arts and humanities. In particular, his proposals on national health insurance and welfare reform were so far in advance of his time that congressional liberals preferred to oppose them than to allow Nixon to take credit for upstaging them. Myriad studies of Watergate have dimmed memories on these topics, but "tell [us] little about policy formulation" or anything else "in relation to substantive [domestic] policy"[83] during the Nixon administration, especially when it comes to his controversial and comprehensive plans for restructuring the executive branch of government along corporate lines.

2

THE NIXONIAN SYSTEM OF CORPORATE GOVERNANCE

After a third of a century of power flowing from the people and the states to Washington, it is time for a New Federalism in which power, funds and responsibility will flow from Washington to the states and to the people.

—Nixon, message to Congress, August 13, 1969

Before Watergate, few of us paid much attention to one reform aspect of the Nixon phenomenon: government reorganization based on his particular administrative style. Following his resignation, opponents charged that Nixon's "managerial nature" had contributed to producing Watergate because they convinced themselves that certain administrative reforms represented an attempt "to establish fascist dictatorship." To compound matters, Nixon exhibited little interest during his prepresidential career in what was to become almost an obsession once he entered the Oval Office, namely, "to get working control of the Executive Branch of the Federal Government."[1] This compulsion to manage the federal bureaucracy led him to pursue several controversial administrative reorganizational plans.

Rather than bringing to the presidency an innate Machiavellian approach to government, as his critics have charged, Nixon probably started out with a simple "fascination with How Things Work." As John Osborne has noted, he waged a "continuing struggle for neatness" and for "disciplined order and precision." My interview with John Ehrlichman in 1984 confirmed Nixon's concern with the details of complicated governmental operations—a characteristic exacerbated by anything smacking of intrigue, such as secret negotiations with foreign powers or the Watergate cover-up.[2]

In Nixon's search for orderly governing procedures, unpleasant memories of cabinet meetings as vice president in the 1950s and pleasant memories of the political support he had always received from large and small businesses naturally led him away from cabinet government theories toward corporate ones, his campaign rhetoric about "cabinet government" notwithstanding. Immediately after his election he created the Lindsay Task Force on Organization of the Executive Branch. In April 1969, on the basis of its recommendations, he appointed Roy L. Ash, founder and CEO of Litton Industries, to head the President's Advisory Council on Executive Organization (PACEO). Also known as the Ash Council, its members—four top corporate executives and Democratic governor of Texas John Connally—were to brainstorm about the specifics of executive reorganization.[3]

In three months the Ash Council targeted six major areas for reorganization. The administration made successful structural changes in four of these: foreign economic policy, environmental protection, social programs, and the executive branch. Following first the Lindsay Task Force's and then the Ash Council's recommendations, Nixon made a series of governmental reorganization proposals to Congress on March 25, 1971. If adopted, they "would have represented the most comprehensive restructuring of the federal government in U.S. history."[4]

The appointment of Connally to the Ash Council marked the beginning of a series of positions that this Democrat and former protégé of Lyndon Johnson would hold in the Nixon administration, much to the irritation of many Republicans in Texas, including George Bush. Nixon apparently became more and more "impressed by the man's savvy and ruthlessness" as they talked politics after meetings of the Ash Council in San Clemente. Following this appointment, Nixon made Connally a member of the prestigious Foreign Advisory Intelligence Board, and finally convinced him to become his secretary of the treasury from February 1971 to May 1972, with the assurance that he would be the president's "counselor-advisor-friend . . . [and] closest confidant." Although he campaigned for Nixon's reelection, on the president's advice Connally did not formally announce that he had left the Democratic party to become a Republican until May 1, 1973.[5]

Connally, the only politically experienced member of the Ash Council, convinced a less than enthusiastic cabinet to pursue extensive restructuring of the executive branch of government. While the president supported reorganization, he remained very pessimistic about its chances for success because he believed that the issue had no "sex appeal" and would "upset too many apple carts" if submitted to Congress in any comprehensive form.[6] Moreover Nixon's own views on the subject were not highly developed. If he followed any general guidelines about management and decision making before becoming president, they appear to have been based on a "crisis syndrome." With embarrassing candor, he detailed in his 1962 book, Six Crises, how he politicized certain personal events in his career. By 1968, there existed little distinction in his own mind between the two. This mind-set served him unusually well until he faced the most serious crisis of his political career—Watergate.[7]

While substantive administrative ideas and decision-making patterns are distinguished by their absence in Six Crises, the book clearly informed its readers that long before becoming president, Nixon had characteristically exhibited risk taking, street fighting, and attack and overkill tactics in personal situations, correctly or incorrectly deemed to be political predicaments. The Age of Nixon, like the cold war era with which it partly coincides, was born and died in a series of real and perceived crises. In addition to this gut-level crisis approach to making decisions, we also know of several experiences that had shaped Nixon's thinking about management before 1968. First, his impatience with red tape and bureaucratic lethargy dated from his World War II experiences as a civilian with the Office of Price Administration in 1941 and later as a naval officer from 1942 to 1945.[8] Second, his years as vice president account for some of his later administrative style. Under Ike's demeaning tutelage, he believed that he had learned how *not* to operate in the Oval Office. This was particularly true of Eisenhower's National Security Council (NSC) system, which effectively excluded Nixon from the informal decision-making meetings that preceded the formal ones.[9]

Acknowledging this exclusion from NSC meetings, he told me that his ideas about management were "in reaction to, not an emulation of," Eisenhower's. "Cabinet government is a myth and won't work," he said. A president should "never rely on his cabinet . . . no [president] in his right mind submits anything to his cabinet . . . it is ridiculous . . . boring."[10] While his apprenticeship as vice president left him with strong impressions about how the cabinet in general, and the NSC in particular, should not function, his political eclipse in the 1960s did little to hone his administrative skills.

Despite the doubts he harbored since serving as vice president about the effectiveness of cabinets for policy formulation, during the 1968 presidential campaign Nixon coined the term and advocated "cabinet government" in order to criticize the centralization of power within the executive office of the president during the Kennedy and Johnson administrations. (Kennedy had been the first modern president to break with the traditional cabinet-based system for policy making, saying—as Nixon would later—that he was "determined to gain presidential control over the sprawling bureaucracy." After Kennedy's death, Johnson continued the trend toward centralization of policy making inside the White House.)[11]

Nixon campaigned on the promise to decentralize policy-making authority and to restore cabinet members to their status as "Deputy Presidents," the prime policy managers and the president's principal counsel in developing major administration policy options. "I don't want a government of yes men," he told the American people over and over again; "officials of [my] new administration will not have to check their consciences at the door, or leave their powers of independent judgment at home."[12] But Nixon's experiences with cabinet government under Eisenhower were too negative to permit any abiding belief in this form of presidential decision making. All along he intended "to keep cabinet meetings to a minimum," on the grounds that "the better each Cabinet member performed his job, the less time I should have to spend discussing it with him, except for major questions of politics or policy."[13] After winning the election, Nixon's "reorganized and strengthened Cabinet" turned out to be made up of "good managers who could immerse themselves in detail." Instead of appointing independent "stars," he decided that he did not want "people who were too strong-willed to act as part of the team." Instead, he "trade[d] flamboyance for competence."[14] Despite having taken this precaution, Nixon succumbed on occasion to his own attraction for flamboyant advisers with grandiose visions; as a result, some of his first executive appointees had such strongly opposing views that cabinet meetings sometimes degenerated into unproductive adversarial sessions.

To counter this debilitating aspect of cabinet government, the president began to centralize most decision-making power within his White House staff. When this system became too rigid, it produced a "results at any price approach."[15] At worst, Nixon's reorganizational plans resulted on occasion in effectiveness becoming more important than morality or constitutionality. At best, they produced exaggerated expectations about the effectiveness of structural reform. Neither extreme can be blamed on the reforms themselves; each rests with personnel who misused them.

NIXON'S SYSTEM OF OUTSIDER AND INSIDER ADVISERS

As he turned away from cabinet government, Nixon increasingly turned away from cabinet members who did not make good team players. Not entirely abandoning his personal preference to have "swashbuckler, blunt men with an air of command" around him,[16] Nixon put together an effective array of insider and outsider advisers within the White House until Watergate deprived him of several key advisers when he needed them most.

After Nixon's election in 1969 the initial momentum for change in most domestic and foreign affairs came from such freethinking outsiders as Roy Ash, Robert Finch, Pat Moynihan, Henry Kissinger, and later John Connally. All of these men appealed to Nixon's preference for bold action, and grandiose schemes. With the exception of Finch, none had been closely associated with him before his election and so fit the flamboyant "feudal bastard" mold of modern American politics discussed in the introduction. During the first administration Moynihan and Kissinger influenced certain crucial details about, but not usually the broad outlines of, domestic and foreign policies. Encouraged by such advisers during his first years in office, Nixon embarked on a systematic risk-taking course in both foreign and domestic policy that attempted to update American Federalism through government reorganization and revenue sharing; to revamp the entire welfare system with the idea of a guaranteed annual income (which he preferred to call a negative income tax); to expand spending dramatically for both environmental and social service programs; to promote a "grand design" for U.S. diplomacy based on the Nixon Doctrine, on devaluation of the dollar and other foreign economic policies, on ending (after widening) the war in Vietnam, and on establishing rapprochement with China and détente with the USSR.

The impact of the freethinking outsiders on Nixonian policies and attitudes is easy to trace. Ash convinced Nixon that only dramatic reorganization of the executive branch would allow him to concentrate on policy, not process; Moynihan and Finch sparked the president's interest in welfare reform and influenced his thinking (both negatively and positively) on race relations and desegregation. Kissinger's own paranoia coincided with

Nixon's, leading to unnecessary covert actions in carrying out the best and the worst of the president's foreign policy; at the same time, Kissinger brought to the administration an intellectual flamboyance that made the press, the public, and perhaps even the president think that more had been accomplished diplomatically than actually was. Connally, whom Nixon appointed secretary of the treasury in 1971, almost single-handedly talked the president into both wage and price controls and devaluation of the dollar. Connally also played a critical role in two of Nixon's most innovative environmental decisions, favoring creation of the Environmental Protection Agency and a Department of Natural Resources—both against the wishes of the farm bloc.

Perhaps of all his freethinking outsider advisers, Nixon was most impressed by Connally, who usually does not figure prominently in books about his presidency. Nixon wanted Connally for his vice president in 1968, when he was still a Democrat and governor of Texas. From the time they first met, Nixon thought Connally understood him better than any of his other political associates. In turn, when this apostate Democrat became secretary of the treasury, he became Nixon's "greatest salesman." And for good reason. The president, after all, had assured Connally that he was the "only man in [the] Dem[ocratic] party that c[ou]ld be P[resident] . . . [and] we have to have someone in the Cabinet who *is* capable of being [P]resident." Had Nixon completed his second term, he apparently hoped that Connally would succeed him in 1976. Despite disparaging remarks from such important advisers as Kissinger, who thought that "Connally's swaggering self-assurance was Nixon's Walter Mitty image of himself," the president strongly relied on Connally for economic and political advice during the short period he served in his administration. "Only three men in America understand the use of power," Nixon confided to Arthur Burns. "I do. John [Connally] does. And," he grudgingly added, "I guess Nelson [Rockefeller] does."[17]

Nonetheless, the political-broker insiders increasingly gained ascendancy over the freethinking outsiders within the first Nixon administration, and Nixon's plans to reorganize became more corporate in nature and more central to his thinking. These insiders were gray-flannel types, many of whom Nixon had known for years: John D. Ehrlichman and H. R. Haldeman, the president's two closest aides; Leonard Garment, the liberal Democratic counterpart to Moynihan among Nixon's inside advisers; Arthur Burns, counselor to the president and later head of the Federal Reserve Board; Melvin Laird, secretary of defense; John Mitchell, attorney general; and George Shultz, secretary of labor and later head of the Office of Management and Budget. In Nixon's first years in office, Ehrlichman, Garment, Laird, and Shultz (later Reagan's secretary of state) became dominant insiders on policy, while Haldeman concentrated on office procedures and organizational matters. Fewer of these political-broker insiders proved themselves temporary adherents of Nixon, in keeping with modern bastard feudalism, than the freethinking outsiders with whom he also consulted.

Ehrlichman, aided by John Whitaker, deputy assistant to the president and later undersecretary of the Interior Department, significantly influenced the content of Nixon's environmental legislation, especially in connection with land-use policies. Ehrlichman and Garment were instrumental in the formulation of both his civil rights and Native American policies. Burns became the unexpected champion of revenue sharing within the administration. Shultz confined his advice largely to economics and labor, but proved remarkably influential in desegregation matters and countering discrimination in the work force as well. Before Kissinger's ascendancy, Laird could be seen brokering on a wide variety of topics, from foreign policy to the volunteer army, revenue sharing, government reorganization, and Vietnamization. If there is a single underestimated, understudied influential figure in the first Nixon administration, it is the most diffident of the political-broker insiders, Melvin Laird—one of the few key persons, in addition to John Mitchell, who died without having written a memoir about his controversial role in the rise and fall of Richard Nixon.

But this emerging system of insider and outsider advisers did not always work. During his first year in office, for example, Nixon became increasingly irritated with his failure to control the actions of the secretaries of both Health, Education and Welfare and Housing and Urban Development, and those they appointed to administer certain programs. Equally dissatisfying were Nixon's relationships with Secretary of the Interior Walter Hickel and HUD Secretary George Romney. All proved more liberal than the president on certain issues, but his problems with them went beyond political ideology into the less clear-cut realm of how independently cabinet members and their appointees should function.

Romney (and to a lesser degree Finch) appointed subordinates who exceeded the White House policy on sensitive issues such as desegregation and the Model Cities Program—an urban renewal program that "was to have been the crowning achievement" of Johnson's Great Society, only to be turned into a pork-barrel operation designed to influence congress-men on important committees. Although Republican conservatives in Congress had targeted it for cancellation under the new administration, Romney and Floyd Hyde, his assistant secretary in charge of the Model Cities Program (and to a lesser degree Moynihan), sided with big-city mayors in trying to preserve it. For example, when Nixon told Moynihan he wanted the program "killed," the head of the Urban Affairs Council purportedly replied: "Now you worry about our treaties in Southeast Asia and I'll worry about our treaties with the cities."[18]

Two separate White House task forces evaluated the Model Cities Program, and both concluded it should be continued. Faced with these reports and opposition from his own cabinet members, Nixon approved $2.3 billion to fund the Model Cities Program from 1969 to 1973. In 1974 it was made part of special revenue sharing for community development, and funding continued "at a rate that was consistent with the target fig-ures the Johnson Administration had originally given to Congress." Romney may have won on this issue, but he lost the president's confi-dence in the process.[19]

Although Romney did not leave the administration until 1973, when he was replaced by a Nixon loyalist, John Lynn, Nixon threatened to fire him several times; but he apparently feared that it might create the same political fallout as had the forced resignations of Leon Panetta, director of the HEW Office for Civil Rights, and Secretary of the Interior Hickel when he moved too independently on environmental and antiwar matters. Other disagreements Nixon had with Romney included the latter's oppo-sition to the original Family Assistance Program (discussed in chapter 4); his criticism of the Ash Council's report on government reorganization; and his early support of wage and price controls, before Nixon became persuaded on this issue. The fact that Nixon disagreed with Romney on so many issues in addition to the Model Cities Program and still retained him is an indication of how difficult it is for modern presidents to control their own cabinet members, let alone the burgeoning executive-branch bureaucracy.

CORPORATE REORGANIZATION, NIXON-STYLE

Almost all of the transitional task forces appointed during the interreg-num period indicated to Nixon that he had inherited unwieldy White House and executive office staffs, with major departments resembling badly managed companies. That Nixon should have turned to corporate management techniques is not surprising given the composition of the Ash Council and Topsy-like growth of the president's own bureaucracy, with its overlapping jurisdictions and interchangeable personnel. This executive bureaucracy grew from four agencies employing 570 people in 1969 to twenty agencies and more than 6,000 employees by 1972.[20]

Through a combination of legislative and administrative actions during his first four years in office, Nixon had made unprecedented progress toward creating a corporate government, including reorganization of executive agencies by function; creation of the Urban Affairs Council (UAC), which was subsumed into the Domestic Council; transformation of the Bureau of the Budget into the Office of Management and Budget (OMB); establishment of the Office of Energy Policy; restructuring of the National Security Council; and subtle, limited manipulations of the civil-service personnel system. On February 27, 1970, the *New York Times* reported that of fifty-seven actions taken by the president to reorganize government programs, forty-three were administrative and only fourteen required congressional approval.[21]

Operating on advice from the Ash Council, Nixon reorganized the federal government, one of his most lasting achievements. By the time he resigned from office he had replaced the Department of the Post Office with a public corporation less subject to political patronage; merged the Peace Corps and Vista into one agency called Action; and created six new domestic advisory boards: the UAC, which became the Domestic Council; the Council on Environmental Quality (this was established at the initiative of Congress, but was effectively utilized by Nixon); the Rural Affairs Council; the Council on Executive Reorganization; the Council on International Economic Policy; and the Council on Economic Policy. Nixon also approved of establishing the Environmental Protection Agency and recommended that the functions of the Atomic Energy Commission be divided into two new agencies, the Nuclear Regulatory Commission and the Energy Research and Development Administration—both of which came into existence under President Ford. He also created the Office of Child Development and the National Oceanic and Atmospheric Administration.[22]

Roy Ash had convinced Nixon early in his presidency of the necessity of bold government reorganization, but it did not become a crisis issue until the beginning of his second term. Each of his subsequent reorganizational attempts from 1970 to 1973 brought him closer to a corporate ideal, but he never did achieve it fully.

To understand the corporate nature of Nixon's proposals, it must be understood that a noticeable managerial change occurs in businesses once four hundred people are employed. It stands to reason that drastic increases in personnel will force organizational changes in government also. After the 1920s the largest, most diversified corporations in the United States began to restructure along horizontal or functional, rather than vertical, lines. Once these large, vertically integrated firms experimented with decentralized strategies, it was only a matter of time before the government in Washington, as it expanded during and after World War II, would also consider organizing departments horizontally by function. Under Truman and Eisenhower, the two postwar Hoover commissions introduced these decentralized, functional concepts, which the Ash Council simply carried to their logical conclusions.

Nixon received two kinds of advice from the Ash Council. The first recommended horizontal *and* decentralized corporate designs, and stressed the "values of economy and efficiency, span of control, policies-administration dichotomies, straight lines of authority, and accountability." The second consisted of such advanced corporate theories as management by objectives (MbO), which Nixon ultimately adopted in 1973 to transform the Bureau of the Budget into the Office of Management and Budget— almost a year after he tried to collapse traditional departments along functional lines. This transformation came on the heels of the failure of the Performance Measures System launched in 1971 as a spinoff from the Planning Programming Budgeting System (PPBS), originally introduced in 1965 under the Johnson administration. Although the Ash Council adapted MbO to accommodate the differences between government and private business management, there are some who still claim that it was an ill-conceived and impossible task since the procedure had worked only imperfectly in the private sector.[23]

The MbO system was not intended to save money, to decide among competing programs, or even to be a means for the White House to mandate priorities for individual departments. It simply allowed the president more influence in facilitating the achievement of budgetary objectives, and thus OMB represented the most important structural change instituted by the Nixon administration. It could even be viewed as his most "imperialistic" achievement, because "OMB is on paper the single most powerful managerial unit in the government." Since Congress failed to establish a countervailing force to OMB by creating the Congressional Budget Office in its 1974 budget reform legislation, only the CIA and the

Defense Department have successfully challenged OMB's budget-setting powers.[24]

The establishment of the Office of Management and Budget remains one of the most influential management changes initiated by Nixon, even though the Ash Council's Reorganizational Plan No. 2 of 1970, which suggested it, initially gave more power to the Domestic Council. While the power of the Domestic Council declined rapidly once Ehrlichman was no longer a presence in the White House, OMB's review procedures based on central clearance of all department, agency, and commission budgets *before* they are submitted to Congress have been institutionalized by Nixon's successors because of their power to evaluate program performance and to control spending. David Stockman's prominence as budget director in the first Reagan administration was not an accident or the invention of supply-side economists. It was a reflection of a basic structural change that Nixon had brought about when he replaced the old Bureau of the Budget with the Office of Management and Budget. OMB had monitoring and investigatory powers that gave it greater influence than ever before on the budgets of all government agencies and departments.[25]

A much more controversial but, in the long run, less substantive aspect of Nixon's suggested governmental reforms involved the reorganization of the Office of Economic Opportunity (OEO). By July 1969 the Nixon administration planned to send legislation to Congress on four major domestic issues: welfare reform, revenue sharing, comprehensive manpower policy, and the OEO, the agency established under President Johnson to aid the poor. All emphasized work, rehabilitation, retraining, and better standards of living for individuals and families at local community levels.[26] All ran into liberal opposition to the president's attempt to turn OEO into a research and development agency by transferring ongoing programs into other agencies and, aside from his handling of desegregation, probably triggered the most partisan response.

SHOWDOWN OVER THE OFFICE OF ECONOMIC OPPORTUNITY

During his 1968 presidential campaign, Nixon had been generally critical of Johnson's antipoverty programs. In his first month in office, it became clear that OEO would be targeted as an example not only of the Great Society's waste and inefficiency but also of its organizational incoherence in addressing the poverty problems facing the nation. Most of Nixon's aides, especially those working on reorganizing the executive branch, reinforced his suspicions about OEO. For example, all preliminary and final recommendations from the interregnum Lindsay Task Force and later the Ash Council consistently called for removing all OEO activities from the executive office, except for those "policy making and management functions appropriate to the Presidential level of attention." Even these development functions of OEO would be transferred to the Domestic Council, where they would be relegated to evaluations of federal social programs. In March 1969 Nixon requested exact information about the number of OEO appointments he could make. As it turned out, the president should have been able to control OEO functions through careful reassignments and new appointments—an option he only partially used because insider advisers such as Bryce Harlow kept telling him: "At present the entire [OEO] operation functions virtually independent of your administration; [it is] as if the previous administration were still in command." To which Nixon replied: "I want immediate action on these characters . . . give me a plan."[27]

Unfortunately, most of the plans he reviewed targeted the OEO Legal Services Program, a sacred cow of congressional liberals. All of Nixon's public statements on this controversial program, those of his aides, and those of the Lindsay Task Force and the Ash Council praised its work as a "unique federal program which extends the benefits of the adversary process to those who do not have the ability to seek legal aid."[28] With the exception of Howard ("Howie") Phillips, Rumsfeld's successor at OEO, however, both the public and private rhetoric of Nixon and his aides insisted on the value of the Legal Services Program, in contrast to their much more negative comments about the Peace Corps and even Head Start.

So it is difficult to prove through documentation whether their determined effort to destroy OEO contained a "hidden agenda" also aimed at destroying the Legal Services Program. There is no doubt that the Nixon administration suspected the political motivation of Legal Services lawyers, and desired to avoid embarrassing confrontations involving class action or individual suits against executive branch agencies and departments. Not a single White House staffer thought that lawyers, often Democratic holdovers, working for OEO's Legal Services Program should be a party to litigation against executive branch departments.

According to a top-secret transcript of the second meeting of the UAC on February 3, 1969, the president ordered a council member to "move ahead at full speed on the final resolution" on the future of the poverty program and the Office of Economic Opportunity, with the intent of "spinning off matured OEO programs to the line departments."[29] Late in February, Nixon personally wrote to Finch that he was transferring certain special OEO programs such as Head Start to HEW, "not for housekeeping but housecleaning purposes." The president concluded: "The purpose of the reorganization is to do more for our children, but also to eliminate overstaffing, overlapping, and inefficiency in administration." When Finch responded with an analysis of Head Start's failures, recommending increased funding in several specific areas, Nixon tersely wrote: "no increases in any poverty program until more evidence is in." Around the same time he told Haldeman: "I want some action taken immediately to clean up this [OEO] outfit. (Moynihan objects but Burns thinks it is essential and I agree.)"[30]

Believing that the functions of OEO "should be spun off into other departments," the president appointed Donald Rumsfeld as OEO director. Nixon had agreed to a two-year extension of OEO in June 1969, so that Rumsfeld could proceed with reorganizing the agency, appointing new personnel, and reviewing all its previous activities, but House conservatives (including Gerald Ford) complicated this task by introducing an amendment at the end of 1969 that would turn all grant-making for OEO over to the states. Liberals immediately charged the administration with favoring this approach over a two-year extension.[31] Part of the problem was that OEO reorganizational plans kept being leaked to the press—to the point where Nixon scribbled rhetorical questions in the margins of news summaries from 1969 to 1973: "Why can't they keep this quiet until I approve?" and "Can't we do a better job in keeping such plans out of [the] papers until we're ready?"[32]

But the main problem was that the White House often moved without consulting Rumsfeld, or left him dangling before congressional committees. For example, in November 1969 Rumsfeld believed that the White House was not supporting his opposition to the so-called Murphy amendment, which would have given each governor veto power over the OEO Legal Services Program funded by that state without the OEO directors being able to override the veto. This issue arose over Nixon's proposal to turn the Office of Legal Services into a separate government corporation chartered by Congress and funded at the local level with revenue-sharing funds. Since it was evident that local officials might choose not to use federal funds for such antipoverty programs, critics feared for its survival. Women and Native American leaders were particularly concerned about continued legal aid for their constituents. The White House went to great lengths between 1969 and 1973 to respond that the president's intent was to "make sure that every citizen has access to legal services," while correcting "the abuses which went on under this program" and removing "legal services from the recurring political controversy which has attended it." Nixon claimed, for example, in an August 11, 1969, statement to Congress about restructuring OEO that legal services to the poor would be "strengthened and elevated" by having independent status. He even argued that by trying to ensure that OEO would no longer function as an "arm of the White House," he was actually "reducing White House power." Civil rights advocates and antipoverty activists questioned both the motives and intent of the White House and, like Rumsfeld, were against the obvious intent of the Murphy amendment to allow governors to cut back funding for legal services benefiting the poor. This prompted Ehrlichman, in a carefully worded action memorandum, to point out to Nixon that "in view of Don's [Rumsfeld] public stance and the nature of the opposition to Murphy's amendment you cannot favor the amendment. I suggest you say nothing . . . letting Congress judge whether we really support him."[33]

Just in case, however, Frank Carlucci, a respected Nixon aide on civil rights, was chosen to defend the idea of a separate legal services corporation and to "refute charges that the . . . proposal is an effort to destroy Legal Services as we know it."[34] After successfully vetoing two extension bills, Nixon ultimately supported Rumsfeld over those in favor of the Murphy Amendment and in 1972 signed a bill extending the life of OEO for three years.

On other occasions the administration made budget requests that Rumsfeld simply did not agree with, forcing him to protest to OMB publicly. Finally, the White House transferred such OEO programs as Head Start to HEW, and the Job Corp and Manpower Training Programs to the Labor Department.[35] Nonetheless, Nixon was pleased enough with Rumsfeld's performance at OEO that in December 1970 he appointed him as counselor to the president, leaving the final, and ultimately unsuccessful, attempt to dismantle OEO to Howard (Howie) Phillips. As acting director, Phillips ruined his own career in the process by alienating Republican as well as Democratic supporters of the agency.[36] Unfortunately for Phillips, his inept efforts were not appreciated by White House aides, let alone his critics at large, who wrote about him in ways similar to those describing Clarence Thomas's (Bush's 1991 appointee to the Supreme Court) performance as head of EEOC. Thus Phillips was described as a "White House minion" who would "cheerfully" preside over the demolition of OEO because he was an "implacable foe of advocacy programs for the poor." It did not help when Phillips allegedly said of Nixon just as Watergate revelations began to plague the White House: "I believe RN epitomizes the American dream and represents all that is great in US. . . . Every country needs its Cato because every country has its Carthage. Well I'm going to be this country's Cato. Carthage was destroyed because it was rotten. I think Legal Services is rotten, and it'll be destroyed."[37]

Such statements lowered even further Phillips's reputation among White House staffers. In an administratively confidential memorandum, White House aide Ken Clawson pulled no punches when he said:

> Howie Phillips has been instructed to drop out of sight following his testimony Friday before the McGovern Committee. . . . Prepare set statements of Presidential policy vis-à-vis OEO for insertion into Phillips's mouth each time he speaks and for insertion into all press releases regarding the dismantling of OEO. . . . When the above material is completed, notify me, and we will set up an intensive briefing of Phillips by Jim Cavannaugh, Ken Cole and John Ehrlichman before he returns to battle.[38]

While Phillips was being so severely criticized inside the White House during the spring of 1973, a lawyers' group and four community action agencies filed a class-action suit against him.

Time and time again Nixon cabinet members and White House staffers reminded him of the misuse of OEO funds for "politically motivated" purposes. "Frankly, I grow weary of seeing government money used to finance some jack-leg lawyers who initiate nuisance suits of this kind against the Department," Secretary of Agriculture Earl Butz wrote in 1972 about the twenty-one OEO-funded lawsuits pending against him and the USDA. "It utilizes an inordinate amount of manpower in our Department, as well as in the Office of [the] Attorney General. . . . When we're looking for places to reduce governmental expenditure, the OEO is one of my primary candidates." Unlike his aides, who thought that Phillips had gone too far, the president thought that the acting head of OEO was correct in attacking "middle level burocrats [sic]" who channeled money for political purposes to the American Indian Movement and the National Welfare Rights Organization. When he read in one of his daily news summaries that this constituted a "diversion of funds away from representing poor people in the courts," Nixon argued, writing to Haldeman: "This type of attack is *correct*. Stick to hard facts."[39]

The attempt to destroy OEO through reorganization was actually well within the legal jurisdiction of the administration—except for the Legal Services Program, the Community Action Program, and the Community Economic Development Program, all of which Congress had mandated could not be delegated to any other agency. By June 1973 Ken Cole reported to the president that "[p]lans are on track to dismantle OEO," but it was never done. For nineteen months Rumsfeld succeeded in reorganizing the bureaucracy and realigning the bureaucrats of the agency without unnecessarily antagonizing either moderate liberals or conservatives. He accomplished this primarily by streamlining OEO's bureaucratic structure; merging, farming out, or transferring some of its programs into other cabinet departments or government agencies; lowering its public profile; and weeding out the most obvious "advocate types," such as Terry Lenzer, the head of OEO's Legal Services.[40] While Rumsfeld partially succeeded, Phillips totally failed. In the end, Nixon was only able to reduce the programs controlled by OEO because a court order in 1973 prevented him from abolishing it completely. As with his earlier red-baiting attacks on Jerry Voorhis and Helen Gahagan Douglas, Nixon was never forgiven by his liberal critics for taking on OEO (despite its demonstrated inefficiencies by the time Johnson left office) or for impounding government funds for projects he ideologically opposed or thought did not require such high levels of spending.

THE NEW FEDERALISM

Nixon's New Federalism was an attempt to resolve a paradox as old as the Constitution itself. Too often, as Senator William Fulbright noted in his famous March 27, 1964, speech, "we are inclined to confuse freedom and democracy, which we regard as moral principles, with the way in which these are practiced in America—with capitalism, federalism and the two-party system, which are not moral principles, but simply the preferred and accepted practices of the American people."[41] Nixon did not. His brand of federalism (like his brand of détente) was a pragmatic, not a moral, concept. He thought that pragmatism was a necessary modus operandi for any president dealing with contemporary American problems. Nixon's New Federalism, as Richard Nathan has noted, was "a political program . . . [not] an academic treatise."[42]

In contrast to the Founders' concept of federalism, Nixon's was not a static but a fluid approach to the powers of the state versus those of the federal government.[43] Nor did it place as much emphasis on American military interventionism in international affairs as traditional cold warriorism had. Instead, Nixon's New Federalism, both at home and abroad, was based on ascertaining where the predominant responsibilities logically lay and then determining the level of domestic or international power that should handle a specific function or activity. Welfare, for example, was brought under the jurisdiction of the federal government, whereas manpower training devolved to the states. Likewise, some international problems such as the Middle East required decentralized and multilateral negotiations, whereas opening up relations with China did not.

To implement the New Federalism, Nixon and his advisers distinguished between federal functions and state or local ones, between activities requiring large cash transactions and those primarily involving services. Nixon attempted to return to the states some power over service issues (what social scientists call "distributive" issues) such as education, manpower training, and public health, while retaining control at the national level over cash transfers or "nondistributive" issues, such as welfare, energy, and the environment. Above all, unlike Reagan's, Nixon's New Federalism was *not* intended to cut federal spending programs. In contrast to Reagan, Nixon supported an expansive and generally successful revenue-sharing program, while Reagan urged the elimination of this program in 1986, relying instead on free-market, supply-side efforts to satisfy state and local funding needs.

In a word, under his New Federalism Nixon addressed national problems by spending more and by redistributing power away from Congress and the federal bureaucracy, toward local, state, and presidential centers of control.[44] As a result, Nixon is currently credited or criticized for taking significant steps toward centralized planning and structural decentralization in domestic affairs. According to Otis L. Graham, Nixon personally began to "preside over a more rapid evolution toward planning than any other President since FDR."[45]

The final essential element of Nixon's New Federalism was the desire to preserve or restore a sense of socioeconomic community structures. As James Reichley has pointed out, the Nixon administration recognized "that contemporary American society required satisfaction of paradoxical sets of needs: 'a need for *both* national unity and local diversity; a need to protect *both* individual equality at the national level and individual uniqueness at the local level; and a need *both* to establish national goals and to decentralize government services.'" Nixon believed that this type of increased centralization would help him implement many of the decentralized features of his New Federalism, such as shifting from categorical grant programs (with their complicated application process) to block grants, through special and general revenue sharing with states and local communities; shifting from a service strategy to an income strategy in aiding welfare recipients; and planning new community development under a national growth policy.[46]

Since the objective of Nixon's New Federalism was to circumvent the bureaucracy in Washington by increasing the power of the White House, implementation of this goal naturally alienated a good portion of the federal bureaucracy.[47] The hostility between the White House and the federal bureaucracy had already reached dangerous levels over Nixon's attempts to restructure the executive branch, and his New Federalism simply exacerbated these feelings because certain aspects of it were inextricably involved with organizational reform. It is Haldeman's contention that reorganization in all its forms, including its New Federalist features, constituted the "secret story of Watergate." According to Haldeman and others, as Nixon moved "to control the executive branch from the White House . . . the great power blocs in Washington" turned against him and were ready to take advantage of Watergate in any way possible by the beginning of his second term.[48] (Unfortunately, these attempts to combine centralization and decentralization also facilitated the impounding of federal funds earmarked for projects Nixon opposed and other, less than positive features of New Federalism, such as the attempt by federal and state agencies to cooperate in the systematic, often extralegal, surveillance or harassment of allegedly subversive groups or individuals who opposed the administration's policies.)

Leonard Garment, the only Democrat to serve on the Nixon White House's legal staff, correctly observed that the "central paradox of the Nixon administration was that in order to reduce *federal* power, it was first necessary to increase *presidential* power." Or as Nixon more bluntly described this paradox to me: "Bringing power to the White House [was necessary] in order to dish it out." At no time was Nixon's intent to diminish all government power—only that of Congress and the federal bureaucracy.[49] Naturally this made Nixon even more enemies than he had before becoming president.

In an abstract sense Nixon's diplomatic policies were also a form of New Federalism. They, too, were based on the realization that the national and international community had to be pursued and local or regional cultural diversity honored at the same time. They, too, tried to accommodate centralized and decentralized loci of power. Thus, although the Nixon administration emphasized the importance of state and local jurisdiction within the United States, it also espoused a dispersed concept of international relations under a "pentagonal," or five-power, approach to foreign policy. Likewise, the Nixon Doctrine, proclaimed in July 1969, was a strategy of devolution that was designed to maintain U.S. commitments abroad at reduced costs by limiting American response when nations were threatened by Communist aggression to military and economic, but not personnel, assistance. "Domestic revenue-sharing was like the Nixon doctrine abroad," the president told Theodore White in a March 1973 interview. "The American government helps, but local governments have got to do it on their own." Thus, Nixon's domestic New Federalism has been appropriately referred to as "national localism," while his diplomatic New Federalism can be considered an example of "regional globalism." William Safire created the term "national localism" in order to convey the New Federalist sense of national unity and local diversity. My term "regional globalism" is a shorthand way of describing a development in international economics increasingly evident since the 1970s, namely, the significance of regional economic blocs. Nixon understood that "pragmatic regionalism rather than ideological or idealistic internationalism [was] the key to understanding geopolitical economic practices."[50]

Just as domestic relationships were linked in an overarching federal pattern (some requiring top-down, others bottom-up, approaches), so "linkage" became an essential concept in Nixon's geopolitical design. For example, arbitrary covert or overt actions by any of the major powers in the Middle East or the Third World would automatically affect superpower relationships; yet small nations within any particular major power's sphere of influence could not independently play off the superpowers against each other and expect any outside help. Thus, "linkage" would inhibit and contain conflict among major nations similar to the way in which federalism channeled potential conflict between national and state spheres of power.

The major differences in the application of his New Federalism at home and abroad are quite evident: the term was not used to describe foreign affairs; domestically the policy *appeared* less successful because no single domestic adviser emerged with the influence, prestige, or gusto that Henry Kissinger brought to the conduct of foreign policy; and the unpopularity of the Vietnam War effort hampered Nixon's ability to influence Congress on certain domestic reform issues more than it hampered his foreign policy initiatives, which he could often set in motion unilaterally.

Historically, the decentralizing and centralizing functions of government have been the key to any concept of federalism. As it tried to sort out the three basic components of domestic government—financing, policy making, and administration—the Nixon administration assigned predominant, but never full, responsibilities to state and local governments whenever possible.

Nixon as Santa Claus: Revenue Sharing

The most popular and substantive of all the programs to come out of Nixon's New Federalism was revenue sharing. The 1972 State and Local Fiscal Assistance Act set up a program for matching federal and state funds through revenue sharing that ultimately distributed $83 billion to states and local government units between 1972 and 1986 ($16 billion, or almost one-fifth, under Nixonian budgets for 1973 through 1975). This bonanza to governors and mayors in the long run "helped to build the modern Republican party." At the time, it also played an extremely important political role in reconciling Nixon with Nelson Rockefeller and other recalcitrant and skeptical GOP governors and mayors, except for Ronald Reagan, who opposed this new spending program as governor of California and later as president. Like Nixon's welfare reform, the idea for sharing federal revenue directly with states without a lot of red tape surfaced first among Democrats whose views were ultimately rejected by the Johnson administration. In this instance Walter Heller, chair of the Council of Economic Advisers under JFK and LBJ, along with the economist Joseph Pechman from the Brookings Institution, deserves credit for devising the original concept. By the end of the 1960s similar ideas were being proposed by a variety of economists and by members of both parties.[51]

While campaigning in 1968 Nixon had said: "I plan a streamlined federal system, with a return to the states, cities, and communities of decision-making powers rightfully theirs." Nonetheless, he apparently had to be convinced by Ehrlichman that revenue sharing should become the economic centerpiece of his New Federalism, along with welfare reform. Within the administration varying degrees of support for revenue sharing came from Caspar Weinberger, head of HEW; Murray L. Weidenbaum, assistant secretary of the Treasury; Richard Nathan, assistant director of OMB; George Shultz, OMB director; and Paul M. W. McCracken, chair of the Council of Economic Advisers. Among Nixon's closest advisers in 1970–71, only Robert Finch, Donald Rumsfeld, and Raymond Price seriously questioned its feasibility. Ehrlichman considered revenue sharing such a high priority that he designated the initial material about it "secret," and gave White House advisers and cabinet members only two days to prepare their initial policy recommendations.[52]

Ehrlichman, with the aid of Raymond J. Waldmann, a member of the Domestic Council staff, summarized these views for the president on December 19, 1970, recommending that he take a middle course in shifting from the old "categorical" grants that had originated under the New Deal. These grants required the state and local recipients to compete with one another and follow complicated guidelines to obtain money that often had strings attached. The simplicity of the "block" grant made it immediately popular in and out of Washington. Administrative costs and discretion were minimized because no applications had to be reviewed; recipients could set their priorities, and spend the money as they saw fit; and the number of state and local units receiving funds increased dramatically—for many, such grants opened the door to federal funding for the first time. Clearly revenue sharing was an idea whose time had arrived, and the president knew it.[53] Nixon's papers do not indicate, as had been asserted before they were opened in the late 1980s, that he "provided the original suggestion, set guidelines, and made the key decisions." Instead, primary documents show that Nixon heeded Ehrlichman's advice on this matter, as he did on many other domestic issues. Nixon said as much in his memoirs. Nonetheless, the president could portray himself as a "political Santa Claus," according to the political commentator Theodore White, and "his historic revenue sharing plan" accounted, in part, for his landslide reelection in 1972.[54]

This is not to say that Nixon faced few political problems after he decided to approve general revenue sharing as the major means to supplement strained state and local budgets. While the program underscored his New Federalist commitment to redirecting power away from Congress and the federal bureaucracy and back to the states and local communities, it also raised several serious questions. First and foremost, congressional opposition proved so strong that Nixon's support wavered. According to Ehrlichman, he single-handedly had to stand up to the president to save the revenue-sharing program. Nixon then held a press conference on February 17, 1971, indicating he realized that "all reforms have rough sledding," but that he believed "that the favorable reaction that . . . we have had at the grassroots and among governors and mayors and county officials . . . will be the decisive factor in getting [revenue sharing] through." In the same press conference he specifically linked opposition to revenue sharing to "dug-in establishmentarians fighting for the status quo," a clear recognition that, if adopted, it would diminish federal bureaucratic control over state, city, and local community activity.[55]

Nevertheless, the opposition from Democratic Congressman Wilbur Mills, perennial chair of the House Ways and Means Committee, and the skepticism of his new treasury secretary John Connally, who allegedly said that revenue sharing "has about as much sex appeal . . . as a cup of coffee,"[56] gave Nixon reason to reconsider. Despite Connally's low opinion of the issue, Nixon and Ehrlichman considered using him as an "Administration admiral" for it because of his prestige and persuasiveness with Congress. Nixon's only reservation about this idea was that he feared overexposing Connally. "[W]e want to remember," he told Ehrlichman, "there's a big gun: we don't want to pop it too often."[57] Nixon has refused to comment on how wrong Connally proved to be on the popularity of revenue sharing.

Ehrlichman's papers indicated that Mills's opposition threatened passage not only of the revenue-sharing program but also of the president's controversial welfare reform. Specifically, Ehrlichman feared that Mills might "attach . . . a proposal to the President's welfare reform bill . . . [in] the form of a $5–10 billion federal assumption of welfare costs now borne by the states, some counties and a very few cities." Among other things, Mills initially refused to meet with anyone except Nixon himself about the issue. After turning down three invitations to come to the White House to meet with Nixon's aides, telling them that "they know where Mills' office is," Mills finally met with Nixon on January 25, 1971. This meeting only reinforced fears among Nixon's advisers on congressional relations that nothing should be done

to take Chairman Mills to task publicly for not understanding the President's revenue sharing proposal and for having open hearings but a closed mind.

If Mills is embarrassed publicly or feels he's backed in a corner, he'll fight with everything he's got, including zapping other proposals before his committee, such as welfare reform, not raising the debt ceiling, increasing social security to 15 or 20%, etc. etc. Also, Wilbur might just stake his whole career on this fight if he's forced to.

I recommend quiet persuasion not to win his lost support but to keep his opposition to a minimum. In the past, the Chairman has been "rolled" on popular programs, but not when the issue has been escalated to major war with Mills in a position of being the major loser.[58]

When Mills finally did agree to meet with several welfare experts in HEW and later with Shultz and Ehrlichman, the picture did not improve. John G. Veneman and Robert Patricelli reported back that in the middle of a discussion over the administration's welfare and health proposals, Mills asserted that Nixon's revenue-sharing proposal was "the only issue that had come before him in his 28-year career on which he was *UNABLE* to compromise." Mills wanted the meeting kept "secret," and it exacerbated Shultz's and Ehrlichman's fears that Mills would proceed with a "counter-threat"—offering governors and mayors federal payment of their welfare costs if they would only oppose the administration's proposal to switch from categorical to block grants. Mills also threatened to substitute a tax-credit program for revenue sharing, whereby anyone filing a federal income tax return could deduct from the federal tax payment part or all of the state (and sometimes local) taxes. The administration dismissed this approach because its distributional effects would be uneven unless complex regulations were developed to ensure that rich states did not receive a disproportionately large share of such funds, which were more needed in poorer states and regions. Tax credit proposals also tended to leave out local governments entirely.[59]

Although other problems arose to complicate passage of what became the 1972 State and Local Fiscal Assistance Act,[60] political opposition from Democrats in Congress worried Nixon and his aides most. Nixon's revenue-sharing program did not benefit as much in the short run from a Vietnam "peace dividend" as the president and his advisers had anticipated, nor did it promote public involvement or political participation at the state and local levels as much as they had hoped. It did, however, reduce bureaucratic discretion, by creating a formula-based standard for funding and lessening federal bureaucratic involvement (except in terms of civil rights requirements) in state and local spending. Additionally, revenue sharing set in motion a change in "the nature of American Federalism" that was completed by the Reagan administration in ways unintended by the Nixon administration. Instead of the New Federalism Nixon envisioned, based on better-funded, decentralized decision making and on community participation in state and local projects, the concept was reduced to an illusion under Reagan, whose rhetoric stressed that "government in general, regardless of the level, could not solve economic or social problems and, in fact, that attempting to do so, it often made the problems even worse." What had started out as an incrementally comprehensive set of domestic programs for redistributing federal and state power and funds through government reorganization as well as fiscal policies became, under Reagan, an exercise "guided more by ideological considerations than by a rational sorting out of administrative functions," which ended in the termination of the general revenue-sharing program in 1987.[61]

CORPORATE REORGANIZATION AFTER REELECTION

Because Congress delayed or turned down several of his major proposals for reorganizing the executive branch, following his landslide reelection in 1972 Nixon decided to call for the summary resignation of his entire cabinet and to create a set of four special counselors to the president, or supersecretaries, to take charge of certain domestic bureaucracies. The heads of HUD, HEW, and the Treasury and Agriculture departments were to be given responsibility for community development, human resources, economic affairs, and natural resources, respectively. These supersecretaries were to have direct and frequent access to the president and his White House staff. In addition, Nixon wanted to create a second line of subcabinet officials consisting largely of former or current White House aides, to act as presidential assistants responsible for such broad functional areas as domestic affairs, economic affairs, foreign affairs, executive management, and White House coordination. As reviewed for the president by Roy Ash right after the reelection, this plan also called for these supersecretaries and presidential assistants to operate as a supercabinet in order to enhance White House control over the bureaucracy.[62]

By the end of his first term in office, Nixon had clearly decided to place loyal "politician managers" in these key supersecretariats, as well as in many of the more than two thousand plum managerial jobs in the executive branch. He hoped to appoint loyalists to posts throughout the top levels of government to ensure implementation of the decentralized aspects of his New Federalism, such as sharing revenue with states and local communities, welfare reform, and the impounding of federal funds earmarked for projects in excess of the president's recommended ceilings.

None of the aspects of this final comprehensive reorganization became institutionalized because Watergate events generated unwarranted criticism and suspicion about its intent. With Haldeman's help Nixon hoped that he could complete his corporate design of the executive branch even while he fought Watergate charges. All of his reorganizational plans, whether submitted to Congress or instituted administratively, evolved from the Ash Council's original horizontal, functional design. A more successful corporate model can be seen in his procedures for conducting foreign policy. To varying degrees, both of these corporate models have been emulated by subsequent presidents, including Reagan, Bush, and most notably Clinton.

The same is true of Nixon's use of his appointive powers. He had endorsed the idea of using appointed generalists (policy politicians) to oversee the work of civil service specialists (experts) from the very beginning of his presidency, knowing that generalists would provide him with more moderate and less self- (or agency-) interested advice. The value of this approach was subsequently impressed upon him by the Ash Council. Initially, however, Nixon thought that he could appoint generalists who were *both* strong agency and department heads, and strong White House staff people to monitor them. After the two inevitably clashed in the course of his first administration, he decided to move members of his White House staff (and other generalists who had proved loyalists on policy) out into key positions within the executive branch.[63]

This notion about appointing Republican generalists to restrain or replace holdover Democratic specialists did not originate with Watergate, but many continue to think that it did because the president abruptly called for the resignation of his entire cabinet after winning reelection. Ehrlichman's handwritten notes for the initial meetings after the election contain brutal descriptions of who should go and why. "Only [Earl] Butz, [agricultural secretary], Attorney General [Richard Kleindienst], and [George] Shultz [treasury secretary] stay." All other resignations were to be accepted until further notice. At one point the president wanted every politician eliminated from consideration except George Bush. Nixon said Bush would "do anything for the cause," so it was suggested that he become deputy secretary of the Treasury. Herb Klein, White House director of communications, was described as a "tenacious bastard." Romney was to be "offered nothing," while it was said that Charles Colson (of dirty tricks and later Watergate fame) "must leave *now*—in the next 2 mo[nths]." Although he once described Colson as "ingenious," Nixon thought it would be "less harmful" to the administration if he left now that the election was over. When Henry Kissinger's name came up, the president desperately expressed the need to replace him because of their disagreement during the campaign over the delay in obtaining an end to the war in Vietnam, by saying, "get someone!" These meetings were also full of aphorisms uttered by the president or his aides, such as "genius needs to be recognized" and "boys run for office to be somebody; men run for office to do something." At one point Ash informed the president that at Litton Industries the motto was: "It's OK to be a prima donna, as long as you can sing." In the end, Nixon, Ash, Fred Malek, Haldeman, and Ehrlichman agreed to try the new system of supersecretaries for a year to see if it worked before sending it to the Hill for approval; otherwise "they'll defeat it and we are put in the position of defying the Congress."[64]

Both Nixon and Haldeman have since admitted that this request for mass resignations and reassignments was a mistake: it had a "chilling effect . . . on morale" and appeared too "cold blooded and ungrateful." After time, they defended it on the grounds that it was fairer and more evenhanded than selecting a few for dismissal and the only way, finally, to accomplish a comprehensive, across-the-board reorganization of the executive branch of government.[65]

Critics did not view the process so benignly. "Nixon's attempt to control the bureaucracy by placing loyalists in key positions was more than an ideological effort to change government policies and programs," the journalist Haynes Johnson insisted as late as 1980. "It was a blueprint for political subversion and executive tyranny."[66] Such criticism doesn't seem to have prevented Nixon's successors from quietly utilizing most aspects of his corporate reorganization of the executive branch. Indeed, his successors in the Oval Office have discovered that Nixon made "life . . . much more comfortable for them." According to I. M. Destler,

it is far easier for a chief executive to deal through a few "loyal" aides almost totally dependent on himself, than to conduct extensive personal efforts at bargaining and persuasion which will frequently prove frustrating and occasionally be directly rebuffed. . . . Those who have not been consulted need not be informed, much less heeded. . . . [The president] is encouraged to act as if he has, not a Neustadtian license to persuade, but a "mandate" to decide things and have his decisions obeyed. He leads less than he orders. Those who obey are "loyal"; those who do not are enemies.[67]

The recommendations Nixon received from the Ash Council did not differ significantly in content from those his predecessors had received from similar advisory bodies. Through a combination of legislative and administrative actions, however, Nixon's reorganizational plans were more extensive than any president's before or after. The degree to which those Nixonian administrative tactics that were legal and constitutional (and we tend to forget that most of them were) became the corporate model for his Democratic and Republican successors constitutes another reason why Nixon is more than Watergate. This fact, along with his surprisingly positive civil rights record, will help to explain the importance of the Nixon phenomenon to future generations.

3

CIVIL RIGHTS
INVIGORATED

*History should say ... about Richard Nixon that his domestic programs extended
opportunities of America to ... Americans who live outside the mainstream of
America's life.*

—Frank Gannon, White House aide, January 18, 1973

Perhaps the domestic area in which Watergate dimmed or skewed memories of the Nixon years more than anywhere else was civil rights. Many became rightly concerned with the civil rights violations of those the Nixon administration deemed enemies or threats to national security. But long before investigations shed light on what even John Mitchell called "White House horrors,"[1] few wanted to give Nixon, who appeared to wear so uncomfortably the affirmative action mantle of LBJ, any benefit of the doubt on this issue. Yet he proved an unexpected agent for change even in this most difficult area of domestic reform.

Most Americans have found it easy to forget that as vice president in the 1950s, Richard Nixon was a stronger supporter of civil rights than Eisenhower, Kennedy, or Johnson. When he presided over the Senate, his rulings consistently favored those who opposed the use of filibusters to block civil rights legislation. He chaired a committee that oversaw enforcement of nondiscrimination provisions of government contracts, recommending in his final report the establishment of "a positive policy of nondiscrimination" by employers, which he later supported as president. Nixon told me that he supported civil rights for blacks and equal rights for women, not because it would "help" members of either group, but because "it was fair" and good for the nation by preventing "wasted talent."[2]

Nixon has always denied being a conservative on civil rights, and in fact, his record in this area shows less aprincipled political expediency than his critics allege. There is some indication, for example, that although he finally adopted a white-oriented southern strategy for the Republican party in the late 1960s, in the 1960 campaign Nixon had expected to increase black support for the Republican party beyond Eisenhower's 39 percent in 1956 because of his previous civil rights record and Martin Luther King, Jr.'s, personal promise to register African-Americans for the Republican party in the South. He also had the support in 1960 of prominent African-American athletes such as Jackie Robinson. After the Democrats nominated Kennedy, whose Catholicism brought an unexpected number of white southern Protestants over to the Republican party, Nixon appealed more carefully to both blacks and whites in the South than he had originally intended. As it turned out, Kennedy's highly publicized intervention after King's arrest in October won over a crucial number of black voters, including Robinson. But before this incident, King (and Robinson) had openly praised Nixon above all other presidential candidates in 1960 for caring about the race issue. Despite Kennedy's grandstanding on King's arrest and subsequent jailing, Nixon still captured 32 percent of the black vote in 1960, but in such a close election that was not enough. As a very public private citizen in the 1960s, Nixon, unlike George Bush, supported the Civil Rights Acts of 1964 and 1966—not southern segregationist planks in Republican state platforms. Nixon also consistently opposed the poll tax and supported antilynching legislation.[3]

Far from being a bland supporter of civil rights, Nixon's record was better than any of the political opponents he ran against for Senate, vice president, and president (with the exception of Hubert Humphrey). Nevertheless, between the Goldwater debacle of 1964 and his bid for the Republican nomination in 1968, Nixon had once again played the role of party unifier, centrist moderate, and "needed voice of sanity" as the Republican party tried to rebuild itself. While members of the emerging New Right, especially in the South, still did not trust him, they needed him in 1968 as much as he needed their support. Consequently, to blunt the appeal of George Wallace in the South, his campaign statements implied that if elected, he would slow down enforcement of school desegregation policies because he had never favored compulsory federal legislation to remedy de facto segregation.[4]

In one of my interviews with Nixon, he denied having had "a southern strategy." This contention has been disputed by people inside and outside his administration, especially after Harry Dent, a former administrative assistant to Senator Strom Thurmond, became a special counsel to Nixon and began to advise him on southern politics. At the time even Dent denied the existence of such a political strategy, although he later published a book about it. "This administration has no southern strategy," Dent privately informed Nixon at the end of 1969, "but rather a national strategy which, for the first time in modern times, *includes* the South, rather than *excludes* the South from full and equal participation in national affairs."[5]

In truth, as Hugh Davis Graham has noted, "Nixon's 'southern strategy' was really a border strategy" aimed not at the "Deep South" but at the "Rim South." As early as the presidential election of 1960, Nixon demonstrated increasing strength among voters in the southern rim, an area that Kirkpatrick Sale defined in 1976 as an imaginary line stretching from the northern border of North Carolina west to San Francisco. This support allowed Nixon to operate from a politically centrist position, in contrast to his opponents in 1968 and 1972—Hubert Humphrey, George Wallace, and George McGovern. It was also reminiscent of Herbert Hoover in 1928, the last Republican president who tentatively courted both black and white southern voters.[6]

However Nixon's "southern strategy" is defined, it was remarkably short-lived. After Dent failed to deliver enough votes to confirm Harrold Carswell as a Supreme Court justice in the spring of 1970, and the president's other aides became more involved in domestic reforms requiring northern votes in Congress, the political liability of courting only the South on conservative issues became evident, despite the lip service the administration paid such a strategy. On September 22, 1969, Nixon sent a memorandum to Ehrlichman, which told him to make "sure that Dent puts at a high priority our project of continuing to build Southern understanding and support for our Family Assistance [Welfare] Program," and a second memorandum to Haldeman, indicating that he wanted a copy of the *New York Times* report on the administration's slow progress on civil rights to be given to Dent for "the proper circulation."[7] The president wanted as much from the South as he gave it. After all, he needed northern and southern votes on all his domestic programs, especially on the environment, national health insurance, welfare, and, of course, his diplomatic initiatives.

By the end of 1971, what was left of his southern strategy appeared to be mostly goodwill. He somewhat wistfully told Haldeman that he wanted to meet with and thank southern Democrats like Senator John Stennis (Dem.-Mich.), "who on vote after vote do stick with us." He said he was tired of meeting, on the advice of the state department, with congressmen such as Senators Mike Mansfield (Dem.-Mont.) and George Aiken (Rep.-Vt.), whose votes were critical on matters of national security.[8] As a moderately progressive Republican, Nixon could carry a southern strategy only so far before it would hurt him on other issues, especially foreign policy.

By 1968 the dilemma over how to handle the political issue of race had become complicated not only by Nixon's ostensible southern strategy in his bid for the presidency and in the first year of his administration but also by rising civil rights expectations in general. According to Moynihan, "Civil Rights had triumphed" in the 1960s. Yet by the end of the decade, "racial problems were widely perceived to have grown worse." In other words, the promise of civil rights had made African-Americans *more* discontent with their unequal status in U.S. society. While Nixon's campaign had not been antiblack, racists such as Senator Strom Thurmond of South Carolina supported him, and the outgoing Johnson administration continued "to convey a sense of commitment" to blacks even though the civil rights movement had peaked in 1965 with rioting at home and war abroad.[9]

The country may have not been "moving forward on civil rights" by 1968, but white and black civil rights leaders still felt that even symbolic support from a Democratic White House was better than the Republicans would offer under Nixon, regardless of his previous record. L. Patrick Gray, Finch's executive assistant at HEW, articulated the problem that the Nixon administration faced from the outset when he wrote in a note to Robert Finch, HEW secretary, sometime in June 1969: "How do you (we) make good on campaign statements which when uttered were not supported by sound research and not based upon the 1st hand look we now have into the perils of Pandora's box of civil rights questions?"[10] During his first term Nixon never was able to overcome widespread African-American suspicion and hostility. Just before his reelection, Julian Bond described the president's "black supporters as 'political prostitutes.'"[11]

Nixon needed calm and astute advice on racial matters, but he did not always receive it. One of Nixon's closest closeted advisers on race questions was Moynihan, the liberal Democrat. Moynihan chose not to call attention to his role as adviser on racial matters because of his negative reputation among African-Americans from his 1965 report to President Johnson about the crisis in the black ghettoes. In this much-publicized document, Moynihan had assigned the problems of the urban poor to "a tangle of pathology" resulting from the high incidence of female-headed families. In this blame-the-victim analysis, Moynihan concluded that such households were contrary to nature, since "the very essence of the male animal, from the bantam rooster to the four-star general, is to strut."[12]

Any administration following Johnson's was bound to suffer from the fallout over rising expectations and worsening conditions of the African-American community, Moynihan later reflected, because "reality had to catch up with pretense and there would inevitably follow a sense of letdown." Moynihan and the president both understood that his administration could not avoid trouble on the race question and at the same time could not benefit from "the smallest gestures" with "a stroke of the pen," as his immediate predecessor had done.[13] With race a no-win issue by 1969, Moynihan was not about to act as a public lightning rod (as he had in 1965 under Johnson) during the first week of the Nixon presidency, and as he ultimately would on welfare reform, discussed in chapter 4. Even the most self-serving, flamboyant "feudal bastards" have self-protective instincts, after all.

The longest (over 125 pages) of Moynihan's many private reports to the president, the one on race consisted of seven parts. One part, titled "The Lower Class Negro Male: Defeat and Defiance," was apparently so intemperate and inflammatory that it has not been made available for research. In his cover letter to Nixon, Moynihan informed the president that his thoughts on the "present state of race relations . . . are meant neither to alarm—much less to intimidate!—nor to reassure, but only to present as best I can the information that seems most relevant, and to suggest the larger implications such information has for the administration program." What followed were pages of anything but calming advice, with controversial and problematic conclusions about blacks.[14]

Moynihan expressed to Nixon in his report of March 19, 1969, his frustration over deteriorating race relations in New York City, among other things. Ranging widely and sometimes illogically over many race-related topics, Moynihan talked about low IQs among blacks, growing Jewish-black antagonism, the increasingly "politically correct" position found in Black Studies programs and among African-American professors, and the specter of blacks demanding quota hiring amounting to "Eleven Percent of all public places and services—in universities, civil services, legislatures, military academies, embassies, judges." He also wrote that, although middle-class blacks really wanted to be "co-opted into the system," they were "volcanoes of hate" and "rage—self-hate as much as anything else." Therefore, they would, if necessary, use the threat of lower-class black urban violence to obtain assimilation into white society. He argued for welfare reform to "dissolve the great black urban lower class (and the rural slums that feed it)," so that the country would not be held hostage by middle-class militant black leaders relying on lower-class black violence and "support from white elements seeking to use Negro unrest to unsettle society generally." In conclusion Moynihan sadly noted: "This was not what the civil rights movement expected to come about, or hoped to see, but it does appear to be the outcome nonetheless."[15]

It is not clear what Nixon thought of this lengthy salvo from Moynihan on race (atypically, he made no handwritten comments on his copy), but much of it no doubt fed his concerns over ghetto violence and the ultimate intentions of the early civil rights movement. When Moynihan had first mentioned the conflict between Jews and blacks to the president in January, Nixon took it seriously enough to forward the memorandum to Kissinger. Moynihan explained African-American anti-Semitism largely in economic terms, that is, the resentment of Jewish businesses in black ghettoes. Again, as with so much of his socioeconomic advice to Nixon (and Johnson), Moynihan relied almost exclusively on New York City for his analysis.[16]

Almost a year later, Moynihan again surveyed a wide variety of racial topics, reiterating the fact that the "position of Negroes . . . had been *the* central domestic political issue" for a decade. While documenting the "extraordinary" quantitative progress of African-Americans in the areas of employment and education in this January 16, 1970, memorandum, which was leaked to the press in March, Moynihan told the president that "there would seem to be countercurrents that pose a serious threat to the welfare of the blacks, and the stability of the society, white and black."[17]

The most controversial aspect of this memorandum (and the section that caused the most difficulty for Moynihan among black and white activists after it was leaked to the press) had to do with his suggestion to the president that "[t]he time may have come when the issue of race could benefit from a period of 'benign neglect,'" to which Nixon responded, "I agree." Moynihan meant this administrative neglect to apply to "hysterics, paranoids, and boodlers *on all sides*," by avoiding situations that gave "extremists of either race . . . opportunities for martyrdom, heroics, histrionics, or whatever." Unfortunately, the only examples Moynihan pointed out to Nixon were those of African-American extremism associated with the militant Black Panthers—not the extremism of Vice President Agnew's speeches about radical groups. He advised that "provocations" from the Panthers be ignored so as not to "transform them into cultural heroes for the white—and black—middle class," citing a cocktail party given by Leonard Bernstein's wife to raise money for the Panthers. Nixon wrote in the margin that Kissinger should note this anecdote because it showed "the complete decadence of the American 'upper' class intellectual elite."[18]

Clearly, whoever leaked this memorandum to the press was no friend of either Moynihan or of the Nixon administration, which was in the process of doing what neither Eisenhower's nor Kennedy's had done: desegregate southern schools. Enforcement of school desegregation had been painfully sluggish since the 1954 *Brown v. Board of Education* decision. By 1968 only 20 percent of black children in the South attended predominantly white schools—largely due to the efforts of Lyndon Johnson. Moreover, the most dramatic improvement under Johnson's administration did not take place until 1968, because HEW deadlines for desegregating southern schools were postponed four times by LBJ following passage of the 1964 Civil Rights Act. By the spring of 1968, however, a few lower court rulings and finally the Supreme Court decision in *Green v. Board of Education* no longer offered any president the luxury of arguing that freedom-of-choice plans were adequate for rooting out racial discrimination or that de facto segregation (caused by residential patterns) was not as unconstitutional as de jure segregation (brought about by state or local laws).[19]

RELUCTANT DESEGREGATION OF SOUTHERN SCHOOLS

There is no denying that Nixon personally was unprepared to go beyond what he thought the decision in *Brown* had mandated, because he believed that de facto segregation could not be ended through busing or cutting off funds from school districts. This was essentially the same position held by President Johnson, the latter's more unequivocal civil rights rhetoric notwithstanding. Nine days after taking office, however, Nixon's administration had to decide whether to honor an HEW-initiated fund cutoff for five southern school districts, originally scheduled to take place in the fall of 1968 but conveniently delayed by the Johnson administration until January 29, 1969—right after Nixon's inauguration. On the day of the deadline, Secretary Finch, one of Nixon's more liberal domestic advisers, announced that the funds would be cut off but that he would allow the states retroactively to claim them if they came into compliance with HEW guidelines within sixty days.[20]

Finch's offer of retroactive payment represented a change from the last set of HEW guidelines, developed in March 1968, but which Johnson had never formally endorsed by signing. At the heart of this debate over various HEW guidelines in the last half of the 1960s were two issues: whether the intent of the 1964 Civil Rights Act had been simply to provide freedom of choice or actually to compel integration in schools; and whether freedom-of-choice agreements negotiated by HEW or lawsuits brought by the Department of Justice constituted the most effective way of achieving desegregation. Under the Johnson administration the HEW approach, based on bringing recalcitrant school districts into compliance by cutting off federal funding, had prevailed. Under Nixon, Justice Department litigation became the primary way of achieving desegregation in schools. Arguing that the "laws have caught up with our consciences," Nixon insisted in his first inaugural address that it was now necessary "to give life to what is in the law."[21] The president wanted to change dramatically the entire system of enforcement on school desegregation from HEW compliance agreements to Justice Department actions. This procedural change proved very controversial between 1968 and 1971, but until attacks on judicial activism during Reagan's second term, Nixon's approach would become standard practice.

The new school desegregation guidelines were announced jointly on July 3, 1969, by Robert Finch and John Mitchell—an odd, but effective, combination of Nixonian outsider and insider advisers—both of whom were old friends of the president. Much has been written about where and when the guidelines originated, but until the National Archives began to open Nixon's presidential papers in the late 1980s, most scholars had to rely on firsthand accounts representing the self-serving opinions of those associated with the process who held the most extreme views at the time.[22] The Nixon papers indicate that as early as May 15, 1969, an informal agreement had been reached between Nixon and Finch about desegregation in the schools. Finch was the only freethinking outsider adviser whom Nixon knew and trusted before becoming president; it is therefore reasonable to believe that a private agreement between them on such a controversial topic was reached in the first months of the administration. Unfortunately, the agreement itself and any other possible references to it remain classified, so there is no way of knowing how close the final public text of the guidelines was to the Nixon/Finch understanding.

In retrospect, the new guidelines appear quite moderate, although in the five months it took to write them, rumors abounded about the purported roles that hard-line conservatives were playing to bring an end to desegregation of schools in the South. "No matter what is written in the statement," one of Nixon's speechwriters, William Safire, gloomily predicted, the headlines would read: "Desegregation Deadlines Dropped."[23] At least seven different drafts of the document exist in the Nixon White House Central Files. Contrary to newspaper reports and most published works on these guidelines, Nixon personally revised one, and possibly two, drafts, and many more moderates on the White House staff and in the HEW and the Justice Department contributed to different versions.[24] John Ehrlichman, Nixon's liberal insider adviser, proved instrumental in brokering this process.

As a result of the domination of moderate advice inside the White House, the most extreme memoranda on both sides usually did not get to the president or the cabinet members. For example, memoranda from Leon E. Panetta, director of the HEW Office for Civil Rights, usually did not go beyond Finch's executive assistant, L. Patrick Gray—although Panetta's leaks to the press (including, in all likelihood, the January 1970 Moynihan memorandum) make it appear as though he were a major player in the decision-making process over civil rights in the first year of the Nixon administration. Panetta played a highly publicized obstructionist role that had conservatives in Congress "frothing in frustration," when, in fact, he did not set policy.[25] Because Panetta was forced to resign from HEW in February 1970, and because he came out with a ghostwritten book on desegregation just a year later, the media exaggerated his importance in the controversy. Both Finch's and Nixon's papers, however, clearly document how far from the actual decision-making process Panetta was.

In contrast to Moynihan, however, Panetta's capacity for making headlines seems to have been in inverse proportion to his ability to influence policy. His language is much more intemperate but less stylistically compelling than Moynihan's. When his initial opposition to changing the guidelines failed,[26] Panetta attempted, according to Gray, to "overrule the Secretary of HEW, the A.G. [Attorney General] and the President," by issuing to regional civil rights directors his office's "working, practical interpretation" of the statement issued by Finch and Mitchell. Panetta's two-page interpretation stated unequivocally that the "'school policies' issued by this Department in March, 1968, are still in effect." Gray told Finch that the "A.G. is aware of this [insubordination] through his attorneys in the field and is wild." Dent later told Gray that Panetta's interpretation of the guidelines "reduces to sheer hypocrisy," and that any endorsement of busing by HEW could "violate the President's word."[27]

Panetta did not limit his activities to opposing the new desegregation guidelines and promoting busing; he also lobbied Finch to take a stand against tax exemption for segregated private schools on the grounds that they were "essentially a subterfuge, an attempt to circumvent the law of the land which manifests itself as another form of resegregation." This letter and an earlier memorandum written by Panetta so outraged Haldeman that he began to send handwritten notes to Gray opposing Panetta's position on "private schools and taxes." Gray, in turn, told Finch that he questioned Panetta's "proposed 'simple' solution . . . to a *very* complex question," and that he "recommend[ed] W[hite] H[ouse] clearance" on the matter. Agreeing with Panetta, Finch ignored Gray's advice and wrote a letter (drafted by Panetta) to Treasury Secretary David M. Kennedy about his concern over tax exemptions for segregated schools. In January 1970—only hours before a federal district court in Washington, D.C., issued a temporary injunction stopping the IRS from granting such tax exemptions to private segregated schools in Mississippi—the IRS rejected Finch's request for a reconsideration of its 1967 policy under Johnson.[28]

Panetta's insubordination (and Finch's occasional collusion with him) did not go unnoticed at the White House, as Haldeman's notes to Gray indicate. Secretary Finch stood by his controversial director of the HEW Office for Civil Rights, however. In October 1969, in the wake of Panetta's failure to undermine the desegregation guidelines (but before his successful attempt to make tax exemptions for private schools more difficult), Finch wrote a confidential letter to Ehrlichman that contained a letter of resignation from Panetta. In frank language Finch reminded Ehrlichman of their "previous conversations" in which he had defended retaining Panetta over the summer because it was "in the best interests of this Administration."[29]

Now he wanted to make sure that the risks concerning the *"timing"* of Panetta's departure had been carefully considered. Denying that he was writing for "self-serving" reasons, Finch first noted that "rightly or wrongly, the Director of the Office for Civil Rights in this Department has become a symbol. . . . His resignation alone will be seized upon by the media to further develop their line that we are softening on our obligations in this field and paying off political debts." Second, he said that Panetta's leaving would affect morale among young bureaucrats throughout HEW. Third, he told Ehrlichman, "to put it bluntly, my credibility is seriously compromised," meaning that White House personnel were openly discussing "the fact that Panetta was being forced to resign." Therefore, there was no way to pass it off as "voluntary."[30]

Finally, Finch agreed that "Panetta has made mistakes, but they were mistakes not of loyalty but of judgment. I have certainly made mistakes but where I have given him specific orders . . . Panetta has programmed. In fact, in recent weeks, with our new approach I have had many compliments from Southern Congressmen with whom he has been working." He pleaded with Ehrlichman to consider Panetta's personal situation (his wife had just had a baby) and his own credibility as head of HEW before the White House forced his resignation. Finch concluded on a much sterner note, which presaged his own departure from HEW in June 1970: "I can only conclude by saying I would certainly hope no other matter between the White House and this Department would be handled in this manner again or I can be of no value to the President."[31] The fact that even the freethinking outsider Finch had to go through the political-broker insider Ehrlichman on this matter to reach the president is yet another indication of Ehrlichman's control over information reaching the president about desegregation.

Despite Finch's defense, Panetta submitted an undated, handwritten, one-sentence letter of resignation ("as requested") to the president on February 5, 1970. Nixon accepted it in a February 10 letter that was softened by a paragraph added by Ehrlichman. But this was not enough for Harry Dent, who complained to Haldeman when he learned that "'Loyal Leon' plans to stay until March 1. After all he's said, should he be left around for further blasts and to gather more ammo against the

Administration? . . . Why not get rid of other disloyalists and limit their access to info that will be used against us eventually—when they go." To which Haldeman replied in the margin: "I sure agree!"[32] Nonetheless, Dent was relegated to venting his antidesegregation views indirectly to Nixon through either Haldeman or Ehrlichman, and only the former appeared to sympathize with them.

This process held true even for the presidential speechwriter Pat Buchanan and for Bryce Harlow, perennial White House congressional liaison. Harlow, in particular, was quickly outmaneuvered or ignored from the very beginning of the Nixon administration by more liberal aides such as Ehrlichman, Kenneth Cole, Leonard Garment, and Raymond Price. Buchanan was outraged by this process, but nonetheless he (along with his young protégé, Tom Huston) was relegated to ranting to Ehrlichman, insisting that the guidelines would represent "hemlock to the civil rights, and to the left-wing press," no matter what language was used. He wanted the president to chuck the guidelines and state simply and directly that he was turning back the clock on desegregation in order to build up the Republican party in the South. Dent, who agreed with this point of view, nonetheless tried more logically to convince Nixon that desegregation should be indefinitely sidetracked by sending him (via Ehrlichman) polls indicating that the public wanted less, not more, integration.[33]

Two drafts were prepared on the morning and afternoon of June 23, 1969: the first by Raymond Price and Ehrlichman in consultation with HEW and the Department of Justice; the second by Jerris Leonard, Mitchell's assistant attorney general for civil rights. The next day it was revised twice by Finch's assistant L. Patrick Gray. Garment sent Ehrlichman this version and another draft, which he described as "a product of this Department alone." The dense legalese of Garment's second version was essentially ignored in the final statement.[34]

On June 26, Nixon abruptly told Ehrlichman that he had heard enough from everyone on the issue; that he did not want the "Departments to tinker any further with it"; that desegregation "has had a history of hypocrisy [because] we have seen unrealistic guidelines and deadlines imposed with tongue in cheek"; and finally, that previous "methods chosen to carry out the law have all failed." The next day Safire and Garment made further changes in the draft begun by Ehrlichman and Price. It was this version that Nixon corrected by hand on June 28, making much more moderate changes to what would become the final version. A year later, however, Nixon was still bitterly complaining to his advisers about the need to "hit two decades of hypocrisy" over desegregation and his not having received enough credit for taking effective action where previous presidents had not.[35]

Nixon has been justifiably criticized by civil rights advocates for employing delaying tactics in the South and particularly for not endorsing busing to enforce school desegregation in the North after the April 20, 1971, Supreme Court decision in *Swann v. Charlotte-Mecklenburg Board of Education*. In fact, at a meeting in the Oval Office the day the decision was handed down, the president and his attorney general agreed that the administration should not submit any legislation to Congress to enforce busing. Rather, the states should be told that it was the obligation of the local schools and district courts to carry out the mandate in *Swann*. Ehrlichman (probably thinking about the negative publicity generated when Finch lost control of Panetta) insisted that the White House make sure that HEW did not "screw us on [this] court decision." In particular, he wanted HEW Secretary Elliot Richardson thoroughly "programmed" to take no initiatives on busing.[36]

The busing question refused to go away, however, and in March 1972 the president proposed to Congress two bills: one to provide more funds for improving poor-quality schools, and the other to "stop excessive busing" and to establish "uniform *national* standards for school desegregation, in which busing would be a remedy of last resort." Herbert G. Klein suggested to Finch that a poll should be conducted to find out "exactly where we stand with the press over the bussing issue." The results were roughly even, for and against. In a lengthy press conference on March 17, Ehrlichman, Shultz, Richardson, and Richard Kleindienst, deputy attorney general, all tried with little success to rationalize the president's position and legislation.[37] By August the Congress had not acted on either his moratorium on "all new and additional busing" or his funding proposal for poor students.[38] In a press statement Nixon castigated Congress for its inaction. Even during the height of the Watergate crisis in 1974, he exhorted Harlow to "lean [on] all our people to take a strong anti-bussing position," although he preferred legislation to an antibusing constitutional amendment.[39]

Despite the bitterness of the battle in Congress, and between Congress and the executive branch, after *Swann* the administration found itself dragged into producing an impressive statistical record on school desegregation. In 1968, for example, 68 percent of black children in the South attended all-black schools, and 40 percent of black children in the entire nation attended all-black schools; by the end of 1972, those numbers had fallen to 8 percent and a little less than 12 percent, respectively.[40] Comparative budget outlays are equally revealing. President Johnson had expended $911 million for civil rights activities, including $75 million for civil rights enforcement during the 1969 fiscal year. For the fiscal year 1973, the Nixon administration's budget called for $2.6 billion in total civil rights outlays, of which $602 million was earmarked for enforcement through a substantially strengthened Equal Employment Opportunity Commission (EEOC).[41] The increased outlays cannot be dismissed as inexorable growth due to inflation or nondiscretionary budgetary commitments.

Although the EEOC was specifically created to enforce Title VII of the 1964 Civil Rights Act, prohibiting employment discrimination on the basis of race, color, religion, sex, or national origin, it took over a decade to make the commission effective. During that time, administrative guidelines evolved for enforcing affirmative action. Two Johnson administration executive orders were particularly important. In 1965 Executive Order No. 11246 prohibited racial, religious, and ethnic employment discrimination by federal contractors, and in 1967 Executive Order No. 11375 added sex discrimination to this list. Executive Order No. 11478, issued by Nixon in 1969, strongly exhorted federal agencies "to establish and maintain an affirmative action program of equal employment opportunity for all civilian employees," and during his administration the EEOC conducted the first compliance reviews of hiring policies toward women by institutions of higher education receiving federal grants. By August 1972 over 350 sex discrimination suits had been brought against such schools across the country.[42]

EXPANDING EQUAL OPPORTUNITY: THE PHILADELPHIA PLAN AND TITLE VII

While Presidents Kennedy and Johnson had employed the term "affirmative action," it "did not have much bite" until the Nixon administration announced a revised version of LBJ's Philadelphia Plan in 1969, requiring federal contractors in the construction industry of that city to hire minority workers. Secretary of Labor George Shultz later extended this plan to nine other cities. He also issued the first guidelines requiring businesses with federal contracts to draw up "action plans" for hiring and promoting women.[43] In other words, not until the Nixon administration did "affirmative action" begin to become coterminous with "civil rights." When the Rehnquist court decided in *City of Richmond v. J. A. Croson* in 1989 that "set-asides" for minority construction workers were unconstitutional, much to the surprise of most Americans, legal specialists recalled that that practice of guaranteeing work for minorities had been initiated with the Philadelphia Plan twenty years earlier by the Nixon administration.

Contemporary ignorance of this fact cannot simply be blamed on Watergate; it also stems from greater acceptance among scholars of Johnson's reputation as the "unanticipated hero" of the civil rights movement, when that title could just as appropriately be applied to Nixon.[44] Recent monographs and newly released documents show the consistency of Nixon's views on civil rights over his entire political career as well as his success where Johnson had failed to implement the Philadelphia Plan.[45] In doing so he alienated more conservative allies than he gained liberal ones. The Supreme Court may have forced Nixon into desegregating the nation's school system, but he championed the Philadelphia Plan on his own.

Under LBJ the Office of Federal Contract Compliance (OFCC) had experimented on a hit-or-miss basis with ways of ensuring greater equal-opportunity practices among white contractors in St. Louis, San Francisco, Cleveland, and Philadelphia. The method specifically employed in Philadelphia required a meeting with low bidders *before* awarding contracts, to review their affirmative action plans and to obtain agreements for on-the-job compliance reviews. In the fall of 1968 the comptroller general of Congress, Elmer B. Staats, declared this policy in violation of fair and competitive bidding guidelines. So Nixon came to office under no pressure to move on minority hiring in the construction industry. Moreover, Democratic leaders in Congress were suspicious of the bureaucrats under Johnson who had launched the original Philadelphia Plan, and even more suspicious of any affirmative action plans designed by Nixon aides to give the executive branch more control over affirmative action.[46]

Indeed, the president had appointed several men who fought for a White House–dominated civil rights program: Secretary of Labor George Shultz, Assistant Secretary of Labor Arthur Fletcher, and OFCC Director John Wilks. Instead of abandoning the Philadelphia Plan, they revised it to ensure as much executive-branch control as possible, an idea perfectly in keeping with Nixon's emerging New Federalism. The revision also allowed the Nixon administration to keep the focus on the racism of the northern craft unions in the construction industry, rather than switching it to the equally racist hiring practices of southern textile industries. But some prominent Democratic senators, such as Edward Kennedy, would have preferred Nixon to concentrate on practices in the South, thereby not allowing Dixie Democrats to be won over by Nixon's southern strategy. Specifically, Kennedy knew that if the Republican administration could be forced to implement nondiscriminatory federal contracts primarily against white southern textile owners and workers, such whites would stay in the Democratic camp.[47] Currently available documents do not reveal Shultz's exact intentions, but some commentators (including J. Larry Hood, who conducted private interviews with him) appear to confirm that the role of the secretary of labor was crucial—and so was Nixon's long-standing commitment to minority hiring.[48]

During the more recent controversy over both affirmative action goals and set-asides of the late 1980s and early 1990s, Nixon took a strong stand on civil rights at a private dinner with prominent Republicans. He said it would be a "bad mistake" if President Bush were to continue to use his opposition to racial quotas as grounds for attacking civil rights legislation. The Republican party had left an "indelible" pro–civil rights record in the 1950s and 1960s, Nixon said, and "there would be no political reward for going after the anti-quota vote." This is not to imply that Nixon favored quotas while president any more than he has since leaving office. Again and again from the Oval Office he wrote to concerned constituents that "with respect . . . [to] affirmative action programs, I agree that numerical goals, although an important and useful tool to measure progress which remedies the effect of past discrimination, must not be allowed to be applied in such a fashion as to, in fact, result in the imposition of quotas."[49]

While political considerations played a role in Congress and the White House, the administration successfully defended the right of a Republican president to exercise the same authority as previous Democratic presidents (dating back to FDR) to require that equal employment opportunities be complied with in government contracts. Thus, Nixon not only stood solidly behind Johnson's Executive Order No. 11246 and his own Philadelphia Plan (which affected only construction contracts in excess of $500,000 in one five-county area) but he expanded that plan in January 1970 with Order No. 4 to include all government contracts of $50,000 or more in all areas of employment. In December 1971, this order was further expanded to include women, and finally in May 1974 it specifically stated that a potential contractor's affirmative action programs had to have as their goal "prompt and full utilization of minorities and women at all levels in all segments of its work force."[50] Nixon had put in place a nationwide plan by 1971, laying the groundwork for the minority set-aside programs and specific affirmative action goals for hiring within the construction industry that the Supreme Court believed constitutional until 1989. Moreover, Order No. 4 gave the OFCC legal authority through Title VI of the 1964 Civil Rights Act to become a major vehicle for redressing discrimination against women by 1972, compared to Title VII, whose enforcement by EEOC had been feeble due to underfunding and understaffing during the Johnson administration. These actions could be considered examples of reverse southern strategy, whereby the administration gave notice to the North that it also had civil rights problems that needed to be addressed.

The other major area in which the Nixon administration expanded enforcement of affirmative action during his first term in office came in March 1972, after a three-year debate over how to increase EEOC's powers under Title VII. Hugh Graham has detailed this struggle within the administration and between Congress and the White House over whether to combine EEOC and OFCC and whether to give EEOC the power to issue judicially enforceable cease-and-desist orders under Title VII, in addition to enforcing its orders through court proceedings. To make a complex legal and political story short, Jerris Leonard and William Rehnquist, both assistant attorneys general at the time, gave Nixon aides conflicting advice on this issue. Leonard favored giving more power to EEOC by its absorption of OFCC (and its legal authority under Title VI) from the Labor Department and both types of enforcement, while Rehnquist opposed strengthening EEOC authority. With passage of the Equal Employment Opportunity Act of 1972, the administration successfully opposed combining EEOC with OFCC and the cease-and-desist method of enforcement, preferring EEOC to use the court-enforced judicial approach it had already endorsed for implementing desegregation.[51]

Most important, between 1969 and 1972 the EEOC staff had risen from 359 to 1,640, and its budget from $13.2 million to $29.5 million. Nixon's fiscal 1973 budget for civil rights enforcement represented an eightfold increase over Johnson's for fiscal 1969. Enforcement funds for fiscal 1974 doubled those of 1972, with the EEOC budget increasing from $20.8 million to $43 million, and the budget for the Civil Rights Division of the Justice Department increasing from $10.7 million to

$17.9 million.[52] Although not always on the cutting edge of this controversial issue, the Nixon administration indisputably put money into civil rights enforcement.

One of the most unexpected highlights of Nixon's civil rights record took the form of the 1972 Voting Rights Act. Rather than simply propose an extension of the 1965 Voting Rights Act passed under Johnson, Attorney General John Mitchell challenged and angered liberal Democrats by proposing a bill that would "nationalize" voting rights, by providing for uniform residence requirements and banning literacy tests all over the country, not simply in the South. Since the 1965 legislation afforded voting rights protection in only a relatively small number of southern states—seven, to be exact—the administration's bill would have removed the stigma of the South's being the exclusive area of the country where African-Americans were denied the right to vote and would no longer have required southern states to submit any changes in their voting laws to the Justice Department for approval.[53] This also represented the reverse southern strategy of the administration.

Once again, however, the administration had to answer the charge by Democrats that this so-called evenhanded application of the law was really a Republican retreat on voting rights in disguise. Nixon's papers now show that his most liberal insider advisers, such as Ehrlichman and Garment, did not think this was the case.[54] At one level, Mitchell was simply carrying the Supreme Court decision in *Gatson County v. United States* to its logical conclusion by denying the nationwide validity of literacy tests because blacks did not receive equal educational opportunities; at another, he was casting liberal Democrats in Congress in the role of defenders of the status quo when they supported simply an extension of the 1965 legislation; and finally, it was a clear message to the South that this region of the country was no longer going to be singled out as the only discriminatory one in the country. Not surprisingly, the end result of the administration's bold initiative was a compromise that kept the "original, regionally targeted, 1964-based formulas for pre-clearance," thus continuing to stigmatize the South, but approved Nixon's nationalization of voting rights and banned all literacy tests until 1975.[55] On a tangentially related civil rights issue, his administration also established "home rule" (local voting rights) in the District of Columbia, Guam, American Samoa, and the Virgin Islands.

MINORITY BUSINESSES

Nixon's support for small businesses dates back to Eisenhower's creation of the Small Business Administration (SBA). While campaigning for his party's nomination in 1969, he wrote to the president of the National Association of Small Business Investment Companies reinforcing his commitment "to closing the small business equity gap" and praising the success of the SBA. And in the spring of 1968, with the influence of his law partner Leonard Garment and aide Raymond Price, Nixon had given two radio addresses setting forth a compelling case for federal encouragement of black-owned enterprises. In the first he had referred to "black capitalism," but quickly changed the wording to "black capital ownership" because of criticism of the former term by militant community activists—but the first term lingered in the minds of the public because reporters perpetuated its use. By the end of the year, after Nixon had become president-elect, his staff was besieged with letters to support a legislative package favoring the establishment of a Small Business Capital Bank, tax breaks for small businesses, and a more lenient SBA loan policy. Initially Haldeman fielded these requests (many of them sent at the urging of Finch's aide, Pat Gray).[56]

Despite the SBA's reputation for mismanagement and defaulted loans,[57] it was Nixon's belief in its purpose that apparently led him to expand the concept to include "blacks, Mexican-Americans, Puerto-Ricans, Indians, and others," with the creation of the Office of Minority Business Enterprise (OMBE) by Executive Order No. 11458 in March 1969. Nixon was under no illusion in establishing this office. He privately wished Secretary of Commerce Maurice H. Stans "good luck" but underscored "the enormous problems in our minority enterprise program," with such start-up businesses having a failure rate of 90 percent. The recommendation to establish the OMBE by presidential decree rather than by legislative authority came from a cabinet committee chaired by Stans, who became responsible for administering the program without any operating funds during the first year. Stans later defended that lack of funding on the grounds that it provided time "to develop a feel for necessary programs." Even with Nixon's and Stans's personal endorsement, however, the program floundered for most of 1969, as Stans tried to tap the resources of existing government agencies and as its new director, Thomas F. Roeser, found himself in direct competition with the head of the SBA, Hilary Sandoval (the highest-level Hispanic appointment in the new administration). Sandoval had been following his Democratic predecessor's attempt to promote minority enterprises by calling on a previously ignored section 8 of the SBA regulations that authorized set-asides for minorities.[58]

Liberal critics of OMBE inside and outside Congress did not help the fledgling enterprise, although it's hard to think they would not have supported it under Democratic presidential leadership, despite its funding and turf problems. House Democrats in particular viewed it as a "cosmetic device to lull minority Americans into acquiescence while corporate America carves up the national pie." Even Moynihan reportedly introduced Roeser at a 1969 meeting of the Urban Affairs Council as the new head of "a program we all know will fail." Others inside the White House strongly endorsed the program, including Garment, who inherited SBA and OMBE matters from Haldeman; Robert Brown, liaison with African-Americans; John Roy Price, counsel for the UAC; Ehrlichman aide Bruce Rabb; and of course Stans, who went directly to Budget Director Robert Mayo for additional SBA funding for minority small business investment companies (SBICs) and issued two major reports on the project in the fall of 1969. After issuing his executive order in March, Nixon did not personally become involved in the infighting over formulating OMBE policy and funding levels, but by the end of the year he felt it necessary to intervene and encourage more interdepartmental cooperation with OMBE, SBA, and the special task force on minority procurement set-asides headed by Garment.[59]

During Nixon's first term in office, the Office of Minority Business Enterprise may have generated too much grassroots expectation that went unfulfilled, and in the short run increased the cynicism of civil rights leaders. But, as with desegregation of southern schools, the statistical results are impressive, considering that the first year and a half of OMBE's existence was largely "exhortational." By mid-1972, before Stans left the Commerce Department to head Nixon's reelection campaign, he had established over fifty SBICs, largely with $18 million of corporate funding. By fiscal 1974 the budget for OMBE had increased to $242.2 million, or 3,000 percent. In October 1972 Nixon personally wrote to Shultz praising his efforts "to assist minorities in finding a profitable role in our economic system," confirming that it was a high priority of his administration: "we have years of discrimination to overcome." Nixon and his immediate staff believed that the administration's efforts in this area, as with many of his other minority programs, received too little publicity and credit. In particular, Secretary of Commerce Peter G. Peterson was faulted in 1972 for failing to promote the minority business enterprise programs more.[60]

White House staffers and cabinet members such as Garment and Laird realized that OMBE was far from perfect, but independent surveys conducted by *Nuestro Business Review* and *Black Enterprise* in 1981 "showed that 45 of the top 100 Latino businesses had been formed between 1969 and 1976" and that 56 of the top 100 black firms had been established "between 1969 and 1976, 30 of them in the years of 1969 through 1971 when the federal minority enterprise program was being launched." In 1985, one thousand black businessmen and -women gave a testimonial dinner in honor of Nixon and Stans for establishing the OMBE (now the Minority Development Agency). Unfortunately, the funding level of $60 million established by the Nixon administration in 1972 was not increased significantly throughout the 1980s.[61]

HISPANICS

Although the word *minority* meant "black" to most Americans in 1969, during Nixon's first term the civil rights of Hispanics and women also received varying degrees of attention. Of the three groups, only Hispanics continued under Nixon as they had under Johnson to be treated with "gestures in political symbolism," largely because their internal divisions over national origins, regional differences, and language problems prevented them from presenting a united front for lobbying purposes. But Nixon expected Hispanics to benefit from his expanded SBA and OMBE programs. He approved a congressionally created Cabinet Committee on Opportunity for the Spanish-Speaking (CCOSS) in December 1969, but it did not officially convene until June 8, 1971, and Nixon did not appoint a CCOSS chair until August 5.[62]

Before that first meeting of CCOSS, Hispanics did receive attention from internal White House reports, the Civil Rights Commission, and the EEOC, as did African-Americans and women. Curiously, given his disregard for civil rights as a Nixonian hatchetman during the 1972 presidential campaign, Charles ("Chuck") Colson came into the White House charged with attracting ethnic votes to the Republican party by suggesting ways to improve their socioeconomic and political status. In a fifty-two-page confidential memorandum to Ehrlichman at the end of 1971, entitled "Issues for Spanish-Speaking Americans," Colson accurately and persuasively argued for substantial and symbolic Hispanic programs, stressing housing, economic development, and education. The Civil Rights Commission and the EEOC had already issued reports showing discrimination against Hispanics in 1970, and Ehrlichman had warned Nixon as early as April of that year that relations with Hispanic leaders could become confrontational. By January 1972 Ken Cole stressed to Ed Morgan the president's interest in developing programs for Hispanics, especially in the area of housing.[63]

Even before Colson wrote his suggestions for encouraging "movement in the voting preferences of Spanish-surnamed Americans" at the end of 1971, Nixon assigned Garment the task of winning minority votes through civil rights measures and ordered his staff to make sure that "Italians, Cuban Americans, Poles and Mexicans . . . be included on the names of every commission formed hereafter." He also launched a program to enlist more Hispanics into the civil service and insisted on having a list of "brilliant Black, Spanish-speaking, and Indian achievers" to consult for making appointments.[64]

Some of these initiatives cannot be separated from an overall strategy to put together a new Republican coalition of "have-nots" for the 1972 presidential election, but they also indicate more than a passing concern on the part of certain presidential advisers and Nixon himself for the civil rights and socioeconomic plight of Hispanics. While leaders of Brown Power, a Hispanic organization for civil rights, remained as cynical about Republican intentions as spokespersons for African-Americans, they also remained more fragmented. They would not find a unified voice over voting and language discrimination until the Ford administration. Hispanic civil rights was an idea whose time had not arrived while Nixon was in office.

THE WOMAN QUESTION

The Nixon administration's record for women's rights was also stronger in terms of both litigation and legislation than is generally recognized.[65] Nonetheless, there were initial complaints inside and outside the White House about the slow pace it set on women's issues. Such criticism had faced Presidents Kennedy and Johnson as well. At first Nixon emulated JFK's rather than Eisenhower's and LBJ's method for handling the "woman question," by not choosing to give appointments to even prominent Republican females. Instead, after eight months in office he created a task force charged with addressing a broad range of women's issues. Although JFK had not appointed his commission on women until eleven months into his presidency, Nixon's delay of eight months has been much more criticized.[66]

By the end of May 1969, fewer than a dozen of the thousand top political appointments made by the new administration had been given to women. By September 1971, despite White House claims to the contrary, the record of these full-time and part-time "high positions" was only marginally better, according to Republican women who were keeping score.[67] But two years into his presidency, Nixon had made more full-time female presidential appointments (fourteen out of four hundred at grade GS-16 and above) than either Kennedy or Johnson at the midway points of their first administrations. (By the end of 1972 the Nixon administration claimed to have promoted or appointed 118 women "to top-level policy-making positions . . . compared to 27 during the previous administration.") As chair of the economic advisers, Herbert Stein claimed this was more "than ever before in the Nation's history . . . [with over] one-half of the appointees serving in jobs *never* before held by women."[68]

Republican women continued to believe, however, that "Republican government leaders [did] not consider women their equals" and that, rhetoric aside, the administration was "positively anti women," in part because "none of Nixon's Cabinet Officials and immediate White House Staffers has ever had an assertive woman working with them or had their wives and daughters in administrative positions so that they are not aware of the capabilities of a woman in high office." Finally, Democratic women apparently convinced their Republican counterparts that JFK and LBJ had had "demonstrably superior records" in the appointment of women (at least to lower-level positions) and in the "area of women's interests."[69] While this may have been true of Johnson, who was responsible for laying all the groundwork for Kennedy's Presidential Commission on the Status of Women, it definitely was not true of his predecessor, whose notorious private interest in women prevailed over his public interest in women's issues.

Unlike the well-organized civil rights movement, the resurgence of a women's movement was just beginning to take place as Nixon took office. Therefore, neither the president nor his staff was prepared for the pressure they received to address women's rights. At one of his very first press conferences, for example, Vera Glaser, the Washington bureau chief for the North American Newspaper Alliance, sharply questioned Nixon about women being a "lost sex" among his all-male cabinet. Moreover, none of the task forces he had appointed during his interregnum focused on women's issues. As a result, the Burns Report (Robert Burns was the aide in charge of summarizing all task force reports) to the president summarizing the domestic recommendations from these task forces completely ignored women.[70]

Yet it fell first to Burns, whose interest in feminism was nonexistent, to cope with irate Republican women such as Glaser, who documented for him in writing the absence of women in top federal government jobs. Her litany of discrimination ended with the following specific recommendations for action: ask Congress to support the Equal Rights Amendment (ERA); ask Congress to authorize cease-and-desist authority to EEOC; ask Congress to add sex discrimination to Title VI for OFCC enforcement so it could be applied particularly to educational institutions; ask Congress to add sex discrimination to the jurisdiction of the Civil Rights Commission; appoint a White House adviser on women's issues;[71] ask the Justice Department to bring sexual discrimination suits under Title VII of the 1964 Civil Rights Act; ask the Labor Department to include sex discrimination in OFCC guidelines (an action successfully blocked by labor unions under Johnson).[72]

Ultimately Nixon complied with all these recommendations; however, his support of the ERA was never as strong as Glaser and other Republican women hoped it would be, given his long-standing support of the amendment before becoming president. But compliance could not be wrung out of the Nixon administration until women's issues were forced on the largely male White House staff. As early as May 1969, Rita Hauser, a New York City lawyer whom Nixon appointed a member of the American delegation to the UN, issued a "rousing call to arms to women to fight sex discrimination in jobs and other areas," combined with the flat statement that "the Administration has not [done] well enough in giving women top jobs." Representative Florence Dwyer (Rep.-N.J.) also wrote Nixon with specific suggestions about which women to appoint.[73]

Nixon's personal opinion of the status of women in society is much more difficult to assess than his public stand in favor of rights for women. By the time he became president, some of his offhand remarks about women had been no more or less patriarchal and sexist than most politicians in their fifties at that time—varying from praise for individual women leaders at home and abroad to praise for the wives of his cabinet members: "women who do not hold office, but who hold the hands of their husbands who do hold office."[74] His staff was no better. None of them, for example, anticipated that Nixon's invitation to "one of the finest groups of Cabinet wives I have ever seen" to attend a cabinet meeting along with their husbands would be perceived as an "empty gesture" by Republican congresswomen, in particular, and prominent Republican professional women, in general.[75]

In the spring of 1969, while the president was acting publicly in both a congratulatory and a condescending way toward women, Ehrlichman smugly noted that a number of male Nixon aides, especially Patrick Buchanan, thought that the women he hired, such as Bobbie Kilberg, were either too liberal or simply out of place on the White House staff. While this is probably true, it is also true that Ehrlichman's early assignment of women to work on his staff, and even his support for the appointment of a special adviser to the president on women's issues, did not turn him into a supporter of the ERA. (And for all Ehrlichman's talk in *Witness to Power* about hiring women, a listing of White House staff positions in April 1971 shows only one woman on the large domestic council staff he headed.)[76]

Of all Nixon's White House advisers, outsiders Pat Moynihan and Leonard Garment exhibited the most interest in the woman question at the beginning of the first administration. Predicting in August 1969 that "female equality will be a major cultural/political force of the 1970s," Moynihan wrote the president one of his more flamboyant memoranda, attacking the hypocrisy of higher education for perpetuating "the notion that women have equal rights, but not really equal potentialities," and insisting that "male dominance is so deeply a part of American life that males don't even notice it." With typical hyperbole, he warned that there would be *violence* if women are not granted equality [because] . . . by all accounts, the women radicals are the most fearsome of all." He concluded by urging the president to take advantage of the issue not only in his appointments to office but also in his public statements because "this subject is ripe for creative political leadership and initiative."[77]

Support among other staffers within the White House varied depending on the circumstances and the specific issue. Most significantly, Ehrlichman refused to take a personal stand on Moynihan's memorandum. At best, most of Nixon's top male advisers (whether insiders or outsiders) recognized the potential political advantages of women's issues without changing their condescending, sexist attitudes or behavior. This was especially true of Harlow, Ron Ziegler (White House press secretary) and

Haldeman when dealing with female presidential aides.[78] For example, Ziegler publicly referred to Constance Stuart, the First Lady's staff director and press secretary, as having a "menopause problem." Haldeman once remarked that a meeting about Native American and women's problems "was a 100% waste of time" and refused even to consider a suggestion from Anne Armstrong, a presidential counselor, in 1973 that Nixon make a sixty-second commercial in behalf of the ERA; he wrote "*No!*" across her memorandum.[79]

Nixon appointed his Presidential Task Force on Women's Rights and Responsibilities on October 1, 1969, after some highly publicized outsider pressure led by Vera Glaser. Democrat Elizabeth Duncan Koontz, appointed by Shultz to head the Women's Bureau in the Labor Department, and Virginia R. Allan, former president of the National Federation of Business and Professional Women and organizer of state commissions on the status of women in the 1960s, supported Glaser and determined the composition of this uniquely Republican task force, thus avoiding the anti-ERA bias of the Democratic-dominated CACSW. Nonetheless, most of the thirteen women appointed agreed with Congresswoman Dwyer, who told Nixon in July 1969 that "our attitude should not be that of feminists. . . . [N]one of us are feminists. We do not ask for special privileges. We seek only equal opportunity."[80]

After being briefed by most of the federal agencies with any concern for or jurisdiction over women's affairs, reports from the Task Force on Women's Rights and Responsibilities, the Committee on Population and Family Planning, and the Citizens' Advisory Committee on the Status of Women, also appointed by Nixon, reinforced most of the demands of the emerging women's movement, especially on abortion and the ERA. These reports had their greatest impact on those of Nixon's advisers who were already favorably disposed to improve the status of women in the administration and the country. Among Nixon's top political-broker advisers, only his first and second secretaries of Health, Education and Welfare, Robert Finch and Elliot Richardson, and Secretary of Labor Melvin Laird strongly urged him to follow the traditional practice of Presidents Eisenhower and Johnson of appointing a few highly placed women. In the first two years of the administration, Shultz and Finch independently continued to press for female appointments within their own departments and throughout the executive branch. Likewise, political-broker insider Richardson, who succeeded Finch at HEW, accepted and implemented the recommendations of the report from the Women's Action Program, a special project of Finch's.[81]

Nixon's confidential statements indicate his political concern about making "some progress in working with women . . . in the way of bringing women into the Administration or in working with women to see whether we make some political hay." As he told Finch in September 1970, "we have failed to grab the ball on the whole women's business and we need to do some things to see that women are properly recognized and that we get credit for the things we do carry out with women." By that time the president was "again" considering appointing a "special assistant to his personal staff for dealing with women's interests."[82]

On October 17, however, Finch turned in a "rather discouraging report" on the involvement of women in administration work. It was especially evident in this confidential report that the Domestic Council under Ehrlichman had not made women's issues a priority. Then, in another confidential memorandum on December 4, Finch confirmed that the "President's concern about the relation of this Administration to women appears justified at present." Noting the criticism of the small number of female appointments, Finch supported the idea that a national "talent bank" be established, but also pointed out that the recommendations of the president's task force on women had been the "subjects of discussion, but not much more." He also reminded Nixon that the Citizens' Advisory Council on the Status of Women, which he appointed in August 1969, had unequivocally come out in favor of the ERA, and that ICSW recommended to the president that he "immediately request passage of the proposed Equal Rights Amendment by the Congress."[83]

A number of Finch's recommendations received White House approval. In April 1971, for example, Nixon issued a strong presidential directive to all executive departments "to increase the number of women in administration positions." At the same time, Finch was able to make a much more positive report to Nixon about "enhancing the role of women in the administration" in order "to really make a difference in the minds of women voters." Once again the HEW secretary stressed the importance of "high level, visible appointments" and recommended a goal of twenty-six to fifty-two such appointments in the next year. He then listed the most recent female appointees, including Barbara Franklin as full-time recruiter, primarily, but not exclusively, of women on Fred Malek's staff. Her main functions were to travel, give interviews, and speak to women's groups. Although Malek was then the official White House liaison for women, Franklin did not become the special assistant to the president that Republican women had recommended.[84] The other appointments made by the Nixon administration did not overly impress these prominent Republican women, and by May 1971 Nixon himself had begun to question whether the effort to recruit women was worth it, saying privately: "I seriously doubt if jobs in Government for women make many votes from women." Rather than being a totally negative comment simply rationalizing the president's reluctance to appoint women, it could have been, suggested the columnist Tom Wicker, a "hard political calculation; or it conceivably was a view somewhat ahead of its time that women generally wanted effective measures against sex discrimination rather than highly visible 'token' jobs in government for a select few."[85]

Ironically, some of the strongest criticism of Nixon on the woman question came from inside the administration just as Finch submitted his most optimistic report to the president. On April 12, 1971, Hauser wrote a memorandum to the president entitled "Emergent Responsible Feminism—Why We Are Missing the Boat for 1972." Only the remaining White House Democrat, Leonard Garment, categorically supported Hauser's memorandum (Moynihan having left the administration at the end of 1970). The varying degrees of bewildered responses to it from Nixon's top male aides indicate that even his most liberal Republican aides, such as John Ehrlichman, still did not think of feminism as a top-priority issue for the administration.[86]

An even stronger indication of the sexist shortcomings among White House staffers can be found in a July 28, 1972, memorandum from Roy Morey, staff assistant for the Domestic Council, to Kenneth Cole, then deputy assistant to the president for domestic affairs, in which he tried to play down the political importance of catering to women in any way on the grounds that (1) women were "substantially less interested in federally imposed solutions [as proposed by the Democrats] to local problems"; (2) they exhibited a "profound lack of understanding of the concept of revenue sharing," regardless of "socioeconomic standing, age, or political identification"; and (3) they expressed "a significantly lower understanding of issues related to foreign affairs." As high as the level of sexism was within the White House, it reached new heights after Alexander Haig became chief of staff in 1973 in the wake of the resignations of Haldeman and Ehrlichman over Watergate. Haig had already established his sexism by remarking about why Nixon's private secretary, Rosemary Woods, had described the eighteen-and-a-half-minute gap on one of the Watergate tapes as being only five minutes: "I've known women who think they have talked on the phone for five minutes who have talked an hour." He compounded that reputation by refusing to allow women to use the gym facilities in the Executive Office Building.[87]

If anything, the Nixon administration's policy on women became less rather than more aggressive after Ann Armstrong (who signed all of her communiqués Mrs. Tobin Armstrong) was appointed the first female counselor to the president on January 3, 1972. When Glaser and Hauser lobbied the White House for the creation of such a position, neither ever dreamed it would go to someone less vocal and assertive on women's issues than they. Armstrong's correspondence consists largely of thanking people and organizing innocuous meetings of top-level women appointees or women elected to Congress. The same is true of the correspondence of her special assistants, Jill Ruckelshaus and Jean Spencer. Their influence was further diminished under Haig's watch, and both women began spending more time on Watergate matters and less on women's issues.[88]

Leadership on women's issues inside the White House came from some of the men Nixon appointed—not from the women, because neither his aides nor the president hired strong, assertive Republican feminists as staffers. Although Garment, Finch, and Shultz became advocates for hiring more women and appointing women to executive positions, neither of these men strongly favored passage of the Equal Rights Amendment. This fact alone better explains why Nixon did not more actively support the ERA before its passage by Congress in 1972 than does the standard argument, which assumes either a change in his position or a lack of genuineness about his earlier commitment to the ERA.

Nixon had sponsored and worked for the ERA in both the House and the Senate in the last half of the 1940s and the early 1950s, and again as vice president and presidential candidate in 1960. As early as 1946, for example, Nixon had written to Josephine V. Terrill, chair of the Southern California branch of the National Women's Party, that he favored the ERA. In 1949 he told Congresswoman Katharine St. George that "I shall be glad at all times to give you any assistance you may want me to for advancing the [ERA] Resolution toward favorable consideration by the House." Although Alice Paul, founder of the National Women's Party and author of the ERA in 1923, detected a decline in Nixon's advocacy of the ERA in the 1950s after he became vice president, he reaffirmed his support when campaigning for the presidency in 1960 and 1968. "It is my hope that there will be widespread support for the Equal Rights for Women Amendment," Nixon flatly declared in July 1968, "which will add equality between the sexes to the freedoms and liberties guaranteed to all

Americans." By the time he became president, his position on the ERA was more long-standing and consistent than most nationally known politicians. Yet by January 1972, his State of the Union Message did not mention the ERA by name, though it contained three paragraphs about women's rights.[89]

While President Nixon continued to support the ERA nominally, he made no serious effort to secure its passage, despite the fact that his Task Force on Women's Rights and Responsibilities, his Citizens' Advisory Committee on the Status of Women, and his Committee on Population Growth and the American Future all endorsed it and urged the president to reaffirm his leadership in behalf of the proposed Twenty-seventh Amendment to the Constitution.[90] In the first months of his presidency, he continued to assure women of his "concern for the advancement of the American woman" and of the need for his administration to have "a general advisory council" on women's issues. Even Rosemary Woods encouraged the president to think along these lines.[91] When it came to the ERA, however, initially there was considerably less enthusiasm among White House aides, except from Leonard Garment, Barbara Franklin, and, belatedly, Ann Armstrong.

The ambiguous congressional testimony of William H. Rehnquist, then assistant attorney general, on behalf of the Justice Department in April 1971 brought matters to a head. According to Rehnquist's statement, there was no "national consensus for compelling all levels of government *to treat men and women across the board as if they were identical human beings.*" Although Rehnquist opened by saying that "President Nixon and this administration wholeheartedly support the goal of establishing equal rights for women," he dwelled on the fact that "opponents of . . . [the ERA] have raised significant questions which deserve serious consideration" and then detailed the "reservations of the Department of Justice."[92] If anything, Rehnquist argued more for H.R. 916—a bill sponsored by the administration based on the recommendations of the Presidential Task Force on Women's Rights and Responsibilities—than he did for the ERA in his twenty-nine-page statement.

This official position of the Justice Department not only angered such vocal Republican feminists as Hauser and Gutwillig but also prompted more moderate women activists within the administration and Congress to write Nixon to "take the initiative on this issue prior to the debate on the house floor [because] we know it will be a major issue in the 1972 Election."[93] The attempt by prominent Republican women to get Nixon to reaffirm his support for the ERA before the House of Representatives considered it one last time failed. Their argument was echoed by Barbara Franklin in August, when she told Malek that "if we wait until after the House acts, chances are we'll be on the defensive—and that's a posture we can't afford." In September, Ehrlichman hand-carried a rather mild-mannered action request memorandum written by Garment to Nixon about the impending House debate on the ERA. For some reason this memorandum undercut both the urgency and the relevancy of the president's reaffirming his support for the ERA. Although Clark MacGregor, John Russell Deane III (both White House aides), Garment, Finch, Rumsfeld, Ray Price, and Franklin all previously approved the idea of an exchange of pro-ERA letters with House minority leader Gerald Ford, Garment concluded by telling Nixon: "It is very likely that the Amendment will not get out of the House and Senate. You should therefore reserve yourself the option of proposing substantive legislation dealing directly with the more obvious forms of legal discrimination against women."[94]

Ultimately, without Ehrlichman's committed support, the ERA, like most domestic issues, would not receive quick or strong presidential action. Since Ehrlichman had not turned the ERA into a crisis issue, Garment's memorandum easily led the president to believe he need not take action on it in the fall of 1971. There simply was not sufficient male staff support within the White House for women's issues to prevail over other domestic concerns. (For example, in 1970 Nixon approved the appointment of an "Adviser on Women Affairs" only to have "the idea killed at the last moment" for no apparent reason.)[95]

Nonetheless, Nixon did agree to an exchange of letters with Ford.[96] Garment sent a special action memorandum by courier (with a draft of a letter to Ford for him to sign) to the president while Nixon was away from the White House in early October. In this memorandum Garment concurred with Mitchell, Ehrlichman, and John Wesley Dean III (counselor to the president) that Nixon should not sign the letter to Ford as previously recommended by some of his other domestic advisers, in part because of the four hundred constitutional amendments on twenty-two subjects then pending. This was the first time Garment linked the ERA to other amendments and to the fact that

there is a sense of developing disquiet in the country—of changes coming too fast, of government that can't adapt to their consequences. The addiction to panaceas is still with us: the imputing of substance to slogans

("End the War"), the wrapping of the most complex dilemmas into easy phrases ("Fair Housing", "Busing"). . . . In my opinion, most if not all of the Constitutional Amendments now pending have this slogan quality about them. Your commenting on any one of them will tend to weaken your ability to resist commenting on all of them during the federal legislative process. Taken together, this group of Amendments represents a large-scale move into the Constitutional alteration process, bypassing the longer but more careful method of legislative enactment or court precedent. . . . [E]ven the floor consideration by Senate or House of these Amendments may start to convey a very special message to the nation: That the Constitution isn't working adequately any longer.[97]

Garment simply suggested to the president that he have Ziegler state that "since the process of amending does not legally require the President's participation, there will be nothing beyond [your] 1968 Statement until Congress acts." Garment further suggested that Nixon rationalize this lack of active support through an announcement by Ziegler that, since the language of the amendment was still not settled, the president was "defer[ring] to Congressional debate before commenting on the Amendment." This same memorandum indicated that Armstrong, MacGregor, Franklin, and Gladys O'Donnell (Armstrong's aide) all continued to support the exchange of letters between Nixon and Ford. The earlier (and presumed continued) concurrence of Finch, Rumsfeld, Ray Price, and John Russell Deane III (not to be confused with John Wesley Dean III of Watergate fame) is not mentioned.[98]

As a result of this remarkable memorandum, Nixon did not sign the letter to Ford that had been prepared for him. When Nixon did send a letter supporting the ERA, on March 18, 1972, it went to Senator Hugh Scott. The ERA passed the Senate four days later, and the administration lost whatever initiative and encouragement it might have shown the ERA in the fall of 1971. The fact that the exchange of letters with Ford fell through and the letter to Scott was sent so soon before passage does not "confirm the insincerity of [Nixon's] professed conviction [about the ERA]." Instead, the real culprits in this situation were Ehrlichman himself, who apparently did not support the ERA; the request action memorandum to the president in September, written by Garment but delivered by Ehrlichman, which was curiously unenthusiastic about all options; and Garment, who reversed his support of the exchange in his October action memorandum and asked the president to reconsider his.

Garment was not the only Nixon adviser no longer adamant in his support for the ERA.[99] Even Robert Finch, as counselor to the president, adopted that position in the spring of 1971.[100] At the same time, Republican women inside and outside the administration had become more outspoken and adamant on all feminist issues, but especially the ERA. Ironically, by the fall of 1971 the common factor motivating these two groups—presidential aides and GOP women—was probably the lukewarm position of the Justice Department as formulated by Assistant Attorney General Rehnquist. As a result, the president was no longer receiving as strong or consistent advocacy memoranda about the ERA—except from prominent Republican women, whom he had never relied on for advice in the past.

Nixon told me in 1983 that his family (his wife and two daughters) favored the ERA, but he had come to believe after 1963 that the Equal Pay Act would achieve equality for women—apparently not realizing that this legislation could never end the pay differential between women and men or the sex-segregated nature of the U.S. labor force. This view may have had validity in 1969 when Nixon came into office, but he argued the point with me as though twenty years had not passed and proved him (and many others, including Democratic women who had supported the Equal Pay Act) wrong. Nonetheless, he correctly asserted that effective application of Title VII of the 1964 Civil Rights Act could serve the same purpose for women as passage of the ERA. Nixon admitted to me, however, that as president he had not done as much for women as he would have liked.[101]

The abortion issue was much more controversial inside and outside White House circles than the ERA during Nixon's first term in office. Nixon had for years disapproved of unrestricted abortions, but he realized as president that it had become a "difficult and touchy problem which had divided national opinion." Although the president received one task force report, one commission report, and two committee reports, all favoring abortion—in the name of responsible family planning, if not freedom of choice for individual women—he hedged until 1971. Then he acted on his "strong personal" antiabortion sentiments by issuing an unpublicized directive to the Defense Department indicating that the termination of pregnancies must conform to state law in military medical facilities. "In those States where the State criteria on termination of pregnancies are more restrictive than the above policy," this March 31, 1971, memorandum read, "procedures in military facilities in those States shall be in accordance with the more restrictive criteria."[102]

Nixon could have addressed abortion indirectly by extending federal planning, if not regulation, into another area, namely, population control and national growth policy. This option became less viable when the administration failed to present a comprehensive legislation package to Congress on national growth policy—in part because by 1972, when the Commission on Population Growth and the American Future brought its report and action memoranda on the subject before the president, he and his staff began to think that family planning issues would be too controversial in an election year. Despite making a special message to Congress, appointing a commission on population growth, and spending endless hours with the Urban Affairs Council (later Domestic Council) discussing the national growth policy, Nixon was never urged by his immediate staff to connect abortion with population control. Finally, on May 5, 1971, the White House issued a press release in which Nixon said that he "consider[ed] abortion an unacceptable form of population control."[103]

When Nixon's staff finally had to face the abortion issue head-on, during discussions over the women's plank for the 1972 Republican party platform, even Rita Hauser expressed relief to Ehrlichman on August 28 that it had been "handled very well in that everyone felt an opportunity was there to express views and no one seemed particularly concerned that it did not make its way into the Platform." Although Hauser noted that a "sizable majority of Americans, including Roman Catholics, now favor[ed] liberal abortion laws," she recommended to Ehrlichman that "nothing further should be said by the President on this issue one way or the other for the duration of the campaign."[104] Thus, Nixon left office with the same position on abortion that he had brought to it—much to the consternation of many Republican and Democratic feminists, none of whom had had enough of the president's attention or sympathy to change his mind on this issue of such profound importance for women, even after the landmark decision in *Roe v. Wade* (written by Justice Blackmun, a Nixon appointee to the Supreme Court).

On other women's questions, however, Nixon proved much more liberal than expected. During his first term, for example, Congress passed the Equal Employment Opportunity Act; approved Title IX of the Education Amendments Act; and prohibited sex discrimination by educational institutions receiving federal aid. Nixon personally insisted that Congress broaden the U.S. Civil Rights Commission mandate to include sex discrimination and amend the 1971 Revenue Act, making child care expenses tax-deductible when both parents worked. In addition, Congress attached a number of anti–sex discrimination provisions to such federally supported programs as health training, revenue sharing, Appalachian redevelopment, and environmental protection.[105]

Of all of these actions taken by Congress and ultimately approved by Nixon, the one he least liked and understood was Title IX, which he once called a "monstrosity" when an aide misleadingly told him that it would "virtually end athletic scholarships." The one in which he took the most active interest was the Civil Rights Commission. Not only did he favor the "extension of the life of the Commission by 5 years," but he also "support[ed] expanding the scope of [its] activities to cover women," despite the strong opposition of Caspar Weinberger, when he was deputy director of OMB, and with only the lukewarm support of Secretary of Labor George Shultz and Associate Director of OMB Frank Carlucci. These internal memoranda clearly indicated that the "controlling factors" for including women's issues under the jurisdiction of the Civil Rights Commission were "political," and that it was "probably inevitable and not worth the flack to oppose it." They also strongly hinted that the president of Notre Dame University, Father Hesburgh (and presumably the Catholic hierarchy in the United States), opposed expanding the mandate of the Civil Rights Commission to include women because of the abortion issue.[106]

The Ninety-second Congress (1971–73) also passed a Child Development Act that would have provided free day care for poor families and a sliding fee scale for higher-income families, but Nixon vetoed this legislation on budgetary and administrative grounds. Unfortunately, child care became the political victim of a struggle between the Democratic-controlled Congress and this Republican president over two other issues: welfare and the Office of Economic Opportunity (OEO). Nixon's own significant reform of the welfare system contained $750 million annually to construct and operate federally funded welfare (including child care) facilities for welfare recipients and the working poor. By calling for $2 billion in the first year, which the administration projected would mushroom into $20 billion annually, Congress went far beyond what Nixon thought was needed (since his Revenue Act already gave a child care tax break to families in which both parents worked).[107] Two-thirds of Nixon's December 1971 veto message dealt with the Democratic-sponsored "comprehensive child development services, patterned after the Head Start Program." Democrats incorporated this into the third section of the Economic Opportunity Amendments of 1971 as a deliberate ploy to make the president appear to be an opponent of child care because they knew that he would not approve the other two provisions of Congress's OEO legislation. However, the extremely profamily tone of the veto message was not in the first draft considered by Nixon. It had been written primarily by the speechwriters Ray Price and John Andrews, with strong support from HEW Secretary Elliot Richardson. The final version was substituted at the last minute to satisfy conservatives in the party who, according to Charles Colson, "have made it very plain to us that if the veto message is not on principle, we will get absolutely nothing. If it's on principle [that is, profamily] . . . it may be precisely what we need to buy ourselves maneuvering room with the right wing." Because the Republican National Committee happened to be meeting in Washington during the week of the veto message, Nixon also expressed concern to Colson that "conservatives [be] on board . . . [because] we will take a lot of heat from the left" over the veto. Colson assured him that there had been discussions with "[conservative Senator James] Buckley and Co.," and that Colson "was certain that if we made our case the right way, it would score big with the conservatives."[108]

Courting right-wing Republicans outweighed all other considerations in the final draft prepared by Pat Buchanan. Up to the last minute, however, Buchanan was not sure that the president would accept his version. "If the president decides not to go with something along these lines," Buchanan told Haldeman the day before the veto message was delivered, "could I see the final of what he is going with? Perhaps it can be laundered a bit."[109] In the end, the ultraconservatism of Pat Buchanan, the Haldeman aide Larry Higby, and Colson prevailed over Richardson and Nixon's more moderate in-house speechwriters. As a result, Nixon did not attack in this message the real object of his veto—the Office of Economic Opportunity (OEO)—as much as he did child care, an emphasis that did not reveal his true position on either issue. As with the ERA, Nixon's public position on child care was determined by which set of advisers won the battle over policy statements.

In this instance, however, his veto derailed the possibility of a national child care program at a moment when an unusual coalition of moderate forces, aided in part by the president's own child care proposals, had succeeded in obtaining congressional approval.[110] Even though both parties supported quality day care services in the 1972 election, a unique opportunity had been lost in 1971 because of partisan politics that Nixon's most conservative advisers took advantage of to promote their own stereotypical views about child care outside the home.

Unlike the vetoed child care legislation, most of the congressional activity on behalf of women approved by Nixon during his first term had been ignored by his critics, not only because it did not fit their image of him but also because so much of it was incremental in the sense that it "involved amendments to or parallels of minority civil rights legislation." Not until the Ninety-third Congress (1973–75) was antidiscrimination legislation passed for women that had no racial antecedents—with the support of both Presidents Nixon and Ford. They approved the Equal Credit Opportunity Act (ECOA), originally passed in 1975 as an amendment to the 1970 Consumer Credit Protection Act, and the Women's Educational Equity Act (WEEA), and created a National Center for the Control and Prevention of Rape and a Foreign Assistance Act amendment favoring "programs, projects, and activities which tend to integrate women into the national economies of foreign countries." In 1975, after much pressure from women inside and outside government, the State Department initiated a Mid-Level Affirmative Action Program and a Junior Office Affirmative Action Program designed to increase the women and minority Foreign Service Officers.[111]

Underneath these invigorated civil and political rights programs, several accomplishments stand out. The Nixon administration desegregated southern schools; significantly increased funding for the enforcement of both group and individual civil rights; achieved court approval of goals in hiring practices rather than quotas; and clearly transformed the power and responsibility for civil rights to a court-enforced approach based on recommendations of permanent government affirmative agencies within the executive branch. That these achievements did not endear Nixon to conservatives of either party goes without saying, and, like his welfare program, they did not ingratiate him with Democratic liberals, civil rights leaders, or union leaders in the North either. While scholars differ on the reasons, there is no denying, as with desegregation of southern schools and public institutions, that Nixon's advances in civil and political rights for women and minorities far outweighed those of his predecessors, belying the "divisive public rhetoric" his administration employed in the process.[112]

Nixon remains the only modern president whose personality, rhetoric, and image can be used with impunity to dismiss or ignore his concrete achievements, especially in the area of expanding civil rights enforcement in particular, and domestic reform in general. Like most modern presidents, some of his positions on these issues were determined as much, if not more, by his choice of advisers than by his own personal views. Nowhere is this more evident than with respect to Nixon's radical domestic proposal for reforming the welfare system of the United States.

4

BOLD ATTEMPTS AT WELFARE, HEALTH, AND ECONOMIC REFORM

Only societies that believe in themselves can rise to their challenges. Let us not, then, pose a false choice between meeting our responsibilities abroad and meeting the need of our people at home. We shall meet both or we shall meet neither.

—Nixon, remarks at the Air Force Academy, June 4, 1969

Nowhere was the influence of Nixon's two quite different sets of advisers more evident than in the formulation of the most radical of all his attempts at domestic reform—a restructuring of the American welfare system. In addition to such freethinking outsiders as Robert Finch and Pat Moynihan, Robert Burns, Melvin Laird, George Shultz, and especially John Ehrlichman played important roles as political-broker insiders when it came to the final formulation of the president's special address to the nation on August 8, 1969. In this speech the president asked for an end to the services approach to welfare through Aid to Families with Dependent Children (AFDC), Medicaid, food stamps, and school lunches. Nixon proposed instead direct cash payments, not only to families with no male heads of households but to the "working poor," including male breadwinners. The recommendation for turning from a services strategy to income maintenance would have helped three times as many children as did AFDC and its ancillary programs, while avoiding the hypocrisy of forcing poor women to say that husbands or lovers had deserted them in order to claim benefits.

This radical welfare proposal constituted a negative income tax, or guaranteed annual income, for all heads of poor households.

How did such a revolutionary idea emerge during Nixon's first administration, when most Americans did not expect him to recommend any significant social reform? Johnson and Carter had expressed much more interest in social issues than the man whose presidency they flanked, but neither had attempted such radical reform of the welfare system. Why do Nixon's welfare proposals, like his national health program, remain relevant for the 1990s?

Unlike his well-known views on such issues as civil rights and government bureaucracy, Nixon's ideas on welfare are difficult to trace. They seem to be connected with antigovernment Lockean statements made early in his career about communities functioning best when individuals are free to work out their own problems, "building their businesses, asking nothing from their government except an opportunity to live a free, decent life."[1] For a long time his views on welfare remained highly unfocused. While campaigning for the nomination in 1968, he said that "at the present time, I do not see a reasonable prospect that I will recommend . . . a guaranteed annual income or a negative income tax." This was in keeping with a Gallup poll indicating that most Americans opposed a guaranteed annual income, but those making under $3,000 a year favored it.[2] Since 1953, however, Nixon had made a distinction between general welfare and the welfare state: "In the welfare state the government absorbs the citizens and private groups. It may smother them with honey, but nonetheless it smothers them. They are regulated from cradle to grave. In the general-welfare state the government is the servant of the citizen. It seeks to help, not to control. It promotes rather than absorbs the free energies of labor, business and the farmer."[3]

As a presidential candidate for the second time, in 1968, he did not relate any of these general ideas to welfare reform, although in his acceptance speech at the Republican convention he spoke of "government programs for unemployed, the cities, [and] the poor . . . [resulting in] an ugly harvest of frustration, violence and failure." His only recommendation for remedying the situation at the time was to refer vaguely to government tax and credit policies to encourage private enterprise.[4]

Later in the campaign Nixon said that welfare should be based on "national standards," should preserve "the dignity of the individual and the integrity of the family," and should provide incentives for moving people "onto private payrolls." He was known to distrust social workers, and he thought that Johnson's "welfare system was an 'utter disaster' [that] required fundamental change." These predispositions conceivably made him prefer cash transfers rather than increased services as a primary means of providing public assistance in the future. One of the brash young liberal Republican founders of the Ripon Society advised Nixon that the only issues over which GOP liberals and conservatives might unite were a negative income tax and a volunteer army. Nixon, nonetheless, managed to become president without having clarified his views on either issue.[5] Yet he endorsed both just three months into his first term.

As president-elect he set an unexpectedly fast pace on welfare, demanding from his aides an investigation into what a newspaper story alleged was corruption in New York City's Human Resources Administration. "This New York mess," he wrote, "is probably typical of a problem which exists all over the country. . . . I want a thorough investigation made. . . . The American people are outraged, and in my view they should be. . . . I do not want this swept under the rug or put aside on the grounds that we want to have an 'era of good feeling' with the bureaucrats as we begin. This whole thing smells to high heaven and we should get charging on it immediately."[6]

Another indication of early interest in domestic affairs, if not specifically welfare, came three days after he took office, with the creation of the Council of Urban Affairs (later the Urban Affairs Council). As his first executive action, the Council and its colorful executive secretary, Pat Moynihan, received unusual publicity. There was speculation about whether this made Moynihan the Kissinger of domestic policy, since the UAC was loosely modeled after the National Security Council. Given Moynihan's temperament and his indifference to management skills, such comparison proved misleading. Moynihan's position from the beginning was more tenuous than Kissinger's because criticism of his liberal views prompted Nixon to appoint Arthur Burns as counselor for domestic affairs. Burns's views diametrically opposed those of Moynihan. Moreover, unlike Moynihan, the maverick liberal Democrat, Burns had access to the president as an insider adviser on domestic matters, access based on years of friendship. The president perceived Burns as "wise and honest, but like most economists often a bore." As a flamboyant outsider adviser, Moynihan, like Kissinger, quickly ingratiated himself with Nixon by wit and histrionic statements. Nixon once told me he thought of Moynihan as "an activist and progressive (not liberal)."[7]

At the second meeting of the Urban Affairs Council, Nixon directed everyone to "move ahead at full speed on a final resolution of the issue of the future of the poverty program." He privately informed Burns, Moynihan, and HEW Secretary Finch that he had decided on minimum federal standards for aid to the indigent. Burns tried to forestall this decision by telling the president that the American people wanted to reduce welfare, and that "setting up national welfare standards" would produce the opposite effect. Nixon impatiently requested a status report on the work of the UAC welfare subcommittee chaired by Finch. He was assured there would be a staff paper ready "no later than March 15." Nixon's handwritten notes at this time indicate frustration over the fact that many ideas could be found "for solutions of Technical problems—few can be found for Human problems." After an inconclusive meeting of Finch's subcommittee the president, to the dismay of Burns and his chief aide, Martin Anderson, continued to place his trust in a guaranteed annual income. It may be that over Easter, when the president was vacationing in Key Biscayne, he decided to revamp public assistance in America completely. Nixon implied as much in a message to Congress, relating that "tinkering with the present welfare system is not enough. We need a complete re-appraisal and re-direction of programs."[8]

The president clearly pressed on welfare matters from the beginning. Whether it "absorbed more of his interest than any other domestic issue," as Moynihan claimed, is debatable, and the direction he was heading remained unclear for months. "I wanted to be an activist president in domestic policy," Nixon said in his *Memoirs*, "but I wanted to be certain that the things we did had a chance of working." He warned members of his cabinet: "Don't promise more than we can do, but do more than we can promise."[9] The most effective evidence of Nixon's personal interest in welfare as a "compassionate conservative" was found in a memorandum to a speechwriter, Raymond Price, suggesting he put the idea in "human" terms for a future presidential address:

Paint a picture of what a terrible mark [welfare] leaves on the child's life. Point out that [Nixon's proposed reform] takes away the degradation of social workers snooping around, of making some children seem to be a class apart. . . .

Point out that the greatest [problem] of the present welfare program is the effect it has on children, and that the greatest benefit of all families in America is to stand proud with dignity without being singled out as those who are getting food stamps, welfare, or what have you.

[I]n the depression years I remember when my brother had tuberculosis for five years and we had to keep him in a hospital, my mother didn't buy a new dress for five years. We were really quite desperately poor, but as Eisenhower said it much more eloquently at Abilene in his opening campaign statement in 1952, the glory of it was that we didn't know it.

The problem today is that the children growing up in welfare families receiving food stamps and government largess with social workers poking around are poor and they do know it. . . .

[T]his is our chance now to see that every child, at least, will grow up in a family where he will not have the fact constantly thrown in his face that his father never married his mother and doesn't live at home, and that therefore in common parlance he is a bastard and further that he is on welfare, while his school mates can point with some degree of pride to the fact that their fathers at least are taking care of the family and have a little pride. The need for dignity, pride, character to be instilled in those first five years of life is something that could well be [included].[10]

Despite his sensitivity to poor and disadvantaged Americans, Nixon and his speechwriters never did succeed in projecting this image to the public.

MOYNIHAN THE MEMO MAN

One of the answers to welfare problems that the president received as an explanation for the welfare "mess" in New York City was in a memorandum from Moynihan. Since he had not committed himself to any course on reform, this first and in many respects most substantive of Moynihan's memoranda on the subject appears to have been what prompted the president's quick acceptance of establishing national standards. The ebullient Moynihan began: "Like the girl and the book about crocodiles, I fear that I may end up telling you more about welfare in New York than you want to know." Information followed along with recommendations based on conventional New York wisdom about welfare, couched in unconventional language and designed to appeal to Nixon's weakness for ideas justified with historical hyperbole.

Such verbiage, playing on the president's darkest suspicions about the Great Society's welfare program and the Washington bureaucracy, became standard fare in subsequent communications from Moynihan. His first memorandum contained extreme statements about the failure of the Great

Society. Moynihan urged Nixon to declare that "welfare as we know it is a bankrupt and destructive system." Then in capital letters he recommended: "THE SINGLE MOST DRAMATIC MOVE YOU COULD MAKE WOULD BE TO SEND A MESSAGE TO CONGRESS CALLING FOR NATIONAL MINIMUM STANDARDS IN WELFARE. THIS SHOULD BE ACCOMPANIED BY THE APPOINTMENT OF A NATIONAL COMMISSION TO FIND OUT WHAT IS GOING ON."[11]

Underlying Moynihan's statistical assumptions was the idea that a welfare crisis existed in New York City and therefore would soon appear in the rest of the country. In 1967, welfare recipients in New York City had nearly tripled in under ten years. A crisis developed, according to Moynihan, because "correlation between unemployment and welfare recipients had . . . ceased to exist among the urban poor." As he did with the advice he gave Nixon about race relations, Moynihan used figures from a controversial study of the black family he had prepared for the Johnson administration. He told Nixon that, unlike in the 1950s, as Aid to Families with Dependent Children cases increased, non–white male unemployment actually decreased. This was the heart of the national welfare crisis as far as Moynihan was concerned: not the increase in traditional poverty but the creation of welfare dependency, especially among minority groups, unrelated to employment.[12]

Fortunately for Moynihan, the president already had indicated that he, too, assumed the situation in New York reflected conditions throughout the country. This assumption made Nixon susceptible to theories about a "crisis in welfare" based on the far-from-typical situation in New York City. Nixon's other advisers would cultivate such predispositions of Nixon as they vied over welfare reform programs because they sensed he was willing to listen not only to Moynihan's theories about a crisis but to their ideas for resolving it. Ironically, subsequent statistical research cast doubt on the catastrophic conclusions drawn by Moynihan; not until the 1980s and 1990s did welfare dependency materialize as he predicted.[13]

Regardless of the accuracy of his facts at the time, Moynihan later claimed authorship of Nixon's welfare program. The evidence shows it did not originate with him. Although he did sound the crisis alarm, his ideas about welfare extended only to vague suggestions about family allowances. Other advisers appeared as much influenced by Moynihan's crisis approach as Nixon, among them John R. Price, Jr., counsel for the UAC, and Richard Nathan, a fiscal-policy expert and research associate at the Brookings Institution whose Task Force on Antigovernmental

Fiscal Relations made the first recommendations on welfare to the Nixon administration. Most important, one of Nixon's most liberal outsider advisers—the only one who could claim to be the president's friend, Finch—accepted the idea of a welfare crisis. In the process of dealing with it, however, all four of these men—Moynihan, Price, Nathan, and Finch—lost control of the decision-making and policy-formulation processes over what was called at first the Family Security System (FSS) and later the Family Assistance Program (FAP).

THE CALIFORNIA CONNECTION

At forty-three, Finch was the youngest member of Nixon's cabinet and, next to John Mitchell, Nixon's closest political adviser, despite the fact that Mitchell was a conservative insider and Finch a liberal outsider. Unfortunately, as head of HEW he was also one of the most ineffective of Nixon's cabinet officers. Due to lack of previous Washington experience, naïveté, and ill health, he left HEW in June 1970 to become counsel to the president, then left Washington in December 1972 to resume his political career in California.

Finch's papers do not indicate whether he ever understood either the bureaucratic labyrinth in which he operated or how much of the advice he received came directly from lower-echelon Democrats. At the beginning of 1969, his views on welfare reform appeared even fuzzier than the president's, despite the fact that in California, as lieutenant governor under Reagan, he had had a reputation for supporting programs for minorities and urban areas. Like Nixon, Finch criticized the welfare system and the social-worker class it bred without offering solutions.[14]

In California Finch had always relied on the California state assemblyman John G. Veneman for advice about welfare programs, so it came as no surprise when he made Veneman undersecretary at HEW. Veneman in turn appointed the man he had relied on for advice on California's welfare problems, Tom Joe, as his assistant. A blind Hawaiian, Joe had become an expert in obtaining federal funds for social services while serving as the state assembly's senior research specialist on welfare.[15]

Ultimately Veneman, whose job it was to oversee HEW "policy planning and the administration of services and other welfare programs," controlled all welfare issues under both Finch and his successor, Elliot Richardson. Likewise, Joe became resident expert on services spending, as well as the catalyst behind the enormous expansion of public assistance funds to finance social services for the poor at the state level. In the spring and summer of 1969, however, Veneman and Joe were still feeling their way through the bureaucratic maze known as HEW, and both new-comers became willing participants in the negative-income-tax issue network of LBJ's holdover appointees. Because Veneman and Joe had a direct line to Finch's office, within weeks the secretary also inadvertently became part of a Democratic web of influence.[16]

THE ISSUE NETWORK TAKES OVER

When Finch appointed Veneman head of a subcommittee task force requested by Nathan, Veneman put the HEW deputy assistant secretary for planning and evaluation, Worth Bateman, in charge of a "working group" of welfare policy specialists. Bateman immediately chose as one of the members an old friend, James Lyday, an OEO economic analyst who was another bureaucratic holdover. Bateman and Lyday belonged to an issue network of welfare specialists who had sought to replace public assistance with a negative-income-tax program. (An issue network is a group of Washington bureaucrats from different departments who special-ize in one area.) Bateman harshly criticized the Nathan-Price plan that Joe privately had given him. Bateman and Lyday prepared a preliminary report suggesting a national standard for adult categories consisting of aid to the old, blind, and disabled and the abolishing of AFDC, to be replaced with a negative income tax for families with children, financed with federal funds.[17]

Supporting what Nixon liked to call the "working poor" represented a historical shift from the AFDC services strategy of all previous adminis-trations. Under Johnson there had been talk of a change to a negative income tax or a guaranteed annual income, as it was also called, but it never materialized. Nixon did not use either term in public, although advisers privately adopted the abbreviation NIT. In 1973, Moynihan used the term "guaranteed income" prominently in the title and text of his book on welfare, to call attention to his part in the attempt to revamp the New Deal welfare system.

Bateman and Lyday, ignoring the new UAC-committee structure, went directly to Veneman with their idea about a negative income tax. He helped them prepare a briefing for Finch on March 3. Finch exhibited his usual reliance on Veneman's advice about welfare and approved the Bateman-Lyday plan contingent on Nathan's acceptance. It remains unclear, however, just how much, if anything, Nathan knew about the dual activities of the working group, or whether he ever officially approved of the NIT approach before Finch's subcommittee met again, on March 24, to consider a modified Nathan-Price plan and the Bateman-Lyday one, then known as the Family Security System.[18] In any case, radical welfare reform did not originate with Nixon appointees, although several were very receptive to it; it came from Johnson appointees working only marginally within the UAC structure.[19]

By April 1, Finch had drafted a position paper for domestic policy called "A Nixon Alternative," which showed how quickly his views had developed since his first tentative television interviews. In general, Finch urged Nixon to "announce an end to the pile-on, political approach to domestic legislation" that had taken place since the New Deal: "Let us challenge the Congress and constituent groups to join with us in a common constituency to get the job done, rather than to preserve specific institutions or programs which are not doing their job."[20]

In his role as freethinking outsider, Finch called for a "revolutionary reform of the welfare system." The three recommendations he made to Nixon were taken from Bateman and Lyday's report and discussions at a subcommittee meeting. "The political support for this proposal should be widespread," the secretary overoptimistically predicted. He pointed out that his proposal was "not a Negative Income Tax Proposal, since it only covers families with children and does not do away with all income and service mechanisms, and is not a guaranteed annual income program unrelated to need or the ability to work." Finch also noted that "the proposed expansion of the food stamp program should be closely integrated with welfare reform since both are aimed at providing forms of income maintenance . . . [and that] the heart of the attack on dependency must be improved efforts of job training and employment."[21]

In the debate over welfare that swirled around the president, Moynihan came to accept first the Family Security System and later the Family Assistance Program, primarily through the efforts of the UAC counselor John R. Price, Jr. As a founder of the Ripon Society, Price had endorsed a NIT plan and previously tried to convince Moynihan that "it was better than [his earlier support for] family allowances." Once Moynihan saw the FSS outline, he became a convert and champion of the issue. He presided over the discussion, avoiding use of the terms negative-income-tax program or guaranteed income. Things became heated between Moynihan and Burns and Burns's aide Martin Anderson, and no decision was reached on whether to recommend FSS to the president. Finch scheduled another meeting but all leading proponents and opponents of FSS, despite lack of the welfare subcommittee's approval for their plans, started to bypass the UAC structure and appeal directly to the president.[22]

Years later it is still not clear whether Moynihan actually educated Nixon about welfare. He certainly did get the president's attention and kept him interested, if not particularly well informed. In retrospect, this liberal Democrat's role as a freethinking outsider and catalyst seems less significant now than it did in 1969 to those working with him in the White House. Despite (or because of) Moynihan's mentoring, Nixon had to look elsewhere for order, mediation, and synthesis before announcing FAP to the American people on August 8. Moreover, Moynihan's disorganized conduct of UAC meetings proved too time-consuming, not only for the president but also for cabinet members. Nixon presided over six of the first eight UAC meetings, spending as much as three hours at some of them. While all proved lively because of Moynihan's presence, they were not task- or decision-oriented, and invited the kind of behind-the-scenes machinations so evident in the formulation of FSS. Moynihan symbolized the disorganization that prevailed in the formulation of domestic policy during Nixon's first year in office.[23]

The president reentered the decision-making picture by requesting welfare proposals from Burns, Finch, and Moynihan for consideration over the Easter weekend, but again reached no decision on details. Burns was infuriated that Nixon did not reject the Family Security System idea outright. "It ran counter to everything I knew about Dick Nixon," he said later. "It seemed that he might do the unthinkable." Unknown to anyone but Ehrlichman, the president decided at the end of that weekend "to go ahead on this program." The problem of leaks led him to instruct Ehrlichman: "Don't tell Finch and Moy[nihan] et al.; but get a plan ready for implementation by the first of next week." This proved impossible, but it demonstrates how early Nixon committed himself to dramatic welfare reform, despite substantive disagreements among his advisers.[24]

The battle of memoranda continued, with Burns determined to develop an alternative to the Family Security System. Nixon began to solicit (and distribute) advice on welfare from people in and out of government. "To my knowledge," one official said, "the president had not done this on any prior issue and he hasn't done it since. . . . He was very involved in the [welfare] decision." He asked members of his cabinet to comment on the various welfare proposals and sent private letters "all over the country" asking a variety of people their opinions. All the time and effort on the part of the president reflected a breakdown in the UAC system itself under Moynihan's leadership and accounted for his remark to me: "I would still have *a* Moynihan, but maybe not *that* Moynihan."[25]

IN SEARCH OF A POLITICAL BROKER

By the middle of April 1969, Nixon needed someone to mediate among his insider and outsider advisers, especially between Burns and Moynihan. The UAC could not provide neutral ground under Moynihan's leadership, and neither could Finch's subcommittee on welfare because Finch was also a partisan of FSS. The president had become the focal point of all major memoranda on the subject of welfare. However, Nixon did not resort to an effective political-broker insider to mediate the situation until July—enduring the confusion and bickering over welfare for almost two additional months. This more than anything proves the president's personal commitment and interest in the issue at the beginning of his first term.

From the beginning Burns and Anderson opposed national standards. They were aided by Nathan and Assistant Secretary of the Treasury Murray L. Weidenbaum. When it became apparent that the president, in keeping with his campaign statement, had opted for minimum standards for welfare payments, Burns and Martin countered by insisting that such standards be linked with revenue sharing and work requirements. Weidenbaum, in an April 19 policy paper, apparently convinced them of the compatibility between federal welfare standards and revenue sharing.[26]

When I asked Nixon about this trade-off that Burns had forced between national welfare standards and revenue sharing, he did not remember it, although existing memoranda clearly establish the connection. In this way Burns and Martin entered the issue network of Nathan and Weidenbaum—both long-standing advocates of revenue sharing. As a congressman, Melvin Laird had also lent credibility to Weidenbaum's theory.[27]

These rationalizations placed both national welfare standards and revenue sharing well within the parameters of Nixon's New Federalism; in fact, they made welfare reform one of the cornerstones of his New Federalism because of its combination of centralization (minimum welfare payments set and administered by the federal government) and decentralization (revenue sharing placing funds for other than welfare purposes directly under the control of the states). At the time, Burns simply complicated the decision-making process, forcing the president to make a hard decision between incremental reform, which did not change the old AFDC system of services, and the radical alteration of providing cash benefits.

Burns opened a concerted attack on the FSS when he submitted a long document, accepting the Nathan task force recommendations he had previously opposed. He now suggested national welfare standards, as long as states meeting those standards would receive monies from revenue sharing. Burns wanted mandatory welfare for unemployed fathers, expansion of work-training programs, as well as job placement and day care centers. Work components figured prominently in his proposal, and for the rest of the summer he fought to ensure their inclusion. Evidence suggests, however, that Burns's battle for work-related elements was more show than substance. Nixon apparently had assured him sometime earlier in the spring that if a negative-income-tax strategy was employed, work would be required, so that opponents could not maintain that Nixon's welfare reform constituted a guaranteed annual income. (Much to the president's disappointment, requiring work from certain welfare recipients did not prevent both proponents and opponents of FAP from saying that it amounted to a guaranteed annual income.) A three-and-a-half-hour cabinet meeting on April 26 failed to resolve issues involving political considerations, family breakup, work incentives, and "cashing out" food stamps as they related to the two opposing programs.[28]

After Burns presented his memorandum, Nixon faced two other positions on welfare: those of two flamboyant outsiders—Moynihan and Finch—in opposition to the gray-flannel insiders Burns, Anderson, and Weidenbaum, and Nathan, a short-lived outsider adviser. Finch presented the president with a refutation of Burns's proposal. Pointing out that "both schemes involve revenue sharing ... [and] national standards," he insisted that Burns and his supporters did not understand the basic difference between "the increase in *dependency* as opposed to the increase in welfare rolls." Finch noted that Burns did not want to replace AFDC with FSS or any other new welfare scheme, but wanted to add funds to AFDC through revenue sharing. This, he told the president, was not enough. Only switching from an inefficient service approach to direct income allotments would transform the existing welfare mess.[29]

Secretary of Defense Laird, a longtime congressional expert on welfare, also told Nixon that the adoption of Burns's approach would essentially "lock the . . . administration into an affirmation of the past," which he described as "badly in need of reform" and the "product of nearly forty years of patchwork." He recommended that a study group prepare a "thoroughly thought-out welfare package," concluding: "On the relative scale, it seems to me, the issues involved in going to volunteer [military] forces are less complex than those involved in the crossroads decision of what U.S. policy ought to be in the welfare and income-maintenance field." Lyday wrote an internal HEW-OEO memorandum protesting Laird's suggestion for another task force, and by the end of May Nixon turned temporarily to Secretary of Labor Shultz for arbitration.[30]

Shultz had raised the issue of the working poor, and now the president asked him what course he should follow. Shultz assigned Jerome Rosow, his assistant secretary for policy development and research, to the problem. Eventually Shultz recommended a modified FSS that would include stronger work incentives in the form of disregarding twenty dollars a week earned by the employed poor. The original FSS adopted by Finch and Moynihan did not include such a work incentive. Shultz apparently was unaware that Congress had already approved a thirty-dollars-a-week "earnings disregard," plus a one-third write-off of the remaining monthly earnings and of some work-related expenses. This new cash incentive was scheduled to take effect on July 1, 1969, but it contained so many loopholes due to sloppy committee work that it soon gave rise to the stereotypical horror story about how mothers on welfare were able to manipulate the system to receive incomes in excess of ten thousand dollars a year. Although Nathan had informed Burns about this pending legislation on June 10, this presidential counselor did not apparently know how to use it to his advantage to show how his work incentive really meant taking a job and would not lend itself to welfare cheating, as the disregard system did. Those favoring the FSS did not raise the issue, as an earnings disregard would increase the cost of their welfare reform plan. For reasons that remain unclear, Shultz and Rosow came up with an earnings disregard that would have been less than the poorly drafted congressional one about to go into effect. In the long run, Shultz's contribution to the welfare debate was not so much that of a "creative synthesizer" as of a creative blunderer. But his suggestion for an earnings disregard, though badly conceived, ultimately provided the bridge between the two opposing welfare camps.[31]

After analyzing the "many uncertainties surrounding the future effects of a Family Security System on the social and economic behavior of poor families," Shultz recommended a work incentive in the form of an earnings disregard instead of the flat 50 percent reduction in FSS for all outside earnings; transition from welfare to work through training and a more ambitious child care program; and that the working poor should go first to FSS and then into job training.[32]

The day after Shultz submitted his memorandum, Finch agreed that some form of work requirements, as desired by Burns, should be incorporated into FSS. Nixon had to decide whether to compel work or to reward it with an earnings disregard. After mulling over the problem, he abruptly asked Ehrlichman to broker draft legislation that would combine FSS with *both* work requirements and work incentives. Burns was not informed of this presidential decision until July 7. By that time Ehrlichman had given his assignment to Edward Morgan, a staff lawyer, who described himself as "a babe in the woods" on welfare. This did not prevent him from cooperating with one of Finch's deputy assistant secretaries, Robert E. Patricelli, a founder of the Ripon Society and former staffer for Senator Jacob Javits, who brought Nathan, Rosow, and Anderson into the final drafting.[33]

In this circuitous manner, a group of low-level antagonists set to work ostensibly to draft legislation along conflicting lines they had already imposed on the president through his top-level advisers. Little wonder that the original battle lines reemerged within the design group, creating even more confusion and delay. Finally, on July 10, Ehrlichman set down Nixon's basic aims. By riding herd on the design group, it was Ehrlichman, not Shultz, Moynihan, or Finch, who emerged as the most effective domestic policy manager on welfare prior to Nixon's informing the nation about FAP. Arguments were strongly voiced at a cabinet meeting as late as August 6—two days before the presidential announcement. Nixon reportedly remarked that if a vote had been taken, it would have been eleven to four against—only Finch, Shultz, Rumsfeld, and Laird supporting it, in addition to Moynihan and Ehrlichman.[34]

As presented to Congress, the administration's bill called for anywhere from $1,600 (proposed in 1969) to $2,500 (in 1971) annually for a family of four. States were expected to supplement this amount and all able-bodied heads of recipient families, except mothers with preschool children, would "accept work or training." If such a parent refused to accept work or training, only the parent's payment would be withheld. FAP unconditionally guaranteed children an annual income and would have tripled the number of children then being aided by AFDC.[35] Nixon's legislation would have revolutionized welfare by switching from providing services to providing income.

THE NUMBERS GAME: WHAT PRICE WELFARE?

All the figures used by both sides essentially came from the Lyday-Bateman data bank. It became impossible for the president to distinguish between impressionistic and substantive advice from his staff. Each adviser based his ideas on systems analysis—an art that left much to be desired and gave to the few who seemingly held a monopoly on computerized information an advantage over those who did not. Nathan has noted that systems analysis was not as widespread in domestic agencies of the government in 1969 as it later became, but that "numbers were the game" with respect to opposing welfare plans. Whoever controlled the database controlled policy. But during sessions of both the original working group and, later, the design or drafting group, Nathan and other welfare generalists such as Finch, Moynihan, and even Burns lost control of the numbers specialists such as Bateman and Lyday, who had a hidden agenda of their own. This far-from-accurate "numbers game" continued after Nixon's August 8 announcement of FAP, as proponents and opponents among Nixon's advisers continued to fight inside the White House over welfare policy while refining the legislation to be presented to Congress.[36]

The numbers game took many forms in the spring and summer of 1969, beginning with Nathan's arbitrary figure of $1.5 billion to $2 billion. This forced Lyday and Bateman to come up with the low minimum-income FAP figure of $1,600 for a family of four, in order to keep within the administration's spending limit. Even though Nixon accepted the higher annual income figure of $2,500 per family in 1971, it made little difference because his liberal opponents called for as much as $6,400—far beyond what the administration, Congress, or the country wanted to spend for each family on welfare. Despite later disputes over details, initial editorials across the country hailed Nixon's August 8 message as a "genuine revolution," equivalent to FDR's Social Security legislation in the 1930s.[37]

The fundamental switch from services to income payment that FAP represented proved too much for liberals and conservatives alike in Congress, and they formed strange alliances for and against it. The "pro-Fappers" were welfare reformers led by two conservatives in the House,

Wilbur Mills (Dem.-Ark.) and John Byrnes (Rep.-Wis.), and a liberal in the Senate, Abraham Ribicoff (Dem.-Conn.), formerly HEW secretary. The "anti-Fappers" were generally conservative opponents of all welfare reform, and were supported outside Congress by the U.S. Chamber of Commerce, the American Conservative Union, and the weekly libertarian publication *Human Events*, which claimed to be "biased in favor of limited constitutional government, local self-government, private enterprise and individual freedom." Then there were the liberal spoilers, who opposed FAP while proposing their own exaggerated versions of it with the outside support of Americans for Democratic Action (ADA), American Friends Service Committee, the National Council of Churches, and most African-American congressmen from the North, who belonged to either the NAACP or the National Welfare Rights Organization (NWRO). Although some of these liberal spoilers initially called FAP a "step in the right direction," they ended up condemning it as an "attack on the poor" because its income guarantees were not high enough. In addition to the NWRO led by George A. Wiley, the International Brotherhood of Teamsters, the Methodist Church, and the NAACP all lobbied Congress against FAP, as did their conservative counterparts.[38]

With "the liberals say[ing] it is not enough [and] the conservatives say[ing] it's a guaranteed income," it took Mills and Byrnes until mid-April 1970 to obtain approval in the House, 243 to 155. They had to sweeten the measure by increasing cash benefits to adults and cash to governors in forty-two states whose payments to AFDC families were less than the proposed annual amount of $1,600. In the Senate, however, no such compromise was ever worked out among the three diverse groups of supporters and opponents of FAP, because Senator Russell B. Long (Dem.-La.), chair of the Senate Finance Committee, conducted hearings long enough to allow special interest groups to argue against it or propose unworkable changes. In particular, white liberals who logically should have favored FAP's basic principles were easily guilt-tripped by largely black liberal groups such as NWRO, which charged, among other things, that the bill was racist when, in fact, it would have benefited southern blacks on welfare for the first time in history. NWRO, largely a New York City–based group representing African-American welfare mothers, feared its own raison d'être might be threatened if FAP succeeded in eliminating the worst poverty among the poorest black families throughout the nation. NWRO Director Wiley predicted "civil disorder" among the poor if the administration's proposal passed, because the $1,600 would barely cover food costs for a family of four. Arguing along these same lines, liberal Senator Eugene J. McCarthy (Dem.-Minn.) dubbed FAP the "Family Annihilation Plan" for starving America's poor.[39]

Labor also did not distinguish itself in the congressional battle over FAP, largely because, since it surfaced in 1946, most economists viewed a negative income tax or guaranteed annual income as an alternative to a minimum wage. Having fought for minimum wages successfully during World War II, the AFL-CIO was not about to endorse a NIT without safe-guarding minimum wage legislation. Ultimately it succeeded in gaining this concession from the administration during the Senate debate. Nevertheless, organized labor did not ever enthusiastically endorse FAP when Senate votes were most needed, in part because a powerful AFL-CIO affiliate, American Federation of State, County, and Municipal Employees, knew that state welfare workers who administered welfare services would either lose their jobs or receive pay cuts when the federal government took over paying their salaries under FAP. Thus, employed middle-class union members prevailed over unemployed welfare recipients.[40]

The work requirements of FAP met opposition in the Senate for contra-dictory reasons. Some claimed that able-bodied women with children should not be "forced" to work, while working middle-class women did not see why they shouldn't. NWRO finally opposed all versions of FAP, opting for the status-quo AFDC program because it could not resolve its own internal inconsistencies about welfare. Then the White House, know-ing welfare would not be a popular issue in the 1972 election campaign, decided not to compromise any further by dealing with the changes pro-posed in the Senate by either conservative Russell Long (Dem.-La.) or liberal Abraham Ribicoff. H.R. 1 passed in 1971 by fewer votes than the 1970 bill. It raised the guaranteed income level from $1,600 to $2,400 for a family of four and strengthened the work requirements. Nixon held to a characteristically "middle position" by supporting the measure when he probably should have gone along with Ribicoff's proposals, which would have raised the basic family-of-four minimum to $3,000 and then reduced it to $2,600, as HEW Secretary Elliot Richardson and Labor Secretary James D. Hodgson recommended.[41]

Democratic presidential candidate George McGovern eventually retracted his proposal to give every American living in poverty $1,000 a year, but this ill-advised suggestion had created such a negative public reaction about any guaranteed annual income that it tainted the negative-income-tax features of FAP, "making it politically impossible to fight it out."[42] For the rest of the campaign, McGovern retreated to an even stricter approach to resolving the welfare problem than Senator Long (who wanted FAP reduced to $2,400 annually in return for thirty-two hours of work each week). Ironically, after a three-year struggle, FAP died anti-climactically in the Senate on October 15, 1972—just weeks before Nixon's landslide second-term victory.

There was an even more subtle, and in the long run more critical, problem with citing average and maximum monthly payments in the numbers game that raged over Nixon's welfare reform. This was the stunning revelation at the end of the 1970s that the alarming increase in welfare dependency shown in Moynihan's statistical trend was an aberration. According to Moynihan's now-famous chart, the crisis existing in welfare by 1969 was based on divergence from 1963 to 1969 between new AFDC cases and unemployment among nonwhite males. Prior to 1963 a decrease in the latter was followed by a decrease in case openings. In the 1970s the relationship between AFDC cases and unemployment returned. In other words, the sense of urgency and crisis that pervaded the Nixon administration in 1969 over welfare was based on a fallacy.[43]

If, indeed, the divergence of AFDC case openings from the unemployment rate from 1963 to 1969 was an aberration, then welfare represented one of several "false" crises that Nixon dealt with as president. This one, however, was not of his own making, nor was it created for partisan purposes. He inherited this "crisis" from the welfare issue network that had come into existence under the Johnson administration and then been exaggerated by Moynihan. Despite his early role as catalyst, Moynihan's influence as head of UAC declined as Ehrlichman's rose after successfully brokering the final welfare policy inside the White House. (In 1969 Moynihan left UAC to become counselor to the president, and by the end of 1970 had returned to a teaching post at Harvard.)

The most comprehensive welfare reform ever proposed by a United States president, FAP was a dramatic attempt to reverse thirty-five years of incremental welfare legislation—which probably contributed more to its defeat than Nixon's temporary loss of interest with the approach of the 1972 presidential election. The president's lack of enthusiasm for welfare reform by 1972, according to Ehrlichman, did not mean a loss of interest on his part or the part of respective staff or cabinet members. Although Nixon did not publicly advocate welfare reform again until his 1974 State of the Union Message, when it was too late because of Watergate, his papers indicate continued activity on the issue inside the White House and at HEW. Much momentum was lost after Ehrlichman resigned in April 1973, but Melvin Laird in particular, as domestic counselor to the president replacing Ehrlichman, and to a lesser extent Al Haig, as assistant to the president replacing Haldeman, kept the issue alive, if not on the front burner. In the fall of 1973, for example, Nixon scribbled on a memorandum from Haig: "Let us put the *long range* broader problem [of welfare reform] in the Domestic Council for further consideration—I feel we are rushing too fast on such a profound program."[44]

Moynihan entered the welfare fray again in 1973, then ambassador to India, with a long memorandum to Laird in which he commented on a meeting with Nixon. The president "was not less enthusiastic," he recalled. "I had begun my account by asking him not to throw me out of the room, meaning only that I assumed he was weary of the ups and downs of FAP. He took it to infer that he had turned against the idea, *and was at pains to assure me otherwise*, stating several times that to his mind FAP was still the best thing we could do to get rid of poverty and bring some sanity to the welfare system." Moynihan correctly predicted that "*a guaranteed annual income will never be enacted while President Nixon is in office*," because the "crisis atmosphere which surrounded welfare at the end of the 1960s has now pretty much vanished." Nonetheless, he recommended that Nixon "continue to associate himself with the idea. It is a place he has earned in history." In the same memorandum, Moynihan incorrectly predicted that "a guaranteed income will be enacted under a Democratic President in the course of the 1980s." In 1992, once again on the welfare trail, he somehow managed to forget that economics had dominated the debate over welfare under Nixon, saying: "Cost was not a concern back then, the question was whether it [a guaranteed annual income] was a good idea."[45]

By the 1980s, however, the alarming increase in the "feminization of poverty" demonstrated the gendered relationship between unemployment and welfare caseloads. Both liberals and conservatives who opposed FAP ignored the increase in black and white female-headed families with children, where welfare dependency has since become strongest. From 1969 to 1976, such families with children under eighteen increased 60 percent, from 3,374,000 to 5,403,000. Then as today, these women existed largely outside of normal labor-market conditions; their numbers are largely unaffected by the unemployment rate, because single female heads of households are almost always either underpaid or underemployed, regardless of business cycles.[46] AFDC mothers are still unaffected by labor-market conditions, in contrast to unemployed or low-paid fathers receiving AFDC, although more men may find themselves in the same position as women if high unemployment rates continue to characterize economic recovery under the Clinton administration. While FAP would have provided assistance to poor households with children whether headed by a woman or a man, Moynihan and other Nixon advisers focused on putting more unemployed and low-paid men on the welfare payrolls in order to preserve the traditional family unit. As a matter of fact, so little attention was given to providing retraining programs, adequate-paying jobs, federal funding of abortions, and child care for single mothers that the welfare crisis of the 1990s is in large measure the direct result of the intransigence of sexist views about welfare.[47]

The defeat of FAP in the Senate in 1972, nonetheless, led to impressive examples of incremental legislation that may not have come to pass had it not been for the boldness of FAP. Congress finally approved a Supplementary Security Income (SSI) on October 17, 1972, which had been part of the president's August 8, 1969, address on domestic programs, including his welfare proposals. Unlike FAP, SSI sailed through Congress, even though it represented the Nixonian idea of federalizing part of the welfare system and posed administrative problems because it would replace state and local programs. This program did not go into effect until January 1, 1974, by which time it had been modified by Congress, largely to protect Medicaid recipients from loss of eligibility because of changes in other government assistance programs.[48] It constituted a guaranteed annual income for the aged, blind, and disabled.

The passage of SSI and the defeat of FAP can only be explained in partisan terms. Because it offered some immediate relief to states with budget problems and because the aged, blind, and disabled were considered more "deserving" in the minds of congressmen than welfare mothers, SSI attracted little publicity and was not touted as a welfare reform or a guaranteed annual income.[49] This was a bitter pill to those who believed that the Senate passed FAP work requirements without FAP guaranteed income when in October 1972 it required AFDC mothers "upon penalty of loss of benefits" to register for work when their children were old enough to go to school. This work requirement (so disputed by all sides in the FAP debate) went into effect on July 1, 1972—four months before the same Senate killed the comprehensive FAP package. Clearly, partisan politics prevented reform of the country's welfare system.

The demise of FAP also led Nixon to support uniform application of the food stamp program,[50] better health insurance programs for low-income families, increased federal funding for students from low-income families, and automatic cost-of-living adjustments (COLA) for Social Security recipients to help them cope with inflation. Of all these expanded programs, the only one that Nixon told me he later regretted supporting was the pegging of Social Security benefits to the cost of living. He did not anticipate the runaway inflation of the late 1970s.[51] His advisers were so sharply divided over COLAs in 1970 that Ehrlichman specifically asked the president to sign an action memo indicating that "the administration continues to support the cost of living escalator." Finch, Harlow, William Timmons (assistant to Harlow), and Morgan favored COLAs, while Mayo, Peter Flanigan (White House political-economic adviser), and Burns did not.[52]

At the time Nixon believed that COLAs would be better than arbitrary congressional increases, as had occurred in 1971 (10 percent) and 1972 (20 percent).[53] Representing a way to replace legislative control over Social Security benefits with some measure of administrative supervision, COLAs were in keeping with Nixon's desire to use executive devices to restrict congressional discretion. At least this was how Wilbur Mills, Democratic chair of the House Ways and Means Committee, originally viewed the indexation of Social Security payments. Because Mills's lack of support for FAP contributed so much to its failure, one could only assume that Social Security indexing would have failed in the House had Mills not changed his mind about it in the face of strong lobbying efforts by groups representing the elderly and his own desire to appeal to this constituency in his bid for the Democratic party's presidential nomination in 1972. It also helped that the COLA legislation was attached to a 15 percent increase in Social Security payments, which in turn was attached to a bill raising the debt ceiling, thus making it less likely that Nixon would veto it on inflationary grounds.[54]

That Nixon experienced these legislative successes only *after* FAP had been defeated is important. Nixon's attitude toward working through Congress on domestic reform in general was negatively affected by congressional disapproval of FAP. Moreover, in the process the acrimonious welfare debate in Congress indirectly contributed to politicizing the Social Security system. As Martha Derthick has noted, the campaign for FAP and its ultimate failure "encouraged the expansion of the social security program in two ways. It lent momentum to welfare legislation generally, and because social security was the popular and feasible form of such legislation, it won support when more controversial forms were stymied. . . . Incremental changes in well-established programs do not attract attention."[55] In addition to passing legislation that federalized aid to the old and handicapped, and the COLAs for Social Security, the Nixon administration succeeded in expanding aid to education through revenue sharing, through a National Student Loan Association to help students from low-income families attend colleges and universities, through a Career Education Program to aid community colleges in teaching critically needed skills, and finally through the National Endowment for the Humanities. When Nixon's increased funding for elementary and secondary schools, beginning with the Education Amendments of 1972, was added to his other social welfare spending programs, the expenditures increased from 49 percent of the GNP in 1965 to almost 60 percent in 1975.[56]

From the first to the last of the Nixon budgets—1970 through 1975— spending on human resource programs exceeded spending for defense for the first time since World War II. Clearly he realized a "peace dividend" by removing U.S. combat troops from Vietnam, and he spent it for peaceful purposes. Despite the contention that some of this social service spending "was due primarily to the inexorable growth in [previous] commitments under human resource programs," Nixon initiated new programs and spent proportionately more on many old ones. Funding for social welfare services under Nixon grew from $55 billion in 1970 to almost $132 billion in 1975, making him (not President Johnson) the "last of the big spenders" on domestic programs. This represented an increase from 28 percent of all federal outlays to 40.4 percent, compared to a decrease in defense spending in the same period from 40 percent of all federal outlays (or $78.6 billion) to 26.2 percent (or 85.6 billion).[57]

In retrospect, while the Nixon administration lost the welfare battle over FAP, some Republicans such as Martin Anderson have absurdly claimed that it won the war on welfare through other means, including the politicizing of Social Security. These, however, were not the means Nixon preferred, nor have they proved adequate for dealing with the massive feminization of poverty now facing the country. Nevertheless, in his 1974 State of the Union message, Nixon announced that he would make a "major new effort" to reform the country's welfare system. While saying that he "did not intend to resubmit a new version of the Family Assistance Program," he nonetheless outlined points that embodied the negative income tax and work incentives of his original legislation. But

Watergate-related events were to dominate the few months he had left in office. The prevalence of his preoccupation with Watergate became painfully evident in that same address when Nixon misspoke, asking Americans to "join me in mounting a new effort to replace the discredited President—discredited welfare system."[58]

The nation's thirty-seventh president left office believing what he had told a private gathering at the White House on Christmas Eve, 1969, concerning the chances of FAP in Congress: "The important thing is we will have established the principle." Unfortunately, that principle has been ignored by Nixon's successors. In 1970, according to the historian James T. Patterson, welfare reform by income maintenance "seemed an idea whose time had come," but the 1970s and 1980s "were not conducive to major social reforms."[59] Nixon had seized a historic moment for welfare reform only to be defeated by liberals and conservatives in Congress—a defeat that has proved irreparable.

MIXING HEALTH AND ECONOMIC REFORMS WITH POLITICS

As I note throughout this book, when he became president Nixon appeared to reverse himself on some of his views, or at least on some views that others had attributed to him. Nowhere was his aprincipled pragmatism more evident, however, than on national health insurance and domestic economic issues. In contrast to traditionally Republican health and economic policy, his administration attempted to extend federal regulation in five major areas: energy (specifically, oil prices), the environment, occupational safety, health care, and consumer production safety. In each instance of extended government regulation, especially with respect to environmental legislation, Nixon imposed limits on the amount and expense of regulation but usually failed to convince enough members of Congress, who also mixed politics and economics without always anticipating their unintended long-range consequences.[60]

Nixon's ideas about national health care may date from his Senate campaign against Helen Gahagan Douglas in 1950 and his years as Eisenhower's vice president, but once again the most direct influence on his thinking in this area came from his set of liberal insider advisers. He had advocated a voluntary plan of health insurance in the early 1950s to counter President Truman's call for a national health insurance system, but both he and Eisenhower found that the American Medical Association opposed even this proposal.[61] During Nixon's first two years in office, he took a traditional view of the nation's health problems, advocating the fight against malnutrition and supporting occupational and consumer safety standards. In 1971, however, he outlined a plan for a National Health Insurance Partnership, including private, employment-related health insurance, a government-sponsored health insurance plan for low-income families, and health maintenance organizations (HMOs) for better delivery of services. Not since Truman (and not again until Clinton) had a U.S. president proposed such a comprehensive national health program.[62]

Congress dutifully took the president's and several other national health insurance plans under consideration, and by October 1972 the administration was cautiously optimistic that its bills on national HMOs and insurance were making reasonable progress. But no legislation ever emerged from congressional hearings. In 1973 Nixon resubmitted his insurance and health care delivery system, but for a combination of political reasons (not unlike the negative reception given his welfare reform ideas by liberals and conservatives), to say nothing of the AMA's influence, this bold initiative became a victim of Watergate and partisanship. Throughout his exhortations to Congress about the need for such legislation, Nixon always distinguished between a *national partnership* and *nationalization* of the health insurance and delivery system, sounding very much like those in the 1990s who make the same argument.[63] This stand represented Nixon at his pragmatic, liberal best—again, much to the consternation of conservatives in both parties.

The president's most un-Republican economic reform occurred when he dramatically announced his New Economic Policy (NEP) on August 15, 1971, at the close of a secret Camp David meeting with sixteen economic advisers. Nixon's failure to obtain more revenue through tax reform legislation in 1969, combined with rising unemployment and inflation rates in 1970, precipitated the NEP. It was an attempt to balance U.S. domestic concerns with wage and price controls, and international ones by devaluating the dollar. (As a slogan and acronym, the NEP became an embarrassment and was almost immediately abandoned when his speechwriters belatedly discovered that Lenin had used it for one of his programs in the early 1920s.)

Nixon had been concerned with foreign and domestic economics from his first months in office. Faced with an inflation problem as early as the fall of 1969, he did not make balancing the budget a major object of policy.[64] First, he tried to deal with it in typically conservative fashion by tightening the money supply. When this approach did not work and the economy appeared by 1970 to be heading into a recession, the administration had to turn to fiscal policy solutions.[65] On the advice of his Council of Economic Advisers (CEA), headed by Paul McCracken, Nixon became the first president to submit a budget based on "the high-employment budget standard." As he said in his 1971 State of the Union message, this budget was "designed to be in balance if the economy were operating at its peak potential. By spending as if we were *at* full employment, we will help to *bring about* full employment." This full-employment budget actually justified an "acceptable" amount of deficit spending—specifically, the amount that would result if expenditures did not exceed the hypothetical revenue that would accrue if full employment existed. By setting such a limit on fine-tuning the economy and on expansion, Nixon proclaimed himself a conservative Keynesian.[66]

With the exception of McCracken, individual members of the CEA did not greatly influence the president's domestic economic policies. Instead, one political-broker insider, Secretary of Labor and later OMB Director George Shultz, and one freethinking outsider, Treasury Secretary John Connally, tended to prevail on economic matters. Not even Arthur Burns was as influential as Shultz and Connally, except on one controversial issue: wage and price controls. Here, support from Burns was absolutely essential because of his reputation as a conservative and close friend of Nixon's. As early as June 1969, Nixon had asked McCracken "what our answer should be" to a suggestion by the Keynesian economist Walter Heller that the president "should insist on voluntary wage and price restraints to avoid contributing [further] to inflation."[67]

Another complicating factor in the decision-making process on monetary and fiscal policy during Nixon's first year in office was that the Urban Affairs Council under the leadership of Pat Moynihan (who was already in competition with Burns over welfare legislation, as noted earlier) wanted to prepare legislation on such economic matters as urban finances and revenue sharing. Both Shultz and Connally absolutely opposed this interference with "highly complex financial issues, [which] are now being handled satisfactorily by *qualified experts.*" Thus, Haldeman firmly told Ehrlichman (who himself was in direct competition with Moynihan for control over domestic policy and with OMB over domestic budgetary matters) that "these subjects simply do not belong in Moynihan's shop."[68] This internal jousting for influence inside the White House did not make dealing with powerful economic interests across the country any easier for

Nixon. Then Connally entered the picture and ingratiated himself, as most of Nixon's flamboyant outsider advisers had, with flattery and bombastic demeanor. Nixon's unusually close relationship with Connally has been described as his "falling in love" with his new secretary of the Treasury.[69]

While U.S. business and financial communities were unenthusiastic about Nixon's full-employment budget, they were in favor of some kind of incomes policy. By 1971 they were more worried about the breakdown of the international economic system established in 1944 with the Bretton Woods agreement and the introduction of the gold standard. For the first time, therefore, they were ready to consider variable rates for international currencies, ending the dollar's convertibility into gold at $35 per ounce. Faced with a gold drain and a trade deficit, the United States allowed the dollar "to float" on international markets to increase markets abroad and stop any more speculative pressures against the dollar. This could not be done without causing even more domestic inflation and had to be offset by some deflationary action to placate unions in the form of wage and price controls.[70]

In fact, economic leaders in the United States accepted the latter only because they so desperately wanted the former. In this sense Nixon's NEP represented the first time an administration responded to the drain the cold war was having on the American economy with coordinated domestic and international action. This drain prompted businessmen and financiers to consider variable rates for international currencies—that is, they were willing to risk destroying the modicum of international currency stability that this post–World War II and cold war–driven agreement had brought into existence, thinking the United States could continue to control variable currency exchange rates because a "floating" dollar would promote more trade.

Under Treasury Secretary Connally's influence, Nixon agreed to the following trade-off between wage and price controls and devaluation: if foreign countries continued to demand ever-increasing amounts of gold for the U.S. dollars they held, the United States would go off the gold standard but would at the same time impose wage and price controls to curb inflation at home. When I interviewed him a dozen years later, Nixon insisted instead that he and Connally were simply convinced for political reasons that "Congress would roll on them" (that is, enact its own wage and price controls) and that ending the convertibility of dollars for gold, along with a surcharge on imports, would "stick it to Japan."[71]

According to Connally's biographer, Nixon and his secretary of the Treasury agreed in the spring of 1971 "to deal dramatically and comprehensively with the ill health of the economy" because "it was simply good politics." Then, just a few days before the secret Camp David meeting in August, Connally presented the entire plan to Nixon, purportedly saying: "I'm not sure this program will work, but I'm sure that anything less will *not* work." This interpretation denies any staff or CEA input or trade-offs within the White House, contending that the entire decision-making process over economic policy from May through July was simply a charade. This is not how Burns, Shultz, McCracken, Ehrlichman, Herbert Stein of the CEA, or Paul Volcker and Peter Peterson of the Council of International Economic Policy viewed the situation at the time. It is true, however, that Nixon and Connally did generally agree in the spring that halfway measures would not do. Only Shultz and McCracken knew of the decision not to take any intermediate steps, according to CEA member Herbert Stein.[72] Both the popularity of the wage and price controls, as indicated by Gallup polls, and the specificity of Nixon's confidential agreement with Connally in the spring of 1971 have probably been exaggerated as determining factors in the formulation of the NEP. Nixon's (and Burns's) papers indicate that the process was much more complicated, and that debate among his aides contributed important details to its major points: nonconvertibility of the dollar, wage and price controls, a temporary surcharge on foreign imports, a repeal of the 7 percent excise tax on automobiles, more personal tax exemptions, and a 10 percent tax cut for new investments.[73]

There were four phases to the domestic part of Nixon's NEP, each originally designed to last ninety days. Phase I, through 1971, "was the most popular move in economic policy that anyone could remember" because the economy stabilized. Then Phase II, with the strong endorsement of Defense Secretary Laird, extended controls to April 1972. By the spring it was evident that inflation continued at a low but steady pace, as did bureaucratic support for the controls that were working less and less well. This created the need for a disengagement period, known as Phase III, but it also failed as prices of internationally traded commodities not subject to domestic controls continued to increase. In June 1973 Nixon imposed a price freeze before Congress could enact its own, over the opposition of most of his economic advisers, and so Phase IV began and ended badly, with political tolerance for domestic wage and price controls at an all-time low. By 1973 world economic conditions were vastly different from 1971, demonstrating that economic controls often took on a political and bureaucratic life of their own long after they had outlived their usefulness.[74]

Implementation problems notwithstanding, the president's NEP perfectly reflected the "grand gesture" Connally thought he should make on economic problems, and the post–Camp David television broadcast simply added drama to economic issues most Americans thought boring until the presidential election of 1992. It is worth noting that neither Secretary of State William Rogers nor National Security Adviser Henry Kissinger were at the August Camp David meeting, even though the NEP was to have more long-lasting international than domestic economic impact. Kissinger was in Paris secretly negotiating with the North Vietnamese, but even had he been in the United States, it is unlikely that he would have attended, for two reasons: its economic orientation and the fact that it was Connally's "show." Two competing "grand designers" at a single meeting would have been one too many. In Rogers's case, his absence is just another indication of how far out of the loop he was as secretary of state.[75]

One thing is clear: all the disparaging remarks that have been made about Nixon's lack of interest in or knowledge of economics as president—based largely on a remark he made about not giving "a shit about the [Italian] lira"—are wrong. No one would have known about Nixon's "lira" remark and used it to denigrate his interest in international economics had he not made it on one of the "smoking-gun" tapes that showed him obstructing justice—almost a year after he had decided on his New Economic Policy. The remark has been quoted out of context ever since 1974. Haldeman had just told Nixon that the British had floated the pound in response to his NEP—a subject in which the president was very interested. By comparison, when Haldeman also informed him that Burns was concerned "about speculation about the lira," Nixon replied as he is often quoted.[76]

Nixon's creation of the Council on International Economic Policy (CIEP), discussed in chapter 7, and his numerous handwritten comments upon and questions about the economic reports that passed over his desk all belie an indifference to economic matters. As Nixon once told me, he had developed this interest in part as vice president, when his travels to U.S. embassies abroad had convinced him that Foreign Service personnel did not understand the economic base of American political foreign policy.[77]

Although the high-handedness of the NEP with respect to traditional U.S. trading partners, especially Japan, left long-term scars, it was a short-term domestic success. The NEP initially worked so well that by early 1972 output rose sharply, unemployment fell, and inflation remained low but on the increase, making Nixon the only president since World War II to bring about an economic upturn in a presidential election year—something he believed essential for solidifying a new coalition of Republican voters throughout the country. Since the Democrats remained even more disorganized behind the leadership of peace candidate George McGovern than they had under Hubert Humphrey, Nixon's economic policies added to, but were not entirely responsible for, his victory margin of 18 million votes, or 60.8 percent of the popular vote. A recent study of incumbent presidents' bid for reelection in relation to economic conditions indicated that the NEP may have been a greater factor in Nixon's landslide vote in 1972 than political pundits thought at the time. With the exception of Dwight Eisenhower's in 1956, parties in control of the White House lost in 1952, 1960, 1968, 1976, and 1980—all years when the economy was in recession.[78]

Long-term implementation of wage and price controls, however, revealed not only how politically motivated Nixon's original commitment had been but also how impossible it would have been to abandon them without exacerbating inflationary trends within the economy and helping to precipitate, after the oil crisis began, a 42 percent decline in the stock market between 1973 and 1975. There were several unanticipated consequences from Nixon's NEP. One was more inflation and more federal regulation of the economy than during any other presidency since the New Deal. The president and most of those involved in approving the NEP, with the exception of Connally, have admitted that one of his greatest domestic economic mistakes was to approve wage and price controls, despite their temporary political and economic success. Moreover, the NEP did not bolster business confidence. Then, when an even greater decline in business confidence occurred because of the market contraction and oil crisis, the result was a temporary reduction in the gap between the wealthiest 1 percent and the poorest Americans to the lowest it had ever been in U.S. history.[79]

Still another unintended consequence arose from the decision to abandon the Bretton Woods system. This aspect of the NEP represented a deregulation of international currencies. Since then, economic regionalism has flourished because three rival trading blocs emerged. Each established a separate regional monetary order based on the yen, mark, and dollar—a situation that has contributed to exchange rate instability and currency speculation since then.[80] The increased tension among these three major regional trading blocs will continue until the current global recession is over. What the world learned following the collapse of the Bretton Woods system is that floating exchange rates and freer trade do not go hand in hand. In fact, instability of the former almost always produces complaints about unfair trading practices and pressures for protectionism.[81] Yet the intensification of regional international competition based on competing currencies—even with the end to the Uruguay Round of GATT talks—could result in a worsening of worldwide economic conditions in the 1990s. There is little doubt that the world needs another Bretton Woods system to stabilize currency exchange rates. To date, no one in the Nixon administration, including the president, has admitted the integrative international function that Bretton Woods served before the United States unilaterally killed it.

When Nixon reshaped global economics or took action before Congress could act and upstage him on regulatory issues, he often did so with deregulatory programs based on free-market assumptions. Deregulation has traditionally been a tenet of conservative Republicanism. The administration not only ended gold convertibility for the dollar but also, in the name of economic freedom,[82] ended the draft and made deregulatory recommendations for the production of food crops, for the reduction of tariff and other barriers to international trade, and for interest rates paid by various financial institutions.

By and large, politics made Nixon more liberal than conservative in economic matters, confounding both his friends and enemies, as he also did on other issues of domestic reform, especially civil rights and welfare. As a Republican, he was willing to move beyond the twin boundaries of the New Deal and Great Society, both set by Democratic presidents.

Ultimately, these domestic programs may be remembered longer than his currently better-known activities in the realm of foreign policy, and they may even minimize his negative Watergate image. In any case, they represent the most positive characteristics of the Nixon phenomenon. In fact, the Age of Nixon that would end in the denouement of disgrace, actually reached its climax in the area of domestic reform.

PART II

REEVALUATING NIXON'S FOREIGN POLICIES

5

AN OVERVIEW OF "NIXINGER" DIPLOMACY

Do we leave the memory only of the battles we fought, of opponents we did in, of the viciousness we created, or do we leave possibly not only the dream but the reality of a new world?

—Toast by Nixon, July 31, 1973

The area in which Richard Nixon's leadership style and ethically questionable judgment have least obscured his achievements is foreign policy. The geopolitical and structural approaches he brought to foreign policy in a time of transition—marked by the ending of the bipartisan cold war consensus—have generally been praised, with the exception of his conducting of the Vietnam War. Although fewer of his foreign policy decisions were reached in a crisis atmosphere than his domestic ones, and therefore theoretically better thought out, Nixon's diplomatic legacy is weaker than he and many others have maintained.

Since 1960, one of the most basic decisions presidents have had to make is whether to assign primary responsibility for foreign policy to the State Department or to the National Security Council (NSC). If they choose the latter, they will try to centralize and manage policy from the White House. President Truman created the National Security Council in 1947, but not until the Kennedy administration did serious contention develop between the secretary of state and the head of the NSC. At the same time, a less evident battle has raged over whether and how to separate policy from operations. Often these disputes have stemmed as much from the management style of the particular president as from substantive arguments between the secretary of state and the national security adviser.[1]

In the case of Nixon's secretary of state, William Rogers, and his national security adviser, Henry Kissinger, their conflicts usually ended with Kissinger and Nixon allied against Rogers. When the long-suffering secretary of state finally resigned in September 1973, Nixon replaced him with Kissinger, who also retained the post of special assistant for national security affairs. Nixon had chosen Rogers not because of his knowledge of foreign policy but because of his strong administrative and negotiating skills. "Rogers was one of the toughest, most cold-eyed, self-centered and ambitious men," Nixon purportedly told Kissinger. As such, he could take on both the Soviets and "the little boys in the State Department" who designed a "eunuch-like, faceless, formless, basically weak approach" to foreign policy.[2] In the long run, this description of the man who could be tough with State Department bureaucrats best fit Kissinger, not Rogers. The secretary of state ended up so far out of the White House loop when it came to the administration's secret diplomacy that Nixon seldom wrote Rogers any of the impromptu memoranda and comments he often jotted on his daily news summaries. The president wrote to many others, however, criticizing Rogers's inability "to keep a secret" (although it was probably Kissinger or his aides who did most of the "leaking" of foreign policy matters), lack of initiative, and general "dovishness."[3]

The absence of a working relationship between Rogers and Nixon, despite their long association under Eisenhower—Rogers as deputy and then attorney general, Nixon as vice president—allowed, in part, for Kissinger's ascendancy on foreign policy matters. It may also have indirectly contributed to prolonging the negotiations over ending the Vietnam War because, according to Haldeman's memoranda and handwritten notes, the antagonism between the NSC and the State Department disrupted top-level policy meetings and became a topic of speculation in the press.[4]

Any revisionist approach to Nixon's management of foreign policy must begin by attempting to place in perspective the complex interaction that developed between Nixon and Kissinger, whose "advanced megalomania" remains legendary.[5] In retrospect, I believe that one of the most unfortunate decisions the president-elect made during the interregnum was to appoint Kissinger, about whom he knew only that, as a Nelson Rockefeller supporter, Kissinger had been openly disdainful of Nixon and his bid for the Republican nomination in 1968. If Nixon thought Kissinger's views on U.S. policy were important, he could have employed him as consultant to the NSC, as the Kennedy administration had briefly done. This opinion, however, is not shared by Nixon or most of his former advisers, one of whom defended Kissinger's appointment by saying that "the care and feeding of Henry" was worth all the paranoia, backbiting, leaking, rumor-mongering, and pseudo-intellectual posturing that he brought to the White House.[6]

Many of the wiretaps and much of the obsession with covert actions that Nixon exhibited in his first year in office can be attributed to Kissinger's ingratiating presence and self-aggrandizing influence. The combination of these two men, while occasionally resulting in dazzling achievements, had a dark, devious underside, from which to date only one of them has walked away unscathed. During the early Nixon years, for example, it was Henry Kissinger, not the president, who entertained at cocktail parties, to the delight of liberals and conservatives alike, with popular one-liners such as: "The illegal, we do right away; the unconstitutional takes a little longer."[7]

A strong circumstantial case has been made for Kissinger's close involvement in initiating the first wiretaps (see chapter 9) and early knowledge of the illegal activities by the Plumbers (who plugged up the "leaks") by such prominent investigative reporters as Jack Anderson, Roger Morris, William Shawcross, Seymour M. Hersh, and, most recently, Len Colodny and Robert Gettlin. Yet he walked away from the stench of devious pre- and post-Watergate projects generated within the Oval Office. Kissinger may have "come out on top, only slightly soiled," but, as Theodore Draper has reminded us, he emerged high on the heap "of a political dunghill."[8] This feat of magic may ultimately supersede the ability he showed in creating the illusion that Nixon's foreign policy was his own.

THE ODD COUPLE OF U.S. FOREIGN POLICY: NIXON AND KISSINGER

On the surface Nixon and Kissinger—an American Quaker and a German-American Jew—appear to have been the odd couple of U.S. foreign policy. Given his long personal and professional association with the Rockefeller family and his blunt criticisms of Nixon, Kissinger apparently did not think he would last even six months in the new Nixon administration. Yet when these two men came together in 1968, they actually shared many viewpoints and had developed similar operational styles.[9] Both relished covert activity and liked making unilateral decisions; both distrusted bureaucracies; both resented any attempt by Congress to interfere with initiatives; and both agreed that the United States could impose order and stability on the world only if the White House controlled policy by appearing conciliatory but acting tough. While neither had headed any complex organization, both thought "personalized executive control" and formal application of procedures would lead to success. Even more coincidental, perhaps, each had a history of failure and rejection, which made them susceptible to devising ways of protecting themselves and their positions of power. Often the concern for protection appeared as obsession with eavesdropping, whether wiretaps or reconnaissance flights. They even eavesdropped on themselves: Nixon by installing an automatic taping system in the Oval Office, Kissinger by having some of his meetings and all of his phone conversations taped or transcribed from notes. In a word, instead of compensating for each other's weaknesses and enhancing strengths, Nixon and Kissinger shared their worst characteristics.[10]

Some experiences and ideas this odd couple did not share. Kissinger's covert monitoring system has not negatively affected his reputation, even though Roger Morris, a member of the NSC staff, reported that from the beginning Kissinger insisted that his aides listen in on conversations between him and the president *without* Nixon's knowledge, and U. Alexis Johnson (an influential deputy undersecretary of state for political affairs) later realized that Kissinger had taped (without his knowledge) some of the U.S. Verification Panel meetings as late as 1973 in preparation for the SALT II talks. In contrast, the White House taping system, installed in 1971 (which, in turn, recorded Kissinger without his knowledge), has been scrutinized and condemned. Kissinger has also escaped censure for protecting himself from a hostile press by leaking information—often through his personal aide and deputy, Lawrence Eagleburger. "If anyone leaks anything," Kissinger purportedly told his NSC assistants at their very first staff meeting, "I will do the leaking."[11]

Such leaks haunted the first Nixon administration, while ensuring Kissinger's popularity with the Washington press corps from then on. As Leslie Gelb later noted: "the most powerful thing to a newsman is information . . . Kissinger began gradually cutting other people of the information flow . . . if they really wanted to know what was going on [in foreign policy] there was only one place to go."[12]

Kissinger may have cinched his appointment in Nixon's administration during the presidential campaign when he leaked information to the Nixon people about Johnson's negotiations with the Vietnamese; or it may have been that John Mitchell, who also had close ties to Rockefeller, recommended Kissinger; or it may have been the aura of his Harvard reputation; or maybe it was simply Nixon's desire to strike a blow at Rockefeller by "stealing" someone close to him—or a combination of all these factors.[13]

Kissinger did not share Nixon's optimistic approach to diplomacy and proclivity for taking risky, far-reaching foreign policy actions. As vice president under Eisenhower, Nixon had said: "I am not necessarily a respecter of the *status quo* in foreign affairs. I am a *chance taker* in foreign affairs. I would take chances for peace." Along these same lines, Nixon told Kissinger in August 1969: "just because [I] supported [something] as a private individual does not mean [I] will as president."[14] In contrast, practically every analyst of Kissinger's ideas points out their essentially conservative (and profoundly pessimistic), nineteenth-century European roots. When he joined the Nixon administration, Kissinger seems not to have changed his ideas (and dense writing style) much from the time he wrote his Ph.D. dissertation, in which he recommended the Metternichian system of alliances among conservative regimes to check the forces of revolution in the modern, Western world. Kissinger's early writings presaged what his memoirs confirmed: the mind of "a middle-level manager who has learned to conceal vacuity with pretentious verbiage."[15] His pre-1968 political science writings convey very conventional cold warrior ideas about Vietnam, anti-Communist views that opposed ideologically driven grand designs in foreign policy and at best paid only occasional lip service to the necessity for some risk taking. And as an "inveterate conceptualizer," he was seldom on top of specific contemporary issues in his search for global solutions.[16]

Prior to 1968 Kissinger also opposed most of the geopolitical views he would later espouse under Nixon, such as détente with the Soviet Union, "partnership" with Europe (he thought NATO was in a state of "disarray"), and the need to shift the focus of U.S. foreign policy to Asia. In contrast to Nixon's positive views on these topics when assuming the presidency, Kissinger's remained conceptually and tactically grounded far back in the 1950s and 1960s, which he misleadingly projected onto Nixon, saying after the 1968 Republican convention: "I'm very worried that Nixon's cold war outlook has remained frozen since his vice-presidential years in the fifties and that therefore in the seventies, in the waning military pre-eminence of American power, it could lead him into taking undue risks." About the only diplomatic ideas shared by Nixon and Kissinger in 1969 that can be documented were their distrust of bureaucracy in formulating policy and their belief that it was time to get out of Vietnam, although neither had any specific notion about how to accomplish the latter.[17]

It remained for the president to lead the way toward genuinely innovative, grand designs for redirecting of U.S. diplomacy. As the chapters in part II will demonstrate, Henry Kissinger was a geopolitical follower rather than a leader, although his talent for dramatic, back-channel diplomacy may have made the execution of some of Nixon's policies exemplary rather than simply ordinary. The scholar Richard Falk, among a variety of contemporary commentators, noted specifically that "Nixon deserves the main credit, and bore the main responsibility, for shifts in political direction implicit in the moves toward accommodation with China and détente with the Soviet Union. In both instances there had been receptivity on the Sino-Soviet side . . . [but] it was Nixon who decided to respond affirmatively." In addition, Washington aficionados as politically and socially diverse as Elliot Richardson and Ralph de Toledano (biographer of the rich and famous) agreed that Nixon's diplomacy was, indeed, "his own." "When I was involved [in the government]," Richardson has recalled, in at least two separate interviews, "I was directly exposed to the development of the Nixon foreign policy. I constantly saw Kissinger. But it was the *Nixon* foreign policy." The president "drew on Henry Kissinger as a knowledgeable, sophisticated source of historic learning . . . [but] Nixon was, from the outset, the principal architect of a foreign policy resting on a series of quite clearly formulated strategic aims." Other White House aides and cabinet-level officers agreed with the assessment that Kissinger "was taking orders, not creating policy." One went so far as to say that Kissinger was the "student" and Nixon, the "foreign policy professor."[18]

Ralph de Toledano realized that Kissinger "was strictly Nixon's messenger boy . . . it was Nixon who made the policy." Contrary to Kissinger's claims, he was "not a great conceptualizer but . . . a brilliant tactician, the negotiator nonpareil, the supreme practitioner of the art of bureaucratic politics."[19] Nonetheless, many newspaper people accepted (then and now) Kissinger's "lone cowboy" projection of himself as the sole force behind Nixonian foreign policy, when his entire career before 1969 was constructed upon the safe premise of never acting alone or being too far out of step with the eastern establishment. In truth, "the cowboy doesn't have to be courageous," Kissinger said in a notorious 1972 interview with Oriana Fallaci that caused him to be banished from Nixon's inner circle for the next month; "all he needs is to be alone to show others that he rides into town alone and does everything himself. . . . This amazing romantic character suits me precisely because to be alone is part of my style, if you like, my technique."[20]

Contrary to Kissinger's public relations coup in this interview, he remained the Tonto, not the Lone Ranger, of U.S. foreign policy. Without Nixon's broad initiatives, international credibility, and, most important, ability to provide at least minimum domestic political consensus for his foreign policy until the fall of 1973, Kissinger, when finally on his own as both national security adviser and secretary of state, "was caught intellectually naked"—a messenger boy without a message. But members of the American press corps never realized that his macho, playboy image impressed them more than it did foreign heads of state, who were looking for more consistent and less idiosyncratic foreign policies and actions. As Leslie Gelb correctly observed in 1977: "Kissinger understood better than most men who come to Washington that politics is theater . . . he had to be seen and heard." And heard he was—ultimately to the dismay of Nixon and his closest aides.[21]

Some of Nixon's advisers, including Haldeman and Ehrlichman, clearly distrusted Kissinger and had little tolerance for his headline grabbing, arrogance, "counterfeit anguish," and indiscriminate threats to resign. In particular, they were critical of the national security adviser's "tendency to ups and downs." Kissinger "was quite enthusiastic and euphoric when things were going well," Haldeman told Mike Wallace in a 1975 interview, "quite despondent and outraged when things were not going well." Just the opposite was true of Nixon, according to his aides, which is probably why the president and his national security adviser operated so well as a team. "Richard Nixon is at his best when things aren't going well," Haldeman recalled, "and at his worst when they are."[22]

It was not, however, until the Watergate scandal forced some of them out of office that Nixon's aides said these things publicly. Ehrlichman now claims that Nixon himself worried about Kissinger's mental state, especially late in 1971 and into 1972, when he was under considerable stress over the leaking of the Pentagon Papers and criticism of the policy failure in the December 1971 India-Pakistan war—when the United States backed the corrupt Pakistani military dictatorship against a long-time democratic ally—precipitating another of Kissinger's many threats to resign. Nixon purportedly indicated to Ehrlichman that Kissinger may have needed psychiatric help. Nixon's chief concern, according to Ehrlichman, "was that the Joint Chiefs of Staff had tapped Kissinger or someone in his office because they, like Nixon, questioned his stability." Both before and after his attachment to the Nixon administration, Kissinger spread unsubstantiated rumors about the president's drinking and diminished ability to take rational, decisive action—saying, among other things, that he had "never known another man who combined such great gifts with such a capacity for depravity and such a drive toward self-destruction."[23]

. (In connection with this purported drinking problem, Ehrlichman and Nixon himself have both indicated that the president had a low tolerance for liquor and therefore imbibed very little in private and not at all in public. According to Ehrlichman, Nixon had gotten drunk at the 1964 Republican convention. When he asked Ehrlichman to join his presidential campaign team in 1967, Ehrlichman had "exacted a promise from Nixon [about his drinking] before coming on board." Ehrlichman said Nixon kept this promise the entire time he was in the administration. Nixon simply said to me: "I had reason to have a drinking problem [after Watergate], but did not.")[24]

Thus, another striking difference between Nixon and Kissinger is the way they have spoken about each other. As one of the most prominent "feudal bastards" in the Nixon administration, Kissinger had supported Nelson Rockefeller as the Republican candidate for president. Finding himself out on a limb in March 1968 when Rockefeller withdrew from the race, he was willing to switch allegiances, even if it meant working for a man he "profoundly distrusted" and had described as a demagogue who did not "have the right to rule" and was "not fit to be President." As late as the Republican convention in August 1968, Kissinger was reported as saying: "Richard Nixon's being nominated by the Republican party is a disaster and thank God he can't be elected president or the whole country will be a disaster area."[25]

Contrary to the tradition of bastard feudalism, Kissinger continued to benefit from the patronage of the Rockefellers. During his first year as head of the NSC, Kissinger received money from the Rockefellers, convincing the president's counsel that "the contemplated gift" was in return for "work . . . done for the [Rockefeller] family rather than on a consulting basis to any governmental agency." In January 1969, Nixon's legal counsels declared this "money from Governor Rockefeller . . . and his brothers" exempt from conflict-of-interest statutes because it was based "solely on your close personal friendship [and] . . . high personal esteem in which they hold you." Despite this informal exemption, Kissinger was reluctant to submit the conflict-of-interest forms required of all White House employees, preferring to talk privately with Ehrlichman and others about his unusual financial arrangement with the Rockefellers. He was specifically asked to return the form in February. Finally, on May 6, Kissinger received a confidential letter from the president's counsels formally declaring that no conflict of interest existed.[26]

Kissinger's comments about Nixon became even more derogatory in the post-Nixon years, referring to his former boss as "this lonely, tortured and insecure man" who was paranoid, "flawed," "very strange," "weird," with a "monomaniacal" preoccupation for public relations (that Kissinger neglected to point out was exceeded only by his own—in fact, most of these criticisms seem to be a projection of Kissinger's own personality onto Nixon). Kissinger has also described Nixon as "my drunken friend," as "petty" and "small-minded," and he apparently joked about the president "contemptuously" to his NSC staff from the very beginning of his association with the new Republican administration. After 1974 he also became the major source of comments about Nixon's supposed emotional breakdown during the Watergate crisis.[27]

Yet, while serving under Nixon, Kissinger also sent notes to the president, obsequiously telling him "your serenity during crisis, your steadfastness under pressure have been all that has prevented the triumph of mass hysteria. It has been an inspiration to serve [you]." And on the eve of Nixon's landslide 1972 victory, Kissinger wrote him: "what a privilege the last four years have been." You have "take[n] a divided nation, mired in war, losing its confidence, wracked by intellectuals without conviction and give[n] it a new purpose and overcome its hesitations . . . [and this] will loom ever large in history books. It has been an inspiration to see your fortitude in adversity and your willingness to walk alone. For this— as well as for unfailing human kindness and consideration—I shall always be grateful."[28]

Despite considerable goading on my part, the most I could get Nixon to say about Kissinger during our interviews was, "I will be fair to Henry, even if he isn't always to me," although he presumably told one of Kissinger's rivals early in his first year that "I don't trust Henry, but I can use him." The best thing to do with advisers, he told me, was "to drain them dry and appoint them Ambassador to India"—but clearly he never thought of doing this with Kissinger, whom, until their falling out over the

Christmas bombings of Vietnam at the end of 1973, he insisted was a "genius" in "looking at the world in political terms." Nixon himself saw foreign policy as being "much broader than politics." In a 1977 television interview with David Frost, Nixon called Kissinger "moody, secretive, capable of outrageous private remarks and intensely protective of official prerogatives," but in his memoirs Nixon was mild-mannered in all of his references to his former aide.[29] This reluctance to evaluate critically a man who served him both ill and well is curious to say the least, since Nixon's former aides no longer pretend that Kissinger was the intellectual genius or the one untainted force in an administration increasingly unable to distinguish right from wrong.

As they both aged, it was no longer so evident that Kissinger and Nixon had, "for years, circled warily and jealously around each other like sharks, each conscious that he could destroy the other but each knowing that some of the blood in the water would be his own." We have forgotten Kissinger's negative pre- and postpresidential remarks and vicious rumormongering while serving in the administration. Scattered throughout his memoirs, Kissinger can be found alternately praising and damning the president with such statements as "success seemed to unsettle Nixon more than failure. He seemed obsessed by the fear that he was not receiving adequate credit." When praising Nixon's "boldness in his historic opening to China," Kissinger added, "it illustrates, however, . . . [his] tendency for illusion to become reality, a brooding and involuted streak that, together with starker character traits, at first flawed, and later destroyed, a Presidency so rich in foreign policy achievements.[30] However, they were able to work together despite the fact that they did not like, and definitely did not trust, each other, because they shared certain foreign policy goals, modes of operation, and psychological needs.

The president's "special relationship"[31] with his national security adviser went so far beyond other classic examples in twentieth-century U.S. history of collaboration on foreign policy—Woodrow Wilson and Colonel Edward M. House, Franklin D. Roosevelt and Harry Hopkins—that it is possible to speak of a "Nixinger" diplomacy. The two men met or spoke by phone continually and began, as time went on, to bring out the worst in each other and to exhibit no small degree of paranoia about their dealings with each other and with others. Still, together Nixon and Kissinger appeared capable of significantly changing the conduct of U.S. foreign policy in a time of transition. Despite their combined personal determination and expertise and their success in instituting some structural reforms in bureaucratic processes, however, Nixon and Kissinger were never able to institutionalize their "grand design" approach to foreign affairs. Their idiosyncratic personal relationship, which appeared to transform "the conduct of diplomacy into a perpetual *tour de force*," was only temporarily successful, and their foreign policy proved more tenuous and ephemeral than either man has yet to admit.[32]

THE WHITE HOUSE AS STATE DEPARTMENT

Shortly after Nixon and Kissinger joined forces, they began "to create the first full White House–dominant system for the management of foreign policy." That Nixon intended the White House to function as State Department cannot be doubted, and during his first year in office the "White House–centered organization model of foreign-policy making" became the "most centralized and highly structured model yet employed by any president." In the first months of his administration, when former Republican national chairman Leonard Hall visited Nixon in the White House and asked the president how he was getting along with the State Department, Nixon pointed in the direction of the Oval Office and said: "There's the State Department."[33]

Nowhere did the centralized corporate presidency of Richard Nixon manifest itself as a closed system more clearly than when he and Kissinger reorganized the National Security Council, turning it into *the* foreign policy forum within the White House. In theory, the State Department was to implement NSC policy, but often in practice, Nixon's and Kissinger's personal management merged policy formulation and operational functions inside the NSC system. This was especially true of the Washington Special Action Group (WSAG)—the all-powerful NSC subcommittee that Kissinger chaired and about which he and the president agreed: "WSAG is [an] action body—not [a] policy [body]." In fact, this conflation of policy and action remains the greatest strength (and weakness) of the Nixonian structural legacy for conducting diplomacy.[34] After the Iran-contra scandal became public at the end of 1986, Henry Kissinger insisted all the more that Nixon's NSC staff and WSAG in particular had engaged only in policy, not operational, matters.

This claim is contradicted by Kissinger's own descriptions of the NSC in his memoirs and, more important, by a full-scale investigation of the NSC from 1973 to 1975 by the Murphy Commission on the Organization of the Government for the Conduct of Foreign Policy.[35] Writing in 1974,

I. M. Destler observed that Nixon's and Kissinger's "'two-man' system for conducting our foreign policy 'blurred' the once-emphasized distinction between 'policy' and 'operations.'" Moreover, he noted that Nixon and Kissinger assumed at the time that they "could dominate the operational decisions that count." And, for better and sometimes worse, they did. Ultimately, even this "system of closed policy-making is limited by the limits of Presidential power at home."[36] What Destler did not point out was that Nixon and Kissinger also intended to bypass the NSC whenever they did not need bureaucratic support to carry out policy.

In Kansas City on July 6, 1971, Nixon announced his five-power, or "northern tier" strategy, which he hoped would replace the bipolar, confrontational aspects of the cold war. Instead of continuing to deal only bilaterally with the Soviet Union, Nixon wanted to bring the five great economic regions of the world—the United States, the USSR, mainland China, Japan, and Western Europe—into constructive negotiation and mutually profitable economic competition. Admitting that the United States could not long maintain its post–World War II position of "complete preeminence or predominance," Nixon outlined a "pentagonal strategy" for promoting peace and economic progress by linking the interests of the major regional powers. Kissinger never officially endorsed this plan, preferring the more exclusive Rockefeller "trilateral" approach that included only the U.S., Japan, and the Common Market nations of Western Europe (including the United Kingdom).

Before joining the administration, Kissinger also had not accepted the manner in which Nixon wanted to link global interests, especially the linking of Moscow to any successful settlement of the war in Vietnam. Ultimately, however, it was Kissinger who coined the word *linkage* for this strategy and who broadened it to include other issues such as trade, food policy, arms control, and Third World competition with the Soviet Union.[37] Linkage became associated more with Kissinger than Nixon during the years they formulated policy together, and the concept certainly fit Kissinger's penchant for grandiose schemes described in impenetrable language. As a political plan, it posed more problems than it resolved. First and foremost, it never worked with respect to the Soviet Union in negotiations with Vietnam or the SALT I talks, and it made Nixinger policy look indifferent to Third World concerns, except insofar as they could be linked to relationships between major powers.

This meant, of course, that from the beginning of the Nixon administration, entire areas of the Third World—southern Asia, the Middle East, Africa, Latin America—occupied a secondary place in the president's (and his national security adviser's) political approach to foreign policy. In particular, Nixon and Kissinger largely ignored economic foreign policy considerations in dealing with the Third World, preferring instead to link events in such countries to power relations among the major nations. "Linkage," therefore, accounts for many of the seemingly erratic aspects of U.S. foreign policy in Third World areas that fell outside the parameters of pentagonal strategy. Nixon was more interested in maintaining American spheres of influence in the Third World than in the economic needs of these developing nations. Thus, the United States promoted the overthrow of Allende in Chile; restrained Egyptian and Syrian aggression in the Middle East, while ignoring the potential instability of the shah's regime in Iran and indirectly encouraging the rise in OPEC oil prices; continued to oppose Castro in Cuba; and supported Pakistan against India. The "grand design" may have been grand by superpower standards, but it remained ineffectual with respect to the Third World.

Nixon's and Kissinger's respective geopolitical divisions of the world became compatible, regardless of how poorly linkage served them. Both assumed it was the responsibility of major regional powers to keep order in their respective spheres of influence and not to intrude in areas dominated by others. Thus Nixon thought that détente based on linkage would prevent small Third World nations from setting the great powers against one another, by making the possibility of outside aid more remote if they did. He and Kissinger also thought that détente would help the United States deal simultaneously with the USSR and the People's Republic of China by taking advantage of their differences to create a triangular relationship in which American leverage could be exerted. Circumstances in all five (or three) areas of the world simultaneously fostered détente between 1969 and 1972.[38] Consequently, the United States and the Soviet Union capitalized upon the favorable international atmosphere that developed during the first Nixon administration to improve Soviet-American relations.

REORGANIZING THE NATIONAL SECURITY COUNCIL

Kissinger's first official task for the incoming Nixon administration was to reorganize the National Security Council. He gleaned from his initial meetings with the president-elect that Nixon was even more determined than he and his consultants to undercut the State Department's preeminence in foreign policy. Nixon insisted on eliminating the Senior Interdepartment Group (SIG), chaired by the undersecretary of state.[39] The final reorganization plan replaced SIG with interdepartmental groups headed by State Department assistant secretaries, who were then subordinated to either the Review Group, chaired by Kissinger, or to five other top-level review committees, also headed by him. These committees prepared policy studies subject to review by a committee also chaired by Kissinger *before* they were presented to the NSC or the president. This new structure and procedure undercut the State Department's influence over policy making, because only policy (as opposed to planning) committees remained chaired by the undersecretary of state or his designated representative from the State Department.[40]

On January 19, one day before inauguration, Nixon signed National Security Decision Memorandum 2, authorizing the newly reorganized NSC system. As its head, Kissinger became the "special assistant to the president on national security affairs"—not simply the president's "national security adviser," the title used by previous administrations. This change in title was not cosmetic, but represented the creation of "a type of super-official" who had complete access to the president and whose appointment was made without statutory base or review by the Senate.[41] Ultimately Kissinger chaired six special committees operating just below the NSC level, including the controversial 40 Committee, which oversaw all covert CIA activity.

On February 17, 1970, Nixon issued National Security Decision Memorandum 40, advising the director of Central Intelligence to "obtain policy approval for all major and/or politically sensitive covert action programs through The 40 Committee," giving "specific operational mission" review authority over Defense Department actions. When asked about this committee, which continued the questionable cold war precedent of giving "the CIA its singular [policy-making] role in American foreign" affairs (as had its predecessor, the 303 Committee), Kissinger has "emphatically" always denied it actually "ran" or "ordered" covert operations, blaming the press for misrepresenting the 40 Committee's purely "review" function. In March 1975 he also asserted—in the face of overwhelming evidence to the contrary then being produced by congressional investigating committees—that "there has been a downward curve of covert activities since the middle '50's."[42] To make matters worse, this fabrication by Kissinger was not challenged by anyone on the Murphy Commission then investigating Nixon's foreign policy procedures.

The reorganized NSC created a "conceptual framework" for diplomacy by establishing the series of policy studies I have been referring to, the National Security Study Memoranda, or NSSMs. These were drafted by the NSC staff and signed by Nixon or by Kissinger on behalf of the president. During the first four months of 1969 the NSC staff submitted to the president approximately fifty-five detailed position papers based on responses from interdepartmental committees (twenty-two papers in its first month of operation). By the end of 1969, Nixon had received eighty-five NSSMs—more than the total for all of 1970 and 1971, demonstrating both the important role these documents played in foreign policy during his first year and Kissinger's rapid rise as the president's chief foreign policy adviser.[43]

The NSSMs directed agencies and interdepartmental groups within the government to prepare detailed policy or "area" options, *not policy recommendations,* which were then passed on by Kissinger to the National Security Council and sometimes argued in front of the president. NSSM 1, for example, asked the Joint Chiefs of Staff to respond to six pages of detailed questions designed to update information on Vietnam.[44] Since the studies from these NSSMs included "formal options," which were written out, Nixon did not usually personally hear or participate in NSC debates over issues. After reading or hearing the pros and cons presented in these reports, Nixon often issued National Security Decision Memoranda (NSDMs). Between 1969 and August 1974, a little over 200 NSSMs were prepared for the president, and he issued over 250 NSDMs. Slightly more of the NSDMs have been declassified than the NSSMs, but the bulk of both sets of documents, particularly the detailed reports resulting from NSSMs, remains classified despite the fact that most of them have been requested by researchers since the mid-1970s under the Freedom of Information Act.[45]

During his first year in office—that is, before Kissinger consolidated his power as the president's number-one foreign policy adviser—Nixon seems to have relied heavily on these NSSMs. "The fact remains," Kissinger attested, "that the NSC machinery was used more fully before my authority was confirmed, while afterward tactical decisions were increasingly taken outside the system in personal conversations with the president." One of Kissinger's aides put it more bluntly: "A decisionmaking structure originally designed to assure dissent later served only to strengthen the control of men who soon would brook no opposition to their policies." Nonetheless, these NSSMs continued to serve a procedural, if not always a substantive, purpose. The system was intended to prevent respondents—the State Department and other executive departments—from becoming advocates for any particular policy option. It relegated them to analysis rather than decision making.[46] Thus, all cabinet-level departments and their bureaucratic personnel were supposedly put in their place under the new NSC system; the first major decisions made under this reformed structure did not always please its creators, however, nor did they always rely on it when making policy.

THE NIXINGER NSC SYSTEM AT WORK

Looking back on the Nixinger National Security Council system as a debating forum for presenting options to the president, we can see that it was *not* utilized to decide the policies of Vietnamization, the Nixon Doctrine, the secret Kissinger negotiations with North Vietnam, Nixon's New Economic Policy (NEP), the intervention in Chile that culminated in Allende's overthrow, or the planning of Nixon's trip to China to redirect our Asian policy vis-à-vis the Soviet Union. All of these were presented to the NSC, if at all, as faits accomplis. Indeed, one might wonder when the NSC system *was* used. During Nixon's first year as president, the NSC decided to begin the secret bombing of Cambodia and to respond to the shooting down of a U.S. Navy plane by North Korea (the EC-121 incident). Later in his administration it played a role in other events: the attempt to keep Taiwan in the United Nations with a "two China" policy; the decision to conduct incursions into Cambodia and Laos; the détente agreements with the Soviet Union; Middle Eastern policy *before* the 1973 October war; and policy in Angola and southern Africa in general.

In the absence of aggregate classified material on most of these issues, no definitive evaluation of the NSC can be undertaken. It is now known that from January 1969 to August 9, 1974, eighty-three NSC meetings were held, all but five of them before 1973. Only two NSC meetings were convened in 1973 (on March 1 and April 1) and only three before August 9, 1974 (on January 1, March 13, and June 6). Clearly there appears to be a relationship between Nixon's mounting Watergate problems and the diminishing number of NSC (and cabinet) meetings,[47] but probably more important from a decision-making perspective is that there also appears to be a relationship between certain NSC and non-NSC decisions that is crucial for understanding how the system actually worked in the formulation of some, but not all, foreign policies. This relationship existed long before Watergate demanded most of the president's attention in his last year and a half in office. The carefully guarded secret to bomb Cambodia has to be viewed in relation to those actions that did not arise from NSC debates, but that were undertaken *around the same time*. These included the policy of Vietnamization (that is, turning the bulk of the fighting and management of the war over to the South Vietnamese), the unilateral withdrawal of American troops from Vietnam, and stepped-up negotiations with the Vietcong in Paris.

Consequently, the Joint Chiefs of Staff (JCS) had more bargaining power on the question of whether to bomb and/or invade Cambodia, not only because of the president's expressed desire for changing policy there but especially because of other Nixonian tactical and strategic diplomatic goals: Vietnamization (including his private commitment to a gradual pullout of U.S. soldiers and a determination to end the draft); the short-term goal of negotiating a quick end to the war; and, above all, his long-term desire for better relations with China, which precluded bombing enemy sanctuaries in North Vietnam. Early secret contacts with the North Vietnamese and the Chinese also automatically made Cambodian sanctuaries ideal substitutes with which to placate the JCS, who disapproved of rapid Vietnamization in general and of even token troop withdrawal in particular (see chapter 7). Also, the covert bombing of Cambodia offered Nixon and Kissinger the opportunity to bring pressure to bear on the North Vietnamese to talk with U.S. representatives, which, if successful, would enhance their respective reputations as diplomats, as well as possibly keep the JCS from sabotaging these negotiations. Yet the exact reasons why the bombings became a top-secret action of the Nixon administration appear, in retrospect, to have been primarily political rather than military or diplomatic.

The need to placate the JCS aside, the first two of these new initiatives—Vietnamization and unilateral troop withdrawal—are now attributed to Secretary of Defense Melvin Laird's influence on Nixon. Laird's role *before* the Cambodian invasion has been neglected by researchers, perhaps partially because he has chosen not to write or even testify about his experiences as secretary of defense, and also because many who lived through the late 1960s as adults remember him as being a congressional hawk. This image drastically colored assumptions about him when he became a member of the first Nixon cabinet. Despite cartoons depicting Laird's bald head in the shape of a missile, bomb, or bullet, from the beginning he assumed a moderate position among the president's top advisers. According to an assistant secretary of the navy who observed him at the time, Melvin Laird's two primary goals as secretary of defense were to end the war and to end the draft. These goals made him one of the few true believers in the policy of Vietnamization (a term he coined) and the behind-the-scenes architect of the Nixon Doctrine. Vietnamization and the Nixon Doctrine were logical extensions of each other, and Laird deserves credit for promoting the best aspects of both policies. He not only wanted to withdraw American troops from Vietnam faster than the Pentagon thought the South Vietnamese forces could be trained to replace them, but he also wanted U.S. allies to realize that they could no longer depend upon American manpower to defend them in conventional war. These views made him question the extension of the war into Cambodia and Laos. Therefore, unlike Nixon and Kissinger, Laird was more interested in *ending* the war in Vietnam than in *winning* it.[48]

Since neither Vietnamization nor the Nixon Doctrine were products of the formal NSC system, there are, to date, insufficient data available to trace their exact origins or their adoption as policies. Although Vietnamization had been presented in January 1969 at top-secret meetings of the NSC, the general policy, but not the terms, had actually been formulated in advance to conform with the president's preinauguration decision to withdraw American troops gradually and unilaterally from Vietnam. The formulation and announcement of the Nixon Doctrine were even further removed from the reformed NSC system. Nixon unexpectedly presented it to a group of reporters on July 25, 1969, on a "nonquotation basis" at a background press briefing in Guam, the first stop on an around-the-world trip.[49]

Years later, when I asked Nixon why he had announced this important doctrine in such an offhand manner, he said that it was for the same reasons that two years later, on July 6, 1971, he introduced his pentagonal global economic concept: to avoid having it leaked in advance by State Department bureaucrats and to avoid telling Kissinger, which would have entailed NSSMs on the subject and thus a National Security Council discussion before his proclamation. In both instances he has also specifically denied that he had gotten these particular diplomatic ideas from Kissinger or that they had "originated in the bureaucracy" and were simply presented to him like choices on a menu. Despite Kissinger's claims to the contrary, eyewitness accounts indicate beyond any doubt that Nixon's pronouncement took Kissinger so much by surprise that "Henry quarrel[ed] with RN when he came off the stage about it . . . [and] was not happy with what RN said." According to this observer, Nixon conde-scendingly replied to Kissinger: "you'll learn, relax." Kissinger was no more pleased with Nixon's unilateral pronouncement about a "pentagonal balance of power."[50]

While the Nixon Doctrine was initially aimed at "southern tier" Third World countries in East Asia as "essentially a rationale for retrench-ment," it came to represent the formal institutionalization of the policy of Vietnamization, that is, U.S. support for regional security and local self-sufficiency generally in the Far East; it also had important international implications for the Atlantic Alliance because, like détente, it embodied "a genuine American acceptance of the implications of nascent multi-polarity—the so-called 'new pluralism.'" The Nixon Doctrine was, in fact, the corollary, in particular, to détente between the U.S. and the USSR and, in general, to the president's pentagonal approach to world affairs. As such, it allowed the United States to begin to resolve the con-tradiction that had plagued its foreign policy throughout the cold war con-tainment years: how to maintain its commitments abroad while at the same time reducing its direct military involvement. "The local efforts suggested by the Nixon Doctrine were not narrowly conveyed as an adjunct to the global *modus vivendi* achieved at the super power level," according to Robert S. Litwak. "Rather, they were to serve as a kind of regional safety-net, presumably consonant with American interests should there develop a local crack in the stable structure."[51]

The Nixon Doctrine also "repudiated the rationale under which the United States had first become involved in Vietnam." It therefore trans-formed that conflict from a "strategic contest between the proxies of two great powers—the United States and China—into a dirty little war that could . . . be lost or settled in a way that would not gravely damage Amer-ican interests or increase threats."[52] The Nixon Doctrine was thus more necessary from an American perspective as a foundation block upon which to build the later détente agreements with the Soviet Union (and China) than was the anti-ballistic missile (ABM) legislation, despite the greater domestic attention that the latter received in the United States during the spring and summer of 1969.

By 1970 the Nixon Doctrine had evolved into the internationalization of the policy of Vietnamization or, at the very least, its blanket application to the Far East. The purpose of this new presidential foreign-policy doc-trine became, according to Nixon, "to provide a shield if a nuclear power threatens the freedom of any nation allied with us. . . . [I]n cases involving other types of aggression we shall furnish military and economic assistance when requested in accordance with our treaty commitments. But we shall look to the nation directly threatened to assume the primary responsibility for the manpower for its defense."

In a word, Nixon wanted "to ensure that there were no more Vietnams in the future."[53] The subsequent invasions of Cambodia and Laos violated the intent if not the letter of the Nixon Doctrine. When Laird and others pointed out this contradiction at NSC meetings, Kissinger, characteristically taking credit for policy he neither initiated nor liked, reportedly insisted: "We wrote the goddamn doctrine, we can change it."[54] Consequently, Vietnamization led to the covert as well as overt expansion of the war in Indochina, a result that had not been anticipated by either the opponents or the proponents of the concept in the first months of the new administration. This is but one of many unanticipated results of the Nixinger approach to foreign policy. For a grand design, it contained many loose ends and loopholes. One of its most interesting features was economic.

NIXON AND ECONOMIC FOREIGN POLICY

Nixon's strongest critics often credit him with a great number of diplomatic successes. Usually, however, they do not include his successes (or failures) in the area of foreign economic policy. In that financial realm Nixon employed far fewer questionable tactics (with the exception of the economic warfare his administration conducted against Salvador Allende's government in Chile) and followed the suggestions of a much broader group of advisers than he did with other aspects of his diplomacy. In fact, with respect to international economics, Nixon acted similarly to the way he did in the field of domestic reform: listening to a variety of opinions, authorizing sensible functional reorganization based on the recommendations of the Ash Council, and trying to lead both Congress and public opinion on this topic. Additionally, as noted in chapter 2, he practiced a type of New Federalist regional globalism more consistently with respect to foreign economic policy than when traditional political diplomacy was at stake. His successes in this area were much shorter-lived than those in domestic policy, but a few, such as the New Economic Policy (NEP), initially appeared as dramatic and significant as the changed political relations with the Soviet Union and the People's Republic of China.

Although John Connally dominated the economic views of the Nixon administration during his short service in the administration as secretary of the treasury from February 1971 to May 1972, largely through the formulation and implementation of the NEP, the president ultimately found more sustained support and advice in the person of George Shultz. Shultz succeeded Connally in 1972 with the unofficial title "deputy president for economic matters." By the end of the year, Nixon had appointed him to head the new cabinet-level Council on Economic Policy (CEP) and he appeared well on his way to becoming the "economic policy czar." Shultz's foreign economic expertise never equaled his domestic, however, and when it did he had stronger views on monetary policy than trade. Even though he had the confidence of the president and respect among other senior officials in the administration, Shultz was never able to use the two new economic councils Nixon created or the reports of a Task Force on International Development and a Commission on International Trade to maximum advantage.[55] This was partly because Shultz preferred to operate informally, rather than through established structures, so his influence on Nixon remained diffuse.

Nixon attributed his interest in international economics to Eisenhower's secretary of state and diplomat John Foster Dulles. As vice president in the 1950s, Nixon had wanted to create a Foreign Economic Council. Failing this, he has said that his travels abroad in the 1950s only confirmed his belief that foreign leaders understood economics better than leaders of the United States and he was determined to remedy this situation as president. Nixon faced two obstacles in this effort: Kissinger (as he has put it: "international economics was not Henry's bag") and the State Department, whose members saw "economic policy as government to government," which limited their diplomatic view of the world and made them so suspicious or cynical (or both) about the private sector that they refused to promote international commerce to the degree that Nixon thought they should. "Unlike the ignoramuses I encountered among economic officers at various embassies in the 1950s and 1960s," Nixon told me, "I wanted to bring economics to the foreign service."[56]

Nixon's interest in and knowledge of international trade increased after 1962 when he was between public offices, practicing law in New York. With the Wall Street firm of Nixon, Mudge, Rose, Guthrie, and Alexander, which merged in 1967 with Caldwell, Trimble, and Mitchell, he specialized in international economics and multinational corporations. Interestingly, given his later troubles as president, he argued one case before the Supreme Court defending privacy rights.[57] It was from these two decades of experience with international and domestic economic matters that Nixon attempted as president to rationalize the formulation of foreign economic policy—definitely not Henry Kissinger's area of expertise. Partially because they were not a "team" on foreign economic policy and partially because Nixon bypassed the NSC entirely in formulating his New Economic Policy in 1971, the president relied not on his national security adviser but on other freethinking outsiders when formulating foreign economic policy. Even the Rockefeller brothers, Kissinger's mentors/patrons, were not able to exercise the influence on economic policy they would have liked because they could not use Henry as a conduit on this issue.[58]

Next to Connally, Nixon was most impressed with the economic views of Peter G. Peterson, who, after starting out in 1971 as assistant to the president for international economic affairs, became secretary of commerce in January 1972. Although Connally and Peterson appeared to agree on such early foreign economic initiatives of the Nixon administration as the NEP and the "get-tough" policy toward Third World countries, which nationalized U.S. companies abroad, as Secretary of Commerce Peterson ultimately proved much more sophisticated and sensitive than the secretary of the treasury about the United States's changed economic role in the world. In a December 27, 1971, position paper defending Nixon's NEP, Peterson remarked that the new global situation in which the United States found itself demanded "shared leadership, shared responsibility, and shared burdens." The reform of the international monetary system, he said, must fully recognize and be solidly rooted in "the growing reality of a genuinely interdependent and increasingly competitive world economy whose goal is mutual, shared prosperity—not artificial, temporary advantage." At no point did Peterson believe, as Connally apparently did, that "the simple realignment of exchange rates" would adequately address the economic problems facing the international economy. Peterson and others, such as his successor in the Commerce Department, Frederick B. Dent, and Secretary of the Treasury George Shultz, also thought that the NEP was a radical departure that "marked the beginning of a new era in postwar international trade and finance."[59]

In January 1971 Nixon, on the advice of the Ash Council and with the approval of the Council on Economic Policy, headed by Shultz, convinced Congress to establish an entirely new cabinet-level Council on International Economic Policy (CIEP), with Peterson as executive director. This was not so much a reorganization of functions as it was an alternative to fill an existing void in the federal structure "to achieve a clear top-level focus on the full range of foreign international economic issues, and to maintain close coordination with basic foreign policy issues." Nixon thought the CIEP so important that he initially chaired its meetings as it attempted to "deal with international economic policies (including trade investment, balance of payments, and finance) as a coherent whole." After its first meeting in April, at which Peterson gave a brief on the twenty years of trends and developments in international economics, Nixon came away believing that all "key White House Staff" should receive the same briefing because "the facts presented and their policy implication were sufficiently important to our foreign policy, foreign economic policy, and our domestic politics."[60]

This centralized approach to foreign economic policy could have been reconciled with the decentralized aspects of the president's New Federalism, as so many others were. According to I. M. Destler, however, "decentralization is inevitable" in a field so fraught with complexity, which is why CIEP did not work as well as Nixon and Peterson (the "economic Kissinger") had hoped. Since three presidents (Nixon, Ford, and Carter) and their economic advisers thought that effective centralization would help the United States compete abroad, it is difficult to accept this conclusion. In retrospect, the real problem appears to be (and Destler also suggests this) that no international economic adviser, council, or board ever became a "primary day-to-day issues manager" for Nixon or his two successors in office. A strong personality who was knowledgeable about international economics probably could have made the CIEP approach a success under Nixon, and Shultz was the only likely candidate because Connally did not have the in-depth knowledge and was too ethnocentric about foreign economic policy. Moreover, Shultz's mode of operation was not as egocentrically aggrandizing as that of either Connally or Kissinger.[61]

Even if Shultz had decided to make CIEP the cornerstone of his control over economic policy, it would have faced criticism from a structural as well as substantive point of view. At one level it appeared to add still another layer to policy making; at another it seemed to encroach on NSC dominance over U.S. foreign policy. While Shultz and Peterson denied both charges, it was clear that the CIEP would have rough sledding within the executive branch of government. Roy Ash recommended its creation after considering whether its coordinating functions could be performed by the Special Trade Representative (STR), the Council of Economic Advisers (CEA), the NSC, and the OMB. Its purpose was "to achieve consistency between domestic and foreign economic policy. . . . Presently, no single high-level body holds the responsibility for the development of international economic policy and its relation to domestic economic policy. . . . Where the Council's responsibilities overlap with that of the National Security Council, as in the case of foreign aid, . . . the CIEP will operate within the general framework of national security policy developed by the NSC."[62] In contrast to Shultz's 1975 description of the ambiguity of CIEP, Ash originally proposed that CIEP not be subordinate to either the NSC or the Domestic Council, and that the word *international* rather than *foreign* be used because CIEP would "take account of the interdependence between nations and . . . avoid the connotation of an antagonistic 'we and you' relationship." In keeping with this charge, CIEP issued a report on September 13, 1971, that the White House hailed as the "first thorough review of United States internal economic policies conducted by any administration since 1954."[63]

U.S. economic foreign policy took on new meaning not only because of the international aspects of Nixon's 1971 New Economic Policy but also because of the energy crisis precipitated by the Organization of Petroleum Exporting Countries (OPEC) in October 1973 in retaliation for U.S. support of Israel during the October war. Both the NEP and the oil crisis became major concerns of the Murphy Commission on the Organization of the Government for the Conduct of Foreign Policy during its hearings from 1973 to 1975. Almost all the witnesses who testified to the commission, for example, were asked about the relation of the October war to the OPEC rise in oil prices, regardless of their area of expertise. Thus, Nixon's foreign economic policies stood out for both negative and positive reasons by the time he resigned.

Kissinger's lack of interest in economics before and while he served in the Nixon administration has never been doubted or denied—not even by Kissinger. In 1971 he wrote to the economist C. Fred Bergsten at the Brookings Institution thanking him for having sent a chapter of a book on international monetary policy: "You have been a great teacher—the question is whether I will learn fast enough to affect events." Events finally overtook Kissinger in the form of the energy crisis beginning in 1973. "I was so uninterested in economics . . . when I was Assistant to the President for National Security Affairs," he unabashedly told the Murphy Commission in 1975, "I not only acquiesced but I encouraged creating what they called CIEP." Kissinger's ignorance of economics did not prevent him from trying to take credit for CIEP, even though there is no documentary evidence for this assertion. Then, between 1971 and 1973, he sporadically tried to undermine its functions. For example, often when Nixon expressed interest in resolving serious international economic problems such as the trade deficit and energy problems with economic advisers like Peterson, they agreed that CIEP "hasn't worked out [because of] the Kissinger problem." Yet because Kissinger was the president's favorite, none of Nixon's economic advisers suggested practical ways to eliminate the problem. Finally, in 1975 Kissinger tried to get the CIEP abolished. Although he unashamedly admitted in this same 1975 testimony that only the oil crisis had forced him "to spend an increasing amount of my time on economic questions," Kissinger arrogantly recommended the abolishment of CIEP and the "return" of international economic policy to the National Security Council.[64]

Secretary Shultz's view of the CIEP was much more ambivalent than Kissinger's. Although the NSC at one time had had a deputy director for economic affairs, its staff under Kissinger did "not develop itself very much in the area of economics," and neither did the State Department. Consequently Shultz (and Peterson and Peter M. Flanigan, who succeeded Peterson as head of the CIEP) believed that the combination of the Council on Economic Policy and CIEP was necessary and provided "adequate machinery for long-range planning with respect to international economic problems." They also agreed that the NEP had initiated a new order in foreign economic relationships that required as much attention as the political aspect of U.S. diplomacy. Without formal membership on the NSC, however, it was difficult for Shultz (or Peterson or Flanigan) to ensure that economics would not be given short shrift. All knew that it took forceful personalities to keep economics in the forefront of decision making, especially after Kissinger formed an ad hoc group within the NSC to deal with the energy crisis precipitated by the oil embargo and began to recommend that the CIEP structure be folded back into the NSC.[65]

For a variety of reasons—not the least of which was Kissinger's general disinterest in, and disdain for, the unglamorous aspects of international economics—in 1975 the Murphy Commission recommended (with Kissinger's wholehearted support) that the CIEP be abolished, despite the fact that it "played a central role in [economic] policy formation" between 1971 and 1975, including the Trade Reform Act of 1973, the president's Expropriation Policy Statement of 1972, preparation and follow-up on economic issues for the 1972 summit meeting with the Soviets, the ongoing lend lease settlements, all commercial and maritime agreements, and international investment policy. In part because Shultz preferred to formulate economic policy in an ad hoc, rather than systematic fashion, the Council did not meet regularly and so its overall performance was difficult to defend against critics like Kissinger because its "paper trail" left much to be desired. In fact, Kissinger was able to claim that periodically he established ad hoc groups on foreign economic matters that functioned as well as the CIEP.[66]

Another reason for the CIEP's perceived weakness was that its goals and functions were never effectively coordinated with those of the Commission on International Trade and Investment Policy (known as the Williams Commission), created in May 1970 on the recommendation of a March 4 report of the president's Task Force on International Development (TFID). This interregnum task force underscored Nixon's personal interest in international economic issues. Accordingly, Kissinger told all cabinet secretaries on October 6, 1969, that "the president attaches high priority to this project" because he wanted "a new approach to these fundamental foreign [economic] problems." Subsequently, the Williams Commission released the first comprehensive review of U.S. international policies sponsored by the White House since 1954. This report emphasized the increasing economic interdependency of the United States in a global economy and called for a "new realism" on the part of the government and private businesses in international economic matters. Its report was designed to coincide with, and bolster support for, the international components of Nixon's NEP.[67] Despite (or because of) the uncoordinated recommendations of the Task Force on International Development and the Williams Commission, the CIEP faltered and finally failed after Nixon left office. For a while it was merged with the Office of the Special Trade Representative. President Ford created the Economic Policy Board (EPB) with many of the same coordination functions of the CIEP, but Kissinger interfered with its operations as well. Carter established the Economic Policy Group (EPG) with the same intent as Ford, but it never had the attention of the president to the degree that the EPB had under Ford and especially the CIEP under Nixon. President Carter simply allowed the CIEP's statutory authorization to lapse in 1977.[68]

The CIEP's rapid decline into obscurity seems to have been hastened by Kissinger's recommendation to the Murphy Commission on the Organization of Government for the Conduct of Foreign Policy that it be eliminated, despite the fact that others, including Peterson, testified in its behalf. Despite CIEP's failure to centralize U.S. foreign economic policy, the Nixon administration dealt successfully with a number of international economic issues, such as the expropriation of U.S. property by foreign countries, on a case-by-case basis. Here again, however, jurisdictional problems were encountered involving the CIEP, the Commission on International Trade and Investment Policy, and the National Advisory Council of the Treasury Department. Even though the CIEP created an interagency staff coordinating group to try to resolve the overlapping authority of the State, Treasury, Commerce, and Defense Departments, there was no centralized way to formulate policy when foreign governments nationalized the property of American multinational corporations. So when the energy crisis exploded in 1973, the administration was incapable of dealing with it in any systematic way. Thus, the high hopes and recommendations of the Ash Council, the president's Task Force on International Development, the Williams Commission, and Nixon himself were far from realized when he left office. Centralization of decision making proved much easier on political, rather than economic, foreign policy issues.

FIRST TEST OF THE NSC: SHOOTDOWN OVER KOREA

Within four months of taking office, Nixon faced his first major foreign policy crisis, that is, the first diplomatic event he did not inherit from previous administrations. On April 15, 1969, North Korea shot down a United States Navy EC-121 reconnaissance plane, killing all thirty-one men aboard. For our purposes here, the importance of this incident is not whether the EC-121 was 45 or 90 miles off the North Korean coast (and hence over international waters, as the U.S. claimed), or whether it was within the 12½-mile territorial limit claimed by the North Koreans. It is not even crucial that, "in addition to routine monitoring of North Korean military communications, [the plane] was electronically eavesdropping on Soviet and Chinese forces facing each other across the border." This additional surveillance had been ordered because, in the spring of 1969, both Henry Kissinger and CIA Chief Richard Helms suspected that the USSR might be planning a preemptive strike against China.[69] The key importance of this incident lies in the fact that it triggered a series of actions within the administration that make it an important way of analyzing early Nixonian policy making.

Given Nixon's campaign criticism of the way President Johnson had handled North Korea's seizure of the *Pueblo* spy ship fifteen months earlier, one might have expected him to react to the EC-121 incident in a dramatically punitive fashion. Such an expectation seemed all the more likely since many American lives had been lost on board the plane. But as president, Richard Nixon had gained a distinctly different perspective from the one he had held as a presidential candidate. When a "fourth-rate military power like North Korea will seize an American naval power on the high seas," he had said in August 1968, "it is time for new leadership to restore respect for the United States of America." Nixon's criticism of Johnson so "upset" Pentagon officials at the "very highest level" that one of them offered to brief L. Patrick Gray in the hope that he could convince Nixon to stop.[70] Although Nixon used the theme of "remember the *Pueblo*" as a "cheer-line" throughout his presidential campaign, he now changed his rhetoric dramatically when faced with his own *Pueblo* incident. At an April 18 press conference, after announcing the resumption of reconnaissance flights with military protection, Nixon responded to a reporter's question about what further action was contemplated by saying: "Looking to the future, as far as what we do will depend upon the circumstances . . . and any other developments that occur as we continue these flights." In his memoirs, Nixon further justified his unexpected caution and final failure to take any significant retaliatory action by saying that "intelligence reports indicated that shooting down the EC-121 was an isolated provocation like the seizure of the *Pueblo*."[71]

However, declassified military documents now clearly indicate that Nixon initially favored the idea of striking the North Korean airfield responsible for the attack on the American plane. This contradicts Kissinger's assertion in *White House Years* that the president gave no indication of what action he preferred.[72] These same documents indicate that Laird proposed seizing a North Korean cannery ship that supposedly was in the area. Others on the NSC talked about seizing or capturing a North Korean military vessel, but this proved impossible because none had left port since the capture of the *Pueblo*. Kissinger's NSC staff was, according to him, "amazingly hawkish" and recommended an immediate air strike. Attorney General John Mitchell and Vice President Spiro Agnew agreed.[73]

Secretary of State Rogers, Laird, Helms, U. Alexis Johnson, and even the Joint Chiefs of Staff opposed retaliatory bombing—all for slightly different reasons: it would tax our already overextended military situation in Southeast Asia; the country could not risk another war in the area should North Korea decide to respond in kind against South Korea; and politically it made no sense because domestic peace groups would only increase their antiwar protests and because, in the spring of 1969, there was no demand for retaliation from Congress or from what Nixon would later call his silent majority.[74]

Most of these antibombing rationalizations coincided with the realization that a swift, reactive air strike was logistically impossible. During the twenty-four hours before the NSC meeting, military advisers determined that the United States simply did not have enough planes or ships immediately available in the area. The Pentagon estimated that at least 150 planes would be necessary, and that using either South Korean or Japanese bases would be out of the question because neither nation wanted to become involved in a potential shootout between North Korea and the United States. This meant that the bombers and escorts for them would have to come from either Guam or Okinawa, since there were no aircraft carriers in the immediate vicinity of North Korea. It would have taken up to a week to mount an effective air strike, with sufficient backup power, in case North Korea decided to deploy its 400 MIG jets.[75]

The only viable option to emerge from the April 16 NSC meetings was that of continuing reconnaissance flights with escorts. Nixon ordered this action taken on April 17, and announced it the next day to the American public at a regularly scheduled press conference. Much to the president's anger and dismay, however, the Pentagon did not implement this order for three weeks, primarily because of the unavailability of enough escort planes. To this day Kissinger refuses to believe this argument or the one about why an air strike was not militarily practical or possible.[76]

Nixon privately issued two other orders on April 17. One called for the deployment to the Sea of Japan of two aircraft carriers, ostentatiously referred to as the 7th Fleet Task Force 71, ostensibly for "possible retaliatory attacks"; another called for an official protest at the April 18 Panmunjom armistice agreement meeting between North Koreans and Americans. This protest included a staged walkout by the U.S. representative. An outright cancellation of the meeting was overruled because that would have placed the United States in technical violation of the 1953 armistice and subsequent negotiation agreements reached with North Korea. Finally, on April 18, after reconfirming with Kissinger that all of his top security advisers (again, with the exception of Mitchell and Agnew) opposed a retaliatory bombing strike, Nixon issued his final order. It called for new raids against North Vietnamese sanctuaries in Cambodia. This operation went by the specific code name LUNCH, and was part of the secret MENU bombing missions that the administration had begun a month earlier.[77]

Of all the public and private actions undertaken by the president in the EC-121 incident, Kissinger approved only of this last one, but thought that even it was too little, too late. Kissinger's dissatisfaction with the policy-making process during this three-day crisis knew no bounds. Commenting later in *White House Years*, he said: "We made no strategic assessment; instead, we bandied technical expedients about. There was no strong White House leadership. We made no significant political move; our military deployments took place in a vacuum." This disagreement within top levels of the administration over the adequacy of U.S. military intelligence in general and how to handle this situation specifically was leaked to the press, prompting Nixon's much-quoted order to his press secretary Ron Ziegler "not to have our people talk to [the] *Post Dispatch—N.Y. Times* and [the] *Washington Post*—Knock it off!"[78]

Timing and logistical factors effectively killed support for an air strike, except from Kissinger, a few members of his staff, Mitchell, and Agnew. Kissinger, in particular, did not think that the North Koreans would counterattack. Moreover, he advised the president that the Soviet Union, China, and North Vietnam were all watching to see what the United States would do. In his memoirs, Nixon quotes Kissinger as telling him: "If we strike back, even though it's risky, they will say, 'this guy is becoming irrational—we'd better settle with him.' But if we back down, they'll say, 'This guy is the same as his predecessor, and if we wait he'll come to the same end.'"[79] Nixon did not accept the idea of acting like a "madman" to scare nations not directly involved in the EC-121 crisis. Kissinger's comment, however, should not be taken lightly; his dissatisfaction with how Nixon handled the EC-121 incident determined that he would overreact when advising President Ford about using force during the *Mayaguez* incident in 1975 when the Khmer Rouge captured a U.S. merchant ship and its forty-man crew.

Following Kissinger's advice, Ford precipitately decided to attack the island of Koh Tang, where it was thought the ship and crew were being held. Although a total of five NSC meetings took place between May 12 and May 15, Kissinger's initial statement at the first one asserting that "the United States must draw the line" or suffer "a serious blow to our prestige around the world" determined the ultimate decision to use force after sixty hours of negotiating had failed. Unfortunately, the marine and air assault was badly carried out and forty-one Americans were killed, fifty more wounded. There were much higher casualties among the Cambodians on the island, largely because the U.S. troops detonated a

15,000-ton bomb as they evacuated. If Ford had waited and tried to use UN or neutral channels after direct U.S. negotiations with Cambodia had failed, he would have discovered that the government had decided to release the crew *before* the U.S. attack began. By the time the marines landed, the *Mayaguez* crew members were no longer there, having been freed a few hours before.[80]

In light of Kissinger's overreaction in both incidents, it is worth looking more closely at the origins of the so-called madman theory in connection with the Nixon administration's conduct of foreign policy. Robert Haldeman claimed in *The Ends of Power* that Nixon used the term one day during the 1968 campaign when they "were walking along a foggy beach after a long day of speechwriting." According to Haldeman's account, Nixon was ruminating about how he would end the war in Vietnam during his first year in office, just as Eisenhower had ended the war in Korea—by covertly threatening to use nuclear bombs. At one point Nixon allegedly turned to Haldeman and said: "I call it the madman theory, Bob. I want the North Vietnamese to believe I've reached the point where I might do *anything* to stop the war. We'll just slip the word to them that, 'for God's sake, you know Nixon is obsessed about communism. We can't restrain him when he's angry—and he has his hand on the nuclear button'—and Ho Chi Minh himself will be in Paris in two days begging for peace."[81]

When I asked Nixon about this often-quoted statement, he said that he seldom talked with Haldeman about substantive foreign policy matters, and certainly did not remember using the term "madman theory." He indicated that had he discussed the concept or principle of threatening to use excessive force, it would have been with others in connection with employing Kissinger in the role of the "good messenger" to play off against his own well-known anti-Communist views when negotiating with Communist nations.[82] I have looked in vain for any other documentation for the madman theory; yet many journalists, historians, and political scientists have accepted Haldeman's hearsay account as documented fact, assuming that Nixon regularly threatened to act like an irrational anti-Communist in order to achieve his foreign policy objectives.[83] Moreover, the president so consistently criticized the "irrationality" of antiwar demonstrators that he could not afford to describe his own diplomacy in similar terms.

My guess is that the term originated with Kissinger, not Nixon, because as early as 1959 Daniel Ellsberg had given two lectures before Kissinger's Harvard seminar on "The Political Uses of Madness." At that time Ellsberg used Hitler as a specific example of the successful "conscious political use of irrational military threats," and told Kissinger's class that such a strategy was reckless and irresponsible. Although there is some indication in even his earliest books that Kissinger accepted such an approach as diplomatically feasible, one cannot find confirmation for authorship in his own memoirs, perhaps because the madman theory does not exalt the former secretary of state's role as negotiator to the mythical heights to which he is still trying to raise it. To date, with the exception of Haldeman, none of either Kissinger's or Nixon's closest aides has indicated any knowledge of the president's use of the term or concept in relation to the use of nuclear weapons in Vietnam, Cambodia, or Laos. Nevertheless, most journalists and many historians have implied, if not actually asserted that he did, because Haldeman, and Haldeman alone, has said so. If anything, the handling of the EC-121 incident demonstrates that Kissinger, rather than Nixon, personally supported the "madman theory."[84]

In his memoirs, Kissinger remains convinced that "in the absence of clear-cut directives, planning was desultory" at the first meeting of WSAG over the EC-121 incident. "There was no real determination to use force: all discussions were theoretical and no concrete operational plan was ever put forward." Nonetheless, he also views the entire affair as a "blessing in disguise," because "it made us dramatically tighten our procedures. Future crises were handled crisply and with strong central direction."[85]

I have discussed Kissinger's reaction at length because it is at such odds with those of other participants in these deliberations, especially Secretary of State Rogers. In contrast to Kissinger, Rogers recalled the decision-making process during the EC-121 incident as the most open and honest one of the entire time he was head of the State Department. Noting that it was "one of the biggest decisions we made," Rogers later told a presidential commission investigating the conduct of American foreign policy that at the NSC meeting on April 16, there was a "real hoe-down in terms of arguments. In that case I actually had a chance to—I mean the decision hadn't been made, it was quite clear." The impression conveyed by this verbatim testimony of Rogers is that this was one of the few times that he participated in a full and candid discussion of foreign policy options over an issue that had not been decided in advance by Nixon and Kissinger. According to the former secretary of state, "the fact of the matter was that toward the end the president really didn't use the NSC at all to speak of. I mean he hadn't used all of the staff of the NSC. . . . Quite often . . . decisions were made by two or three or four people."[86]

The president's views on the outcome of the EC-121 affair remain ambivalent. On the one hand, he was apparently convinced by the logic of the moderate positions taken by Rogers and Laird, but he regretted that the response could not have been tougher. "Frankly, I tilted toward [an air strike]," Nixon told David Frost in 1977; but then the NSC debates changed his mind. "I still agree," he later wrote in his memoirs, "that we had to act boldly; I was just not convinced that this was the time to do it." He also claimed to have told Kissinger: "They got away with it this time, but they'll never get away with it again." The public, of course, heard or read only Nixon's mild-mannered words at his April 18 press conference: "I have ordered that these flights be continued. They will be protected. This is not a threat; it is simply a statement of fact."[87]

THE LEGACY OF NIXINGERISM

What conclusions about the management of foreign-policy making under Nixon can be drawn from this first diplomatic crisis? First, it is absurd to claim, as Tad Szulc did, writing under the influence of revelations about Watergate and the secret bombings of Cambodia, that Nixon brought us to the brink of war with the North Koreans in April 1969. Second, the event clearly indicates that Nixon was much more willing than Kissinger to admit that we did not have the necessary military capacity to retaliate, and therefore should not risk provoking a counterattack by the North Koreans. Third, once again, both Rogers and Laird espoused moderate positions, with the latter perhaps exceeding his authority as head of the Department of Defense by canceling other reconnaissance flights to ensure that no precipitant action would be taken. Fourth, the newly reconstituted NSC structure did not function to anyone's satisfaction (with the possible exception of Rogers). Fifth, Kissinger was clearly maneuvering to ingratiate himself with the president at the time, by not appearing too far out of step with the moderates. Sixth, while the policy making went on in secret, it did not smack of the excessive precautions characterizing the decision a month earlier to bomb Cambodia, or to engage in the subsequent double-bookkeeping method adopted to cover up those bombings (see chapter 7). Seventh, there was a vindictiveness to Nixon's final order to lash out at North Korea and its Communist supporters by stepping up the secret air strikes along the Cambodian border. Such calculated retribution showed up again in the next four years when the North Vietnamese refused to compromise at the negotiating table. But the bombings of Vietnam and surrounding countries should not be confused with the acts of a mad bomber. They were carefully designed to impress China and the USSR with America's resolve on other international issues having little or nothing to do with the situation in Indochina.

Finally, and equally important, the entire EC-121 incident reinforced Nixon's and Kissinger's suspicions about hostile or lethargic bureaucracies. In this case Rogers, representing the State Department, did not turn out to be the worst culprit—Secretary of Defense Laird did. At the same time, the secretary of defense also emerged as a formidable obstacle in Kissinger's battle to become Nixon's primary adviser on foreign policy. In the course of 1969, only Laird successfully challenged Kissinger's self-appointed role as number-one foreign policy formulator for the president. However, after the overt invasion of Cambodia in the spring of 1970, Kissinger had completely consolidated his position.

Thus, within a month, in March and April 1969, the NSC reached two important, but quite dissimilar, decisions: to bomb the hell out of selected North Vietnamese sanctuaries in Cambodia, using a devious double-bookkeeping method; and not to overreact to the shooting down of an American EC-121 spy plane with thirty-one men aboard. The former has been generally castigated by the press and public, while the latter has been generally praised. Was one a mistake of the NSC system and the other not? That seems unlikely. I think that the discongruity between the two decisions can best be explained by how much private consultation took place between Nixon and Kissinger, rather than by any inherent flaw in the NSC system itself.

Since the EC-121 incident occurred unexpectedly, the two men had little or no time to consult with each other. The Cambodian sanctuary situation, on the other hand, was inherited from the Johnson administration. They had discussed the problem several times before the North Vietnamese launched a small-scale offensive in February 1969. Thus the decision to bomb the sanctuaries was not made in a crisis atmosphere. Yet it was intimately related to the other changes in U.S. policy toward Vietnam that I have already mentioned. At heart, however, it represented a policy based on the exaggerated expectation that North Vietnam could be cajoled into being more reasonable in its peace demands through a combination of bombings, improved U.S. relations with China, Vietnamization, and unilateral withdrawal. This expectation was never realized. In the end, after four more years of war, the United States accepted essentially the same terms that the Vietcong had offered in 1969.

Yet, as I will demonstrate in chapter 7, the bombing of Cambodia was one of the few truly covert foreign policy undertakings of the Nixon administration that received *full* NSC consideration, even if it was after the fact. Most of the other covert actions bypassed the NSC. This says something quite significant about policy making under Nixon and the legacy he left in foreign affairs. *When a decision could be carried out that did not depend on the civilian or military bureaucracy for implementation, the NSC was ignored, whether the action was covert or not. It was utilized, however, whenever the covert or overt policy required large-scale bureaucratic support.* This has become a practical rule of thumb for all subsequent administrations' use of the NSC.

The NSC has been an easy target for attacking the Nixinger foreign policies, but it is really only the symbol of a much more complex decision-making process, one that became increasingly capricious between 1969 and 1974. In the final analysis, the NSC system, or any other government system, is only as good as the people who staff it, and no amount of tinkering or reorganization can change that.

6

DÉTENTE, NATO, AND RAPPROCHEMENT

The United States of America is the only nation in the free world that has the power and the influence that can determine whether freedom does survive in the world over the next twenty-five years.

—Nixon, remarks to Presidential Scholars, June 4, 1970

Improved relations with the Soviet Union and the People's Republic of China are often cited as the most successful diplomatic achievements of Nixon's presidency. There is no doubt that they were important components of the Nixinger "grand design." While triggering relations with Communist China remains a major achievement, détente with the Soviet Union, for all its innovativeness at the time, did not survive the Ford administration. The reasons for these two outcomes are not difficult to describe in retrospect, although both Nixon and Kissinger continue indiscriminately to claim accolades for both. Significantly, in both of these major cold war areas, the president and his special assistant for national security affairs chose back-channel contacts whenever possible to achieve their foreign policy goals. Short-lived as it proved to be, détente with the Soviet Union remains an excellent example of their preference for covert rather than open diplomacy.

Through a byzantine diplomatic process, détente came to represent as much symbol as substance in the Nixon administration's evolving foreign policy. The literal meaning of the word *détente*, from the French and Russian, is "relaxing or easing of tensions between nations." At one level it became more important as a domestic political struggle between the president and Congress than as a debate over the actual details of either the antiballistic missile (ABM) agreement or the strategic arms limitation talks (SALT I); at another it was symptomatic of the covert modus operandi of the president and his national security adviser; and at still another, it symbolized White House control of foreign policy above and beyond Congress and the State Department. As an executive-branch creation, détente also became associated with both the Nixon Doctrine and Kissinger's convoluted concept of linkage, which the Soviets refused to accept.[1]

Finally, détente reflected Nixon's belief that "there could never be absolute parity between the U.S. and the USSR in the area of nuclear and conventional weapons." It was time for the United States to seek *sufficiency* rather than *superiority* in describing its arms-control goals. This acceptance by the president of "strategic parity" as a basis for negotiating a détente with the Soviets is all the more remarkable in light of the fact that "there was virtually no national public discussion of the issue in the United States." On June 16, 1969, Nixon simply informed Kissinger that he wanted the State and Defense Departments, as well as the CIA, to provide him with "their best judgment as to what our force level should be . . . in order to provide sufficiency. . . . These recommendations should be made to me personally, on an eyes only basis, and will not be disclosed in an NSC meeting." In this fashion a great opportunity was lost to educate the American public with respect to the "real" meaning of détente within the context of sufficiency, as opposed to unnecessarily raising popular expectations by concentrating on its more simplistic and symbolic aspects. It should be remembered, however, that the very nature of American foreign policy formulation requires a certain amount of overselling. And détente was no exception.[2]

From a Nixinger perspective, détente represented nothing more or less than a political and an economic means, strategy, or process (as opposed to goal or condition) for: (1) avoiding nuclear war; (2) "building a network of mutually advantageous relationships"; and (3) modifying Soviet behavior by gaining its de facto acceptance of international cooperation and competition (sometimes referred to as "competitive coexistence"), in order to preserve international stability by according the Soviet Union a greater stake in the status quo. To a lesser degree than some have argued, détente also reflected the domestic and international economic problems the United States faced as a result of the Vietnam War. At the time, the one thing détente did not represent under the Nixon administration was a continuation of the traditional cold war policy of containment, although the former president has equivocated on this point since resigning from office.[3]

Détente was very dependent on the personal interactions between individual leaders and their perceptions of their respective nation's relative strength or of any tangible benefits accruing from relaxed tensions. For example, the Soviet Union never viewed détente as a static condition or status quo concept, the way the United States did. For Soviet leaders the perceptual factors promoting détente by the beginning of the 1970s included the Marxist belief that history was on their side; their fear of improving Sino-American relations; their approval of U.S. unilateral troop withdrawals from Vietnam; Nixon's acceptance of strategic parity; certain economic considerations; and the friendly personal relationships among Nixon, Kissinger, General Secretary Leonid Brezhnev, and Soviet Minister of Foreign Affairs Andrei A. Gromyko. In a thirty-seven-page document about a March 26, 1974, meeting, not declassified until 1993, Kissinger can be found joking with both Brezhnev and Gromyko. Many of the general secretary's remarks indicate his close and informal relationship with Nixon as well. Kissinger is at his bantering best in this document, because he knew that his aide Peter W. Rodman was taking verbatim notes of the conversation. When, for example, Brezhnev jokingly told Kissinger he had just received a coded message from Nixon expressing displeasure with his secretary of state, Kissinger replied: "It happens every Tuesday." To which Brezhnev responded: "It must be something you told him [and] he must have taken an objective view of the situation."[4]

By 1976, much of this personal intimacy had diminished because of differences over the stalled Conference on Security and Cooperation in Europe (CSCE) and mutual and balanced force reductions (MBFR) talks, congressional obstacles to Soviet-American trade, and the double-standard code of conduct that the United States applied to its own interference into the affairs of such Third World countries as Angola, compared to what it was willing to accord the USSR. And, of course, Nixon was no longer on the international (or domestic) scene.

Even though Nixon formulated U.S. foreign policy during the summer of 1969 largely in secret (including the bombing of Cambodia), congressional opposition loomed large in his mind. He and his aides tried to outmaneuver diplomatic initiatives on the part of the Senate in ways that forced Nixon into a delicate political balancing act that ultimately shaped his and Kissinger's plans more than they wanted at the time and more than they have admitted since. Their "grand design" thus became more a "balancing act" than a blueprint for U.S. diplomacy and, much like détente, its centerpiece, remained a process rather than a fixed policy.[5] It is in these ever-shifting sands of domestic political considerations (which increased after details of the Watergate break-in and cover-up became known in 1973 and 1974) that one must look for both the strengths and the weaknesses of Nixon's détente policies—especially in relation to NATO, the North Atlantic Treaty Organization—the cold war military alliance established under U.S. leadership in 1949 to protect Western Europe against Soviet attack.

DÉTENTE AND NATO

Long before Nixon and Kissinger formally adopted the word *détente* to describe their diplomatic strategies and goals,[6] the president's use of the term in early foreign policy statements and in private notes for speeches clearly indicates that he thought the relationship between NATO and détente with the USSR problematic. This uncertainty was considerably exacerbated when the bilateral, back-channel methods used to achieve rapprochment with China and détente with the Soviet Union bypassed the North Atlantic Treaty countries. In particular, both the ABM and SALT I agreements were negotiated with a minimum of consultation with NATO nations. The same was true of the New Economic Policy announced by Nixon in August 1971. Among other things, the NEP unilaterally "floated" the U.S. dollar on international financial markets, setting the stage for its subsequent devaluation and ending the post–World War II Bretton Woods international monetary system.[7]

In preparation for his first presidential trip to Europe from late February to March (scarcely a month after assuming office), Nixon's private handwritten notes convey the distinct impression that while he recognized the complex relationship among adequate NATO defenses, disarmament, and détente, he thought that U.S. relations with Europe stood "at a great watershed. Now is the time to move. We must seize the moment. I shall do it." Moreover, in his predeparture notes Nixon repeatedly reminded himself to stress that the United States was initiating "a new era of consultation" with its European allies and that "no demonstrations shall deter me at home or abroad. . . . [T]he demonstrators cannot hurt me—only themselves and the cause of peace . . . [which is] too important to be derailed by irresponsible [demonstrators]."[8]

It would also appear, however, that by the spring of 1969 Nixon thought that the 1968 intervention into Czechoslovakia by the USSR made continued European and Soviet proclamations favoring détente somewhat hollow, even though he believed that up to then moves toward "détente [had] produced less fear." Upon his return from Europe, Nixon told legislative leaders that he recognized how "dangerous" détente would be if it were not based on something "real," and that there could be no reduction of U.S. support to NATO or arms negotiations between America and the Soviet Union until there had been "progress on political issues . . . because most wars start as [the] result of political issues." In the interim, however, he maintained that talks "should go forward on all fronts."[9] According to these private notes, Nixon also returned from his first trip abroad as president ostensibly convinced that NATO member countries should be consulted "in advance of East-West negotiations," but at the same time he became more selective about dealing with individual NATO nations. In a March 2, 1970, "eyes-only" memorandum, for example, Nixon outlined his priorities in foreign policy, indicating that with respect to Western Europe he would direct his attention only to those problems "where NATO . . . and where major countries (Britain, Germany and France) are affected. The only minor countries in Europe which I want to pay attention to in the foreseeable future will be Spain, Italy, and Greece. *I do not want to see any papers of the other countries unless their problems are directly related to NATO.*"[10]

Nixon's and Kissinger's official involvement with NATO began at a crucial time in the arms-control talks left over from the Johnson administration. LBJ had already signed the Treaty of Non-Proliferation of Nuclear Weapons. Even though the president and his national security adviser were not particularly enthusiastic about this treaty, believing that technical knowledge about nuclear power could not be contained or limited only to major powers, they inherited the far more important issues from the previous administration of deteriorated relations with NATO and inconclusive disarmament talks with the Soviet Union. According to a February 1969 issue of *U.S. News & World Report,* Nixon came into office determined to repair the damage that President Johnson and his secretary of defense, Robert S. McNamara, had done to the NATO Alliance by not consulting with its members and by opposing the development of British and French national nuclear deterrents. The administration's policy of negotiating secretly with the Soviet Union over terms of the nuclear non-proliferation treaty had "generated resentment and confusion" among Alliance members. The news magazine predicted this would be remedied during the Nixon administration because it would not "doctor" intelligence information about the relative military strengths of the NATO nations and the Warsaw Pact of Eastern European forces, as had the Defense Department "whiz kids" under Johnson in order to rationalize bilateral talks.[11]

Contrary to these optimistic predictions, Nixon almost immediately resorted to sporadic back-channel dealings with, or neglect of, NATO nations. For example, he told Kissinger on February 4, 1969, that he wanted "to go forward with a heads of government meeting" during the NATO twentieth-anniversary gathering in April, but that this plan should be "very closely held until we complete our European trip. I will discuss this matter of other NATO heads of government and then make the announcement on my return from the trip." Not until he and Kissinger proclaimed 1973 to be the Year of Europe did the president concentrate on concrete ways to improve relations with NATO. By that time they thought they had secured relations with both China and the Soviet Union and successfully ended the war in Vietnam.[12]

THE ABM AND THE NIXON DOCTRINE, 1969

The United States was on the verge of developing a defensive antiballistic missile system just as LBJ and Soviet Premier Alexei Kosygin had agreed in the summer of 1967 to discussions about reducing their countries' respective nuclear arsenals.[13] It was obvious to both Nixon and Kissinger that the ABM might prove counterproductive if it resulted in an increased number of missiles (as did indeed occur later with the multiple independently targeted reentry vehicles, or MIRVs), but the president, in particular, was convinced that he had to have the ABM as a "bargaining chip" because intelligence reports indicated a buildup in Soviet offensive nuclear weapons. Unable to reveal these reports, the administration had to rationalize the ABM system to critics on Capitol Hill on other grounds. Consequently, Nixon publicly said that opposition from Congress to the ABM system threatened the possibility of détente and continued U.S. conventional arms support for the North Atlantic Treaty nations. Liberal, Democratic senators who opposed ABM tended to be the same senators who wanted to reduce U.S. troop contributions to NATO through what was known at the time as the Mansfield amendment. So he ordered the Departments of Defense and State to close ranks behind the ABM, instead of encouraging more dissent among senators with "informed sources leaks."[14]

The administration also did not place as much emphasis as its opponents within Congress and the arms-control community on the danger of the ABM system jeopardizing the ongoing negotiations between Gerard C. Smith, head of the U.S. Arms Control and Disarmament Agency (ACDA), and his Soviet counterpart, Valdimir Semenov, who were meeting in Vienna. As head of the U.S. SALT delegation as well, Smith wanted the development and deployment of MIRVs and ABM systems to be limited. This placed him immediately in opposition with Nixingerism on two counts because the administration was in the process of striking a private bargain with the Joint Chiefs of Staff in which they would receive MIRVs in exchange for their agreement to limit ABM sites. (Smith was to add a third point of opposition in 1972, when he disagreed with specific provisions of SALT I.) But in 1970 the administration tried its best to downplay disagreement with Smith because he could sway so many congressional votes.[15]

Facing Smith's criticisms, difficulty with the JCS, and intelligence reports saying that the USSR was deploying more intercontinental ballistic missiles (ICBMs) and building its own ABM system around Moscow, Nixon decided that he had to initiate back-channel talks directly through Kissinger with Soviet Ambassador Anatoly Dobrynin. This approach would outflank both the State Department bureaucracy (of which he considered Smith but the tip of the iceberg) and Congress in the formulation of foreign policy. Arms control, like all other diplomatic endeavors, was to be the preserve of the White House, even if it meant avoiding needed expert advice on this technically complicated topic. Nixon's only public concession on the issue was to downgrade the "extensive ABM coverage" known as Sentinel under the Johnson administration to a "reduced version" he called Safeguard. As with so many of Nixon's other foreign policy initiatives, Kissinger, who had never been an advocate of arms control because he thought that nuclear weapons had both a strategic and a tactical usefulness, became the secret conduit between Dobrynin and the president and, paradoxically, between the president and the arms-control community, with whom Kissinger had been at odds since the 1950s.[16]

During the spring and summer of 1969, Nixon dealt publicly and privately with NATO nations and his gradually emerging détente policy while battling senators over the ABM. The president's handwritten comments and memoranda testify to his personal involvement in the domestic political fight over the ABM issue. From telling his staff to "raise hell with CBS" for its anti-ABM television coverage when polls showed 64 percent of the American public in favor, to criticizing members of his own cabinet, like Secretary of Defense Laird, for not "doing enough," he alternately cajoled his supporters and berated his opponents. After informing Congress on March 14 of his decision to go forward with a "substantial modification in the ABM system submitted by the previous administration," Nixon privately called Senator Edmund Muskie's proposal to use the $6.6 billion proposed for the ABM on hunger and poverty at home and abroad "unbelievable nonsense from a national leader!" When he read that Senator John Glenn, the former astronaut, had called the ABM a "false hope" because "no one knows if it works," the president sarcastically asked: "did he know the first space shot would absolutely work?" These private outbursts notwithstanding, Nixon, always the hardball politician, told Haldeman, "this is war," and issued heavy-handed orders to his staff to "concentrate on those [senators] who are on the fence and *only* on those where we have a chance to win." Nonetheless, on August 6 he only narrowly won the battle on this antiballistic missile system in three separate amendment votes, with Vice President Agnew breaking a tie on the crucial amendment providing "spending for Safeguard deployment." The struggle left bitterness on both sides that did not bode well for future White House–Capitol Hill cooperation on other foreign or domestic issues, and the press treated it "as an anticlimactic victory for the administration."[17]

While carefully monitoring and refusing to compromise his basic ABM proposal, Nixon authorized back-channel meetings between Kissinger and Anatoly Dobrynin, garnered support for the ABM from NATO nations, and decided to go ahead with MIRV testing despite the opposition of nonmilitary experts—all before leaving for his June 8 meeting with South Vietnamese President Nguyen Van Thieu on Midway Island in the Pacific.[18] Then a month later, on July 25, at the beginning of a trip around the world, the president informally presented to reporters what became known as the Nixon Doctrine, noting that the United States would no longer commit U.S. troops to East Asia, although it continued to support regional security and national self-sufficiency in the area. Hence, the Nixon Doctrine was more necessary from an American perspective as a foundation block upon which to build the détente agreements with the Soviet Union (and China) than was the ABM legislation, despite the greater domestic attention that the latter received in the United States during the spring and summer of 1969.

The unexpectedness of the unilateral Nixon Doctrine also caused problems for Kissinger and his NSC staff. Among other things, the president originally presented it on a "nonquotation basis," so it was not an official part of the public record until he summarized it in an address on Vietnam in November 1969 and again at a press conference in December, but press reaction was generally favorable. Nixon's most complete explanation of it can be found in a report to Congress on foreign policy on February 25, 1971. The NSC staffer Robert Osgood was particularly disturbed by the Doctrine's vagueness and the fact that the new "low posture" that it implied was being mistaken among journalists and academics for "inaction or lack of imagination." The fact that it also upstaged the "Review of the World Situation," which he had written on July 7 for Kissinger and the president, contributed to Osgood's concern about what the Doctrine meant.[19]

As a defense system, the ABM was more important to Soviet foreign policy than it was to the American grand design. The relative unimportance of the ABM issue for Nixingerism became more evident after Kissinger and Dobrynin agreed to divide the issues of the defensive weapons (the ABM) and offensive weapons (ultimately SALT I) in May 1971. By that time, the president and his national security adviser had decided that it would be easier to come to an agreement over future deployment of their respective ABM systems, which primarily existed only on paper, than it would be to conclude a treaty limiting the deployment of existing nuclear weapons. After campaigning against congressmen who opposed the ABM in the 1970 midterm elections, Nixon continued his "war" against Capitol Hill in the spring of 1971 by deciding it was time to "break the back of the establishment and Democratic leadership . . . [and] then build a strong defense in [our] second term."[20] When the president wrote this to Kissinger, he faced stiff opposition in Congress over three military issues: U.S. NATO troop commitments, suspicion about a Soviet ABM system, and, of course, the ongoing Strategic Arms Limitation Talks. Even under this domestic political duress, the president did not forget the dual nature of détente; from his perspective, despite its public call for arms limitations and economic exchanges with the USSR, it privately meant continued military buildup—except in Vietnam.

In the end Nixon was forced by the Mansfield amendment, calling for the reduction of U.S. NATO troop strength, to deal publicly with disarmament—even though arms reduction had not originally been part of his grand design. The other two issues he chose to have Kissinger negotiate privately and directly with Dobrynin, telling his cabinet not to "speculate on where" the negotiations might go now that SALT I and the ABM had been separated. "The less said regarding what is going on the better," Nixon warned members of the cabinet; "the more we talk, the less chance of an agreement."[21] As usual, the president and Kissinger agreed to operate in secret whenever possible.

NATO TROOP REDUCTIONS, 1971 TO 1974

While European and Soviet conditions favored détente during Nixon's first term, an unfavorable congressional climate toward continued U.S. troop support of NATO complicated things for Nixon. Beginning in 1966 Senator Mike Mansfield (Dem.-Mont.) had periodically introduced "a sense of the Senate resolution" to reduce substantially the number of American soldiers stationed in Europe. Support for Mansfield's NATO Troop Reduction Amendment to the Military Selective Service Act grew during the last half of the 1960s in direct proportion to the rise of the anti-Vietnam/peace movement. Thus, two years into his presidency Nixon faced the distinct possibility that the Mansfield amendment, calling for an outright reduction of U.S. troops by one-half, or 150,000, by the end of the year, would pass.[22]

The president's staff closely monitored the various troop reduction amendments that arose during the spring and summer of 1971. The president himself personally made telephone calls to individual senators to ensure a negative vote, and even wrote to former occupants of the White House asking them to reassert their support for NATO, while Kissinger desperately drew upon the support of such notables of American foreign policy as Dean Rusk and listened to advice (and criticism) from individual senators such as Charles Mathias, Jr. (Rep.-Md.).[23]

Part of the administration's problem with Congress stemmed from its refusal to rely on the 1967 Harmel Report in formulating NATO or détente policies. This NATO report, entitled "The Future Tasks of the Alliance," not only called for a "détente in East-West relations" but also specifically argued that "military security and a policy of détente are not contradictory but complementary." This report produced the first NATO studies on troop reductions, which by the early 1970s had turned into a formal NATO call for negotiations on mutual and balanced force reductions (MBFR) with the nations of the Warsaw Pact. Individual congressmen seemed to pay more attention to this NATO material than the White House did.[24]

During the same time, the Warsaw Pact nations began advocating a conference on European security. Both sides were aware (and wary) of the other's proposal, and reciprocal acceptance was considerably delayed by the intervention into Czechoslovakia by the USSR and some of the Warsaw Pact nations. Then, in the course of 1970–71, Willy Brandt, West Germany's chancellor, initiated a policy of *Ostpolitik* by entering into a treaty with the Soviet Union that officially recognized the existence of two Germanys. This gave new life to these mutual force reduction proposals and made Nixon and Kissinger worry that West Germany would achieve détente with the Soviet Union before the United States. So when Mansfield used Brandt's *Ostpolitik* (in addition to the U.S. balance-of-payments problem) to justify his 1971 Nato troop-reduction amendment, they tried to thwart both. Because Nixon and Kissinger understood that NATO support of MBFR was cynically designed to guarantee the existence of a large number of American troops in Europe, they made sure that at a November 19, 1970, meeting of the National Security Council a decision was reached not to reduce U.S. forces in Europe, "except in the context of mutual reductions negotiated with the East."[25]

The administration was also prepared to prevent passage of the Mansfield amendment (which required unilateral withdrawal of American troops from NATO) with a Republican counteramendment introduced by Senator Mathias that requested the president to negotiate a MBFR agreement "consistent with balance of payments situation and to report to Congress the results every six months commencing September 15, 1971." Mansfield had already accepted a friendly amendment to his resolution, saying that his called-for U.S. troop reductions would "become inoperative if prior to December 30, 1971, representatives of the Warsaw Pact countries . . . entered into negotiations, or . . . entered into formal discussions, regarding a mutual reduction by such organizations of their military forces stationed in Europe."[26]

Before the final vote on the Mansfield amendment in May 1971, the administration received some unexpected help toward its defeat from Soviet Premier Leonid Brezhnev—for which Kissinger later tried to give the administration credit. In March and again in May 1971, Brezhnev indicated that the Soviet Union was willing to begin discussing mutual arms reductions in central Europe. While the administration took advantage of his May statement to undercut support for the Mansfield amendment by arguing that a unilateral withdrawal of U.S. troops would preclude taking Brezhnev up on his MBFR offer, there is no documentary proof for Kissinger's assertion that "carefully calibrated measures of the Administration toward the Soviet Union . . . [and] our willingness to discuss détente had lured Brezhnev into an initiative about mutual force reductions that saved our whole European defense structure from Congressional savaging." This was simply one of many of Kissinger's attempt after the fact to imply that "linkage" was working when it wasn't. For his part, Mansfield tried to downplay Brezhnev's announcement by saying the proposal was similar to one made a year earlier, but at the time he, too, grudgingly gave the administration credit for the Soviet initiative. In fact, Soviet officials were more concerned about the "unpredictable consequences of a sudden massive American military withdrawal [from NATO]," than they were influenced by the back-channel contacts between Kissinger and Dobrynin.[27]

With his usual propensity for exaggerating achievement and turning coincidence into calculated success, Kissinger claimed that "the debate over the Mansfield amendment was a benchmark in the American domestic debate over foreign policy, though none of the participants understood this at the time. Until then the Administration had been on the defensive on the whole range of its policies. . . . With the SALT announcement on May 20 we seized the initiative. It was followed by my secret trip to Peking, the announcement of the Moscow summit, and a nearly uninterrupted series of unexpected moves that captured the 'peace issues' and kept our opponents off balance."[28] Kissinger's claims notwithstanding, what is significant about the defeat of the Mansfield amendment and similar ones until 1973 was Nixon's ability to outmaneuver a Democratically-controlled Congress between 1969 and 1971—not his (or Kissinger's) ability to outmaneuver the Soviet Union, which, after all, had been pursuing détente longer than the United States.

By the next time a similar troop-reduction resolution, such as the Jackson-Nunn amendment to the 1973 and 1974 Defense Appropriations Authorization Acts, became a problem for the administration's foreign policy, the president's political power in Congress had been so weakened by the unfolding Watergate scandal that his arguments about the debilitating effects on "the confidence of our allies in the U.S.

[NATO] commitment and . . . [on] the likelihood of further progress in SALT, European Security and MBFR negotiations" no longer carried the day. In March 1973, NSC staffers were frantically pointing out to Kissinger that "we are behind the eight ball once again on the NATO Troop Cuts," and Nixon was privately admitting to his national security adviser that NATO G.I.s in Germany were so expensive that "we can't stay forever" at current military levels. So the proclaimed Nixinger 1973 Year of Europe ended, even by Kissinger's admission, with "the effort to revitalize America's alliances with its fellow democracies . . . run[ning] into unexpected obstacles," including the uncooperative attitude of most NATO nations during the October war in the Middle East.[29]

In May 1974, Kissinger submitted to Nixon the second report on the Jackson-Nunn amendment, requiring written information at ninety-day intervals "on the progress that has been made . . . to have our Allies fully offset the balance of payments deficit incurred as a result of our troop deployment in NATO Europe." The Jackson-Nunn amendment called for mandatory unilateral cuts of U.S. troops, designed to go into effect automatically "if full offset of U.S. NATO balance of payments was not achieved." It was in keeping with congressional resolutions passed in 1973 calling for NATO allies to contribute more to the cost of their own defense.[30]

Nixon reported to the NATO Council on its twenty-fifth anniversary in June 1974, two months before he resigned from office, that he had succeeded in maintaining U.S. forces in Europe and would continue to do so until there was a reciprocal reduction in troop force on the part of the Warsaw Pact nations. He also affirmed that without the Alliance, he doubted that détente would have begun or continued. Otherwise, however, his remarks echoed those he had uttered on NATO's twentieth anniversary—a tacit admission that not much progress had been made toward cementing better NATO relations through consultation. Moreover, little had been accomplished by the many meetings of the Conference on Security and Cooperation in Europe and mutual and balanced force reductions talks.[31]

RAPPROCHEMENT WITH CHINA:
A COLD WAR REVERSAL BY A COLD WARRIOR

From 1949 until 1979 the United States refused to recognize the Communist government of the People's Republic of China. Not until the early 1970s, during Nixon's first administration, did the U.S. government begin to reverse this standard cold war policy of nonrecognition with a number of unilateral gestures of reconciliation, which ultimately brought about rapprochement (the establishment of friendly relations) under Nixon and recognition under Jimmy Carter in 1979. Setting in motion a process that ended in recognition of China remains one of Nixon's longest-lasting diplomatic accomplishments. Normalization of U.S. relations with China was part of Nixon's grand design to bring this giant Communist nation into the ranks of the superpowers. Long before Nixon sent Kissinger on a secret mission to Peking in July 1971 to arrange the details of his own visit there the following year, the president had used the State Department and other government agencies to make various unilateral gestures of reconciliation, indicating that he wanted fundamental improvements in relations between the United States and the People's Republic of China. It remains one of the best examples of a "Presidentially imposed, Presidentially-initiated policy."[32]

Opening relations with China also appears to have been on Nixon's mind from the beginning of his presidency. By the mid-1960s China specialists had openly begun to complain about continuing to isolate the People's Republic and, even though anti-Chinese sentiments loomed large in the public mind because of China's support for the North Vietnamese, China had been gaining international credibility for over twenty years and was recognized by over fifty countries when Nixon assumed office. As leader of the nonaligned nations, China challenged the superpowers' right to dictate to Third World nations. Its ties with the Soviet Union had been severely strained, if not actually broken, by 1969. And the cultural revolution inside China had subsided.[33]

Thus, conditions were propitious for rethinking Chinese-American relations—a fact not lost on Nixon. It was time to bring China into the international fold of civilized nations, along with the Soviet Union, through rapprochement. There was even the slight possibility that, despite Soviet and U.S. military advantages over China, that country might launch an irrational attack against one of them. In rationalizing his new approach to the Chinese, Nixon argued to his top foreign policy adviser in April 1969 that "the tragic fact of history [is] that most of the great wars were not started by responsible men and that we have to base our assumptions on what potentially irresponsible or irrational men may do, rather than simply on what we, as responsible leaders, might do." Rapprochement might help make "irrational" Communist Chinese leaders more rational, or so the president ethnocentrically implied.[34]

As early as 1954 Nixon had spoken of the importance of ending "the isolation of China gradually and to do this by reopening trade relations and cultural exchanges." In 1967, with the help of his speechwriter and aide Raymond Price, Nixon published a groundbreaking article in the journal *Foreign Affairs* in which he compared the People's Republic of China to an African-American ghetto that "should be ... induce[d] to change." Nixon believed that "any American policy toward Asia must come urgently to grips with the reality of China. ... [W]e simply cannot afford to leave China outside the family of nations." He proposed a short-term policy of "firm restraint," but a long-range one of "pulling China back into the world community—but as a great and progressing nation, not as the epicenter of world revolution." Of course, he had spoken out harshly against Communist China in 1958 when the People's Republic bombarded the islands of Quemoy-Matsu, which Chiang Kai-shek had fortified with his anti-Communist Nationalist troops. He took the same critical stand in his 1960 presidential campaign, and in 1964 he publicly rebuked Senator J. William Fulbright (Dem.-Ark.) for calling for a "review" of Sino-American policy despite the growing split between the Chinese and the Soviets because of the former's support for North Vietnam.[35] Nonetheless, the 1967 article indicated that Nixon was rethinking the unthinkable, despite his long association with the anti-Communist Republican China lobby—again confounding those who maintained that his anti-Communist views dominated his every waking hour.

By the time Nixon became president he had decided to establish a new policy toward the People's Republic of China in several stages. First, American anti-Chinese rhetoric had to be toned down in order to bring about a more rational discourse than had prevailed in fifteen years of discussion largely conducted through the mediation of Poland. Second, trade and visa restrictions needed to be reduced. Third, the number of U.S. troops at bases surrounding China and in Vietnam would be reduced. Finally, Nixon wanted the Communist leaders to know that he would personally consider revising the rigid cold war position of the United States on Taiwan and its heretofore unstinting support of Chiang. These attitude changes and low-level diplomatic actions initially took place without fanfare. Nixon underscored this approach in a memorandum to Kissinger on February 1, 1969, wanting "to give every encouragement to the attitude that this Administration is 'exploring the possibilities of rapprochement with the Chinese.' This should be done privately and under no circumstances get into public prints from this direction." Around the same time, Nixon privately told Senate majority leader Mike Mansfield that he wanted to involve China in "global responsibility." Then, on February 18, 1969, he instructed Secretary of State William Rogers to make a public announcement that the United States now favored a program of cultural and scientific exchanges with the People's Republic.[36]

The Chinese ignored all these private and public signals until 1970. By that time Nixon had repeatedly commented publicly on the "what a dangerous world . . . and . . . unhappy world it would be if those seven hundred million [Chinese] people [continued to] live in angry isolation from all the rest of the world." In a rambling monologue, he even told uncomprehending students demonstrating at the Lincoln Memorial over the Kent State student killings that he hoped one day China would be opened up so they could visit "one of the most remarkable people on earth."[37]

Peking's slow response was fortunate in that it allowed Kissinger to come up to speed on Nixon's rapprochement policy. In August 1969, Kissinger finally invited Allen S. Whiting, a former State Department specialist on China, to brief him personally about Sino-Soviet border clashes that had occurred in March. Up to this point Kissinger had only generally endorsed Nixon's idea of rapprochement, but did not contribute specifically to it. Whiting convinced Kissinger that the administration had reacted to these military skirmishes much too casually, and that it was inaccurate to think that China would attack Russia. In fact, China so feared a Soviet attack that this was a historic opportunity to change traditional U.S. cold war policy, which had been more "favorably" disposed toward the USSR than toward China. "Belatedly, Kissinger became a convert—a latter-day Marco Polo discovering the new China," according to Marvin and Bernard Kalb, "and he plunged into his subject with all of the eagerness and occasional naiveté of the newcomer to Asia."[38]

Kissinger's memoirs do not convey that he was playing catch-up on Chinese policy. Instead, we read that Nixon "was indeed somewhat schizophrenic" about China, simultaneously opposing recognition of Peking by any more European governments and holding out the possibility that if "some changes" occurred in China, U.S. policy would positively respond. Kissinger accounted in detail the military encounters between the Soviet and Chinese troops along the Ussuri River in the spring and summer of 1969 as though he kept meticulous track of them during his first months as national security adviser, saying that all ambiguity about Chinese policy up to March 1969 "vanished" with these Siberian border clashes "and we moved without further hesitation toward a momentous change in global diplomacy." At the first National Security Council meeting about

Sino-American relations, on August 14, 1969, Nixon announced "his revolutionary thesis" about the Soviets being more aggressive than the Chinese in their recent military encounters and said that it was in the interest of the United States to see to it that Communist China survived. Kissinger insisted in his memoirs that he "strongly shared" the president's view, with no mention that this was also Whiting's position. Kissinger concluded the first section of his memoirs by referring to "our China initiative," giving himself equal credit with Nixon. As late as April 1971, however, one of Kissinger's strongest defenders noted that his "inclination . . . was to distrust Chinese motives" and to react suspiciously to the Communist-inspired "ping-pong" diplomacy that spring.[39]

The Chinese agreed to resume the discontinued Warsaw talks, but after the first meeting in January 1970, they canceled the next two—one when a Chinese diplomat defected and another over the extension of the Vietnam War into Cambodia. By May, however, Peking had begun tentatively to respond positively to Nixon's first Foreign Policy Report to Congress which had been issued in February 1970. Nixon, in turn, had been trying to reassure the Chinese through two unlikely (and, as it turned out, unsavory) contacts: the Romanian leader, Nicolae Ceauşescu, and the president of Pakistan, Yahya Khan. By October indirect contact had been established. The next month the president issued the following memorandum to Kissinger:

> On a very confidential basis, I would like you to have prepared in your staff—without any notice to people who might leak—a study of where we are with regard to the admission of Red China to the UN. It seems to me that the time is approaching sooner than we might think when we will not have the votes to block admission.
>
> The question we really need an answer to is how we can develop a position in which we keep our commitments to Taiwan and yet will not be rolled on by those who favor admission of Red China.
>
> There is no hurry on this study but within two or three months I would like to see what you come up with.[40]

The stage was set for a breakthrough in Sino-American relations. An encouraging message from China through Romania at the beginning of 1971 prompted the United States in March and April to terminate all restrictions on American travel to the Chinese mainland and the twenty-year-old embargo on trade. Following the highly publicized Ping-Pong games between Chinese and American teams in April, the Pakistan ambassador to the United States also delivered a message from Chinese Premier Chou En-lai to Nixon (replying to one from the president on January 5), asking him to send a representative to China for direct discussions. The message noted that "the Chinese government reaffirms its willingness to receive publicly in Peking a special envoy of the President of the United States . . . for direct meetings and discussions."[41]

It has never been made absolutely clear by either Nixon or Kissinger why the contacts after this note had to be conducted in secret. The obvious reasons are that the mission might have failed and that it might have provoked both the Russians and the Japanese—neither of whom knew about the previously secret contacts with the Chinese. Thus secrecy bred secrecy. Additionally, Nixon paid lip service in his memoirs to the realization that there would be conservative opposition to open, direct contacts; Kissinger gives no reason for keeping his mission secret. He does, however, manage to exaggerate both his initial role in the policy and its potential danger: "I felt immense relief [at being chosen as envoy] after so long a preoccupation with its design I would be able to bring the enterprise to fruition. . . . Assisted only by his security adviser, without the alibi provided by normal processes of bureaucratic clearance, [Nixon] authorized a mission that, had it failed, would surely have produced a political catastrophe for him and an international catastrophe for his country."[42] More likely, covert foreign policy operations had simply become so common that Kissinger was the obvious choice as secret envoy, even though others mentioned for the mission were more qualified. Secrecy certainly made Nixon's July 15, 1971, announcement of Kissinger's undercover trip and of his own decision to visit China early in 1972 more dramatic.

In planning for the China trip, however, problems arose among members of Nixon's cabinet. One was simply the fact that the president and his national security adviser had bypassed Secretary of State Rogers when pursuing secret contacts with both Russian and Chinese leaders and preparing for presidential visits to their respective countries. Rogers had also been left out of the planning for Nixon's New Economic Policy, discussed in chapter 4. How to inform Rogers of all these new initiatives required finesse. Rogers was planning a trip to Israel, but Kissinger had already undercut the secretary's role in formulating Middle Eastern policy to the point that Nixon told his staff: "Kissinger has to quit running Rogers down to the Israelis." Kissinger was also jousting with Secretary of the Treasury John Connally because the latter had seized the lead on economic matters. To make matters worse, Rogers had reservations about the China policy because of the fact that the UN was unlikely to admit China and continue to recognize Chiang Kai-shek's government in Taiwan as the legitimate representative of the Chinese people. To meet this objection, Nixon was pursuing a so-called "two-China" policy, hoping that the UN would recognize both governments. At the end of 1971, the UN expelled Taiwan when it admitted the People's Republic of China, confirming the worst fears of Rogers and others loyal to Chiang.[43]

This ongoing problem of personality and ego among some of his top advisers was overshadowed by a second one that developed exclusively between Kissinger and Nixon and it presaged the falling-out they would have over events just before the end of the war in Vietnam. It arose over who should get the credit for the diplomatic breakthrough on China. Just before Kissinger made a second, this time public, trip to Peking in October 1971, Haldeman's lengthy handwritten notes indicate that the president and his staff worried about Kissinger grabbing the spotlight by giving too many backgrounders to the press. At one point Nixon said bluntly, we "need to get Kissinger under control. . . . [I] don't want to escalate Kissinger's trip." Nixon already knew that the "press will try to give Kissinger the credit and say the President had nothing to do with it." (Ironically, Kissinger's lack of knowledge about China was painfully revealed on this second trip when he met in Peking with the former U.S. diplomat John Service. He dismissed Service with some perfunctory remarks, apparently not knowing that he "had campaigned for Chinese Communist–American détente twenty-five years before Nixon and Kissinger.")[44] The president had no more success in containing Kissinger at the end of 1971 over China, however, than he would over Vietnam at the end of 1972.

Despite the obvious importance and success of rapprochement with the People's Republic of China, Nixon believed that the media never gave it as much credit as it deserved. As late as 1988 he was still trying to claim as much personal credit for rapprochement as possible: "We changed the world. If it had not been for the China initiative, which only I could do at that point, we would be in a terrible situation today with China aligned with the Soviet Union and with the Soviet Union's power."[45]

THE SOVIET RESPONSE TO RAPPROCHEMENT

Although various government officials denied that Nixon courted China in order to bring pressure to bear on the Soviet Union, the president's triumphant visit to the People's Republic of China in February 1972 (with its attendant joint "Shanghai Communiqué") was clearly part of the Nixinger "triangularization" policy. Moreover, in July 1971 when Nixon announced the visit, there is some indication that possible Sino-American rapprochement made the Soviets more amenable to moving ahead with détente in the fall of 1971. It is often forgotten, however, that the original purpose behind improved relations with both China and the USSR was to bring leverage to bear on both nations to improve the situation for the United States in Vietnam. Like so many other attempts at linkage, this one did not prove successful.[46]

There is no direct evidence that because of Soviet concern over the results of Nixon's trip to China, rapprochement became indirectly linked to the success of negotiations leading to the ten formal summit agreements signed in Moscow between the United States and the USSR in May 1972. Once again Secretary Rogers and the State Department had no more to say about their content than they had with the Shanghai communiqué. Instead, the NSC Senior Review Group and the CIEP prepared and coordinated these agreements.[47] They provided for prevention of military incidents at sea and in the air; scholarly cooperation and exchange in the fields of science and technology; cooperation in health research; cooperation in environmental matters; cooperation in the exploration of outer space; facilitation of commercial and economic relations; and, most important, the Anti-Ballistic Missile Treaty, the Interim Agreement on the Limitations on Strategic Arms (SALT I), and the Basic Principles of U.S.-Soviet Relations.

In the area of arms control, Nixinger détente policy contained the potential not only to substitute for containment—the standard way the United States had fought the cold war against the Soviet Union since the late 1940s—but also to transcend the procrustean ideological constraints at the very heart of the post–World War II conflict between these two nations. This potential was never fully realized, in large measure because Nixon and Kissinger chose to give priority to SALT talks over MIRV talks. To a smaller extent it was never realized because, until the collapse of communism in central and eastern Europe and the Soviet Union almost thirty years later, their immediate successors proved unable (or unwilling) to build upon the delicate distinction between containment and détente that they left behind. Also, there was no changed leadership or structural base in the USSR (or the former Soviet bloc countries) to reinforce the concept of détente inside or outside its borders during the last half of the

1970s, as there began to appear at the end of the 1980s. It must be remembered that the Nixon-Brezhnev détente remained essentially tactical because the cold war had not yet significantly begun to recede. Hence, there was no basic change in conflicting cold war strategies under Nixingerism—only a temporary blurring of hostilities that Reagan revived to a fever pitch in the early 1980s.[48]

SALT I, conducted in Helsinki in 1969 and Vienna in 1970, led to two arms-control documents at the 1972 Moscow summit—both in keeping with the tactical aspects of Nixon's détente. These included a treaty limiting the deployment of antiballistic missile systems (ABMs) to two for each country, and an agreement freezing the number of offensive intercontinental ballistic missiles (ICBMs) at the level of those then under production or deployed. Unlike SALT I, the ABM Treaty was of "unlimited duration . . . and not open to material unilateral revision," despite attempts by the Reagan administration to do just this beginning in 1985. Until the Strategic Defense Initiative (SDI) efforts in the last half of the 1980s, however, the ABM Treaty essentially succeeded in relegating deployment of conventional ballistic missile defense systems to minor strategic significance.[49]

SALT I, on the other hand, was an agreement of limited, five-year duration that attempted to establish a rough balance or parity between the offensive nuclear arsenals of the two superpowers, despite the "missiles gaps" that continued to exist between them in specific weapons. For example, when Nixon signed SALT I, the United States had a total of 1,710 missiles: 1,054 land-based ICBMs and 656 on submarines (sub-launched ballistic missiles, or SLBMs). The USSR had a total of 2,358 missiles: 1,618 land-based ICBMs and 740 SLBMs. SALT I not only recognized the strategic parity of the USSR but gave it a numerical edge in missiles and a slight throw-weight advantage. The United States retained a numerical advantage in warheads and a superiority in strategic bombers—460 in 1972 to 120 for the Soviets. SALT I by no means stopped the nuclear arms race, but it recognized that unregulated weapons competition between the two superpowers could no longer be rationally condoned. By freezing further missile buildup, SALT I meant that by the time SALT II was signed in 1979, total American-Soviet missile strength remained essentially unchanged: 2,283 to 2,504, respectively. From 1972 until the mid-1980s, therefore, SALT talks were regarded as a barometer of relations between the two countries, contrary to the claims of critics, even though the "MIRVing" engaged in by both sides has tended to obscure their generally parallel buildup since 1972.[50]

While it is relatively easy to generalize about the meaning of SALT I so many years after its announcement, there was much controversy and confusion at the time over specific terms. The controversy was largely partisan, but the confusion was legitimate because, in terms of sheer complexity and scope, this summit meeting between Nixon and Brezhnev was an unprecedented contrast from the previous five summits following World War II. Complicating matters, we now know from those who participated in the multilevel negotiations and in the drafting of the various technical provisions that Nixon and Kissinger did not completely understand all the terms, let alone the implications, of arms control, especially the sections concerning submarine-based missiles. This was because Kissinger had erred during his initial back-channel negotiations by not insisting that these missiles be included in SALT I. By the time they were added, the Soviets had benefited from the agreed-upon formula. Additionally, as just mentioned, MIRVing, which allowed the Soviets (and the U.S.) to modernize their missile fleets, was not limited in any way by SALT I, and the original protocol had to be rewritten and signed again by Nixon and Brezhnev after the formal ceremony.[51]

THE DECLINE OF DÉTENTE

Nixon and Kissinger returned from the May 1972 Moscow summit meeting triumphant, but more vulnerable than ever on three fronts: military, economic, and moral and ideological. All three boded ill for the SALT II talks that would begin six months later. Critics immediately asserted that the United States had been "hoodwinked" by the Soviet Union into a disadvantageous military deal with respect to SLBMs. With Helsinki CSCE agreements still three years away and no mutual and balanced force reductions in sight, as negotiations over SALT II dragged on into the 1970s, an additional military criticism became that the Soviets were violating the terms of both the ABM and SALT I agreements. Trade arguments against détente were ultimately translated in 1973 and 1974 into congressional legislation in the form of the Jackson-Vanik amendment to the Trade Reform Bill. Moral criticism of Nixingerism based on ideological hostility to the USSR became more credible in the wake of Watergate, but had always been strong in the minds of particular Republican and Democratic conservatives in Congress and across the country. It was this criticism that Nixon and Kissinger found the hardest to answer, because their approach to détente had not, in fact, been based on moral or ideological considerations, but on very pragmatic ones.

The situation did not improve with Nixon's resignation. In the summer of 1975, with Gerald Ford as president, Kissinger went on a national speaking tour to convince people that détente was more important than "blind assertions of moral absolutes."[52] But the time had passed for such Nixinger arguments to carry the day. Between 1972 and 1974, there was a decline in popular support for détente despite all the hard-sell tactics used to promote it, including a controversial grain deal with the Soviets in 1972, which caused domestic prices of grain to rise.

While Nixon took the economic importance of détente for the United States seriously, it was probably even more important to the Soviet Union. Brezhnev took pride in the fact that trade between the two countries had recently doubled, and pushed Kissinger during a meeting in March 1974 to concentrate on a "long-term agreement on economic, industrial and technological cooperation," in keeping with Nixon's address to the American Trade and Economic Council. He seemed particularly concerned about developing gas and oil deals with American companies, expressing disappointment in the administration's statements about energy independence, despite the OPEC crisis. At the time Kissinger tried to assure the general secretary that "we believe a general improvement in economic relations is an essential component of [our political] relationship," but, at least during this conversation, he was not as concerned as Brezhnev, saying wearily at one point: "Mr. General Secretary, we have had many talks on economic matters."[53]

Such talks, however, did not prevent officials from mishandling the first wheat sales with the Soviet Union. This gave the administration the opportunity to combine its New Economic Policy with détente in order to develop a more systematic food and trade policy for the United States. Neither succeeded because Secretary of Agriculture Earl Butz never completely successfully coordinated U.S. grain production with foreign demand, and because of competition between Butz and Kissinger over who was in charge of making food aid a more integrated part of American diplomacy. Nonetheless, the second grain deals with the Soviets, in 1974 and 1975, corresponded better with American agricultural production schedules.[54]

Beginning in 1972 certain members of Congress insisted that in return for most-favored-nation treatment (MFN), the Soviet Union should liberalize emigration policies affecting Jews. As late as March 1974, Kissinger referred to "domestic obstacles, some of a highly irresponsible nature," after Brezhnev brought up Senator "Scoop" Jackson's opposition to granting MFN status to the USSR. When Brezhnev said that Jackson was linking "something [the question of Jewish migration] that bears no relation to this entire matter [MFN]," Kissinger agreed, saying: "We don't consider this a proper subject of inquiry by the United States Government." The general secretary's fears, which he had expressed the previous year to George Shultz, proved more realistic than the secretary of state's optimism on this question.[55]

Once again, as on NATO troop reductions and arms control, Senator Jackson orchestrated a Senate amendment to counter the Soviet-American trade agreement. After two and a half years of haggling over various versions of the Jackson-Vanik amendment, which was extended in 1974 to include a ceiling on loans to the Soviet Union from the Export-Import Bank, Ford signed the Trade Reform Bill with the amendment on January 3, 1975, and the Soviet government officially refused to comply with it on January 10. Later that month the president withdrew his support for the MFN treatment of the USSR because of Soviet intervention into the Angolan civil war. Thus ended the move toward liberalizing trade with the Communist world (at least as represented by the Soviet Union) in the name of détente that had begun so optimistically under the Nixon administration with the passage of the Export Administration Act of 1969, liberalizing export controls.[56]

In the interim, the October 1973 war in the Middle East not only misleadingly contributed to the popular impression in the United States that détente was not working with the Soviet Union; it also exacerbated all the underlying differences between the European and American conceptions of détente—placing even more strain on the Atlantic Alliance. The October war (discussed in chapter 8) constituted a short but intense NATO crisis because, of the NATO nations, only Portugal allowed U.S. planes to refuel during the American airlift of supplies to Israel.

In July 1975, with American-Soviet trade relations temporarily on hold and NATO allies restive over having been bypassed at the Moscow summit and uncertain over how the United States would respond to talk of increasing Soviet military strength, the long-awaited Conference on Security and Cooperation in Europe began. The declaration of ten principles signed by thirty-five nations at Helsinki on August 1 was important to the United States and the Soviet Union for different reasons. Consequently, they differed over how best to implement the Final Act of the CSCE because they each emphasized different sections of it. This had not been the case in 1974 when Kissinger and Gromyko frankly agreed to thwart the "impossible proposals" for "military détente" being put forward by the

Western allies of the United States at CSCE and MBFR meetings. The Soviet Union, for example, opposed supplying such information about troop maneuvers. "I have told you we will not support this proposal," Kissinger assured Gromyko with Brezhnev listening, adding, "we can weaken these proposals substantially." Kissinger even assured the Soviet foreign minister and secretary general in this 1974 meeting that the United States would "use its influence [at CSCE meetings in Helsinki] not to embarrass the Soviet Union or raise provocative issues" with respect to Basket III, which called for humanitarian and cultural cooperation, including the freer movement of people, which the Soviets opposed.[57]

By the time President Ford traveled to Helsinki to sign the CSCE agreements before the election of 1976, Basket III had been not only included in them but "linked" to further East-West economic cooperation at the insistence of Western Europe. Significantly, Ford's political opponents within the Republican party, such as Ronald Reagan and members of his own staff, implied in press statements that the Helsinki Accords represented "another Kissinger deal that was forced down the President's throat."[58] They simply didn't understand how much these agreements differed from the promises Kissinger had made to Gromyko in 1974. Gone were the halcyon days of détente under the Nixon administration.

To save face the Soviets insisted that the Helsinki Accords were a triumph because they recognized the post–World War II boundaries of eastern Europe that Moscow had long sought. They also involved, however, serious risks for the USSR because of the human rights and freedom of movement and information provisions. In the face of the widespread perception in the United States of Helsinki as victory for the USSR, there was mounting political criticism of détente. Kissinger found himself supporting the human rights declaration at Helsinki to offset such criticism, even though he had always eschewed moral restraints in the pursuit of détente. He has since rationalized his position by saying that he thought it would encourage the Soviets to be more forthcoming in SALT II talks. This was risky for a variety of reasons, not the least of which was the fact that Kissinger was much less intimately involved in the writing of the Helsinki texts than he had been with those for ABM and SALT. At one point in 1974, for example, he admitted to Brezhnev that he had "not studied" the three Basket proposals being supported so vigorously by Western European countries.[59]

The U.S. government, especially under President Carter, stressed the human rights provision of the CSCE and used it as a standard by which to measure the treatment of citizens in foreign countries, including the USSR and its satellite nations. This principle became a bone of contention between the United States and the Soviet Union in ways not anticipated by the Nixon administration. Moscow, on the other hand, logically preferred to focus on those segments of the Final Act that granted implied recognition of Soviet hegemony in eastern Europe. A major legacy of Nixinger foreign policy from 1975 until the disintegration of the Soviet Union has been manifested by agreement to disagree over the importance of the Helsinki Accords. Little wonder that Nixon's successors (including Ford) quickly retreated from a defense of Nixon's brand of détente to the point of dropping the use of the word. Yet, in light of the fall of communism, it deserved more credit than it received before Nixon's death. Détente was more than "deals with Moscow in return for no demonstrable Soviet restraint," as some commentators in the early 1990s asserted.[60]

The same defense cannot be made of Nixingerism in Vietnam and other parts of the Third World.

7

VIETNAM: WITHOUT
PEACE OR HONOR

Whether I may be a one-term President is insignificant compared to whether by our failure to act in this crisis the United States proves itself to be unworthy to lead the forces of freedom in this critical period in world history. I would rather be a one-term President and do what I believe is right than to be a two-term President at the cost of seeing America become a second-rate power and to see this Nation accept the first defeat in its proud 190-year history.

—Nixon, national address, April 30, 1970

It was clearly in Nixon's psychic and political self-interest to end the war in Vietnam as soon as possible. "It is essential that we end this war, and end it quickly," he said while campaigning for his party's nomination in 1968, only to add the fateful words: "But it is essential that we end it in such a way that we can win the peace."[1] Although Nixon came to office committed to negotiating a quick settlement to a massive undeclared war that his administration had inherited from Kennedy and Johnson, he ended up expanding and prolonging the conflict in the name of peace and honor.

In the process, he could never build the domestic consensus he needed to continue the escalated air and ground war (even with dramatically reduced U.S. troop involvement) and to ensure passage of some of his domestic programs. For Nixon (and Kissinger), Vietnam became a symbol of influence in the Third World, which, in turn, was but one part

208

of their geopolitical or grand-design approach to international relations. The war in Southeast Asia had to be settled as soon as possible so as not to endanger other elements of Nixonian diplomacy and domestic policy.

According to his book *No More Vietnams* (1985), Nixon viewed that conflict as military, moral, and multinational in scope. Consequently, he first sought to bring military pressure to bear on the North Vietnamese in order to speed up the negotiating process. There is little indication, however, that this approach succeeded. The Communist Vietcong forces correctly counted on opposition in the United States to the announced bombing and invasion of Cambodia in April 1970 and of Laos in February 1971. Likewise, Nixon's commitment to the war as a "moral cause" did not ring true, as the carnage in that civil war increased despite American troop withdrawals. Finally, the president never succeeded in convincing the country that quick withdrawal from Vietnam would "damage American strategic interests" all over the world. So ending the draft and bringing the troops home did not end Congress's opposition to the Vietnam War (although these actions did diminish the size of antiwar demonstrations beginning in 1971) because Nixon had failed to convince that branch of government (and many Americans) that the conflict in this tiny Third World country warranted the military, moral, and multinational importance he attributed to it. Neither he nor Kissinger has ever admitted that their policies destabilized most of Indochina and led to horrific events in Cambodia, Laos, and Vietnam in which hundreds of thousands of people lost their lives.[2]

Instead, Nixon allowed Kissinger as special assistant to the president for national security affairs to become egocentrically involved in secret negotiations with the North Vietnamese from August 4, 1969, to January 25, 1972 (when they were made public, over Kissinger's protestations).[3] As a result, only marginally better terms were reached in 1973 than had been agreed to in 1969. The significance of the 1972 agreement by Hanoi (capital of North Vietnam) that President Nguyen Van Thieu, the president of South Vietnam, could remain in power in return for allowing its troops to remain in South Korea palls when compared to the additional 20,552 American lives lost during this three-year period. Moreover, by 1973, despite or because of Vietnamization, the government in Saigon (capital of South Vietnam) was inherently weaker than it had been in 1969.[4] The most embarrassing evidence of this weakness occurred when President Ford was forced to order an emergency evacuation of the last remaining U.S. troops from Saigon in April 1975.

On the tenth anniversary of the peace accords ending the war in Vietnam, Nixon admitted to me that "Kissinger believed more in the power of negotiation than I did." He also said that he "would not have temporized as long" with the negotiating process had he not been "needlessly" concerned with what the Soviets and Chinese might think if the United States pulled out of Vietnam precipitately.[5]

A more likely scenario is that Nixon had no clear idea in 1969 of how to end the war quickly. His immediate options seemed to be the initiation of secret negotiations with the North Vietnamese and/or the resumption of overt, massive bombing attacks over North Vietnam. At the same time he was probably more worried about the reaction of the general public or antiwar movement to a renewal of the bombing of North Vietnam than about that of the People's Republic of China or the Soviet Union. Both countries had, after all, tolerated Johnson's bombings of North Vietnam. So he chose to pursue secret negotiations *and* secret expansion of the war into Cambodia and Laos, thus destabilizing all of Indochina, not simply Vietnam. As a result there was neither peace nor honor in Vietnam by the time the war was finally concluded on January 27, 1973. Another plausible, but not entirely convincing, argument can be made, in retrospect at least, that Nixon's (and Kissinger's) initial concern about public relations—more than concern about diplomatic relations with China and the USSR—locked them into the same compromise on military strategy that Johnson had pursued, ultimately prolonging the war and resulting in unintended negative consequences for all of Indochina.

WIDENING THE WAR COVERTLY

Under President Johnson, the Joint Chiefs of Staff had repeatedly requested permission to bomb Communist sanctuaries in Cambodia. The last of the requests was to the outgoing Democratic administration on December 13, 1968, when the JCS asked for "standby authority . . . to pursue North Vietnam Army Viet Cong (NVAVC) Forces into Cambodia following major enemy offensives mounted and supported from Cambodia." They reiterated this position to the incoming Republican administration when Nixon, on January 21, 1969, asked General Wheeler in NSSM 1 to provide a "study of the feasibility and utility of quarantining Cambodia against the receipt of supplies and equipment for support of Viet Cong and North Vietnamese Army."[6]

Early in 1969, in response to this memo, the JCS recommended "military actions which might be applied in concert or incrementally, subject to their political acceptability."[7] In light of such proposed Nixonian innovations as renewal of the Paris peace talks, troop withdrawals, and Vietnamization, this request may have seemed a more reasonable way to ensure an orderly replacement of American units with forces from the Army of the Republic of Vietnam than it had during the last months of the Johnson administration.

President Johnson had refused to consider a mutual, let alone unilateral, withdrawal of troops. On December 21, 1968, his secretary of defense, Clark M. Clifford, had requested from the JCS a reassessment of the situation in Cambodia in relation to the air and naval bombardment of North Vietnam, and said that the reply "would provide a basis for review of military operations in Cambodia and their possible relation to the broader question of US diplomatic objectives in Southeast Asia." In an analysis of the JCS response, Secretary Laird was told that in view of the "political ramifications" of the recommendations, the National Security Council would have to consider these proposals.[8] Given Clifford's reason for this reassessment, Johnson administration officials perhaps might have been more inclined toward the bombing of Cambodia than was the president. At least this is how the JCS chose to interpret Clifford's memorandum for Nixon's secretary of defense, Melvin Laird.

Nixon's attitude did prove quite different from Johnson's. On January 8, 1969, while still president-elect, Nixon informed Kissinger in a note that he wanted "a precise report on what the enemy has in Cambodia and what, if anything, we are doing to destroy the buildup there." He concluded these early thoughts on the matter of bombing Cambodia with the words: "I think a very definite change of policy toward Cambodia probably should be one of the first orders of business when we get in."[9] Later that month, top military officials had to face the unhappy prospect of significant troop withdrawals. General Wheeler indicated at the January 25 NSC meeting that the military was doing everything it could in Vietnam except bombing the Cambodian sanctuaries, but he added that "a small reduction of US forces . . . would help Nixon domestically and convey the image of a self-confident South Vietnam." Subsequently he wrote to General Creighton Abrams, Commander, United States Military Assistance Command, Vietnam (COMUSMACV), that on the basis of this meeting and later conversations with Secretary Laird, troop reductions were imminent. "At the present time," Wheeler told Abrams, "public discussion of withdrawals or troop reduction in Vietnam should be limited to mutual withdrawal within the context of the Paris negotiations. I myself propose to keep silent." Wheeler strongly urged Abrams to "quietly put the damper on any public discussion [of troop withdrawals] by senior U.S. officers," and to request this same silence from General Cao Van Vien, President Thieu's chief of staff, and from other top South Vietnamese officials.[10]

By February 6 President Thieu had publicly agreed to a "sizable" reduction in American troops. By March 28 (ten days after the first bombs were secretly dropped on Cambodian sanctuaries) the NSC used (with Abrams in attendance) Laird's term *Vietnamization* to describe the "de-Americanization" of the war based on significant troop withdrawals. On April 10 departments and agencies began planning schedules for Vietnamizing the war, and in June the first of many U.S. troop reductions was publicly announced by Nixon from Midway Island after a crucially important meeting in which he obtained (once again) Thieu's reluctant support for the beginning of these cutbacks of American military personnel.[11]

Nixon faced public as well as military skepticism about the policy of Vietnamization being nothing more than a sophisticated form of appeasement. "Mr. President," wrote one disgruntled resident of Salt Lake City, "your current trip to Midway and your press releases has [*sic*] finally ended your political career as president. . . . If you are afraid to end the war that the United States has a superiority in you are selling the American people down the river of false hopes. . . . How can you possible [*sic*] live with the fact that a release of 25,000 Americans from Vietnam is a contribution to anything bewilders me."[12]

At the beginning of the Nixon administration, Secretary of Defense Laird (and, to a lesser degree, Secretary of State Rogers) adamantly opposed the bombing of both North Vietnam and Cambodia because it would not be popular in Congress, the country, or the UN, let alone the attacked countries. In the first weeks of March, however, Laird endorsed the bombing of Cambodian sanctuaries as a better alternative to bombing North Vietnam—an option initially under consideration by the Nixon administration—even after the NVAVC increased attacks in February against major South Vietnamese cities.[13] Cambodia, in other words, became a surrogate for the more drastic option of bombing North Vietnam (or, later, North Korea, as some commentators suggested, after the EC-121 incident, discussed in chapter 5).

At no time, however, did Laird believe that the bombing of Cambodia should be kept a secret. Much to the disdain of Ehrlichman and others close to Nixon, Laird seemed too much the politician on most issues and particularly on this one, because he was convinced that the United States had to pull out of Vietnam before losing any more domestic support. Curiously, Nixon's closest aides attributed even Laird's moderately consistent position on getting out of the war through Vietnamization purely to what Ehrlichman pejoratively called "constituency politics"—meaning that Laird was excessively beholden to Congress and the Pentagon.[14] In fact, the greatest weakness of Laird's position was not his personal concern about congressional or military opinion but the fact that his Vietnamization program would take more time to implement than Nixon could spare, considering how public opinion stood on the war by the time he assumed office. Laird may have been excessively concerned about Congress and the Pentagon, but the president had much broader constituencies to satisfy.

By 1969 it would have been next to impossible to court *both* Congress and the Pentagon. Therefore, criticism of Laird for being too politically oriented in trying to serve two masters is difficult to accept. Ehrlichman in particular seemed to harbor strong hostility toward Laird for being "impossible to rely on . . . never delivering on a promise . . . in it for himself . . . [and] ingenious to a fault."[15] The impact of such attitudes ultimately weakened Laird's influence within the administration—a condition later exacerbated when Nixon and Kissinger began to deal as much as possible with the JCS and the NSC behind the backs of both Laird and Rogers. Nixon's increasing lack of confidence in Laird, according to my interviews with him, was based on the fact that the president thought of him as a typical Republican "isolationist" who wanted to end the fighting quickly "because it was their [the Democrats'] war."[16] Moreover, others within the administration thought that Laird wanted to end the war rather than win it. Faced with such overwhelming internal opposition, the secretary of defense chose to speak his mind rather than try to ingratiate himself with the president by continuing to assert that the secret bombing of Cambodia, if ever made public, would ultimately only further undermine the administration's credibility at home on the war issue and to document his position as fully as possible.

In March 1969, Laird was the only one to call for a full NSC review of the policy. The secretary's request reflected the advice he had received on March 12 from Acting Assistant Secretary of Defense Ralph Earle II. After summarizing for Laird the JCS response to the president's inquiry about the practicality of neutralizing Cambodia "against the receipt of supplies and equipment or the support of the Viet Cong and North Vietnamese," Earle said that he agreed with all the military recommendations except the one for conducting raids "in sparsely populated areas of Cambodia along the South Vietnamese border, and in southern Laos," because the JCS "did not address . . . the political and legal implications" of their recommendations. "Obviously, our preferred course of action is to negotiate their [Viet Cong/North Vietnamese Army VC/NVA] withdrawal of US forces," Earle told Laird, but "if improved relations with Cambodia do not substantially alter the situation, then the military actions recommended by the JCS will probably be the only means by which this situation can be altered." In conclusion, Earle noted that the JCS had neglected in its response to Clifford's December 21, 1968, review request to provide a specific "listing of various military actions which might be undertaken against enemy forces in Cambodia along with an appraisal of the military effects and risks of each alternative action." In addition to conveying Earle's information in requesting a full NSC review of plans to bomb Cambodia, Laird told the president that "because of the political implications of bombing Cambodia, the entire NSC should review the policy."[17]

Laird's March 18 memorandum provided an important insight into the secretary of defense's thinking on the subject, and it forced the NSC members to listen one more time to his objections to keeping the bombing of Cambodia a secret. In addition to forwarding the JCS review to the president, Laird noted that while the military had suggested actions "subject to their political acceptability . . . there are international political and legal implications of blockade or quarantine operations" that they did not address. The secretary of defense further informed the president that "to assist in this review," he had asked the JCS for more specific information than they had provided for his predecessor about the respective "military effects and risks of each action."[18]

The NSC meeting on the bombing of Cambodia took place on March 18, the same day that Laird delivered his own memorandum to the president based on information contained in one he had received from the head of the JCS, General Earle G. Wheeler. This was *two days after* the command decision was made to implement the secret bombing of the Cambodian sanctuaries, at a March 16 meeting attended by Rogers, Laird, Wheeler, and Kissinger. At this meeting only Laird opposed the bombing of Cambodia, and he continued to do so for domestic, not foreign policy, reasons.

Since General Wheeler authorized a strike on the Communist head-quarters presumed responsible for the guerrilla war in South Vietnam—known as Central Office for South Vietnam (COSVN)—before Laird wrote the president, one can assume that Nixon decided to approve the secret bombing of Cambodia without the additional information that Laird had requested from the JCS.[19] It can further be assumed that the NSC review of policy was indeed intended by the secretary of defense to set the historical record straight from his point of view and to apply political pressure on the JCS to obtain more specific military information.

Nixon probably made his two initial decisions in February and March to bomb Cambodian sanctuary areas where, according to General Creighton W. Abrams's data, the least number of civilians were located. The president apparently retracted these decisions twice, not finally implementing his third decision until the middle of March. Nixon's resolve was reinforced (as, indeed, it evidently needed to be) by the reported increase in North Vietnamese attacks in the intervening weeks on South Vietnamese cities. Nixon became increasingly impatient with top-secret military reports (and newspaper accounts) that continually noted "extensive evidence of enemy plans and preparations for large scale offensive operations [into South Vietnam]," telling Kissinger that he thought the United States and not the Communists should take the initiative.[20]

While Nixon formally authorized the secret bombing of Cambodia as a result of the March 18, 1969, NSC review, the command decision had actually been issued on March 16 and, according to Kissinger, the president had made his decision on March 15.[21] The secret B-52 sorties over Cambodia lasted from March 18 to May 26 under the general code name MENU, with exact target areas given the unsavory titles of BREAKFAST, LUNCH, DINNER, SUPPER, DESSERT, and SNACK. A secret dual-bookkeeping system was used to report on the covert bombing of Cambodia until February 17, 1971. According to a September 1970 Department of Defense "White Paper," the purpose of MENU "was to protect American lives during the preparation for and actual withdrawal of U.S. military personnel from Southeast Asia by pre-empting imminent enemy offensive actions from the Cambodian sanctuaries into South Vietnam and against U.S. servicemen and women."[22] But this does not explain why it was conducted in secret.

Some have attributed the secrecy of the bombings to Nixon's observation of Eisenhower privately threatening to use nuclear weapons if necessary to end the unpopular Korean War. This thesis is not very convincing, however, because there is no documented evidence that Nixon ever sent secret nuclear threats to either the North Vietnamese or the Chinese. Moreover, Eisenhower did not suppress information about the escalated bombings he ordered over North Korea in the spring of 1953. More convincing is the argument that fear of triggering new demonstrations and destroying the honeymoon period Nixon unexpectedly experienced until the fall of 1969 influenced the new administration's decision to cover up the initial bombing of Cambodia. Because Nixon's (and Kissinger's) concerns over public relations apparently prevented them from seriously pushing for the bombing of North Vietnam, they opted to bomb Cambodia and to keep it a secret.

COVERING UP THE BOMBING OF CAMBODIA

According to Kissinger's undocumented assertion, Nixon ordered Colonel Haig and an air force colonel, Ray B. Sitton, to meet with him on February 23 in Brussels, where he had flown to begin a tour of European nations. Gathering for this meeting on *Air Force One* (where the presidential accoutrements so impressed Kissinger that he meticulously described the push-button chairs and table in the middle of the only paragraph of his memoirs detailing the formulation of secret bombing plans) were Henry Kissinger, Alexander Haig, Ray Sitton, and H. R. Haldeman. Colonel Sitton had briefed administrative officials in January about bombing options in Vietnam. Haldeman, according to Kissinger's memoirs, was representing Nixon because the president's presence would have attracted too much attention. According to Seymour Hersh's account, however, Haldeman did not attend, leaving Nixon, who had called for the meeting, unrepresented. In this setting of three or four men (depending on whose story one accepts), the details of the bombing of a neutral, sovereign nation were worked out, although no independent documentation of this fact exists down to the present. All we have are a single paragraph in Kissinger's memoirs and Sitton's belated oral admission to Hersh that he, indeed, was the brains behind the double-bookkeeping system.[23]

The inability of congressional committees or the Pentagon's own White Report team to identify or fix responsibility for devising and authorizing this system boggles the mind, since Sitton would have been a perfect scapegoat for everyone, including Nixon, during the Watergate investigations and impeachment inquiry of 1973–74. Yet Sitton's name never surfaced until he "readily described his activities" to Hersh, who contacted him on a tip from a "senior Pentagon official in mid-1979." Since the House Judiciary Committee considered, but voted down, the possibility of making the concealment of the bombing of Cambodia an article of impeachment against Nixon, it is all the more curious that Kissinger's and Haig's personal involvement in setting up the secret system has not discredited them for public office.[24] At the time, of those who learned of the deceitful bookkeeping plan once the information was transmitted to Washington in February 1969, apparently only Laird cabled his reservations about it to Nixon.

General Wheeler's March 16 order authorizing a strike on COSVN headquarters contained detailed information about answering press releases and questions about the bombings evasively. Similar instructions became standard for all orders directing secret flights over Cambodia throughout the spring of 1970. For example, almost a year after the strikes inside Cambodia began, a memorandum from General Wheeler authorizing certain targets contained standard wording for a news release, along with the following advice: "In the event press inquiries are received following the execution of these operations . . . U.S. spokesman will confirm that B-52s did strike on routine mission adjacent to the Cambodian border but state that he has no details and will look into this question. Should the press persist in its inquiries or in the event of a Cambodian protest concerning U.S. strikes in Cambodia, US spokesman will neither confirm nor deny reports of attacks on Cambodia."[25] Although the journalist Bill Beecher had reported the bombings on May 9, 1969, in the *New York Times*, the administration did not officially acknowledge this violation of Cambodia's sovereignty until the spring of 1972, and the public did not become fully aware of these covert strikes until a year later.[26]

Individual or agency responsibility for the back-channel communications system that was employed to ensure optimum security of the MENU operation remains blurred. According to a Department of Defense "White Paper" issued on September 10, 1973, MENU flights ended in May 1970, but the dual-reporting system initially used in the field continued undetected for other covert strikes until February 1971, when duplicate information showed up on a downed aircraft operating under the code name FREEDOM DEAL outside designated target areas in Cambodia. This "error" resulted in the discontinuance of all such special reporting on subsequent special air (that is, cover) operations over Cambodia and Laos, proceeding under such code names as GOOD LUCK and PATIO.

Since there were pro forma requests from the Cambodian government for U.S. air support between February 17, 1971, and August 15, 1973, sorties flown during this period became part of the official record. It was not until the summer of 1973, when the Senate Armed Services Committee opened hearings on the bombing of Cambodia, that the public first learned about the dual-reporting system used for covert land and air operations—a system for which no military or civilian official has yet taken responsibility.[27]

Finally, on September 10, 1973, the Department of Defense issued its "Report on Selected Air and Ground Operations in Cambodia and Laos," which corrected all previous testimony and unclassified statistics presented to Congress by secretaries of defense Melvin Laird, Elliot Richardson, and James Schlesinger. Prior to this report, Congress had been systematically misled by top government officials, who presented false or misleading figures on the war's progress, never mentioning covert activity. A few members of Congress may have been informed by the Department of Defense about MENU and other covert military actions in Laos and Cambodia: Senators Richard Russell, John C. Stennis, and Everett Dirksen; Representatives Mendel Rivers, Leslie Arends, George H. Mahon; and the future vice president and president Gerald Ford.[28]

To this day, however, no one has admitted that he personally ordered the falsification of figures or the double recordkeeping, which was allegedly devised by Sitton with the approval of Kissinger, Haig, and possibly Haldeman. "The necessity to minimize the likelihood of public speculation or disclosure was established within the NSC," according to the White Paper. "NSC guidance issued for the first MENU mission . . . remained representative of the guidance for all MENU missions. . . . The responsibility for development of detailed MENU procedures was delegated to the levels in DoD [the Department of Defense] that normally controlled these procedures."[29] No direct answer has ever been given as to how far up (or down) the civilian and military chains of command knowledge about Sitton's double-entry system went.

Although there is no evidence that it was discussed at the March 18 meeting, Laird has implied that the responsibility lay with the NSC, which directed him and General William C. Wheeler "to implement the use of cover targets."[30] The White Paper, however, stated that the "procedures to obtain necessary reports and to preserve security were developed and authorized by MACV [Military Assistance Command, Vietnam]," strongly implying that it was designed in the field by anonymous individuals. General Wheeler indicated that "it just grew up within the system."[31] A DoD representative concurred, saying:

> That answer it seems to me represents the best thing that we know. There was a directive worked out in the National Security Council process. It directed special security precautions, to include the use of cover targets. Those directives were transmitted to the Secretary of Defense and to the Chairman of the Joint Chiefs. In implementing those directions, as General Wheeler said, the JCS system implemented a cover target system and in doing that, that action made it necessary that you not have in the secret-level computers information that was being held at higher levels of security. By the act of implementing a directive to use cover targets, you in fact built into the system one set of reporting at the secret level and a further set of reporting at the special-access level.[32]

Thus, a military policy cover-up—for which no one issued orders, which the NSC never explicitly discussed, but which Sitton now says he designed—presaged a domestic political cover up.

In retrospect, the "illegal and criminally concealed" bombings and the subsequent overt invasion of Cambodia can be seen to have been multiply flawed policies. They did not bring psychological pressure to bear on negotiations, as hoped; they did not result in destruction of the COSVN headquarters; they needlessly angered a segment of the American population already suspicious of Nixon, and made Congress determined not to permit such unilateral, undemocratic exercise of executive authority in the future; they were initially inadequately funded through secretly diverted funds; and, finally, they never became major military objectives of the United States, but only a "short-term objective of insuring the success of Vietnamization."[33]

Consequently, the Joint Chiefs of Staff's initial jubilation over the civilian political decision to move into Cambodia waned quickly in the light of military reality. In a word, politics did not make for good military decisions, as General William W. Palmer's 1975 "End of Tour Report" documents in detail.[34] The secret bombing of Cambodia failed, as did Nixon's general policy in Vietnam; but this particular policy failure should not be used to indict the entire NSC system. In other situations it performed adequately, and sometimes admirably, as in the EC-121 incident. The problem was that Nixon and Kissinger used it at their convenience rather than systematically.[35]

THE HOME FRONT

Nixon never changed his attitudes or policies on Vietnam but, faced with an antiwar movement that some say toppled his predecessor in the Oval Office, he was forced to consider the timing and the publicity given to his military and diplomatic moves more carefully than otherwise would have been the case for a wartime president. Whenever he took action in Vietnam, Nixon faced three "publics" at home that varied in size and influence: (1) a tiny group of East Coast intellectuals and journalists, many of whom were influential opinion makers; (2) college students in the antiwar movement; and (3) the general public at large, who approved of him as president but who became increasingly ambivalent or negative about the war.[36]

In contrast to LBJ, who personally anguished over each bombing run and daily fatality report, Nixon (and Kissinger) saw U.S. involvement in Vietnam as an abstract symbol of influence in the Third World, just one part of the grand design for international relations. To most Americans, however, this war became a marathon of television coverage during the dinner hour, complete with stylized, but disjointed, accounts of the conflict, the body count, and the occasional atrocity. By not ending the war sooner, Nixon not only endangered the most abstract elements of his diplomacy and domestic policy but subjected an increasingly restive public to its nightly coverage and to the loss of more and more American lives. How well he disentangled these various elements in the formulation of foreign policy during his first months in office remains unclear, but the home front certainly figured into Nixon's thinking.

With the exceptions of ending the draft, creating an all-volunteer army, and publicly endorsing the return of U.S. POWs as a major condition of peace, practically every action taken by Nixon with respect to Vietnam (including the Vietnamization program for withdrawing U.S. troops) created resentment, suspicion, and opposition from intellectuals and journalists who opposed the war. The dissatisfaction of this powerful, but relatively small, number of upper- and middle-class Americans proved a more significant factor in the steady decline in public approval of the Vietnam War than did the much more numerous and visible members of the antiwar movement, fueled primarily by a variety of equally upper- and middle-class college students. In any case, the most intense and confrontational activities of the antiwar demonstrators took place between 1965 and 1971, thus affecting the presidency of Lyndon Johnson more than that of Richard Nixon.[37] Moreover, polls showing disapproval of the war must be weighed against Nixon's relatively high approval ratings as president until Watergate began to affect them in the spring of 1973, after the Paris Peace Accords had been signed, ending American participation in the war. These public opinion polls tell only part of the story about the domestic problems created for Nixon by his prolongation of the Vietnam War and the three publics he faced as long as the war continued.

The only area in which the administration consciously and successfully courted general public opinion over the war turned out to be the prisoner-of-war issue. Nixon did not consider the POWs or MIAs (those missing in action) a major public relations possibility when he took office. He had pledged to bring "an honorable end to the war in Vietnam" when accepting the Republican nomination in 1968, but the POWs/MIAs had not figured prominently in his calculations for a negotiated peace. His handwritten comments during the spring and summer of 1969 indicate that he worried most about the public's treatment of, and availability of government services at home for, *returning* veterans. But that fall two major antiwar demonstrations took place, on October 15 and November 3, and the press began to print the first information about the incident at My Lai on November 12, when the court-martial of Lieutenant William L. Calley, Jr., got under way.

Although Calley and the infantrymen he led had gunned down unarmed Vietnamese civilians in My Lai in March 1968, while Johnson was still president, Nixon had to contend with the fallout, in part because the Department of Defense (with Laird's strong support) had been investigating the incident since April and the president had known about it since at least August. Nixon turned to his conservative and liberal domestic advisers, instead of to Laird or Kissinger, on this issue because of its sensitive political nature. They differed on how to handle the uproar over Calley, especially after he began to be lionized in the South (with a little help from such different southern governors as Jimmy Carter and George Wallace).

Pat Buchanan suggested superficial ways in which the president could effectively "fudge" the dates of the Department of Defense investigation and his knowledge of the incident so as not to appear to be ignoring the issue. Instead, the president made such a strong statement on December 8 about its "certainly [being] a massacre" and in favor of prosecution of this "isolated incident" that he appeared to be prejudging the case against Calley. Pat Moynihan's views apparently led Nixon to take this judgmental position. While Moynihan pointed out the obvious—Calley "look[ed] and sound[ed] like a Southern psychotic"—he also noted that liberals could use the military trial to turn the war from one of "liberal anticommunism" into one of "conservative anticommunism." Nixon was so concerned about the political implications of losing his argument that the liberals had started the war that he asked Kissinger for his reaction to Moynihan's memorandum. By the time a court-martial jury found Calley guilty, in March 1971, Nixon considered bolstering his flagging southern strategy by intervening on the behalf of a southern war "hero" for what appeared to be purely political reasons. However, John Dean advised him not to take any such action because the "facts of the case show particularly aggravated conduct on the part of the accused . . . therefore, Presidential involvement at this time could have an adverse effect on world opinion." Nixon personally took the case under review and placed Calley under house arrest instead of stockade confinement until his sentencing. Appeals resulted in several reductions of his sentence (twenty years in 1971; ten years in 1974). Nixon said in 1974 that his own review had indicated no further action was "necessary or appropriate." After an acquittal was overturned, Calley was paroled in November 1975 and dishonorably discharged, having served almost no jail time for his actions.[38]

THE POW/MIA CONTROVERSY: MYTH AND REALITY

Neither the war hawks nor the peace doves acquitted themselves well in the Calley incident involving brutality by U.S. soldiers against Vietnamese civilians because both tried to exploit it for their own purposes. More moderate "doves," for example—not generally associated with the antiwar demonstrators—were trying to make Calley a victim of the war, not unlike the way they were already portraying the prisoners of war. Between the October 15, 1969, Moratorium Day antiwar demonstration and the beginning of the My Lai trial in November, the POW issue turned into a doubled-edged sword inside and outside the Oval Office: Had there been U.S. military mistreatment of Vietnamese civilians, as well as North Vietnamese mistreatment of American POWs? For the growing number of opponents to the war, the answer became yes, while Nixon and most of his civilian advisers said no—and the public generally agreed.

In the fall of 1969 the press and Congress began spotlighting the activities of the relatives of MIAs, and Congress unanimously passed a bill declaring a national day of prayer for POWs. The businessman H. Ross Perot, then one of the directors of the Richard M. Nixon Foundation, had established the United We Stand organization, which advocated immediate release of POWs. In December, the Senate unanimously denounced "the ruthlessness and cruelty of North Vietnam," and Perot led 152 wives and children to Paris carrying Christmas presents for their missing or captured relatives. According to Charles Colson, special assistant to the president, Nixon was "absolutely taken by this guy [Perot]" who kept promising to deliver millions in support of a POW public relations campaign. He apparently never delivered the money he promised (some $30 million), using it primarily as a carrot to gain personal access to Nixon for his own purposes. At least this was Colson's interpretation of Perot's effectiveness: "He never put up a nickel. He parlayed that offer . . . into access, which ended up costing him nothing. It [was] one of the most effective con jobs I ever saw in the White House."[39]

Nixon could not have orchestrated the POW issue more successfully (with or without Perot) had he tried, but his administration had, in fact, kept a low profile on POWs until the end of 1969. Department of Defense officials had met privately earlier that spring with families of MIAs, but then Secretary Laird announced that the MIA question was a humanitarian, not a political, one, and that is how Nixon and Kissinger approached the POW/MIA problem in their initial negotiations with the North Vietnamese. At best it could be used as a public "propaganda offensive" against the North Vietnamese—and in this sense as an effective countermeasure against the most militant antiwar demonstrators; at worst, if used as a major bargaining chip at the peace table, both of them realized it could backfire—as it did, in December 1972, when Le Duc Tho, the North Vietnamese member of the politburo who had been designated Kissinger's counterpart in these protracted secret negotiations, withdrew the concession he had made in October about releasing American POWs without requiring the release of Vietcong civilians held by the South Vietnamese. Nixon also wanted the large number of American civilians in Saigon to be reduced to eliminate the possibility of their becoming prisoners of war, in addition to those that the U.S. bombing raids continued to produce.[40]

Return of POWs had always been a condition in negotiations with the North Vietnamese under Johnson before the peace talks in Paris began to break down, as in any previous peace settlement in which the United States had participated. Under Nixon it became a more emotionally charged and publicized issue than the president had intended, but one he took full advantage of after the fact. There is no evidence for the charge that five days after his inauguration Nixon ordered the introduction of the POW/MIA issue for the first time at the Paris Peace talks or that it became "an ingenious tool for building insurmountable roadblocks within the peace talks." Nixon's first bargaining position after taking office was the same as what had been established by the Johnson administration in 1966, the so-called Manila formula: once the North Vietnamese forces withdrew from South Vietnam, the U.S. would withdraw its forces six months later. In January the president told Ambassador Henry Cabot Lodge to call for prompt POW talks, but the administration did not undertake a review of the POW policy until March.[41]

Not until a May 14, 1969, meeting of the National Security Council did Nixon announce a modification of this original U.S. offer, indicating that one year following the signing of a peace agreement, both sides should simultaneously withdraw their troops. Then there would be supervised elections in South Vietnam and a POW exchange "at the earliest possible moment." While this offer by Nixon and Kissinger may have been for public consumption only, one thing is clear: "the fate of American POWs had not yet become a major issue" for the public or the White House, in part because as of January 1969, there were only 326 or 329 (depending on whose figures are used) POWs and the White House had received only 620 letters about them.[42]

From January until October a Democratic Congress and bipartisan support across the country used the media to turn the POW issue into an emotionally popular one that the president was perfectly willing to capitalize upon for domestic political reasons. There is no evidence, however, that either the president or his national security adviser approved of any so-called go-public campaign on March 1, 1969, to "marshall public opinion" in order to obtain "the prompt release of all American prisoners of war." When Secretary of Defense Laird publicly supported this effort on May 19, he was criticized for doing so by Henry Kissinger, who was even then anticipating the secret negotiations with the North Vietnamese that would begin in August and last into 1973.[43]

As late as October 2, 1969 (two weeks before the Moratorium Day demonstration that had the administration so worried), the president's major concern was that the more prominent the POW issue became, the more it would be used by the North Vietnamese in negotiations with Kissinger—not that it was a particularly good bargaining chip for the U.S.

to exploit. Kissinger, for example, recommended that Nixon *not* meet with wives of POWs who were going to Paris to meet with representatives of the Democratic Republic of (North) Vietnam (DRV). Nixon agreed, saying that there should be no government involvement with "the ladies" so as not to jeopardize their chances of learning about their husbands. Nixon agreed with Pat Buchanan that the purpose of the Moratorium Day demonstration was "to force a unilateral bug-out of American troops from Vietnam" and thus represented a Democratic party–sponsored "peace-at-any-price movement." After House minority leader Gerald Ford told the president that the demonstration "fell flat," however, Nixon agreed to meet with a random group of POW wives as "a good follow up" to attract "silent Americans" to the administration's position following the October march on Washington and before he delivered what turned out to be his very successful address on November 3, in which he appealed to the "great silent majority" of Americans. The president proclaimed November 9 a National Day of Prayer and Concern and took the POW issue to the UN Human Rights Committee. (The president did not meet with an organization officially representing POW/MIA family members until December 1969.)[44]

By the end of the year, the POW issue had become a top priority in both the public and the private negotiations—not because both proponents and opponents of the war had taken it up but because the North Vietnamese had made it one of their strongest bargaining chips by literally turning the POWs into hostages. Thus, Nixon and Kissinger (whether they realized it then or not) were becoming trapped by their worst fears about highlighting the POWs in the negotiations with North Vietnam: it was an issue that undercut their bargaining power on other peace issues. Nixon did not need to initiate the public relations possibilities of the POW/MIA issue; a bipartisan coalition of liberal doves and conservative hawks did that for him for most of 1969. (As late as 1990, he continued to assert that in the fall of 1969, the POW issue as touted by antiwar demonstrators represented a peace-at-any-price approach to ending the war. Then—and later—he said that he could not tolerate this approach because of the negative impact it would have on other aspects of U.S. foreign policy.)[45]

On February 2, 1970, Nixon asked Kissinger to prepare a report about "all of our operations in Laos to free U.S. persons known to be, or suspected of being, held captive in Laos." But eight months would pass before the president significantly modified the negotiating terms by offering North Vietnamese a cease-fire "in place" (all troops staying where they were), monitored by international peacekeeping teams and accompanied by continued U.S. troop withdrawals, with no call for an equivalent withdrawal by the North Vietnamese forces from South Vietnam. Nixon also proposed "that all prisoners of war [and all journalists and other innocent civilian victims], without exception and without condition, be released now to return to the place of their choice." After this peace initiative failed, the administration authorized on November 21 an unsuccessful rescue attempt of some POWs by the army and air force special units at Son Tay, North Vietnam. As early as February, Ross Perot had urged the president to turn U.S. airdrops of foodstuffs over Laos into POW rescue operations. Almost 90 percent of the letters received about this failed raid were favorable, with some 58 percent coming from relatives of POWs or MIAs.[46]

In March 1971, with over 1,600 POWs or MIAs (the numbers increased with each bombing raid), Nixon pleaded with the American people to give their "continued dedication and continued public understanding, for the sake of the prisoners, for the sake of their families, and for the sake of human decency." By November, Kissinger and Nixon "belatedly" recognized that the POWs had become an inextricable component of the negotiating process.[47]

In the course of 1970 and 1971, the POW issue became increasingly more important in the Paris negotiations. While Nixon and Kissinger tried to use it to their advantage in secret talks with the North Vietnamese, it became evident that all the leverage over the POWs was on the side of the Vietnamese. Beginning in March 1970, for example, Nixon publicly instructed the U.S. Paris peace delegation to bring pressure to bear weekly on North Vietnam about the POW/MIA problem. The more the president and his national security adviser insisted on the immediate release of the POWs or at least an exchange before peace had been reached, the more obdurate the North Vietnamese became—it was their best guarantee that they would get what they wanted (the end of Thieu's regime in the South) before agreeing to any other terms. To obtain even minimum advantage from the POW issue, the Nixon administration was reduced to arguing that it would keep a residual armed force in South Vietnam.

By the beginning of 1972, Nixon showed how caught up he was in his own circular argument, as he tried to explain to the newsman Dan Rather the position of the POWs in the negotiations: "If the POWs are still retained by North Vietnam, in order to have any bargaining position at all with the North Vietnamese, we will have to continue to retain a residual force in Vietnam, and we have to continue the possibility of air strikes on the North Vietnamese." By this time he and Kissinger had also discussed the POW problem with both China and the Soviet Union. In May Nixon had Kissinger tell the North Vietnamese that in return for an immediate cease-fire and return of the POWs, the United States would withdraw all its troops from Vietnam in four months, only to have this new proposal rejected out of hand. This rejection, in turn, led Kissinger to begin to hedge on the public commitment the administration had made not to stop the air war over North Vietnam until the POWs were returned.[48]

At the end of 1972 both the administration and the doves used the POWs to rationalize their positions: Nixon said he would withdraw U.S. troops in exchange for American POWs, but that he could not stop supplying the Army of the Republic of (South) Vietnam (ARVN) at the same time; the doves insisted that all the United States needed to do to get its POWs back was to set a firm date for withdrawing troops. Both were wrong. The North Vietnamese had long since determined that they would not release the POWs until the United States ceased all aid to South Vietnam—not simply removed its troops.[49] For this reason the POW/MIA issue became an overwhelming liability in the negotiating process, but not one that Nixon and Kissinger initiated or deliberately popularized among the American people in 1969. The last thing they wanted, especially during their first year in office, was for any aspect of their grand design for foreign policy, particularly the end of the war in Vietnam, to be decided by what they considered street mobs or uninformed popular opinion.[50]

NIXON AND THE ANTIWAR MOVEMENT

Although Nixon appears to have paid as much if not more attention to general public opinion as to the antiwar movement, in reaching his decision not to bomb North Vietnam in his first months in office he and his advisers took the antiwar movement seriously, for two reasons. First, Nixon and Kissinger were convinced that the protesters were harming their attempts to negotiate a settlement, because the antiwar demonstrations indicated to Hanoi that the United States wanted out of the war. Having discussed student unrest with Kissinger "from time to time," Nixon concluded in April 1969 that "this was the heart of matter." Second, some of his advisers, including Attorney General John Mitchell, economic adviser Arthur Burns, and Pat Buchanan's ultraconservative aide Tom Charles Huston, believed that student demonstrators in the United States and other countries were being "bankrolled" and coordinated by Communist groups in China and Cuba. His more liberal advisers, such as John Ehrlichman and Leonard Garment, insisted to the president that "the conclusion of the intelligence community is that our Government does not have specific information or 'ironclad proof' that Red China or Cuba is funding campus disorders."[51]

Nixon refused to accept this opinion, and in June 1969 wanted to "give Huston (or someone of his toughness and brains) the job of developing hard evidence" of Communist infiltration of antiwar groups. And he repeatedly asked for reports on such different organizations as the Students for a Democratic Society (SDS), the Women's Strike for Peace, and the Socialist Workers party, on the grounds that they were front organizations and should be exposed as such. The president indicated in one handwritten note to Ehrlichman that this information might have to be used, especially if campus disorder spread to Latin America.[52]

Despite Nixon's belief that Communists were behind the antiwar movement, opinion among his advisers (and the intelligence community) remained divided on this question. As a result he followed a three-track policy with respect to student demonstrators. First, whenever possible he tried to discredit antiwar groups as Communist fronts. Second, he approved of meetings between some of his staff and young Republicans who were concerned with the "liberal drift" the administration was making on domestic policy but who were still supportive of the administration's efforts in Vietnam. Third, he tried to tighten the coordination of intelligence information about antiwar leaders, especially those who took their messages abroad, like the Black Panther leader Stokely Carmichael. This led him on July 14, 1970, to approve of the infamous, but unimplemented, Huston Plan, discussed in chapter 9. Temporarily thwarted by J. Edgar Hoover, who opposed the Huston Plan, Nixon withdrew his support for it just two weeks later. Almost immediately he began intensive use of the special domestic FBI unit Operation CHAOS, established by the Johnson administration for monitoring whether antiwar groups were financed by foreign enemies. Subsequently the Nixon administration initiated surveillance of domestic antiwar and other protest groups through a variety of extralegal means. Several other tactics were suggested to him, such as taking legal action against pacifist groups in the United States that were sending supplies to North Vietnam (which Nixon refused to do, even though Kissinger favored it).[53]

Instead of Nixon's opposition to antiwar demonstrators and other critics of the war having triggered secret domestic surveillance and wiretaps, this type of activity came directly out of Nixon's and Kissinger's initial conduct of the war in Vietnam. *It was the secret way in which Nixon chose to conduct his foreign policy that determined how and why he finally tried to deal with domestic dissent through wiretaps and surveillance—not the other way around, as is usually argued.*

By the end of 1969 the president appeared, unlike LBJ, to have faced down the antiwar movement with a combination of extralegal surveillance; his Vietnamization policies, including an end to the draft; and a defense of his peace initiatives combined with systematic criticism of the opponents of the war. His particularly eloquent "silent majority" speech on November 3, 1969, proved very effective in temporarily quelling the antiwar movement. After revealing heretofore private aspects of his pursuit of peace through Soviet and Chinese contacts and emotionally stating his personal reasons for wanting to end the war as much as the administration's opponents did, Nixon said: "Let historians not record that when America was the most powerful nation in the world that we passed on the other side of the road and allowed the last hopes for peace and freedom of millions of people to be suffocated by the forces of totalitarianism." It took the members of the antiwar movement six months to recover from Nixon's skillfully orchestrated campaign against them during his first year in office.[54]

The president lost this advantage, however, when he announced to the public at the end of April 1970 that American and South Vietnamese troops had crossed into Cambodia with air support to attack Communist sanctuaries. He tried to rationalize this widening of the war by saying that there were POWs in some of these target sites who might be rescued during the bombings of Communist factories, airstrips, and munitions dumps. Campus opposition to these "incursions" into Cambodia resulted in the shooting deaths of four students by National Guardsmen at Kent State University in Ohio on May 4, and of two students at Jackson State in Mississippi on May 14. As universities all over the country closed and students planned a major demonstration in Washington for May 9 and 10, the president reacted personally as well as officially to the impending "invasion" of the capitol.[55]

After calling campus demonstrators "bums" just before the Kent State deaths, Nixon met awkwardly, to put it mildly, with a group of students in the White House on May 8 and then conducted an unsatisfactory press conference. Abruptly, at 4 A.M. on May 9, he decided to go to the Lincoln Memorial (accompanied initially by his valet, Manolo Sanchez) for an informal meeting with students who were camping there in preparation for the demonstration. Herbert Parmet has described in great detail this strangely poignant and pointless act by Nixon, as has one of the president's speechwriters, William Safire. The president himself dictated a fourteen-page memorandum to Haldeman about it. "That night . . . turned out to be the most traumatic and most uplifting of his first term," according to Safire: "It was the strangest, most impulsive, and perhaps most revealing night of Nixon's Presidency." But in the end it was all for naught. The press had a field day with the incident. For the president, it confirmed that what had been a "memorable event" for him was simply distorted and misinterpreted by the media—as usual. Personally, however, it represented for Nixon one of the few times in his public career that he attempted to talk about "matters of importance—qualities of the spirit, emotion, of the depth and mystery of life . . . [and] to lift them [the students with whom he spoke] out of the miserable intellectual wasteland in which they now wander aimlessly around."[56]

The president weathered the protests (including the deaths of students at Kent and Jackson State) that accompanied the overt bombing of and incursion into Cambodia without serious political consequences. By the fall of 1972, he had also managed to halt the casualties and so eliminate body counts from the evening news through the steady withdrawal of U.S. troops. On September 21 the first week since March 1965 passed without a U.S. combat death. Kissinger happily reported to Nixon in November that there had been no U.S. combat deaths during Thanksgiving week. (In the midterm elections of that year, the Republicans gained two Senate seats, and lost only twelve in the House.) At the end of the year, U.S. troop total in Vietnam stood at 24,200—down from a peak of 543,400 in the spring of 1969.[57]

Nixon may not have understood equally well all three of his home-front "publics" on the Vietnam issue but he did not succumb to any of them, with the very major exception that bombing Vietnam was ruled out by the administration in February and March 1969 because of concern about general public opinion. It has also been asserted, but not proved, that Nixon timed the Christmas bombings to coincide with the semester break at most colleges and universities. There is strong evidence to support the idea that these bombings were more closely related to Kissinger's faltering negotiations with both North and South Vietnam than with the fact that campuses would be deserted then.[58]

In the end, Nixon subdued the antiwar movement by ending the draft in September 1971 and slowing U.S. casualties through Vietnamization. He also assuaged the general public with his January 1973 Peace Accords, the return of "all" POWs, and Kissinger's promise of a "full-scale investigation" into the fate of the MIAs.[59] However, Nixon never came close to ending the criticism and suspicions of his career-long critics, namely, the left-of-center intelligentsia. And in the four-year process it took to end U.S. participation in the war, his domestic programs suffered because it was during his first term in office that he proposed most of his innovative legislation on domestic problems. Some have insisted that he went to Congress with liberal domestic reforms only to encourage Republican and Democratic moderates to support his foreign policies, but if that was his purpose, it did not work. While his domestic record remains remarkably impressive, his reforms at home were not generally supported by those Democrats or Republicans in Congress who were most critical of his handling of the war in Vietnam.

HOW NOT TO END A WAR

On October 8, 1972, Kissinger's secret negotiations with the North Vietnamese ended in an agreement that began to fall apart almost immediately because of South Vietnam's opposition to it. As a result, both Nixon and Kissinger resorted to political maneuvering just before the presidential election to ensure that only one of them would be perceived as the "chief" peacemaker—but neither focused on the POWs as a way of doing this. In any case, Nixon was upstaged by Kissinger, who telegraphed General Alexander Haig from Saigon on October 22, suggesting a way to produce a (pre–Election Day) "October surprise." In his message he second-guessed Nixon and presaged his own later insubordination with respect to the injection into the 1972 presidential campaign of the prospects for peace:

It is hard to exaggerate the toughness of Thieu's position. His demands verge on insanity. . . . He stated that we have been colluding with Moscow and Peking for months against him and that there has been an organized press campaign in America against him. He insisted that he would settle for nothing less than a document which legally recognizes the two Vietnamese states with the DMZ [demilitarized zone] as their border. . . . To take him on publicly would demonstrate that our opposition was right all along. . . . I see two choices. . . . The first . . . is for me to go through with [the] final leg, discuss our difficulties with the North Vietnamese . . . and offer to immediately negotiate a bilateral agreement which we should sign after the election. . . . [This] would give us a face-saving formula for stopping the bombing which I believe to be an inevitable part of any scenario. Further it would give us a big boost in American public opinion. . . . I know the president's objections to ending the bombing, but I do not think they apply to the present situation. Ending the bombing would support the public impression *that an agreement is near.* Failure to end it would ask Hanoi to endure several more weeks of punishment because of refusal by Saigon to go along with an agreement in which the DRV made almost unbelievable concessions.[60]

The only concession of any note in the October (and January 1973) agreement when compared to Hanoi's original Ten Point Program of 1969 was that the North Vietnamese had dropped their insistence on having a Communist-approved coalition government in place *before* any cease-fire. But this was a concession in name only, because the military and political weaknesses of the Saigon government were greater in 1973 than in 1969. So it was only a matter of time before a de facto Communist government would control South Vietnam.

Nixon told Kissinger to delay the signing (set for October 31) until Thieu came on board, but the North Vietnamese thwarted this attempt by Nixon to stall for time by unilaterally publicizing the terms of the agreement. Kissinger then committed insubordination when he tried to make the best of this embarrassing situation by paraphrasing his telegram to Haig, saying on October 26 that *"peace is at hand . . .* what remains to be done can be settled in one more negotiating session with the North Vietnamese." Thus he grabbed the spotlight yet again and made it look as though Nixon had agreed to an October surprise, on the eve of the election—when the president had not approved Kissinger's statement and, in fact, had specifically told him not to discuss the timing of the peace agreement. To make matters worse, on his return to the United States Kissinger selectively leaked information about the proceedings in Paris, angering Nixon to the point that he purportedly said: "I suppose now everybody's going to say that Kissinger won the election." While rejecting Kissinger's suggestion of bypassing Thieu for a bilateral treaty with North Vietnam, on November 2 Nixon appeared to follow his advice by authorizing "some relaxation of the restriction on B-52 raids over North Vietnam that had been in effect since October 13," in order to bring pressure to bear on Hanoi to sign the agreement after the election. By that time, he also concurred with Kissinger's mistaken insistence that in the October agreement North Vietnam "had virtually capitulated and agreed to everything we required." On November 4, too late to affect election returns, North Vietnam agreed to meet in Paris later in the month.[61]

At a November 20 meeting, Tho remained as intransigent as before the letup in bombings, rejecting all of Thieu's demands and even a few points he had agreed to in October with Kissinger. After more delays in the talks, Nixon said he would agree to a separate peace with North Vietnam on the basis of the October terms, but that if Hanoi did not agree within seventy-two hours the bombing would resume with more intensity than ever before. The deadline passed, but the bombings did not begin until December 18, continuing around the clock for twelve days, right through Christmas. Nixon and Kissinger apparently disagreed over whether these attacks should be publicized in advance, with Nixon deciding not to "go public" with the reasons for stepping up the military pressure on North Vietnam. As a result, Kissinger could publicly imply that he did not agree with the tactic of renewed bombings, while privately saying the opposite to Nixon. In this way he let the opprobrium of being a "mad bomber" fall exclusively on the president.

Their memoirs give contradictory accounts of whether Kissinger actually recommended and supported the Christmas bombings and who was bringing the most pressure to bear on the North and South Vietnamese to agree to the October terms, but Ehrlichman's terse handwritten notes for a December 6 meeting with the president and Haldeman precisely document Kissinger's support for the bombings, his mental state, and his continued insubordination.[62] Erhlichman read Kissinger's cables to the president for December 4–6, and Nixon asked Ehrlichman if he agreed with their recommendation that Nixon "go on TV to rally public support for resumed bombings and a suspension of negotiations." Ehrlichman said he did not agree, and Haldeman then summarized the situation, implying that Kissinger was undergoing psychiatric treatment and had been "doing some very strange things":

K[issinger] very down; under care; while in Saigon K cabled N[orth] Viet[namese] twice accepting 10/8 deal as [an] act of π [the president]— *Done over Haig's objection & beyond any πal [presidential] authority.*

JBC [John Connally], Colson, Z[iegler] and H[aig] urge π to finesse failure, not going on TV, letting HAK[issinger] tell press it's another NViet
maneuver. Sunday 12/3 both Russ[ia] and Chinese enlisted Russia note
via Dobrynin to Col. R. Kennedy assur[ing] they are "working on it" and
D[obrynin] urges "one more" session in Paris.

Ehrlichman's notes also indicate that Nixon blamed Kissinger's weak bargaining position on his "peace-is-at-hand" statement, his controversial
interview with Oriana Fallaci in November, and the fact that the "NViets
size[d] him up, knew he must make a deal or lose face—[thus] they shift[ed]
their offer to [a] harder position." At this point in the meeting the president
decided to "finesse" the situation and advised Kissinger's aide Colonel
Richard T. Kennedy that his boss do the same. "There are no good choices,"
Nixon said, but "we won't let them humiliate us." He also requested the
delivery of the "bombing renewal contingency plans," noting that there was
"no point going on TV to ask [the] Amer[ican] people to support more of the
same." In a final colloquy on the matter, Nixon unrealistically predicted that
ultimately Congress would come to the aid of Saigon. The "U.S. people
wouldn't support cessation of military action *and* of economic support in
return for POWs [because] this would doom [the] SViets."[63]

Since at least October 1972, the president and his national security
adviser had competed with each other to receive credit for ending the war
on terms that left much to be desired, despite their rationalizations about
them. Kissinger later arrogantly remarked that "the publicity [after his
'peace-is-at-hand' statement] I received caused [the president] to look for
ways of showing that he was in charge *even while usually endorsing the
strategy I devised.*" It was around this same time that Kissinger's interview
with Oriana Fallaci appeared, in which he described himself as the lone
cowboy directing U.S. foreign policy. Despite all Nixon's efforts to put a
"lid on Kissinger" by limiting his backgrounders to the press and contacts
with politicians in the last months of the year, by the beginning of 1973 he
bitterly remarked that Kissinger had become the "hottest property in the
world." According to Colson, the president even ordered the Secret Service to begin keeping a record of the phone calls Kissinger made from his
home in Palm Springs. Nixon told Colson that "Kissinger will be leaving in
six or eight months. It is not good for a man to stay in that [NSC] position;
it will be better for Henry. Time for him to get back to other things."[64]

The stage was set for the war to end, but it remained to be seen whether
Nixon or Kissinger would get the credit for "winning" it. Kissinger won this

public relations battle because the president continued to vacillate over whether Kissinger had "exceeded his authority" in the final months of the peace negotiations. Nixon finally told Colson that "Henry had made a mistake" in handling the Christmas bombings, especially in terms of public relations with Congress, and that he was "getting a little tired of him. I really am."[65]

But in order to save face, Nixon insisted privately, in a handwritten note to Thieu's representative in Paris on November 29, that the "negotiations have been at my personal direction. K[issinger] and Haig have not made one move I have not personally authorized. I am frankly distressed to see stories to [the] effect they exceed[ed their] authority." In no uncertain terms, he indicated in this note that there could be no settlement at this time requiring the North Vietnamese to withdraw their troops from the South. Nixon also dispatched Haig to Saigon on December 19 to inform Thieu personally in the strongest language possible that the president would proceed with or without his cooperation. Without saying why, the North Vietnamese resumed negotiations on January 8. Nixon had to threaten the ever reluctant Thieu again on January 16 with the "immediate termination of U.S. economic and military assistance" if he did not "go along with a settlement that could save his country as well as himself." On January 20 the president of South Vietnam capitulated to terms he knew were suicidal for his country, in part because of two secret pledges Nixon had made to him, on November 14 and January 5, assuring U.S. military enforcement of the agreement. The Paris Peace Accords were initialed by Kissinger and Le Duc Tho on January 23, 1973 (for which they shared the Nobel Peace Prize), and formally signed by Secretary of State William Rogers and representatives of North and South Vietnam on January 27, 1973. Although Kissinger later misleadingly used the word *treaty* to refer to these accords, they were never submitted to the Senate for approval and, combined with the secret pledges, showed, according to McGeorge Bundy, foreign policy adviser to Kennedy and Johnson, the president's and his secretary of state's "contempt for the clear opinion of the Congress, and ultimately contempt for democracy itself."[66] But then, Nixingerism had been based on such contempt from the very beginning.

So many members of Congress feared that Nixon and Kissinger would take the country back into war to save South Vietnam and Cambodia from new Communist invasions that in May 1973 the House of Representatives outlawed any more bombing in Indochina as of August 15—even though as late as June, the president naively seemed to think that he and his secretary of state could ward off passage of such legislation. With the cessation of bombing, the administration "decided to honor all Cambodia requests for ammunition," thereby "spending more in military assistance to Cambodia in 1974 [$350 million] than it had in 1973 [$150 million]." Through April and May 1974, in a series of memoranda under the heading "Presidential Determination on Cambodia," Nixon and Kissinger can be seen continuing to try to obtain more military assistance for Cambodia through the president's "drawdown" authority under the Foreign Assistance Act. By this time, however, they both admitted the obvious: this would "probably provoke a negative Congressional reaction."[67]

Ultimately, President Ford was left to pick up the pieces of the failed Nixinger policy in Vietnam. By the spring of 1975, the State Department had contingency plans for evacuating civilians from Vietnam and Cambodia in the face of indigenous Cambodian Communist guerrillas, the Khmer Rouge, marching toward the capital, Phnom Penh, and the North Vietnamese military closing in on Saigon. After considering the consultation provisions of the 1973 War Powers Act, intended to prevent unilateral military action by the executive branch, the State Department advised Ford against consulting Congress about these plans, even though it would require American troops to carry out. Kissinger seemed to think that Ford personally might have to inform some members of Congress, but even this was not done. According to Ford, he ordered the evacuation of some Vietnamese refugees as early as March 26, even though he had not been able to get in touch with the leaders of Congress because of its annual recess. Consequently, when Congress reconvened, some of its members accused Ford of violating the War Powers Act (which he had opposed in 1973, when still a member of the House of Representatives). In a last-ditch effort to place the blame for the fall of Saigon to the Vietcong on Congress (as Nixon and Kissinger had), Ford asked for $722 million in military aid and another half million for social and economic aid to forestall a total collapse of South Vietnam. When it was not forthcoming, Ford initiated Operation Frequent Wind to evacuate some 50,000 Vietnamese who had either fought or cooperated with the U.S. war effort.[68]

The Saigon evacuation turned into chaos as military helicopters left the roof of the American Embassy in Saigon with refugees clamoring to get aboard before the Communist takeover. Only 6,500 South Vietnamese friends of the United States succeeded in escaping. Ford's memoirs defend the way the war ended in 1973 as strongly as though it had been by his own design, adding that he "felt deep satisfaction and relief that the 1975 evacuation had been a success."[69] This final and humiliating military action in Vietnam, accompanied as it was by little public outcry in the United States, confirmed the hollowness of the "peace with honor" settlement of 1973, except for those involved in carrying it out.

Watergate cannot be blamed for the failure of the Paris Peace Accords to work; they were unworkable the day they were signed, and so were the secret pledges that were supposed to make them workable. Between 1973 and 1975, Congress displayed unusually strong opposition to unchecked executive authority in the conduct of U.S. foreign affairs. Unfortunately, congressional resolve as reflected in the War Powers Act did not prevent unilateral military and diplomatic actions by other presidents or violations of the Constitution and the democratic process under Ronald Reagan, which far exceeded those for which Nixon was almost impeached.

THE POW/MIA CONTROVERSY REVISITED

When the first of the POWs began returning home on February 12, 1973, the White House imposed strict security and press restrictions on the grounds that these men and their families had a "right not to be exploited." (To set an example, the president refused to fly to Travis Air Force Base in California to greet the first POWs personally when they arrived or to allow any other high government officials to greet them: "they deserve[d] some time to themselves.") The press immediately criticized restraints on coverage, but Nixon held firm (and instructed his staff and cabinet members to do likewise) in part because of fear about the possible condition and statements of the men, only to be overjoyed when they all praised him for ending the war as they stepped off the planes. The administration, of course, basked in such fortuitous good publicity.[70]

Nixon himself was personally affected by their words of patriotism and praise more than perhaps any other event of his administration. In May the White House hosted a huge extravaganza in honor of the POWs and their families. Sweet as this victory party was at the time for all connected with the Nixon administration's foreign policy, even it would come back to haunt the president during Watergate. In investigating his tax returns, the IRS disallowed the 650 corsages he had personally purchased for the wives and mothers of the POWs (poetic justice in many ways, because he had used the IRS to harass his political opponents).[71]

For the general public, the POW/MIA issue was the most popular aspect of the war at the time it ended. A Harris poll for May 1973 showed that bringing home the POWs ranked first among all foreign policy issues, above relations with the USSR and China, with 81 percent approving of how Nixon had handled this issue with the announcement of the Paris Peace Accords ending the war.[72] Little did Nixon suspect that twenty years later the POW/MIA issue, which he thought the Paris Peace Accords had lain to rest, would still haunt the American psyche, which was waiting to be politically manipulated by hawks and doves in both parties, just as it had been during his administration. The 80,000 missing from World War II and the 8,100 missing from the Korean War were not publicly mourned and privately believed to be alive for as long as the much smaller numbers of POWs/MIAs in Vietnam, for one simple reason: it remains the only war the United States has lost. Thus, friends and relatives found it harder to justify those killed or missing. The Vietnam POWs and MIAs became a popular cultural phenomenon in the 1970s and 1980s despite Pentagon and congressional investigations indicating that there were no more than 200 unresolved MIA cases out of the 2,266 the Defense Department officially listed as missing, and around a dozen unaccounted-for POWS. (Approximately 300,000 North and South Vietnamese are still considered MIAs.) With the American victories in the cold war and Gulf war, incredulousness over POWs/MIAs in Vietnam resurfaced in the early 1990s. This time the cause was aided by a former KGB officer's testimony that as late as 1978, the Soviets had interviewed American MIAs in North Vietnam; by renewed congressional interest in the issue during the 1992 campaign; and by the presidential candidate Ross Perot, for whom the POWs have been a personal hobbyhorse for two decades.[73]

As the scapegoat for most of the nation's unresolvable political problems since he resigned, Richard Nixon would inevitably be blamed for the POW/MIA phenomenon at some point. One such attempt occurred in 1977 when it was revealed that Kissinger and Tho had secretly negotiated a pledge of $3.25 billion by the United States to "contribute to the postwar reconstruction of North Vietnam without any political conditions." The existence of this agreement in the form of a letter from Nixon to the North Vietnamese Prime Minister, Pham Van Dong, had been denied by Kissinger, Philip Habib, and other high State Department officials until it was finally declassified in 1977. Although Nixon's February 1, 1973, letter appears to be a codicil to Article 21 of the Paris Peace Agreement dealing with postwar reconstruction and designed to set up a Joint Economic Commission, POW/MIA mythmakers decided that it had been a "done deal" to pay North Vietnam reparations and that when the U.S. reneged, the Vietcong decided not to return all the POWs.[74]

In 1992 a much more serious charge of indifference or complicity was levied. This time the focus was on POWs in Laos, where U.S. military personnel 'had been captured by North Vietnamese Pathet Lao forces as early as 1964. Although the Victory in Vietnam Association (VIVA) and other pro- or antiwar groups had maintained for some time that there were POWs in Laos, evidence had been slim, in part because the Pathet Lao had usually turned its captives over to North Vietnam.[75] Several Department of Defense memoranda from 1973 surfaced in August and September 1992 at hearings of the Senate Select Committee on POW/MIA Affairs, chaired by John F. Kerry (Dem.-Mass.), indicating that by 1972 "approximately 350 U.S. military and civilians [were] missing or captured in Laos." Particularly disturbing was an action memorandum from Lawrence Eagleburger (prepared by none other than then Lieutenant Colonel Richard V. Secord, of Iran-contra fame) to Secretary of Defense Elliot Richardson. While commenting on the impreciseness of the voluminous intelligence data, Eagleburger told Richardson—who, in turn, informed Kissinger—that the return of only 10 of the estimated 350 POWs in Laos after the signing of the Paris Peace Accords "is considered unacceptable." Eagleburger further recommended that the North Vietnamese and their surrogates, the Lao Patriotic Front (LPF), be informed the "U.S. will no longer play games with the POW issue in Laos" and be given a deadline of March 28, 1973, by which to respond. When it passed, Richardson suggested to Kissinger other diplomatic actions that should be taken (all of which involved "little physical risk" and no use of force) "to gain some accounting of our men held/missing in Laos."[76]

Although the secretary of defense asked Kissinger to inform the president about this matter, it is not known whether he did. In August 1992, Nixon, Kissinger, and Eagleburger, as deputy secretary of state, were asked to give depositions to Kerry's Senate Select Committee about these memoranda and whether they had "abandoned" another 600 American servicemen when North Vietnam returned fewer than half of them—591 out of 1,205 prisoners, according to a previously secret Russian document estimated to be held at the end of the war. In September three former secretaries of defense under Nixon—Melvin Laird, Elliot Richardson, and James R. Schlesinger—all testified that "there was a possibility that some Americans were left behind." As late as May 1973, Schlesinger said that Kissinger was still trying to get Le Duc Tho to sign a statement saying that no more Americans were being held.[77]

Presumably these statements about POWs left behind did not refer to the *confirmed* number of POWs held by the North Vietnamese—all of whom were returned—but to the alleged POWs in Laos who were not specifically included as a condition of the peace terms, since the United States had conducted primarily a covert war in that country. It would appear that Secord and Schlesinger were talking about at most twenty or thirty more Americans, not hundreds.[78]

Yet the Russian top-secret report said North Vietnam actually held over 600 additional American soldiers. "Officially, until now, we published a list of only 368 prisoners of war, the rest we have not revealed," wrote the presumed author of this report, General Tran Van Quang, deputy chief of staff of the North Vietnamese Army in 1972. "The government of the U.S.A. knows this well, but it does not know the exact number of prisoners of war, and can only make guesses based on its losses. This is why we are keeping the number . . . secret, in accordance with the Politburo's instructions." Within days of having been authenticated in Moscow after its release in 1992, this report was called a "clear fabrication" by Vietnam's senior diplomat dealing with U.S. affairs because, among other things, General Quang was not attached to the North Vietnamese general staff and so would not have had any reason to write such a report. Quang finally told U.S. envoy John W. Vessy, Jr., in April 1993 that the report had to be a forgery because he had not written it. American officials have since agreed that it is riddled with erroneous statements, such as names that do not correspond to any on our MIA list—and even that three of the names on the Russian list were those of American astronauts. Nonetheless, POW/MIA activists accepted this document and another one translated from Russian and released by the Pentagon in September 1993, which alleged that at a Vietnam Communist party meeting it was stated that 735 POWs were then being held. Proof that the Nixon administration had abandoned scores of American soldiers to the enemy in 1973 is far from conclusive, but it is clear that the president wanted to "get Vietnam out of the way" because it was becoming embarrassing for him to alternate between statements about the war and about Watergate.[79]

In March 1973, in the same speech in which Nixon said that "all of our American POWs are on the way home," he also indicated some "problem areas" such as inadequate accounting for MIAs in Indochina—but he did not specifically mention the possibility of any more Americans being held in North Vietnam or Laos. The question now is whether Nixon and

Kissinger did all they could to free servicemen "knowingly" left behind, or whether they were so desperate to end the war in Vietnam that they sacrificed POWs to do it. Both Nixon and Kissinger maintain that it was the doves in Congress who prevented any effective military action to find out the truth when it was still possible, in the spring and summer of 1973.[80]

Despite the publicity given these documents and statements in 1992 and 1993, they did not corroborate the charge that Nixon's and all subsequent administrations may have covered up the existence of POWs in Indochina. Likewise, the bulk of available declassified evidence from the years 1969 to 1973 do not substantiate Stephen Ambrose's or E. Bruce Franklin's assertions that "within weeks after taking office . . . Nixon and his senior aides embarked on a campaign to incite national outrage over North Vietnam's treatment of U.S. servicemen taken prisoner during the war," or that "throughout President Nixon's first term, the issue of POWs and MIAs would serve mainly as an indispensable device for continuing the war." Yet both allegations have been widely cited in press accounts and by relatives of the missing.[81]

Neither is there any evidence in the released Nixon White House tapes for the assertion made by the historian Stanley Kutler (on ABC TV's "Nightline," August 10, 1992) that the president hoped to use the returning soldiers in his second term to take people's minds off the revelations of Watergate. In fact, these taped conversations with his aides indicate that the two issues were simply not discussed together. Transcripts for the tapes available as of the end of 1993 do not contain any references to MIAs. POWs appeared once on three separate tapes (all one-sentence comments about the peace and pride flooding the nation) and prisoner references in general occurred twice. None of these comments was made before the peace accords went into effect. The only connection to Watergate came when Colson told Nixon on February 14, 1973, that people were telling him, "Congratulate the President on the [return of] the prisoners," and this prompted Nixon to make a reference to the suffering of the jailed Watergate burglars.[82]

One can always read between the lines of these often less than accurate transcriptions, but in this instance it would be stretching even the limits of Nixon-hating to substantiate the interpretations about using the POWs to delay the war or to divert attention from Watergate. The emotionalism on this issue defies previous U.S. handling of POWs and MIAs following all the wars in this century, and the partisan overtones it has assumed—because of documents released abroad as a result of the end of the cold war, attempts to improve relations with North Vietnam, and hearings held during the 1992 presidential election—only fuel the fires of illogic and exacerbate the pain of still-grieving relatives.

In September 1992 Kissinger protested in characteristically flamboyant language that Nixon's former secretaries of defense who testified before the Kerry Committee were "tear[ing at] the scabs of Watergate" (his perennial shibboleth for any criticism of the failed Nixinger policy in Vietnam) and committing "unforgivable libel" because they were being haunted by a ghost of their own creation. "It is the ultimate irony that our Herculean efforts to get an accounting in 1973 should be twisted 20 years later into 'evidence' that we knew POWs had been left behind."[83] Both the doves, represented by Vietnam War hero Senator John Kerry, and the hawks, in the person of Kissinger and Haig, missed the opportunity at the 1992 hearings to stop attacking one another and to admit that the war was lost by the South Vietnamese, not by the dove-inspired constraints on the U.S. military. From the beginning it had been Saigon's war to win or lose— a fact neither side in this unending and futile debate is yet willing to admit. Personally, I am still waiting for an apology from the U.S. government and military officials for the Vietnam War. Even Soviet officials had the courage to apologize in the aftermath of their fiasco in Afghanistan.

It is perhaps fitting that the POW/MIA issue may be resolved during the administration of a president who opposed the war in Vietnam. With the support of the Senate and the American business community, Clinton removed the nineteen-year trade embargo against Vietnam on February 3, 1994. Although such groups as VIVA, the National Alliance of Families for the Return of America's Missing Servicemen, opposed the action, many on both sides of the issue began to argue that more information could now be obtained with the enhanced cooperation of the Vietnamese (and Laotians) through improvement in trade relations. Even though 57 percent of Americans still believe that some U.S. soldiers missing in action in Vietnam are still alive, they favored ending the embargo by a margin of 46 to 40. Moreover, a majority of Vietnam veterans are no longer active in the POW/MIA campaign.[84] Motivated by dimming hopes of finding out more about missing relatives without access to all relevant locations in Vietnam, and the economic potential of the 71 million consumers residing there, the United States finally admitted that the only war it ever lost was over and that, in keeping with traditional practice after all other military conflicts this century, it was better to trade with a former enemy than to continue to fight it with the ghosts of POWs and MIAs.

8

BALANCING THE FOREIGN POLICY SCALE

The Third World is the battleground on which much of the present phase of World War II is being fought. It is in the interests of Third World peoples and nations, as well as our own, that our side prevail.

—Nixon, *The Real War* (1980)

While Nixon's foreign policy has generally been praised, I have pointed out its basic flaws throughout this section. In addition to Vietnam, nowhere are these more evident than in other areas of the Third World. A recently declassified document shows that some of his administration's most advanced views on foreign policy were not applied to the Third World or the Middle East. On July 7, 1969, Robert E. Osgood, a NSC senior staff member, circulated a secret memorandum to the National Security Council. Osgood had been a graduate school friend of Kissinger's, and his widow has said that, although he stayed on the NSC staff only eighteen months, Kissinger "gave him free rein" to conceptualize and "never bore down on him."[1] Osgood's 109-page "inventory" of the world situation represented a response to a presidential request that became the first of Nixon's unprecedented four annual reviews of global affairs. It was based on a number of the early NSSMs, particularly NSSM 9, in which Nixon had ordered a "review of international situations," and on other government documents, including assessments provided by the National Intelligence

Estimates (NIEs) and the State Department Bureau of Intelligence Research Reports (INRs). Additionally, Osgood candidly noted in his cover memorandum to the NSC staff that "there are some data, a number of generalizations, and many inferences and analytical conclusions in the overview that are not in the government documents."[2]

Containing thirteen detailed sections on every part of the world, along with specific analyses about economic, political, and structural trends, this document came close to being a blueprint for all the most innovative aspects of Nixon's foreign policy. Written a little over five months after Nixon took office, it left no doubt about the innovative diplomatic ideas circulating within the administration. Unfortunately, both the president and Kissinger have waffled about many of them since leaving office. It began, for example, with a "reappraisal of containment" that made it clearer that Osgood, at least, had reached the conclusion that traditional "containment no longer adequately describes the organizing concept of American foreign policy."[3]

Lack of cold-warrior fear of communism permeated this remarkable secret document. An entire section emphasized that the United States faced a "transitional period of international politics in which the familiar structures of power and patterns of conflict and alignment are eroding in some respects or disappearing altogether." In the process the cold war itself was transformed from its original "Europe-centered bipolar order" into Third World conflicts as postwar colonial empires crumbled that actually had little to do with the basic interests of the superpowers—the exceptions being Vietnam, Cuba, and Chile.[4]

The emergence of politically independent and active states in colonial areas, according to this enlightened view, would "not prove to be a decisive arena of great-power conflict." Third World countries were simply "too heterogeneous, disorganized, and resistant to external control and influence ... [and] ideological affinities seem relatively unimportant except as levers of competition over personal or organization power." Thus, in most lesser developed countries (LDCs) "the capacity of local communist parties to subvert or gain control of unstable states by 'wars of national liberation' or any other means has proved to be quite limited ... even when such parties [were] supported by an adjacent communist power." Unfortunately, these non–cold warrior insights about LDCs encouraged Nixon and Kissinger to ignore most of the Third World nations of Asia and Africa in their grand design because, despite the "vulnerability of the LDCs to external influences," they exhibited "invulnerability to external control."[5] If direct military or political control of LDCs was impossible in the future, then indirect linkage would have to suffice.

THIRD WORLD MISTAKES

Diminished cold warriorism and "Nixingerism" in general usually did not apply in the Third World, where indifference and geopolitical calculations led to actions that often underplayed economic reality and/or the human dimension of individual situations. This proved particularly true for U.S. diplomacy from 1969 to 1974 in already established or emerging small nations. In a very revealing memorandum, Nixon once said that Kissinger "must not let members of his staff or members of the establishment and the various Departments think that I do 'not care' about the under-developed world. I do care, but what happens in those parts of the world is not, in the final analysis, going to have any significant effect on the success of our foreign policy in the foreseeable future.[6] Nixon and Kissinger often pursued policies that the State Department under William Rogers opposed. Haldeman's notes document the endless wrangling between the secretary of state and the head of the national security council that took place in many White House meetings.

Their honest disagreements often degenerated into petty bickering and can be seen again and again over such policies as the "tilt" toward Pakistan in 1971 in its war with India; the racist "tar-baby" policy adopted for all of Africa in 1970 and subsequent misguided intervention into the Angolan civil war; the use of the CIA and American businesses to destabilize the democratically elected Communist regime of Salvador Allende in Chile beginning in 1971, which contributed to his downfall in 1973; inaction in the face of starving Biafrans during the Nigerian civil war of 1969–70; and tactics favoring the rightist military junta that overthrew Archbishop Makarios in 1974 and encouraging the subsequent Turkish invasion of Cyprus. In each of these instances, the administration acted globally without considering the unique local and historical aspects of the situation. For example, relations with India deteriorated because Pakistan served as the conduit to China in the early, secret stages of rapprochement and led not only to Pakistan's suppression of Bangladesh's independence but also to India's decision to develop nuclear weapons—all because Nixon and Kissinger decided that the United States "could not let an American/Chinese friend [Pakistan] get screwed in a confrontation" where the Soviets seemed to be allying with India.[7]

While Rogers and the State Department opposed many of these actions, with respect to only one of these diplomatic decisions was there any indication that Nixon wanted some policy other than the one that evolved. Nixon had criticized the State Department during the 1968 presidential campaign for siding with the British in not insisting that more be done to get food and medical supplies to members of the Ibo tribe in Biafra, who were trying to secede from Nigerian rule. His NSSM 11 reviewed U.S. Nigerian policy but essentially upheld the prevailing American position. From that point Nixon wavered between doing nothing to oppose the State Department (which was in compliance with the NSC decision) and secretly pursuing a White House plan for aiding and recognizing Biafra. Kissinger initially did not act on any of the president's off-and-on-again recommendations, snidely telling his NSC staff that Nixon was "a little crazy" on this subject. Finally Nixon ordered Kissinger to attempt to mediate an end to the civil war and also requested a plan for aid to Biafra to "ameliorate the situation." In particular, he wanted the emphasis on "nonrecognition of Biafra" changed because over a million Biafrans, rebel propaganda maintained, faced death through starvation. William Shawcross has suggested that because so many private, international (often religious) relief agencies set up night airlifts of humanitarian supplies to the successionist leader General Ojukwu, the administration was able to delay a negotiated settlement and successfully convey the impression to the world that the Ibos faced genocide, when this charge may have been more the result of a successful propaganda campaign than reality. If so, Nixon bought the Ojukwu version of reality in 1968 and 1969, as did many others.[8]

The Nigerian food situation attracted world attention after General Yakubu Gowon in Nigeria insisted that all humanitarian supplies be distributed by the central government and Ojukwu rejected this plan. Nonetheless, Undersecretary of State Elliot Richardson continued to promulgate the official U.S. position that nothing needed to be done to aid the Ibos, either during or immediately after the civil war ended in their defeat early in the 1970s. As a result, the White House began meeting with both sides in the summer of 1969 without informing the State Department. In September Nixon wanted Kissinger to "needle State" into appearing to play a more active role in bringing about a cease-fire. Nothing substantial came of Nixon's order to mediate the situation or his marginal comments to Kissinger on his daily news summaries about providing more aid. Part of the problem was that Kissinger did not want to oppose Richardson and thus alienate one of his few allies in the State Department. Later, after he had become secretary of state, Kissinger toyed off and on with making food a factor of U.S. diplomacy, testifying in 1975 that food was "one of our most important assets in foreign policy." In this same testimony, however, he frankly admitted that it was often wasted on "countries that can do us the least good." Biafra was clearly one of these.[9] (Despite the lip service Kissinger paid to food in global relations, the United States did not develop a systematic or humanitarian way of dealing with incorporating agricultural commodities into foreign policy, as the grain deals with the USSR in 1972, 1974, and 1975 all attest.)[10]

As with all issues, Nixon also understood that aid to the Ibos had domestic political overtones: the Biafrans were Catholic. So his staff suggested to him that he should receive credit for trying to get food to them "for two reasons (one because it is right morally and secondly politically)." Not even Nixon's political instincts could prevail over Kissinger's obdurance and Richardson's indifference on this question. It has also been suggested on the basis of an undocumented conversation that racism influenced Kissinger's and Nixon's lack of resolve on this issue and other foreign policy questions involving Africa. According to Richard Morris, when Nixon prepared his first message to Congress on foreign policy, he asked Kissinger to make sure that "there's something in it for the jigs." (As discussed in the next chapter, this derogatory word and other racial and ethnic slurs attributed to Nixon do not show up on his released tapes. Whether they exist on the unreleased tapes remains a matter for speculation.) Obviously race influenced foreign policy between 1969 and 1974. Racism has been a characteristic of American foreign policy since the American Revolution; Nixon and Kissinger did not invent or initiate it.[11]

A final obstacle to American aid to the Ibos was the fact that Nixon lost interest in the issue in January 1970 as he began to work on his first State of the Union address. Consequently, when Richardson gave his perfunctory report to the president on January 20, saying that things were not so bad in Biafra, Nixon knew that the time to aid the Ibos had passed. After the undersecretary left the Oval Office, the president purportedly turned to Kissinger and said: "They're going to let them starve, aren't they, Henry?" To which Kissinger answered, "yes." Nigeria simply was not geopolitically important enough in their grand design.[12]

Angola was important enough, however. An armed revolt had been in progress against the Portuguese there since 1961. In the course of the fighting, three national independent organizations developed: the National Front for the Liberation of Angola (FNLA), the National Union for the Total Liberation of Angola (UNITA), and the Popular Movement for the Liberation of Angola (MPLA). During the 1960s the FNLA received some covert funding from the United States and China; the MPLA from the Soviet Union. On the basis of NSSM 39, dated April 10, 1969, the Nixon administration reevaluated American policy toward the white governments not only in Angola but also in Rhodesia and South Africa.

This is one of the few NSSMs whose full text has been made available to the public. It established the so-called tar-baby policy of the Nixon administration, which stated in essence that change without radical upheaval could be achieved only in cooperation with the white minorities in these countries and so aid to the FNLA was reduced. Other spinoffs of NSSM 39, when it was finally adopted in January 1970 by the NSC, were that the United States relaxed its arms embargo against South Africa, thus reinforcing its apartheid system, and undermined its economic sanctions against Rhodesia by permitting the purchase of chrome and other rare metals. In retrospect, Kissinger's aide Roger Morris later concluded, NSSM 39 was "a disaster, naive in concept, practically impossible for the government to execute, and thus a ready cover for pursuing the most reactionary and short-sighted U.S. interests in the region."[13]

When Kissinger decided to abandon this tar-baby diplomacy in 1975 under the Ford administration, he compounded the problem by deciding to back the anti-Communist black groups: the FNLA and the UNITA, led by Jonas Savimbi, against the Soviet- and Cuban-backed MPLA. Thus, Angola became but a pawn in the superpowers' cold war competition and entered a period of civil war that appeared to end in 1990 as both sides agreed to hold elections. However, when the bellicose and charismatic UNITA leader lost his 1992 presidential bid to José Eduardo dos Santos, a Soviet-trained engineer who ran as a peacemaker, Savimbi led his UNITA guerrillas into revolt against the government that the United States formally recognized in May 1993. By the end of 1993, his forces controlled 65 percent of Angola, including four of eighteen provincial capitals and approximately a third of the population. This was more territorial control than he had had during the civil war when he was backed by the United States. Although American officials denied any responsibility for the situation, the duly elected government criticized the Bush and Clinton administrations for not recognizing the dos Santo government sooner and providing it with military aid to contain the undemocratic military efforts of this former cold war client.[14]

Perhaps the worst example of cold war interventionism on the part of the Nixon administration occurred in Chile. While CIA intervention on behalf of the U.S. government and business interests in Chile has been well documented,[15] there has never been conclusive proof that the CIA (or the Nixon administration) played any direct role in the assassination of President Salvador Allende, a pro-Castro Marxist; but they did do everything possible to destabilize his government. In addition to examining the proof of the unsuccessful attempt to prevent Allende's election as president and then the successful attempt to undermine his government, it is worth noting the way both Nixon and Kissinger defended their actions in Chile.

Allende failed to win in three presidential elections before 1970, in part because under the Kennedy and Johnson administrations the CIA had spent almost $4 million to thwart his candidacy. Nixon rationalized his own authorization of CIA funds in 1970 (to prevent the Chilean Congress from proclaiming Allende president on the basis of the plurality he had won) by referring to the policy under JFK and LBJ. "We live in a far from ideal world," he wrote in his memoirs: "As long as the Communists supply external funds to support political parties, factions, or individuals in other countries, I believe that the United States can and should do the same and do it secretly so that it can be effective." Nixon then implied that after Allende's election, no more money went into CIA destabilizing efforts in Chile. This is simply not true.[16]

In testifying before the congressional Commission on the Organization of Government for the Conduct of Foreign Policy in 1975, Kissinger vehemently denied that covert CIA activities had "destabilized" the elected government of Chile under Allende:

> I have to tell you quite candidly, and you can draw whatever conclusions you will about my moral fitness from this, in normal times if we had not been beaten to death on the Chile operation we would have explored Forty Committee operations last year in Portugal. . . . And let's get clear what we did in Chile. You can go to any cocktail party in Washington and use the word "destabilize" and there will be clucking of outrage. What did we do? There was a government in power in Chile of which the Communists were the more moderate element which had Castro-ites and revolutionaries to the left that was systematically squeezing the democratic

parties out of office and out of control by confiscatory taxation of newspapers, radio stations, and so forth. We supported the democratic, the alternative forms, in order to be ready for the '76 election.

As it turned out, we failed. This is why the military moved. We didn't generate the military move. The democratic opposition proved so weak that the military felt Allende would establish a dictatorship. The argument you can make is Chile isn't important enough for us to have done that. That is an arguable proposition, and I am not going to go into that now. All I want to say is there must be countries in the world that are so important to us that we will try [covertly] to give the democratic forces or the forces friendly to us an opportunity where we can not do it by diplomatic means and we do not want to do it [overtly] by military means.[17]

At this crucial juncture (and several other times) in Kissinger's testimony to some of the more hostile members of the Murphy Commission, Vice President Nelson Rockefeller, Kissinger's hero and patron, came to the rescue of his former protégé by taking his side or leading him into another area of discussion. In this instance Rockefeller tried to neutralize the use of the word *covert* with respect to action taken in Chile (which Kissinger had indicated he wanted to duplicate in Portugal in 1974) by asking how long Portugal had been under a dictatorship. Upon receiving the answer of forty years, Rockefeller continued: "It seems to me what this country stands for is democracy and to help people organize democratic government or help people organize parties—there's nothing sinister about this. This is right down the alley of what we are trying to do, which is to preserve the world from going either to dictatorships of the right or the left. So I can't understand why we are not helping the Portuguese democratic forces learn how to organize democracy." To which Kissinger gratefully agreed: "That is the sort of situation in which with covert capability we would have acted differently."[18]

The remarks by Kissinger and Rockefeller defending secret contributions to foreign elections were contradicted several weeks later in the testimony given to the Murphy Commission by former Secretary of State William Rogers. Even when pushed by the Commission's chair, Robert Murphy, to agree with the Kissinger/Rockefeller position, Rogers insisted:

I have never thought that the financial contribution to elections in foreign countries is very important. . . . I think that financial contributions to the elections in other countries is counterproductive, and I think it is a mistake. In the first place, it is usually know[n]; and in the second place, I don't think you get your money's worth any more than you do in elections in this country; and third, I don't believe we should interfere in internal affairs in other countries. If we are going to do it that is the worst possible way to try to do it. So I don't favor political campaign contributions by the United States in another country. . . .

I suppose you can always think up situations like that why a contribution might have succeeded and might have been worthwhile. [Murphy had said that Allende had won the election in Chile by only 38,000 votes because the United States had cut off covert funds to the opposition forces too soon.] . . . But you can also think of places where if you get caught doing it [it] is so embarrassing to the country and flies in the face of all the statements we have made about noninterference that I am not sure it is worthwhile. I am not speaking about political contribution. . . .

I think that like anything else in foreign policy it is important to have people trust you, and if they don't then it is hard to deal with other countries. So if I am correct, if trust is worth anything in the conduct of foreign policy, then I think it is essential over the long run. We say we are prepared to let countries determine their own future and we will not interfere with them, then if we fly directly in the face of our statements, if we do something just the opposite to what we have said, I think it is harmful to our country in the long run.[19]

Once again, there was a clear division among Nixon, Kissinger, and Rogers over policy in Chile, and once again the president sided with his national security adviser. The Rogers/Kissinger split went far beyond the personality and petty ego differences that the press reported from 1969 until Rogers's resignation in the fall of 1973, when he had finally decided that his advice and presence had been ignored too much and for too long. Nowhere is Rogers's untenable position within the Nixon administration more evident than in the formulation of Middle Eastern policy, discussed in the next section.

All these seemingly random cold war foreign policies in the Third World have one thing in common beside their failure or wrongheadedness: they represent examples of Kissinger's concept of linkage (discussed in chapter 5). In this sense they attest to decentralized global regionalism at its worst. Linking U.S. reaction to Third World events based on relations with the Soviet Union tended to backfire. Curiously, such actions also contradicted the rather sophisticated analysis and recommendations of the Osgood report when discussing Third World countries, and they reflect Nixon's and/or Kissinger's disagreement with previously established U.S. policy. With respect to Israel, however, even the Osgood report viewed the Middle East as being in a hopeless "rising trend of violence." Convinced that "Israel can withstand this hostility," the Osgood report predicted deepening "Arab frustration." It viewed any further action by Israel to "seek security in expansion" with as much alarm as it viewed what appeared in the summer of 1969 to be everspreading Soviet influence in the area.[20]

MUDDLE IN THE MIDDLE EAST

One of the most important foreign policy discussions during Richard Nixon's first year as president concerned National Security Study Memorandum 2, dated January 21, 1969—the first full review of U.S. Middle East policy since the 1967 Six-Day War. The long overdue full-scale NSC debate over American policy in the Middle East took place at an all-day session on February 1. Two other NSSMs on the Middle East followed in the next two months; two more in 1970—before and after the Jordan crisis; none in 1971 or 1972; and an unknown number in 1973 after the outbreak of war in October.[21] Subsequently, there was no similarly comprehensive review of U.S. Middle East policy until President Carter's 1978 Camp David Accords, although President Ford considered conducting a complete reassessment in 1975 when negotiations over the Sinai II agreements temporarily broke down.

While the February 1 meeting established the basic goals of the United States for the 1970s—namely, substantial Israeli withdrawal from occupied territory in exchange for contractual and practical security arrangements with Egypt—the NSC adopted the least successful means of the entire decade for achieving these goals. The tactic agreed upon was the Rogers Plan, which called for American-Soviet agreement on a comprehensive peace settlement in the Middle East and for a more evenhanded public posture toward both the Israelis and the Arabs. This policy of "evenhandedness" was tentatively proposed by Governor William Scranton (Rep.-Pa.), Nixon's special preinauguration envoy to this area of the world. No American president or secretary of state formally disavowed this general principle until the end of 1983, when President Reagan and his secretary of state, George Shultz, affirmed a statement of joint military-political cooperation with Israel. In the intervening fourteen years, however, the principle of evenhandedness was breached more than it was honored, one example being the application of the Nixon Doctrine after 1972 in the form of increased arms sales to Israel and especially to Iran, in a futile attempt to maintain peace in this area of the world.[22] Even the original attempt at evenhandedness through the Rogers Plan lasted only a year.

There are several reasons why this plan of Nixon's first secretary of state probably would have failed even if Kissinger had not undermined the negotiations of the secretary of state. The Rogers Plan was based on three assumptions that were untenable for that era: (1) that the USSR would agree to become a joint peacemaker with the United States (by the time Moscow was willing to accept this role in 1973, Washington had abandoned the idea) and would pressure Egypt's President Nasser into accepting a compromise peace based on UN Resolution 242; (2) that a publicly impartial stance toward Israel and the Arabs would enhance the American bargaining position with both sides in a way that previous pro-Israeli statements by the United States had not; and (3) that Israel would comply with Rogers's endorsement of a substantial withdrawal from occupied territory in return for a contractual peace.[23]

Nixon's first press conferences were alternately optimistic and pessimistic about achieving peace in the Middle East. "I consider it a powder keg, very explosive. It needs to be defused," he told reporters on January 27, 1969. "I am open to any suggestions that may cool it off and reduce the possibility of another explosion, because the next explosion in the Mideast, I think, could involve very well a confrontation between nuclear powers, which we want to avoid." On February 6 he remarked that both unilateral and multilateral initiatives were being taken, and by March he said he was "cautiously hopeful" about the progress being made, but warned that the major powers interested in the Middle East could not "dictate to the small nations" in the area. He told me (and I was able to confirm this using Haldeman's notes) that he had wanted to declare 1973 the Year of the Middle East, but that Kissinger and other advisers prevailed in making it instead the Year of Europe.[24]

If this indeed is true, Nixon waited too long to focus systematically on Middle Eastern problems; by the fall of 1973 he was preoccupied with unfolding Watergate events. Obviously, Nixon could not have equally addressed all diplomatic fronts at once, and he clearly chose to concentrate on Vietnam, China, and the USSR during his first administration. So it made sense for him personally to have put the Middle East on a back burner until some of his other foreign policy initiatives were achieved.

Also, like all modern presidents he probably despaired of bringing order to the area, and hoped that the problems there would somehow resolve themselves before he got around to them. Perhaps Secretary of State Rogers was, indeed, the only top official who had a concrete plan for handling Middle Eastern affairs during Nixon's first term in office.

Kissinger certainly did not have a plan. Initially he insisted on seeing only the big geopolitical picture in the Middle East—not individual countries, just the United States and the Soviet Union. In the end he was reduced to pursuing the tactical interim agreements, just as Rogers had. Most important in 1969, however, Kissinger feared getting embroiled and bogged down in an area of the world that posed only risks of failure, not the chance for flamboyant success. During the summer of 1973, Kissinger remained curiously reluctant to concentrate on the Middle East. "Not until I am Secretary of State," he presciently remarked, "and more my own man."[25]

Moreover, both Nixon and Kissinger shared doubts about his effectiveness, as a Jew, in negotiations with Arabs, and even feared that he could become the target of anti-Semitic propaganda or threatened acts of terrorism from Egyptian, Syrian, Iraqi, or Palestinian groups, which had plagued Arthur Goldberg and Eugene and Walt Rostow in an earlier time. Precautions were taken to protect Kissinger during the Jordanian crisis of 1970, which began in September when Palestinians hijacked three international planes and landed them in Jordan. The incident should have ended after Israel released 450 Palestinian prisoners, but instead it escalated into a potential cold war conflict when Iraq and Syria (a client nation of the USSR) threatened to invade Jordan (a client state of the United States). The White House, for example, arranged for a "full-time round-the-clock [military] bodyguard who would be responsible both for Kissinger's personal safety and for the security of the documents he frequently has in his possession." By the end of the year, rumors about "possible plots of kidnapping" the national security adviser were so rampant that Kissinger instructed Nixon: "If such an attempt should succeed, I would like to ask you to meet no demands of the kidnappers, however trivial. I would assume that any demand that is met would establish a precedent which is against the national interest. If you should receive any communication from me to the contrary, you should assume that it was made under duress."[26]

Undermining the Policy of "Evenhandedness"

While William Rogers and Joseph Sisco, an assistant secretary of state for Near Eastern and South Asian affairs, hammered out a plan to present to the Soviets, Kissinger met separately with Ambassador Anatoly Dobrynin. There is strong circumstantial evidence suggesting that Kissinger indicated to Dobrynin that the White House had lost interest in the Rogers Plan, thereby ensuring its eventual official rejection by the Soviet Union.[27] However, it remains evident that the USSR did not view this offer to become a joint peacemaker with the United States as favorably in 1969 and 1970 (when it appeared to be benefiting from greater polarization in the area) as it would in 1973 (the year following the expulsion of twenty thousand Soviet technicians from Egypt by then president Anwar Sadat). Regardless, when the Rogers Plan became public at the end of 1969, both Israel and Egypt opposed it as an obvious attempt by the Big Two (or in this case the Big One) to impose a settlement.

A number of questions are raised by this spectacle of the national security adviser (and possibly the president himself) working to defeat a formally approved NSC policy for the Middle East. If Kissinger was so convinced that Rogers's comprehensive final settlement was premature, erecting the "architecture before fashioning the foundation," why did he not try to oppose the secretary at early NSC meetings? After all, when he succeeded Rogers as secretary of state in 1973, he pursued the same goals, but through a series of interim agreements rather than a single settlement. Why did the president allow Rogers to proceed so far with a plan that he later wrote in his memoirs "could never be implemented"? Why was Rogers excluded from the secret talks with Dobrynin? Did Nixon and Kissinger have an alternative plan for Middle East policy to warrant undermining Rogers's activities? There are a number of possible answers to these questions. In the early months of the Nixon administration Kissinger was still unsure of his position, and on several occasions, including during the Middle East debate, he chose not to assert himself for fear of alienating Nixon and because he correctly suspected that any new comprehensive policy in the area would fail. "I will never get involved in anything unless I'm sure of success," he told an Egyptian diplomat in the summer of 1971. "And if I do get involved, it means I'm going to succeed. I hate failure." He often remarked during the early years of the Nixon administration: "The Middle East isn't ready for me."[28]

In retrospect, it appears that Kissinger preferred a stalemate in the

Middle East so that he could take credit for stepping in and picking up the pieces. At the time, however, both Nixon and Kissinger claimed that the president thought his national security adviser's Jewish background "would put him at a disadvantage during the delicate initial negotiations for the reopening of diplomatic relations with the Arab states." Clearly not a Zionist, and often diffident about his own Jewishness, Kissinger apparently accepted Nixon's disqualification of him on ethnic grounds. More important to the president than Kissinger's ethnicity, however, was the belief that the Middle East question deserved full-time, expert attention, and Kissinger not only lacked expertise but also had his hands full with the Vietnam negotiations, SALT and other discussions with the Soviets, and issues involving Japan and Europe. Kissinger suspected that Nixon wanted to stimulate rivalry between him and Rogers (as though the president could generate any more competition than Kissinger had already precipitated). "I never treat crises when they're cold," Kissinger once told a friend, "only when they're hot. This enables me to weight the protagonists one against the other, not in terms of ten or two thousand years ago but in terms of what each of them merits at the moment."[29] In the Middle East this ultimately meant the 1973 Yom Kippur war, now more commonly known as the October war.

As had Rogers and Kissinger, Nixon assumed office convinced that the "key to peace in the Middle East lay as much in Moscow as it did in Cairo or Damascus." But unlike them, by July 1969 the president had developed a partial alternative plan should the Big Two or even Big Four settlement prove unrealistic. This alternative plan came to be known as the Nixon Doctrine, and was the product of neither NSC discussion nor even consultation with Kissinger. The Nixon Doctrine called upon regional powers to maintain their own security with U.S. military aid, but warned that they could no longer expect the United States to commit its troops as it had in Vietnam. The Nixon Doctrine would result in the increased arms sales to Israel, and especially to Iran, ostensibly in order to maintain stability.[30]

It is conceivable that the president permitted his secretary of state to carry on to the bitter, embarrassing end with the Rogers Plan not because he believed that the Big Two talks would succeed in 1969 but because he thought such talks were the quickest way to convey to the "Arab world that the United States did not [any longer] automatically dismiss its case regarding the occupied territories or rule out a compromise settlement of the conflicting claims" on the basis of what was "balanced and fair."

Nixon presumed that, with the Rogers Plan firmly on record, "it would be easier for the Arab leaders to propose reopening relations with the United States [including acceptance of the Nixon Doctrine] without coming under attack from the hawks and pro-Soviet elements in their own countries."[31] Exclusion of Secretary Rogers from negotiations with Ambassador Dobrynin also makes sense if one remembers that Kissinger had already carved out the USSR as his own personal bureaucratic territory within the executive office. With Nixon's approval, Kissinger pursued secret contacts with the Soviets that would lead ultimately to détente.

Consequently, the Nixon administration's early Middle East policy followed a two-level pattern that would come to characterize much of its diplomacy throughout the world: public actions through the State Department and secret back-channel contacts supervised by Kissinger. Finally, it can be argued that by giving Rogers enough rope to hang himself, so to speak, Nixon and Kissinger placated the pro-Arab elements within the State Department until the president and his national security adviser could come up with a Middle East policy of their own—one that would not be dominated or directed by the bureaucrats within the State Department, whom they viewed with suspicion and disdain.

Behind the scenes, of course, "evenhandedness" served a number of nondiplomatic ends, as top officials within the American government vied with one another for a variety of bureaucratic, political, and personal purposes. The complexity of the process was exacerbated by the fact that State Department and NSC documents often referred to "domestic political considerations" when discussing the Middle East. This euphemistic reference to the so-called Jewish lobby and American-Jewish interest in keeping U.S. relations with Israel on a favorable footing prompted Nixon to write the following to Rogers and Kissinger: "Under no circumstances will domestic political considerations have any bearing on the decisions I make with regard to the Mideast."[32]

Stalemate as Policy

In October 1969 the Soviet Union officially rejected the Rogers Plan, leaving the new Republican administration with no apparent positive alternative until after the October war—aside, that is, from the Nixon Doctrine, whose excessive application in Iran has been commonly criticized. From the 1970 crisis in Jordan through the 1973 October war, the United States appeared to pursue a policy of stalemate. As Kissinger remarked in confidence about the failure of the Rogers Plan to two journalists (who published the comment anyway): "My view has always been that you have to know when to be active and when not to be active. I always thought there had to be a period of stalemate in which the various parties recognize the limits of what they could achieve. That didn't mean one shouldn't make an effort to defuse it. But I was always less optimistic about the possibilities of a real breakthrough than some others."[33]

Subsequently Kissinger went to great lengths in both volumes of his memoirs to make a virtue out of what may have been the vice of having no policy at all. As with many of Kissinger's convoluted rationalizations, it will take historians years to sort out the truth. The stalemate policy, at most, seemed to consist of applying sporadic behavior-modification techniques to Israel beginning in 1969. For example, promises to Israel of more A-4 Skyhawks and F-4 Phantoms were deferred on two occasions in the hope that this would encourage an Arab-Israel cease-fire along the Suez Canal and implementation by the Israeli government of UN Resolution 242 calling for territorial concessions. This tactic was often accompanied by theatrics and exaggerated statements in Washington. On June 26, 1970, for example, in direct contradiction of Rogers's continued efforts to negotiate calmly with all parties over the Middle East, Kissinger announced that it was the goal of American policy to "expel" the Soviets from the Middle East. Although both the White House and the State Department issued statements qualifying the meaning of "expel," Kissinger refused to back down, thus further undermining the credibility of Secretary Rogers in his attempts to obtain an American-Soviet settlement in the Middle East.[34]

On August 7, Rogers and Sisco arranged an uneasy cease-fire along the Suez Canal among Jordan, Israel, and Egypt, which was violated literally within seconds. For four weeks, however, personal competition and antagonisms among Kissinger, Rogers, and Sisco delayed verification of these violations. By that time Jordan's slow disintegration into civil war had reached a new crisis point, allowing Nixon and Kissinger to enliven their stalemate approach with another element of theater. In a belated but dramatic move, Nixon ordered the rush delivery to Israel of eighteen F-4 supersonic aircraft, the latest electronic-countermeasure (ECM) equipment, and conventional Shrike air-to-ground missiles so that the Israeli air force could neutralize Soviet surface-to-air-missiles (SAMs) in the Suez Canal. As before, when Kissinger had undermined Rogers's private attempts to restrain the Egyptians, Syrians, and Iraqis by negotiating with the USSR, their major arms supplier, this time he held a theatrical meeting in Washington with Golda Meir, Israel's prime minister. The charade was not as complicated as their 1969 encounter had been, but it did end with an interrupted fund-raising banquet in New York, with Ambassador Yitzhak Rabin rushing to fly back to Washington to confer with Kissinger and Meir before returning to Israel. The next night, September 21, President Nixon finally assured the ambassador that the United States would intervene in Israel's behalf against the Egyptians and Soviets should Israel come to the aid of Hussein, the beleaguered king of Jordan.[35]

The faulty cease-fire along the Suez Canal and the Jordanian crisis of 1970 totally discredited Rogers and the State Department, setting the stage for the bilateral, personal, often secret "shuttle diplomacy" of Henry Kissinger following the October war. It also effectively ended any remaining doubt about the death of "evenhandedness" associated with the Rogers Plan. Instead of returning to the openly pro-Israeli diplomacy of previous administrations, however, this administration preferred a devious cat-and-mouse approach more in keeping with the personalities of Nixon and Kissinger. Consequently, whenever it was deemed necessary, they enticed Israel and the Arab nations (particularly Jordan, Iran, and Saudi Arabia) with military supplies to offset similar arms shipments by the USSR to Egypt, Syria, Iraq, and Libya. A free-market policy for arms exports to the Middle East peaked in 1976 at $15 billion, up 400 percent from 1970.[36] This policy continued under Ford, Carter, Reagan, and Bush, until the Gulf war unearthed old criticisms of it.

While one result of the failed Rogers Plan appeared to be simply a return to traditional regional polarization policies, there were actually two new twists to it: one covert and the other overt. The first consisted of a secret agreement between the shah of Iran and Nixon in May 1972. In keeping with his commitment to the Nixon Doctrine, the president, according to one account, "personally gave the Shah permission to buy any conventional weapon in the American arsenal. In the four years beginning in 1973 the Shah spent $15 billion on weapons, making him the world's leading arms buyer. From 1973 until 1977, therefore, more than half of U.S. arms sales abroad went to Iran, including weapons more advanced than anything then introduced into America's own [non-nuclear] arsenal."[37] Many reports have surfaced claiming that the major accomplishment of the Nixon Doctrine in the Middle East was to encourage the shah to initiate, without fear of American opposition and over the initial objections of the Saudis, an inflationary spiral in OPEC oil prices to pay for his exorbitant purchases.

The second twist was the emergence in the wake of the 1970 Jordanian crisis of a special Kissinger-Rabin relationship. Unlike the less publicized special arms arrangement with Iran, Kissinger received much attention in the international press as the "good friend" of Israel. Privately, however, he continued to view the Jewish state as only one, albeit a special, part of a much larger strategic struggle with the Soviet Union. Kissinger solidified his position with Israel by interceding with Rogers on Rabin's behalf when the secretary of state attempted to pressure Israel into unilateral concessions during negotiations for reopening the Suez Canal in return for jet plane deliveries. Yet this was the same "kickass" behavior-modification policy for keeping Israel on a "short leash" that he and Nixon had agreed upon earlier. In this fashion Kissinger further undermined the secretary of state and also secured Rabin's support for Nixon's reelection in 1972.[38]

These two results—increased arms sales to Iran and better relations with Israel—indirectly led to two unfortunate developments: they contributed to the OPEC embargo ("oilgate") and encouraged Israel's development of nuclear arms and the frightening possibility that the Israelis would use them if they were "abandoned by the United States and overrun by Arabs." (This modern-day reenactment of the biblical figure who killed himself and his enemies has been dubbed the "Samson option").[39]

From the beginning of his presidency, Nixon worried about increasing the oil revenues of Iran so that the shah could close the gap between oil sales and the financial needs of his "well executed development program," which increasingly in the 1970s emphasized military rather than humanitarian concerns. Nixon told one of his economic advisers, Peter Flanigan, to bring pressure to bear on the U.S. members of the Iranian Oil Consortium to increase Iranian oil purchases, and even gave consideration to a proposal whereby Norway would buy Iranian oil and resell it to Cuba. "Knowledge of the Iranian [Norwegian-Cuban] arrangement would be taken as an indication of U.S. willingness to soften our stand on Cuba . . . [and] stimulate initiatives for a rapprochement," Flanigan and Kissinger warned the president in an action memorandum in 1970, and so he rejected the idea. The administration's desire to help the shah balance his budget took a much more dangerous turn than a "softening of the U.S. attitude toward Cuba" ever would have.[40]

Details about the "blank military check" that Nixon and Kissinger issued to the shah were known as early as the late 1970s because of Senate hearings and reports, but it was not until the 1979 overthrow of the shah, the taking of U.S. hostages under the Ayatollah Khomeini, and the Iran-contra arms-for-hostages scandal under Reagan ("Irangate") that the wrongheadedness of the Nixinger policy toward Iran hit home. Iranian radicals released fifty-eight volumes of documents taken from the U.S. embassy that proved beyond a doubt just how blank the blank check to the shah had been, even though both Kissinger and Nixon have continued to deny that it was. In a word, the president of the United States through his national security adviser informed the Department of Defense that "[d]ecisions on the acquisition of military equipment should be left primarily to the government of Iran." A year later, Kissinger reiterated to Nixon that "we adopted a policy which provides, in effect, that we will accede to any of the Shah's requests for arms purchases from us."[41]

After their visit to Tehran in May 1972, Nixon and Kissinger gave Mohammad Reza Pahlavi, the shah of Iran, this "military carte blanche" because they believed that there had to be another "trusted local power," in addition to Israel, in the Persian Gulf. This triangularization policy— the United States, Israel, and a third Middle Eastern nation—had become characteristic of U.S. policy as the British withdrew their military presence in the Gulf area from 1968 to 1971. Between 1972 and 1978, this policy was carried to its logical extreme with respect to arming Iran. U.S. military sales approached $17 billion in those years; Iranian defense spending increased 670 percent—from $1.4 billion in 1972 to $9.4 billion in 1977. Such military purchases made up 40 percent of the Iranian budget by the late 1970s. In the fall of 1973, OPEC took advantage of the October war to quadruple oil prices, which, in turn, increased the shah's coffers from $4 billion annually to almost $20 billion, making Tehran a mecca for arms sales.[42]

While Nixon's later comments on the obvious connection between Iranian arms sales and increased oil prices have been somewhat circumspect to say the least, he was no less impressed by the shah than his national security adviser was, calling him a "revolutionary monarch," "talented and hardworking, a man who produced progress with stability . . . but [who] did not strike the emotional chord in his people that Nasser did." Nixon's unexamined attitude toward the shah as the "protector" of the Persian Gulf apparently stemmed from his experiences as vice president under Eisenhower, whose administration had supported a covert American-British military operation that restored the shah to power. He was so impressed with the shah when he first met him in 1953 that it blinded Nixon to what was happening in Iran by the time he became president. In later writings he invariably referred to the shah favorably in comparison to three other strong Arab leaders, Gamal Abdel Nasser and Anwar el-Sadat of Egypt and King Faisal of Saudi Arabia.[43]

Kissinger lavished even more praise than Nixon on the shah—both before and after his fall from power—as a "friend of our country and a pillar of stability in a turbulent and vital region ... a dedicated reformer ... wrestling perhaps with forces beyond any man's control, he was for us that rarest of leaders, an unconditional ally, and one whose understanding of the world situation enhanced our own."[44] Kissinger continued to insist to a Senate committee in 1976 that, despite the shah's leadership role in the raising of oil prices and the oil embargo, which precipitated a worldwide energy crisis, "on all major international issues, the policies of the United States and the policies of Iran have been parallel and therefore mutually enforcing."[45]

A year earlier, before the Murphy Commission, Kissinger denied any U.S. government responsibility for the oil embargo, such as its resupply of arms to Israel during a crucial point in the October war or its misplaced trust in the stability of the shah's regime. Kissinger also later asserted that "the Shah's overthrow had little to do with his purchases of military equipment," denied that he had sacrificed either domestic reform or internal economic development for those purchases, and said that the administration did not favor higher oil revenues for Iran so that the shah could purchase more military hardware.[46] Nothing could be further from the truth, as books by Barry Rubin, Jack Anderson, Gary Sick, and James A. Bill have all shown.[47]

There is some evidence indicating that Nixon had second thoughts about this pro-Iranian, pro-Israel policy before the October war. Secretary of Defense Laird wrote Nixon a memo after Sadat had expelled the Soviets from Egypt, saying that secret negotiations should begin with Sadat. In the margin of this memo Nixon wrote: "K[issinger]—lean to Laird's view." Unfortunately, nothing came of Laird's suggestion or Nixon's own desire to make 1973 the Year of the Middle East instead of the Year of Europe. Moreover, Sadat and Saudi Arabia's King Faisal gratuitously offered the Nixon administration "the chance to avert the consequences of almost four years of reverses in oil affairs" in the summer and fall of 1972, which U.S. oil companies favored. Given Nixon's long-standing political indebtedness to American oil interests, the favoritism he had shown them before becoming president, and his own demonstrated interest in, and knowledge of, international economics, it is difficult to understand why he let opportunities in 1972 and 1973 slip away.[48]

Meetings between Sadat's representative Hafiz Ismail and Kissinger were put off again and again until February 1973—two years after Sadat and Faisal had signaled that their countries wanted a better relationship with the United States and seven full months after Soviet military and civilian advisers left Egypt. While Kissinger tried to blame this delay on Nixon's greater interest in domestic policies—namely, the 1972 presidential election, saying that "Middle East diplomacy was a loser"—there is no indication that Kissinger saw any geopolitical necessity for substituting Egypt and/or Saudi Arabia for Iran in their Middle East triangle. The U.S. oil consortium, Arabian-American Oil Company (ARAMCO), in particular, tried to impress White House, State Department, and Defense Department officials that time was running out for accepting Faisal's "positive use of oil" offers that favored U.S. companies. Instead, Faisal joined OPEC in a pro-Arab "negative use of oil" in 1973. While all this was going on, the White House thought that the main concern of the consortium should be to take "action designed to punish the radical [oil-producing] Arabs."[49]

On October 12, 1973 (the same day Nixon says he made his "last major foreign policy decision": to begin the 550-mission airlift of arms to Israel), the four American companies making up ARAMCO told Nixon through Haig:

> We have been told that the Saudis will impose some cutback in crude oil production as a result of the United States action taken thus far [support of Israel in the United Nations]. A further and much more substantial move will be taken by Saudi Arabia and Kuwait in the event of further evidence of increased U.S. support of the Israeli position. . . . We are convinced of the seriousness of the intentions of the Saudis and Kuwaitis [who would between them account for more than half of the oil cutoff] and that any actions by the U.S. government at this time in terms of increased aid to Israel will have a critical and adverse effect on our relations with the moderate Arab oil-producing countries.[50]

This misguided Nixinger arms-sales policy skewed the shah's domestic and international priorities, and in the process an executive agreement exempted such sales from the review policies of both the State and Defense Departments, "creat[ing] a bonanza for U.S. weapons manufacturers." It ultimately included an arrangement whereby CIA listening posts in Iran were removed, which contributed to a lack of intelligence information about the internal conditions that led to the overthrow of the shah in 1979.[51]

Additionally, this excessive courting of the shah resulted in the sending of $16 million in CIA funds between 1972 and 1975 to the Kurds, a mountain people living in Iran, Iraq, Turkey, and the Soviet Union who had been fighting for autonomy from Iraq since 1961. According to a leaked congressional report (known as the Pike Report), "even in the context of covert action, ours was a cynical enterprise," because neither the United States nor the shah wanted the Kurds to succeed against Iraq. They simply wanted to sap Iraqi resources and used aid to the Kurds to achieve this. Although Kissinger promised in the first volume of his memoirs that he would explain in another book this inhumane policy on the basis of primary evidence about "White House decisions and reasoning," his second volume does not do so. We are left with Kissinger's rationalization of the Kurdish affair in one long footnote published in 1979.[52] Nixon's subsequent writings entirely ignored this misuse of the Kurds as a geopolitical pawn—a fate still plaguing them in the 1990s.

The Oil Crisis

Major U.S. oil companies with holdings in the Middle East encountered a series of negative developments in the region beginning in 1969 as the bargaining power shifted away from them in favor of producing nations. The reason was simple. World demand had exceeded production. All of them—Standard Oil Company (New Jersey), Occidental Petroleum Company, and Royal Dutch-Shell Group (Shell)—immediately contacted representatives in the congressional or executive branches of government about rising oil prices, especially in Libya. Among the various companies, Shell took the lead in recommending a united front. Writing to Senator Frank Church, head of the Subcommittee on Multinational Corporations of the Senate Foreign Relations Committee, Shell's chief executive, Sir David Barren, said that Shell's view "was that the avalanche had begun and that our best hope of withstanding the pressures being exerted by the members of OPEC would lie in the companies refusing to be picked off one by one in any country and by declining to deal with the procedures except on a total, globe basis."[53]

In retrospect, even Shell failed to recognize how much the handwriting on the wall had changed in terms of OPEC's power and what measures would be required to counter its potential to control oil prices. So did the 1969 Cabinet Task Force on Oil Import Control chaired by Shultz when he was secretary of labor. Moreover, within the State Department some, most notably James Akins, thought Libya and other oil-producing nations in the Middle East deserved higher prices. As a result, in September 1970 oil companies "submitted" to higher Libyan prices following the government's policy recommendation of "cooperation, not confrontation." While Kissinger generally criticized the "romantic view" of the State Department toward Third World radicalism, he did not specifically oppose the pro-Arab oil policy it fostered. This only confirmed the suspicion of oil company leaders that Kissinger thought their concerns represented nothing more than greedy self-interest. The general public also held this view of oil companies.[54]

But the president was another matter. He had built his political career, in part, with the support of U.S., especially California, oil interests. Why did he not heed the warnings of oil executives, especially since his administration favored big business in antitrust and some civil rights suits? Instead, as early as the summer of 1970, he began telling "key people in the oil business" that "nothing is going to be done now or later regarding their problem" about oil imports.[55] Perhaps this was because he was not paying attention, particularly in 1973, as Watergate consumed more and more of his time. Another reason might be that by forsaking Secretary Rogers's plan for evenhandedness in the Middle East back in 1970 and not developing any alternative policy, he had no choice but to favor Iran and Israel over U.S. oil interests in 1973.

Despite repeated meetings between CEOs of oil companies in the U.S. and abroad and Arab representatives of OPEC at the beginning of 1971, under the shah's "moderate" leadership, prices began to edge inexorably upward on February 3, 1971, after a formal OPEC meeting in Tehran. This 1971 Tehran Agreement, and one in Tripoli later that year, "represented for the international oil companies a practical end to their influence over prices." Yet the administration optimistically viewed these and another agreement with Iran in 1972 as a "major plus in our oil relations with the Middle East"; besides being "very beneficial to Iran" they point to the "development of Middle Eastern oil in a direction dramatically opposed to that taken by other oil-producing countries." From that point, relations between OPEC and American and foreign oil companies deteriorated until the United States decided to begin an arms airlift to Israel on October 13, 1973. This precipitated a dramatic OPEC cut in production by 5 percent two days later and a total embargo of oil to the United States within a week. This embargo would last for five months, ending temporarily only after Nixon and Kissinger agreed privately to (but denied publicly) a request from Egyptian and Saudi foreign ministers Ismail Fahmy and Omar Saqqaf (representing Arab leaders) for the United States to use its "best influence" to bring about a Syrian-Israeli military disengagement—one of the few "linkages" over which they apparently disagreed: Nixon, for political reasons, wanted the embargo lifted almost regardless of the quid pro quo, while Kissinger apparently wanted the impossible— an unconditional end to the embargo. Instead, the president sent him shuttling to Damascus to work for a "permanent" peace in return for lifting the embargo. As it turned out, the United States had to enlist the personal support of Egyptian president Sadat to obtain a permanent end to the oil embargo.[56]

While American oil firms dealt innovatively with the resulting energy crisis, the era of foreign domination of Middle Eastern oil prices had ended. The boycott proved less difficult to manage than the continued restriction of production by OPEC from that time forward. By the end of the 1980s, many still believed that this "revolution of the 1970s resulted directly from the failure of their government to pursue any consistent overall policy in the Middle East . . . [or] support [for] U.S. [oil] business abroad, as had been traditional." Twenty years after OPEC imposed an oil embargo, the United States has still not modified its energy consumption and is more dependent than ever before on Middle Eastern oil.[57]

Kissinger's personal and bureaucratic victory over Rogers (and Laird) in the battle to influence Middle East policy before the October war had one devastatingly negative and long-term effect: White House underestimation of the emerging economic power of OPEC. Incredible as it may seem now, Nixon's 1971 foreign policy report to Congress, which was drafted by Kissinger's staff, failed to mention anything about oil or OPEC. Even after the embargo was imposed, Kissinger continued to view the Middle East primarily as a geopolitical problem between the United States and the Soviet Union, not as a dangerous and potentially debilitating economic or resource problem for the United States and its Western allies. The eighty pages he devoted to the energy crisis and related issues in the second volume of his memoirs do little except talk around the topic and deny any responsibility for energy policy because he "had no expertise on the subject"—which is contradicted by the fact that he established a special NSC ad hoc committee to deal with the oil crisis in 1973 in order to make sure that he and not Secretary of the Treasury George Shultz controlled foreign economic policy in the Middle East.[58] The years 1969 to 1973—the crucial years when control of oil prices shifted inexorably toward the producing nations—constitute an unfortunate and expensive incubation period for the Nixon administration's Middle East policy. Instead of promoting the expansion of domestic production (or the unthinkable: conservation), Nixingerism concentrated on more important geopolitical matters. At the end of the October war, Kissinger's step-by-step disengagement policy, otherwise known as shuttle diplomacy, emerged full-blown but too late to prevent or resolve the oil crisis, even if the newly appointed secretary of state had made it his top priority. Although Kissinger's frantic shuttling about gave the false impression of creating meaningful multilateral arrangements, this approach was piece-meal and stopgap in nature. It was also essentially bilateral and did not address the question of oil prices.[59]

In the wake of the October war, Kissinger soon fell into the habit of telling the Israelis and Arabs what they wanted to hear, sometimes exceeding both congressional and White House intentions. But he finally retreated from his earlier reckless call for the expulsion of the Soviet Union from the area. Realizing that this simply had the effect of further polarizing the Arabs and driving the more militant factions into buying Russian arms, the administration deemed it possible that Arab national-ism would assert itself against Soviet imperialism.[60] And, indeed, Sadat's 1972 independent expulsion of Soviet personnel had demonstrated just this to other Middle Eastern nations. Even these changes in U.S. policy came too little, too late—a fact that the cosmetic addition of shuttle diplomacy could not change. Flawed as it already was, Nixingerism in the Middle East easily succumbed to the sham of Kissinger's shuttling as Watergate occupied more and more of the president's time.

SHUTTLING IN THE VACUUM CREATED BY WATERGATE

Paradoxically, Watergate first threatened and then ensured Kissinger's tenure in office, as a politically preoccupied and psychologically debili-tated Nixon came to rely on him more and more. "It tied me to the job," Kissinger once told reporters, "because this was one area that hadn't been essentially touched by Watergate."[61] The confluence of the October war and Watergate resulted in Kissinger's promotion to secretary of state in 1973. While he also remained head of the NSC until December 1975, when President Ford replaced him as national security adviser, occupy-ing two major government jobs instead of one did not give him any more personal power or control than he was to exercise during the brief outbreak of another Middle Eastern war, when Egypt and Syria attacked Israel in October 1973. During those three weeks, Henry Kissinger came the closest he ever would to being president of the United States.

After appointing Kissinger secretary of state on October 19, Nixon gave him diplomatic "power of attorney" to end the war by negotiating with Brezhnev in Moscow. As the president was still too embroiled in the political fallout of the "Saturday Night Massacre"—the White House's firing of Special Prosecutor Archibald Cox and Deputy Attorney General William Ruckelshaus, and the resignation of Attorney General Elliot Richardson—to devote full attention to foreign policy, upon Kissinger's October 24 return from Moscow, Nixon "empowered" him to formulate the American response to a new Soviet threat to take unilateral action to enforce the cease-fire in the Middle East.[62]

At this unique and opportune time, Kissinger made the controversial decision during the October war to put U.S. military forces on a worldwide alert, known as a grade-3 DEFCON (defensive condition) or DEFCON III. The October 24 alert ostensibly was in response to a Soviet note that implied the USSR was contemplating unilateral military action to stop Israeli violations of the cease-fire. Nixon now takes full responsibility for ordering this high-level alert, unequivocally claiming that the "alert worked" because Brezhnev backed down.[63] This explanation, as well as Kissinger's later rationalizations about the alert, obscure the fact that the United States and the Soviet Union had in essence been in agreement about achieving a cease-fire throughout the October war. Without the alert, this Middle Eastern conflict would have been viewed more accurately at home and abroad as an example of U.S./USSR détente functioning, rather than faltering.

Although both Kissinger and Nixon have vehemently and repeatedly denied that the president's preoccupation with Watergate or the desire to take the public's mind off the "Saturday Night Massacre" had anything to do with the alert, suspicions about this still linger. In answer to congressional inquiries, classified responses from the Department of Defense leave the distinct impression that the alert was an excessive reaction on Kissinger's part for reasons that have not yet been adequately explained. Either the alert represented a deliberately exaggerated response to divert attention from the Saturday Night Massacre *or* it was an equally deliberate attempt by Kissinger to assert his own new power and authority.

Kissinger became unusually defensive at his October 25th press conference when it was suggested that the alert reflected the president's domestic difficulties more than being a true reading of the Middle East situation. "It is a symptom of what is happening to our country that it could even be suggested that the United States would alert its forces for domestic reasons," the secretary of state angrily told reporters: "I am absolutely confident that the President had no other choice as a responsible national leader." Although Kissinger promised to reveal the "ambiguous developments" (such as how many people participated in the decision), as well as the full text of the Brezhnev message that had prompted the action, he never did.[64]

Most tellingly, Secretary of Defense James Schlesinger's press conference the next day contradicted some of Kissinger's remarks, particularly about how many people had been involved in the decision, whether it had been unanimous, and how much the president had participated directly. Schlesinger strongly implied that Watergate had been a factor in the decision. "I think it was important," he said, "in view of the circumstances that have raised a question or may have raised a question about the ability of the United States to react appropriately, firmly and quickly. . . . [The alert] certainly scotched whatever myths may have developed with regard to that possibility." Later, in closed testimony before the Murphy Commission on the Organization of the Government for the Conduct of Foreign Policy, Schlesinger implicitly criticized the way the alert had been decided upon—"some of the senior decisionmakers are men who like to do things in an individual . . . and private way"—but defended the publicity the alert received. He said the Defense Department could not have carried out a DEFCON III in secret, since it involved moving two million military personnel.[65]

Kissinger later smugly confided to aides that the alert was "our deliberate over-reaction." By this he apparently meant that he wanted to warn the Soviets that the United States would not tolerate a unilateral intervention, and to warn the Israelis that they must not attempt to destroy the Egyptian Third Army by violating the cease-fire. Nixon, in a rambling press conference of his own, simply said that the only thing the Soviets understood was power, and that Brezhnev had to be impressed with the fact that the president of the United States "would do what was right . . . regardless of pressures at home." Nixon concluded by calling the whole affair the "most difficult crisis we have had since the Cuban confrontation of 1962."[66]

Watergate and the October war were inextricably interwoven in the minds of top American policy makers. Some, such as Nixon and Kissinger, even suspected that the Soviets and their client nations in the

Middle East may have taken advantage of the domestic turmoil it caused to test the resolve of the United States. In his *Memoirs,* Nixon alternated back and forth between Watergate and the Middle East in discussing the fall months of 1973, and his public statements and reactions on both issues became hopelessly intertwined. For example, in his October 19 announcement of displeasure with Special Prosecutor Archibald Cox, the president began with a reference not to Watergate but "to the extremely delicate world situation at that very moment" by saying:

> What matters most in this critical hour is our ability to act—and to act in
> a way that enables us to control events, not to be paralyzed and over-
> whelmed by them. At home, the Watergate issue has taken on overtones
> of a partisan political contest. Concurrently, there are those in the inter-
> national community who may be tempted by our Watergate-related diffi-
> culties at home to misread America's unity and resolve in meeting the
> challenges we confront abroad.[67]

The same day, Nixon dispatched Kissinger to Moscow with full power to negotiate a cease-fire resolution, and the following day Nixon sent a stern note to Brezhnev about the Soviet airlift. Later that afternoon, Cox held a press conference insisting that the president turn over the subpoenaed Watergate tapes. Nixon immediately related this demand to the negotiations in Moscow:

> I strongly felt that I could not allow Cox to defy openly a presidential
> directive. I thought of Brezhnev and how it would look to the Soviets if in
> the midst of our diplomatic showdown with them I were in the position of
> having to defer to the demands of one of my own employees. Furthermore,
> I thought that Cox had deliberately exceeded his authority; I felt that he
> was trying to get me personally, and I wanted him out.[68]

When Attorney General Elliot Richardson threatened to resign rather than carry out Nixon's order to fire Cox, the president had General Alexander Haig appeal to him to wait until the Middle East crisis had been settled. According to Nixon's memoirs, Haig appealed to Richardson's patriotism by telling him that "the impact of his resignation during this crisis while Kissinger was meeting with Brezhnev might have incalculable effects, not just on the Soviets' assessment of our intentions and our strength, but on the morale within our government." Along the same lines Nixon later complained to one of his defense attorneys, Len Garment, "If I can't get an order carried out by my Attorney General, how can I get arms to Israel?"[69]

The October war broke the stalemate that had substituted for American policy in the Middle East since 1969. "It took the war to unfreeze the positions" on both sides, Kissinger later told an aide. By the time this breakthrough occurred, the stalemate had cost the United States more than Kissinger could ever gain back, even though it freed him to play hopscotch diplomacy among Middle Eastern countries. In fact, adopting the role of "Henry of Arabia" enabled Kissinger to survive Watergate without appearing to have lost any personal influence. It is debatable, however, whether U.S. policy in the Middle East improved once he took overt control of it. Seyom Brown and others have documented that there was little substance to show for all of Kissinger's shuttling.[70]

His flamboyant dominance over Middle Eastern policy until 1977 was not based on any comprehensive strategy; it was all tactical and hence did not contribute to stability in that area of the world. Instead, it led to a condition of "dependence without responsibility." From 1967 until the Gulf war, the more Israel and other Middle Eastern nations became dependent upon the United States, the less they had to fear (other than verbal admonitions) about obtaining military aid.[71] This is because it is in the Middle East that the Nixon Doctrine of July 1969 has been most systematically applied. Under its aegis the United States has insisted that regional powers maintain security in their geographical areas. Before the shah of Iran's overthrow, the two powers that could stabilize the Middle East were Iran and Israel. Beginning with the May 1972 secret agreement with the shah, the American government under three presidents opened its vast arsenal of weapons to a nation that became obsessed with purchasing military hardware.

The neutralization of Egypt and the world oil crisis in 1973–74 initially created a situation in which the United States had a much greater interest in quickly solving the Palestinian problem than it would feel through the 1980s, with falling oil prices and a genuinely more anti-Arab attitude in Congress. But the military might of the shah's Iran or Egypt or Saudi Arabia or some other major Arab nation was still required by the triangularization of U.S. policy because Israel could not act alone without American backing as a general force for stability in the Middle East. Recognizing this, Nixon waived payment on $1.5 billion of debts contracted by Israel to military equipment during and after the October war and extended credit to Israel at concessional rates to allow it to make another $1.2 billion in military purchases. Publicly the administration justified these actions by saying they "will contribute substantially to the avoidance of major economic dislocation." Privately, however, Kissinger told the president that "our studies do not confirm that severe economic dislocation would result if we do not waive the repayment" and that both the Office of Management and Budget and the Treasury Department agreed. "The crucial factor in this decision is not so much economic considerations," Kissinger continued, "as it is our interest in a close and trusting relationship with Prime Minister Rabin's new government. . . . At the same time there has been little critical reaction from Arabs, who appear resigned to U.S. aid to Israel when U.S. diplomacy is crucial to maintaining the momentum of [the postwar] settlement." Nonetheless, Nixon told Haig: "Don't allow any [Israel aid] to slip by me without my attention."[72]

Whether U.S. evenhandedness could ever be asserted in the area seemed doubtful until the collapse of the Soviet Union and the break in Arab unity against dealing with Israel during and following the Gulf war. At least the Bush administration appeared to abandon the sham of Secretary of State James Baker's shuttle diplomacy for the face-to-face Israel-Palestinian peace talks of 1991–92. This may, indeed, have been the long-awaited opportunity to return to an evenhanded U.S. policy in the Middle East based on cooperation with Russia—as Secretary of State William Rogers envisioned almost a quarter of a century earlier. Nixon admitted in January 1992 that with the Soviet Union out of the picture, the United States should be able to progress more easily toward real peace in the area, in large measure because it would be to Israel's advantage to come to terms with Arab nations while it still held a monopoly on nuclear weapons. Thus, the Samson option continues to figure in any Middle Eastern peace settlement.[73] With the demise of communism at the end of the 1980s, the steps Nixon and Kissinger took away from traditional containment seem less impressive than they did over twenty years ago when it looked as if the "evil empire" would last forever.

At another level, however, Nixon's legacy in foreign affairs goes far beyond his or Kissinger's attempts to control the bureaucracy by restructuring the executive branch of government. Nixon's broad foreign policy concepts remain the only comprehensive attempt to construct a new cold war consensus for the 1970s. His early postpresidential books, *The Real War, The Real Peace,* and *No More Vietnams,* all implied that détente and other geopolitical maneuvers of his administration were only examples of containment by another name. But at the time, regardless of Nixon's later reassessment of them in light of the Iranian and Afghanistan crises, these policies held out the hope that the United States could wage the cold war differently than it had since 1945. Instead, those who managed U.S. foreign policy for the remainder of the 1970s, including Ford and Kissinger, Carter and Brzezinski, proved unable to build this delicate balance between containment and détente into a new national foreign policy consensus before problems in the Middle East during the fall of 1979 encouraged a return to traditional cold warriorism. Under Reagan's "evil empire" view of the Soviet Union, détente disappeared entirely from the landscape of American diplomacy. Until the USSR began to crumble internally and loosen its grip on eastern and central Europe, détente remained, like Nixon himself, a ghost from the past, waiting in the wings to be resurrected by changing world and domestic circumstances.

Nonetheless, Nixon's diplomatic legacy is weaker than he and many others have maintained. For example, the pursuit of "peace and honor" in Vietnam failed; his Middle Eastern policy, because of Kissinger's shuttling, ended up more show than substance; he had no systematic Third World policy (outside of Vietnam); détente with the USSR soon floundered in the hands of his successors; and, likewise, the Nixon Doctrine has not prevented use of U.S. troops abroad. Only rapprochement with China remains intact. It laid the foundation for recognition, even though Nixon failed to achieve a two-China policy in the United Nations and relations between the U.S. and China continue to be problematic. This "sleeping giant" remains not only the largest Communist country in the world but also the largest market and the nation most likely to dominate the twenty-first century, despite its record on human rights. As Charles de Gaulle told Nixon in 1969: "It would be better for you to recognize China before you are obliged to do so by the growth of China."[74]

This summary is not meant to discredit Richard Nixon as a foreign policy expert both during and following his presidency; his most recent books, *In the Arena, Seize the Moment,* and *Beyond Peace,* all attest to this expertise. It is simply a reminder that the lasting and positive results of his diplomacy faded more quickly than some aspects of his domestic policies. Now that the cold war is over, his imaginative ways for fighting it from 1969 to 1974 have lost their importance as precedents, in part because they were not followed by his successors in the White House and in part because they were never designed to end the cold war—only to contain it through new tactics.

PART III

REEVALUATING
WATERGATE

9

PRELUDE TO WATERGATE: CIVIL RIGHTS VIOLATED

We are in the midst of a historic assault upon the constitutional powers of the Presidency, and unless we meet this assault directly and rebuff it, we will have presided over a constitutional revolution.

—Tom Huston to Henry Kissinger, May 23, 1970

While both the failures and the successes of the Nixon phenomenon can be explained in a variety of ways connected with his personality and flaws in the modern American presidency and political system, two other factors—the wartime mentality inside the White House and widespread domestic unrest in the United States—must also be taken into consideration. From the moment he entered the Oval Office, Nixon received alarmist advice about domestic discontent that was largely, but not exclusively, a product of the civil rights and antiwar movements. All of his closest advisers presented him with information about the situation in the country that exacerbated his normally embattled mind-set. The dominant message seemed to be that the nation faced domestic crisis and chaos in 1969.

The administration modeled its response to domestic unrest largely on precedents it had set early in 1969 for dealing with foreign policy issues. Nixon and Kissinger developed a highly centralized, often covert response mode in foreign affairs that they quickly transferred to perceived and real domestic threats. This resulted in the restriction or violation of the civil rights of antiwar demonstrators and anyone deemed an "enemy" of the administration, in the name of national and international security. *Yet, at the same time, Nixon and some of his domestic advisers were expanding the civil rights of other groups of Americans, so these advisers appeared to play schizophrenic roles—encouraging the president to violate or invigorate civil rights, depending on the situation.* Given his aprincipled nature, it was to be expected that Nixon would demonstrate the same schizoid behavior on civil rights.

As a wartime president, Nixon and his aides trampled again and again on the civil rights of antiwar protesters and other groups and individuals critical of the government. Many works have described these actions in detail.[1] While they constitute one of the most vivid memories of the Nixon administration, the Watergate Special Prosecution Force's (WSPF) investigation of these alleged misuses of federal agencies and mistreatment of demonstrators in fact found "insufficient evidence and/or substantial legal problems mitigating against the bringing of any criminal charges."[2] This investigation focused on federal agencies such as the Internal Revenue Service and the White House "Responsiveness Program," designed in 1972 to "channel Federal grants, contracts, loans, subsidies, and other benefits to persons and organizations supporting President Nixon's reelection campaign, and to withhold such benefits from those opposing his candidacy." Subsequently, the WSPF concluded that Sam Ervin's (Dem.-N.C.) Senate Select Committee "had exaggerated the effect of the 'Responsiveness Program,'" and no criminal charges were ever filed in connection with its activities.[3]

Even before establishing the Responsiveness Program, however, the president and those closest to him regularly talked of using the IRS to audit or look into the tax-exempt status of groups, educational institutions, and think tanks opposed to the administration's policies. Murray Chotiner, an early campaign manager and old friend of Nixon's, for example, provided White House staff members with lists of names, "largely Democrats," "for the purpose of having audits commenced." And organizations ranging from the Amendment to End the War Committee to the Massachusetts Institute of Technology to the Brookings Institution were subjected to harassment by the IRS or to interference with their research contracts by the Office of Management and Budget. In the most matter-of-fact, nonchalant manner, counsel to the president John W. Dean III wrote to Egil ("Bud") Krogh, a White House assistant to Ehrlichman, about cutting off government money to Brookings: "If you want me to 'turn the spigot off' please let me know; otherwise I will assume that you are proceeding on this matter." Of course, the White House Special Investigative Unit, commonly known as the Plumbers, regularly misused IRS files for their own investigative and harassment purposes.[4]

Such abuse by the Nixon administration of the IRS to obtain the tax records of individuals in order to harass them cannot be justified, regardless of whether such activity could be successfully prosecuted or of how besieged the president might have perceived himself. Nixon later rationalized these activities by implying that the Democrats had gained access to his tax records to use against him in 1962 when he ran for governor of California and again in the 1968 presidential election. He clearly approved of this misuse, however, telling Dean in September 1972 that "I'll look forward to the time that we have the entrance to the Department of Justice and IRS totally under our control. . . . [W]e have to do it artfully so that we don't create an issue by abusing the IRS politically. . . . And, there are ways to do it. God damn it, sneak in the middle of the night."[5]

Nixon later claimed that his predecessors in the White House did the same thing and that he faced unusual bureaucratic and press hostility, but the fact is that Nixon's abuses of the IRS and other violations of civil rights began almost immediately after he took office. In one rambling conversation with L. Patrick Gray right after he had nominated him to become the permanent head of the FBI in February 1973, the president recalled his first years in office:

> you see these past four years have not been . . . easy—we've had almost
> the entire bureaucracy, including many in Defense who were opposed to
> what we were doing in Vietnam, opposed to [the secret bombing of] Cam-
> bodia, opposed to Laos, opposed to [the] May [1970 Invasion of Cambodia
> even though] it worked, and . . . incidentally, most of the White House
> staff was against . . . the December [1972 "Christmas"] bombing[s]. [M]y
> point is that with the media against you, with the bureaucracy against
> you, uh, with the professors, uh, with the church people and the rest, let
> alone Congress, it's a hard damn fight. . . . Let me tell you, there were
> times an-an-and [stuttering] and, and Lyndon Johnson told me this same
> thing, when I felt that the only person in this goddamned government who
> was standing with me was Edgar Hoover. He was the only one.[6]

It is hard to sympathize with this statement, because as a seasoned politician Nixon knew as well as anyone that the presidency would not be an easy job. What he didn't seem to know, as an aprincipled politician, was that misusing the IRS and violating the civil rights of others would not make his tenure in office any easier. Nonetheless, he remains the only modern wartime president of the United States whose administration fell, in part, because of assumed as well as actual violation of individual rights. Obviously it also fell because of the criminal and civil prosecutions of some of those working for the White House and because the president obstructed justice.

That Nixon could not "get away with" such activity as his predecessors had, even though the country was at war and all but twenty months of his five and a half years in office were spent, does not excuse his constitutional transgressions. That members of Reagan's administration, and Reagan himself, could "get away with" even more egregious constitutional violations in the Iran-contra affair in time of *peace* says much about the disintegration of the American political system since Nixon occupied the White House.

The constitutional specialist Michael Belknap has argued that "Johnson and Nixon were merely following in the footsteps of Lincoln, Roosevelt, and Truman. They were implementing concepts accepted, and even applauded by most lawyers, scholars, and politicians before the Vietnam debacle itself called them into question. Thus condemning Johnson and Nixon for unconstitutional conduct is scapegoating—it personalizes responsibility for a national mistake."[7] Whether one agrees with this specific argument about Vietnam, a "semi-war" in the name of the cold war had been conducted for almost three decades on a "semi-constitutional basis" before Nixon became president.[8]

Until the mid-1960s only a few knowledgeable Americans knew about constitutional violations incurred in the battle against communism under various presidents since World War II, and they were, for the most part, either morally indifferent or ideologically enthusiastic. Most Americans, however, remained largely ignorant of the escalating illegal activities of the CIA, the increased spying on U.S. citizens by the FBI, and the clandestine plans for overthrowing foreign governments or assassinating their leaders under Presidents Truman, Eisenhower, Kennedy, and Johnson. As the war in Vietnam dragged on with no clear-cut victory in sight, more and more Americans became aware for the first time of the inherent dangers to the Constitution in the methods for conducting U.S. foreign policy that had evolved over the decades of the cold war.

The United States has never fought a war without violating the constitutional rights of its citizens. Vietnam was no exception. What was exceptional was the increased sensitivity of people toward violations of the Constitution in the conducting of foreign and domestic policy. Many had their consciousness raised about such violations because of their association with the civil rights movement of the late 1950s and 1960s. Nixon assumed office as a wartime president. As far as the White House was concerned, a wartime atmosphere prevailed that warranted traditional wartime violations of the Constitution.

It is easy to forget that a wartime atmosphere prevailed *in the White House as well as across the country* at the beginning of the Nixon administration. Unlike other military conflicts, Vietnam became the first war since the Civil War that seriously divided public opinion and, more important, divided the elite opinion makers under Johnson. Nixon realized he had a great domestic and foreign policy opportunity because the post–World War II consensus had broken down by the end of the 1960s. What he did not appreciate was that, because of divisions at the highest levels of government and society, he could not enjoy this opportunity for innovative action in wartime with the same constitutional immunity as earlier wartime presidents had.

By 1969 the fighting in Vietnam had been going on inconsequentially for too many years. Thus a significant and vocal portion of the population began to question the White House and Congress about it. The scattered, often regionally isolated cases of antiwar protests begun during Johnson's administration became nationally coordinated and epidemic by the time Nixon took office. More important than the demonstrations was the fact that public-opinion leaders across the country and an elite group of opinion makers during the second Johnson administration began to disagree with one another. It would prove easier for Nixon to unite the American people behind his efforts to end the war, and even behind certain domestic policies, than it would to reunite these elite opinion makers as he wound down the war. Nixon's real problem, and the reason he could not get away with wartime actions that disregarded the Constitution, as other presidents had, was that his opposition consisted of a substantial group of influential bureaucrats, policy makers, opinion leaders, and, of course, students. Largely white and middle class with draft-exempt status, these students also constituted an elite group of future American leaders.

One of the least analyzed ironies of the Nixon administration is that Vietnamization did bring American soldiers home, but the war became even *more* unpopular as fewer and fewer American lives were lost. Among other things, antiwar groups thought that Vietnamization was a way to prolong rather than end the war. Of course, this angered the president and made him even more paranoid about his various opponents. The opposition solidified rather than diminished as the war dragged on. If Nixon had ended the war in Vietnam as soon as possible, he might have also ended his harassment of these groups and undercut a major source of opposition to his other foreign and domestic policies. (Why he didn't is discussed in chapter 7.)

If he ever intended to deal successfully with these opinion leaders and opinion makers, Nixon had to reestablish consensus at both the public and elite levels. His election victory in 1972 represented a partial success with the former, but it did nothing to bring around the disaffected elite groups that every president has to have behind him, especially in time of war. The fact that most of these disaffected elites came from the ranks of Democrats made their antiwar efforts all the more suspect. As the political commentator Nicholas von Hoffman has said: "Nixon was the first American President since Lincoln to guide the nation through a war that fundamentally divided the ruling classes."[9] Lincoln, after all, had closed down newspapers and suspended writs of habeas corpus to keep Copperheads, or Peace Democrats who opposed his war policy, in jail during the Civil War. Nixon did not have the luxury of such direct unconstitutional actions because the civil war he faced was in Vietnam, not the United States. His paranoia about antiwar activists was no less than Lincoln's, however, and some would claim that Nixon acted as though those in opposition to the war were, indeed, fomenting civil war in the United States. He probably came to believe that it would be easier to fight an incipient civil war at home than the one in Vietnam.

In fact, there was a civil war going on among the American opinion leaders. Since Lincoln wartime presidents had traditionally silenced dissent and attacked with impunity such powerless groups as first- and second-generation European immigrants, self-proclaimed Socialists and Communists, and Japanese-Americans. Nixon, in contrast, had to take on the so-called best and brightest among powerful policy-making groups. His unique situation raises an interesting question: What realistic avenues are open to any president who challenges an influential segment of the eastern establishment? The better part of wisdom would have been to end the Vietnam War quickly, to neutralize the dissension among and criticism by the best and brightest. Instead, Nixon chose a much more problematic course: to engage them in overt and covert combat. Before

Watergate he and his subordinates developed three basic ways to do this: through intelligence gathering and harassment, black-bag jobs, and cover-up. These tactics made Watergate an accident waiting to happen.

COUNTERING CHAOS WITH CHAOS
AND DOMESTIC SURVEILLANCE

It is difficult to convey the myriad counterculture attitudes of the 1960s that culminated in massive demonstrations against both the Johnson and Nixon administrations. Neither president, nor their advisers, appeared to understand the depths of legitimate disaffection over foreign and domestic policy that had arisen in the course of the decade. One of Nixon's most liberal advisers, Pat Moynihan, for example, told the president that the "primary problem of American society continues to be . . . the eroding authority of the principal institutions of government and society." Citing the trial of the Chicago Seven, who led the mass demonstration at the Democratic National Convention in 1968, as "an almost total victory for the forces of disorder," Moynihan asserted that there was an increase in "organized terrorism, of a more or less classic Nihilist pattern of upper-class youth blowing up symbols of their parents' authority." Then he warned the president: "Do not doubt that there is a struggle going on in this country of the kind the Germans used to call a *Kulturkampf*. . . . [There] is the growing conviction among critics of the left that the present era [in the United States] can be compared to the Weimar Republic in Germany. . . . It may be that the traditional culture of the nation['s silent majority] is so demoralized that it will never fight back."[10]

By the time Moynihan wrote these words to Nixon, in November 1970, the president had already decided to take action on behalf of the silent majority with a series of illegal actions in the name of international, national, and local security. He had heard the same kind of description about the state of the country from FBI director J. Edgar Hoover and Henry Kissinger, to say nothing of lesser advisers such as Patrick Buchanan and Tom Huston. Nixon was bombarded with statements about the American people being unwilling to admit that "their children could wish to destroy their country," and about the government's need for a "plan which will enable us to curtail the illegal activities of those who are determined to destroy our society." The student radical was "a paradox because he is difficult to judge by the normal standards of civilized life. At heart, he's a revolutionist, an anarchist, a nihilist. His main reason for being is to destroy, blindly and indiscriminately, to tear down and provoke chaos. . . . They conceive of themselves as the catalyst of destruction—bring to death a society they so bitterly hate." Or, as Kissinger summed the situation up for the president: "What was at stake here was the problem of authority in this society altogether."[11]

The alliteration "from Whittier to Watergate," referring to Nixon's California hometown,[12] might more appropriately have been "from Weimar to Watergate" because both Kissinger and Nixon (and others in the White House) made the negative comparison between the weak political leadership and cultural disarray in Germany in the 1920s and that of the United States in the 1970s. It is too bad they did not also consider what happened to Germany in the 1930s when Hitler and the Nazis began to scheme and plot in undemocratic and illegal ways to fight those who opposed them and their policies.

The emotionally fearful atmosphere that permeated the halls of the White House, the Pentagon, and the FBI in the late 1960s and early 1970s under both Johnson and Nixon was generated largely by the words: leaks to the press and demonstrations. "Leaks can kill you," LBJ told Nixon in a private briefing on December 12, 1968, "and even with all the precautions I take, things still leak." Nixon, with the help of the FBI and Hoover, hoped to stop both during his first administration. He was ultimately much more successful in handling antiwar demonstrations, largely because of withdrawal of U.S. troops from Vietnam, than he ever was with the problem of leaks. According to Nixon's own estimation, during his first five months in office there were twenty-one serious leaks from National Security Council files, and a total of forty-five his first year in office. He faced foreign policy as well as domestic policy leaks, according to Huston, by "people attempting to use the press to embarrass the president from doing something which they find ideologically offensive." Nixon's personal files, the memoranda he wrote Haldeman, and many of the released tapes are fraught with references to leaks, the urgent need to stop them, and the need to stop the press from reporting them.[13]

Nixon invented his own extraconstitutional ways of harassing individual members of the media, such as Joseph Kraft and Daniel Schorr,[14] but it was Johnson who provided him with one of the first vehicles he used to combat not only leaks but the other major problem: demonstrations sponsored by "national leftist groups or individuals." In 1967 the CIA had created, with Johnson's approval, a program called Operation CHAOS. Although the original purpose of the group was to ferret out information about foreign support for dissident groups in the United States, by the time Johnson left office it had gone beyond the "clandestine collection abroad of information on foreign . . . efforts to support/encourage/exploit domestic extremes and dissidence in the United States."[15] Under Nixon, Operation CHAOS became a CIA tool for obtaining information indirectly on domestic dissident groups, especially after the Huston Plan failed to become operational. Another Johnson creation that Nixon used with relish was the army's domestic intelligence system, known by the computer acronym CONUS (Continental United States).

The Kissinger Wiretaps

By the summer of 1970, national security leaks still abounded despite heightened background checks, physical surveillance, and seventeen White House–authorized wiretaps installed by the FBI, without court-ordered warrants, on the telephones of friends and associates of Kissinger. Alexander Haig acted as the liaison between the head of the NSC and the FBI in delivering the names of those suspected of leaking foreign policy information. Four of these so-called Kissinger wiretaps were put on the phones of newsmen and the other thirteen on those of staff members of the NSC and the State and Defense Departments. In 1969 and 1970 these taps were technically legal, according to the 1968 Omnibus Crime bill (and Attorney General Mitchell advised Nixon of their legality), under presidential power to protect national security. A Watergate Special Prosecution Task Force report ultimately concluded that "none of seventeen wiretaps can be shown to be based solely on national security grounds. . . . For the most part these taps appear to be an exercise in bureaucratic infighting and, in some cases, partisan, intelligence gathering."[16]

The working papers of the Watergate Special Prosecutor Force contain the most damning summary of Kissinger's and Haig's roles in these warrantless wiretaps against individual citizens. In 1972 the Supreme Court declared the presidential doctrine in the crime bill unconstitutional when applied to individual citizens. In contrast to Kissinger's statements in his memoirs and under oath—in which he hedged his direct involvement and denied having read the letters prepared from the logs of these taps or the logs themselves—in a May 20, 1969, letter to Hoover, William C. Sullivan, head of the FBI's Domestic Intelligence Division, wrote that Kissinger and Haig had come to his office, where

Kissinger "read all the logs." Kissinger then commented to Sullivan: "it is clear that I don't have anybody in my office that I can trust except Colonel Haig here." He further told Sullivan that he was under great pressure to adopt a soft line on foreign policy, but that he was not going to do so. Before leaving Sullivan's office, Kissinger said that he wanted the taps to continue on four of the people and that he would be adding two more to the list because "what he is learning [from the taps] as a result of this coverage is extremely helpful to him while at the same time disturbing."[17] He has claimed under oath that he had little interest in this information, that no analyses of these reports were made by his staff, and that he did not initiate any of these wiretaps, discuss them, or use the information they contained in any substantive way, despite Haig's testimony to the contrary.[18]

However, the problem of proof for the lawsuits brought against those who initiated the wiretaps rested on showing "criminal intent" on the part of the participants (none of whom were about to confess to such intent). Since the White House tapping system had not yet been installed whereby such intent could have been shown, the WSPF closed its investigation of the Kissinger wiretaps.[19] Needless to say, no information of any significance about leaks or anything else was ever obtained from these early wiretaps or any of the subsequent bungled break-ins by the Plumbers. Yet Nixon's obsession with leaks (both those he controlled and those he did not) knew no bounds, and his papers and tapes are replete with references to them.[20]

The country seemed to be disintegrating in 1970. The FBI reported three thousand bombings and fifty thousand bomb threats; campuses remained in uproar for several months over Nixon's invasion of Cambodia and the subsequent student deaths at Kent State and Jackson State universities. Against this background of increasing paranoia about societal disorder and about foreign policy leaks because so much secret diplomacy was being conducted, a "siege mentality" was fed rather than tempered by all of Nixon's major and minor advisers. Little wonder that the president decided that the FBI was not doing an adequate job in tracking down leakers or obtaining information about individuals or groups opposing the administration's policies.

Hoover had always considered the Kissinger wiretaps so "dangerous" and potentially "explosive" if ever discovered that he did not enter them on the department's electronic surveillance computer system (ELSUR). When Hoover refused to tap the phone of the journalist Joseph Kraft, Haldeman hired his own private investigator—Jack Caulfield, a former New York City police officer who had served in a security capacity for the 1968 Nixon campaign—to carry out the president's orders. Despite the fact that Hoover had used the FBI since 1968 to harass and disrupt the antiwar, black militant, and radical student groups through several COINTELPROs, his efforts were not enough for the Nixon White House by the summer of 1970. The very secrecy of, especially, the Black Panther COINTELPRO (*Counter Intel*ligence *Pro*ject) prevented Hoover from considering further expansion of this already intensely "dirty war" against African-American radicals that had begun under Johnson. By the fall of 1971, Nixon was privately talking to Attorney General Mitchell about how they could persuade Hoover to resign. They agreed that he was "too old" and "getting senile," but the president noted that, like Vice President Agnew, who was becoming "a liability more than an asset," both men had to resign voluntarily—"to go of his own volition . . . and that's why we're in a hell of a problem."[21]

Hoover's expansion of the domestic intelligence system in the 1960s had always occurred within the well-defined parameters of the FBI director's own anti-Communist philosophy. For Hoover, "the real threat to the country [w]as a radical upswing aided by the Soviet Union." So his entire surveillance system was designed as a permanent bulwark against foreign espionage and the long-term threat of a resurgent international Communist movement. It had little to do with domestic partisan politics or protection of the covert diplomacy of the Nixon administration. Hoover's philosophy had outer limits that he would not breach for fear of destroying the FBI through shortsighted misuse of its already questionable antiradical tactics. Also, he had been FBI director too long (almost fifty years) to put his intelligence-gathering powers at the disposal of other agencies of government or, as it turned out, the White House. These philosophical and territorial limitations also guaranteed that Hoover would refuse a final attempt by the White House in March 1972 to engage the FBI in its purely domestic political intrigues. Consequently, a little less than two months before his death, Hoover refused to "doctor" FBI documentary evidence in an antitrust suit revealing that Mitchell had told the ITT lobbyist Dita Beard that the suit could be "fixed" for a campaign donation of $400,000.[22]

The Huston Plan for Domestic Surveillance

Long before this last act of defiance, however, Nixon had decided that the FBI was not cracking down hard enough on domestic radicals. Following the campus outbursts and deaths over the invasion of Cambodia, Nixon called together the directors of all the intelligence agencies to tell them they were performing so badly that he had approved a reorganization plan designed by a twenty-nine-year-old midwestern lawyer named Tom Charles Huston—who had been trained, interestingly enough, at the army's intelligence school at Fort Holabird, Maryland, where the CONUS blacklist files on "subversives" were generated. After moonlighting during the 1968 campaign by helping to set up the Nixon Youth Program while serving in the army as an intelligence officer, he was hired by Pat Buchanan to prepare news summaries for the administration. He ultimately rose to the position of associate counsel to the president. This former head of the Young Americans for Freedom soon began to do odd jobs for Haldeman, including organizing the administration's attempt to use the IRS illegally against its presumed enemies.[23] Among other things, he (like John Dean after him) aspired to become the Henry Kissinger of domestic intelligence, because "intelligence gathering was clearly the key to power in the Nixon White House," as clearly demonstrated by Kissinger, Haig, Haldeman, and Ehrlichman. Huston devised a plan for coordinating the work of all the intelligence agencies (Hoover no longer even communicated with the CIA) against the forces of the "New Left," and one of the first jobs Haldeman gave Dean when he started working for the White House was to evaluate it.[24]

Why Nixon (or anyone else) ever listened to Huston's half-baked ideas had always been a mystery to me until Nixon's recently released papers began to show how well ensconced Huston was within the most paranoid elements of the White House hierarchy of advisers. Huston's obvious emulation of Kissinger also stood him in good stead, as did his close relationships with Sullivan and Robert Mardian, the assistant attorney general in charge of the Justice Department's internal security division. The Huston Plan was not simply Nixon's or even Huston's paranoia run amok. It represented a segment of Republican establishment whose fear of social and political chaos outweighed their normal respect for individual rights free from government interference—after all, Huston claimed to be both a Jeffersonian Republican *and* a strict constructionist when it came to interpreting the U.S. Constitution on other issues.[25] Perhaps that was the problem. Like Jefferson once he became president, Huston did not practice what he preached about the Constitution once inside the White House.

After receiving Nixon's reprimand on June 5, the heads of the government's intelligence community representing the FBI, the Defense Intelligence Agency (DIA), the National Security Agency (NSA), and the CIA dutifully began to consider a report to the president recommending "an integrated approach to the coverage of domestic unrest," otherwise known as the Huston Plan. There is no doubt that at one level it represented an attempt to channel what was perceived to be waning anticommunism (prompted in part by the Nixon administration's rapprochement with China and détente with the USSR) into a broad mainstream cultural campaign aimed at alleged internal subversion. Although it was not explicitly stated, the CIA's role in this reorganization "would have been to contribute foreign intelligence and counterintelligence" in violation of the National Security Act of 1947, which stated that the CIA had no "police, subpoena, law-enforcement powers, or internal security functions." Since 1967 the CIA had been violating this directive by complying with a request from the NSC under Johnson to assess the "possible foreign links with American dissident student groups," such as the Students for Democratic Society (SDS). This was the CIA's Operation CHAOS.[26]

Beginning in January 1970, reports began to be leaked in New York and Washington that the U.S. Army had been used since 1966 to spy on practically every politically active group outside the Democratic and Republican parties. This information came from Christopher Pyle, a former military intelligence officer. According to Pyle, the CONUS operation included over one thousand undercover agents working out of more than three hundred offices nationwide, and kept thousands of files on secret computers at the army's intelligence school at Fort Holabird. This facility went so far as to circulate a pamphlet (nicknamed "Blacklist") of some of these names to its operatives in the field in order to help identify "people who might cause trouble for the Army."[27]

Nothing might have come of Pyle's exposure of this domestic surveillance system set up by the army under Johnson had Senator Sam Ervin not decided to conduct a public investigation when the Nixon administration did not respond cooperatively to his inquiries about it. Attorney General Mitchell used the same arguments that he had when justifying the earlier wiretaps: spying on domestic political activity was in the purview of the federal government's duty to protect internal security. Inside the

White House, Huston used Ervin's criticisms and inquiries to push for greater "coordination within the intelligence community." This proved to be a major mistake; such stonewalling motivated Ervin to begin the first congressional investigation of intelligence agencies whose powers had increased during the cold war with presidential approval. Had the Nixon administration not been involved in so many other covert activities, it might have welcomed Ervin's attempt to "bring out evidence of how the Democratic administration [of LBJ] had permitted the Army to spy on civilians."[28] But such was not the case.

The formal investigation of CONUS that Ervin launched from the Senate in 1971 allowed him to pursue several lifelong goals of his own. As a conservative and strict constitutionalist who defended a very narrow combination of civil and privacy rights in the name of liberty (as long as these concepts were not extended to women or African-Americans), he wanted to use the hearings to promote public awareness of the importance of protecting against attempts at "political control and intimidation which is alien to a society of *free men.*" He also had long championed limiting the expanding cold war powers of the president, which had taken place at the expense of Congress. Finally, Ervin became unhappy with the administration over certain domestic issues such as its proposal for welfare reform, its handling of school desegregation in the South, and the fact that in the course of 1970–71 Nixon had, for all intents and purposes, abandoned any serious pursuit of the southern strategy with which he had initially courted Ervin and other conservative senators such as Barry Goldwater, John Tower, Strom Thurmond, and J. William Fulbright. More important, these investigations set this reactionary, racist, and sexist senator on a path that would make him the darling of liberals during the famous Senate Watergate hearings, which he also chaired.[29]

From these earlier hearings Ervin learned both the tactics and the strategy he would employ to investigate Watergate. The issues were essentially the same: violating privacy rights through surveillance, blacklisting, and pulling partisan tricks ranging from dirty to illegal. As a conservative, Ervin must have enjoyed the irony of receiving political accolades from liberals while playing the hero in the theatrical drama of a down-home, country lawyer investigating an "imperial" Republican president for authorizing a domestic-surveillance policy originally established by a liberal Democrat.

After inheriting Johnson's policy of investigating the foreign ties of student groups through CHAOS and his creation of the army's domestic surveillance program, CONUS, Nixon expanded the activities of both into a massive domestic spy system, convinced that the demonstrations, leaks, and bombings warranted such action. Just about everything he read or heard from his advisers reinforced his suspicions about the civil war he faced at home, especially from Communist instigation of campus unrest. For example, the *Wall Street Journal* on May 27, 1969, recommended that the administration take strong steps to quell campus disorders. Referring to Lincoln's attempts to keep the nation together before the Civil War, this publication said that Nixon faced an even harder task because he, unlike Lincoln, "must save the Union not from a civil but a guerrilla war." Nixon had been confronted, after all, with antiwar demonstrators on the day of his inauguration, before he had even assumed power and responsibility as president. Immediately afterward he ordered John Ehrlichman to give him a report about why and how things got so "screwed up" in the police action taken against those protesters. In particular, Nixon thought that "an opportunity was missed" when the demonstrators at his inauguration were not removed before they got out of hand, because "people would have supported strong action."[30]

By the fall of 1969 he and his staff (along with the D.C. police and the National Guard) were better prepared for the Vietnam Moratorium demonstration, one of the largest antiwar marches in Washington, D.C. From its perspective, the Nixon administration made few "screw ups" in countering the antiwar movement for the remainder of 1969 (and, indeed, through 1972)—except for the volatile May Day protests of 1970 (in the wake of the incursion into Cambodia and the student deaths at Kent State and Jackson State), when over ten thousand people were arrested in Washington, D.C., over a four-day period and placed in stadiums and other large holding areas in the district. Most of these arrests were thrown out by the courts on the grounds that they violated the demonstrators' civil rights. But generally the tactics of systematically removing or excluding opponents of the Nixon administration from public appearances by the president, of infiltrating radical organizations, and of using tear gas and other crowd control tactics against demonstrators contained the protests. While all these charges were investigated by the WSPF, *none were prosecuted.*[31] When Nixon and some of his advisers endorsed the Huston Plan, they obviously had students in mind even though the president's 1971 announcement ending the draft probably had more to do with breaking the cycle of protests than any of the administration's extralegal plots and plans. Moreover, at extremely emotional demonstrations, like those of May 1970, none of the administration's crowd control or other purported antidemonstrator schemes worked and it had to resort to mass arrests.

Ironically, as the activities of Hoover's COINTELPROs intensified in the late 1960s in the name of saving the country from communism, the resulting CIA assessment concluded that "there is no convincing evidence of control, manipulation, sponsorship, or significant financial support of student dissidents by any international Communist authority." This did not prevent the CIA, however, from gathering counterintelligence information on almost ten thousand Americans at home and abroad, which it turned over to the FBI. In March 1974 this program was terminated because "some CIA employees" had "misinterpreted [the agency's counterintelligence functions] as being more focused on American dissidents than on their possible connections with foreign governments." In a few individual cases the CIA actually "recruited or inserted individuals into American dissident circles to establish their credentials for operation abroad against those foreign elements which might be supporting, encouraging, or directing dissidence in the United States."[32]

On June 8, 1970, the heads of the intelligence agencies met once again to work out the details of the Huston Plan. In the next two weeks a proposal for a "permanent interagency committee on intelligence" was fleshed out that would have placed few legal restrictions on the president's options for dealing with domestic unrest, including mail opening, burglaries, electronic surveillance, and campus informants. Huston and Sullivan also recommended that the former head the new secret interagency committee, which would have made Huston director of domestic intelligence. When Hoover saw the details of the Huston Plan on June 23, he said he would not sign it because of the lack of restrictions on various surveillance activities. He was no longer willing to "accept the responsibility" for carrying out activities authorized by the White House alone. He also adamantly opposed the idea that the new intelligence committee would "coordinate intelligence originating with this committee in the same manner as Dr. Henry Kissinger, Assistant to the President, coordinates foreign intelligence on behalf of the President." Two days later, the day set for the formal signing of the Special Report Interagency Committee on Intelligence (Ad Hoc), Hoover insisted on going over the forty-three-page report page by page, footnoting his own comments. No one listening to his objections had any way of knowing that the FBI director was already rethinking his own surveillance operations and would terminate all the COINTELPROs less than a year later "for security reasons because of their sensitivity."[33] The heart of the FBI's domestic security system since 1956, the era of COINTELPROs was passing, only to be exposed soon after by the Watergate investigations.

Despite Hoover's "footnotes" objecting to most of the Huston Plan's major provisions, Huston and Sullivan strongly recommended it to the president. Nixon approved its most extreme segments on July 14, because he "felt they were necessary and justified by the violence we faced." But he did not formally sign the Huston Plan, possibly to keep himself "legally uninvolved" with the report. This sealed its fate as much as Hoover's objections to it and Attorney General Mitchell's concurrence with them. When Nixon and Haldeman told Huston to sign the order implementing the plan, it became clear to the intelligence community "what a hot potato it was," and with Mitchell speaking for Hoover, the president withdrew his approval on July 28. All that Huston and Sullivan were able to salvage from their efforts was the establishment on December 3, 1970, of a powerless Interagency Evaluation Committee, coordinated by John Dean but chaired by Mardian. Nixon followed this up with a memorandum on December 21, once again expressing his concern to all intelligence directors over the proliferation of sensitive intelligence data through the news media. Hoover refused to cooperate with this committee too, and Huston left the White House staff on June 18, 1971, after a departing meeting with Nixon, conveniently arranged by Dean.[34] With visions of Henry Kissinger dancing in his head, Dean continued to use this Interagency Evaluation Committee to build an intelligence power base from which to serve his own needs and ambitions, as well as those of the 1972 presidential campaign.

Nixon's subsequent rationalization for initially approving the Huston Plan pale beside the extremism of the document for carrying out unrestricted domestic surveillance. Insisting that the "program did not involve the use of any measures not previously employed under federal law," he tried to compare the debate its revelation caused to Roosevelt's incarceration of the Japanese and Lincoln's suspension of habeas corpus. "The irony of the controversy over the Huston Plan," he later wrote in his memoirs, "did not become apparent until a 1975 investigation revealed that the investigative techniques it would have involved had not only been carried out long before I approved the plan but continued to be carried out after I had rescinded my approval of it."[35] In the atmosphere of chaos and crisis that had been established in the White House by the end of

1970, however, the stage had been set for overreaction. Little wonder that when Daniel Ellsberg, government consultant and former Vietnam War hawk, leaked the Pentagon Papers to the press in June 1971, hysteria prevailed among Nixon's advisers.

THE PENTAGON PAPERS AS CATALYST FOR CRIMINAL ACTIVITY

As just discussed, the first wiretaps of the Nixon administration on the friends, acquaintances, and employees of Henry Kissinger, and a few members of the press, were undertaken in the name of national security. Likewise, the first break-in by the Plumbers at the office of Ellsberg's psychiatrist had nothing to do with partisan politics, but with the release to the press of four thousand pages of classified documents critical of U.S. policy in Vietnam from the 1950s through the Johnson administration, commonly known as the Pentagon Papers. To meet the almost hysterical demands of Nixon and Kissinger to punish Ellsberg for photocopying and leaking this information, the Plumbers' unit undertook its first illegal "black-bag" job with Ehrlichman's specific approval. He gave the go-ahead to Bud Krogh and David Young—a former member of the Domestic Council staff and Kissinger protégé who had become co-commander, with Ehrlichman, of the Plumbers—when he said to them on August 11, 1971: "If [it can be] done with your assurances that it is not traceable." The idea for the proposed break-in came from Young on the advice of E. Howard Hunt, one of the original Plumbers, and Charles Colson, a special assistant to the president.[36] On September 3, 1971, the Plumbers burglarized the office of Dr. Lewis Fielding in the hope of obtaining Ellsberg's psychiatric files. This burglary was the first in a string of criminal actions undertaken by the Plumbers—most of which ended in failure.

When the *New York Times* began publishing the Pentagon Papers in June 1971, Sullivan's relationship with J. Edgar Hoover at FBI headquarters, which had started to deteriorate in the wake of the abortive Huston Plan, continued its downward spiral. Sullivan had attached himself to Alexander Haig, then a brigadier general and Kissinger's deputy, and began to try to discredit his longtime boss. Although the FBI quickly ascertained that the Pentagon Papers had been leaked by Daniel Ellsberg acting alone, the White House did not believe Hoover was pushing the investigation hard enough. In particular, Kissinger, probably overestimating his importance as a part-time adviser on Vietnam policy for both

Kennedy and Johnson, feared that the Pentagon Papers would reveal the quite different advice he now gave Nixon. Also, Ellsberg was a former student and academic colleague of Kissinger and later an NSC staffer who became a RAND Corporation consultant on the NSSM 1, evaluating U.S. policy in Vietnam. Because of their previously close association, Kissinger felt obliged to wage a "furious campaign" against him within the White House to prove his own trustworthiness. He described Ellsberg to the president as the "brightest student" he had ever had, who had "flipped [from a] hawk to a peacenik" and "always was a little unbalanced." Additionally, Kissinger feared that the publicity generated by the publishing of the Pentagon Papers would have a negative impact on his own covert and overt negotiations with China, the USSR, and North Vietnam. For a variety of self-interested reasons, therefore, Kissinger stressed that this leak constituted an extreme national security risk—although the documents did not deal with the Nixon administration or the president personally.[37] Once again, it can be asked whether this national security adviser served Nixon's best interests.

On the other hand, Nixon did not need much convincing about the national security risk posed by the publication of the Pentagon Papers. Ellsberg and his purloined documents symbolized all the leaks plaguing Nixon since he took office. In July, when the *New York Times* carried a leaked story about the U.S. bargaining position at the SALT I talks by William Beecher, the same reporter who had revealed the secret bombing of Cambodia two years earlier, Nixon became livid. In a repetitious and almost incoherent diatribe, he ordered Haldeman, Ehrlichman, and Krogh to begin conducting polygraph tests of all government bureaucrats with top-security clearance. While this presidential edict was never carried out, it set a tone within the White House that encouraged illegal activities on the part of the Plumbers. In contrast to his decidedly paranoid reaction at the time, Nixon later calmly rationalized his opposition to the publication of the Pentagon Papers by giving these three reasons for it: (1) antiwar critics would use evidence about the Kennedy and Johnson policy in Vietnam "to attack my goals and my [other] policies [such as the secret negotiations with China and the Soviet Union]"; (2) the documents were classified and would set a bad precedent for other disgruntled government officials to release similar documents; and (3) their release could harm past or present CIA informants and have a chilling impact on obtaining future information.[38]

In the summer of 1971, while Nixon and especially Kissinger were reacting frantically to the leak of the Pentagon Papers, Sullivan reported to both Mardian and Haig that Hoover was about to fire him and might use the "Kissinger wiretaps" to blackmail the White House if Nixon tried to remove him as director of the FBI. These wiretaps had become a prime concern because one of them, on Morton Halperin (another NSC staffer), contained several "Ellsberg overhears"—that is, Ellsberg had walked in and been taped along with Halperin. Since these tapes were not in the FBI's ELSUR (electronic surveillance) computer system, they did not show up in the Justice Department investigation of Ellsberg. The WSPF later reported that there was "some evidence to the effect that Kissinger, Haig, Haldeman and Ehrlichman as well as Sullivan and [Bernard] Wells at the FBI [a supervisor in the domestic intelligence division] would have recalled that Ellsberg had been overheard on the Halperin tap . . . due to the unusual nature of one of the two overhears . . . reported in letters to Nixon and Kissinger dated September 3, 1969."[39]

Thus, as many as six top White House and FBI personnel knew about Ellsberg's presence on the Halperin tap but withheld the information to protect the secret of the Kissinger wiretaps. This same WSPF report indicated that, indeed, a "Hoover 'threat' or 'blackmail'" possibly did occur early in August 1971, and that Mardian discussed this with Kissinger after Nixon had already ordered Mardian to retrieve these wiretap logs from Sullivan and put them in Ehrlichman's safekeeping. Hoover apparently began "tearing the place [FBI headquarters] up" after Mardian obtained the material from Sullivan, but before it was transferred to Ehrlichman, Mitchell told Nixon that he feared Hoover would "blow the safe" in Mardian's office because he "feels very insecure without having his own copy of those things because, of course, that gives him leverage with Mitchell and you."[40]

In the meantime the FBI created a false memorandum stating that Halperin had never been the subject of a wiretap.[41] The handling of the Pentagon Papers was key to the transformation of the Plumbers into an illegal unit within the White House and led White House staff to lie under oath and even to the president himself.[42] It also set the stage for the administration to undertake a cover-up—not of its activities directed at external enemies but of an embarrassing case of spying within the executive branch itself.

THE EXECUTIVE BRANCH SPIES ON ITSELF

As if the leaking of the Pentagon Papers and details of the SALT I negotiations were not enough to rattle nerves and common sense within the White House, on December 14, 1971, Ehrlichman and two of his Domestic Council aides, Krogh and Young, made a startling discovery. Yeoman Charles Radford of the U.S. Navy had pilfered hundreds of documents from NSC files and turned them over to Admiral Robert O. Welander, a liaison between the NSC and the JCS. Welander, in turn, gave them to the chair of the JCS, Admiral Thomas Moorer. Ehrlichman and his aides then became even more paranoid about leaks of top-secret foreign policy information. Krogh apparently thought this spying activity in behalf of the JCS might mark the beginning of a military coup because of the interference it represented "into the deliberations of duly-elected and appointed civilians to carry out foreign policy."[43] According to Radford, an aide to both Haig and Kissinger, the Joint Chiefs of Staff spied on the National Security Council (NSC) during 1970–71 as part of a military intelligence operation aimed at "bringing Nixon down. Really, getting rid of Kissinger—Kissinger was a real monkey wrench in things."[44] Whether this is true, the incident set in motion a cover-up. Once again, without Kissinger's highly visible and controversial presence in the Nixon administration, the complex web of spying and wiretapping might not have become such standard procedure by those inside and outside the White House.

The Radford-Moorer incident highlighted the conflict Nixon already knew he faced: government departments, including the military, totally distrusted him and his top foreign policy adviser. Instead of confronting the JCS directly after Admiral Welander confessed (twice) to ordering Radford to spy on the NSC, Nixon decided not to fire or discipline Moorer, primarily for political and diplomatic considerations. Basically he did not want a military scandal to upset the foreign policy triumphs he had planned for 1972 or his reelection, which he thought depended on them. Since his diplomacy had come to depend so much on Kissinger's back-channel activities, any exposure of spying on the part of the JCS could possibly reveal these covert diplomatic moves—one of which was that Pakistan was serving as a conduit to the People's Republic of China. Nixon also worried that exposure would further undermine morale in the military, already depressed by his Vietnamization policy and the antiwar movement. Finally, exposure of military surveillance of the NSC would be embarrassing, to say the least, in an election year.[45]

Haig, who tried to protect Welander (and himself) throughout the White House's investigation of the matter, ended up being protected from Kissinger's wrath by the president, who told Ehrlichman, "Don't let K[issinger] blame Haig." But Nixon did not suspect that Haig's first allegiance—according to Len Colodny and Robert Gettlin—was not to Nixon but to the military establishment, as represented by the Joint Chiefs of Staff. In *Silent Coup,* Colodny and Gettlin document that Haig's friend and colleague Fred Buzhardt interviewed Welander a second time (after he had admitted assigning Radford to spy on Kissinger), in order to eliminate compromising references to Haig in the admiral's first confession. Not knowing this when he covered up the Radford-Moorer incident, Nixon later appointed Haig his chief of staff, on the advice of Colson, among others, in 1973 when the president was involved in the much bigger cover-up of Watergate.[46] A fox guarding the henhouse, Haig was determined not to let any investigation of Watergate expose his involvement in the early wiretap or his spying connections to the JCS. This would considerably complicate his role after Nixon's resignation, when Haig became an adviser to President Ford.

One thing is perfectly clear (to use a Nixonian expression today's students no longer recognize), and that is that the White House, the NSC, and the Joint Chiefs of Staff should never have used wiretaps or private investigators or double agents in any capacity to spy on other members of the administration for national security or other reasons, because all this activity, regardless of its legality, had to be covered up again and again—which, in turn, encouraged more and more such actions and more and more opportunities for leaks. The cover-up of the Ellsberg break-in, for example, set the entire byzantine process in motion that climaxed with the Watergate break-in. This cover-up succeeded until February 1973, according to Colodny and Gettlin, when Haig told Bob Woodward and Carl Bernstein of the *Washington Post* about the Halperin-Ellsberg tap as part of the White House's investigation of the Pentagon Papers leak. He did this in order to "lead the reporters away from the NSC [spying incident]," since Haig's role in the Radford-Moorer affair would have damaged him more in the eyes of the president than the one he played in the Kissinger wiretaps. Another way in which Haig consolidated his own position as Nixon's chief of staff following the resignations of Haldeman and Ehrlichman consisted of bringing Buzhardt into the White House to assist Leonard Garment in Nixon's defense. As long as Buzhardt remained general counsel to the Defense Department, he controlled his own confidential Pentagon file that contained all reports on the Radford-Moorer spy incident. These included his own interview with Admiral Welander without the compromising remarks made about Haig in Welander's first confession.[47] Haig's involvement with the Kissinger wire-taps and his cover-up of the attempt to spy on the NSC prompted him to deal in the same circuitous way with Nixon's secret White House tapes when the WSPF began to subpoena them and he was acting as the president's chief of staff, but without the same success.

So the cover-up circle over the Radford-Moorer matter was complete, as far as Haig was concerned, by the spring of 1973. For Nixon the incident was never over. He continued to refer to it as proof that "this country . . . this bureaucracy . . . [i]s crawling with . . . at best unloyal people and at worst treasonable people."[48] The remaining loose end was the president himself and, of course, the disposition of his presidential papers. Long before Haig publicly proclaimed himself "vicar" after President Reagan was shot, he probably felt the same way at the height of President Nixon's Watergate problems. Just as Nixon had been obsessed early in his administration with foreign policy leaks—many of which could be traced directly to Kissinger—now he was plagued with Watergate leaks to Woodward and Bernstein, which probably could be traced to Haig. In both instances, but particularly the later one, the president became dependent on two men who isolated him from less self-interested advisers and who dealt with reporters behind his back.

Many times on the recently released tape transcripts, Nixon can be found struggling to keep the details of all these covert activities straight (even the ones he knew about, let alone those he did not), especially after Haldeman and Ehrlichman began lying to him about their involvement. Many times he simply could not remember who had told him what; other times he would angrily say in various ways, as he and his two top aides tried to figure out how to wiggle out from under Watergate: "the problem of my position up to this time has been, quite frankly, nobody ever told me a goddamn thing." (It has been suggested that Nixon said these things simply because he wanted to present himself in the most innocent light on the tapes. No doubt he is self-serving in many instances because he knew he was being taped. This was especially evident in his tense conversations with John Dean. But examples of genuine confusion are also so abundant, and largely useless if meant to be used later in his own defense, that self-interest cannot explain all such statements before July 1973, when the tapings stopped. At one point, for example, Nixon, the consummate politician, could not remember whether the California presidential primary in 1972 had occurred before or after the Watergate break-ins.)[49]

In the long run, Nixon reaped what he had sown: secret machinations, aprincipledness, and a seamless web of lies and half-truths. The transcribed conversations convey a Nixon wasting considerable time and talent on matters that were beneath the office of the president, no matter how threatening he perceived the domestic political situation or how important he believed his foreign policy plans to be when he encouraged excessive and ultimately criminal activities on the part of his aides—just as Reagan was to do during the Iran-contra controversy. "Men of great power do not commit crimes," according to the historian Walter Karp; "they procure crimes without having to issue incriminating orders. A word to the servile suffices."[50]

The responses of the president and his subordinates in these three instances—the attempt to counter perceived domestic chaos, especially student unrest, with the CIA's CHAOS and the army's CONUS programs of spying and domestic surveillance and with the Huston Plan; the illegal use of the Plumbers to investigate the leak of the Pentagon Papers; and the cover-up of the embarrassing incident involving the Joint Chiefs of Staff spying on the National Security Council—presaged how (and why) Nixon and his advisers would mishandle the Watergate scandal. It cannot be doubted that these early examples of the relationship between foreign policy and civil rights violations paved the way to Watergate. Yet at the same time that the administration was digging its own grave with these tactics, it was formulating one of the most comprehensive programs for domestic reform in U.S. history and laying the groundwork for one of the most innovative periods in American foreign policy. This erratic pattern of progressive and reactionary policies continues to confound any balanced evaluation of the Nixon presidency. Clearly Nixon's use of foreign policy, specifically the cold war shibboleth of national security arguments, to rationalize violations of civil rights provided the modus operandi that ultimately led to his forced resignation over a petty partisan domestic break-in that mushroomed into Watergate. Thus, when the Nixon phenomenon ran headlong into the Watergate phenomenon, he learned the hard way that there were limits even to the enhanced power of the modern presidency.

10

WATERGATE REVISITED: POLITICS OR SEX?

We won't be happy until we cut Richard Nixon's heart out and hold it high on the summit of the Presidential pyramid while an ooh goes up from the crowd.
—Norman Mailer, May 20, 1974

W atergatitis" swept the country in 1973 and 1974 as no scandal involving the highest officials of government had since the Teapot Dome scandal in the 1920s. And for good reason. The cover-up by the president and his top aides of the original break-ins and bugging at Democratic National Committee (DNC) Headquarters located in Washington's Watergate complex in May and June 1972, and related corrupt or criminal political activities, ultimately resulted in the indictment, conviction, and sentencing of twenty men. These included the top White House aides to Nixon (John Ehrlichman and H. R. Haldeman); counsel to the president (John W. Dean III); a special assistant to the president (Charles Colson); a former cabinet member (Attorney General John Mitchell, Jr.); and others who worked for the Committee to Re-elect the President (CRP, usually referred to derogatorily as CREEP) and/or the White House Special Investigative Unit, commonly known as the Plumbers, whose members, largely under Ehrlichman's supervision, engaged in break-ins before Watergate.

Most of these men participated in the Republican reelection campaign or were presidential advisers in whom public trust, or at least Republican party trust, had been placed. A few Plumbers such as E. Howard Hunt, James McCord, and G. Gordon Liddy—all former CIA or FBI agents—were specifically employed by the White House with private funds to carry out political espionage. They in turn hired four Cubans, who were arrested in the second break-in at the Watergate complex. All served time for their participation in the burglary and bugging of the national offices of the Democratic party. The arrest of James McCord, Bernard Baker, Virgilio Gonzalez, Eugenio Martinez, and Frank Sturgis after Frank Wills, the night watchman at the Watergate, discovered adhesive tape not once, but twice, on basement doors of the expensive office and apartment complex in Washington, D.C., set off a series of events and investigations unprecedented in U.S. history. This break-in culminated in a series of political dirty tricks authorized by the CRP beginning in the fall of 1971, although it is still disputed whether the two Watergate break-ins were approved by Attorney General Mitchell or Presidential Counsel Dean. President Nixon learned of the burglars' connections with the CRP and White House personnel on June 20, 1972, and on June 23 he privately agreed with a recommendation that he thought came from Mitchell and Haldeman, but which probably originated with Dean, that the CIA should prevent an FBI investigation on grounds of national security. The CIA did not comply with the president's attempt to obstruct justice in a criminal matter and the investigation moved forward, after being delayed until the 1972 presidential election took place.

Even before the "smoking-gun" tape of June 23, 1972 (which was not released by the White House until August 5, 1974), revealed how early Nixon had been involved in the cover-up, the Watergate Special Prosecution Force (WSPF) headed by the Texas attorney Leon Jaworski had concluded (in February 1974) that "beginning no later than March 21, 1973, the President joined an ongoing criminal conspiracy to obstruct justice, obstruct a criminal investigation, and commit perjury (which included payment of cash to Watergate defendants and influence their testimony, making and causing to be made false statements and declarations, making offers of clemency and leniency, and obtaining information from the Justice Department to thwart its investigation) and that the President is also liable for substantive violations of various criminal statutes."[1]

All these actions had taken place in the space of two years—from the summer of 1972 to the summer of 1974. Early in 1973, Federal Judge John J. Sirica, using heavy-handed legal tactics, threatened the Watergate defendants with tough sentences unless they told the truth. As McCord and others began to talk about payoffs from the White House, evidence of illegal campaign contributions (unassociated with the Watergate break-in) began to surface and be investigated by the WSPF. The WSPF ultimately set up five different task forces to investigate the variety of charges surfacing against the administration, ranging from the Watergate cover-up, campaign contributions, the IT&T antitrust suits, and the Plumbers' other break-ins, to Nixon's tax returns and mistreatment of demonstrators. Nixon essentially fired Haldeman, Ehrlichman, Dean, and Mitchell by formally accepting their resignations on April 30, and announced on May 22 that they had been involved in a White House cover-up *without* his knowledge. Dean then decided to testify before the Senate Select Committee on Presidential Campaign Activities (headed by the conservative Sam J. Ervin, and so known as the Ervin Committee), and between June 25 and 29 accused the president of being involved. Among other things, nationally televised testimony before this committee disclosed to millions of mesmerized Americans the existence of a White House "enemies list" of prominent politicians, journalists, academics, and entertainers, who had been singled out for various types of harassment, including unnecessary IRS audits. In July 1973 it was revealed that Nixon had installed a voice-activated taping system in the Oval Office in 1971.

Various attempts to obtain unedited transcripts of these White House tapes failed until July 24, 1974, when the Supreme Court ruled in *United States v. Nixon* that the president could not retain subpoenaed tapes by claiming executive privilege. During this year-long legal struggle, Archibald Cox, the first special prosecutor appointed to investigate Watergate, acting on behalf of a federal grand jury, also tried to gain access to the tapes. When Cox rejected a compromise proposed by Nixon, the president ordered both Attorney General Elliot Richardson and Deputy Attorney General William D. Ruckelshaus to fire the special prosecutor. Refusing to do so, they resigned. On October 20, 1973, Acting Attorney General Robert Bork (later unsuccessfully nominated by President Reagan to the Supreme Court) finally carried out Nixon's order, but this "Saturday Night Massacre" was subsequently ruled an illegal violation of Justice Department procedures in *Nader v. Bork*. This incident also created such negative public opinion that the president agreed to turn over nine subpoenaed tapes to Judge Sirica, only to announce on October 31 that two of them did not exist and on November 26 that a third contained an eighteen-and-a-half-minute gap—an erasure that remains unexplained to this day. On October 30, the House Judiciary Committee, headed by Peter Rodino, began preliminary investigations, and in April 1974 it launched a full-scale impeachment inquiry. This led to a vote on July 27 recommending the impeachment of the president to the entire House of Representatives, even before the release of the smoking-gun tape. Nixon resigned from office on August 9, rather than face almost certain conviction in an impeachment trial.

Despite multiple investigations and books, many fundamental questions remain unanswered about the Watergate incident itself and its historical significance. This chapter does not attempt to review all the disputed facts or lacunae in the evidence uncovered since 1972, but simply to discuss certain theories about the origins of the break-ins and the subsequent cover-up that so rocked the nation a quarter of a century ago—all of which relate to the importance of government accountability in a democracy. This issue of accountability will continue to make Watergate more important than Nixon well into the next century.

UNPROVED THEORIES

The reasons for the Watergate break-ins on May 28 and June 17, 1972, still remain in dispute. Like the Kennedy assassination, the many investigations never proved the motivation behind them. Originally most accounts emphasized the connections among the ubiquitous financier and industrialist Howard Hughes, Nixon, and Larry O'Brien, chair of the DNC. Hughes had generously contributed to the campaign chests of both parties in the past, and at different times it had been rumored that both Nixon and O'Brien acted as lobbyists on retainers for Hughes's multifaceted business interests. To complicate matters, Hughes had contributed an unreported $100,000 for the 1972 campaign to Charles ("Bebe") Rebozo, a confidant of Nixon. Within the White House it was feared that O'Brien might have information about the cash contribution to Rebozo— or, worse yet, about the rumor that Rebozo had kept a portion of this money for himself or given it to Nixon family members or friends for their personal use. According to this theory, the break-ins took place in order to determine whether O'Brien knew about any of these rumored transactions or other information about Nixon's dealings with Hughes that could be used to threaten the president's reelection. While the fear that O'Brien had knowledge about the Nixon/Hughes/Rebozo financial connections may have been one of the peripheral reasons for the May and June break-ins, no indictments ever resulted from the several Watergate investigations. In particular, the Senate Watergate Committee, the IRS, and the WHSF all concluded that the evidence against Rebozo did not support legal action.[2]

Another theory connecting O'Brien with Hughes stems from the fact that the Democrats had resurrected and released information about a 1956 loan that Hughes had made to Nixon's brother Donald. In 1961 the Justice Department under Bobby Kennedy had investigated this transaction. To counter any partisan use of this loan during the campaign, in a January 1971 memorandum to Haldeman, Nixon expressed a strong desire to know as much as possible about any private deal between O'Brien and Hughes and about Hughes's contributions to the Democratic party, in order to "worry O'Brien." A couple of months after the Watergate break-ins, Nixon found out through a questionable IRS investigation of the Hughes Tool Company that payments for lobbying had indeed been made to O'Brien. The White House was never able to use this tainted information effectively against the Democratic party, even though John Connally strongly supported the idea.[3]

The major problem with the various theories involving Hughes's financial dealings with O'Brien and Nixon is that the Watergate burglars did not initially bug, nor were they subsequently caught in, O'Brien's office; rather, they initially bugged and were later arrested in the offices of his subordinates at the Democratic National Headquarters. Again, similar to the various conspiracy theories about the Kennedy assassination, this glaring factual discrepancy did not prevent practically every investigative reporter from Woodward and Bernstein on down and most Watergate buffs from subscribing to warmed-over versions of the O'Brien/Hughes political espionage interpretation down to the present.

A third theory focuses on the paranoid and sinister political views of Charles Colson, a close Nixon aide, and Howard Hunt, one of the original members of the infamous Plumbers group established by John Ehrlichman that began to carry out black-bag jobs when the White House decided that the FBI was not pursuing its investigation of the Pentagon Papers aggressively enough. According to this theory, Colson and Hunt used Mitchell, Haldeman, and Ehrlichman as fronts while they usurped H. Gordon Liddy's (another Plumber who had been transferred to the CRP)[4] amorphously naive plan, named GEMSTONE, to bug Democratic Headquarters for any and all information that might be obtained, specifically to "find or plant evidence linking the democrats to left-wing radicals and to install phone taps." Colson and Hunt apparently wanted such information because they intended to instigate violence at the Republican convention and then blame it on radical groups with connections to the Democratic party. They apparently harbored the delusion that this would prompt Nixon to declare martial law on the grounds that a state of domestic emergency existed.[5] The purpose of this remains unclear.

A fourth theory is much simpler. It claims that the White House had inside information that the Supreme Court was about to hand down a ruling against broad administrative powers to issue wiretaps, so the June 17 break-in took place in order to remove wiretaps planted the previous month. This explanation is no longer considered valid for two reasons: some of those involved in the break-in, such as Liddy, still mistakenly thought their purpose was to find out what derogatory information O'Brien had on the Republicans or to obtain similar information on the Democrats; and no bugs existed at DNC Headquarters by the time of the second break-in, for reasons I will explain shortly.[6]

A fifth theory involves the CIA connections and intentions of two ostensibly retired CIA agents—Hunt and McCord. (Nixon's animosity toward the CIA dated back to his unsuccessful presidential campaign in 1960, when he thought the agency had provided John Kennedy with misinformation about the so-called missile gap between the United States and the Soviet Union.) This theory claims that Hunt and McCord, acting as CIA operatives, deliberately botched the second break-in at the Watergate complex because the agency feared that, if reelected, Nixon intended to weaken the agency's power and/or use it for political purposes and to discredit longtime CIA supporter Howard Hughes. Indeed, the president considered replacing Richard Helms as CIA director at the beginning of 1970, but decided against it by November, on Kissinger's advice, saying instead that he simply wanted a "thorough housecleaning at other levels at CIA . . . [and] a good thinning down of the whole CIA personnel situation, as well as our Intelligence activities generally."[7]

Both McCord and Colson contributed to the idea that the CIA was behind the Watergate break-ins—the former by denying it and the latter by supporting it. In a famous letter to Judge John Sirica on March 19, 1973, McCord claimed that those arrested at DNC Headquarters had committed perjury because they had been pressured by the White House to remain silent. In statements to the WSPF, McCord vehemently denied any CIA connection to Watergate, insisting that "at no time did anyone from the CIA direct him to destroy any papers subsequent to his arrest."

Instead, he alone among the Plumbers caught in the Watergate complex referred to the break-in as the Mitchell Operation, thus fingering the attorney general (without any proof).[8] His denials about CIA involvement, however, laid out the thesis later propounded by Colson. Among other things McCord said that:

> the way in which his defense had been handled had convinced him that the White House had fired CIA Director Helms in order not only to put its own man in control at CIA, but as well to lay the foundation for claiming that the Watergate operation was a CIA operation, and now to be able to claim that "Helms had been fired for it." . . . Further, based on an earlier discussion with Robert Mardian in May, 1972, it appeared to me that the White House for some time [had] been trying to get political control over the CIA assessments and estimates, in order to make them conform to "White House policy." One of the things this meant to me was that CIA estimates and assessments could then be forced to accord with DoD estimates of future U.S. weapons and hardware needs. Among other things, this also smacked of the situation which Hitler's intelligence chiefs found themselves in, in the 1930's and 1940's, when they were put in the position of having to tell him what they thought he wanted to hear about foreign military capabilities and intentions, instead of what they believed. . . . When linked with what I saw happening to the FBI under Pat Gray—political control by the White House—it appeared then that the two government agencies which should be able to prepare their reports, and to conduct their business, with complete integrity and honesty in the national interest were no longer going to be able to do so.[9]

Among Nixon's former aides, Haldeman and Colson remain the primary source of information about CIA involvement in Watergate. Haldeman's information about the CIA apparently came from Colson and the CBS broadcaster Daniel Schorr, while Colson's probably came from his close association with both McCord and Hunt. After he was indicted for participating in the Watergate cover-up, he arranged to plea-bargain and was finally convicted of only one charge of obstructing justice in connection with the trial of Daniel Ellsberg, who had leaked the Pentagon Papers. Colson described his position in the White House as "basically to establish liaison with people outside of government," such as his attempt to improve relations with the Hispanic community, discussed earlier. At this time he also admitted that the "job grew into . . . being sort of the generalist trouble-shooter," especially with respect to labor unions, and "running what was known as the administration's attack and counterattack program [in the 1972 election]." During the summer of 1972 he began meeting with Haldeman, Ehrlichman, and press secretary Ziegler in so-called "nine-fifteen [in the morning] meetings of the 'attack' group" to plan daily public relations tactics.[10]

In the summer of 1971, Colson recommended to Ehrlichman that he hire Hunt "to do research on the 'Pentagon Papers.'" From that point, it is not clear whether Hunt directly reported to Colson or to Ehrlichman (through his assistant "Bud" Krogh). But it is clear that Colson tried to pass off as jokes his most outlandish recommendations—for example, "firebombing" the Brookings Institution because the Plumbers could find no way to break into it to retrieve leaked NSSMs—and comments, including being "willing to run over my own grandmother" if it would help reelect Nixon. He also denied any anti-Semitic overtones to the White House practice of compiling lists of liberal Democratic Jews who worked for the Bureau of Labor Statistics. Neither, he insisted, did he compile the "enemies list" of twenty names—which, in any case, he added, was nothing more than part of a general "opponent priority activity list" so that the White House would know who "not to invite to White House functions" or not to appoint. In general, since Colson cut his own deal with the WSPF (and subsequently found God), he has played down the importance of his involvement in Watergate matters, especially any CIA conspiracy, in his WSPF and National Archives interviews and in his book, *Born Again*.[11]

A sixth reason offered for the break-in maintains that the CIA had established a prostitution operation in Washington and that O'Brien's Democratic Headquarters might contain information about prominent Republicans (and Democrats) who used the illicit service. In his 1984 book, *Secret Agenda*, Jim Hougan maintained that McCord and Hunt deliberately sabotaged the second break-in to prevent its uncovering the call-girl ring, and that their purpose was *not* to plant more wiretaps or to repair previous ones. In fact, it is Hougan's contention that the Democrats planted the bugs later found by the FBI in order to build a better case against five burglars working for the Committee to Re-elect the President. Hougan also noted that the office of R. Spencer Oliver, the national president of the Young Democrats and executive director of State Democratic Chairmen, was the target of the original bugs, not the office of Larry O'Brien.[12]

A final theory about the break-in is more obtuse and complicated than these others. Called the Greek Connection because it focuses on Elias P. Demetracopoulos, a newspaperman exiled by the dictatorship that had come into power in 1967 after a military coup in Greece. This hypothesis also has both CIA and O'Brien overtones because it alleges that O'Brien might have known that a CIA intelligence front group, called the Greek KYP, had transferred money to the 1972 Republican campaign through businessman Thomas Pappas, who supported the new military junta and had connections with both the CIA and the KYP. Demetracopoulos's opposition to Pappas threatened to embarrass the administration, whose foreign policy also favored the military takeover, and so, according to this theory, the Nixon administration wanted to know how much O'Brien knew about Pappas's contributions to CRP.[13]

Of all the theories to surface claiming to explain the reason for the Watergate break-ins, none has been adequately documented. One theory supported by strong circumstantial evidence is the subject of a heated litigation initiated in 1992 by John and Maureen Dean against the authors of *Silent Coup*, Len Colodny and and Robert Gettlin, as well as their publisher, St. Martin's Press. The Deans, seeking over $50 million in damages, complain that they were defamed by Watergate theories of Colodny and Gettlin in their 1991 book, *Silent Coup*. Building on the idea first propagated by Hougan, the authors question whether the traditional interpretation of Watergate as a politically motivated crime is correct.

In the first half of the 1980s, as the result of the release of an obscure FBI investigation,[14] it became evident that there were no bugs on the phones of the DNC at the time of the second break-in. It also began to be suggested that both McCord and Hunt, while employed by CRP, were still working for the CIA independently, trying either to preserve or to investigate a sex-ring operation that would have compromised certain prominent Democrats. Gradually evidence began to indicate that the Committee to Re-elect the President and even Liddy himself were unaware that someone might have wanted to find out more about the purported prostitution ring operating out of Democratic National Headquarters. If true, this would mean that sexual, not political, intelligence was the object of the Watergate break-ins.

In *Silent Coup*, Colodny and Gettlin more thoroughly investigate the existence of a high-priced call-girl service at the Democratic National Office, but they do not subscribe to Hougan's idea that McCord and Hunt functioned unilaterally as CIA agents to expose it. Instead, they document that a prostitution ring was indeed operating informally out of an office at

Democratic National Headquarters, largely under the independently enter-
prising auspices of a Washington attorney, Phillip Mackin Bailley, who had
an as yet unidentified female contact inside the DNC Headquarters. The
most interesting facts about this prostitution operation were that the offices
it utilized were those of R. Spencer Oliver and of the head of the State
Democratic Governors organization, because they were often vacant. These
offices apparently became the object of the two Watergate break-ins—not
Larry O'Brien's office, as is usually claimed. The authors of *Silent Coup*
note that, in the early 1970s, John Dean's girlfriend (and future wife) Maureen ("Mo") Biner lived off and on with the woman who purportedly ran the
call-girl operation for Bailley—Erika L. Heidi Rikan, alias Cathy Dieter.
Colodny and Gettlin contend—and the Deans deny—that Maureen Dean
was referred to as "Clout" in Bailley's little black book of telephone numbers because of what Rikan thought were her powerful political connections. On April 6, 1972, materials in Bailley's law office were confiscated
by the FBI, and he was later charged with violating the Mann Act. The lawsuit denies the book's claim that Dean's interest in the Bailley case
prompted him to meet with local prosecutors and ask to see the address
book being used as evidence, apparently to see whether his girlfriend's or
her occasional roommate's name were in it. The subsequent disposition of
the Bailley case on a plea bargain without a trial (he was sentenced to five
years) effectively suppressed evidence seized at his home and office that
allegedly might have tarnished the reputation of John Dean's future wife.[15]

According to *Silent Coup*, the target of the second break-in likewise
turned out not to be O'Brien's office, as Liddy thought, but the office area
used by Oliver and his secretary, Ida Maxwell ("Maxie") Welles. Between
the two break-ins, the one operating transmitter had been removed so that
no bugs were found *until September*. Hougan suggested in 1984 that these
bugs had been planted either by the Democrats themselves to revive
interest in Watergate before the 1972 elections, or by other CIA operators
who wanted to allow the prosecution of Watergate burglars to go forward
as a political espionage case unrelated to the agency's interest in the
prostitution operation.[16]

It is from this set of circumstantial evidence that Colodny and Gettlin
query whether Dean masterminded the break-ins to find out whether
there was any compromising information about Democrats using a call-
girl ring at Democratic National Headquarters. Then, according to
Colodny and Gettlin, but challenged by the Deans, he also instigated the

various attempts at cover-up. In the first instance, involving the break-ins, he allegedly acted through Magruder, who gave instructions to Hunt and McCord; in the second, involving the cover-up, he again acted through Magruder, who instructed Liddy to tell the attorney general to "get McCord out of jail immediately." Later, according to Colodny and Gettlin, Dean also suggested the idea of using the CIA to thwart the FBI's investigation of Watergate. In accepting this suggestion, thinking that it originated with Mitchell, Nixon and his aides began to cover up Watergate by obstructing justice.[17] (Mitchell died in 1988 at the age of eighty-eight, still denying that he had approved GEMSTONE or authorized the cover-up.)

The lawsuit—additionally against Liddy and Bailley—about *Silent Coup*'s various theories is pending, embroiled in discovery and other disputes. Although it contains many evidentiary gaps, nonetheless, in my opinion *Silent Coup* has surpassed other books about the origins of Watergate—especially the well-known but largely unsubstantiated accounts by Bob Woodward and Carl Bernstein. Among other things, *Silent Coup* attempts to resolve factual contradictions in the testimony of all the participants about the break-ins and cover-up.

McCord's inept performance as a burglar remains another unanswered question about the second Watergate break-in. For example, he had taped open the doors in the basement of the Watergate complex not once but twice, after the first ones had been removed by the night watchman, in such an obvious way as to invite discovery. As noted, there is circumstantial evidence indicating that both McCord and Hunt continued to work for the CIA and that McCord deliberately botched the break-in to embarrass the Nixon administration, but we still don't know exactly why. One theory is that it was to protect what was a CIA sex-ring operation inside the DNC Headquarters, but there is no evidence to support this argument. Another is that it was to prevent the White House from undertaking any more actions of sabotage against the DNC because the CIA wanted a monopoly on information obtained about those using the Democratic party call-girl services. Still another is that the CIA simply wanted to embarrass the administration to prevent Nixon from asserting any more control over the agency. Regardless of why he bungled the attempt, McCord succeeded beyond his wildest dreams.[18] The irony of it all may be that he was simply a former CIA electronics expert who found himself in over his head in the field on a black-bag job, taking orders from Magruder, Dean, Hunt, and Liddy for their own various purposes. If so, then McCord's role is only that of a disgruntled, secondary figure who blew the whistle on the White House for petty personal reasons rather than for professional, conspiratorial ones.

What light, if any, do the released Nixon papers and tapes cast on all these unanswered questions about old or new theories purporting to explain the Watergate break-ins? Not much, so far, except that they do confirm that Nixon and his aides knew nothing beforehand about the June break-in at the Watergate complex. Publication of the Haldeman diaries and the release of other tapes may change this view. And the tapes available as of 1994 are interesting and important for other reasons.

THE INFAMOUS TAPES

During its first year, the Nixon administration engaged in technically legal wiretapping in the name of national security. Then in 1971 the president installed a secret, albeit legal, taping system in the White House for purely personal reasons: he wanted to create an "objective record" to counter "revisionist histories—whether from within or without his administration." This recording system was disclosed in July 1973, when Alexander Butterfield, a former White House assistant, revealed inadvertently while responding to questions from staffers from the Ervin Committee that Nixon had installed a voice-activated taping system in the Oval Office on February 11, 1971. Both Haldeman and Rosemary Woods, Nixon's private secretary, according to Hougan, thought that Butterfield was a CIA "plant" in the White House.[19]

These tapes became the butt of jokes and ultimately produced the "smoking gun" that forced the president to resign, even though Nixon believed that these tapes would allow him to rescue himself from charges of obstruction of justice. The columnist Art Buchwald was at his comedic best in a July 3, 1973, syndicated column when he wrote the following fictional conversation between Nixon and Press Secretary Ron Ziegler:

> Now I know there are some people who are going to say "Tricky Dick" is up to his dirty tricks. . . . But when I took this office. . . , I vowed I would never do the easy thing, the popular thing, the political thing. Ron, the toughest decision I ever had to make was whether I would tape some of the people all of the time, or all of the people some of the time. It was only when I talked with Butterfield that I found out I could tape all of the people all of the time. It was probably the greatest day of my life.

Of the four thousand hours of tapings, only sixty-three hours have been released at the time of this writing. There are no transcripts for the last three hours released on May 17, 1993. Of the original sixty hours released in 1991, there are transcripts for eighty-five of the eighty-eight individual entries. *There are no transcripts for the remaining 3,937 hours of taped conversations.* Only two of the eighty-eight entries were not released by the National Archives and Records Administration, because of sound problems or for national security reasons. Less than half of 1 percent of the transcripts were censored by the National Archives, according to standard guidelines governing privacy or national security. These transcripts vary considerably in physical quality because they consist of several generations of photocopies, often made from the hastily typed original transcripts whose readability leaves a lot to be desired. Because of the multiple transcribers involved, they also contain many spelling variations and syntax errors. Most important, they have not always been accurately or completely transcribed from the original tapes. Some of these transcribing discrepancies are due to the exceedingly poor quality of the sound-recording system used at the White House. In a word, scanning the transcripts and using a computer to search them, as I did, is no guarantee of accuracy, but it comes closer than anyone yet has to gaining a comprehensive view of this invaluable primary source. While I listened to a number of these tapes to check the accuracy of the transcripts, I did not listen to them all. What follows represents a combination of computer runs and verification of the transcripts by listening to the most controversial ones and cross-checking them against both Ehrlichman's and Haldeman's extensive handwritten notes and their own published works for these same meetings.[20]

This is no easy task. Even if all the White House tapes were released tomorrow, it would take years to make sense of them because of the numerous discrepancies that would emerge in transcribing them. Sometimes Haldeman's and Ehrlichman's handwritten summaries capture the essence of the conversations better than the currently transcribed ones. On April 26, 1973, for example, Nixon called Henry Petersen, the assistant attorney general who was in charge of the Watergate investigation because his boss, Richard Kleindienst, had recused himself from the case a few days earlier. Nixon wanted advice about FBI Acting Director Patrick Gray's revelation that he had destroyed some documents belonging to Howard Hunt that were unrelated to Watergate. Nixon did not know how he should instruct Ziegler to handle the disclosure. In two or three sentence fragments, Haldeman's notes summarized the dilemma the president faced better than three transcript pages of a one-sided phone conversation. "Needless casualty doing a dumb thing," Haldeman wrote. At two other points in this transcript there are references to whether Dean held a "trump card or blackjack" and whether Nixon feared he would try to blackmail the White House; these do not agree with Haldeman's notes.

In another instance, Ehrlichman read the transcript and then listened to the tape of a March 22, 1973, meeting in which the transcript said he had coined the phrase "a modified limited hangout" when advising the president to make a "sham disclosure." He discovered that the voice was Haldeman's, not his. "The authors of the transcripts didn't know the players," he concluded, "so they attributed words and thoughts to the wrong people.[21] No one writing about Watergate has yet undertaken the enormously time-consuming task of cross-checking the accuracy of the transcripts of the released tapes. Computer analysis by no means solves the question of accuracy, but it can show patterns and trends.

No more smoking guns have emerged from either the Nixon Presidential Papers released to date or the initial batch of transcripts from the secret tapes made during the Nixon administration. These transcribed tapes represent what the Watergate Special Prosecution Force considered the best evidence of abuse of power by the Nixon administration to be used for his impeachment and for his subsequent trial. Assistant Archivist for Presidential Libraries John T. Fawcett insisted that these sixty hours released in the summer of 1991 represent all of the "integral file segments" related to Watergate, but others have estimated that anywhere from three hundred to four hundred more hours of abuse-of-power conversations may exist on the tapes relating to Watergate.[22] An August 1993 federal court decision barred the release of any more taped conversations until the personal material is culled from them.

In the first transcripts we began to hear and read about in 1974, the speakers appeared to talk both grammatically and logically—without hesitation or ambiguousness—about obstruction of justice and other unconstitutional and illegal events. These many years later, the original transcripts do not read with such clarity or single-mindedness of purpose. For example, there are three versions of the "smoking-gun tape" (not simply one, as we normally think)—all recorded on the same day, June 23, 1972, and each containing a more elaborate version of the original cover-up scheme agreed to by Nixon. From them it is clear that the president was not the creator of the cover-up story—using the CIA to thwart the FBI investigation of the break-in—although he contributed incrementally in the course of the day to its final details. The cleaned-up version of the smoking-gun tape that the White House relinquished in August 1972 did not convey this sense of progression or lack of precision about what exactly Nixon, Ehrlichman, and Haldeman were doing or that they were dealing with complicated domestic and foreign policy matters in the same conversations.[23]

My computer runs revealed other interesting characteristics of these tapes. First, there is what I call the guerrilla-like speech pattern that makes the president and his aides appear less than astutely conspiratorial, but rather illogically and often inarticulately intent on covering their asses as they slowly (and I stress *slowly*) began to perceive the magnitude of the Watergate break-ins and their precipitous decision to cover it up. By "guerrilla-like," I mean that their conversations were punctuated throughout with numerous uhs, ahs, huhs, hums, um-huhs, and yeahs. Excluding the yeahs, these grunting noises and expressions occurred roughly ten thousand times or at least three times on each of the 2,700 pages of transcripts. By itself, *yeah* was used over three thousand times, usually not to mean "yes" but in the sense of "uh-huh," meaning "I am listening."

Such guttural expressions are so numerous among all voices on the tapes as to make one wonder whether most private conversations are this hesitant and fragmented in nature. The sanitized versions published to date usually complete every sentence and leave out these interminable audible breaks in thought processes, so that one is left with the impression that Nixon and his aides were communicating with one another precisely and efficiently.

Second, the swearing patterns exhibited in the tapes appear to be linked to unfolding Watergate events, including the type and number of swear words used by Nixon and those with whom he consulted about Watergate. In general there is an internal and external rhythm to their swearing. If they start out swearing on a tape, especially the longer ones, they end up swearing more and more. If there is little or no swearing at the beginning, the expletives usually do not reach a crescendo level. There is very little swearing on the tapes made in 1971, before Watergate, and even less in the tapes of April 1973, when Nixon, Haldeman, and Ehrlichman discuss in a rather desultory manner the inevitability of the two of them leaving White House service. (The tapes contain no reference to the possibility than Nixon himself might have to resign.)

The most intense swearing can be found not in the smoking-gun tape but in tapes from the beginning of 1973 as Nixon and his advisers tried to elaborate on the cover-up and as its ramifications became more complex and forced them to try to construct ever more complicated rationalizations for the unraveling sequence of events threatening to expose the cover-up they had created. Only a dozen profanities were used consistently, such as damn, goddamn, Jesus, bastard, Christ, shit, and similarly mild-mannered curses, leaving it to our imaginations (or at least my imagination) to think that every "expletive deleted" represented the usage of much stronger four-letter words. It may come as a surprise to learn that the president and his aides never used "the f word" unless quoting someone else, and then only four times in the 2,700 pages so far released.

Each of the major speakers on these tapes favored certain terms when they blasphemed. Nixon's favorites were damn or goddamn and Jesus Christ or Christ's sake, while Charles Colson, who became a "born again" after serving time for Watergate and who won the million-dollar Templeton Prize for Progress in Religion in February 1993,[24] used hell, damn or damnable, and God almost exclusively, except for a few times when he described people as assholes or bastards. Haldeman and Ehrlichman employed the terms shit, shitty, half-cocked, or cold-cocked more often than the others. Mitchell, Ehrlichman, and Dean swore the least on the tapes.

Third, one can trace the changing perceptions these men had of Watergate, from seeing it as unimportant in the great political scheme of the campaign to becoming the major problem of Nixon's second administration. This changing perception of the seriousness of Watergate also changed Nixon's attitudes toward some of his most trusted aides, including Kissinger, Mitchell, and Colson. For example, Nixon went from referring to Colson as "Chuckie" and admiring his fighting qualities to wondering whether he was a liar, concluding in April 1973: "Colson is closer to this group of robbers than anybody else. That's the problem with Colson." Nixon had lauded Colson's ability to think up dirty political tricks to play against the Democrats in 1971 and early 1972 and his stonewalling on the issues, until his indictment for conspiracy, obstruction of justice, dirty tricks,, and lying about all of the above. Facing fifteen years in prison, Colson pleaded guilty to a lesser charge and became a government witness to save himself. Then Colson became someone who "was up to his ass" in the cover-up and who got his "tit caught in a wringer," as the president and Haldeman and Ehrlichman tried to recap Colson's reasons for having raised with the president the issue of clemency for the burglars.[25]

Similarly, Nixon expressed real sympathy at the beginning for Mitchell, only to question why he and his aides ever tried to protect "the clever son-of-a-bitch" in the first place. Initially, Nixon anguished over forcing Mitchell to resign, saying that it was harder than firing Secretary of Interior Walter J. Hickel or the decisions to bomb Cambodia and North Vietnam. The president turned to Secretary of State William Rogers, whose reputation was above reproach, rather than to Henry Kissinger when he wanted someone to talk to Mitchell about resigning. Rogers "is clean," the president said, and "from the public point of view the Dean of the Cabinet." Nixon even considered postponing a scheduled foreign trip by Rogers because Watergate matters took precedent: "Kissinger must understand [there are] bigger things here." In the end the president concluded that Rogers "was not tough enough," and the unpleasant task of talking to Mitchell about resigning over Watergate fell to Ehrlichman. As of April 16, 1973, Rogers did not yet "know the facts" about Watergate, but Kissinger had already been briefed about it by Nixon's counsel, Leonard Garment.[26]

Those involved in Watergate but not personally close to Nixon—such as Jeb Magruder and Patrick Gray, acting FBI director from May 1972 to April 1973, who passed information in secret to Dean and destroyed documents during his initial investigation of the June break-in—devolved into "clowns" or "horses' asses," or were considered just plain "dumb."[27] Liddy, in particular, received little personal sympathy from the president and his aides, even when they discussed the possibility that he might be willing to be the fall guy for the entire Watergate break-in and thus limit its political consequences during the presidential campaign. In describing Liddy to the president, Haldeman noted: "Apparently he is a little bit nuts. . . . He sort of likes the dramatic. He said, 'if you want to put me before the firing squad and shoot me, that's fine.'" In recommending the "Liddy scenario," Haldeman told Nixon that after he took the rap for the crime, "then we could ask for compassion: 'this is a poor misguided kid who read too many spy stories, a little bit nutty, and obviously we got rid of him, made a mistake having him, and that's too bad.'"[28]

Even while Nixon considered making Liddy the fall guy, he continued to indicate that he did not think Watergate was such a big deal: "Breaking and entering and so forth without accomplishing anything is not a helluva lot of crime." The president said he disagreed with Press Secretary Ron Ziegler's characterization of the break-in as a "third-rate burglary." Instead, Nixon said, it should be called a "third-rate attempted burglary."

Nixon noted in his memoirs that Watergate in June 1972 was an "annoying problem, but it was still just a minor one among many."[29] The ethical and political indifference Nixon and his closest aides initially expressed over the Watergate arrests can be traced back through taped conversations to just four days after the break-in when Nixon can be heard saying:

> Anything that's as bizarre as this and interesting is going to be national
> story. . . . In terms of reaction of people, the reaction is going to be pri-
> marily in Washington and not the country because I think the country
> doesn't give much of a shit about bugging when somebody bugs somebody
> else, you see. Everybody around here is all mortified about it. [*Mockingly*]
> "It's horrible to bug." Of course it isn't and most people around the coun-
> try think it's probably routine, everybody's trying to bug everybody else,
> it's politics. That's my view.[30]

Almost a year later, when Nixon, Ehrlichman, and Haldeman were discussing how to deal with the Watergate cover-up, all three revealed how cynically they viewed the political process in the United States. In one transcribed conversation, after Nixon referred to the "dirty-tricks crap"—designed by Haldeman and his aide Dwight Chapin to disrupt the Democrats' campaign in 1972, only to be replaced by Liddy's and Hunt's black-bag jobs—the following exchange took place. Haldeman started to say that a "man wouldn't be as good an investigator if he hadn't been in . . . trouble a couple of times," but the president interrupted to say "unless he knew how to bug." Haldeman went on to say that a "man wouldn't have been a true campaigner if he hadn't had a prank or two once in a while," and Nixon then returned to the question of giving the Watergate burglars "full pardons" after "a reasonable time had expired." To which Ehrlichman agreed, indicating that he did not consider illegal break-ins any more serious than political pranks or tricks and that neither did the president or Haldeman.[31]

Their descriptions of the last Watergate break-in stand in stark contrast to the fact that their cover-up of it began to consume an inordinate amount of the president's and his top aides' time from the beginning of his second term. They move inexorably from referring to it as a "caper," something they would look back on and wonder what it was all about, to its being an example of the double standard in the treatment of Nixon by Congress and the press and of a Democratic vendetta. Colson perhaps captured this dismissal of Watergate as unimportant at best, and typical of politics as usual at worst, when he said jokingly to Hunt on the telephone in November 1972: "Well, I always thought when I write my memoirs of this book—of this campaign—that I'm gonna say that . . . Watergate was brilliantly conceived as an escapade that would, uh, divert the Democrats' attention from the real issues, and therefore permit us to win a landslide that we probably wouldn't have won otherwise."[32]

Finally, it is interesting to note how infrequently such terms as *cover-up* (or the word *aftermath*—a euphemism I discovered that they substituted for the word *cover-up*), *obstruction of justice, executive privilege,* and *national security* were actually used on the tapes, as opposed to how often we suspected at the time that these words must have been used. With the exception of *cover-up,* these words were used fewer than a hundred times. *Cover-up* was used fewer than two hundred times, but a quarter of the time with no connection to Watergate. John Dean first uttered the words *obstruction of justice* in March 1973. After that, they appeared almost exclusively in connection with him, while Nixon, his political aides, and his legal advisers all denied that those closest to the president could be proved to have obstructed justice.

It has also been claimed that profanity and ethnic slurs abounded in the Nixon White House. My search of the tapes released as of the end of 1993, for which there are transcripts, does not reveal any of the most common epithets for African-Americans, Hispanics, Irish, Italians, or Jews. The *Washington Star-News* reported at the time that, despite the rumors about such statements, "sources with access to the tapes given to the [House Judiciary] committee and the prosecutors say that as far as evidence on the tapes themselves [as opposed to the preliminary drafts of the transcripts, is concerned] . . . both rumors have some substance but both have been overstated." This newspaper friendly to Nixon also said that most of the deleted expletives were "actually milder than might be imagined," and my research has confirmed this point.[33] Whether the remaining tapes, largely covering non-Watergate subjects, would contain such vernacular references remains a matter of pure conjecture, although the charge has been made again and again.

Even hostile newspaper accounts from the period, however, agree that there were no racially pejorative remarks about African-Americans. They were referred to throughout the transcripts as "blacks."[34] The most negative remark I found was on a tape from June 4, 1973. In reference to the excessive sentences that Judge Sirica had imposed on the Watergate burglars, Nixon said to Haig in a telephone conversation: "'Thirty-five-year sentence . . . this is just a very flagrant thing. . . . For example, if a black held up a store with a gun, uh, he'd get perhaps two years.' And Dean kind of—'Yeah, he'd get two years, and he'd get a suspended sentence.'" Immediately following this remark, Nixon turned to the subject of Supreme Court appointments and said to Haig that he had told Dean he was thinking about appointing Jewels LaFontaine: "'There you kill two birds with one stone. You've got a black and a woman.'" Dean replied: "'Brilliant—she's great. She'd be fine.'"[35]

The word *Jew* appears in one-sentence references on six different tapes and two references on another. Two are strictly diplomatic in nature, with Nixon and his aides talking about Jews and Arabs in the Middle East and the visits by Jewish leaders to the United States. One of the others consists of Haldeman laughing and saying that when he heard that Jeb Magruder, deputy director of CRP, was bringing two lawyers with him to talk about Watergate matters: "Probably one Jewish and one Gentile." Another refers to the "Jewish seat" on the Supreme Court after the resignation of Justice Abe Fortas.[36]

Three of the references to Jews are much more suspect. On May 5, 1971, for example, the president asked Haldeman: "Aren't the Chicago Seven all Jews?" On October 5, 1971, when Nixon was anxious for the transcripts of the so-called Kissinger wiretaps carried out by the FBI to be removed from J. Edgar Hoover's office, he referred to Robert Mardian, assistant attorney general, as a "Lebanese Jew"; Ehrlichman agreed, because he had "treated with the enemy"—referring to the fact that the assistant director of the FBI had given these transcripts to Mardian to keep Hoover from using them against the administration in some future dispute. During one of the smoking-gun tapes, Nixon made the passing remark: "The Arts, you know, they're Jews, they're left wing, in other words."[37]

The most lengthy reference to Jews came on June 4, 1973. In a rambling conversation about obtaining justice for the seven people arrested in connection with the Watergate break-ins and making appointments to the Supreme Court, the president related to an agreeing Alexander Haig a conversation he had had with Dean:

> "How would you like Teddy Kennedy to propose the judges?" [unintelligible] I said, "I want you to know that appointments are not going to go on the basis of—they, they're saying that you need a Jewish seat." And I

said, "Now look, there's no Jewish seat on that Court." I said, "There are Jews all around this White House." I said, "You've got Arthur Burns; you've got Henry Kissinger; you've got [unintelligible]." And I said, "What we have to do, we've got to re-realize we've got to appoint some [unintelligible]. They may not be quite up to what we think is the standard, but we've got to get them and pull them up." I said, "That's the way our system works." Uh, uh, I said, "Republicans are worse than the Democrats in this respect, because they're snobbish. And here's Nixon telling him, 'We've got to spread the base.'"

Finally, when the name of Mark Felt, assistant FBI director, came up, Nixon reported to Haig that Dean had told him Felt was "known as the 'White Rat' at the, at the, uh, FBI. And, uh, the question, uh, I think he raised, is he, uh, is he Jewish. And, uh, Dean said, 'He, he could be.'"[38]

In 1974 (and again in 1992) the reporter Seymour Hersh charged Nixon with using *wop* in reference to Judge Sirica and making anti-Semitic remarks on the tapes of February 28 and March 20, 1973. At the time, the transcripts in question were checked by James Doyle, chief press officer for Special Prosecutor Leon Jaworksi, who said he found no such references. Fred Buzhardt forcefully denied Hersh's charges, saying that he had listened to almost forty tapes, and "I don't remember the word Jew. I do remember the word Jewish being used. . . . Somebody may have said somebody was Polish." Buzhardt added that these fabrications were "malicious and vicious attempts to poison the public mind against the President by any means." Despite this denial, Buzhardt's own notes show that for the March 20 tape, he had written on his daily calendar some of the slurs attributed to Nixon. But it is not clear whether he wrote them down to check for their existence on the tapes or took them directly from the tapes, and they are not on the released transcriptions. Woodward and Bernstein later said in *Final Days* that what sounded like the president calling Sirica a "goddamn wop" actually turned out to be "That's the kind I want." They also noted that the phrase "Jewish boys" was not uttered by the president, but by Dean.[39]

There is no doubt that the White House made a fatal mistake in expurgating the swearing and occasional ethnic slurs used by the president. This censorship made the sentences more grammatical (and hence more conspiratorially damning). The voices on the tapes constantly interrupt and "talk over" one another. It is possible that the use of racial and ethnic slurs will be discovered when and if more tapes are released. It is also possible that Haldeman's published diary will confirm or deny their existence. In any case, deconstructionists will have a field day comparing these full transcripts with the sanitized versions we read twenty years ago.

As for the cover-up itself, Ehrlichman told me that he attributed it to what he called the "Ed Meese syndrome." Since there is no basic "institutional apparatus" in the White House for dealing with political mistakes, presidents come into office knowing that their predecessors have successfully hidden things from the public. It really does not matter whether someone close to the president is innocent or guilty. If it simply looks like he is, that is reason enough to cover up. He also noted that Nixon simply "couldn't leave it alone," meaning that the president found "intrigue attractive as a hobby" and, once the Watergate events unfolded, could not ignore them. Nixon indicated to me that none of his advisers ever asked him to denounce the burglary and, therefore, from the moment he learned about the break-in, he did not know how far up on his staff knowledge of the affair had gone. The president's uncertainty about the involvement of his top aides is evident on a number of the tapes.[40] As discussed in chapter 9, the Radford-Moorer incident had also set the precedent within the White House for covering up incidents of highly questionable spying and espionage when Nixon judged that exposure would cause political embarrassment. (It also set an inadvertent precedent for desultory congressional investigations, as the Senate Armed Services Committee looking into this matter never got beyond Kissinger's, Haig's, and Buzhardt's stonewalling it because they did not want the issue brought into Watergate matters.)[41]

When Nixon learned of the break-in on June 17, he responded very much like he did in 1971 after learning that the Joint Chiefs of Staff had been spying on the National Security Council, hoping "to limit investigations and to prevent political damage."[42] Had he any inkling that sexual rather than political espionage might have prompted the Watergate break-ins, at Dean's and not Mitchell's instigation, would he have so readily agreed to a cover-up? Would these and the unanswered questions about Watergate been resolved long before now had Gerald Ford not pardoned Richard Nixon, after succeeding him as the thirty-eighth president of the United States, thus preventing any further litigation against the former president? We shall never know.

THE UNPARDONABLE PARDON

Nixon's resignation thwarted the process of justice over Watergate, and Ford's pardon of him just one month later, on September 8, 1974, delivered the coup de grâce. Nixon had appointed Ford vice president after Spiro Agnew resigned on October 10, 1973—in the midst of, but for reasons unrelated to, Watergate. After taking over as president, Ford unconditionally pardoned the former president for all federal crimes he may have committed or been a party to, freeing Nixon from any federal criminal or civil liability in the Watergate affair. Questions about whether a "deal" had been struck between Ford and Nixon over this pardon before the latter resigned contributed to Ford's defeat by Democrat Jimmy Carter in the 1976 election. Despite lingering suspicions among the public at large, no scholar or investigative reporter has found evidence of a "pardon deal" between Nixon and Ford.

Of the four major Nixon aides whom Ford retained—Fred Buzhardt, Leonard Garment, Alexander Haig, and Henry Kissinger—Garment and Haig were most involved in the pardon process and, of these, Haig personally had the most at stake, as shown by his insistence on connecting Nixon's pardon with his Presidential Papers. Not until the opening of the Nixon and Ford Presidential Papers, however, was it possible to document Haig's role in shaping both the terms of the pardon itself and the initial disposition of Nixon's controversial tapes and other presidential materials, because he wanted to cover his own paper trail of involvement in the Kissinger wiretap and spying for the JCS (discussed in chapter 9). At the time, Haig's personal motivation was not clearly perceived by those closest to either Nixon or Ford. Had Haig not been involved in the pardon process, that proclamation probably would not have included the infamous Nixon-Sampson agreement, which would have allowed the former president unprecedented latitude for destroying his tapes and papers.[43] Suffice it to say here that Haig exercised no less a proprietary interest in Nixon's Presidential Papers than he did later, more successfully, over his own.

Fortunately for Haig, no one on Ford's staff sufficiently understood the importance of keeping these papers out of Nixon's control. This was especially true of Philip Buchen, Ford's close friend and counsel, who viewed the Nixon presidential material as an unnecessary storage and litigation problem imposed on the legal counsel of the new president. When asked about the Sampson agreement at a press conference whether "any consideration was given to the right of history," he replied: "I am not sure the historians will protest, but I think historians cannot complain if evidence for history is not perpetuated which shouldn't have been created in the first place." As late as 1989, Buchen still complained about the space these files took up at the Executive Office Building, across from the White House, and said his main concern was to "get the [Ford] White House out of the line of fire" on the disposition of the Nixon papers. He never seemed to appreciate the negative impact that the Nixon-Sampson agreement, if carried out, would have had on future Watergate litigation and scholarly research. In fact, Buchen believed that the compromise it contained—a vague promise by Nixon to deed his papers, if not the tapes, back to the public domain at some unstated time and a "two-key" system of protection, with a representative of the General Services Administration and Nixon having the keys—was adequate.[44]

Buchen never apparently comprehended that the Nixon-Sampson agreement was negotiated by GSA without consultation with the National Archives, and that GSA had no more understanding than he did of the scholarly and litigious value of Nixon's papers. In reviewing the situation for Ford in 1975, Buchen continued to describe the Nixon-Sampson agreement, which had by then been voided by congressional legislation, as representing an "effort to relieve [the] White House from the burden of custody and from the responsibilities of responding to subpoenas for particular material." Buchen viewed requests from committees in Congress for access to certain Nixon materials with the same irritated cost-analysis, workload approach as he did those from the special prosecutor's office. Buchen had the most knowledge about Ford's decision to pardon Nixon, but his recently opened papers proved disappointing. They neither revealed any deal between Ford and Nixon, as asserted by Seymour Hersh in a 1983 article, nor shed any light on the more likely deal between Haig and Nixon about his pardon, as suggested by Colodny and Gettlin.[45] Buchen was probably rightly criticized for being a "small-time lawyer" who had badly advised Ford about the pardon. As late as 1976, for example, he did not yet know whether Nixon could still be indicted after he had resigned and been unconditionally pardoned![46]

The controversy over Nixon's papers bore no logical relationship to his pardon, but immediately after he resigned the disposition of the records of his presidency became a highly publicized issue. Ford had instructed his staff to prevent any more destruction of Nixon's papers, but his press secretary, Jerry F. terHorst, told the press that, based on a Justice Department ruling provided him by Buzhardt, both the tapes and papers were Nixon's personal property to be disposed of as he wished (although the special prosecutor did not concur). The negative fallout from this announcement caused Ford to fire Buzhardt as counsel. He replaced him with Buchen, who never seemed completely on top of the issues he dealt with—especially the pardon.

One of Ford's aides, Robert T. Hartmann, noted Haig's fury over Buzhardt's dismissal but at the time it did not seem important because Attorney General William Saxbe confirmed that Presidential Papers were traditionally considered personal property. In the interim, however, William Becker, another legal counsel to Ford, had intervened to prevent Haig from shipping White House documents to San Clemente, where Nixon lived after resigning (something Buzhardt had apparently arranged before his dismissal), only to find that Haig had already removed his own papers from the White House. Becker had also researched the question of whether Ford could pardon Nixon, since the ex-president had not been charged with or convicted of any crime, and concluded that he could. At Ford's first news conference, on August 28, the issues of the pardon and the papers were raised interchangeably, even though Ford's major concern was the pardon.[47]

According to Ford White House memoranda, it was not until August 30 that Ford began to consult in secret with Haig, Kissinger, Hartmann, Buchen, and John O. Marsh, another aide, about the "possibility of a pardon." Sometime between September 4 and 5, Ford finally decided in favor of an unconditional pardon, having received legal advice on September 3 about presidential power to grant reprieves and pardons. Moreover, Jaworski had told Buchen that to try Nixon would take "from nine months to a year, and perhaps even longer." Ford continued to go through the motions of bargaining with Nixon, but he initially did not want to link the pardon with any agreement about Nixon's papers. Haig, however, apparently kept telling him to grant Nixon both a pardon and control over his papers, while Becker and Hartmann remained adamant that the papers and tapes should not be transferred to the former president, despite the Justice Department ruling. Haig took the position that the papers were Nixon's problem, not Ford's. Becker flew to San Clemente on September 5, with Herbert J. Miller, Jr., Nixon's new attorney, with instructions not to discuss the pardon until the issue of the papers had been resolved and then to get a statement of contrition as a condition of the pardon. Haig disagreed with these instructions. By the time Becker arrived in California, Ziegler (and presumably Nixon) already knew about his secret instructions.[48]

Colodny and Gettlin, citing Becker as their source, maintain that Haig was Nixon's back-channel connection in the Ford administration. Haig apparently informed Ziegler, who told the ex-president, that the pardon was his without an act of contrition and to be firm on the status of his papers. This is exactly what Nixon's representatives did. Becker returned to Washington with a pardon statement and an agreement on Nixon's papers that became known as the Nixon-Sampson agreement.[49] Both were announced to the country on the same day— September 8, 1974. In this circuitous fashion, the pardon and the papers became inextricably linked. For the moment it looked as though Haig had once again succeeded in covering his own paper trail of wiretaps and spying for the JCS.

The historian Stanley Kutler has documented that, while Ford was under considerable pressure from former Nixon aides such as Haig, Garment, and Buzhardt, his pardon of the former president was based primarily on practical and moral considerations.[50] Ford's general clemency behavior with respect to granting amnesty and pardons compares very favorably with that of other presidents. In fact, Ford had the highest pardon record of any of the modern presidents, and tied with FDR and Carter in granting amnesty (only Truman's was better). Nixon, on the other hand, had the third highest pardon record among modern presidents, but had taken no amnesty actions as president.[51]

While it is unlikely that there had been a deal between Ford and Nixon, when the Ford White House tried to reconstruct events leading to the pardon in order to answer requests for information by reporters Woodward and Bernstein in 1975 and 1976, it could not completely reconcile the discrepancies in Ford's public statements about when and who first raised the issue of pardoning Nixon with him. Representative Elizabeth Holtzman (Dem.-N.Y.) remained convinced in 1989 that members of the subcommittee of the Judiciary Committee who questioned Ford about the pardon did not try hard enough to get at the truth—particularly the role that Haig played in encouraging the pardon of Richard Nixon. Holtzman cited this as an example of the same desultory kind of congressional investigation that had plagued the initial investigations of Watergate. She continued to question why Haig's role was never fully investigated and whether the pardon might have been agreed to in order to ensure Nixon's resignation, thereby avoiding the embarrassment to the Republican party of an impeachment trial. (It is in this additional sense, therefore, that the investigations *both before and after* Nixon's resignation did not show the system working at its best.)

Ford held his ground after deciding to pardon Nixon, despite polls showing that almost 60 percent of Americans opposed the action. Ford's reasons were that: (1) the trial of the former president over whether Nixon should be punished further (in addition to having been forced to resign) could not take place for over a year, during which national divisiveness would continue; (2) Nixon's health was failing; (3) he and his family had suffered enough; and (4) it was Christian to show mercy. In his autobiography, Ford added a final reason: he believed that Nixon's resignation from office was "an implicit admission of guilt."[52] Nixon did not. Ford never overcame the damage to his political credibility generated by his "full, free, and absolute pardon" of Richard Nixon, and Congress intervened to abrogate the Nixon-Sampson agreement. Objections to the pardon and the political cost to Ford aside, one of its most interesting features remains Haig's role in bringing it about for reasons that were unknown to Ford at the time.

Nixon's initial response to his unconditional pardon is worth quoting in its entirety, since it became the basis of many of his early postpresidential statements in which he admitted to committing mistakes but not to being guilty of obstructing justice:

> I have been informed that President Ford has granted me a full and absolute pardon for any charges which might be brought against me for actions taken during the time I was President of the United States. In accepting the pardon, I hope that his compassionate act will contribute to lifting the burden of Watergate from our country.
>
> Here in California, my perspective on Watergate is quite different than it was while I was embattled in the midst of the controversy, and while I was still subject to the unrelenting daily demands of the Presidency itself.
>
> Looking back on what is still in my mind a complex and confusing maze of events, decisions, pressures, and personalities, one thing I can see clearly now is that I was wrong in not acting more decisively and more forthrightly in dealing with Watergate, particularly when it reached the stage of judicial proceedings and grew from a political scandal into a national tragedy.
>
> No words can describe the depth of my regret and pain at the anguish my mistakes over Watergate have caused the Nation and the Presidency—a Nation I so deeply love, and an institution I so greatly respect.

I know that many fair-minded people believe that my motivations and actions in the Watergate affair were intentionally self-serving and illegal. I now understand how my own mistakes and misjudgments have contributed to that belief and seemed to support it. This burden is the heaviest one of all to bear.

That the way I tried to deal with Watergate was the wrong way is a burden I shall bear for every day of the life that is left to me.[53]

Given this response to what many thought a suspiciously rushed, unconditional pardon, vindictiveness against Nixon reached a fever pitch in the fall of 1974. For example, the House of Representatives amended the public law statute that defined the term *former president* in such a way that Nixon would not be allowed to use it; attempts were made to prevent him from receiving the briefings on classified information accorded all former presidents, on the implicit grounds that his performance as president had made him a security risk; and there were many questions raised over the cost and duration of his transition staff at San Clemente.[54]

Ford's pardon of Nixon continues to symbolize the double standard of justice that exists for presidents and other high government officials and to convey the "ineluctable impression at that time that there may have been a deal."[55] Unfortunately for the future of democratic politics in the United States, matters involving legal and ethical standards do not raise the indignation or ire of as many Americans as they did in 1974. Bush's "midnight" pardon of those associated with the Iran–Contra affair at the end of 1992 clearly demonstrated increased public tolerance of this dual level of justice.

CONCLUSION: WATERGATE IS MORE THAN NIXON

If we have peace over the next fifty years, I think Nixon will go down in the history books as one of our truly great Presidents. The Watergate episode will then receive a mere footnote in the history books.

—Arthur Burns, remarks at a public forum, October 29, 1985

If, indeed, the Watergate break-in had more to do with sex than politics, then Nixon's unsuccessful attempt to cover it up was more incongruous than he, or any of us, thought at the time. Instead of covering up a black-bag job designed to gather political intelligence, Nixon may have unwittingly been trying to cover up a plan designed to retrieve sexual information about a prostitution ring operating out of Democratic National Headquarters. The irony of either petty scenario bringing down a presidency can only be appreciated if it is understood that ultimately Watergate was about the accountability of top government officials to the people in a democratic system. This issue of government accountability in a democracy will continue to make Watergate more important than Nixon well into the next century. In this sense Watergate offered an unusual opportunity for the country to reevaluate its political system and reinforce its democratic principles. The outcome of that process remains mixed at best.

The most important positive legacy should have been the demand it produced for accountability on the part of top politicians and for greater access to government information. Thus, Watergate directly or indirectly precipitated a series of reforms for elections, for financing political campaigns, and for ensuring more public access to secret or classified documents. These reforms specifically included the establishment of the Federal Election Commission, the Congressional Budget Office, the War Powers Act, the 1974 and 1978 Presidential Materials and Preservation Acts, the 1974 amendments to the Freedom of Information Act, the 1976 Sunshine Act, the 1978 Inspector General Act, and the 1978 Ethics in Government Act.[1] In addition, Congress agreed to open conference committees to public scrutiny, and the Democratic party continued its efforts (which had begun before Watergate) to reform the primary system, with the Republican party following suit. Unfortunately, most of these congressional acts and party reforms have since been violated, watered-down, or contradicted by presidential actions, or else have created unforeseen additional problems, such as the uncontrolled financing of candidates by political action committees (PACs), overly complicated ethical standard requirements, and the automatic triggering of special-prosecutor investigations in response to trivial incidents.[2] These Watergate reforms failed to make government and the electoral process more accountable and democratic.

Nixon should not be excused for obstructing justice and temporarily getting away with it. But if he and Watergate remain primarily historical aberrations in the public mind, then little will have been learned from this productive, as well as painful, period in the history of the U.S. presidency. As one American wrote to Ford after he pardoned Nixon: "Watergate must not be allowed to become a basis for self-righteous moralizing but should serve as a lesson that even small crimes can lead to larger ones, and undo even the greatest odds."[3] Unfortunately, the most negative legal legacies of Watergate are that our highest officials of government (and business) are above the law and that there is no single standard of justice.

THE REAL LESSONS OF WATERGATE

Two decades after the break-in at the Democratic National Committee Headquarters in the Washington, D.C., Watergate complex, what lessons can be drawn from the event? A few obvious questions and answers come to mind. To what degree was Watergate the logical extension to domestic politics of the surreptitious practices that characterized American foreign policy? To what degree did it reflect the callous attitude the government routinely exhibited toward civil rights and antiwar protesters in the course of the 1960s? Conversely, to what degree did it represent the climax of a series of disillusioning experiences of students and other reformers? Was it glaring proof of the decline in grassroots democratic politics in the United States? Or was it simply Democratic and Republican partisanship as usual, as Nixon claimed again and again? Was Watergate, in the final analysis, an example of the legal and political systems working or not working?

To answer any of these questions, we must decide what is meant when we refer to "Watergate." If we view it simply as a "sordid episode in our history, something to be lived down or blotted out; a bad thing itself, and the cause of other bad things . . . [we will have missed] the whole point of Watergate." Yet this is how many still think of it. Everything from the controversial policies in Vietnam, Cambodia, and Iran to media disrespect for the office of the president and the POW/MIA myth has been blamed on Watergate.[4]

In this age of deconstructing symbols, it is worth noting that, since biblical times, the term *water gate* (a source of water for a city) meant "a point of weakness." This is a direct reference to an eastern section of the ancient wall of Jerusalem where there was a Water Gate and a tower guarding the Temple (near a part of the city once called Ophel, where Temple workers lived). This and other gates came to symbolize power if one conquered or controlled them, danger or defeat if controlled or conquered by one's enemy. Water images abounded in the Nixon administration before Watergate became the most famous one. After all, it all began with the Plumbers trying to plug leaks.[5]

How can we begin to place Watergate into historical rather than histrionic perspective? While we may remember Watergate in a variety of frivolous and serious ways, despite the additional facts now available, the ways to interpret it have not changed much since 1974—with the possible exception of seeing it in relation to a sex scandal.[6] First, there is the literal and least important meaning, referring to the break-ins at the Watergate office and apartment complex. Second, there is a generalized meaning, since the term has become shorthand for all the subsequent investigations and legal proceedings leading to Nixon's resignation.[7]

Third, there is a political atmosphere evoked by the name Watergate—a lingering stench, if you will—that is most commonly associated with the general disillusionment and cynicism that had tarnished the idealism of 1960s' activists by the early 1970s. After all, they had not been able to do away with segregation or the war or even to make lasting curricula or other changes on most campuses. This group was ripe for a national scandal of unprecedented proportions that would confirm their worst fears and suspicions about American society and government officials. Their manic state of euphoria over Watergate quickly turned into depressed alienation about "the system" in general and into president-bashing—particularly Nixon-bashing. This attitude has been carefully nourished by a small group of journalists and scholars—most of whom came of age in the 1950s and who have never forgiven Richard Nixon for dominating their political consciousness for almost half a century.

A fourth way to view Watergate "goes beyond and behind the '60s to include the range of official abuses that came to light in the course of post-Watergate investigations—the illegal activities of the FBI and the CIA, the truth about spying on our own citizens and attempting to assassinate foreign leaders."[8] In this sense Watergate has come to represent the lawless power of lawless modern presidents during the years of the cold war. Such lawlessness was on the increase because of the semi-state of war the nation had waged since 1945 under the rubric of the cold war. Although the cold war in general permanently increased the potential for constitutional violations by presidents, only those in the midst of a full-scale war (whether declared or undeclared) have exercised with impunity what Garry Wills has called "semi-constitutional" actions. Similarly, others have suggested that "the cynicism that has always pervaded a large sector of American politics" since World War II is in part the product of "prolonged acceptance of wartime standards of behavior [which] helped erode moral and ethical sensitivities."[9]

No matter which interpretation of Watergate is emphasized, we must clearly avoid the trap of simply asking whether Nixon got caught doing what other presidents did. It is as easy to create a hierarchy of "bad deeds" among presidents as it is to create a hierarchy of oppression among disadvantaged groups. For example, bugging Larry O'Brien's Watergate office for damaging political information that wasn't there may not be considered perhaps as pernicious as bugging the motel room of Martin Luther King, Jr., for sexual information that was there; "just as sabotaging the campaign of Edmund Muskie probably does not rank with overthrowing a foreign government."[10] This approach is not fruitful except to confirm that the Watergate break-in was not unique; in other words, questionable if not actually criminal actions on the part of the American government at home and abroad did not start nor did they end with Watergate.

On the more positive side, as noted earlier, Watergate did initiate a series of reforms, even if many of them were ignored or eliminated by subsequent administrations, especially Reagan's. For this reason, some have viewed Watergate as a cure for a seriously diseased political system, since post-Watergate legislation appeared (at least temporarily) to restore constitutional procedures in the conducting of domestic and foreign affairs by the United States. Thus, it has often been argued that the investigation of Watergate and these subsequent reforms taken together constitute an example of the system working at its best, an "eloquent testimony that the nation had a serious commitment to rule of law."[11]

But was it? Congress showed itself so reluctant to act when it came to investigating the lawlessness of the Nixon presidency that it was only after the Saturday Night Massacre and one million letters demanding the impeachment of the president that the Democrat-dominated House Judiciary Committee reluctantly began "an inquiry into *whether* to begin an inquiry into possible grounds for recommending impeachment to the House." At the same time, Republicans seemed to favor the resignation of the president because, as Senator George Aiken (Rep.-Vt.) noted: "many prominent Americans, who ought to know better, find the task of holding a President accountable as just too difficult. . . . To ask the President now to resign and thus relieve Congress of its clear congressional duty amounts to a declaration of incompetence on the part of Congress."[12]

In retrospect, it appears just as likely that if those advising Nixon had not prepared such an inept defense for him, Congress might never have acted. It took ten months of revelation after revelation of criminal acts and political misconduct and presidential deceit before the House authorized the Judiciary Committee to investigate possible grounds for impeachment on February 6, 1974. In June a Gallup poll showed that the percentage of Americans who thought Nixon should be tried for the bewildering plethora of interconnected misdeeds had fallen from 60 to 50 percent, and the *New York Times* complained on July 7 that the "official investigations seem beset by the semitropic torpor" of the humid Washington summer. Granted, much was going on behind the scenes once John Doar, special counsel for the House Judiciary Committee, began at the end of 1973 organizing his own staff and conducting multipronged investigations of the Plumbers, Nixon's finances, alleged improper use of government agencies for political purposes, impoundment of funds, and even misconduct of foreign policy such as the bombing of Cambodia.[13]

Even the special prosecutor's office under Jaworski seemed to be moving more cautiously than necessary when it recommended in February 1974 to the Watergate grand jury, which had been serving since June 5, 1972, that instead of indicting a sitting president, it simply give its report to the House Judiciary Committee. The grand jury did, however, secretly name Nixon as an unindicted co-conspirator—a fact that Jaworski did not tell Haig until early May. Seven of Nixon's aides were publicly indicted by this same grand jury on March 1, 1974.[14] The wheels of justice turned slowly in the nation's capital, with Nixon, following the advice of Haig and Buzhardt, abetting the process with mistake after mistake in handling the release of subpoenaed tapes.[15] Ford's pardon simply froze this slow-moving process before justice took place.

Moreover, Colodny and Gettlin have provided disturbing evidence that almost all the seven men charged in the initial grand jury indictment (most notably Mitchell) "had not actually committed the specific acts with which they were charged, and on which they were later convicted." The first and foremost act that triggered the charges of conspiracy and obstruction of justice against them was their supposed involvement with Mitchell's initiation of the Watergate cover-up. According to the charges brought by the Watergate Special Prosecution Force (WSPF), Mitchell allegedly ordered Liddy to instruct Attorney General Richard Kleindienst to obtain McCord's release from jail after the Watergate break-in so that his connections with the CRP would not be discovered. Colodny and Gettlin theorize, however, that Dean and Jeb Magruder, as deputy director of CRP, were responsible for this first attempt at covering up and that Liddy acted on their instructions *before* Mitchell even knew about the break-in. The same is true of the second and more serious cover-up involving an attempt to use the CIA to thwart the FBI investigation of Watergate. In both cases Mitchell was blamed. Dean may have been the real source, but he apparently lied to the Ervin committee about when he learned of the break-in. This and other discrepancies in his testimony (and Magruder's) were overlooked at the time because of the overzealous investigation of the cover-up rather than the break-in and because Dean was telling investigators what they wanted to hear.[16]

This is not to say that five of the seven men finally convicted were not guilty of obstructing justice, conspiracy to violate civil rights, or perjury on other matters. It is simply that, twenty years later, new evidence suggests that they may not have participated in the initiation of the cover-up. It is this mindless reliance on the veracity of Dean's testimony that has dominated all previous studies of Watergate.

THE REAL LEGACY OF WATERGATE

If it is true, as I believe, that Watergate has proved more a palliative or placebo than a genuine cure for festering weaknesses within the American political system, it is all the more important that we stop portraying it as "the system working" at its best, dismiss it as an aberration, or, with simplistically negative comments, blame it for all that has gone wrong in U.S. foreign and domestic policy since 1972. If we continue to look at Watergate as an isolated incident involving only a peculiar group of men around Richard Nixon, then in the long run it will be no more important to future generations of Americans than the Teapot Dome scandal of the 1920s. The system worked so poorly both during and after Watergate, especially in terms of the effectiveness of post-Watergate reforms, that it was not able to work again when called on to do so during the Iran-contra affair. Just as the New Deal did not end the Great Depression, so "the system" did not put an end to the problems of accountability and access to information that had plagued the political and legal systems before Watergate. If anything, Nixon's resignation and his pardon (both of which were encouraged by "the system") ended the national agony known as Watergate without addressing its root causes or enhancing democratic accountability. Instead, these acts condoned the idea of a two-tiered system of justice—one for top government officials and one for everyone else.

Watergate and the unsuccessful end to the war in Vietnam have also skewed domestic and foreign policies and internal partisan politics from 1974 to the present. Without Watergate, Nixon would probably have been succeeded by another progressive, middle-of-the-road Republican. Without Watergate and the "stagflation" caused by the impact of the war on the economy, there would not have been a Carter administration to further discredit the presidency (and liberalism). This perceived "failure" of Carter allowed fundamentalism and neoconservative Reaganism to dominate the 1980s, giving neither substance nor sustenance to a dying political system. Watergate, in essence, perverted what should have been a fairly progressive period of conservatism following the end of the war in Vietnam into a regressive one under Reagan and Bush.

In addition to skewing American politics in the 1970s and 1980s, another unintended tragedy of Watergate is that it stifled significant reform of the U.S. electoral system and paralyzed the process whereby presidents are held constitutionally accountable, in part because of the lingering idea that Nixon was personally responsible for all the political and constitutional problems of the nation. At the same time, sleight-of-hand media politics has increasingly substituted for real discussion of issues. The Iran-contra controversy alone has proved, if anything, that only superficial constitutional lessons were learned from Watergate. This distorted view of Watergate as an exclusively Nixonian phenomenon helped to *prevent rather than promote* an effective prosecution and public condemnation of Colonel Oliver North, Admiral Poindexter, and their commander-in-chief Ronald Reagan, on the grounds that the country (and the presidency) could not afford another congressional recommendation for impeachment. Reagan's administration was not alone in adopting the unspoken but unmistakable strategy of making sure that the Iran-contra affair did not become another Watergate; it became the modus operandi of Congress, the press, and ultimately scholars, and is partially responsible for the fact that North, who lied to Congress and destroyed government documents, could credibly run for the U.S. Senate.[17]

Consequently, Watergate has *not* "revitalized and nourished the tradition of constitutional responsibility ... [or] elevated moral considerations in the judgment of public officers and in the conduct of public business." In the Iran-contra affair, Reagan's personal popularity prevailed over justice, private morality, trust, and public conscience—only a little over a decade after Watergate presumably "established historical forces as standards for future political behavior ... [and] reflected an understanding that public officials must themselves adhere to the same rule of law they so piously demanded that the governed obey."[18]

This misreading of the impact of Watergate reflects the determination of certain scholars to exaggerate its importance in order to ensure that nothing connected with Nixon's presidency be positively interpreted. Insisting on such an interpretation, their vindictiveness toward Nixon simply mirrors the vindictiveness they attribute to him without enhancing our understanding of his years in office as the best and worst of recent presidencies. Most important, it implies that "the system worked" to expose Watergate without making clear that this was in part because so many influential people disliked Nixon. The system has yet to work in the same way when a popular president violates congressional legislation and/or the Constitution itself. This makes Watergate much more important than the man who was responsible for adding that word to our vocabulary.

The study of the Nixon presidency is not a struggle "for the soul of history or the souls of historians," unless one believes Nixon to be the devil incarnate.[19] For example, in 1984, on the tenth anniversary of Nixon's resignation, Robert Sherrill maintained in *The Nation* that "Nixon was our Hitler," and a column written under a pseudonym for *Radical History Review* three years later compared Nixon to both Hitler and Stalin, implying that his actions as president approached those taken during the Holocaust and the Communist purges. The scholars and journalists who insist on making these comparisons trivialize the devil, the Communist purges, and the Holocaust. This interpretation was carried to its logical extreme in the 1989 television movie "Final Days," based exclusively on the largely undocumented and extensively criticized 1976 book of the same name by Bob Woodward and Carl Bernstein.[20] The same interpretation dominated all the TV documentaries commemorating the twentieth anniversary of the Watergate break-ins in 1992, despite the publication of more credible accounts questioning both the sources and the conclusions in Woodward and Bernstein's book.

In 1992 some scholars, as well as journalists, began to acknowledge for the first time that "the road from Watergate had been paved with good intentions," and that the attempts to reform the political system since then had largely failed or in some instances "unintentionally spawned a different set of abuses." Yet at the same time, many continued to blame Watergate generally and Nixon personally for "radically transforming American politics" and for the widely held view that politicians are corrupt (with Nixon being the most corrupt), ignoring the fact that public ethics and private morality have been on the decline in this country and abroad for most of the twentieth century, and that scandals involving U.S. government and business officials have risen dramatically *since* 1974.[21] Watergate is more than Nixon because the potential for future Watergates is as great as ever.

Such continuing vacillation and exaggeration over the meaning of Watergate is the result not so much of lack of research or vagaries of collective memory as lack of historical commitment on the part of scholars in general, and historians in particular, to rise above conventional wisdom on controversial contemporary topics. With the scholarly deck stacked against him at a variety of ideological levels, and with the aging, angry

1950s intellectuals still savoring the taste of Watergate, is a revised view of Richard Nixon likely to come from the remaining group—namely, post-Watergate investigative journalists, many of whom still pursue the illusion that headlines and money can be made in Woodward and Bernstein fashion from denigrating him? Probably not.

HOW NIXON VIEWED WATERGATE

While time has stood still for most intellectuals and journalists with respect to Nixon, he did not. His views about Watergate, in particular, evolved. With his resignation addresses—to the nation on August 8, 1974, and to his staff the next day—Nixon even in disgrace showed his talent for using television. In one of his most dramatic television performances, Nixon resigned to avoid impeachment proceedings that would almost certainly have found him guilty of obstructing justice as president of the United States. Both of Nixon's televised resignation speeches represent remarkable performances by a man whose entire career was characterized by effective use of television—from his 1952 "Checkers" talk to his 1956 "kitchen" debate with Nikita Khrushchev. Yet the fact that John F. Kennedy "won" their first televised campaign debate in 1960 continues to convey the impression that Nixon was "not good" on television. Although Nixon's emotional farewell remarks to his staff are difficult to watch even today because he and those close to him were so close to breaking down, there was an underlying order to what he was saying—whether he was talking about the quality of greatness or his parents or a quotation by Theodore Roosevelt. This farewell cannot be written off as the rambling of a broken man. It was in some ways as skillfully crafted as his much more formal resignation speech the day before.

Already red-eyed and sweating, with an even more forced than usual smile on his face, Nixon began his farewell to his staff. He admitted, as he would for several years after resigning, that errors had been made by him and his advisers, but insisted that no one had profited materially: "mistakes yes, personal gain—never." He repeated the theme that "government service means monetary sacrifice" and represents something "far more important than money" several times, concluding that it was this type of service that had made "us the leader of the world" and that "with our leadership the world will know peace and security." At this point it was not clear whether Nixon was referring to himself or the United States. He then went on to remember his father as "a sort of little common man" and his mother as a "saint." After clearing his throat and coming closer than he ever had to crying in public, Nixon sighed heavily, put on his glasses, and read a passage from Theodore Roosevelt's diary. It referred to the death of his wife, whom Roosevelt described as "fair and pure" with "saintly unselfishness." His voice hoarse and cracking, Nixon read Roosevelt's words: "the light went from my life forever." But Roosevelt went on, he said, because "he was a man . . . and as I leave let me say that's an example all of us should remember."

Other segments of this talk have been more often quoted, such as "greatness comes . . . when you're really tested"; one can only "know how magnificent it is to be on the highest mountain" after being in the "deepest valley"; and you hate those who hate you, "then you destroy yourself." This was a remarkably coherent speech made under intense emotional pressure—a fact that both Walter Cronkite and Dan Rather ignored when they tried to summarize his remarks. Nixon had also quoted Roosevelt the night before, when he addressed the nation for the last time as president. Both times he turned Roosevelt's words and emotion into his own—even the improbable comparison between a wife's death and a president's resignation from office worked, because leaving office at that moment was a metaphorical death for Nixon. Yet he would go on, as he reminded his staff that Roosevelt had: "always in the arena, always vital . . . sometimes wrong, sometimes right."[22]

In his thirty-minute farewell to the nation, Nixon spent under ten minutes on Watergate, devoting the rest of the address to his foreign policy achievements. Since he left office, Nixon continued to use television effectively. Over the years his rationalizations about Watergate grew rather than diminished. This was more true of his written remarks than those on television. In his preface to the 1979 edition of *Six Crises*, for example, he admitted that "history will justifiably record that my handling of the Watergate crisis was an unmitigated disaster." He said essentially the same thing to David Frost in his March 1977 TV interview.[23] But in his 1990 book, *In the Arena*, Nixon came close to blaming Watergate on everyone else: "[Watergate] was one part wrongdoing, one part blundering and one part political vendetta by my enemies." In reviewing what he called the "myths of Watergate," the former president denied: (1) having any prior knowledge of the break-ins at the offices of either Daniel Ellsberg's psychiatrist or the Democratic National Committee Headquarters; (2) agreeing to offer clemency to the Watergate defendants; (3) that any obstruction of justice took place, even though he "made the inexcusable error of following the recommendations from some members of my staff" to have the CIA interfere with the investigation of Watergate by the FBI; and (4) that he or any of his closest male White House aides erased eighteen and a half minutes of a presumably incriminating conversation from a crucial tape. He also defended his use of the IRS to conduct "politically instigated" audits because the Democrats had done the same and he "was simply trying to level the playing field"; defended the "standard, and continuing, practice" of appointing a handful of principal contributors to choice embassies; denied that he made any statements at press conferences about Watergate that he "did not think were true at the time"; and denied that he "ordered massive illegal wiretapping and surveillance of political opponents, members of the House and Senate, and news media reporters," saying instead that they were "limited and totally legal . . . for reasons of national security," unlike the much greater number of taps ordered without warrants by the Kennedy administration. Once again he denied that he or his White House staff had personally profited while in office, noting that he remains the "only living former President who has never taken honoraria for speeches . . . [and has] voluntarily given up . . . Secret Service protection," saving taxpayers over $12 million since 1985; and denied that he ever cheated on his income taxes, particularly with respect to the postdated deed of gift signed by a White House staffer in 1969 to deduct his Vice Presidential Papers as a donation to the National Archives. Throughout *In the Arena* Nixon insisted that he was subject to "baseless and highly sensationalistic charges" (many of which he rightly insists were never retracted after it became evident they could not be substantiated) and held to a double standard, especially by the press, compared to other presidents.[24]

By the time of his death, Watergate was no longer a regrettable mistake on which he "never look[ed] back," as he said in the 1970s and 1980s,[25] but something from which he had personally distanced himself by making his subordinates and partisan enemies largely responsible for what he never admitted was a constitutional and ethical crisis of unprecedented public proportions. To him it was simply a "political struggle" and a "concerted political vendetta" whose legacy now and then has been overshadowed by what he called the "Vietnam syndrome." He did not even mention Watergate in his books in the 1990s, and few interviewing him about post–cold war foreign policy ever asked him about the event that brought down his administration.[26] Since his resignation, he deservedly continued to be recognized as a foreign policy expert, but in the last twenty years Watergate assumed a financial and ideological life of its own, independent of the thirty-seventh president of the United States.

Whatever the real reason(s) for the break-ins, I believe that Watergate was a disaster waiting to happen, given the decline in political ethics and practices during the cold war. This does not excuse the break-ins or the subsequent cover-up, which resulted in an obstruction of justice for which Richard Nixon should have been impeached; but if we make him an aberration rather than a normal product of the aprincipled American political system, we will have learned little from Watergate. In the last decade of the twentieth century, the details about Nixon's questionable behavior as president are a part of history that will grow dimmer as those of us who lived through Watergate as adults pass from the scene. Obviously, the Nixon phenomenon will also diminish as an issue in the next century as the former president and his lifelong detractors leave the political arena in which they have engaged in mortal combat for almost half a century. But an Age of Nixon may linger as an object of study long after the details of his tumultuous presidency disappear from living memory, just as the Age of Jackson has.

Nixon, of course, hoped to resolve the "problem" he had posed for his political and scholarly enemies in his own lifetime. "What history says about this administration will depend upon who writes history," he told David Frost in 1977. "Winston Churchill once told one of his critics that history would . . . treat him well, and his critic said: 'How do you know?' And he said, 'Because I intend to write it.' And he did and he treated himself quite well." So did Nixon—in the nine books he wrote since resigning the presidency. But some of the things he did as president cannot be redeemed.

This does not mean, however, that Nixon's accomplishments as president will be ignored. On the day Richard Nixon resigned from office as thirty-seventh president of the United States, James Reston wrote in his *New York Times* column: "The journalists have now written his obituary and passed him on to the historians—who will probably treat him more kindly." Up to the mid-1980s historians primarily emulated a standard journalistic approach for researching and writing about his presidency, lending credence to Nixon's own criticism of the profession of history. "The problem is not that history repeats itself," he said to me; "it is the fact that historians repeat other historians."[27]

Indeed, polls of U.S. specialists seem to bear him out. For example, in 1982 a national poll of four hundred American historians rated Nixon a failure as president of the United States, along with Andrew Johnson, James Buchanan, Ulysses S. Grant, and Warren G. Harding. Much to my surprise, in 1990, despite the unprecedented number of prosecutions and convictions of officials in the Reagan administration and the successful stonewalling of the Iran-contra investigation, responses to another poll of historians rated the Nixon administration the third "most corrupt" (with Grant's and Harding's in first and second place, and Reagan's coming in fourth). This same poll ranked Nixon as the "most imperial" of all American presidents (followed very closely by Johnson, and then at a considerable distance by Franklin Roosevelt, Reagan, and Kennedy) and reaffirmed that Watergate remained the "greatest abuse of power in U.S. history." In determining this last ranking, the pollster gave historians a choice of abuses of power from which to choose. Watergate "won" by a large margin, with the following three events virtually "tied" for second in this order: Andrew Jackson's refusal to follow a Supreme Court order on Indian removal policy; Lyndon Johnson's use of executive power in Vietnam; and Reagan during Iran-contra.[28]

By the middle of the 1990s, only one historian and one journalist have attempted in full-length biographies to break out of this mold of repetition.[29] If historians continue to repeat one another about Nixon only in the context of Watergate, they will not only be living down to his assessment of them, but they also will have failed the fundamental calling of their discipline: to reevaluate, not rehash, controversial historical events.

RESTRAINED REHABILITATION

The lingering negative perceptions of Richard Nixon personally, as well as of many of his international and national initiatives, have gone through several stages since he resigned and was pardoned in 1974. As these words are written at the time of his death, the "Nixon phenomenon" is still evolving because it has yet to be resolved. At first liberals in particular and Democrats in general had a heyday in the 1970s and 1980s castigating the former president for fulfilling their dire prophecy about him as the most evil, venal, lying, and imperial politician ever to occupy the White House. Nothing he did or said was given any credit, according to this immediate post-Watergate evaluation, because his most vocal detractors wrote him and his entire administration off as a historical aberration. Such vociferous criticism of Nixon continues among an older, unregenerative group of liberal scholars and journalists—many of whom gained prominence because of their criticism of his presidency.[30]

During the 1980s, this view of Nixon, which ostracized him from mainstream politics, began to be replaced by a more nostalgic view of the man—not among mainstream Republicans, who, if anything, became more conservative under Presidents Reagan and Bush than Nixon ever thought of being, but among some of his long-standing left-of-center opponents. Finding themselves in a state of disarray over how to combat the conservative backlash of the 1980s—the length and depth of which they had not foreseen in 1974 when Nixon resigned in disgrace—some baby-boomer liberals began openly praising his legacy of "rational and systematic pursuit of a new world order" and wishing that they had his farsighted domestic legislation, especially on welfare and environmental issues, "to kick around" again. This liberal nostalgia for the "good old days" of Richard Nixon waned dramatically when the 1992 election of Bill Clinton promised a rhetorical return to Camelot. Yet it could revive if Clinton turns out to be a Bush disguised as Carter or a blurred postmodern case of multiple identity packaging.[31]

When Nixon left office he did not agree that his domestic reforms were more important than his foreign policy initiatives. During my interviews with him a decade later, he clearly preferred to discuss his foreign policies. Yet his "comeback" in recent years is based as much on his own writings and a reevaluation of his domestic achievements as it is on a variety of public appearances beginning in 1978, four years after he left office.

As is to be expected, given his age, many of the photo opportunities that kept Nixon in the public eye for almost twenty years after his resignation had been associated with funerals, beginning with his unexpected attendance at services for Hubert Humphrey in the Capitol Rotunda on January 13, 1978.[32] Then came Anwar Sadat's funeral in Cairo in October 1981, where he and Presidents Ford and Carter led an American delegation. In 1987 he delivered a eulogy to Ohio football coach Woody Hayes, and attended the funerals in 1990 of baseball manager Billy Martin and financier Malcolm Forbes. Perhaps the two most poignant appearances he made were at the funeral of his old friend and political confidant John Mitchell in November 1988 and, of course, at the funeral of his wife, Pat, in 1993. Added to this curious process of "rehabilitation" through internment services are other public appearances that brought Nixon to our attention over the last two decades, such as his interviews with David

Frost in 1977, his refereeing of the 1985 baseball umpires' strike, his 1987 installation as a foreign associate of France's Fine Arts Academy, and all the interviews that accompanied the publishing of his nine post-presidential books.[33]

Bill Clinton confirmed Nixon's reputation as the phoenix of American politics when he met with Nixon in March 1993, partly because the new president agreed with the old president about rebuilding Russia in the aftermath of the cold war—a position Kissinger has played down (as did the Bush administration a year earlier, before Nixon launched an all-out campaign for aid to the former Soviet Union).[34] Although his reputation as a foreign policy "elder statesman" has seldom been denied in recent years, Nixon was notable by his absence from the signing of the historic Israel-Palestine peace accord in September 1993, but then again so was Henry Kissinger—a testament, perhaps, to the insignificance of their Middle Eastern policy.

Nixon's rehabilitation was never complete in life and will never be complete in death. But it will become more and more spontaneous and less controversial as the public's memories of Watergate become even dimmer and as his domestic record is reclaimed. Regardless of his longevity, Richard Nixon did not "outlive" Watergate in his lifetime, and he was not yet widely "respectable, even honored, [or] certainly admired,"[35] eulogies at his funeral notwithstanding.

Moreover, Nixon's rehabilitation in the 1980s found fertile ground for growth abroad, where his resignation and disgrace over Watergate had never been understood in constitutional terms or thought to be as important as his foreign policy record. Given the dramatic events in the Middle East in 1993, and the collapse of Communist regimes in central and eastern Europe and the Soviet Union beginning in 1989, his grand design for American diplomacy may not stand out as much in the 1990s as it did in the 1970s. Yet he relied on his foreign policy expertise to produce two other best-sellers with the advent of the post–cold war world, *Seize the Moment* and the posthumously published *Beyond Peace*.

During the 1980s Watergate became a fainter and much less sinister memory for that quarter of the population who were not born when Nixon resigned in 1974. Despite the much-touted reputation of the reforms and counterculture of the 1960s, for these younger Americans civil rights and antiwar demonstrations, the antics of the flower children, and Nixon are at best oddities. Moreover, the parents of those born after 1974 either strongly opposed or supported Nixon for reasons their children still do not quite understand. "My parents hate him," one of my students responded on a questionnaire asking why she was taking a class on Nixon, "and I want to know why." On these two divergent generational points of view—that of nostalgic liberals (along with genuinely progressive conservatives) and confused teenagers and fatalistic "twentysomethings"—Nixon's potential rehabilitation rests and continues, phoenixlike, to grow, much to the consternation of diehard Nixon critics and more extreme Republican neoconservatives.[36] Only when all of these current viewpoints are transcended will it be fully possible to come to a comprehensive understanding of Nixon that goes beyond Watergate.

There is a final reason for the partial rehabilitation of Richard Nixon, which survived even the pop culture hype of the 1992 presidential election. He remained one of the few politicians in the United States who could still arouse passion—for or against him. He insisted on speaking out on issues, especially foreign policy ones; he looked like a real person, not a talking head, on television; he stood for something rather than nothing or everything, as is now the trendy postmodern fashion. For years his critics complained about who the "real" or "new" Nixon really was, only to find that the American people always "knew" that, for better or for worse, in Nixon they saw themselves "as *they knew they were.*"[37] A September 1981 letter to the editor in the *New York Times* summed up this feeling of identification with Nixon:

> Americans now seem to partake of a peculiarly vindictive spirit in kicking around our former President. . . . Perhaps, though, this profound rage stems from deeper causes than Mr. Nixon's abuse of Presidential power. Put simply, Nixon, throughout his career, merely acted out some of the most subterranean—and sordid—desires of established postwar American society. It is much easier to heap all the blame on a disgraced President than to question those underlying cultural assumptions from which Mr. Nixon acted. . . .
>
> Yes, Richard Nixon deserves repudiation. But he, too, is no monster. His ideas and character differ little from the people who voted him into the highest office of our land.
>
> Perhaps we isolate and blame him because we fear finding the same impulses and thoughts in ourselves. If so, we must come to our senses and begin to re-examine our nation's fundamental values and assumptions.[38]

Others have offered more subtle and psychologically complicated explanations of the "ambivalent attraction felt toward him [because it] mirrored the ambivalent outlook of an individual into himself." The pop psychology of the late 1960s and 1970s was "influenced by a preoccupation with authenticity—i.e., with being one's self, being honest and forthright, overcoming false consciousness, and striving for naturalness." The harder people tried to be authentic, the more they realized how often they did the right things for the wrong reasons or how they were on occasion given credit for doing the wrong thing. Best of all, they realized that it was possible to say one thing and do another, and to receive credit for doing something they had opposed and others had defended. In this sense, Nixon was (and is) "an intrapsychic dream come true." To the degree "that Richard Nixon in some sense epitomized [his] times," we can better understand the public's identification with him. His biggest crime, in the minds of most Americans, may not have been obstructing justice, but rather stimulating "our own unresolved difficulty," that is, our unconscious awareness of the discrepancy between our public and private selves. If it is true that in striving for authenticity, we suspect that "[t]here is a 'Tricky Dick' within us all, so to speak," then continued public preoccupation with Nixon makes more sense than all the tirades against him by a tiny minority of Nixon-haters.[39] If anything, those who were (and are) most enraged by Nixon are probably those whose *ideal* views of themselves in an age of authenticity made them most uncomfortable, and possibly vengeful, toward an exposed version of their *real* inner selves.

It is not clear that Nixon ever fully appreciated the irony of his even greater authenticity in the postmodern world of inauthentic symbols. Like Ross Perot's in the 1992 presidential election, Nixon's potential appeal by the early 1990s because of his own "real" look was lost on him; he once said to me that "blow-dry hair is now as important as brains" when running for office.[40] It is truly a postmodern moment when Richard Nixon, who had to deal with charges of inauthenticity all his public life, became more real and authentic than the totally packaged variety of contemporary politician. Nixon was so much more than Watergate and Watergate so much more than Nixon that his diehard critics can only simplistically conflate them by resorting to political correctness. Thus, they continue to lament rather than learn from Watergate and the Age of Nixon.

ABBREVIATIONS
USED IN NOTES

FREQUENTLY CITED FILES IN NIXON
PRESIDENTIAL MATERIALS (NPM)

ANS   Annotated News Summaries prepared for Nixon, which he read almost every day and on which he wrote numerous comments

CF   Confidential Files

Clapp Files   Files of Charles L. Clapp, a special assistant on the presidential staff of Robert Allen and coordinator of all of Nixon's seventeen task forces (including the one on women)

CO   Countries Files

Cole Files   Files of Kenneth R. Cole, Jr., staff secretary and then deputy director of the Domestic Council

Dean Files   Files of John Wesley Dean III, counsel to President Ford

Dent Files   Files of Harry Dent, special adviser to President Ford on southern politics

Ehrlichman Notes   Handwritten notes of John D. Ehrlichman, assistant to the president for domestic affairs, on meetings with the president on a wide range of topics

Ehrlichman Papers	Assorted memoranda, especially good on domestic policy
EX	Executive Files
FG	Federal Government Files—Organizations
FG 51	Federal Government Files—Supreme Court
FO	Foreign Affairs Files
GEN	General Files
Haldeman Notes	Handwritten notes of H[arry] R[obbins] Haldeman, chief of staff at the White House, on meetings with the president on a wide range of topics
Haldeman Papers	Assorted memoranda, especially good on government reorganization and public relations
HU	Human Rights
HU2–1	Education—School Integration and Busing
HU2–4	Voting Rights
HU2–5	Women's Rights
HU3–2	Campus Disturbances
HWC	Handwritten comments (other than Nixon's) on certain documents
IN	Indian Affairs
IT	International Organizations
JL	Judicial Legal Matters
Krogh Files	Files of Egil ("Bud") Krogh, assistant to Ehrlichman, head of the Special Investigations Unit (the "Plumbers"), undersecretary of the Department of Transportation
MR	Mandatory Review, process whereby under Executive Order No. 12356 requests can be made for declassification of individual documents in presidential libraries because they are not subject to the Freedom of Information Act
NARA	National Archives and Records Administration; located in the main building in Washington, D.C., with repositories all over the country, and under whose jurisdiction the Nixon Presidential Papers have been since 1974

NHC	Nixon's handwritten comments, usually found on his daily Annotated News Summaries (ANS)
NPM	Nixon Presidential Materials; main collection of Nixon's presidential papers, now located at Archive II, College Park, Maryland
NPP	Nixon's Public Papers, six volumes, published for each year of his presidency by the Government Printing Office
NTCA	National Tribal Council Association
	Osgood Report Secret memorandum written by Robert E. Osgood, NSC senior staff member, in 1969 suggesting a complete reappraisal of cold war policies
Patterson Files	Files of Bradley Patterson, Jr., executive assistant to Leonard Garment, mainly on Native American and environmental affairs
POF	President's Office Files, consisting of materials drawn together from the Special Files Unit from several administrative subdivisions within the White House; largely documents with the president's handwriting, Annotated News Summaries, and sensitive papers sent to the Staff Secretary
PPF	President's Personal Files, consisting essentially of Rosemary Woods's files as secretary to the president, in which there are many transcripts of dictated messages from Nixon to his staff
SF	Subject Files
SMOF	Staff Members and Office Files
SS-CF	Staff Secretary-Courier Files; all of the material that was sent to President Nixon when he was away from the White House, including many action memoranda
WHCF	White House Central Files; a permanent unit within the White House of all recent presidents, for cross-filling, cross-referencing, duplication, and preservation of documents
Whitaker Files	Files of John C. Whitaker, staff secretary and then undersecretary of the Department of the Interior, mainly on environmental affairs and natural resources

WHSF

White House Special Files; a Special Files Unit originally created at the suggestion of Haldeman to provide a separate storage location for documents removed from the Central Files and selected staff members' offices because they were considered "sensitive." Under the 1974 Presidential Recordings and Materials Preservation Act, these documents were processed first because they contained more "abuse-of-power" papers, but at no time were these files considered secret either by the White House or by the Office of Presidential Papers Archives, which helped establish this special filing system for them in the White House.

WSPFFS

Watergate Special Prosecution Force File Segment; collection in which the White House Tapes are located, in the Nixon Presidential Materials

FREQUENTLY CITED FILES
IN OTHER COLLECTIONS

Brodie Papers

Papers of Fawn M. Brodie, in addition to her personal papers; consist of tapes and interviews she conducted about Nixon; located in Special Collection Department, Marriott Library, University of Utah, Salt Lake City

Buchen Files

Files of Philip Buchen, counsel to President Ford; located in the Gerald R. Ford Presidential Library, Ann Arbor, Michigan

Burke Materials

Photocopy transcripts of interviews Vee Burke and Vincent J. Burke conducted with leading participants in welfare reform under Nixon; now in my personal possession

Burns Papers

Papers of Robert F. Burns, counsellor to President Nixon (1969), head of the Federal Reserve System (1970–78); located in the Gerald R. Ford Presidential Library, Ann Arbor, Michigan; some of Burns's papers are in the Nixon White House Files (NWHF) at the Ford Library

Buzhardt Papers

Papers of Fred J. Buzhardt, counsel to President Nixon (1973–74), in the possession of his widow, Imogene, at her home in Columbia, South Carolina

Carlson Files	Files of John C. Carlson, deputy press secretary, Office of the Press Secretary (OPS); located in the Gerald R. Ford Presidential Library, Ann Arbor, Michigan
Cheney Files	Files of Richard B. Cheney, assistant to President Ford; located in the Gerald R. Ford Presidential Library, Ann Arbor, Michigan
DoD	Department of Defense
Ehrlichman Materials	Memoranda, handwritten notes, diary entries on daily calendar, and assorted documents of Nixon's counsel and domestic adviser; located in Archives of Artists of New Mexico and the South West, Fenn Gallery, Santa Fe, New Mexico. Material deposited in the archive is numbered in my endnotes; those without numbers consist of photocopied material given to me by Ehrlichman and now in my personal possession.
Finch Papers	Papers of Robert H. Finch, secretary of Health, Education and Welfare; located at Occidental College, Los Angeles. These papers were unprocessed when I researched them, so no box numbers or folder titles can be cited for the copies now in my possession.
FOIA	Freedom of Information Act
Haig Files	Files of Alexander Haig, chief of staff for President Ford; located in the Gerald R. Ford Presidential Library, Ann Arbor, Michigan
JCS	Joint Chiefs of Staff
Murphy Commission	Commission on the Organization of Government for the Conduct of Foreign Policy (headed by Robert Murphy), Record Group [RG] 220, Boxes 1–77; consists of the working papers, reports, correspondence, and original unedited transcripts of testimony heard by the commission from 1973 to 1975, NARA
NWHF	Nixon White House Files; located in the Gerald R. Ford Presidential Library, Ann Arbor, Michigan
RG	Record Group for papers in the National Archives and Records Administration
WSPF	Watergate Special Prosecution Force, established within the

Department of Justice; consists of investigative reports, interviews, memoranda, published and unpublished material, and legal briefs from May 29, 1973, to the middle of September 1975, in Record Group (RG) 460; located in the main building of the National Archives and Records Administration, Washington, D.C.

NOTES

PREFACE AND ACKNOWLEDGMENTS

1. *Ramparts,* November 17, 1968, pp. 35, 40.
2. Author's interview with Nixon, January 26, 1983.
3. For details, see Joan Hoff, "A Researcher's Nightmare: Studying the Nixon Presidency," *Presidential Studies Quarterly* (forthcoming); and David J. Garrow, "The Legal Status of Presidential 'Papers'—Electronic Records and 'Kissing Cousins,'" paper delivered at the Conference on Prospects for Editions: The Papers of Modern Presidents, Princeton University, October 29, 1993.
4. *OAH Newsletter,* Organization of American Historians, May 1993, pp. 9–10; AP press releases, May 17 and August 4, 1993, NPM, NARA.
5. *New York Times,* August 10, 1993, p. A14.
6. The standard of private-political association proved particularly troublesome in the processing not only of documents but also of tapes because, like most presidential papers, the Nixon materials have some political content. Few are concerned exclusively with the private-political association of the person who wrote or received the document. See Hoff, "Researcher's Nightmare"; Maarja Krusten, "The Nixon White House Tapes," unpublished paper, March 1993; AP press release, "Nixon Tries Again to Block Release of Tapes" (byline James Rowley), NPM, NARA.
7. Edward Jay Epstein, *Between Fact and Fiction: The Problem of Journalism* (New York: Vintage, 1975; rep. of orig. 1967 ed.), pp. 3–18 (quotation on p. 8).
8. For these latest charges, see Seymour M. Hersh, "Nixon's Last Cover-up: The Tapes He Wants the Archives to Suppress," *The New Yorker,* December 14, 1992, pp. 82–95, esp. p. 76; and *New York Times,* December 14, 1992, p. A9. See the conclusion of this book for more details about ethnic slurs and the White House tapes.
9. An example of an interview on stressing the "creative aspects to the construction of memory" without any attempt to verify information can be found

in a conversation with Alexander P. Butterfield in 1988 published in the *Journal of American History* 75 (March 1989): 1245–62. Other quotations can be found on pages 1117–29. I hasten to add that this phenomenon is not true of the interviews conducted of participants in the Nixon administration by trained archivists and oral historians working for the National Archives. A much more historically valuable interpretation of Butterfield's various interviews can be found in Len Colodny and Robert Gettlin, *Silent Coup: The Removal of a President* (New York: St. Martin's, 1991), pp. 332–36.

10. This is particularly true of a former Nixon aide, born-again Charles Colson, who appears to be the main source for Hersh's contention that Nixon wanted to plant McGovern campaign material in the apartment of Arthur Bremer, who attempted to assassinate George Wallace on May 15, 1972. This undocumented charge has led the son of former governor Wallace to request a reinvestigation of his father's shooting—a request under consideration by the Clinton administration. See Hersh, "Nixon's Last Cover-up," p. 76; and *New York Times*, December 14, 1992, p. A9.

11. As valuable as these Brodie interviews are, they are all skewed by the fact that she wanted to "prove" that Nixon demonstrated latent homosexual tendencies, especially in his relationship with Charles G. ("Bebe") Rebozo. I found only 2 interviews among the 120 where the subjects agreed with Brodie's hypothesis: Dan Rather and Scott Armstrong.

INTRODUCTION. NIXON IS MORE THAN WATERGATE

1. Arthur B. Murphy, "Evaluating the Presidents of the United States," *Presidential Studies Quarterly* 14, no. 1 (Winter 1984): 117; George Gallup, Jr., *The Gallup Poll: Public Opinion, 1985* (Wilmington, Del.: Scholarly Resources, 1986), p. 168.

2. "The Legacy of Richard Nixon," transcript of Rod MacLeish broadcast for August 9, 1974 (emphasis added), Box 38, Brodie Papers.

3. Author's interview with Nixon, January 26, 1983.

4. Lloyd C. Gardner, *The Great Nixon Turnaround: New Foreign Policy in the Post-Liberal Era* (New York: Viewpoints, 1973), pp. 25–28; Allen J. Matusow, *The Unraveling of America: A History of Liberalism in the 1960s* (New York: Harper & Row, 1984), pp. 376–439; Charles R. Morris, *A Time of Passion: America 1960–1980* (New York: Harper & Row, 1984), pp. 129–34; Richard P. Nathan, *The Plot That Failed: Nixon and the Administrative Presidency* (New York: Wiley, 1975), pp. 14–16; Nelson W. Polsby, *The Citizen's Choice: Humphrey or Nixon* (Washington, D.C.: Public Affairs Press, 1968), pp. 1–69; Richard Rose, *Managing Presidential Objectives* (New York: Free Press, 1976), pp. 48–49; Jonathan Schell, *The Time of Illusion* (New York: Knopf, 1976), pp. 5–14; Tom Shactman, *Decade of Shocks: Dallas to Watergate, 1968–1974* (New York: Poseidon Press, 1983), pp. 285–96.

5. Author's interview with Nixon, January 26, 1983.

6. Lewis Chester, Godfrey Hodgson, and Bruce Page, *An American Melodrama: The Presidential Campaign of 1968* (New York: Viking Press, 1969), p. 236.

7. Herbert Klein, exit interview conducted by John R. Nesbitt and Terry W. Good, January 13, 1973, pp. 30–31, NPM, NARA.

8. Arthur M. Schlesinger, Jr., *The Cycles of American History* (Boston: Houghton Mifflin, 1986), pp. 23–48. Unlike Schlesinger, however, I do not believe that a private interest era—that is, a conservative period—was initiated by the assassination of President John Kennedy. This interpretation does a disservice to the reforms of the post–Kennedy and Johnson years and to the legitimate reform and some enlightened aspects of foreign policy during Nixon's first term. Conservative periods simply follow wars. An extended one began in 1974 as a post-Vietnam phenomenon, having little, if anything, to do with Kennedy's death.

9. Richard Rose, *The Postmodern President: George Bush Meeting the World*, 2nd ed. (Chatham, N.J.: Chatham House, 1991), pp. 1–7, 17–30. While I generally agree with Rose's description of the traditional presidency (what I am calling premodern) and modern presidency, I do not think the postmodern presidency began with Carter, nor do I think it reflects a decline in real presidential power as the hegemonic role of the United States in world affairs has declined. The United States remains, after all, the preeminent single power of the post–cold war world; all the enhanced cold war powers of the presidency remain intact, waiting to be exercised if Clinton or some other postmodern president can only abandon "directionless compromises" long enough to define a post–cold war role for the United States. See Sam Smith, *Shadows of Doubt: A Freethinker's Guide to Politics in the Time of Clinton* (Bloomington: Indiana University Press, 1994), pp. 73–74, passim.

10. Fred I. Greenstein, ed., *Leadership of Modern Presidents* (Cambridge, Mass.: Harvard University Press, 1987), p. xx. Also see Richard Nathan, *The Administrative Presidency* (New York: Wiley, 1983), p. 2, for a description of how the open-ended original language of Article II, Section I, of the U.S. Constitution continues to give the president vast powers despite all attempts by Congress to put its own stamp on important legislation. Among other things, executive orders, a common practice of modern presidents, have the same effect as laws and do not require congressional approval.

11. *International Herald Tribune*, January 23–24, 1993, p. 6 (op/ed).

12. K. B. McFarlane, ed., *England in the Fifteenth Century: Collected Essays* (London: Hambledon Press, 1981), pp. 23–43; Alan Ehrenhalt, *The United States of Ambition: Politicians, Power, and the Pursuit of Office* (New York: Times Books, 1991), pp. 271–72.

13. Hugh Heclo, *Studying the Presidency: A Report to the Ford Foundation* (New York: Ford Foundation, 1977), p. 32; Paul Johnson, *Modern Times: The World from the Twenties to the Eighties* (New York: Harper & Row, 1974), p. 708; *New York Times*, April 22, 1991, p. A15 (op/ed).

14. Sheldon Wolin, *The Presence of the Past: Essays on the State and the Constitution* (Baltimore: Johns Hopkins Press, 1989), pp. 151–207 (quotation on p. 196).

15. Ibid., pp. 151–79; Ehrenhalt, *United States of Ambition,* passim.

CHAPTER 1. BEYOND THE NEW DEAL AND THE GREAT SOCIETY

1. *Ramparts*, November 17, 1968, p. 35 (first quotation); *Wall Street Journal*, April 2, 1969, p. 14, and April 30, 1969, p. 1; *National Review*, February 25, 1969, pp. 159–60. For the origins and use of these political slogans see Richard P. Nathan, *The Plot That Failed: Nixon and the Administrative Presidency* (New York: Wiley, 1975), pp. 17, 32n5, 98, 100n2; *Public Papers of the Presidents: Richard Nixon, 1969* (Washington, D.C.: Government Printing Office, 1970), p. 789 (second quotation); *Public Papers of the Presidents: Richard Nixon, 1971* (Washington, D.C.: Government Printing Office, 1972), p. 95 (third quotation). The refusal of liberals or radicals to give his domestic programs any credence at the time is best represented in Alan Gartner, Colin Greer, and Frank Riessman, eds., *What Nixon Is Doing to Us* (New York: Harper & Row, 1973).

2. Aside from Nathan (in *Plot That Failed*), few scholars gave Nixon credit for significant domestic reform. No survey of Nixon's domestic reforms appeared until the publication of Leon Friedman and William F. Levantrosser, eds., *Richard M. Nixon: Politician, President, Administrator* (Westport, Conn.: Greenwood Press, 1991). Unfortunately, with the exception of my article on welfare and Hugh Graham's on civil rights, none of the articles in the Friedman and Levantrosser collection is based on original research from documents in the Nixon Presidential Materials.

3. Unpublished paper by Paul J. Halpern, "Personality, Politics and the Presidency—The Strange Case of Richard Nixon," August 1, 1973, Brodie Papers.

4. Hugh Graham, *The Civil Rights Era: Origins and Development of National Policy, 1960–1972* (New York: Oxford University Press, 1990), pp. 302, 308, 313, 475. Graham claims that all of Nixon's domestic actions were based on a "slapdash agenda," political expediency and "moral indifference," which led to a "policy vacuum," in turn inviting the "ad hoc pattern of interesting but essentially uncoordinated and incoherent policy initiatives (or inaction)." See also *The Atlantic* 270, no. 3 (September 1992): 4 (in which the editors apply Arthur Schlesinger, Jr.'s, quotations about Kennedy and Nixon to Clinton and Bush).

5. Nixon to Ehrlichman, October 10, 1969 (expressing concern about the foreign perception of U.S domestic policy), PPF, WHSF, NPM, NARA.

6. Meeting of Five O'Clock Group, April 13 and 14, 1969, Haldeman Papers, Box 43. Nixon to Ehrlichman, January 25, February 5, March 1, and March 13, 1969. Nixon to Ehrlichman, Arthur Burns, and Bryce Harlow, March 12, 1969; Nixon to Haldeman and Ehrlichman, April 14, 1969—all in PPF, WHSF, NPM, NARA. John Taylor, administrative assistant to the ex-president until 1990, to author, November 29, 1969.

7. John Orman, "Covering the American Presidency: Valenced Reporting in the Periodical Press, 1900–1982," *Presidential Studies Quarterly* 14 (Sum-

mer 1984): 381–90; John Tebbel and Sarah Miles Watts, *The Press and the Presidency: From George Washington to Ronald Reagan* (New York: Oxford University Press, 1985), pp. 500–515. The four newspapers were the *New York Times, Boston Globe, St. Louis Post-Dispatch,* and *Washington Post.* Nixon's principal magazine enemies were at *Time* and *Newsweek.*

8. Huebner/Safire, suggested remarks to cabinet meeting, December 18, 1969 (second quotation), Box 4, POF, WHSF; Robert Finch, "A Nixon Alternative," April 1, 1969 (position paper, first quotation), "About President Nixon's New Domestic Program," 1969 (n.d.) (position paper), Finch Papers. Also see Graham, *Civil Rights Era,* pp. 301–45, 393–421; idem, "The Incoherence of the Civil Rights Policy in the Nixon Administration," pp. 159–72; Shirley Anne Warshaw, "The Implementation of Cabinet Government During the Nixon Administration," p. 345—these last two in Friedman and Levantrosser, *Richard M. Nixon.* Discussants at the 1987 conference that produced the articles in the Friedman and Levantrosser collection of essays were inside participants from the Nixon administration, and they generally disputed the lack of coherence in his domestic policies that a number of the academic authors stressed. See, in particular, comments by Sallyanne Payton (pp. 176–85), Finch (pp. 132–33, passim), Elliot Richardson (pp. 134–37), Maurice Stans (pp. 239–46), H. R. Haldeman (pp. 353–55), and Roy Ash (pp. 351–52).

9. Author's interview with Nixon, January 26, 1983. As early as 1958, Nixon had said essentially the same thing to Stewart Alsop. A portion of that interview can be found in the *Saturday Evening Post,* July 12, 1958. The entire unedited transcript is in Box 42, Brodie Papers.

10. Author's interview with Nixon, January 26, 1983. Documents about his Supreme Court appointments can be found in NPM, WHCF, FG, EX FG 51A, Boxes 3 and 4, NARA.

11. Author's interview with Ehrlichman, April 9, 1984; John Ehrlichman, *Witness to Power: The Nixon Years* (New York: Simon & Schuster, 1982), pp. 207–8. By 1978, Nixon's own list of "gut issues" was much smaller than it had actually been in 1969, including only "cost of living, busing, drug abuse, and possibly tax reform as it relates to property taxes." See Richard Nixon, *RN: The Memoirs of Richard Nixon* (New York: Grosset & Dunlap, 1978), p. 671.

12. Author's interview with Nixon, January 26, 1983.

13. Jonathan Schell, *The Time of Illusion* (New York: Knopf, 1976), pp. 111–16. For Nixon's rationale of the Huston Plan, see Nixon, *Memoirs,* pp. 473–76.

14. Author's interview with Ehrlichman, April 9, 1984, and with Raymond Price, January 26, 1983; Hazel Erskine, "The Polls: Pollution and Its Cost," *Public Opinion Quarterly* (Spring 1972): 121; *New York Times,* July 13, 1971, p. 33; Tom Wicker, *One of Us: Richard Nixon and the American Dream* (New York: Random House, 1991), pp. 507–14.

15. Author's interview with Professor Sally Fairfax, Environmental Studies Department, University of California at Berkeley, October 21, 1980.

16. John C. Whitaker, *Striking a Balance: Environment and Natural Resources Policy in the Nixon-Ford Years* (Washington, D.C.: American Enterprise Institute, 1976), pp. 27–31, 79–80; author's interview with Raymond Price, January 26, 1980. Ehrlichman's involvement in national-growth and land-use policies is well documented in the private papers of John R. Price, which I was given permission to research in 1980. In addition to the Ehrlichman Papers, the recently opened Staff Member Office Files in the White House Central Files, under the names John Whitaker, Richard K. Fairbanks, and L. Edwin Coate, now constitute the single best source of primary material on formulation of environmental policy during the Nixon years. For poll data gathered by White House aides on environmental issues in an effort to convince Nixon of its growing importance, see Coate to Whitaker, June 1, 1971, Box 153, Coate Files, SMOF, WHCF; and Whitaker memoranda, May 12 and 26, June 21 and 29, 1971, and Thomas W. Benham (president of Opinion Research Corporation) to Whitaker, June 22, 1971, Box 4, Whitaker Files, SMOF, WHCF, NPM, NARA.

17. Ehrlichman, *Witness to Power*, pp. 97–101. Ehrlichman neglected to note, for example, that it was Hickel who in June 1970 banned the use of 16 pesticides, including DDT, on 534 million acres of public land and proposed making Earth Day a national holiday.

18. Author's interview with Raymond Price, January 26, 1983.

19. DeMuth to Whitaker, November 25, 1969, NHW, Box 3, POF, WHSF, and Whitaker Files, Boxes 2 and 3, SMOF, WHCF, NPM, NARA. See also Whitaker, *Striking a Balance*, pp. 27 (first quotation), 48–56, and *New York Times*, January 14, 1969, p. 27; May 30, 1969, pp. 1, 10; January 2, 1970, pp. 1, 12; January 4, 1970, p. 13; and January 23, 1970, pp. 1, 23.

20. William Safire, *Before the Fall: An Inside View of the Pre-Watergate White House* (New York: Doubleday, 1975), p. 592 (second quotation); DuBridge to Nixon, February 1969 (n.d.); author's interviews with Nixon and Raymond Price, January 26, 1983; Wicker, *One of Us*, p. 510 (first quotation). Memoranda on the increasing political importance of the environment are concentrated in Box 4, Whitaker Files, SMOF, WHCF, NPM, NARA.

21. John E. Whitaker, oral history interview conducted by Frederick J. Graboske and Ray H. Geselbracht, December 30, 1987, p. 12, NPM, NARA; author's interview with Ehrlichman, April 9, 1984.

22. *New York Times*, July 13, 1971, p. 33, and July 20, 1971, p. 12; Wicker, *One of Us*, p. 511 (first quotation), 513 (quoting Commoner at the 1987 Hofstra College Conference on the Nixon presidency), 518 (last quotation); "Nixon's First Four Years," press release, December 14, 1972, Box 19, POF, WHSF, NPM, NARA.

23. DeMuth to Whitaker, November 25, 1969, Box 3, POF; ANS, March 14, 1973, NHC, Box 49, POF; Ken Cole to Nixon, March 20, 1974 (quotation), Box 26, POF—all in WHSF, NPM, NARA. April 17, 1969, meeting of the President's Air Quality Advisory Board, Board to Nixon, December 12, 1969, Finch to Nixon, December 17, 1969, Finch Papers.

24. Wicker, *One of Us*, pp. 515, 518 (quotations from taped conversation on these two pages with emphasis added); DeMuth to Whitaker, November 25, 1969, Box 3, POF, and ANS, March 14, 1973, Box 49, POF—both in WHSF, NPM, NARA; April 17, 1969, meeting of the President's Air Quality Advisory Board, Board to Nixon, December 12, 1969, Finch to Nixon, December 17, 1969, Finch Papers.

25. Whitaker to Nixon, December 29, 1969, Box 4, POF; Whitaker to Nixon, February 25, 1970 (both with NHC), Box 5, POF, WHSF. See also Whitaker Files, Boxes 4, 113, 114, and 149, SMOF, WHCF, NPM, NARA; Whitaker, *Striking a Balance*, pp. 79–92.

26. Whitaker, *Striking a Balance*, pp. 88–92; author's interview with Ehrlichman, April 9, 1984. The administration's environmental proposals that were not acted on by Congress include the Toxic Wastes Disposal Control Act; the important National Land Use Policy Act, intended to bring new discipline and foresight to the way the nation prepares for the long-range future; measures to tax emissions of sulfur oxides and to require advance planning of power plant sites; the proposed designation of forty-eight new wilderness areas, which would have added another 6.6 million acres to the National Wilderness Preservation System; a bill to protect Florida's Big Cypress swamp; a proposal to expand protection of endangered wildlife; legislation designed to avoid past mistakes in strip mining; a proposal to stimulate non-toxic control of predators; and new authorities to control water pollution from sediment runoff. See "Nixon's First Four Years," press release, December 14, 1972, Box 19, POF, WHSF, NPM, NARA.

27. Richard M. Fairbanks to Ehrlichman, December 14, 1972 (brackets in original), Box 19, POF, WHSF, NPM, NARA.

28. *Russell E. Train, Administrator, EPA v. City of New York*, 420 U.S. 35 (1975), *New York Daily News*, May 10, 1973, p. A14; Stanley I. Kutler, *The Wars of Watergate: The Last Crisis of Richard Nixon* (New York: Knopf, 1990), pp. 133–37.

29. Nixon, *Memoirs*, p. 1042; *Wall Street Journal*, October 8, 1985, p. 30E. Kutler, *Wars of Watergate*, pp. 594–95; *NPP, 1974*, pp. 587–88 (quotations).

30. *NPP, 1969*, pp. 564–76 (quotations on p. 566); *New York Times*, July 12, 1970, p. 4; *U.S. News & World Report*, September 14, 1970, pp. 68–70. *Commonweal*, September 4, 1970, p. 432; Bradley H. Patterson, Jr., *The Ring of Power: The White House Staff and Its Expanding Role in Government* (New York: Basic Books, 1988), p. 60. In general, Nixon's presidential papers are excellent on Native American policy. See Boxes 1–3, EX IN, and Boxes 8, 14, 75–76, Patterson Files, SMOF, WHCF, NARA, NPM.

31. "White House Fact Sheet," August 18, 1972, Finch Papers; Willkie quoted in *U.S. News & World Report*, September 14, 1970, p. 700; Kilberg to Nixon, November 16, 1970, Nixon to MacDonald, November 16, 1970, MacDonald quoted in Garment to Nixon, November 20, 1970—all in EX IN, Box 1, WHSF, NPM, NARA. For more information on fluctuating trends in federal policy toward Native Americans from the New Deal until the Nixon adminis-

tration, see William A. Brophy and Sophie D. Aberle, compilers, *The Indian: America's Unfinished Business: Report on the Commission on the Rights, Liberties, and Responsibilities of the American Indian* (Norman: University of Oklahoma Press, 1966), pp. 117–37, 179–213; Edward H. Spicer, *A Short History of the Indians of the United States* (New York: Van Nostrand, 1969), pp. 139–46; Theodore W. Taylor, *The States and Their Indian Citizens* (Washington, D.C.: U.S. Department of the Interior [BIA], 1972), pp. 63–73, 195–201; Frances Paul Prucha, *United States Indian Policy: A Critical Bibliography* (Bloomington: Indiana University Press, 1977), pp. 18–23; and David Murray, *Modern Indians: Native Americans in the Twentieth Century,* British Association American Studies (BAAS) Pamphlets in American Studies no. 8 (South Shields, U.K.: Peterson Printers, 1982), pp. 16–20.

32. *New York Times,* February 1, 1970, p. 41; April 4, 1970, p. 18; July 9, 1970, pp. 1, 18; July 12, 1970, sec. 4, p. 3; July 15, 1970, p. 38; December 15, 1970, p. 31. *U.S. News & World Report,* September 14, 1970, pp. 68–70; *Arizona Republic,* July 9, 1970, p. 1, and July 10, 1970, p. 6; *Commonweal,* September 4, 1970, p. 432.

33. Bradley H. Patterson, Jr., exit interview, conducted by Terry W. Wood, September 10, 1974, pp. 23–42, NARA; Checker Finn to Pat Moynihan, September 17, 1969, Finn to Garment, November 21, 1969, Ehrlichman to Nixon, November 3, 1969, and to Dwight Chapin, November 15, 1969, Rumsfeld to Chapin, March 17, 1970—all in Box 1, EX IN, WHCF, NPM, NARA. Chotiner's sporadic interest in Native American matters can be found scattered throughout Boxes 1 and 2 of EX IN.

34. Agnew to Nixon, October 8, 1971, Box 2, EX IN, WHCF, NPM, NARA; Agnew to Nixon, November 10, 1972, Ehrlichman Notes, for meeting with Agnew, November 24, 1972, no. 181, Ken Cole to Ehrlichman, November 16, 1972—all in Ehrlichman Materials.

35. Patterson, exit interview, September 10, 1974, p. 39 (quotation), NPM, NARA. For a positive evaluation of Nixon's policies by a radical Native American leader, see Robert Burnette, *The Road to Wounded Knee* (New York: Bantam Books, 1974), pp. 165–72; for a highly critical view, see Jack D. Forbes, *Native Americans and Nixon* (Los Angeles: American Indian Studies Center, UCLA, 1981).

36. "White House Fact Sheet," August 18, 1972, Finch Papers; Garment to Dennis J. Banks, October 12, 1972, EX IN, Box 2, WHCF, NPM, NARA; *New York Times,* April 14, 1970, p. 18, and July 12, 1970, sec. 4, p. 3; *Washington Post,* August 23, 1973, p. G7; *U.S. News & World Report,* September 14, 1970, p. 68. See also Raymond V. Butler, "The Bureau of Indian Affairs; Activities Since 1945," *The Annals* 436 (March 1978): 50–60; Vine Deloria, Jr., "Legislation and Litigation Concerning American Indians," *The Annals* 436 (March 1978): 86–90.

37. *New York Times,* June 13, 1971, p. 111; December 3, 1970, pp. 1, 40; and December 16, 1970, p. 25. Wicker, *One of Us,* p. 520.

38. Wicker, *One of Us,* p. 518 (quotation); Patterson, exit interview, September 10, 1974, p. 1, NPM, NARA.

39. Wicker, *One of Us*, pp. 519–20. Wicker probably accepted his own interview with Ehrlichman too much at face value in presenting this interpretation without questioning it.

40. Kilberg to Ken Cole, November 5 and 19, 1970, Ken BeLieu to Chotiner, April 22, 1970 (with Anderson's March 12, 1970, letter to Hickel), Garment to Chapin, December 9, 1970—all in Box 1, EX IN, WHCF, NPM, NARA.

41. Wicker, *One of Us*, 518–20; Patterson, exit interview, September 10, 1974, pp. 2, 21, 24–28, 42, NPM, NARA. Again, Wicker is probably placing too much emphasis on Ehrlichman's interpretation about Morton and the Alaska land issue. The Bradley Patterson files shed quite a different light on the situation, as do documents from the Ford Presidential Library cited in notes 62–63 in this chapter.

42. John Whitaker to Hickel, December 3, 1969; Nixon to Pollock, September 24, 1970 (first quotation); William Byler, executive director of the Association on American Indian Affairs, to Patterson, July 23, 1970; Greene (Kilberg) to Patterson, March 13, 1970; Patterson to Don Rice and Garment, February 27, 1971; Wright to Nixon, February 21, 1971; Wright to Agnew (with attachment on "Views of Alaska Native Peoples"), February 28, 1971—all in Box 8, Patterson Files, SMOF, WHCF, NPM, NARA.

43. Garment to Ehrlichman, March 4, 1971, Garment to Dwight Chapin, March 30, 1971, Garment to Ehrlichman and Ziegler, April 5, 1971—all in Box 8, Patterson Files, SMOF, WHCF; Patterson, exit interview, September 10, 1974, pp. 25–29 (quotation), NPM, NARA. In contrast to Ehrlichman's account, Patterson recalled it was Morton who actually proposed the more generous settlement he and others had been working on at the crucial meeting in Ehrlichman's office when it was announced that the president would back the new legislation.

44. *Christian Science Monitor*, September 13, 1971, pp. 1, 2, 8; *New York Times*, February 20, 1971, p. 17, and September 18, 1971, pp. 1–2; AIPA *News Service*, p. 2 (add). Also see Wicker, *One of Us*, p. 518.

45. Quotations by Native Americans against the BIA can be found in *New York Times*, September 22, 1971, p. 20, and September 29, 1971, p. 66. Hickel's intention to do away with the BIA are described in Finn to Moynihan, September 17, 1969, and Whitaker to Garment, October 6, 1969—both in Box 1, EX IN, WHCF, NPM, NARA. See also Wicker, *One of Us*, p. 521.

46. Wicker, *One of Us*, p. 521. For the political problems posed by McGovern on the Native American question, see John Dean to C. D. Ward, June 21, 1972, attached to Ward to Downey draft (n.d.), Box 2, EX IN, WHCF; ANS, March 1, 1973, Box 48, NHC, WHSF, NPM, NARA.

47. Robertson to Agnew and Garment, July 15, 1970, and Garment to Ehrlichman and Shultz, July 28, 1970—both in Box 1, EX IN, NPM, NARA.

48. Ibid.; Patterson, exit interview, September 10, 1974, p. 33 (quotation).

49. *New York Times*, June 1, 1970, p. 19; Murdoch/Greene (Kilberg) to Ehrlichman, August 4, 1970 (first quotation), "Points Concerning Alcatraz" (draft), January 26, 1970 (second and third quotations), Box 1, EX IN; Egil "Bud" Krogh to Ehrlichman, December 11, 1970 (fourth and sixth quotations), Box

3, Krogh Files, SMOF, WHCF; Patterson, exit interview, September 10, 1974, p. 32 (fifth quotation), NPM, NARA.

50. Patterson, exit interview, September 10, 1974, pp. 31–33 (quotation). See also Krogh Files, Boxes 3, 4, 10, 15, SMOF, NPM, NARA, especially Krogh's March 5, 1971, meeting (in Box 15) with Ehrlichman, in which they were still talking about "getting the Indians off and the navigational aids operative" on Alcatraz. At that point Secretary of Transportation John Volpe became involved in the situation, and both Krogh and Ehrlichman hoped he would be able to "pacify [the] Garment-Patterson-Greene" group in bringing the Alcatraz incident to closure.

51. "Briefing Paper: Wounded Knee," Patterson Files, SMOF, WHCF, NPM, NARA; Clyde D. Dollar, "The Second Tragedy at Wounded Knee: A 1970s Confrontation and Its Historical Roots," American West 10, no. 5 (1973): 4–7. Trouble actually broke out on February 12, when 68 U.S. marshals were called in to Pine Ridge before the AIM escalated the situation on February 27. Throughout the incident there were an average of 110 marshals on duty, with 200 being the greatest number deployed during the confrontation.

52. Dollar, "Second Tragedy at Wounded Knee," pp. 8, 59; Geoffrey C. Shepard to Laird, August 27, 1973, Box 3, EX IN, WHCF, NPM, NARA.

53. Patterson, exit interview, September 10, 1974, pp. 33–36. Patterson to Garment, March 2, 1973 (with press conference attachment), Box 75; Patterson to Jerry Warren, March 1, 1973, Garment to Hobart Gates, March 2, 1973, Garment to Cole, March 15, 1973, Patterson to Ehrlichman, March 27, 1973, Garment to Cole, March 13, 1973, Box 76—all in Patterson Files, SMOF, WHCF, NPM, NARA. See also "Decision Summary," December Group Folder, Haldeman Papers, Box 161, WHSF, NPM, NARA. On March 13, 1973, for example, this informal policy and public relations group within the White House discussed "how to reach [the] objective of making it clearer to [the] media and public opinion that the AIM group at Wounded Knee are very unrepresentative of the American Indian community or leadership, that they are acting irresponsibly and wildly."

54. Garment to headsmen and chiefs of the Teton Sioux, May 15, 1973, Box 3, OPS, Carlson Files; Carlucci and Garment to Nixon (report of the task force), August 8, 1973, Box 3, EX IN; Patterson to Warren, March 1, 1973, Box 76, Patterson Files, SMOF, WHCF; Patterson, exit interview, September 10, 1974, pp. 33–37, NPM, NARA. A complete copy of the 1868 Treaty can be found in Patterson Files, Box 75.

55. Garment to Cole, March 15, 1973, and Patterson to Cole, March 13, 1973 (with Cole's handwritten comments vetoing the press conference briefing), Box 76; Patterson to Garment, March 29 (criticizing some of the resolutions of the National Tribal Chairman's Association as "sheer stupidity" because they fell "into the AIM trap"), Box 75—all in Patterson Files, SMOF, WHCF, NPM, NARA. Through the first half of March, the president's advisers working on the Wounded Knee situation worried about the public perceiving that the administration was in a "'do nothing' posture concerning

Indian affairs and that tougher measures to deal with lawbreaking may be appropriate particularly if irresponsible acts continue." See "Decision Summary," March 13, 1973, December Group Folder, Box 161, Haldeman Papers, WHSF, NPM, NARA.

56. Patterson to Garment (n.d.; second week in March 1973), and Patterson to Garment (n.d.; first week in April 1973)—both in Box 75, Patterson Files, SMOF, NPM, NARA.

57. Hank Adams to Nixon, March 13, 1973, and Garment to Bill Rogers and Ralph Erickson, March 19, 1973, "Summary of March 19 Proposals & Statements of Indian People at Wounded Knee" (Adams copy)—both in Box 76, Patterson Files, SMOF, WHCF, NPM, NARA. A full account by Adams of his participation in the negotiations for a settlement at Wounded Knee can be found in this same box in a nineteen-page memorandum to Vine Deloria, May 16, 1973 (last two quotations on p. 3).

58. Patterson, exit interview, September 10, 1974, p. 38 (first quotation); Weinberger to Garment, March 14, 1973 (with attachment), and Garment to Cole, March 15, 1973 (second quotation)—both in Box 76, Patterson Files, SMOF, WHCF, NPM, NARA.

59. Patterson to Garment, April 16, 1973 (emphasis added), Box 76; Patterson's confidential note for the record, September 13, 1974 (confidential status ended 11/4/88), Box 75—both in Patterson Files, SMOF, WHCF, NPM, NARA.

60. Patterson, exit interview, September 10, 1974, p. 39 (quotations), NPM, NARA; American Indian Press Association (AIPA) *Newsletter*, p. 2 (add).

61. Marvin L. Franklin, assistant to secretary for Indian Affairs, Department of Interior, to John Sawhill, associate OMB director, April 23, 1973, Box 14, Patterson Files, SMOF, WHCF, NPM, NARA.

62. Shepard to Laird, August 27, 1973, Box 3, EX IN, WHCF, NPM, NARA. Shepard described the four in the following negative ways:

(1) *The Vice President's National Council on Indian Opportunity* is basically a sounding board for Indian complaints with very little policy input. (2) *OMB Chaired Interagency Task Force on Indian Affairs* is newly created to try to overcome the lack of centralized direction, but no present top level people in OMB have expertise or a clear inclination to "take charge" of the issues. (3) *HEW Ad Hoc Interagency Task Force on Off Reservation Indians* is basically a continuation of Under Secretary Carlucci's interest in urban Indians which began with his work at OEO. (4) *Justice's Office of Indian Rights* was created this past month in the Civil Rights Division by Richardson to enforce Federal statutes regarding the civil rights of American Indians.

These four interagency groups were, in addition to the Garment and Carlucci special task force, "to investigate Indian grievances and report to the President." See note 34 in this chapter. See also Patterson to Whitaker, June 29, 1973 (with NTCA press release), Box 3, OPS, Carlson Files.

63. Laird to Agnew, Ash, Garment, and Carlucci, August 31, 1973; Garment to

Chief Fools Crow and Matthew King, January 8, 1974; Richard L. McGraw, HUD executive assistant, to Tod R. Hullin, June 28, 1974—all in Box 3, EX IN, WHCF, NPM, NARA. See also press release, May 15, 1973, announcing the appointment of a National Advisory Council on Indian Education, Box 3, OPS, Carlson Files.

64. Garment to Traditional Chiefs and Headsmen of the Teton Sioux, May 29, 1973, Justice Department press release, August 13, 1973, Box 3, OPS, Carlson Files. J. Stanley Pottinger to Mary Bye, Friends Peace Committee, September 28, 1973, Roger Morton to Senator Abourezk, November 28, 1973, Patterson to Garment et al., November 19, 1973, Patterson to Garment, January 10, 1974, Box 75; Patterson to Garment recapping situation, October 3, 1973, Box 76—all in Patterson Files, SMOF, WHCF, NPM, NARA.

65. AIPA *News Service* (n.d.), 1975, p. 1.

66. *Time, Inc., v. Hill* 385 U.S. 374 (1967); *New York Times v. U.S.*, 403 U.S. 713 (1971); *U.S. v. Nixon*, 413 U.S. 683 (1974); Martin Shapiro, "The Supreme Court: From Warren to Burger," in *The New American Political System*, ed. Anthony King et al. (Washington, D.C.: American Enterprise Institute, 1978), pp. 183–84.

67. Shapiro, "Supreme Court," pp. 179–211 (quotation on p. 203).

68. Ruth Bader Ginsburg, "The Burger Court's Grapplings with Sex Discrimination," in *The Burger Court: The Counter Revolution That Wasn't*, ed. Vincent Blasi (New Haven, Conn.: Yale University Press, 1983), pp. 132–56; Joan Hoff, *Law, Gender, and Injustice* (New York: New York University Press, 1991), pp. 247–70.

69. ANS, July 1969 (n.d.), NHC, Box 30, POF, WHSF, NPM, NARA.

70. Nixon, *Memoirs*, pp. 418–20; Haldeman Papers, notes for May 7, 1969, Box 40, SMOF, WHSF, NPM, NARA.

71. Dent to Nixon, May 26, 1969, Box 3, EX FG 51A, WHCF, NPM, NARA; Ehrlichman, *Witness to Power*, p. 118 (quotation); John Massaro, *Supremely Political: The Role of Ideology and Presidential Management in Unsuccessful Supreme Court Nominations* (Albany: State University of New York Press, 1990), pp. 78–157.

72. *New York Times*, October 13, 1991, p. E15 (op/ed); Massaro, *Supremely Political*, p. 136; author's interview with Nixon, June 6, 1984.

73. Safire to Haldeman, May 20, 1969, with related material to June 10, 1969, Box 3, EX FG 51A, SF (Fortas conflict with references to Burger), EX FG 51, WHCF, NPM, NARA.

74. Haldeman to Harlow, October 1, 1969, Box 3, EX FG 51A, WHCF; Buchanan to Nixon, May 26, 1969, Box 2, POF, WHSF, NPM, NARA; Ehrlichman, *Witness to Power*, pp. 113–38; Massaro, *Supremely Political*, pp. 135–52.

75. Author's interview with Nixon, January 28, 1983; Malek to Nixon, October 20, 1971, Box 4748, SF, judicial legal, WHCF, list of "Additional Women Candidates for the Supreme Court," Box 70, Dean Files, SMOF, WHSF, NPM, NARA; Beverly B. Cook, "Women and Supreme Court Candidates:

From Florence Allen to Sandra Day O'Connor," *Judicature* 65 (December–January 1982): 324.

76. Safire to Haldeman, May 20, 1969, Box 3, EX FG 51A, WHCF; Buchanan to Nixon, May 26, 1969, Box 2, POF, WHSF, NPM, NARA.

77. Mollenhoff to Nixon (via Ehrlichman), October 11 and 13, 1969 (plus attachments), Box 3, SF, FG, EX 51A, WHCF, NPM, NARA.

78. Massaro, *Supremely Political*, pp. 135–52.

79. Box 40, Haldeman Papers, Part 2; Box 34, Ehrlichman Papers; Box 6, Dent Files, SMOF, WHSF, Boxes 2 and 3, SF, FG, EX 51A, WHCF, NPM, NARA; Bruce Odes, ed., *From the President: Richard Nixon's Secret Files* (New York: Harper & Row, 1989), pp. 60, 69–70, 74–75.

80. Ehrlichman Papers, notes for October 1, 2, and 21, 1969, Box 9, SMOF, WHSF, NPM, NARA; *NPP, 1969*, pp. 814–20.

81. Ehrlichman Notes, February 12, March 10, March 25, March 26, and March 31, 1970, Box 9, Ehrlichman Papers, SMOF, WHSF, NPM, NARA.

82. Ehrlichman, *Witness to Power*, pp. 116–17; Haldeman to Mitchell, October 14, 1969, Box 22, SF, EX (confidential files), FG 51A; Cole to Haldeman, October 23, 1969, Box 34, Ehrlichman Papers, WHSF, NPM, NARA.

83. Ehrlichman, *Witness to Power*, pp. 207–43; John Kessel, *The Domestic Presidency: Decision-Making in the White House* (North Scituate, Mass.: Duxbury Press, 1975), p. viii (quotation).

CHAPTER 2. THE NIXONIAN SYSTEM OF CORPORATE GOVERNANCE

1. Raymond Price's unpublished interview with Haldeman, November 10, 1975, sent to author by Haldeman; Richard Tanner Johnson, *Managing the White House: An Intimate Study of the Presidency* (New York: Harper & Row, 1974), p. 210.

2. Theodore H. White, *Breach of Faith: The Fall of Richard Nixon* (New York: Atheneum and Reader's Digest Press, 1975), p. 62 (first quotation). White had also noted in an earlier book that Nixon's mind was "neat, disciplined, severely sequential, [and] compulsively orderly." See his *The Making of the President, 1972* (New York: Atheneum, 1973), p. 52; John Osborne, *The First Two Years of the Nixon Watch* (New York: Liveright, 1971), pp. 28, 96; and author's interview with Ehrlichman, April 9, 1984.

3. The working papers of the Ash Council were among those opened by the National Archives in December 1986. Those that proved particularly important for this summary of government reorganization under Nixon can be found in Boxes 71 and 72, WHCF, PACEO, NPM, NARA. I have also utilized a 428-page bound, in-house summary of all the recommendations made to Nixon by the Ash Council provided to me by John Whitaker, entitled "Memoranda of the President's Advisory Council on Executive Organization" (hereafter cited as "Memoranda of PACEO").

4. Richard W. Waterman, *Presidential Influence and the Administrative State* (Knoxville: University of Tennessee Press, 1989), p. 62. In addition to White's *Breach of Faith* and Osborne's *First Two Years of Nixon Watch*, the best analysis of the philosophy, work schedule, and recommendations of the Ash Council can be found in Arnold, *Making the Managerial Presidency*, pp. 280–302. See also Roy L. Ash oral history interview by Ray H. Geselbracht and Frederick J. Graboske, January 13, 1988, NPM, NARA.

5. James Reston, Jr., *The Lone Star: The Life of John Connally* (New York: Harper & Row, 1989), pp. 377, 381 (second quotation); Garry Wills, "The Hostage," *New York Review of Books*, August 13, 1992, pp. 24 (first quotation)–26.

6. William Safire, *Before the Fall: An Inside View of the Pre-Watergate White House* (New York: Doubleday, 1975), pp. 332, 333 (quotations), 334–35; Peri E. Arnold, *Making the Managerial Presidency: Comprehensive Reorganization Planning, 1905–1980* (Princeton, N.J.: Princeton University Press, 1986), pp. 272–80.

7. In addition to the events leading up to his "Checkers" speech, Nixon discusses five other "crises" in *Six Crises* (New York: Warner Books, 1979): the Hiss case in 1948; Eisenhower's heart attack in 1955; his visit to Caracas in 1958; his meeting with Khrushchev in 1959; and the presidential campaign in 1960. For a psychological interpretation of Nixon's reactions to perceived crises, see Leo Rangell, *The Mind of Watergate: An Exploration on the Compromise of Integrity* (New York: Norton, 1980), pp. 25–55.

8. See his early negative reference to the OPA, quoted in Earl Mazo and Stephen Hess, *Nixon: A Political Portrait* (New York: Popular Library, 1968), p. 22; Stewart Alsop, *Saturday Evening Post*, July 12, 1958, pp. 26–29, 54, 58, 60, 62, 66, 70, 72; Stephen E. Ambrose, *Nixon: The Education of a Politician, 1913–1962*, vol. 1 (New York: Simon & Schuster, 1987), pp. 101–4, 137–38; Richard Nixon, *RN: The Memoirs of Richard Nixon* (New York: Grosset & Dunlap, 1978), pp. 26–27.

9. Garry Wills, *Nixon Agonistes: The Crisis of the Self-Made Man* (Boston: Houghton Mifflin, 1970), pp. 90–138; Raymond Price's interview with Haldeman, November 10, 1975, sent to author by Haldeman; Anna Kasten Nelson, "'On Top of Policy Hill': President Eisenhower and the National Security Council," *Diplomatic History* 7 (Fall 1983): 307–26.

10. Author's interview with Nixon, January 26, 1983; Nixon, *Memoirs*, p. 338.

11. Arthur M. Schlesinger, Jr., *A Thousand Days* (Greenwich, Conn.: Fawcett Publications, 1965), p. 625; R. Gordon Hoxie, *The White House: Organization and Operations* (New York: Center for the Study of the Presidency, 1971), pp. 72–73; Theodore H. White, *The Making of the President, 1968* (New York: Atheneum, 1969), p. 505.

12. Nixon quoted on September 19, 1968, by both NBC and CBS, pp. 3 and 5 of transcript, Box 40, Brodie Papers.

13. An example of how Nixon's use of this campaign slogan has been mistakenly equated with his personal commitment to the concept can be found in

Shirley Anne Warshaw, "The Implementation of Cabinet Government During the Nixon Administration," in *Richard M. Nixon: Politician, President, Administrator*, ed. Leon Friedman and William F. Levantrosser (Westport, Conn.: Greenwood Press, 1991), pp. 331–36.

14. *New York Times*, September 20, 1968, p. A1 (first quotation); Richard P. Nathan, *The Plot That Failed: Nixon and the Administrative Presidency* (New York: Wiley, 1975), pp. 37 (second quotation), 38–56; Nixon, *Memoirs*, p. 338 (third quotation).

15. A. James Reichley, *Conservatives in an Age of Change: The Nixon and Ford Administrations* (Washington, D.C.: Brookings Institution, 1981), p. 257.

16. Wills, "Hostage," p. 26.

17. Nixon, *Memoirs*, pp. 591, 925–26; Reston, *Lone Star*, pp. 381, 393–394 (first, second, and third quotations); Safire, *Before the Fall*, p. 644 (last quotation).

18. Richard W. Waterman, *Presidential Influence and the Administrative State* (Knoxville: University of Tennessee Press, 1989), pp. 53–54; Christopher C. DeMuth, "Deregulating the Cities," *The Public Interest* 44 (Summer 1976): 115, 124–25 (DeMuth quoting Moynihan from his notes).

19. DeMuth, "Deregulating the Cities," p. 125; Bernard J. Frieden and Marshall Kaplan, *The Politics of Neglect: Urban Aid from Model Cities to Revenue Sharing* (Cambridge, Mass.: MIT Press, 1977); Waterman, *Presidential Influence*, pp. 54–56.

20. Hugh Heclo, *Studying the Presidency: A Report to the Ford Foundation* (New York: Ford Foundation, 1977), pp. 33–37; Richard Rose, *Managing Presidential Objectives* (New York: Free Press, 1976), p. 32; John H. Kessel, *The Domestic Presidency: Decision-Making in the White House* (North Scituate, Mass.: Duxbury Press, 1975), pp. 17–18.

21. John Whitaker, *Striking a Balance: Environment and Natural Resources Policy in the Nixon-Ford Years* (Washington, D.C.: American Enterprise Institute, 1976), pp. 43–47; Kessel, *Domestic Presidency*, pp. 19–23; Marian D. Irish, "The President's Foreign Policy Machine," in *The Future of the American Presidency*, ed. Charles W. Dunn (Morristown, N.J.: General Learning Press, 1967), p. 162; Arnold, *Making the Managerial Presidency*, pp. 282–92; *New York Times*, February 27, 1970, p. 14.

22. PACEO, Boxes 71 and 72, WHCF, NPM, NARA. See also Whitaker, *Striking a Balance*, pp. 43–44; Rose, *Managing Presidential Objectives*, pp. 48–165, passim; and Arnold, *Making the Managerial Presidency*, pp. 293–364, passim. The Domestic Council absorbed not only the Urban Affairs Council but also the Rural Affairs Council and the Cabinet Council on the Environment.

23. Rose, *Managing Presidential Objectives*, pp. 58–66.

24. Glenn P. Hastedt, *American Foreign Policy: Past, Present, Future*, 2nd ed. (Englewood Cliffs, N.J.: Prentice Hall, 1991), pp. 116 (quotation)–17. See chapter 1 of this book for a discussion of the 1974 Budget Reform and Impoundment Act.

25. Ibid., pp. 67–73; Larry Berman, *The Office of Management and Budget and the Presidency, 1921–1979* (Princeton, N.J.: Princeton University Press, 1979), pp. 85, 105–30; idem, "The Office of Management and Budget That Almost Wasn't," *Political Science Quarterly* 92 (1977): 298; Charles Warren, "The Nixon Environmental Record: A Mixed Picture," in *Richard M. Nixon: Politician, President, Administrator,* ed. Leon Friedman and William F. Levantrosser (Westport, Conn.: Greenwood Press, 1991), pp. 198–99.

26. Burns to Nixon, July 21, 1969, Finch Papers.

27. Burns to Nixon, March 21, 1969, and Harlow to Nixon, March 23, 1969—both in Box 1, POF, WHSF, NPM, NARA, p. 330; Report of PACEO to Nixon, November 10, 1970, copy sent to author by John Whitaker, pp. 330–31.

28. Report of PACEO to Nixon, November 10, 1970, p. 331.

29. John R. Price, "Record of Action of the Second Meeting of the Council for Urban Affairs," February 3, 1969 (top secret), Finch Papers.

30. ANS, March 1969 (n.d.), Box 30, POF; Nixon to Finch, February 1969 (n.d.), and Ehrlichman to Nixon, March 19, 1969 (summarizing Finch's analysis), Box 1, POF—all in WHSF, NPM, NARA. Moynihan walked a tightrope on OEO, criticizing "OEO types" in some correspondence with Nixon, but shying away from calling for a complete reorganization. See Moynihan to Nixon, January 31, 1969, Box 1, POF, WHSF, NPM, NARA.

31. Rumsfeld to Nixon, December 6, 1969, Harlow, December 1969 (n.d.), possible answer to question on OEO extension, Box 4, POF, WHSF, NPM, NARA.

32. ANS, March 1969 (n.d.), Box 30, February 19, 1973 (both with NHC), Box 48, POF, WHSF, NPM, NARA. See also *Washington Post,* October 13, 1970, pp. A1 and A13, for another leak about the administration's proposed OEO budget for fiscal 1972.

33. Press release, August 11, 1969, Box 79, PACEO. Quotations are from Armstrong to Gaines Griffin, May 11, 1973, Ehrlichman to Nixon, November 13, 1969, SF, JL, Legal Aid, WHCF, Boxes 47 and 48; ANS, March 6, 1973, NHC, Box 49, POF, WHSF; Ehrlichman to Richard C. Greenberg, April 25, 1973, and J. Alan Mackay, OEO acting general counsel to Barbara A. Lee, April 30, 1973—both in Boxes, 47 and 48, SF, JL, WHCF, NPM, NARA. See also Garment to Ruth Fleming, April 25, 1973, Box 75, Patterson Files, SMOF, WHCF, NPM, NARA.

34. Krogh to Cole, April 8, 1971, Boxes 47 and 48, SF, JL, WHCF.

35. *Washington Post,* October 13, 1970, pp. A1, A13 (reporting on Rumsfeld's opposition to the proposed 50 percent cut in OEO's antipoverty budget for fiscal 1972); press release, August 11, 1969, PACEO, Box 79, WHCF, and Nixon to Shultz, February 1969 (n.d.), Box 1, POF, WHSF, NPM, NARA.

36. White House Central Files material on OEO proved disappointing. See Box 79, OEO, Subject Categories, PACEO, WHCF, NPM; and SF, JL, Legal Aid, Boxes 47 and 48, WHCF, NPM, NARA. See also Price, "Record of Action," Finch Papers.

37. Quotations from ANS, weekend news review, February 19 and 27, 1973, Box 48, POF, NPM, NARA.

38. Clawson to Bruce Herswhensohn, February 27, 1973 (administratively confidential), Box 14, SF, CF, WHSF, NPM, NARA.

39. Butz to Weinberger, Ehrlichman, and John Whitaker, December 5, 1972, EX JL, Box 8, WHCF; ANS, April 30, 1969, Box 30, ANS, March 19, 1973, NHC (emphasis in original), Box 49, POF, WHSF, NPM, NARA.

40. Mary C. Lawton, Deputy Assistant Attorney General, to Dean, December 27, 1972 (administratively confidential), Box 79, OEO, SF, CF, WHCF; Kenneth Cole to Nixon, June 1, 1973, Box 22, POF, WHSF, NPM, NARA.

41. Michael D. Reagan and John G. Sanzone, *The New Federalism,* 2nd ed. (New York: Oxford University Press, 1981), pp. 3–30; James William Fulbright, *Old Myths and New Realities, and Other Commentaries* (New York: Random House, 1964), p. 6.

42. Nathan, *Plot That Failed,* p. 19.

43. Reagan and Sanzone, *New Federalism,* pp. 3–29.

44. Timothy Conlan, *New Federalism: Intergovernmental Reform from Nixon to Reagan,* 2nd ed. (Washington, D.C.: Brookings Institution, 1988), pp. 19–35, 95–149; Nathan, *Plot That Failed,* pp. 17–34; idem, *The Administrative Presidency* (New York: Wiley, 1983), pp. 15–27; Safire, *Before the Fall,* pp. 275–95; Tom Wicker, *One of Us: Richard Nixon and the American Dream* (New York: Random House, 1991), p. 529.

45. Ibid.; Otis L. Graham, Jr., *Toward a Planned Society: From Roosevelt to Nixon* (New York: Oxford University Press, 1976), pp. 187–263 (quotation on p. 256). In addition to Graham, only a few scholars have given Nixon credit for significant national planning: See David E. Wilson, *The National Planning Idea in U.S. Public Policy: Five Alternative Approaches* (Boulder, Colo.: Westview Press, 1980), pp. 64–93; and Arnold, *Making the Managerial Presidency,* pp. 272–302.

46. Reichley, *Conservatives in an Age of Change,* pp. 165–66 (quotation), 167–73. See also Nathan, *Administrative Presidency,* pp. 60–61; *New York Times,* January 31, 1987, p. 7 (evaluating the negative impact of the official end to the revenue-sharing program on September 30, 1987). The best private set of in-house memoranda on the origins of Nixon's revenue-sharing program (which ultimately affected more local governments than any other federal program in history) can be found in the Finch Papers. Unfortunately, the revenue-sharing material opened by NARA in May 1987 does not contain as complete decision-making information about revenue-sharing policy as had been anticipated because of withdrawals of documents by representatives of the former president. This is particularly true of documents in the Ehrlichman Papers. See Boxes 23–25, SMOF, WHSF, NPM, NARA. Also less useful than they should be on the subject of revenue sharing, because his correspondence with Nixon is still classified, at the Ford Presidential Library are the Burns Papers, NWHF, 1969–70, Box A19. However, material in Box A32 clearly shows the trade-off between revenue sharing and welfare that Burns helped forge.

47. Nathan, *Plot That Failed,* pp. 70–76.

48. H. R. Haldeman, *The Ends of Power* (New York: Times Books, 1978), pp. 167–81; Nathan, *Plot That Failed*, pp. 81–89. The latest adherents to this theory to connect Nixon's fall in the Watergate incident in part, at least, to disaffected bureaucrats in particularly powerful agencies are Waterman, *Presidential Influence*, p. 64; and, of course, Len Colodny and Robert Gettlin, *Silent Coup: The Removal of a President* (New York: St. Martin's Press, 1991), who target the CIA as the leading participant in this process.

49. Reichley, *Conservatives in an Age of Change*, p. 259; author's interview with Nixon, January 26, 1983; David A. Caputo, "Richard M. Nixon, General Revenue Sharing, and American Federalism," in *Richard M. Nixon: Politician, President, Administrator*, p. 63. For others who have discussed this same paradox of Nixon's New Federalism, see Nathan, *Administrative Presidency*, pp. 19–21; Arnold, *Making the Managerial Presidency*, pp. 291–93; and Wilson, *National Planning Idea*, p. 162. See also Dorothy Buckton James, "The Future of the Institutionalized Presidency," in *The Future of the American Presidency*, ed. Charles W. Dunn (Morristown, N.J: General Learning Press, 1975), pp. 110–11.

50. White, *Making of the President, 1972*, p. 358; Safire, *Before the Fall*, p. 283; Joan Hoff-Wilson, "Economic Issues and Foreign Policy," in *Guide to American Foreign Relations Since 1700*, ed. Richard Dean Burns (Santa Barbara, Calif.: ABC-Clio, 1983), p. 1145. See also Robert S. Litwak, *Détente and the Nixon Doctrine: American Foreign Policy and the Pursuit of Stability, 1969–1976* (Cambridge, U.K.: Cambridge University Press, 1984).

51. Reagan and Sanzone, *New Federalism*, pp. 81–122; Wicker, *One of Us*, pp. 524–25; Caputo, "Nixon, Revenue Sharing, and Federalism," pp. 59–60, 64–65; John Ehrlichman, *Witness to Power: The Nixon Years* (New York: Simon & Schuster, 1982), p. 208; Murray L. Weidenbaum to Burns, April 16, 1969, "Report on Revenue Sharing and Welfare," Vincent J. and Vee Burke materials in author's possession. By 1969 at least four Republicans and three Democrats had introduced revenue-sharing bills.

52. Weidenbaum to Burns, "Report on Revenue Sharing and Welfare," April 16, 1969 (Nixon quotation); Ehrlichman, *Witness to Power*, pp. 208–10, 259, 336–37; Ehrlichman to Paul McCracken, Bryce Harlow, Bob Finch, Don Rumsfeld, George Shultz, Caspar Weinberger, Ed Harper, Ken Cole, and John Connally, December 12, 1970 (secret), with attached responses from McCracken, Finch, Rumsfeld, Shultz, and Price, Box 24, Ehrlichman Papers, WHSF, NPM, NARA.

53. Ray Waldmann to Ehrlichman, November 10, 1970, and Ehrlichman to Nixon, December 19, 1970—both in Box 24, Ehrlichman Papers, WHSF, NPM, NARA; Wicker, *One of Us*, p. 412; Caputo, "Nixon, Revenue Sharing, and Federalism," pp. 63–65.

54. Paul R. Dommel, *The Politics of Revenue Sharing* (Bloomington: Indiana University Press, 1974), p. 112 (first quotation); Nixon, *Memoirs*, p. 671; White, *Breach of Faith*, p. 424 (second and third quotations).

55. Ehrlichman, *Witness to Power*, pp. 209–10, 336–37; George W. Johnson,

ed., *The Nixon Presidential Press Conferences* (New York: Earl M. Coleman Enterprises, 1978), pp. 150–51.

56. After only four weeks in office, Connally reportedly told a meeting of fifteen of Nixon's major advisers (including Kissinger) at Blair House on March 8, 1971, that:

> [t]he problem of the administration was threefold as he saw it: Nixon was a "hell of a lot better president" than he was getting credit for; he was doing things for which "he's not only getting no credit, but no attention"; and the administration was forcing issues like revenue sharing and the environment that could not be forced and which did not catch the public's imagination. . . . Moreover, with such a [revenue-sharing] program, "you put yourself in the hands of men in public office, and that's always a fatal mistake." No one laughed. The public official, Connally instructed them, "is always going to look out for himself. If he thinks you're going to get him in a little trouble, he'll desert you damn quick to look after himself." The staff should step back from their daily work and consider their overall goals. The chief goal was reelection. Forget about the war, he told them. By 1972 the war should be "in excellent shape," but they should stop thinking that the end of the war would be the end of their problem. He would take bets that there would not be a billion dollars' difference in the wartime and the peacetime budgets.

See Reston, *Lone Star*, p. 392.

57. White House Tapes, conversation nos. 428-017, 482-018, April 29, 1971, pp. 22–23 (quotations), 24–31, WSPFFS, NPM, NARA.

58. William E. Timmons, assistant to the president for congressional relations, via Clark MacGregor, counsel to the president for congressional relations, January 29, 1971 (two memoranda), Box 23, Ehrlichman Papers, WHSF, NPM, NARA.

59. Ehrlichman to Agnew, February 4, 1971, and Nathan to Shultz, February 6, 1971, Box 24; Safire to Ehrlichman, February 1, 1971, Box 25—all in Ehrlichman Papers, WHSF, NPM, NARA.

60. These included the question of whether to include Native Americans on reservations in the revenue-sharing program and questions about what other civil rights provisions in addition to Title VI should be included in the administration's bill. See Weidenbaum to Cole, February 5, 1971; Nathan to Ehrlichman (n.d.); Weidenbaum to Garment, January 28, 1971; Garment to Ehrlichman, January 27 and 29, 1971; Jerris Leonard, assistant to attorney general, to Garment, January 21, 1971—all in Box 25, Ehrlichman Papers, WHSF, NPM, NARA.

61. Wicker, *One of Us*, p. 525; Caputo, "Nixon, Revenue Sharing, and Federalism," pp. 68–72 (first quotation); Waterman, *Presidential Influence*, p. 127 (second quotation); Conlan, *New Federalism*, pp. 221–37 (third quotation).

62. Transcript of Ray Price's interview with Haldeman, November 10, 1975 (sent to author by Haldeman), pp. 10–14; Ehrlichman Papers, no. 171, 192, November 14, 1972; Nathan, *Plot That Failed*, pp. 61–95; Arnold, *Making*

the Managerial Presidency, pp. 295–302. The supercabinet was to be made up of three sets of members: five White House assistants, who would look after White House matters in addition to domestic, foreign, economic, and budget issues; three cabinet secretaries, who would coordinate interagency matters involving the operational aspects of human resources, natural resources, and community development; and a final group made up of the secretaries of State, Treasury, and Defense and the Attorney General, who would carry on their duties as in the past.

63. Richard P. Nathan, "The 'Administrative Presidency,'" *The Public Interest* 44 (Summer 1976): 41–44; Nixon, *Memoirs,* pp. 337–42, 351–56, 764–70.

64. Ehrlichman Materials, nos. 169, 171, 192, November 12, 14, and 16, 1972.

65. Nixon, *Memoirs,* pp. 768–69; Ray Price's interview with Haldeman, November 10, 1975, pp. 25–38.

66. Haynes Johnson, *In the Absence of Power: Governing America* (New York: Viking, 1980), p. 58.

67. I. M. Destler, "The Nixon System: A Further Look," in *Perspectives on the Presidency,* ed. Aaron Wildavsky (Boston: Little, Brown, 1975), p. 313.

CHAPTER 3. CIVIL RIGHTS INVIGORATED

1. Quoted in Stanley I. Cutler, *The Wars of Watergate: The Last Crisis of Richard Nixon* (New York: Knopf, 1990), pp. 9, 81, 200, 209, 365–66.

2. A. James Reichley, *Conservatives in an Age of Change: The Nixon and Ford Administrations* (Washington, D.C.: Brookings Institution, 1981), pp. 174–75; President's Committee on Government Contracts, *Final Report to President Eisenhower, Pattern for Progress* (Washington, D.C.: Government Printing Office, 1960), p. 18; author's interview with Nixon, January 26, 1983.

3. Daniel Patrick Moynihan, *The Politics of a Guaranteed Income: The Nixon Administration and the Family Assistance Program* (New York: Random House, 1973), p. 99; Richard Nixon, *RN: The Memoirs of Richard Nixon* (New York: Grosset & Dunlap, 1978), pp. 435–44; Reichley, *Conservatives in an Age of Change,* pp. 175–76; Jules Witcover, *The Resurrection of Richard Nixon* (New York: Putnam, 1970), pp. 71–72; Tom Wicker, *One of Us: Richard Nixon and the American Dream* (New York: Random House, 1991), pp. 179, 238–42; Herbert Parmet, *Richard Nixon and His America* (Boston: Little, Brown, 1990), pp. 268–70, 374; Stephen Ambrose, *Nixon: The Education of a Politician, 1913–1962* (New York: Simon & Schuster, 1987), pp. 42, 80, 269, 406–7, 474; Garry Wills, "The Hostage," *New York Review of Books,* August 13, 1992, p. 22; *New York Times,* July 14, 1991, p. E19 (op/ed reviewing Bush's civil rights record). For Jackie Robinson's support of Nixon in 1960, see Robinson to Nixon, January 22, 1969, Box 1, Charles L. Clapp, SMOF, WHCF, NPM, NARA.

4. Nixon, *Memoirs,* pp. 264, 316–23; "Nixon on Target," *Indianapolis News,* November 9, 1964, p. 8 (quotation); *National Review,* April 4, 1967, p. 338;

June 13, 1967, p. 640; October 17, 1967, pp. 1115–19; November 14, 1967, pp. 1263–64; and November 28, 1967, p. 1312.

5. Author's interview with Nixon, January 26, 1983; Dent to Nixon, December 8, 1969, Box 4, POF, WHSF, NPM, NARA.

6. Hugh Davis Graham, *The Civil Rights Era: Origins and Development of National Policy, 1960–1972* (New York: Oxford University Press, 1990), p. 303; Kirkpatrick Sales, *Power Shift: The Rise of the Southern Rim and Its Challenge to the Eastern Establishment* (New York: Vintage Books, 1976), pp. 109–10. See also Reichley, *Conservatives in an Age of Change*, pp. 176, 179–80; Stewart Alsop's interview with Nixon in 1958, Brodie Papers; Reg Murphy and Hal Gulliver, *The Southern Strategy* (New York: Scribner's, 1971); and Harry S. Dent, *The Prodigal South Returns to Power* (New York: Wiley, 1978). For Hoover's southern strategy, see Donald J. Lisio, *Hoover Blacks and Lily Whites: A Study of Southern Strategies* (Chapel Hill: University of North Carolina Press, 1985), pp. 115–282.

7. Nixon to Haldeman, September 22, 1969, Box 229, and Nixon to Ehrlichman, September 22, 1969, Box 228—both in Haldeman Papers, WHSF, NPM, NARA.

8. Nixon to Haldeman, November 12, 1971, Box 230, Haldeman Papers, WHSF, NPM, NARA.

9. Moynihan, *Politics of a Guaranteed Income*, pp. 99–100 (quotations), 101, 103.

10. Gray's handwritten note to Finch (n.d.), Finch Papers.

11. Letter to *Chicago Defender* (from the White House), August 14, 1972, Box 4, EX HU2, WHCF, NPM, NARA. This letter complained about Bond's statement and defended the fact that Nixon had promoted "more black officers to the rank of general and admiral in the past three years than in the entire history of this nation"; that he was the first president to obtain federal support for the battle against sickle-cell anemia; that he had tripled the money available for minority businesses; and that he had increased funds for civil rights enforcement eightfold.

12. Daniel Patrick Moynihan, *The Negro Family in America: The Case for National Action* (Washington, D.C.: Office of Planning Research of the U.S. Department of Labor, 1965). Known as the Moynihan report, it was so strongly criticized at the time by civil rights leaders that Johnson dissociated himself from both the report and its author. It has been widely reprinted. See, for example, Peter I. Rose, ed., *Slavery and Its Aftermath*, vol. 1 (New York: Atherton, 1970), p. 375 (quotation). Moynihan has never retreated from his original thesis.

13. Moynihan, *Politics of a Guaranteed Income*, pp. 101, 103.

14. Cover letter to Moynihan report to Nixon, March 19, 1969, Box 1, pp. 1–2, EX HU2, WHCF, NPM, NARA.

15. Ibid., pp. 17–19, 22, 24–28. See also Moynihan memorandum to Nixon, March 10, 1969, Box 1, EX HU2, WHCF, NPM, NARA.

16. Moynihan to Nixon, January 30, 1969, and Nixon to Kissinger—both in Box

1, Clapp Files, SMOF; Moynihan to Nixon, March 19, 1969, pp. 2–4, Box 1, Oversized Area [OA] no. 564, EX HU2, WHCF, NPM, NARA.

17. Moynihan memorandum to Nixon, January 16, 1970, Box 5, POF, WHSF, NPM, NARA.

18. Ibid., emphasis added.

19. *Statistical Abstract of the United States* (Washington, D.C.: Government Printing Office, 1978), p. 151; *Washington Post*, July 4, 1972, pp. A11–12; Reichley, *Conservatives in an Age of Change*, pp. 176–78; *Brown v. Board of Education of Tokepa*, 347 U.S. 483 (1954); *Green v. Board of Edcuation*, 391 U.S. 438 (1968).

20. January 29, 1969, Finch statement, Finch Papers. The Finch Papers contain a significant amount of information on the first months of the Nixon administrations's civil rights policy. For typical early White House response to criticism of relaxed civil rights enforcement, see Harlow to Representative William Clay, April 11, 1969, Box 1, EX HU2, WHCF, NPM, NARA.

21. *Congressional Quarterly*, February 14, 1969, pp. 255–61; New York *Post*, June 20, 1969, p. 14; *NPP, 1969*, p. 3.

22. In particular, see the diametrically opposed positions on civil rights taken within the administration by Harry S. Dent and Leon Panetta—both of whom wrote books on the subject. See Dent, *Prodigal South Returns*, pp. 121–97; and Panetta and Peter Gall, *Bring Us Together: The Nixon Team and the Civil Rights Retreat* (Philadelphia: Lippincott, 1971).

23. New York *Post*, June 20, 1969, p. 14; Safire to Nixon, June 28, 1969, Box 8, EX HU2–5, WHCF, NPM, NARA.

24. See Box 8, EX HU2–5, WHCF, NPM, NARA.

25. Gray's handwritten notes to Finch (n.d.), attached to Panetta to Finch, May 26, 1969.

26. Panetta memoranda to Finch, June 24, July 1 (confidential), and August 7, 1969, Finch Papers.

27. Panetta to Finch, June 24 and August 7, 1969, January 28, 1970; Panetta to civil rights directors, July 8, 1969; Gray's handwritten notes to Finch (n.d.), attached to Panetta to Finch, May 26, 1969, and July 16, 1969, attached to Panetta to regional civil rights directory, July 8, 1969—all in Finch Papers. Dent to Gray, August 21, 1969, Box 7, Dent Files, SMOF: memoranda in EX HU2–1, Box 8, WHCF, NPM, NARA. See also *Washington Post*, July 4, 1969, p. A12.

28. Panetta to Finch, November 19, 1969, and December 3, 1969, Finch to Kennedy, December 1969 (n.d.), Haldeman to Gray, December 23, 1969 (handwritten note), and January 7, 1970 (handwritten note), IRS press release, August 2, 1967—all in Finch Papers; *Wall Street Journal*, January 14, 1972, p. 2; Dent to Ehrlichman, January 14, 1970, Box 23, Ehrlichman Papers, WHSF, NPM, NARA.

29. Finch to Ehrlichman, October 6, 1969 (confidential), Box 23, Ehrlichman Papers, WHSF, NPM, NARA.

30. Ibid.

31. Ibid.

32. Panetta to Finch (n.d.; October 1969 or February 1970), Nixon to Panetta, February 10, 1970, Ehrlichman to Nixon, February 5, 1970 (with two hand-written suggestions for inserting another paragraph)—all in Box 23, Ehrlichman Papers, WHSF, NPM, NARA.

33. Dent to Nixon, April 1, 1969, Dent to Harlow, June 25, 1969, Harlow to Nixon, April 13 and June 10, 1969, Houston memorandum (n.d.), attached to Buchanan to Ehrlichman, June 23, 1969—all in Box 8, EX HU2–1, WHCF, NPM, NARA.

34. All drafts can be found in Box 8, EX HU2–1, WHCF, NPM, NARA.

35. Ehrlichman to Jim Keogh, June 26, 1969 (conveying Nixon's thoughts), Safire to Nixon, June 28, 1969 (with NHC attached), Garment to Haldeman, June 30, 1969—all in EX HU2–1, Box 8, WHCF, NPM, NARA. For Nixon's complaints about hypocrisy with respect to desegregation, see cabinet meeting notes, August 4, 1970, no. 66, and August 13, 1970, no. 69, Ehrlichman Materials.

36. Reichley, *Conservatives in an Age of Change*, pp. 185–99; Haldeman Notes, April 20, 1971 (quotations), Box 43, Haldeman Papers, WHSF, NPM, NARA.

37. Klein to Finch (administratively confidential), March 1972 (n.d.), press conference, March 17, 1972, Presidential Press Statement, August 24, 1972, Finch Papers.

38. Even though federal appropriations for higher education had quadrupled between 1960 and 1970, from $1.1 billion to $5 billion, Nixon wanted to expand opportunities for poor students even more. The Education Amendments of 1972 provided for a three-year, $19-billion extension of existing federal aid programs to higher education, including enhanced programs for Native Americans and for desegregating of racially impacted schools. However, the legislation also included Nixon's antibusing provisions (that is, barring the use of federal funds for busing except when voluntarily requested and no risk to the health or education of the students involved). The bill Nixon finally signed on June 23, 1972 (after successfully vetoing three others that year because they contained appropriations in excess of what he had requested), did not completely satisfy his antibusing proclivities. See *NPP, 1970*, "Special Message to the Congress on Higher Education," March 19, 1970, pp. 276–84; and *Congress and the Nation, 1969–1972*, vol. 3 (Washington, D.C.: Congressional Quarterly, 1973), pp. 515–17, 598, 602–3.

39. Harlow to Nixon (with NHC), February 16, 1974, Box 26, POF, WHSF, NPM, NARA.

40. *Statistical Abstract of the United States*, p. 151.

41. "White House Fact Sheet," August 18, 1972, Finch Papers.

42. Ibid.; *Federal Register* 34: 12985.

43. Samuel H. Beer, "In Search of a New Public Philosophy," in *The New American Political System*, ed. Anthony King et al. (Washington, D.C.: American Enterprise Institute, 1978), p. 35 (quotation); "White House Fact Sheet,"

August 18, 1972, Finch Papers; Richard P. Nathan, *The Plot That Failed: Nixon and the Administrative Presidency* (New York: Wiley, 1975), p. 16.

44. Graham, *Civil Rights Era*, pp. 302, 308, 313, 475. Like Stephen Ambrose (*Nixon: Education of a Politician*), Graham fails to understand the consistency or strength of Nixon's civil rights record as president because he claims that there was no coherence to any of Nixon's domestic actions. See note 4 in chapter 1.

45. See notes 3 and 6 of this chapter.

46. J. Larry Hood, "The Nixon Administration and the Revised Philadelphia Plan for Affirmative Action: A Study in Expanding Presidential Power and Divided Government," *Presidential Studies Quarterly* 23 (Winter 1993): 145–269.

47. Ibid.

48. Ibid. See also Garment to James M. Jones, December 31, 1969, Box 8, EX HU2-1, WHCF, NPM, NARA.

49. *Buffalo News*, December 26, 1990, p. C3 (Evans and Novak column); Nixon to Philip E. Hoffman, president, American Jewish Committee, August 11, 1972, and U.S. Civil Rights Commission to Dennis Garrison, September 27, 1972—both in Box 4, EX HU2, WHCF, NPM, NARA.

50. Hood, "Nixon Administration and Revised Philadelphia Plan"; federal statute 41CFR60-2 (quotation). Again, even though Graham admits the importance of Order No. 4, he refuses to give Nixon or Shultz any credit for the expansive affirmative action aspects of it, preferring to attribute its drafting and issuance to the "arcane technical nature of the modern administrative state . . . [and] bureaucratic boilerplates." See Graham, *Civil Rights Era*, pp. 343, 409–10.

51. Graham, *Civil Rights Era*, pp. 420–45, 448; Dean to Garment, February 26, 1971 (plus attachments), Finch Papers. I have not gone into this matter in greater detail because Nixon's papers do not indicate that he was personally involved in this debate over how to enforce Title VII more effectively.

52. "First Four Years," press release, December 4, 1972, Box 19, POF, WHCF, NPM, NARA; *Business Week*, March 24, 1973, pp. 74–75.

53. Wicker, *One of Us*, p. 492; Graham, *Civil Rights Era*, pp. 346–65.

54. Garment to Ehrlichman, December 8, 1969, Box 4, POF, WHSF, NPM, NARA.

55. For details, see Graham, *Civil Rights Era*, pp. 346–62 (quotation on p. 361).

56. Nixon to Elliott Davis, NASBIC president, July 11, 1968; L. P. Gray III to Haldeman, December 23, 1968 (with attachments); Walter B. Stults, NASBIC executive director, to Gray, December 26, 1968; Charles M. Noone, NASBIC general counsel, to Gray, December 27, 1968; George C. Williams, NASBIC president, to Gray, January 2, 1969; Gray to Haldeman, January 4, 1969 (in which Gray admits to "bombarding" Haldeman with an "amphibious assault against an impregnable objective, storming your citadel, so to speak"—all in Finch Papers. For details of Nixon's radio addresses and change in rhetoric, see John McClaughry, "Black Ownership and National Politics," in *Black*

Economic Development, ed. William F. Haddad and Douglas Pugh (Englewood Cliffs, N.J.: Prentice-Hall, 1969), pp. 38–49; and unpublished paper by John C. Topping, Jr., in author's possession, "A Star-Spangled Success: A Retrospective Look at the Early Years of the Federal Minority Business Program," pp. 10–11. Topping served as counsel to the president's advisory council on minority business enterprise. His paper, written sometime in the early 1980s, was given to me by Walter Sorg, a Chicago printing company executive and veteran of the successful 1966 Republican campaign of Chuck Percy for the U.S. Senate. Sorg became OMBE's liaison with the corporate community. A large number of liberal Republicans involved in Percy's campaign were associated with OMBE, and Percy himself encouraged Stans to be an innovative secretary of commerce and to revitalize the department, in part by promoting minority entrepreneurial development (pp. 15–16). This made a clash of interest with SBA inevitable. (In deciding to establish OMBE within the Commerce Department, Stans anticipated Shultz's March decision to revise the Philadelphia Plan and strengthen the Office of Contract Compliance inside the Labor Department rather than transferring it to EEOC. In both instances these men appear to have acted out of conviction and territorial imperative.) See also Maurice H. Stans, *The Terrors of Justice* (New York: Everest House, 1978), pp. 102–3; and Cole to Chapin, January 29, 1969, and Report on Minority Contractors by Herbert S. Tompkin—both in Box 1, Clapp Files, SMOF, WHCF, NPM, NARA.

57. Note how much less tolerant Nixon was when similar charges were made against OEO, discussed in chapter 3. Criticism of SBA continued unabated from the 1960s through the 1980s for contradictory reasons: it was too cautious or it was mismanaged by overzealous, second-rate managers. Democrats generally supported it only under Democratic presidents. Republicans remained more consistently committed to the SBA because of its origins under Eisenhower, but became increasingly concerned in the 1960s about the decline in large company support for the program. Additionally, certain conservative columnists such as Jack Anderson conducted a personal crusade against the SBA under all administrations, but especially Johnson's, Nixon's, and Carter's, where special efforts were made to extend loans to minorities. See Nixon to Elliot Davis, NASBIC president, July 11, 1968, Finch Papers; Garment to Nixon, April 20, 1970, Box 2, EX HU2, WHCF, NPM, NARA; *Washington Post*, June 8, 1981, p. C15 (Jack Anderson column); and Graham, *Civil Rights Era*, p. 314.

58. *NPP, 1969*, pp. 197–98; Topping, "Star-Spangled Success," pp. 13–15. Topping's January 21, 1981, interview with Stans is the source of this paraphrased quotation by the secretary of commerce. For Stans's latest defense of OMBE, see "Nixon's Economic Policy Toward Minorities," in *Richard M. Nixon: Politician, President, Administrator*, ed. Leon Friedman and William F. Levantrosser (Westport, Conn.: Greenwood Press, 1991), pp. 239–46.

59. The strongest published criticism of OMBE from liberal Democrats can be found in Arthur I. Blaustein and Geoffrey Faux, *The Star-Spangled Hustle*

(Garden City, N.Y.: Doubleday, 1972). See also Topping, "Star-Spangled Success," p. 9 (Moynihan quotation is based on his January 21, 1981, interview with Gary Baden, OMBE's government program head); Stans to Mayo, August 6, 1969, file TI-6/2, series 69.1, Bureau of the Budget, NARA; Nixon to head of departments and agencies, December 5, 1969, Box 2, EX HU2, WHCF, NPM, NARA; Stans, report on "National Program for Minority Enterprise," September 10, 1969, and idem, report on "National Strategy for Minority Enterprise," October 13, 1969, Finch Papers; and Graham, *Civil Rights Era*, p. 315.

60. Topping, "Star-Spangled Success," pp. 7, 20; staff and department briefs, March 10, 1969 (confidential, including Laird's criticism), Box 30, POF, WHSF; Nixon to Shultz, October 2, 1972, Ehrlichman to Peterson, August 10, 1972, John Evans to John Campbell, September 26, 1972—all in Box 4, EX HU2, WHCF, NPM, NARA. For external and internal criticism of OMBE, see Garment to Cole, April 20, 1970 (including Laird's criticism), Box 2, EX HU2, WHCF, NPM, NARA.

61. For the long-run successes of OMBE in terms of black and brown capitalism, see *Nuestro Business Review* 2 (January–February 1981): 5–8; *Black Enterprise* 11 (June 1981): 121–28; Stans, "Nixon's Economic Policy Toward Minorities," pp. 244–45; and *Washington Post*, June 16, 1987, p. 27.

62. For details about Hispanics and the Nixon administration, see Graham, *Civil Rights Era*, pp. 314, 316 (quotation), 317–18.

63. Ehrlichman to Nixon, April 23, 1970, Box 2; Colson to Ehrlichman, December 20, 1971 (confidential), and Cole to Morgan, January 10, 1972, Box 4—all in EX HU2 WHCF, NPM, NARA.

64. Graham, *Civil Rights Era*, pp. 317–18. Flanigan to Harry Flemming, July 5, 1970, and Ehrlichman to Nixon, November 24, 1970, Box 2; Chapin to Garment, December 31, 1970, Box 3; Colson to Ehrlichman, December 20, 1971 (confidential), Box 4—all in EX HU2. Nixon to Desi Arnaz, January 27, 1969, Box 1, Clapp Files, SMOF, WHCF, NPM, NARA.

65. Joan Hoff, *Law, Gender, and Injustice: A Legal History of U.S. Women* (New York: New York University Press, 1991). See charts on pp. 236–44 for a comparison of litigation and legislation affecting women from Kennedy to Bush.

66. For details about these different attitudes toward women between the administrations of JFK and LBJ, see ibid., pp. 231–233; and Graham, *Civil Rights Era*, pp. 400–406.

67. Glazer to Burns, May 23, 1969 (with attachments), Box 39, Clapp Files, SMOF, WHCF, NPM, NARA; Helen Delich Bentley, chair of the Federal Maritime Commission, to Nixon (confidential), 1970 (n.d.), Finch Papers.

68. "Nixon's First Four Years," press release, December 14, 1972, Box 19, POF, WHSF, NPM, NARA; "Women in the Economy," Stein speech, September 21, 1972, Finch Papers; Wicker, *One of Us*, p. 522; Hoff, *Law, Gender, and Injustice*, pp. 231–32.

69. Bentley to Nixon (confidential), 1970 (n.d.), and Finch to Nixon, April 15, 1971—both in Finch Papers.

70. *NPP, 1969,* press conference, February 6, 1969, p. 75; Burns to Nixon, January 18, 1969, transitional task force reports, 1968–1969, Box 1, WHCF; East to Shultz, December 30, 1968, Box 39, Clapp Files, SMOF, WHCF, NPM, NARA; Graham, *Civil Rights Era,* pp. 394–97.

71. Republican congresswoman Florence Dwyer (N.J.) had made this same suggestion to Nixon as early as February 26, 1969. See Glaser to Burns (summarizing Dwyer's letter), May 23, 1969, Box 39, Clapp Files, SMOF, WHCF, NPM, NARA. Nixon did not act on this suggestion until January 1973 for reasons discussed later in the chapter.

72. Graham, *Civil Rights Era,* pp. 397–98; Glaser to Burns, May 23, 1969 (with attachments), Box 39, Clapp Files, SMOF, WHCF, NPM, NARA. White House material on women is concentrated in NPM, WHCF, EX HU2–5, Boxes 21 and 22, and Clapp Files, Task Force on Women's Rights and Responsibilities, Boxes 9, 11, 39, SMOF, WHCF, NARA. The Finch Papers also contain considerable material on women, as, of course, do the working papers of the Committee on Population Growth cited in note 103 of this chapter.

73. Glaser to Burns, May 23, 1969, and Dwyer to Nixon, July 8, 1969—both in Box 39, Clapp Files, SMOF, WHCF, NPM, NARA. For Nixon's and Ziegler's response to Hauser's 1969 statement, see president's ANS, POF, Box 30, May 1969 (n.d.).

74. *NPP, 1969,* pp. 291, 297. Even Finch made similar statements, telling a group of Republican women that "[w]ith a wife like Carol who keeps me in shape at home, and a secretary like Doris who keeps me in shape at the office there is no question in my mind about the importance of women." See draft of Finch speech, September 24, 1969, Finch Papers.

75. *NPP, 1969,* p. 291; Glaser to Burns, May 23, 1969, and Dwyer to Nixon (cosigned by Representatives Heckler, May, and Reid)—both in Box 39, Clapp Files, SMOF, WHCF, NPM, NARA. These same congresswomen had telegrammed Nixon their general concern that he not neglect women's issues before his second State of the Union address, in January 1970. For his relatively noncommittal response, see Nixon's telegram to Dwyer, January 23, 1970, *National Women's Party Papers, 1913–1974,* microfilm reel 3.

76. John Ehrlichman, *Witness to Power: The Nixon Years* (New York: Simon & Schuster, 1982), pp. 82, 239. At a May 20, 1971, meeting in the Oval Office, Kilberg was discussed very negatively. One aide said, "She is cutting us—so bad—get her out before June," and Ehrlichman reported that the president did not want to "have her in any meetings with him." See Haldeman Notes, May 20, 1971, Box 43, Haldeman Papers, WHSF; Krogh meeting with Ehrlichman, March 5, 1971, Box 15, Krogh Files; and listing of staff positions issued by White House press secretary, April 1971, Box 150, Whitaker Files, SMOF, WHCF, NPM, NARA.

77. Moynihan to Nixon, August 20, 1969, Box 21, EX HU2–5, WHCF, NPM, NARA; Graham, *Civil Rights Era,* pp. 406–7.

78. Ehrlichman to Nixon, September 29, 1969, Ehrlichman to staff secretary (Ken-

neth R. Cole), August 27, 1969, Keogh to staff secretary, August 26, 1969, Flanigan to staff secretary, August 25, 1969, Harlow to staff secretary, August 21, 1969, Cole to Nixon, August 30, 1969, Box 21; Spencer to Harlow, December 10, 1973, Box 22—all in EX HU2–5, WHCF, NPM, NARA. In responding to Spencer about Armstrong's suggestion that a major civil service commission study be undertaken on the problems in the federal employment of women, Harlow implied that such a project had already been done and that in any case they should "quietly go over this with Bob Hampton first. He's a great guy."

79. Helen Delich Bentley to Nixon (confidential), 1970 (n.d.), quoting Ziegler, press release, August 18, 1972, Finch Papers; December Group Decision Summary, March 13, 1973, Haldeman Papers, Box 161, WHSF, NPM, NARA.

80. Graham, *Civil Rights Era*, pp. 393–400; Hoff, *Law, Gender, and Injustice*, pp. 206–12, 230–33. Burns to Virginia R. Allen, September 12, 1969, Box 9; minutes of first meeting of Women's Task Force, September 25–26, 1969, Box 39—both in Clapp Files, SMOF, WHCF, NPM, NARA.

81. Dwyer to Nixon, July 8, 1969, Box 39, Clapp Files, SMOF, NPM, NARA.

82. Haldeman to Finch (paraphrasing Nixon's views), September 8, 1970 (confidential), Finch Papers, also in Box 42, SS-CF, P600-P650, SMOF, WHSF; Shultz to Bruce Rabb, June 3, 1970, Box 39, Clapp Files, SMOF; Richardson to Ehrlichman, January 12, 1972, EX HU2–5 21, WHCF, NPM, NARA.

83. John R. Brown III to George Grassmuck, executive assistant to Finch, November 21, 1970, Higby to Haldeman, November 21, 1970, Finch to staff secretary, October 17, 1970 (confidential)—all in Box 42, SS-CF, SMOF, WHSF; Finch to staff secretary, December 4, 1970 (confidential), Finch Papers.

84. Nixon memorandum to heads of executive departments and agencies, April 1971; Finch to office of staff secretary, December 4, 1970, Finch Papers; Malek to Nixon (list of women attorneys serving in high-level positions), October 20, 1971, Box 47, SF, JL, WHCF, NPM, NARA.

85. Confidential memorandum from Jon M. Huntsman to Finch, May 5, 1971 (quoting NHC on Finch's April 15 memorandum), Finch Papers; Wicker, *One of Us*, p. 522. For a negative use of this quotation by Nixon, see Graham, *Civil Rights Era*, p. 411.

86. Garment to Haldeman, April 19, 1971, and Ehrlichman to staff secretary (Kenneth R. Cole, Jr.), August 27, 1969 (in connection with Moynihan's memorandum discussed above)—both in Box 21, EX HU2–5, WHCF, NPM, NARA.

87. Morey to Cole, July 28, 1972, Box 21, EX HU2–5, WHCF, NPM, NARA; *Dallas Morning News*, January 17, 1974.

88. Representative samples of Armstrong's, Ruckelshaus's, and Spencer's letters can be found in Box 22, HU2–5, WHCF, NPM, NARA; *Dallas Morning News*, January 17, 1974.

89. Nixon to Josephine Terrill, November 14, 1946, Terrill to Anita L. Pollitzer, November 20, 1946, Nixon to Katharine St. George, February 1, 1949, state-

ment as vice president, August 26, 1960—all in the National Women's party papers, 1913–1974, reels 90, 94, and 104; Nixon campaign statement, July 1968, *Civil Rights During the Nixon Administration, Part I: The White House Central Files* (University Publications of America), reel 23. In particular, Paul recalled that Nixon became "too busy" as vice president to meet with representatives of the National Women's party. See *Conversations with Alice Paul: Woman Suffrage and the Equal Rights Amendment,* Berkeley Oral History, pp. 387–96. Interestingly, White House press releases and correspondence usually said that Nixon's support for ERA went back only to 1951.

90. "Recommendations of the Committee on Population Growth and the American Future," Box 6, RG 148, NARA; *New York Times,* January 21, 1972, p. 20.

91. Woods to Noble Melencamp, February 10, 1969; Nixon to Claudia Giannini Hoffman, February 11, 1969; Nixon to Margaret Belcher, president of the National Association of Negro Business and Professional Women's Clubs, August 14, 1969—all in Box 21, EX HU2–5, WHCF, NPM, NARA.

92. Transcript, Rehnquist testimony, April 1, 1971, Box 21, EX HU2–5, WHCF, NPM, NARA.

93. Catherine May Bedell, chair, U.S. Tariff Commission; Helen Delich Bentley, chair, Federal Maritime Commission; Mary Brooks, director, Bureau of the Mint; Florence P. Dwyer, member of Congress; Margaret M. Heckler, member of Congress; Patricia Reilly Hitt, assistant secretary for Community and Field Services; Carol M. Khosrovi, assistant director for the Office of Program Development, Office of Economic Opportunity; Charlotte T. Reid, member of Congress; Jayne B. Spain, vice chair, U.S. Civil Service Commission; and Ethel Bent Walsh, commissioner, Equal Employment Opportunity Commission—all to Nixon, July 20, 1971, in Box 21, EX HU2–5, WHCF, NPM, NARA.

94. Franklin to Malek, August 31, 1971, Finch Papers; Garment to Nixon, action request memorandum, September 1971 (n.d.), Dean Files, Box 33, WHSP, NPM, NARA.

95. Colson to David Parker, May 4, 1971, Box 21, EX HU2–5, WHCF, NPM, NARA.

96. Graham incorrectly stated that Nixon did not agree to the exchange. See *Civil Rights Era,* p. 557n90.

97. Hullin to Garment, September 20, 1971, Box 21, EX HU2–5, WHCF; Garment to Nixon, action memorandum, October 1, 1971, Box 36, SS-CF, SMOF, WHSF, NPM, NARA. Garment went out of his way to tell Nixon that John Dean "strongly concurs—with the observation that any short term political benefit from endorsing the amendment with specificity is outweighed by the troublesome precedent of the President being placed in a position of endorsing countless additional amendments that may also emerge through the efforts of small but intense lobbies."

98. Garment to Nixon, action memorandum, October 1, 1971, Box 36, SS-CF, SMOF, WHSF, NPM, NARA.

99. Compare Garment's May 25, 1970, memorandum to Ehrlichman to his September and October 1972 ones to Nixon.

100. Finch to Gutwillig, May 17, 1971, Box 21, EX HU2–5, WHCF, NPM, NARA.

101. Author's interview with Nixon, January 26, 1983.

102. Nixon to Laird, March 24, 1971, Nixon to secretaries of the military departments, March 31, 1971, Laird to Nixon, March 31, 1971—all in Box 1, Carlson Files.

103. Press release, May 5, 1971, Box 1, Carlson Files. The John Roy Price Papers, to which I was given special access, contain a wealth of information about how hard Price, Moynihan, Ehrlichman, and Whitaker worked on developing a rural and later an urban growth policy from 1969 to the beginning of 1972. Also see the Records of the Commission on Population Growth and the American Future, esp. Boxes 1, 2, 6, 30, RG 148, NARA; and David E. Wilson, *The National Planning Idea: Five Alternative Approaches* (Boulder, Colo.: Westview Press, 1980), pp. 64–66.

104. Hauser to Ehrlichman, August 28, 1972 (emphasis in original), Box 21, EX HU2–5, NPM, WHCF, NARA.

105. "Nixon's First Four Years," press release, December 14, 1972, Box 19, POF, WHSF, NPM, NARA.

106. Geoffrey Shepard to Nixon (through Cole), May 17, 1974, Box 26, POF, WHSF; Carlucci to Ken Cole, January 8, 1972, and Shultz to Ehrlichman, January 14, 1972—both in Box 21, EX HU2–1, WHCF, NPM, NARA.

107. "Veto of Economic Opportunity Amendments of 1971," December 10, 1971, document no. 387, *NPP, 1971* (Washington, D.C.: Government Printing Office, 1972), pp. 1174–78; Andrews's draft of veto message, December 8, 1971, Box 21, EX HU2–5, WHCF, NPM, NARA.

108. News conference transcript no. 1274, December 9, 1971, transcript of Frank Carlucci and Stephen Kurzman press conference, December 9, 1971, Colson to Haldeman, December 8, 1971 (two separate memoranda)—all in Box 87, Haldeman Papers, WHSF, NPM, NARA.

109. Buchanan to Haldeman, December 9, 1971, Box 87, Haldeman Papers, WHSF, NPM, NARA. This memorandum makes it very clear that Buchanan was not sure the president would accept his draft, but he continued to insist that "since we are certain to get our lumps from the opposition even with a Milquetoast veto, we ought to reap the rewards of an unequivocal one."

110. Mary Frances Berry, *The Politics of Parenthood: Children, Women's Rights, and the Myth of the Good Mother* (New York: Viking Press, 1993), pp. 139–41.

111. Jo Freeman, "Women and Public Policy: An Overview," in *Women, Power, and Policy*, ed. Ellen Boneparth (New York: Pergamon Press, 1982), pp. 57–59; Joan Hoff-Wilson, "Of Mice and Men," in *Women and American Foreign Policy*, ed. Edward P. Crapol (Westport, Conn.: Greenwood Press, 1988), pp. 175–78. For details of the class action suit brought by female foreign service personnel in *Palmer et al. v. Shultz* and *Cooper et al. v. Shultz,*

Civil 616 F. Supp. 1540 (D.D.C. 1985), *rev'd.*, 815 F. 2d 84 (D.C. Dir. 1987), see Hoff, *Law, Gender, and Injustice*, pp. 257–58, 262.

112. Graham, *Civil Rights Era*, pp. 445–49 (quotation). Graham, for example, separates criticism of Nixon's civil rights record from its solid achievements by as much as a hundred pages in some instances. cf. pp. 314–16 to 448–49.

CHAPTER 4. BOLD ATTEMPTS AT WELFARE, HEALTH, AND ECONOMIC REFORM

Vee Burke generously gave me transcripts of the interviews her late husband conducted with leading participants in welfare reform under Nixon in the early 1970s, while they worked on their book. She also gave me memoranda from Moynihan, as well as from other government officials involved in formulating Nixon's welfare policy. I also had access to the unprocessed Finch Papers at Occidental College, Los Angeles, and so there are no box numbers or folder names. Unless other sources are cited, all memoranda referred to in this chapter are from the Burke Materials now in my possession.

1. Nixon quoted (at a 1946 rally in El Monte, California) in James Koegh, *This Is Nixon* (New York: Putman's, 1956), pp. 80–81. This idea about preserving natural community structures free from bureaucratic interferences reached fruition in Nixon's New Federalism, as discussed in chap. 2. From the early 1950s to the 1970s, however, Nixon seldom talked about the U.S. welfare system in relation to Lockean ideas about individuals living "self-sufficient, solitary, and happy existence . . . before the formation of society or the institution of government." In fact, not until his 1990 book *In the Arena* did he seem to link Locke, with his dislike of federal bureaucratic interference, with the lives of individual citizens. See Richard Nixon, *In the Arena: A Memoir of Victory, Defeat, and Removal* (New York: Simon & Schuster, 1990), p. 298.

2. Rowland Evans and Robert Novak, *Nixon in the White House* (New York: Random House, 1971), p. 224; *Gallup Opinion Weekly*, January 1969, pp. 20–21.

3. Koegh, *This Is Nixon*, p. 89 (a 1953 address).

4. Edward W. Knappman, ed., *Presidential Election 1968* (New York: Facts on File, 1970), p. 153. Ironically, in one year to the day—August 8, 1969—Nixon would be proposing a very specific and radical reform of the entire welfare system.

5. Nixon quoted on October 28 in Daniel P. Moynihan, *Politics of a Guaranteed Annual Income: The Nixon Administration and the Family Assistance Plan* (New York: Random House, 1973), p. 67; Vincent J. Burke and Vee Burke, *Nixon's Good Deed: Welfare Reform* (New York: Columbia University Press, 1974), p. 50n. See also Richard P. Nathan, *The Plot That Failed: Nixon and the Administrative Presidency* (New York: Wiley, 1975), p. 26.

6. Burke and Burke, *Nixon's Good Deed*, p. 45; Moynihan, *Politics of a Guaranteed Annual Income*, p. 80.

7. Moynihan, *Politics of a Guaranteed Annual Income*, p. 79; author's interview with John Roy Price, February 6, 1980; Burke and Burke, *Nixon's Good Deed*, pp. 46, 79–80; author's interview with Nixon, January 26, 1983.

8. "Record of Action of the Second Meeting of the Council for Urban Affairs," prepared by John R. Price, February 3, 1969, Burke Material; Franklin D. Raines, 1971 Harvard senior thesis, "Nixon Task Forces," pp. 23–32; *NPP, 1969*, p. 286. Burns quoted in Burke and Burke, *Nixon's Good Deed*, pp. 52, 63–67. See also president's UAC notes, February 17, 1969, Box 1, POF, WHSF, NPM, NARA.

9. Moynihan, *Politics of a Guaranteed Annual Income*, p. 81; Richard Nixon, *RN: The Memoirs of Richard Nixon* (New York: Grosset & Dunlap, 1978), p. 353.

10. Nixon's description of himself in author's interview, January 26, 1983; Nixon to Price quoted in Tom Wicker, *One of Us: Richard Nixon and the American Dream* (New York: Random House, 1991), pp. 530–31.

11. Moynihan memorandum to Nixon, January 31, 1969, p. 8; Burke and Burke, *Nixon's Good Deed*, pp. 78–80.

12. Moynihan to Nixon, January 31, 1969, pp. 8–9, Burke Material. On February 1, Moynihan sent Nixon a chart illustrating the welfare "crisis," adapted from his 1965 report on the black family, that so impressed the president he wrote in the margin: "Why did this happen? Give me a brief memo on the causes." See Moynihan to Nixon, February 1, 1969, Box 1, POF, WHSP, NPM, NARA.

13. These later reevaluations have ranged from pointing out that in 1971 "there was no sudden new crisis in welfare," to asking in 1977, "what welfare crisis?" to asserting in 1978 that "after 1969 the old positive relationship between [male] unemployment and case openings was restored." See Gilbert Y. Steiner, *The State of Welfare* (Washington, D.C.: Brookings Institution, 1971), p. 94; Moynihan memorandum to Nathan (signed by Price), February 1, 1969; idem, memorandum to Nixon, January 31, 1969, pp. 2ff; Frederick Doolittle, Frank Levy, and Michael Wiseman, "The Mirage of Welfare Reform," *The Public Interest* (Spring 1977): 62–78; Moynihan, *Politics of a Guaranteed Annual Income*, pp. 34–59; Martin Rein and Hugh Heclo, "What Welfare Crisis?—Confusion Among the United States, Britain, and Sweden," *The Public Interest* (Fall 1973): 61–83; P. Royal Shipp and Vee Burke (with the assistance of Carmen D. Solomon), "Unemployment and Welfare Caseloads," *Congressional Research Service Publication* (CRSP), August 25, 1978, p. 6.

14. For the general vagueness of Finch's views on welfare, see March 1969 (n.d.) transcript of a "60 Minutes" interview with Finch conducted by Daniel Schorr, and May 22, 1969, transcript of "Today" show interview with Finch conducted by Bill Monroe—both in Finch Papers.

15. Eleanora W. Schoenebaum, ed., *Political Profiles: The Nixon-Ford Years* (New York: Facts on File, 1979), p. 199; Burke and Burke, *Nixon's Good Deed*, p. 43.

16. Martha Derthick, *Uncontrollable Spending for Social Services Grants* (Washington, D.C.: Brookings Institution, 1975), pp. 35–36, 54–56; Burke and Burke, *Nixon's Good Deed*, pp. 50–51.

17. Worth Bateman and James Lyday, "Confidential Preliminary Report of the Working Group on Welfare Legislation," February 27, 1969, Burke Materials; Burke and Burke, *Nixon's Good Deed*, pp. 53–58; M. Kenneth Bowler, *The Nixon Guaranteed Income Proposal* (Cambridge: Mass.: Ballinger, 1974), pp. 45–46.

18. Author's interview with Nathan, November 4, 1980; Burke and Burke, *Nixon's Good Deed*, pp. 58–63; Bowler, *Nixon Guaranteed Income*, pp. 46–47.

19. Author's interview with Nathan, November 4, 1980; author's interview with John Price, March 8, 1980; Price to Vee Burke, December 5, 1973; Bowler, *Nixon Guaranteed Income*, p. 47; Burke and Burke, *Nixon's Good Deed*, p. 62.

20. Burke and Burke, *Nixon's Good Deed*, pp. 65–67; Finch to Nixon, April 1, 1969, Finch Papers.

21. Ibid.

22. Moynihan, *Politics of a Guaranteed Annual Income*, p. 148; John H. Kessel, *The Domestic Presidency: Decision-Making in the White House* (North Scituate, Mass: Duxbury Press, 1975), pp. 89–90; John Osborne, *The First Two Years of the Nixon Watch* (New York: Liveright 1971), pp. 56–57, 148–54; Burke and Burke, *Nixon's Good Deed*, pp. 61–66.

23. Author's interview with John Price, March 8, 1980; Burke's interview with Nathan, August 20, 1970; Bowler, *Nixon Guaranteed Income*, pp. 66–69.

24. Burns quoted in Burke and Burke, *Nixon's Good Deed*, p. 68; Moynihan to Nixon, April 11, 1969 (with Nixon's confidential handwritten remarks to Ehrlichman), Box 1, POF, WHSF, NPM, NARA.

25. Bowler, *Nixon Guaranteed Income*, p. 50 (quotation); author's interview with Nixon, January 26, 1983; Daniel Schorr, "Behind the Nixon Welfare Showdown," *The New Leader*, August 18, 1969, p. 3.

26. Anderson memoranda to Burns, April 14 and May 5, 1969; Nathan memoranda: to Anderson, April 24, 1969, to Burns, April 14 and May 26, 1969, to Nixon and Burns, June 11, 1969; Weidenbaum memorandum to Burns, April 19, 1969, pp. 2–3. See also Burns to Nixon, April 15, 1969 (with NHC), Box 1, POF, WHSF, NPM, NARA.

27. Author's interview with Nixon, January 26, 1983; Melvin Laird, *Republican Papers* (New York Praeger, 1968), pp. 60–84; Weidenbaum memorandum to Burns, April 19, 1969, pp. 2–3.

28. Burns, "Investing in Human Dignity: A Study of the Welfare Problem," April 21, 1969, unpublished policy paper; memoranda to Nixon, April 24, July 12, 14, 21, 1969; Nathan, *Plot That Failed*, p. 45; Burke and Burke, *Nixon's Good Deed*, pp. 72–75; Bowler, *Nixon Guaranteed Income*, pp. 48–50; Osborne, *First Two Years*, pp. 144–45; author's interview with Nathan, November 4, 1980.

29. Finch memorandum to Nixon, April 30, 1969, pp. 1, 6, 11, passim, Finch Papers.

30. Laird memorandum to Nixon, May 7, 1969; author's interview with Laird, October 15, 1984.

31. Shultz memorandum to Burns, Ehrlichman, McCracken, and Moynihan, June 21, 1969; Burke and Burke, *Nixon's Good Deed*, pp. 24–27, 83–85. The Burkes maintain that the congressional earnings disregard legislation reflected badly on representatives Wilbur D. Mills (Dem.-Ark.) and Russell B. Long (Dem.-La.)—both of whom challenged the committees that drafted and approved it, proving what Nixon was saying: that the federal government had to take control of welfare and could no longer through neglect and confusion leave it to the perogative of individual states (pp. 27–28).

32. Shultz memorandum to Burns et al., June 21, 1969.

33. Author's interview with Ehrlichman, April 9, 1984.

34. Bowler, *Nixon Guaranteed Income*, pp. 52–58; Burke interviews with Ehrlichman, January–February 1971.

35. A. James Reichley, *Conservatives in an Age of Change* (Washington, D.C.: Brookings Institution, 1981), pp. 138–53; Bowler, *Nixon Guaranteed Income*, pp. 83–147.

36. Burke and Burke, *Nixon's Good Deed*, pp. 86–128.

37. Ibid.; editorial/column analysis, August 20, 1969, September 1969 (n.d.), ANS, Box 30, POF, WHSF, NPM, NARA.

38. For details of the popular and congressional debate over FAP on which the next paragraphs are based, see Burke and Burke, *Nixon's Good Deed*, 129–87; and Moynihan, *Politics of a Guaranteed Annual Income*, pp. 236–542.

39. NWRO testimony to U.S. Senate Committee on Finance, *Social Security Amendments of 1971: Hearings Before the Committee on Finance, 92nd Cong., 1st and 2nd sess. on H.R. 1* (Washington, D.C.: Government Printing Office, 1972), pt. 4, pp. 2059–20; ANS, September 1969 (n.d.), Box 30, POF, WHSF, NPM, NARA; Burke and Burke, *Nixon's Good Deed*, pp. 136–38, 159–65 (quotation on p. 152); Moynihan, *Politics of a Guaranteed Annual Income*, pp. 327–29.

40. Theodore R. Marmor and Martin Rein, "Reforming 'The Welfare Mess': The Fate of the Family Assistance Plan, 1969–72," in *Policy and Politics in America: Six Case Studies*, ed. Allan P. Sindler (Boston: Little, Brown, 1973), pp. 20–24; Burke and Burke, *Nixon's Good Deed*, pp. 180–82.

41. Marmor and Rein, "Reforming 'The Welfare Mess,'" pp. 22–23; Burke and Burke, *Nixon's Good Deed*, pp. 185–86.

42. Elliot Richardson, "Discussant," in Friedman and Levantrosser, *Nixon: Politician, President, Administrator*, p. 137.

43. Shipp, Burke, and Solomon, "Unemployment and Welfare Caseloads," pp. 28–35. This was not known, however, until 1978, when a congressional research staff report refuted Moynihan's findings on statistical grounds. Specifically it said that the linkage between male unemployment and wel-

fare proved incorrect in the 1970s for three reasons: (1) increase in single-women households; (2) liberalization of disability by courts and Congress, and increase in benefit levels; and (3) increase in AFDC participation rate of those eligible for welfare because of the increase in female-headed families, administrative liberalization that made the AFDC program more accessible, changing attitudes toward welfare that made it more socially acceptable, and the longer tenure of AFDC families on welfare, especially single mothers. It should be noted, however, that poverty became so much worse in the 1980s that Moynihan's linkage theory came true for women, if not for men.

44. Author's interview with Ehrlichman, April 9, 1984, John Evans to Nixon (via Ed Morgan), August 30, 1971, and Eugene S. Cowen to John Evans, August 30, 1971 (confidential)—both in Box 36, SS-CF, SMOF; Ken Cole to Nixon, October 9, 1972, and Moynihan to Nixon, November 23, 1971—both in Box 19; Al Haig to Nixon, September 14, 1973 (with NHC), Box 23—all in POF, WHSF, NPM, NARA.

45. Moynihan to Laird, September 4, 1973 (emphasis added in first quotation), and Moynihan to Herbert Stein, September 10, 1973—both in Box 23, POF, WHSF, NPM, NARA; New York Times, July 26, 1992, p. 12.

46. Elyce Rotella, "Fact Sheet: Women in the U.S. Economy," in Issues in Feminism, ed. Sheila Ruth (Boston: Houghton Mifflin, 1980; rev. ed., 1991); Lenore J. Weitzman, The Marriage Contract: Spouses, Lovers, and the Law (New York: Free Press, 1981), p. 171; U.S. News & World Report, August 6, 1984, pp. 46–48; Victor R. Fuchs, Women's Quest for Economic Equality (Cambridge, Mass.: Harvard University Press, 1988), pp. 84–89, 92–93; Susan Ware, Modern American Women: A Documentary History (Chicago: Dorsey, 1989), p. 377; idem, The State of Families, 1984–85 (New York: Family Service America, 1984), pp. 7–15. See also Joan Hoff, Law, Gender, and Injustice: A Legal History of U.S. Women (New York: New York University Press, 1991), pp. 252–53, for data on the earnings of working women.

47. "Rethinking Welfare," New York Times, six-part series, July 5–26, 1992; Barbara Ehrenreich and Frances Fox Piven, "The Feminization of Poverty," Dissent (Spring 1984): 162–70; Ford Foundation, "Women, Children, and Poverty in America," working paper, January 1985.

48. NPP, 1969, p. 640; Congress and the Nation, 1973–1976, vol. 4 (Washington, D.C.: Congressional Quarterly, 1977), p. 408.

49. James Patterson, The Welfare State in America, 1930–1980, British Association American Studies (BAAS) Pamphlets in American Studies no. 2 (South Sheilds, U.K.: Peterson Printers, 1981), pp. 35–36.

50. Food-stamp appropriations increased from $610 million in 1970 to $2.5 million in 1973, although if the 1971 version of Nixon's FAP had passed, it would have given cash payments to welfare recipients instead of food stamps. See Congress and the Nation, vol. 3 (Washington, D.C.: Congressional Quarterly, 1973), p. 628.

51. Author's interview with Nixon, January 26, 1983. See also note 36 in chapter 5.

52. Edward L. Morgan memorandum to Ehrlichman, March 11, 1970, and Ehrlichman action memorandum to Nixon, March 14, 1970—both in Box 5, POF, WHSP, NPM, NARA.

53. *NPP, 1969*, pp. 740–45; *Congress and the Nation, 1969–1972*, vol. 3, pp. 612–13, 615, 619.

54. *Congress and the Nation, 1969–1972*, vol. 3, p. 612; *National Journal* 2 (May 16, 1970): 1032–33, and 4 (April 24, 1972): 723–25; Moynihan to Nixon, November 14, 1969 (after meeting with Mills), Box 3, POF, WHSF, NPM, NARA. See also chap. 3 for a discussion of Mills's views.

55. Martha Derthick, *Policy Making for Social Security* (Washington, D.C.: Brookings Institution, 1979), pp. 357–68; idem, *Uncontrollable Spending*, pp. 35–42.

56. For details see Carl Lieberman, "Legislative Success and Failure: The Social Welfare Policies of the Nixon Administration," in Friedman and Levantrosser, *Nixon: Politician, President, Administrator*, pp. 113–15, 118–20; and Alfred M. Skolnick and Sophie R. Dales, "Social Welfare Expenditures, 1950–1975," *Social Security Bulletin* 39 (January 1976): 6, 12.

57. Jodie T. Allen, "Last of the Big Spenders: Richard Nixon and the Greater Society," *Washington Post*, February 24, 1983, p. A15; "Total Federal Outlays, Defense Expenditures, and Defense as Percent of Total Federal Outlays—U.S. Bureau of the Census," *Statistical Abstract of the United States: 1975*, 96th ed. (Washington, D.C.: Government Printing Office, 1975), p. 314, and *Statistical Abstract of the United States: 1979*, 100th ed. (Washington, D.C.: Government Printing Office, 1979), p. 364; Transfer Payments— *Special Analyses, Budget of the United States Government for Fiscal Year 1975* (Washington, D.C.: Government Printing Office, 1974), p. 13; *Special Analyses, Budget of the United States Government Fiscal Year 1977* (Washington, D.C.: Government Printing Office, 1976), p. 31.

58. Burke and Burke, *Nixon's Good Deed*, pp. 221–22; *NPP, 1974*, pp. 68–69. Nixon's misstatement is from James P. Johnson, "Nixon's Use of Metaphor: The Real Nixon Tapes," *Psychoanalytical Review* 66 (Summer 1979): 270.

59. Author's interview with John Price, March 29, 1980; Patterson, *Welfare State*, p. 36 (quotations); Ford Foundation, "Women, Children and Poverty in America," pp. 16–19.

60. Congressional Quarterly, *Nixon: The Fourth Year of His Presidency* (Washington D.C.: Congressional Quarterly, 1973), p. 16 (quotation). The best secondary account of Nixon's domestic economic policies can be found in Herbert Stein, *Presidential Economics: The Making of Economic Policy from Roosevelt to Reagan and Beyond* (New York: Simon & Schuster, 1984), pp. 133–207. The Ford Presidential Library at Ann Arbor also contains significant information in the Arthur Burns Papers, and there is some in the Finch Papers. Most of the information in the following section is taken from these sources in addition to Nixon, *Memoirs*, pp. 515–22; Charles L. Schultze and Arthur M. Okun, *President Nixon's New Economic Policy* (Washington, D.C.: Brookings Institution, 1971); and Alan Blinder, *Economic Policy and the Great Stagflation* (New

York: Academic Press, 1979). Ironically, there are more primary data available on Nixon's foreign economic policies than on some of his domestic economic policies because of the Commission on International Trade and Investment Policy and Task Force on International Development he appointed and whose records (which touch occasionally on domestic economic issues) can be found in RG 220, NARA. See chap. 7 for more details.

61. Herbert Parmet, *Richard Nixon and His America* (Boston: Little, Brown, 1990), p. 189; Stephen E. Ambrose, *Eisenhower: The President* (New York: Simon & Schuster, Touchstone ed., 1985), pp. 157, 199.

62. *NPP, 1971*, pp. 170–86; Congressional Quarterly, *Nixon: The First Year of His Presidency* (Washington, D.C.: Congressional Quarterly Inc., 1970), pp. 43A, 56–57A, 74A.

63. William Timmons to Nixon, October 31, 1972 (with attachment), Ehrlichman Materials; Congressional Quarterly, *Nixon: Fourth Year of His Presidency*, p. 11A; idem, *Nixon: The Fifth Year of His Presidency* (Washington, D.C: Congressional Quarterly, 1974), p. 22A.

64. For Nixon's early attempts to understand and curb inflation, see Ehrlichman to Burns, September 30, 1969, Albert H. Cox to Martin Anderson, October 3, 1969, Burns to Ehrlichman, October 9, 1969—all in Box A10, Burns Papers, NWHF, 1969–1970; ANS, June 1969 (n.d.), Box 30, POF; Shultz to Nixon, October 10, 1969, and Ehrlichman to Nixon, October 15 and November 26, 1969—both in Box 3, POF; Ehrlichman to Nixon, December 20, 1969, Box 4, POF, WHSF, NPM, NARA. Nixon's numerous handwritten comments on all kinds of economic memoranda and his ANS in the POF records demonstrate his interest in, and considerable knowledge about, economics, especially during his first term in office.

65. Burns to Nixon, January 22, 1970, and Peter Flanigan to Nixon, February 2, 1970—both in Box 5, POF, WHSF, NPM, NARA. See also M. Mark Amen, "Macroeconomic Policy Under Nixon," and Ann Mari May and Robert R. Keller, "President Nixon's Political Business Cycle," both in Friedman and Levantrosser, *Nixon: Politician, President, Administrator*, pp. 207–38.

66. Stein, *Presidential Economics*, pp. 139–74; *NPP, 1971*, p. 52 (emphasis in original).

67. Stein, *Presidential Economics*, pp. 145–55, 162–63; ANS, June 1969 (n.d.), with NHC, POF, WHSF, NPM, NARA.

68. Haldeman to Ehrlichman, June 5, 1969 (emphasis added), Box A10, Burns Papers.

69. James Reston, Jr., *The Lone Star: The Life of John Connally* (New York: Harper & Row, 1989), pp. 381–82.

70. George P. Shultz and Kenneth W. Dam, *Economic Policy Beyond the Headlines* (New York: Norton, 1977), pp. 67–69.

71. Stein, *Presidential Economics*, pp. 156–68; author's interview with Nixon, January 26, 1983.

72. Reston, *Lone Star*, pp. 396–410 (quotations on p. 407); Stein, *Presidential Economics*, pp. 163–68.

73. Peter Peterson to Nixon, November 6, 1971, Box 36, SS-CF, SMOF, WHSF, NPM, NARA; Shultz and Dam, *Economic Policy Beyond the Headlines*, pp. 65–85; I. M. Destler, *Making Foreign Economic Policy* (Washington, D.C.: Brookings Institution, 1980), pp. 5, 191; Stein, *Presidential Economics*, pp. 165–87.

74. Stein, *Presidential Economics*, p. 180 (quotation); Shultz and Dam, *Economic Policy Beyond the Headlines*, pp. 72–82.

75. Reston, *Lone Star*, pp. 408–10; Stein, *Presidential Economics*, pp. 176–82.

76. White House Tapes, June 23, 1972, p. 12, conversation no. 741-002, WSPFFS, NPM, NARA.

77. Author's interview with Nixon, January 23, 1983.

78. *New York Times*, October 9, 1991, pp. C1, C6 (citing historian Allan J. Lichtman's and Ken DeCell's study of reelection patterns), in Allan J. Lichtman, *Thirteen Keys to the Presidency* (Lanham, Md.: Madison Books, 1990); *New York Times*, August 16, 1992, p. E3.

79. Author's interview with Nixon, January 23, 1983; May and Keller, "Nixon's Political Business Cycle," pp. 232–33; Stein, *Presidential Economics*, pp. 176–87; *New York Times*, August 16, 1992, p. E3.

80. John Ralston Saul, *Voltaire's Bastards: The Dictatorship of Reason in the West* (London: Sinclair-Stevenson, 1992), pp. 271–72. For details, see papers delivered at the Fourteenth Annual Conference of the National Committee for the Study of International Affairs at the Royal Irish Academy in Dublin, November 20, 1992, by Reinhardt Rummel, "German-American Relations in the Setting of a New Atlanticism," and David Wightman, "Europe and the Dollar." These have been published in the RIA's *Irish Studies in International Affairs* 4, no. 1 (1993).

81. *Irish Times*, November 23, 1992, p. 11, and December 1, 1992, pp. 1, 12, 17–18; David Wightman, "The U.S. and Europe," paper delivered at the Royal Irish Academy, November 20, 1992.

82. This argument was based on the 1970 *Report of the President's Commission on an All-Volunteer Force* (the Gates Commission), which said that laissez-faire economic principles should guide military recruitment. It recommended that "monetary inducements guided by marketplace standards" be used to recruit U.S. troops. Melvin Laird, as secretary of defense, strongly support this concept. See Charles C. Moskos, Jr., "The Marketplace All-Volunteer Force: A Critique," in *The All-Volunteer Force After a Decade: Retrospect and Prospect*, ed. William Bowman, Roger Little, and G. Thomas Sicilia (Washington, D.C.: Pergamon-Brassey's, 1986), pp. 15–22; author's interview with Laird, October 15, 1984.

CHAPTER 5. AN OVERVIEW OF "NIXINGER" DIPLOMACY

1. Alexander L. George, *Presidential Decisionmaking in Foreign Policy: The Effective Use of Information and Advice* (Boulder, Colo.: Westview Press, 1980), pp. 146–47, 151, 162–63.

2. Henry Kissinger, *White House Years* (Boston: Little, Brown, 1979), p. 26; Nixon oral history interview by Richard D. Challener, February 21, 1966, p. 43, John Foster Dulles Oral History Collection, Princeton University.

3. Richard Nixon, *RN: The Memoirs of Richard Nixon* (New York: Grosset & Dunlap, 1978), pp. 339, 433–34. Representative samples of Nixon's comments criticizing Rogers can be found in ANS, May and September 1969, NHC, Box 30, POF, WHSF, NPM, NARA.

4. For representative press samples, see January 14, 1972, Haldeman Notes, Part I, Box 45, John Scali to Haldeman, and December 2, 1971 (declassified February 6, 1986), Box 48, Haldeman Papers. One of the best single collection of memoranda by Nixon (usually to Kissinger) about Rogers can be found in Box 85, SS-CF, SMOF, WHSF, NPM, NARA. See also Theodore Draper, *Present History* (New York: Random House, 1983), pp. 218–19.

5. Secretary of Commerce Peter G. Peterson, press briefing, June 27, 1972, p. 17, Finch Papers. Others have noted Kissinger's megalomania, including Kissinger himself. John Mitchell, for example, once described him as a "psychotic egomaniac," and Max Lerner, in a biographical sketch, said Kissinger "himself confesses that his ego is massive." See Phyllis Schlafly and Chester Ward, *Kissinger on the Couch* (New Rochelle, N.Y.: Arlington House, 1975), p. 13.

6. Draper, *Present History,* pp. 218–22; author's interview with Raymond Price, January 26, 1983.

7. Harold Hongju Koh, "Reflections on Kissinger," *Constitution* (Winter 1993): 40.

8. Draper, *Present History,* p. 218; Schlafly and Ward, *Kissinger on the Couch,* p. 158 (citing the June 14, 1973, column by Jack Anderson); William Shawcross, "Through History with Henry A. Kissinger," *Harper's,* May 1979, pp. 37–38; Seymour M. Hersh, *The Price of Power: Kissinger in the Nixon White House* (New York: Summit Books, 1983), pp. 83–97, 383–401; Roger Morris, *Uncertain Greatness: Henry Kissinger and American Foreign Policy* (New York Harper & Row, 1977), pp. 158–62; Len Colodny and Robert Gettlin, *Silent Coup: The Removal of a President* (New York: St. Martin's Press, 1991), pp. 54–56, 433.

9. Draper, *Present History,* p. 217. Nixon and Kissinger had apparently met briefly in 1967 at a party given by Clare Boothe Luce, but Nixon makes no mention of this meeting or any other direct contact before 1968. See Kissinger, *White House Years,* p. 9; and Henry Brandon, *The Retreat of American Power* (New York: Doubleday, 1973), p. 25. Brandon also refers without documentation to some correspondence between them in the 1950s.

10. A listing of these shared characteristics was compiled from Dana Ward, "Kissinger: A Psychohistory," *History of Childhood Quarterly: The Journal of Psychohistory* 2 (Winter 1975): 287–348; David Abrahamsen, *Nixon vs. Nixon* (New York: Farrar, Straus & Giroux, 1976); and Harvey Starr, *Henry Kissinger: Perceptions of International Politics* (Lexington: University Press of Kentucky, 1984), pp. 34–43, 54–59. See also Walter Isaacson, *Kissinger: A Biography* (New York: Simon & Schuster, 1992), pp. 139–46.

11. Morris, *Uncertain Greatness*, p. 94; Hersh, *Price of Power*, pp. 93, 117; U. Alexis Johnson, *The Right Hand of Power: Memoirs of an American Diplomat* (Englewood Cliffs, N.J.: Prentice-Hall, 1984), p. 592; Colodny and Gettlin, *Silent Coup*, pp. 333, 417–18.

12. Gelb quoted in Martin Agronsky's television program, January 11, 1977, Brodie Papers.

13. Author's interview with John Ehrlichman, April 9, 1984; Hersh, *Price of Power*, pp. 16–24; Kissinger, *White House Years*, p. 10; Nixon, *Memoirs*, p. 323; Tom Wicker, *One of Us: Richard Nixon and the American Dream* (New York: Random House, 1991), pp. 377–81; Clark Clifford with Richard Holbrooke, *Counsel to the President* (New York: Random House, 1991), p. 584; Schlafly and Ward, *Kissinger on the Couch*, p. 139.

14. Nixon interview with Stewart Alsop, *Saturday Evening Post*, July 12, 1958, p. 28 (emphasis added). The risk-taking aspects of Nixon's career are best discussed and analyzed by Leo Rangell in *The Mind of Watergate: An Exploration of the Compromise of Integrity* (New York: Norton, 1980). See also Kissinger to Nixon, August 27, 1969, with NHC, Box 2, POF, WHSF, NPM, NARA.

15. Noam Chomsky, "Deception as a Way of Life," *Inquiry*, April 7, 1980, p. 21.

16. Draper, *Present History*, pp. 174–78. The most comprehensive positive analysis of Kissinger's pre-1968 thinking can be found in a work by his friend and Harvard colleague Stephen Graubard, in *Kissinger: Portrait of a Mind* (New York: Norton, 1973). Even Graubard noted that Kissinger had little to say about contemporary foreign policy issues just before joining the Nixon administration because he "did not know enough about [them]." It is also usually forgotten that Kissinger's article criticizing U.S. policy in Vietnam, "The Vietnam Negotiations," *Foreign Affairs* (January 1969), did not offer any solutions for the problem. Nor did an earlier article in *Look* (August 9, 1966).

17. Henry Kissinger, "Democratic Structures and Foreign Policy" and "Central Issues in American Foreign Policy," both in *American Foreign Policy* (New York: Norton, 1974, expanded version of 1969 ed.), pp. 11–136; idem, *Troubled Partnership* (New York: McGraw-Hill, 1965), pp. 9, 232; idem, in *No More Vietnams*, ed. Richard M. Pfeffer (New York: Harper & Row, 1968), pp. 11–13; Draper, *Present History*, pp. 173–83, 211–13, 231–35; David Watt, "Kissinger's Track Back," *Foreign Policy* 37 (Winter 1979–80): 59; Henry Brandon, *The Retreat of American Power* (New York: Doubleday, 1973), p. 25 (quotation). One has only to compare writings of Kissinger with Nixon's statements and writings in 1967 and 1968 to note their profound differences, especially on China, the Soviet Union, and Europe.

18. Frederick J. Graboske's oral history interview with Elliot Richardson, May 31, 1988 (sanitized), p. 2. See also Richard A. Falk, "What Went Wrong with Henry Kissinger's Foreign Policy?" policy memoranda no. 39, Woodrow Wilson School of Public and International Studies, Princeton University,

July 1974, p. 7; Frederick J. Graboske and Ray H. Geselbracht oral history interview with John C. Whitaker, December 30, 1987, pp. 20–23, NPM, NARA. Whitaker specifically recalls Nixon explaining things to Kissinger "like giving instructions to a child."

19. Brodie interview with de Toledano, August 28, 1975, Brodie Papers; James Chase, quoted in *The New Republic*, November 9, 1974, p. 31. See also Vincent Davis, *Henry Kissinger and Bureaucratic Politics: A Personal Appraisal* (Chapel Hill: Institute of International Studies, 1979), essay series no. 9.

20. "Kissinger: An Interview with Oriana Fallaci," *The New Republic*, December 16, 1972, pp. 17–22.

21. Fawn Brodie interview with de Toledano, August 28, 1975; Gelb quote made on Martin Agronsky's television program, January 11, 1977, Brodie Papers; ANS, February 3, 1973, pp. 10–11, Box 48, POF, WHSF, NPM, NARA (quoting Kissinger saying he could not admit that the stories about him being a "playboy" were exaggerated, but also denying they had negatively affected his ability to deal with foreign leaders).

22. Davis, *Kissinger and Bureaucratic Politics*, pp. 33–35; Mike Wallace's interview with Haldeman, March 30, 1975; tape and partial transcript in Boxes 42, 53, Brodie Papers.

23. Author's interview with Ehrlichman, March 21, 1985; Marvin Kalb and Bernard Kalb, *Kissinger* (Boston: Little, Brown, 1974), pp. 257–64; Colodny and Gettlin, *Silent Coup*, pp. 53–57; author's interview with Nixon, June 6, 1984. For the significance of the JCS's wiretapping of Kissinger, see chap. 9.

24. Author's interview with Ehrlichman, March 21, 1985; author's interview with Nixon, June 6, 1984.

25. Isaacson, *Kissinger: A Biography*, pp. 127–28; Brandon, *Retreat of American Power*, p. 68; Schlafly and Ward, *Kissinger on the Couch*, p. 139; Kalb, *Kissinger*, pp. 15–16. The "distrusted" and "not fit" quotations were also apparently uttered at the Miami Beach Republican convention in 1968. Emmet Hughes recalled the "disaster" quote on a Martin Agronsky broadcast, January 11, 1977, Brodie Papers.

26. Edward L. Morgan and Egil Krogh, Jr., to Kissinger, January 15, February 4, May 6 (confidential), and May 28, 1969; Ehrlichman to Morgan, May 26, 1969 (confidential), Dean Files, Box 98, WHSF, SMOF, NPM, NARA. The February 4 memorandum specifically told Kissinger: "In order to preclude any future question regarding this matter, we would very much appreciate your completing the enclosed form and returning it to us." The matter was not settled internally until May 1969. A crucial memorandum from Morgan to Ehrlichman for May 28, 1969, concerning Kissinger's request for an exemption has been removed from this file.

27. Richard Valeriani, *Travels with Henry* (New York: Berkley Books, 1979), p. 123; Morris, *Uncertain Greatness*, pp. 3, 85, 147–48; Draper, *Present History*, pp. 218–20; Kissinger, *White House Years*, pp. 299, 734, 736, 760, 1086; Starr, *Kissinger: Perceptions* p. 56.

28. Kissinger to Nixon, April 7, 1971, November 1972 (n.d.), Box 10, POF,

WHSF, NPM, NARA. For other examples of Kissinger's obsequiousness, see Isaacson, *Kissinger: A Biography*, pp. 146–47.

29. Author's interview with Nixon, January 26, 1983; Morris, *Uncertain Greatness*, p. 3; Davis, *Kissinger and Bureaucratic Politics*, pp. 34–35 (quotation from Frost interview); Isaacson, *Kissinger: A Biography*, pp. 601–2.

30. Shawcross, "Through History with Henry A. Kissinger," pp. 39 (quotation)–40; Kissinger, *White House Years*, pp. 1094–95.

31. Robert S. Litwak, *Détente and the Nixon Doctrine: American Foreign Policy and the Pursuit of Stability, 1969–1976* (Cambridge, U.K.: Cambridge University Press, 1984), p. 48. Kissinger coined the phrase "special relationship" in 1972 at the end of his successful three-year pursuit during Nixon's first administration to become the president's closest foreign policy adviser. See "Kissinger: An Interview with Oriana Fallaci."

32. Litwak, *Détente and the Nixon Doctrine*, p. 58.

33. Chester Crocker, "The Nixon-Kissinger National Security Council System, 1969–1972; A Study in Foreign Policy Management," vol. 6, Appendices, Commission on the Organization of the Government for the Conduct of Foreign Policy, June 1975 (Washington, D.D.: Government Printing Office, 1976), pp. 79–99 (first quotation); George, *Presidential Decisionmaking*, pp. 155, 177 (second and third quotations); Morris, *Uncertain Greatness*, pp. 77–90; Leonard Hall's interview with Fawn Brodie, August 29, 1975, Box 42 (fourth quotation), Brodie Papers.

34. Haldeman Notes, January 14, 1972, Box 45, Part I, Haldeman Papers, SMOF, WHSF, NPM, NARA.

35. Commission on the Organization of Government for the Conduct of Foreign Policy (Murphy Commission), RG 220 (hereafter referred to as Murphy Commission, RG 220), Boxes 1–77, NARA. Questions to Kissinger and his answers are in Box 43 and do not always conform with his description of the NSC in Kissinger, *White House Years*, pp. 38–48.

36. I. M. Destler, "The Nixon System—A Further Look," in *Perspectives on the Presidency*, ed. Aaron Wildavsky (Boston: Little, Brown, 1975), pp. 304, 308–15.

37. Isaacson, *Kissinger: A Biography*, pp. 165–66.

38. Raymond L. Garthoff, *Détente and Confrontation: American-Soviet Relations from Nixon to Reagan* (Washington, D.C.: Brookings Institution, 1985), p. 31.

39. Morris, *Uncertain Greatness*, pp. 77–78; Kissinger, *White House Years*, pp. 41–43.

40. Morris, *Uncertain Greatness*, pp. 78–85; Kissinger, *White House Years*, pp. 43–44; George, *Presidential Decisionmaking*, pp. 155–56.

41. I. M. Destler, *Presidents, Bureaucrats, and Foreign Policy: The Politics of Organizational Reform* (Princeton, N.J.: Princeton University Press, 1972), p. 28.

42. NSDM 40, February 17, 1970, can be found in the National Security Archive, Washington, D.C. The specific Defense Department projects were

sanitized out of this declassified document; Kissinger's testimony, March 3, 1975, p. 109, Box 43, Murphy Commission, RG 220, NARA. See also Morris, *Uncertain Greatness*, p. 88.

43. Hersh, *Price of Power*, pp. 35–36; Morris, *Uncertain Greatness*, p. 101.

44. A copy of NSSM 1, January 21, 1969, can be found in the National Security Archive, Washington, D.C. However, the report resulting from this six-page inquiry is still classified.

45. Kissinger, *White House Years*, p. 46; Morris, *Uncertain Greatness*, pp. 90–91; Hersh, *Price of Power*, pp. 29, 35. A list of all the NSSMs and NSDMs can be found in the National Security Archive in Washington, D.C. For a much more sinister and exaggerated description of the NSSMs and NSDMs as a "thought-control system," see Schlafly and Ward, *Kissinger on the Couch*, pp. 247–60, esp. 251–53.

46. Kissinger, *White House Years*, p. 48; Morris, *Uncertain Greatness*, pp. 79–81.

47. James E. Connor to Richard Cheney, March 28, 1975, Box 13, Staff Secretary-Subject Files, Ford Presidential Library, Ann Arbor, Michigan. Cheney had requested a breakdown of both NSC and cabinet meetings under the Nixon administration on March 13, but in this report Connor indicated that there were no accurate records for the latter except for 1973 and 1974, when precise documentation for each cabinet meeting began to be kept. In 1973 there are nineteen recorded such meetings, but only seven up to August 9, 1974.

48. Morris, *Uncertain Greatness*, pp. 87–88, 153–54; author's interview with Laird, October 5, 1984.

49. Nixon, press statement, July 25, 1969; Richard Nixon, *Setting the Course: Major Policy Statements by President Richard Nixon* (New York: Funk & Wagnalls, 1970), pp. 300–307.

50. Author's interview with Nixon, January 26, 1983; Nixon to Robert Litwak, June 29, 1984 (document in author's possession); Whitaker oral history interview, December 30, 1987, pp. 21–22.

51. Robert E. Osgood et al., *Retreat from Empire* (Baltimore: Johns Hopkins University Press, 1973), p. 3 (first quotation); Litwak, *Détente and the Nixon Doctrine*, p. 136; Richard W. Stevenson, *The Rise and Fall of Détente: Relaxations of Tension in US-Soviet Relations, 1953–84* (Urbana: University of Illinois Press, 1985), p. 184.

52. Franz Schurmann, *The Foreign Politics of Nixon: The Grand Design* (Berkeley, Calif.: Institute of International Studies, 1987), p. 118.

53. William Shawcross, *Sideshow: Kissinger, Nixon and the Destruction of Cambodia* (New York: Simon & Schuster, 1979), p. 167. In his *Memoirs*, Nixon is much more circumspect about the importance of his doctrine, saying that it "was misinterpreted by some as signaling a new policy that would lead to total American withdrawal from Asia and from other parts of the world" (p. 395). For his view of it in 1970, see Nixon, *U.S. Foreign Policy for the 1970s, A Report to Congress*, February 25, 1971, pp. 12–14 (quotation).

54. Shawcross, *Sideshow*, p. 145 (quotation). Former members of Kissinger's

NSC staff also found Nixon's doctrine problematic. In particular, see Osgood, *Retreat from Power*, pp. 1–27.

55. I. M. Destler, *Making Foreign Economic Policy* (Washington, D.C.: Brookings Institution, 1980), pp. 10–11, 141–42.

56. Nixon Oral History Interview, conducted by Richard D. Challener, February 21, 1966, Princeton University Library, pp. 6–35; author's interview with Nixon, January 26, 1983.

57. Nixon, *Memoirs*, pp. 248, 250, 279; Leonard Garment, "Annals of Law," *The New Yorker*, April 17, 1989, pp. 90–110.

58. On several occasions, for example, the Rockefellers tried to get through to Nixon with questions about the NEP. In September 1971, Nelson Rockefeller forwarded a letter from the vice president and chief economist for Chase Manhattan Bank of New York to Kissinger only to have his NSC secretary remark: "I can't understand the significance of this [for the NSC], but is safe to assume that anything NAR sends to HAK is significant." On another occasion, Haldeman blocked a suggested meeting between David Rockefeller and the president about his concerns involving the "international monetary and trade picture" because Kissinger did not insist on the meeting. Later, when Ehrlichman met with David Rockefeller (instead of Nixon), his views were not given serious consideration; NSC staffer Robert Hormats characterized them with impunity as "not especially innovative." See Box 43, GEN FO, WHCF, NPM, NARA.

59. Peter G. Peterson, *A Foreign Economic Perspective* (Washington, D.C.: Government Printing Office, 1971), pp. 1–2, 47; Dent's testimony, February 25, 1974, p. 73, and Shultz's testimony, February 25, 1974, p. 25—both in Box 41, Murphy Commission, RG 220, NARA.

60. Peter M. Flanigan, CIEP executive director, February 26, 1974, p. 209 (first quotation), Box 41, Murphy Commission, RG 220, NARA; Destler, *Making Foreign Economic Policy*, pp. 213 (second quotation); Haldeman to Chapin, April 22, 1971, Box 43, GEN, FO, WHCF, NPM, NARA.

61. Destler, *Making Foreign Economic Policy*, pp. 10–11, 214–15. (Also see chap. 2.)

62. Press conference by Shultz and Peterson, January 19, 1971, Carton 7, Williams Commission on International Trade and Investment Policy, RG 220, NARA.

63. Report of March 10–11, 1971, CIEP meeting, pp. 2–3, Carton 6; press release, September 13, 1971, Carton 7—both in Williams Commission, RG 220, NARA.

64. Kissinger's testimony, March 3, 1975, pp. 70 (second quotation), 72 (first quotation), 74, 77–79, Box 43, Murphy Commission, RG 220, NARA; Kissinger, *White House Years*, p. 950; Ehrlichman's handwritten notes for a meeting between Pete Peterson and Nixon reviewing the economic picture for the next term, November 17, 1972, Ehrlichman Materials.

65. Shultz's testimony, February 25, 1974, pp. 8–9, 25, 63 (quotation), and Flanigan's testimony, February 26, 1974, pp. 208–10, 221, Box 41; Kissinger's

testimony, March 3, 1975, pp. 74–75, Box 43—all in Murphy Commission, RG 220, NARA.

66. Flanigan's testimony, February 26, 1974, Box 41, pp. 209–10, and Kissinger's testimony, March 3, 1975, Box 43, pp. 72–79—both in Murphy Commission, RG 220, NARA.

67. Quoted in the Papers of the TFID, October 6, 1969, Box 11, RG 220, NARA. See also papers of the Williams Commission, Boxes 1–9, RG 220, NARA; and *U.S. Foreign Assistance in the 1970s: A New Approach*, report to the President from the Task Force on International Development, March 4, 1970.

68. *Commission on the Organization of the Government and for the Conduct of Foreign Policy, June, 1975* (Murphy Commission Report) (Washington, D.C.: Government Printing Office, 1976), chap. 5, pp. 61, 63; Destler, *Making Foreign Economic Policy* pp. 10–11.

69. Tad Szulc, *The Illusion of Peace: Foreign Policy in the Nixon Years* (New York: Viking Press, 1978), pp. 86–89.

70. *New York Times*, February 6, 1969, p. 1, and April 16, 1969, p. 1; Lewis Chester, Godfrey Hodgson, and Bruce Page, *An American Melodrama* (New York: Viking Press, 1969), pp. 497–98; Gray to Robert Finch, April 27, 1968, and Gray to Nixon February 12, 1968 (with Pentagon information)—both in Finch Papers.

71. Nixon, *Memoirs*, p. 383.

72. Kissinger, *White House Years*, p. 316. The following declassified documents from the National Military Command Center, DoD, and Joint Chiefs of Staff were used in summarizing the sequence of events discussed here: Rear Admiral R. L. Baughan, Jr., memorandum for the record, April 15, 1969, DoD; Brigadier General M. W. Kendall, memorandum for the record, April 16, 1969, DoD; Baughan, memorandum for the record, April 16, 1969, DoD; General Bonesteel to General Wheeler, April 17, 1969 (with attachments), JCS; Baughan, memorandum for the record, April 18, 1969, DoD; John P. McConnel to General K. L. Reaves, May 5, 1969, JCS; J. S. McCain, Jr., to JCS, May 27, 1969, JCS; Reaves to Directory for Plans and Policy, June 7, 1969, JCS. Most of these documents were declassified in 1969 and 1980.

73. Author's interview with Nixon, June 6, 1984; Nixon, *Memoirs*, pp. 384–85; Hersh, *Price of Power*, pp. 71–73.

74. Colonel Robert E. Pursley to Kissinger, April 15, 1969 (with attachments, including April 16 press release), JCS, declassified January 14, 1980; Szulc, *Illusion of Peace*, pp. 82–86; author's interview with Laird, October 15, 1984.

75. Ibid.

76. *NPP, 1969*, April 18, 1969, news conference, pp. 298–99; Kissinger, *White House Years*, pp. 316–21.

77. Hersh, *Price of Power*, pp. 69–77; Nixon, *Memoirs*, pp. 382–85.

78. Kissinger, *White House Years*, p. 321; ANS, May 20, 1969, NHC, Box 30, POF, WHSF, NPM, NARA.

79. Nixon, *Memoirs*, p. 384.

80. Gerald R. Ford, *A Time to Heal: The Autobiography of Gerald R. Ford* (New York: Harper & Row, 1979), pp. 275–84 (quotation on p. 276); Brown, *Crises of Power*, p. 111; Hersh, *Price of Power*, pp. 639–40.

81. H. R. Haldeman, *The Ends of Power* (New York: Times Books, 1978), pp. 82–83.

82. Author's interview with Nixon, June 6, 1984. Ehrlichman confirmed that even on domestic issues Haldeman "refused to get into substance" except on organizational matters. See Vincent Burke's interview with Ehrlichman, January–February 1971, Burke Materials.

83. For a recent acceptance of the madman theory as "plausible" and "instructive" only because it appeared in Haldeman's memoirs, see Richard H. Immerman, "Psychology," *Journal of American History* 77 (June 1990): 169–70.

84. Examples of unquestioning acceptance of the madman theory or related "mad bomber" and "irrationality" theories about how Nixon conducted foreign policy include Isaacson, *Kissinger: A Biography*, pp. 163–64; Ambrose, *Nixon*, vol. 2, pp. 224, 256, 258, 463; Hersh, *Price of Power*, pp. 52–53; Lloyd Gardner, *Covenant with Power: America and World Order from Wilson to Reagan* (New York: Oxford University Press, 1984), pp. 180–81; George C. Herring, "Nixon, Kissinger, and Madman Diplomacy in the Far East," paper delivered at annual meeting of Organization of American Historians, San Francisco, April 10, 1980; "Foreign Policy: Men or Measures," *Atlantic Monthly* 234 (October 1974): 48–60. This article by Hughes appears to be the first published account of the "mad bomber" theory in connection with the 1972 Christmas bombings. As early as 1970 there were some oblique references in the press to Nixon's irrationality during the Jordanian crisis, but subsequent works usually cite Hughes's article even though Hughes's sole evidence consisted of a remark by Nixon at a 1970 press conference, which cannot be verified, and notes purportedly taken by the columnist Richard Wilson at a 1972 White House dinner.

85. Kissinger to Nels, April 21, 1969, JCSM, declassified January 14, 1980; Kissinger, *White House Years*, pp. 319, 321.

86. Rogers's testimony, March 31, 1975, pp. 6, 11, Box 43, Murphy Commission, RG 220, NARA.

87. Nixon, *Memoirs*, pp. 384–85; *Public Papers, 1969*, pp. 298–99.

CHAPTER 6. DÉTENTE, NATO, AND RAPPROCHEMENT

1. Raymond L. Garthoff, *Détente and Confrontation: American-Soviet Relations from Nixon to Reagan* (Washington, D.C.: Brookings Institution, 1985), p. 25, 32, 48; Richard W. Stevenson, *The Rise and Fall of Détente: Relaxations of Tension in US-Soviet Relations, 1953–84* (Urbana: University of Illinois Press, 1985), p. 11. Kissinger explicitly endorsed linkage on June 15, 1972, while in Moscow; see Department of State news release, June 20, 1972, p. 31.

2. Richard Nixon, *RN: The Memoirs of Richard Nixon* (New York: Grosset &

Dunlap, 1978), p. 415 (first quotation); Garthoff, *Détente and Confrontation,* pp. 29, 53, 57 (second quotation); Nixon to Kissinger, June 16, 1969, Box 1, PPF, WHSF, NPM, NARA; Stevenson, *Rise and Fall of Détente,* p. 185.

3. Garthoff, *Détente and Confrontation,* pp. 33 (quotation)–36, 47; U.S. Congress, Senate Committee on Foreign Relations, *Hearings on Détente, 93d Cong, 2d sess., August–September, 1974,* pp. 239, 301 (quoting Dean Rusk and Kissinger); Stevenson, *Rise and Fall of Détente,* pp. 6–11, 179–82, 188; Franz Schurmann, *The Foreign Politics of Richard Nixon* (Berkeley, Calif.: Institute of International Studies, 1987), pp. 80–81, 88. For a strictly economic interpretation of détente, see Marshall I. Goldman, *Détente and Dollars: Doing Business with the Soviets* (New York: Basic Books, 1975); and Keith L. Nelson, "Nixon, Brezhnev, and Détente," paper delivered at the 1985 Pacific Coast Branch of the American Historical Association. For the argument that détente simply reflected a continuation of George Kennan's ideas about containment, see John Gaddis, *Strategies of Containment: A Critical Appraisal of Postwar American National Security Policy* (New York: Oxford University Press, 1982), p. 283, passim.

4. "Memorandum of Conversation," March 26, 1974, meeting between Brezhnev and Kissinger (declassified through FOIA, 1993), pp. 2, 13, National Security Archive, Washington, D.C. When Brezhnev asked why Rodman was taking such copious notes of their conversation, Kissinger said: "We need this for our diplomatic language training. . . . We will introduce it into our Foreign Service charm school" (p. 13).

5. Schurmann, *Foreign Politics of Nixon,* pp. 47–64, 84–90, 372–82. Schurmann makes a much more convincing case for Nixon's grand design than C. Warren Nutter does in *Kissinger's Grand Design* (Washington, D.C.: American Enterprise Institute, 1975).

6. See Garthoff, *Détente and Confrontation,* pp. 24–29, for a discussion of when Nixon and Kissinger officially began to use the word *détente* as a general description of their overall foreign policies. Despite this delay of a little over a year, Nixon, at least, was using the term on a regular basis in private and in a less comprehensive fashion in public from the very beginning of his administration.

7. Robert Gilpin, *The Political Economy of International Relations* (Princeton, N.J.: Princeton University Press, 1987), pp. 140, 149, 164–65; Schurmann, *Foreign Politics of Nixon,* pp. 368–74. While there is no dispute over the unilateral aspects of the NEP, there is still considerable debate over how internationalist these economic moves on the part of the United States ultimately were. (Also see chaps. 2 and 5.)

8. February–March, 1969, RN Notes—European Trip (n.d.), President's Speech File, PPF, WHSF, NPM, NARA.

9. Ibid.

10. Nixon to Haldeman, Ehrlichman, and Kissinger, March 2, 1970 (emphasis added), Box 229, Presidential Memoranda, Haldeman Papers, WHSF, NPM, NARA.

11. Seymour M. Hersh, *The Price of Power: Kissinger in the Nixon White House* (New York: Summit Books, 1983), pp. 148–49; *U.S. News & World Report,* February 17, 1969, pp. 46–47. The Soviet Union Created the Warsaw Pact in 1955 to counter an expansion in NATO membership to include West Germany.

12. Nixon to Kissinger, Box 228, January 31, 1973, Box 47, Haldeman Notes; Jeanne Davis to Dave Parker, April 5, 1973 (declassified by NSC in 1986), Box 111, Haldeman Papers, WHSF, NPM, NARA.

13. Garthoff, *Détente and Confrontation,* pp. 25–36.

14. Nixon to Kissinger, Rogers, et al., April 24, 1969 (declassified by NSC in 1990 and for author in 1993), Box 5, PPF, WHSF, NPM, NARA; Nixon, *Memoirs,* pp. 415–18.

15. Colson to Haldeman, August 5, 1970 (declassified 1986), Box 146, Haldeman Papers, SMOF, WHSF, NPM, NARA; Hersh, *Price of Power,* pp. 157–67; Gerard C. Smith, *Doubletalk: The Story of the First Strategic Arms Limitation* (Garden City, N.Y.: Doubleday, 1980), pp. 60–64, 90. See also note 51 in this chapter. In addition to telling Semenov that the ABM could not work, Smith praised his Soviet colleague for having a better understanding of the necessity to reduce nuclear weapons than those trying to direct arms control from the White House.

16. Butterfield to Nixon, June 11, 1969, Box 2, POF, WHSF, NPM, NARA. In his book *Nuclear Weapons and Foreign Policy* (New York: Harper & Row, 1957), Kissinger indicated that nuclear weapons were strategically useful not because they would be used but because they deterred; and in, 1961, in *The Necessity for Choice: Prospects for American Foreign Policy* (Harper & Row, 1961), he actually argued that some small nuclear weapons could play a tactical role under certain combat conditions.

17. Butterfield to Kissinger, April 12 and 25, 1969, Box 50, Haldeman Papers, SMOF; Butterfield to Kissinger, April 8 and 10, 1969, Box 30, ANS, POF; Nixon to Haldeman, April 14, 1969, Box 1, PPF, WHSF, NPM, NARA; Nixon, *Memoirs,* p. 418.

18. Alexander Butterfield to Nixon, June 11, 1969, Butterfield telephone calls, August 1969, Bryce Harlow to Nixon, July 1, 1969, Box 2; NHC, Box 30, April 8, 13, and 24, and May 11, 1969, Box 30, ANS, POF; Nixon to Herbert Klein, March 13, 1969, and Nixon to Ehrlichman, April 10, 1969, Box 1— all in PPF, WHSF. J. Francis Lally to Nixon, June 10, 1969 (telegram), Box 64, GEN FO, WHCF, NPM, NARA. See also Kissinger, *White House Years,* pp. 204–12; Schurmann, *Foreign Politics of Nixon,* pp. 114–18; and *NPP 1969,* pp. 443–44.

19. See chap. 7 for details on the origins of the Nixon Doctrine. See also *NPP, 1969,* pp. 544–56, 905–6, 1003–13; Osgood to Kissinger, November 19, 1969 (quotations, with Osgood's draft of an explanation of the Nixon Doctrine), Box 6, Robert Osgood Papers, Milton S. Eisenhower Library, Baltimore, Maryland; and Nixon, *U.S. Foreign Policy for the 1970's, A Report to Congress,* February 25, 1971, pp. 12–14; Kissinger to Nixon August 29, 1969 (declassified by NSC in 1986), Box 52, Part I, Haldeman Papers, WHSF, NPM, NARA.

20. Haldeman Notes, April 17, 1971, Box 43, Part I, Haldeman Papers, SMOF, WHSF, NPM, NARA.

21. Haldeman Notes, April 17, 1971, Box 43, Part I, Haldeman Papers, SMOF, WHSF, NPM, NARA; Schurmann, *Foreign Politics of Nixon*, p. 204.

22. Garthoff, *Détente and Confrontation*, p. 115.

23. Ken BeLieu to Nixon, May 17, 1971, Clark MacGregor to Nixon, May 17, 18, and June 29, 1971, Nixon to Harry Truman, May 21, 1971, Truman to Nixon, June 7, 1971, Box 10, EX IT 50; Dean Rusk to Kissinger, May 21, 1971, Box 11, GEN IT 50; Mathias to Kissinger, May 20, 1971, Kissinger to Mathias (n.d.), Box 15, CF, FG 6-11-1, SF—all in WHCF, NPM, NARA.

24. "The Future of the Alliance: Report of the Council," in *NATO Final Communiqués, 1949–1970* (Brussels: NATO, 1971), pp. 188–92.

25. John J. McCloy to Kissinger, December 23, 1970, Box 5, CF, CO, WHCF, NPM, NARA; Garthoff, *Détente and Confrontation*, pp. 110–15; Kissinger, *White House Years*, p. 402 (quotation).

26. Garthoff, *Détente and Confrontation*, p. 115; Kissinger, *White House Years*, p. 399; see note 23 of this chapter; MacGregor to Nixon May 17 and 18, 1971.

27. Garthoff, *Détente and Confrontation*, p. 115; Kissinger, *White House Years*, p. 949 (quotation); see note 23 of this chapter; MacGregor to Nixon, May 17, 1971.

28. Kissinger, *White House Years*, p. 949.

29. J. F. Lehman to Kissinger, March 6, 1973 (with attachment, first quotation on p. 5, second in cover letter), Box 11, EX IT 50, and NHC to Kissinger on March 15, 1973 news summary, Box 49, ANS, POF—both in WHCF, NPM, NARA; Henry Kissinger, *Years of Upheaval* (Boston: Little, Brown, 1982), pp. 700, 707–22.

30. OMB Legislative Referral Memorandum to DoD and NSC, June 27, 1973 (re: H. Con Res. 146, 168, 198), W. Marshall Wright to Thomas E. Morgan (n.d.) (attached to OMB memo), Kissinger to Nixon, May 13, 1974—all in Box 11, EX IT 50, WHCF, NPM, NARA.

31. *NPP, 1974*, p. 547; Lester A. Sobel, ed., *Kissinger and Détente* (New York: Facts on File, 1975), p. 165.

32. Gaddis, *Strategies of Containment*, pp. 295–98; Robert J. Art, "Bureaucratic Politics and American Foreign Policy: A Critique," *Policy Sciences: An International Journal* 4 (1973): 482 (quotation), 483.

33. Robert D. Schulzinger, *Henry Kissinger: Doctor of Diplomacy* (New York: Columbia University Press, 1989), pp. 75–77; Michael Schaller, *The United States and China in the Twentieth Century* (New York: Oxford University Press, 1979), pp. 158–65.

34. Nixon to Kissinger, Rogers, et al., April 24, 1969 (declassified by NSC in 1990 and for author in 1993), Box 5, PPF, WHSF, NPM, NARA.

35. Henry Brandon, *The Retreat of American Power* (New York: Doubleday, 1973), pp. 181–82. Brandon was paraphrasing his own diary entry about an interview with Nixon in 1954. Author's interview with Raymond Price, Janu-

ary 26, 1983; Richard Nixon, "Asia After Vietnam," *Foreign Relations* 46 (October 1967): 121–24. For Nixon's anti-Communist China views that were more in keeping with the Republican party's China lobby, see Stephen E. Ambrose, *Nixon: The Education of a Politician, 1913–1962* (New York: Simon & Schuster, 1987), vol. 1, pp. 213–15, 230, 497–99, 597–80; vol. 2, pp. 44, 68, 81. Nixon once said he thought John Foster Dulles's greatest service to American diplomacy "was in the two Quemoy-Matsu incidents rather than Korea which I think would have come anyway at some point." See Nixon Oral History Interview, conducted by Richard D. Challener, February 21, 1986, Princeton University Library.

36. Nixon, *U.S. Foreign Policy for the 1970s: A Report to the Congress,* February 9, 1972, pp. 28–29; Marvin Kalb and Bernard Kalb, *Kissinger* (Boston: Little, Brown, 1974), pp. 219–22; Nixon, *Memoirs,* p. 545; Kissinger, *White House Years,* p. 169.

37. Nixon remarks to Presidential Scholars, June 4, 1970, Patrick E. O'Donnell to Finch with selected presidential quotations, October 16, 1971, Finch Papers; Nixon to Haldeman, May 13, 1970 (recounting his conversation with the students on May 9), Box 229, Presidential Memoranda, Haldeman Papers, WHSF, NPM, NARA; Nixon, *Memoirs,* p. 463; Schaller, *United States and China,* pp. 166–67.

38. Kalb and Kalb, *Kissinger,* pp. 225–27 (quotation); John G. Stoessinger, *Henry Kissinger: The Anguish of Power* (New York: Norton, 1976), pp. 117–18.

39. Kissinger, *White House Years,* pp. 163–94 (quotations on pp. 168, 171, 182, 194); Schulzinger, *Kissinger: Doctor of Diplomacy,* p. 86.

40. Nixon, *Memoirs,* pp. 545–47; Schaller, *United States and China,* pp. 167–68.

41. Nixon, *Memoirs,* pp. 546–52; Kissinger, *White House Years,* pp. 684–718 (quotation on p. 714); Schaller, *United States and China,* pp. 169–70.

42. Nixon, *Memoirs,* pp. 550, 553; Kissinger, *White House Years,* pp. 717–18; Schaller, *United States and China,* pp. 170–71.

43. Haldeman Notes, July 7 and 15, August 13, October 3, 4, and 27, 1971, Box 44, Part I, Haldeman Papers, SMOF, WHSF, NPM, NARA.

44. Ibid., October 4, 26, and 27, 1971; Schaller, *United States and China,* p. 172 (last quotation).

45. See assorted memoranda from Nixon in *From the President: Richard Nixon's Secret Files,* ed. Bruce Oudes (New York: Harper & Row, 1989), pp. 308, 309, 325, 382–85, 396–97, 573, 621 (quoting Nixon on "Meet the Press," April 10, 1988).

46. Hersh, *Price of Power,* pp. 350–82, 489–502.

47. Haldeman to Rogers, March 16, 1972 (declassified 1986), Box 199, Haldeman Papers, SMOF, WHSF, NPM, NARA.

48. Flora Lewis, *New York Times,* May 29, 1988, p. E17 (op/ed), and Leslie H. Gelb June 6, 1991, p. A15 (op/ed).

49. For a discussion of the illegalities (comparable to those involved in the Iran-contra affair) of the attempt under Reagan to reinterpret the ABM Treaty in order to find loopholes for development and deployment of the SDI, see Ray-

mond L. Garthoff, *Policy versus the Law: The Reinterpretation of the ABM Treaty* (Washington, D.C.: Brookings Institution, 1987).

50. Raymond L. Garthoff, *Perspective on the Strategic Balance* (Washington, D.C.: Brookings Institution, 1983), pp. 6–8, 15.

51. Gordon R. Weihmiller, *U.S.-Soviet Summits: An Account of East-West Diplomacy at the Top, 1955–1985* (Lanham, Md.: University Press of America, 1986), pp. 54–65. For details about Nixon's and Kissinger's confusion over whether the SLBMs had been included or excluded in certain drafts of the interim agreement because they bypassed knowledgeable bureaucrats and experts on this and other subjects, their indifference to the military significance of "MIRVing" for modernizing Soviet missiles, and for their generally unprofessional treatment of the SALT delegation, see Garthoff, *Détente and Confrontation*, pp. 155–88; Smith, *Doubletalk*, pp. 371–40; and Hersh, *Price of Power*, pp. 147–56, 529–60.

52. "Why Kissinger Woos Grass-roots Support" and "Kissinger Goes to People to Strengthen His Hand," *Christian Science Monitor*, June 25, 1975, p. 1, and July 17, 1975, p. 4.

53. "Memorandum of Conversation," March 26, 1974, pp. 26–33, National Security Archive.

54. I. M. Destler, *Making Foreign Economic Policy* (Washington, D.C: Brookings Institution, 1980), pp. 36–87, 103–20.

55. "Memorandum of Conversation," pp. 32–35; Shultz to Nixon, two memoranda, October 4, 1973 (declassified for NSC in 1990 and for author in 1992), Box 23, POF, WHSF, NPM, NARA.

56. I. M. Destler, *Making Foreign Economic Policy* (Washington, D.C.: Brookings Institution, 1980), pp. 188–90; Stevenson, *Rise and Fall of Détente*, pp. 170–71; Garthoff, *Détente and Confrontation*, pp. 453–63.

57. "Memorandum of Conversation," pp. 9–11.

58. Garthoff, *Détente and Confrontation*, pp. 478–79 (quotation).

59. Ibid., pp. 473–76; "Memorandum of Conversation," p. 11.

60. Leslie H. Gelb, *New York Times*, June 6, 1991, p. A15 (op/ed), in response to a talk by Nixon about whether to separate economic reform of, and economic aid to, the Soviet Union from "broader political and strategic questions." For the text of Nixon's remarks and others on post–cold war U.S.-Russian relations, see *Washington Post*, June 2, 1991, pp. D1, D4; *New York Times*, November 19, 1992.

CHAPTER 7. VIETNAM: WITHOUT PEACE OR HONOR

1. Nixon NBC radio statement, March 7, 1968, Box 40, Brodie Papers.

2. Paul Johnson, *Modern Times: The World from the Twenties to the Eighties* (New York: Harper & Row, 1983), pp. 654–58; William Shawcross, *The Quality of Mercy: Cambodia, Holocaust, and Modern Conscience* (New York: Simon & Schuster, 1984), pp. 45–69, 385–430; idem, *Sideshow: Kissinger, Nixon, and the Destruction of Cambodia* (New York: Simon & Schuster,

1984). Nixon has always specifically denied that his policies in Indochina led to the excesses there later. See Nixon, *No More Vietnams* (New York: Arbor House, 1985); and Nixon, *In the Arena: A Memoir of Victory, Defeat, and Renewal* (New York: Simon & Schuster, 1990), p. 342.

3. Haldeman Notes, January 14, 1972, Box 45, Part I, Haldeman Papers, SMOF, WHSF, NPM, NARA.

4. Walter Isaacson, *Kissinger: A Biography* (New York: Simon & Schuster, 1992), pp. 483–90; Guenter Lewy, *American in Vietnam* (New York: Oxford University Press, 1978), pp. 418–41; General Bruce Palmer, Jr., *The Twenty-five-Year War: America's Military Role in Vietnam* (Lexington: University Press of Kentucky, 1984), pp. 122–51; Seymour Hersh, *The Price of Power: Kissinger in the Nixon White House* (New York: Summit Books, 1983), pp. 610–38; Shawcross, *Sideshow*, pp. 259–79; Tad Szulc, *The Illusion of Peace: Foreign Policy in the Nixon Years* (New York: Viking Press, 1978), pp. 653–84.

5. Author's interview with Nixon, January 26, 1983.

6. Wheeler to Clifford, December 13, 1968, JCSM 742-68 (declassified under FOIA, November 18, 1977). In this memorandum to the secretary of defense, General Wheeler referred to a September 19, 1968, JCSM (558-68) in which the same request had been made. Quotation from NSSM no. 1, January 21, 1969 is based on copy in the National Security Archive.

7. Wheeler to Laird, February 27, 1969, JCSM-114-69, DoD (declassified through FOIA, November 18, 1977).

8. Ralph Earle II to Laird, March 12, 1969, DoD (declassified through FOIA in 1977).

9. Henry Kissinger, *White House Years* (Boston: Little, Brown, 1979), p. 241.

10. Ibid. pp. 239–42; Shawcross, *Sideshow*, 91–95; Wheeler to Abrams, January 28, 1969, JCS 01181 (declassified through FOIA, May 19, 1977).

11. Other nonclassified material on Nixon's Midway meeting with Thieu can also be found in Box 64, GEN FO, WHCF, NPM, NARA. For more information about this meeting and conflicting interpretations of Thieu's acceptance of U.S. troop withdrawals, see Kissinger, *White House Years*, pp. 271–75; Richard Nixon, *RN: The Memoirs of Richard Nixon* (New York: Grosset & Dunlap, 1978), pp. 392–93; Tom Wicker, *One of Us: Richard Nixon and the American Dream* (New York: Random House, 1991), pp. 575, 581; and Joseph A. Amter, *Vietnam Verdict: A Citizen's History* (New York: Continuum, 1982), p. 169.

12. J. Francis Lally to Nixon, June 10, 1969 (telegram), Box 64, GEN FO, WHCF, NPM, NARA.

13. See NSSMs no. 19, February 11, 1969, and nos. 21 and 22, February 13 and March 12, 1969, National Security Archive.

14. Author's interview with Ehrlichman, April 9, 1984. For a description of Laird's position that is less negative, see Kissinger, *White House Years*, p. 245. Laird went out of his way when testifying at a Senate hearing on POWs in 1992 to reiterate that he had opposed keeping the bombing of Cambodia secret. See *New York Times*, September 22, 1992, p. A6.

15. Author's interview with Ehrlichman, April 9, 1984.
16. Author's interview with Nixon, January 26, 1983.
17. Kissinger, *White House Years*, pp. 243–44; Earle to Laird, March 12, 1969, DoD; Laird to Nixon, March 18, 1969, DoD (both declassified through FOIA, August 18, 1977); Laird to Nixon, March 18, 1969, DoD (declassified through FOIA, April 11, 1977).
18. Laird to Nixon, March 18, 1969.
19. General Wheeler to Generals Abrams, commander, U.S. Military Assistance, Command, Vietnam; to General Holloway, commander-in-chief, Strategic Air Command; to Lieutenant General Hutchin, commander-in-chief, Command Staff, Pacific; and to Admiral McCain, commander-in-chief, Command Staff, Pacific—all on March 16, 1969 (declassified through FOIA, April 11, 1977).
20. Abrams to Wheeler, February 11, 1969, JCS 01836, DoD (declassified through FOIA, April 11, 1977); Shawcross, *Sideshow*, p. 19 (the date of this communiqué is February 9 in Shawcross); Kissinger, *White House Years*, pp. 239–47.
21. Ibid.; Hersh, *Price of Power*, p. 63; Kissinger, *White House Years*, pp. 239–49.
22. DoD, "Report on Selected Air and Ground Operations in Cambodia and Laos (White Paper)," September 10, 1973, p. 5.
23. Hersh, *Price of Power*, pp. 54, 61–63; Kissinger, *White House Years*, p. 243.
24. Hersh, *Price of Power*, p. 62.
25. Wheeler to Abrams, March 16, 1969, JSC 03298, Wheeler to Abrams, February 5, 1970 (with attachments), JCS 01762, DoD (both declassified through FOIA, April 11, 1977).
26. Seyom Brown, *The Crises of Power: An Interpretation of United States Foreign Policy During the Kissinger Years* (New York: Columbia University Press, 1979), p. 55; Roger Morris, *Uncertain Greatness: Henry Kissinger and American Foreign Policy* (New York: Harper & Row, 1974), p. 53; Hersh, *Price of Power*, pp. 86–87.
27. DoD, "White Paper," pp. 19–24.
28. Ibid., p. 30; Isaacson, *Kissinger: A Biography*, p. 179. How "fully" these men were informed by Laird has never been confirmed.
29. DoD, "White Paper," pp. 16–17.
30. DoD, "Morning Briefing," August 29, 1973, p. 13.
31. DoD, "White Paper," p. 11, "Morning Briefing," August 29, 1973, p. 13.
32. DoD, "Morning Briefing," August 29, 1973, p. 13.
33. Wicker, *One of Us*, p. 584; General William Palmer, "End of Tour Report," April 1975 (no page numbers), DoD.
34. Ibid.
35. The ad hoc way in which Kissinger, in particular, arbitrarily used the various committees within the restructured NSC system is confirmed in Vincent Davis, *Henry Kissinger and Bureaucratic Politics: A Personal Appraisal* (Chapel Hill: University of South Carolina Institute of International Studies,

1979), essay series no. 9, pp. 24–30, and discussed in chap. 6 of the present volume.

36. John Mueller, "A Summary of Public Opinion and the Vietnam War," in *Vietnam as History: Ten Years After the Paris Peace Accords*, ed. Peter Braestrup (Washington, D.C.: University Press of America, 1984), charts in appendices, n.p. I separate what I am calling "general public opinion" from antiwar sentiment because the former determined presidential approval ratings, while the latter influenced opinion specifically about the war.

37. Melvin Small, *Johnson, Nixon, and the Doves* (New Brunswick, N.J.: Rutgers University Press, 1988), pp. 1–23. Generally speaking, Nixon's more liberal aides or advisers were more troubled by the antiwar movement than the president himself, and some of them misleadingly tended to attribute their attitudes to him. See Small, pp. 20, 171, 242n81, 82, 83, 86. These last two notes contain reviews of the literature contending that the antiwar movement significantly affected U.S. foreign policy under Johnson and Nixon and the literature saying that it did not.

38. Moynihan to Nixon, November 26, 1969, Box 3, Buchanan to Nixon, December 5, 1969, Box 4, POF; Haldeman Notes, November 25, 1969, Box 40; John Dean to Ehrlichman and Haldeman, April 1, 1971 (declassified 1986), Box 115, Haldeman Papers SMOF, WHSF, NPM, NARA; Rowland Evans and Robert B. Novak, *Nixon in the White House: The Frustration of Power* (New York: Random House, 1971), pp. 394–98; *NPP, 1969*, December 8, 1969, p. 1003.

39. Charles W. Colson, oral history interview, September 21, 1988, conducted by Frederick H. Graboske and Paul A. Schmidt, NPM, NARA; H. Bruce Franklin, "The POW/MIA Myth," *Atlantic Monthly* 268, no. 6 (December 1991): 58.

40. Franklin, "POW/MIA Myth," pp. 54, 58; Kissinger to Nixon, October 2, 1969, and John S. Wold to Nixon, November 6, 1969 (with Nixon's comments to Kissinger)—both in Box 3, POF, WHSF, NPM, NARA; Stephen E. Ambrose, *Nixon: The Triumph of a Politician, 1962–1972* (New York: Simon & Schuster, 1989), 2, p. 32; Szulc, *Illusion of Peace*, p. 641.

41. Franklin, "POW/MIA Myth," p. 54 (first two quotations); Herbert G. Stein, general letter to constituents with statistics on POWs, December 1, 1970, Box 27, Papers and Other Historical Materials of Edward E[mil] David, Jr., Office of Science and Technology Files, SMOF, WHCF, NPM, NARA.

42. Szulc, *Illusion of Peace*, p. 64 (third and fourth quotations); Stein, general letter, December 1, 1970, Box 27, David Files, SMOF, WHCF, NPM, NARA.

43. H. Bruce Franklin, *M.I.A. or Mythmaking in America* (Brooklyn, N.Y.: Lawrence Hill Books, 1992), pp. 48–49 (quotation). Franklin does not seem to realize that Nixon and Kissinger were either bypassing or at odds with both the Departments of Defense and State, and that neither would have been allowed to conduct a major campaign on any foreign policy issue. For Kissinger's criticism of Laird's position, see Douglas L. Clarke, *The Missing*

Man: Politics and the MIA (Washington, D.C.: National Defense University, 1979), pp. 30, 47*n*3.

44. Kissinger to Nixon, October 2, 1969, and Harry Dent to Nixon, October 21, 1969—both with NHC, Box 3, POF; Stein, general letter, December 1, 1970, Box 27, David Files, WHCF, NPM, NARA; *NPP, 1969,* November 3, 1969, pp. 901–9 (quotation).

45. Nixon, *In the Arena,* p. 215.

46. Butterfield to Kissinger, two memoranda on February 2, 1970 (declassified by NSC in 1990 and for author through MR, 1992), Box 1, SS-CF, SMOF, WHSF; Stein, general letter, December 1, 1970, Box 27, David Files, SMOF, WHCF, NPM, NARA; Szulc, *Illusion of Peace,* pp. 161, 344; *Atlanta Constitution,* November 25, 1970, p. 4A; *Wall Street Journal,* November 24, 1979, p. 4.

47. Szulc, *Illusion of Peace,* p. 384.

48. Ibid., pp. 161, 262, 339, 346, 388, 495, 508–9 (quotation), 513, 549, 572; Haldeman Notes, January 14, 1972, Box 45, Part I, Haldeman Papers, SMOF, WHSF, NPM, NARA.

49. Ibid., p. 384; Ambrose, *Nixon,* vol. 2, pp. 480–81, 494–95, 505–6.

50. Franklin, *M.I.A.,* pp. 48–54, 57–64; Kissinger, *White House Years,* pp. 87–88.

51. January 24, 1969, p. 2, ANS with NHC to Kissinger, March 1969 (n.d.), p. 4, ANS with NHC to Herbert Klein, April 1969 (n.d., n.p.), ANS with NHC to Kissinger, May 1969 (n.d.), Nixon to Kissinger, April 10, 1969, Box 30; Ehrlichman to Nixon, June 5, 1970, Box 2;—all in POF, PPF, Box 1, WHSF, NPM, NARA. See also Herbert S. Parmet, *Richard Nixon and His America* (Boston: Little, Brown, 1990), pp. 566, 570–74.

52. ANS, May 1969 (n.d, n.p.), with NHC to Ehrlichman, Box 30, Arthur Burns to Nixon, May 26, 1969 with NHC to Ehrlichman, Box 2; Jack Caulfield to Ehrlichman, October 10, 1969 with NHC to Ehrlichman, Box 3—all in POF, WHSF, NPM, NARA.

53. ANS, March 1969 (n.d., n.p.), Box 30, POF; Haldeman to Kenneth Cole, March 13, 1969, Ehrlichman to Nixon, March 18, 1969, Box 1, POF; Tom Charles Huston to Haldeman, August 12, 1969, Box 51, June 8 and 25, 1970, July 10, 1970, BOX 70, Haldeman Papers, WHSF, NPM, NARA; Jonathan Schell, *The Time of Illusion* (New York: Knopf, 1976), pp. 59–74, 111–27; Tom Shactman, *Decade of Shocks: Dallas to Watergate, 1963–1974* (New York: Poseidon Press, 1983), pp. 259–84; Richard Gid Powers, *Power and Secrecy: The Life of J. Edgar Hoover* (New York: Free Press, 1987), pp. 456–57.

54. *NPP, 1969,* pp. 901–9 (quotation); Amter, *Vietnam Verdict,* pp. 173–74, 228–29.

55. Szulc, *Illusion of Change,* p. 262; Amter, *Vietnam Verdict,* pp. 173–74, 228–29.

56. Parmet, *Nixon and His America,* pp. 1–13; William Safire, *Before the Fall: An Inside View of the Pre-Watergate White House* (New York: Ballantine,

1977), pp. 249, 257–72; Nixon, *Memoirs*, pp. 458–69 (quotation on p. 461). For the full text of Nixon's own description of his encounter with students at the Lincoln Memorial, see Nixon to Haldeman, May 13, 1970, Presidential Memoranda BOX 229, WHSF, Haldeman Papers, NPM, NARA.

57. Kissinger to Nixon, "Vietnam Indicators Report," November 28, 1972, Box 39, SS-CF, WHSF, NPM, NARA.

58. For the assertion that the Christmas bombings were timed to coincide with the semester break, see John Mueller, "Reflections on the Vietnam Antiwar Movement and on the Curious Calm at the War's End," in *Vietnam as History*, p. 153. For a more convincing argument that the timing was determined by negotiating problems, see Amter, *Vietnam Verdict*, pp. 285–90.

59. ANS, February 26, 1973, p. 1, Box 48, POF, WHSF, NPM, NARA.

60. Kissinger to Haig, October 22, 1972 (declassified for author through MR, 1989), Box 10, PPF, WHSF, NPM, NARA. Emphasis added.

61. Nixon, *Memoirs*, pp. 701 (last Nixon quotation)–7; Charles W. Colson, *Born Again* (Old Tappan, N.J.: F. H. Revell, 1977), pp. 75–76; Hersh, *Price of Power*, p. 604 (first Nixon quotation).

62. Colson, *Born Again*, pp. 79–80; Safire, *Before the Fall*, p. 668; Tom Wicker, *New York Times*, December 26, 1972 (op/ed); *Time*, January 8, 1973, p. 14; Nixon, *Memoirs*, pp. 717–48; Kissinger, *Years of Upheaval*, pp. 1420–21.

63. Ehrlichman Notes, No. 194, December 6, 1972 (emphasis added), Ehrlichman Materials. For a much enhanced account of this meeting, see John Ehrlichman, *Witness to Power: The Nixon Years* (New York: Simon & Schuster, 1982), pp. 313–15.

64. Henry Kissinger, *Years of Upheaval* (Boston: Little, Brown, 1982), p. 1409 (emphasis added); Colson, *Born Again*, pp. 79–80; Haldeman Notes, January 14, 1973, Box 47, Haldeman Papers, SMOF, WHSF, NPM, NARA.

65. White House Tapes, January 5, 1973, conversation no. 393-013, WSPFFS, NPM, NARA.

66. Ehrlichman Notes, December 2, 1972, Box 4, Ehrlichman Papers, SMOF, WHSF; "Vietnam Negotiations," NHC, November 29, 1972, Box 82, Haldeman Notes, January 10, 11, 12, 15, 19, 23, 24, 31, 1973, Box, 47, Haldeman Papers, SMOF, WHSF; President's Speech File, PPF, WHSF, NPM, NARA; Nixon, *Memoirs*, pp. 735–38, 749–750. The text of these secret pledges were released by Nguyen Tien Hung, a South Vietnamese official, on April 30, 1975; see *New York Times*, May 1, 1975, pp. 1, 6. Kissinger's transparent rationalization of these secret pledges, given open congressional opposition to any more "two-man" foreign policy because of the Cambodian bombing, has been thoroughly discredited by McGeorge Bundy, "Vietnam, Watergate and Presidential Powers," *Foreign Affairs* 58 (Winter 1979–1980): 397–407.

67. Kissinger to Nixon (n.d.; sometime in January 1974); Scowcroft to Haig, January 4, 1974; Haig to Nixon, January 4, 1974, Roy Ash to Nixon, January 4, 1974, memorandum and attachments on foreign and military assistance for FY 1975; Haig to Nixon, January 5, 1974, Box 25, POF (all these POF documents declassified by NSC in 1990, by DoD in 1991, and for author through

MR in 1993): William E. Timmons to Nixon, June 15, 1973, Box 22, POF; Kissinger to Nixon, April 27, 1974, action memoranda with attachments, Box 41, SS-CF, WHSF, NPM, NARA (both documents declassified by NSC in 1990 and for author through MR in 1992).

68. Robert S. Ingersoll, acting secretary of state, to Ford, March 18, 1975, Kissinger to Ford (n.d.; sometime in March 1975), Box 12, Buchen Papers, Ford Library; Brown, *Crises of Power*, p. 52.

69. Gerald R. Ford, *A Time to Heal: The Autobiography of Gerald R. Ford* (New York: Harper & Row, 1979), pp. 249–56 (quotation).

70. Haldeman Notes, January 16, 23, and 31, 1973, Box 47, Haldeman Papers, SMOF, WHSF, NPM, NARA. Bruce Kehrli to Kissinger, February 3, 1973, Box 85, SS-CF; ANS, February 22, 1969, NHC, Box 20; David Gergen to Nixon, March 14 and 17, 1973, Box 21—all in POF, WHSF, NPM, NARA; Szulc, *Illusion of Peace*, p. 669 (second quotation).

71. Ambrose, *Nixon*, vol. 2, pp. 64–66; Nixon, *In the Arena*, p. 40. Nixon argued that he deducted the corsages because it was a legitimate professional expense, and paying for them personally was cheaper than going through government channels.

72. W. Richard Howard to Nixon, May 15, 1973, NHC, Box 22, POF, WHSF, NPM, NARA.

73. For a review of the popular culture and partisan political resurrection of the POW/MIA issue, see Franklin, "POW/MIA Myth," pp. 45–81; idem, *M.I.A.*, pp. 127–66; "The MIA Industry: Bad Dream Factory," *Time*, January 13, 1992, pp. 10–16; *USA Today*, July 24, 1992, p. 3A, and August 12, 1992, p. 6A; *New York Times*, September 22, 1992, p. A6. In 1993, 82 of the nearly 200 MIAs on the DoD list were confirmed dead. See *New York Times*, February 7, 1994, p. A11.

74. Franklin, *M.I.A.*, pp. 122–26, 182–85 (complete text of Nixon's February 1, 1973, letter).

75. Ibid., pp. 86, 108–13.

76. Press release of Kerry Committee, August 11, 1992; Eagleburger to Richardson, n.d. (replying to a March 13, 1973, query from Richardson); Richardson to Kissinger, March 28, 1973, Roger Shields to Ambassador Hill, May 24, 1973, National Security Archive, Washington, D.C. (declassified through FOIA in 1992).

77. *USA Today*, August 14, 1992, p. 13A. *New York Times*, September 22, 1992, pp. A1, A6; September 25, 1992, p. A8; September 27, 1992, p. 17 (op/ed).

78. *New York Times*, September 25, 1993, p. A8.

79. White House Tapes, conversation no. 423-003 (March 27, 1973), p. 2 (Nixon quotation), WSPFFS, NPM, NARA; Leslie H. Gelb, *New York Times*, September 27, 1992, p. 17 (op/ed), and September 9, 1993, p. A8; *International Herald Tribune*, April 13, 1993, pp. 1, 2, April 14, 1993, p. 5, April 20, 1993, p. 3, April 24–25, 1993, p. 5.

80. *NPP, 1973*, p. 234; Leslie H. Gelb, *New York Times*, September 27, 1992, p. 17 (op/ed); *International Herald Tribune*, December 1, 1992, p. 7.

81. Ambrose, *Nixon*, vol. 2, pp. 505–6; Franklin, *M.I.A*, pp. 48, 124; *Washington Post*, September 24, 1992, pp. A6–7 (Ambrose and Franklin quoted).
82. White House Tapes, February 14, 1973, conversation no. 885-010 (quotation on p. 18); February 16, 1973, conversation no. 862-006, February 23, 1973, conversation no. 862-006; March 22, 1973, conversation no. 422-020; April 14, 1973, conversation nos. 896-004, 005—all in WSPFFS, NPM, NARA.
83. *Washington Post*, September 24, 1992, pp. A6–7.
84. *New York Times*, February 2, 1994, pp. A1, A4; February 3, 1994, pp. A1, A4; February 5, 1994, pp. 1, 5; February 7, 1994, p. A11.

CHAPTER 8. BALANCING THE FOREIGN POLICY SCALE

1. Author's telephone conversations with Gretchen Osgood, December 5 and 9, 1989.
2. Robert E. Osgood to NSC Staff, July 7, 1969 [hereafter Osgood Report], Box 1, EX FO, WHCF, NPM, NARA, emphasis in original. Sanitized version declassified for author on September 15, 1989, through MR.
3. "The U.S. in the International Environment: An Overview," p. 1, attached to Osgood memorandum to NSC staff, July 7, 1969, Box 1, EX FO, WHCF, NARA.
4. Ibid., pp. 6–8.
5. Ibid., pp. 10–12 (first three quotations), 63–77 (last quotation on p. 64).
6. Nixon to Haldeman, Ehrlichman, and Kissinger, March 2, 1970, Box 229, Presidential Memoranda, Haldeman Papers, SMOF, WHSF, NPM, NARA.
7. Rogers's disagreement with the White House during the India-Pakistan war was particularly irritating to Nixon. See Rogers to Nixon, August 10, 1971 (declassified for author through MR in 1990), Box 36, Jon M. Huntsmand to Kissinger, December 6, 1971 (declassified in 1982), Box 85, SS-CF; Haldeman Notes, December 7, 1971 (quotation), Box 44, January 14, 1972, Part I, Box 45, Haldeman Papers, SMOF, WHSF, NPM, NARA.
8. Roger Morris, *Uncertain Greatness: Henry Kissinger and American Foreign Policy* (New York: Harper & Row, 1977), pp. 120–23 (Kissinger quotation); ANS with NHC, July 1969 (n.d.), NPM, NARA; William Shawcross, *The Quality of Mercy: Cambodia, Holocaust and Modern Conscience* (New York: Simon & Schuster, 1984), pp. 424–27.
9. Henry Kissinger, *White House Years* (Boston: Little, Brown, 1979), pp. 416–17; ANS with NHC, July 1969 (n.d.), September 1969 (n.d.), Box 30, POF, NPM, NARA; Morris, *Uncertain Greatness*, pp. 124–30; Kissinger testimony, March 3, 1975, Murphy Commission, pp. 67–68, Box 43, RG 220, NARA.
10. I. M. Destler, *Making Foreign Economic Policy* (Washington, D.C., Brookings Institution, 1980), pp. 19–120.
11. Murray M. Chotiner to Haldeman, January 20, 1970 (declassified in 1986), Box 56, Haldeman Papers, SMOF, WHSF, NPM, NARA; Morris, *Uncertain*

Greatness, pp. 131–32; Michael H. Hunt, *Idealogy and U.S. Foreign Policy* (New Haven: Yale University Press, 1987), pp. 46–91.

12. Morris, *Uncertain Greatness*, p. 129.

13. Ibid., p. 111.

14. For more details, see Anthony Lake, *The "Tar Baby" Opinion: American Policy Toward Southern Rhodesia* (New York: Columbia University Press, 1976), pp. 123–57; Mohammed A. El-Khawas and Barry Cohen, eds., *The Kissinger Study of Southern Africa* (Westport, Conn.: Lawrence Hill, 1976); Morris, *Uncertain Greatness*, pp. 107–20; *New York Times*, September 24, 1993. p. A3.

15. Tom Wicker, *One of Us: Richard Nixon and the American Dream* (New York: Random House, 1991), p. 667–69; Rhodrei Jeffrey Jones, *The CIA and American Democracy* (New Haven: Yale University Press, 1989), pp. 182–83, passim; Seymour M. Hersh, *The Price of Power: Kissinger in the Nixon White House* (New York: Summit Books, 1983), pp. 258–296.

16. Richard Nixon, *RN: The Memoirs of Richard Nixon* (New York: Grosset & Dunlap), p. 490.

17. Kissinger's testimony, March 3, 1975, pp. 93–95, Box 43, Murphy Commission, RG 220, NARA.

18. Ibid., pp. 96–98. Other examples of Rockefeller running interference for Kissinger during this 1975 testimony can be found on pp. 83 and 86.

19. Rogers's testimony, March 31, 1975, pp. 38–41, Murphy Commission, Box 43, RG 220, NARA.

20. Osgood Report, pp. 76–77.

21. Tad Szulc, *The Illusion of Peace: Foreign Policy in the Nixon Years* (New York: Viking Press, 1978), pp. 90–92. See the list of NSSMs at the National Security Archive. None of the ones on the Middle East has been declassified.

22. George W. Ball, "The Coming Crisis in Israeli-American Relations," *Foreign Affairs* 58 (Winter 1979–80): 231–56; Marvin Kalb and Bernard Kalb, *Kissinger* (Boston: Little, Brown, 1974), p. 187; Edward R. F. Sheehan, *The Arabs, Israelis, and Kissinger* (New York: Thomas Y. Crowell, 1976), pp. 15–16, 22; Seyom Brown, *The Crisis of Power: An Interpretation of United States Foreign Policy During the Kissinger Years* (New York: Columbia Univerity Press, 1979), p. 22; *New York Review of Books*, June 26, 1980, p. 19. For the fullest presentation of the Rogers Plan, see Rogers's December 9, 1969, address in Sheehan, *Arabs, Israelis, and Kissinger*, app. 2, pp. 221–27.

23. Ball, "Coming Crisis," pp. 236–40; Kalb and Kalb, *Kissinger*, pp. 190–91; Brown, *Crises of Power*, pp. 73–74.

24. NPP, *1969*, pp. 18, 185; author's interview with Nixon, January 26, 1983; Haldeman Notes, January 14, 1973, Box 47, Haldeman Papers, SMOF, WHSF, NPM, NARA.

25. Kalb and Kalb, *Kissinger*, p. 188; Morris, *Uncertain Greatness*, p. 252 (quotation); Nixon, *Memoirs*, pp. 477–85; Kissinger, *White House Years*, pp. 559–629, 1276–1300.

26. Haldeman to General James D. Hughes, June 29, 1970, Hughes to Halde-

man, July 6, 1970, Box 42, SS-CF, Kissinger to Nixon, December 4, 1970, PPF, WHSF, NPM, NARA.

27. Szulc, *Illusion of Peace*, p. 101; Kissinger, *White House Years*, p. 348.

28. Szulc, *Illusion of Peace*, p. 101; Sheehan, *Arabs, Israelis, and Kissinger*, pp. 17–18 (quotation); Nixon, *Memoirs*, p. 479.

29. Nixon, *Memoirs*, p. 477; Kissinger, *White House Years*, pp. 348, 1289–1300; Szulc, *Illusion of Peace*, pp. 101–2; Sheehan, *Arabs, Israelis, and Kissinger*, pp. 17, 40.

30. Nixon, *Memoirs*, p. 478. (The Nixon Doctrine is discussed in chaps. 2 and 7.)

31. Ibid., pp. 478–79; Szulc, *Illusion of Peace*, pp. 97–98.

32. Nixon to Rogers and Kissinger, February 22, 1969, Box 1, PPF, WHSF, NPM, NARA.

33. Kalb and Kalb, *Kissinger*, p. 188.

34. Haldeman Notes, February 26, 1970, Box 41, Haldeman Papers, SMOF, WHSF, NPM, NARA; Szulc, *Illusion of Peace*, pp. 98–99; Kalb and Kalb, *Kissinger*, pp. 192–93; Brown, *Crises of Power*, pp. 79–82; Kissinger, *White House Years*, pp. 1289–1300.

35. Brown, *Crises of Power*, pp. 82–87.

36. Ibid., "Report on Meir Visit to U.S.," October 7, 1969, Box 3, POF, WHSF, NPM, NARA.

37. *New York Review of Books*, June 26, 1980, p. 19.

38. Szulc, *Illusion of Peace*, pp. 313–14, 329–33; Haldeman Notes, February 26, 1970, Box 41, Haldeman Papers, SMOF, WHSF, NPM, NARA; Kissinger, *Years of Upheaval*, pp. 289–90.

39. Seymour M. Hersh, *The Samson Option: Israel's Nuclear Arsenal and American Foreign Policy* (New York: Random House, 1991), p. 137. The term originally was applied to Israel by Norman Podhoretz in a 1976 *Commentary* article.

40. Nixon to Kissinger, February 4, 1969 (declassified for author under MR in 1990), Box 228, Haldeman Papers, Presidential Memoranda, SMOF; Flanigan and Kissinger to Nixon, February 25, 1970 (declassified for author under MR in 1990), Box 5, POF, WHSF, NPM, NARA.

41. Gary Sick, *All Fall Down: America's Tragic Encounter with Iran* (New York: Random House, 1985), pp. 14–22; Walter Isaacson, *Kissinger: A Biography* (New York: Simon & Schuster, 1992), p. 563.

42. Sick, *All Fall Down*, pp. 21–22; James A. Bill, *The Eagle and the Lion: The Tragedy of American-Iranian Relations* (New Haven: Yale University Press, 1988), pp. 200–3; U.S. Senate Committee on Foreign Relations, Subcommittee on Foreign Assistance, Staff Report, *U.S. Military Sales to Iran* (Washington, D.C.: Government Printing Office, July 1976), pp. vii–xvi; *Hearings on U.S. Arms Sales Policy*, 94th Cong., 2d sess., September 16, 21, and 24, 1976.

43. Wicker, *One of Us*, pp. 138–40, 663–65; Richard Nixon, *Leaders: Profiles and Reminiscences of Men Who Have Shaped the Modern World* (New York: Warner Books, 1982), pp. 289–309 (quotation on pp. 307–8).

44. Kissinger, *White House Years*, pp. 1259–61. Also see idem, *Years of Upheaval* (Boston: Little, Brown, 1982), pp. 667–76.

45. Kissinger quoted in Bill, *Eagle and Lion*, p. 203.

46. Kissinger's testimony, Murphy Commission, March 3, 1975, pp. 71–72, 76–77, Box 43, RG 220, NARA; Kissinger, *Years of Upheaval*, pp. 670, 857; idem, *White House Years*, p. 1260.

47. Barry M. Rubin, *Paved with Good Intentions: The American Experience and Iran* (New York: Oxford University Press, 1980); Jack Anderson, *Fiasco* (New York: Times Books, 1983); Gary Sick, *All Fall Down;* Bill, *Eagle and Lion*.

48. Anderson, *Fiasco*, pp. 315–16 (quotations).

49. Ibid., pp. 313–14; Flanigan to Nixon, July 7, 1972 (last quotation), Box 38, SS-CF, WHSF, NPM, NARA.

50. Ibid., p. 316; Richard Nixon, *In the Arena: A Memoir of Victory, Defeat, and Renewal* (New York: Simon & Schuster, 1990), pp. 335–36 (first quotation); idem, *Memoirs*, pp. 926–27. (It was at this same time that Nixon made the decision to appoint his new vice president and had to deal with an adverse court decision on the Watergate tapes.)

51. U.S. Senate, *Military Sales to Iran*, pp. viii–ix; Sick, *All Fall Down*, pp. 108–9.

52. For details on Representative Otis G. Pike's still unreleased 1976 report, see Bill, *Eagle and Lion*, pp. 205, 207, 484n37; Kissinger, *White House Years*, p. 1265.

53. Quoted in Bennett H. Wall, *Growth in a Changing Environment: A History of Standard Oil Company (New Jersey), Exxon Corporation, 1950–1975* (New York: McGraw-Hill, 1988), pp. 753–57 (quotation). This is the single best source for detailed opinions of the large oil companies and their futile efforts to influence oil policy under Nixon before the 1973 October war.

54. George P. Shultz and Kenneth W. Dam, *Economic Policy Beyond the Headlines* (New York: Norton, 1978), pp. 182–84; Wall, *Growth in a Changing Environment*, pp. 753–63.

55. Haldeman to Flanigan, July 11, 1970, Box 62 (declassified 1987), Haldeman Papers, SMOF, WHSF, NPM, NARA.

56. Wall, *Growth in a Changing Environment*, pp. 768–812 (second quotation); Kissinger, *White House Years*, pp. 947–52; Isaacson, *Kissinger*, pp. 565–66; Flanigan to Nixon, July 7, 1972, Box 38, and Brent Scowcroft to Nixon, two memoranda, May 1, 1974 (declassified by NSC in 1990 and for author through MR in 1992), Box 41—all in SS-CF, WHSF, NPM, NARA.

57. Wall, *Growth in a Changing Environment*, pp. 813–64, 892 (quotation); Shultz and Dam, *Economic Policy*, p. 184; *New York Times*, October 17, 1993, p. 4 (chart).

58. Kissinger, *Years of Upheaval*, p. 854–934 (quotation on p. 856), Kissinger testimony, Murphy Commission, March 3, 1975, pp. 76–81, Box 43, RG 220, NARA.

59. Brown, *Crises of Power*, pp. 104–5.

60. Ibid.

61. Kalb and Kalb, *Kissinger*, p. 445.

62. Kissinger, *Years of Upheaval*, pp. 575–613; Szulc, *Illusion of Peace*, p. 742; Morris, *Uncertain Greatness*, p. 246; Kalb and Kalb, *Kissinger*, p. 490.

63. Nixon, *Memoirs*, p. 930–42.

64. Kalb and Kalb, *Kissinger*, pp. 497–98; Morris, *Uncertain Greatness*, pp. 247–48; Kissinger, *Years of Upheaval*, pp. 593–96.

65. Schlesinger's testimony, December 14, 1973, pp. 60–61 (quotation), 62–64, Box 25, Murphy Commission, RG 220, NARA.

66. *NPP, 1973*, pp. 896–97, 900 (quotation), 901–2.

67. Nixon, *Memoirs*, p. 932.

68. Ibid., p. 933–34.

69. Ibid., p. 934.

70. George W. Ball, *Diplomacy for a Crowded World: An American Foreign Policy* (Boston: Little, Brown, 1976), pp. 132–52; Brown, *Crisis of Power*, pp. 101–5; Kalb and Kalb, *Kissinger*, pp. 500–541; Morris, *Uncertain Greatness*, pp. 256–78.

71. Ball, "Coming Crisis," p. 231; Brown, *Crisis of Power*, pp. 71–101.

72. Kissinger to Nixon (n.d.; sometime in June 1974) (declassified by NSC in 1990 and for author through MR in 1992), Box 41, SS-CF; Roy Ash to Nixon, January 4, 1974, memorandum and attachments on foreign and military assistance for FY 1975 (declassified by NSC in 1990, by DoD in 1991, and for author through MR in 1993), Haig to Nixon (with NHC), January 5, 1974 (declassified by NSC in 1990 and for author through MR in 1993)—both in Box 25, POF, WHSF, NPM, NARA.

73. Nixon on "Nightline," January 7, 1992. See also his book *Seize the Moment: America's Challenge in a One-Superpower World* (New York: Simon & Schuster, 1992), pp. 194–231; Hersh, *Samson Option*, p. 137.

74. Nixon, *Leaders: Profiles and Reminiscences*, p. 74.

CHAPTER 9. PRELUDE TO WATERGATE: CIVIL RIGHTS VIOLATED

1. Two representative samples written over fifteen years apart are Jonathan Schell, *The Time of Illusion* (New York: Knopf, 1976), pp. 50–126, and Stanley I. Kutler, *The Wars of Watergate: The Last Crisis of Richard Nixon* (New York: Knopf, 1990).

2. WSPF Report, pp. 65–70 (quotation on p. 67), passim.

3. WSPF Report, pp. 67–68 (quotations), 70.

4. Within the White House, Colson and Bud Krogh seemed to make the most of the requests for IRS audits, while Dean provided the information to them from the IRS. At the same time, the Plumbers independently misused the IRS largely through the efforts of Jack Caulfield. For representative samples, see Haldeman to Flanigan, September 14, 1970, and Larry Higby to Chotiner and Harry Dent, September 8, 1970—both in Box 64, Haldeman Papers, SMOF; Dean to Colson, May 13, 1971, Dean to Krogh, July 27,

1971, Colson to John Evans and to John Dean, May 30, 1971—all in Box 39, Dean Papers, WHSF, NPM, NARA; interview of Murray Chotiner, April 2, 1974, Plumbers Task Force, IRS Witness for 6-MC, and Plumbers Abuse of IRS, Jack Caulfield Witness File, WSPF, RG 460, NARA. The president can be heard ordering the cutoff of research funds for MIT in released taped conversation between Nixon and Haldeman for June 1972; see Burrelle's news-clipping service for *Virginia-Pilot* editorial, May 21, 1993, NARA.

5. White House Tapes, September 15, 1972, pp. 1, 3, conversation no. 779-002, WSPFFS, NPM, NARA.

6. White House Tapes, February 16, 1973, p. 19, conversation no. 858-003, WSPFFS, NPM, NARA.

7. Michael R. Belknap, "Vietnam and the Constitution: The War Power Under Lyndon Johnson and Richard Nixon," *This Constitution* 10 (Spring 1986): 19. For a similar, but more partisan, interpretation of the double standard used by critics of the war in judging Nixon, see Nicholas von Hoffman, "How Nixon Got Strung Up," *The New Republic*, June 23, 1982, pp. 24–27.

8. Garry Wills, *Newsday*, June 13, 1982, p. 12.

9. Von Hoffman, "How Nixon Got Strung Up," p. 26.

10. Moynihan to Nixon, November 13, 1970, Ehrlichman Papers.

11. Nixon and Hoover quoted in Richard Gid Powers, *Secrecy and Power: The Life of J. Edgar Hoover* (New York: Free Press, 1987), pp. 449, 451; Kissinger quoted in Schell, *Time of Illusion*, p. 115.

12. Leo Rangell, *The Mind of Watergate: An Exploration on the Compromise of Integrity* (New York: Norton, 1980), p. 35.

13. Richard Nixon, *RN: The Memoirs of Richard Nixon* (New York: Grosset & Dunlap, 1978), pp. 357–58 (quotation), 387; Huston to Cole and Krogh, June 24, 1969, Box 8, EX HU2–1, WHCF, NPM, NARA. Ironically, Huston wrote this in connection with conservative opposition in the Justice Department to Nixon's desegregation plans. For more examples of Nixon's invectives against the press and attempts to wage war against them, see John Robert Greene, *The Limits of Power: The Nixon and Ford Administrations* (Bloomington: Indiana University Press, 1992), pp. 130–32.

14. For details of the "hardball" game he played with the press, see Greene, *Limits of Power*, pp. 131–32, and Eric Alterman, *Sound and Fury: The Washington Punditocracy and the Collapse of American Politics* (New York: HarperCollins, 1992), pp. 73–75.

15. June 1, 1972, CIA "eyes-only" memorandum, Box 5, Cheney Files.

16. Frank Martin to William H. Merrill, July 29, 1974, Martin to Files, October 10, 1975, Haig Materials, WSPF, RG 460, NARA. For other details about these wiretaps, see Walter Isaacson, *Kissinger: A Biography* (New York: Simon & Schuster, 1992), pp. 212–29.

17. *U.S. v. U.S. District Court*, 407 U.S. 297 (1972); Sullivan to Hoover, May 20, 1969, in attachments to FBI Director to Leon Jaworski, April 30, 1974, National Security Wiretaps, RG 460, WSPF, NARA.

18. Roger Morris, *Uncertain Greatness: Henry Kissinger and American Foreign Policy* (New York: Harper & Row, 1977), pp. 157–62; Seymour M. Hersh, *The Price of Power: Kissinger in the Nixon White House* (New York: Summit Books, 1983), pp. 83–97; Len Colodny and Robert Gettlin, *Silent Coup: The Removal of a President* (New York: St. Martin's Press, 1991), pp. 417–18.

19. "Kissinger Wiretaps," Haig Files, WSPF, RG 460, NARA.

20. Ken BeLieu, June 15, 1969, Kissinger to Nixon, June 26, 1969 (both declassified 1986), Box 283; Nixon to Haldeman, November 30, 1970, Box 299—all in Haldeman Papers. For representative samples of Nixon's concern over leaks, see Ehrlichman Papers, Box 21; Nixon to Kissinger, Rogers, et al., April 14, 1969, Box 5; Nixon to Kissinger, June 16, 1969 (both declassified by NSC 1990 and for author under MR, 1992 and 1993), Box 1, PPF; Bruce to Kehrli, February 13, 1973, Box 85, SS-CF—all in WHSF. White House Tapes, July 6, 1971, conversation no. 538-015; July 24, 1971, conversation no. 545-003; February 23, 1972, conversation no. 862-006; February 16, 1973, conversation no. 853-003—all in WSPFFS, NPM, NARA.

21. Powers, *Secrecy and Power*, pp. 447–48, 458–61; transcript of conversation, October 8, 1971, no. 587-003, pp. 4–5, WSPFFS, NPM, NARA.

22. Ibid., pp. 462–63 (quotation), 475–76.

23. Schell, *Time of Illusion*, pp. 66, 111; Nick Egleson, "The Surveillance Apparatus," in *State Secrets: Political Surveillance in America*, ed. Paul Cowan et al. (New York: Holt, Rinehart & Winston, 1974), p. 14; memorandum to Nixon, June 18, 1971, Box 98, Dean Papers, WHSF, NPM, NARA.

24. Powers, *Secrecy and Power*, pp. 451–55; Schell, *Time of Illusion*, pp. 111–16; Colodny and Gettlin, *Silent Coup*, p. 98.

25. William Safire, *Before the Fall: An Inside View of the Pre-Watergate White House* (New York: Ballantine Books, 1977; Random House, 1975), pp. 289–90, 379–85; Schell, *Time of Illusion*, p. 111.

26. William E. Colby to Ford, December 24, 1974, Box 13, Cheney Files, summarizing at the president's request the "reported involvement of the CIA in a 'massive' domestic intelligence effort," annexes to this letter declassified through MR in 1985 and 1989.

27. Christopher H. Pyle, "CONUS Intelligence: The Army Watches Civilian Politics," *Washington Monthly*, January 1970, pp. 4–7. See also idem, "Military Surveillance of Civilian Politics, 1967–1970," Ph.D. diss., Columbia University, 1974.

28. *New York Times*, January 16, 1970, p. 27; Huston to Haldeman, July 10, 1970, in *From the President: Richard Nixon's Secret Files*, ed. Bruce Oudes (New York: Harper & Row, 1989), p. 145 (quotation); Athen Theoharis, *Spying on Americans: Political Surveillance from Hoover to the Huston Plan* (Philadelphia: Temple University Press, 1978), p. 88. Ervin quoted in Paul R. Clancy, *Just a Country Lawyer: A Biography of Senator Sam Ervin* (Bloomington: Indiana University Press, 1974), p. 234.

29. Ervin quoted in *Congressional Record*, 91st Cong., 2d sess., p. 26,321 (emphasis added). For a discussion of the meaning and short-lived applica-

tion of Nixon's "southern strategy," see chaps. 1 and 3; Arthur Schlesinger, Jr., *The Imperial Presidency* (Boston: Houghton Mifflin, 1973), pp. 392–411; and Karl E. Campbell, "Just a Country Lawyer: Senator Sam Ervin and the Road to Watergate," paper delivered at the annual conference of the American Historical Association, December 28, 1992.

30. ANS, January 22, 1969 (n.p.), Box 30, with NHC to Ehrlichman, and May 28, 1969 (n.p.), Box 30, POF, WHCF, NARA.

31. Greene, *Limits of Power*, pp. 89–98; WSPF Report, pp. 68–70; Schell, *Time of Illusion*, pp. 54–62, 88, 111–12, 223–24.

32. Ibid.

33. Powers, *Secrecy and Power*, pp. 453–55, 467.

34. Ibid., pp. 455–57, 586n50; Nixon, *Memoirs*, p. 474; Helms to Ehrlichman, August 20, 1971 (declassified in 1989), Box 21, Alpha Subjects, Ehrlichman Papers; Dean to Nixon, June 18, 1971, Box 98, Dean Files, SMOF, WHSF, NPM, NARA.

35. Nixon, *Memoirs*, pp. 471, 475, 476.

36. Powers, *Secrecy and Power*, pp. 467–71; Earl J. Silbert to Archibald Cox, June 7, 1973, pp. 1–5 (Ehrlichman quotation), reviewing pre- and post-Watergate criminal activities, Silbert File, WSPF, RG 460, NARA. In addition to the 4,000 classified pages of documents, the Pentagon Papers contained 3,000 pages of narrative chronology.

37. Ehrlichman Diary, June 1971 (n.d.), no. 119, Ehrlichman Materials; Ehrlichman Notes, June 12, 1971, Box 11, Ehrlichman Papers, SMOF, WHSF, NPM, NARA, Isaacson, *Kissinger*, pp. 162–64, 282–83; Colodny and Gettlin, *Silent Coup*, pp. 112–13; Morris, *Uncertain Greatness*, pp. 250–51.

38. Ehrlichman Notes, July 24, 1971, Box 11, Ehrlichman Papers, SMOF, WHSF; White House Tapes, July 24; 1971, conversation no. 545-003, pp. 2–6, WSPFFS, NARA; Nixon, *Memoirs*, pp. 508–9.

39. Powers, *Secrecy and Power*, pp. 470–72; Frank Martin to Files, interview with Bernie Wells, September 17, 1973, National Security Wiretaps Files; Frank Martin to Files, October 10, 1975, closing memorandum on "Kissinger wiretaps," Haig Files, WSPF, RG 460, NARA.

40. Powers, *Secrecy and Power*, pp. 104–19; White House Tapes, October 8, 1971, conversation no. 587-003, p. 1, WSPFFS; Frank Martin to Files, interview with Bernie Wells, September 17, 1973, National Security Wiretaps Files, WSPF, RG 460, NARA. There apparently was only one set of these logs from the "Kissinger wiretaps"; only letters containing some of the material (marked by Sullivan) were sent to the White House, and most of these had been returned to the FBI after the taps were discontinued in 1971.

41. After leaving the NSC, Halperin initiated a nineteen-year lawsuit seeking damages against Kissinger for the twenty-one-month tap on his phone. This legal action did not come to an end until November 1992, when Kissinger publicly apologized (in a letter written in December 1991) for his role in this particular wiretapping. Kissinger accepted "moral responsibility" in this

apology, but denied that he was the "principal person responsible" for this violation of constitutional rights. "It is something if circumstances were repeated I would not do again," Kissinger said, but maintained that he had simply "acquiesced in the tap" after Hoover identified Halperin as a possible leaker of National Security Council information. He admitted, however, that his "office became part of the process at least to the extent of reading the reports until May 1970." See *International Herald Tribune*, November 14–15, 1993, p. 3.

42. For example, Ehrlichman later perjured himself before a grand jury on May 14, 1973, saying he "had no foreknowledge" of the break-in at Dr. Fielding's office. On April 18 he had lied to Nixon about the nature of the operation, indicating that he did not know a burglary had been contemplated. The next day, Nixon repeated this denial to Richard Moore, another White House special counselor. Ehrlichman's exact words to Nixon about the Fielding break-in were these: "The way the project was finally represented to me was that it was a covert look at some files, which could be read to be that [sic] they walked in when the nurse wasn't looking and they flipped through the file. . . . It wasn't until much later that we learned that they actually conducted a burglary." The day after this Nixon told Moore: "Edgar [Hoover]— just couldn't bring himself to get into it. So we had to do something on Ellsberg and . . . the capabilities up here to try to get information on the Ellsberg case. But . . . there was no bugging. . . . There was this crazy thing where Hunt goes out and breaks into the psychiatrist's office. . . . But Ehrlichman had no knowledge of that particular thing." In July 1974 Ehrlichman was convicted of perjury and of conspiring to obstruct justice and violate the civil rights of Ellsberg. He later insisted in his memoirs that he had been betrayed by the White House because Nixon had personally authorized the Ellsberg caper. Indeed, his notes for a May 2, 1973, conversation with Nixon contain the following exchange: "Did I know sooner?" the president asked. Ehrlichan nodded yes and the president said: "If so, I don't remember." By contrast, Nixon has said, "I do not believe I was told about the break-in at the time, but it is clear that it was at least in part an outgrowth of my sense of urgency about discrediting what Ellsberg had done." Only the release of the tape for this conversation will settle this dispute over who knew what. In this specific instance, the discovery of the Fielding break-in also caused a mistrial in the government's attempt to prosecute Ellsberg for leaking classified information. See White House Tapes, April 18, 1973, conversation no. 900-026, p. 9, and April 19, 1973, conversation no. 429-015, p. 21—both in WSPFFS, NARA; Nixon, *Memoirs*, p. 514; Ehrlichman, *Witness to Power*, pp. 395–96, 399–407; and Ehrlichman Notes, May 2, 1973, no. 224, Ehrlichman Materials.

43. Krogh quoted in Kutler, *Wars of Watergate*, p. 117.

44. Ehrlichman Diary, December 1971 and January 1972, no. 126, Ehrlichman Notes, January 5, 1972, no. 128, Ehrlichman Materials; Radford quoted in Colodny and Gettlin, *Silent Coup*, p. 28.

45. Colodny and Gettlin, *Silent Coup*, pp. 48–68; Nixon, *Memoirs*, pp. 525–31. As discussed in chapter 8, the "tilt" toward Pakistan in its war with India also became a major cause célèbre for the Nixon administration because the president's top-secret orders to the NSC to get "tough" on India were leaked to the press after the Joint Chiefs of Staff planted a spy in Kissinger's office. Colodny and Gettlin, *Silent Coup*, pp. 14–17; Morris, *Uncertain Greatness*, pp. 222–30; Henry Kissinger, *White House Years* (Boston: Little, Brown, 1979), pp. 897, 901*n*, 917; Nixon, *Memoirs*, pp. 531–32; Marvin Kalb and Bernard Kalb, *Kissinger* (Boston: Little, Brown, 1974), pp. 257–64.

46. Ehrlichman Notes, December 23, 1971, Box 6, Ehrlichman Papers, WHSF, NPM, NARA; Colodny and Gettlin, *Silent Coup*, pp. 3–68; Charles W. Colson, Oral History Interview, September 21, 1988, conducted by Frederick H. Graboske and Paul A. Schmidt, p. 28, NPM, NARA. Colson admitted in this interview that he, Haig, and Buzhardt had met several times in 1973 and 1974 to discuss how the Special Prosecutor's investigation was going and the CIA involvement in Watergate (p. 29).

47. Martin to Files, October 10, 1975, Haig Files, WSPF, RG 460, NARA; Colodny and Gettlin, *Silent Coup*, pp. 286–93 (quotation on p. 291).

48. White House Tapes, February 16, 1973, conversation no. 858-003, p. 22, WSPFFS, NARA.

49. White House Tapes, January 8, 1973, conversation nos. 394-021/395-001, p. 1, WSPFFS, NARA. Other representative examples can be found on tapes for April 14, 1973, conversation nos. 428-019, 896-004, 005, 428-028, 038-034, 038-037—all in WSPFFS, NARA.

50. Walter Karp, "The Hour of the Founders," *American Heritage* (June–July 1984): 27.

CHAPTER 10. WATERGATE REVISITED: POLITICS OR SEX?

1. Prosecutive Report (draft), February 7, 1974, Nixon File No. 6, Jaworski to Files, June 28, 1974 (second draft), Watergate Prosecutor's Files, WSPF, RG 460, NARA. The quote in the text is from the second draft, but essentially the same conclusion was reached in February.

2. Watergate Special Prosecution Force (WSPF), *Report* (Washington, D.C.: Government Printing Office, 1975), pp. 82–84.

3. Richard Nixon, *In the Arena: A Memoir of Victory, Defeat and Renewal* (New York: Pocket Books, 1991; Simon & Schuster, 1990), pp. 41–42; Stanley I. Kutler, *The Wars of Watergate: The Last Crisis of Richard Nixon* (New York: Knopf, 1990), pp. 203–6; Stephen E. Ambrose, *Nixon: Ruin and Recovery, 1973–1990* (New York: Simon & Schuster, 1987), pp. 421–23.

4. Box 21 of the Ehrlichman Papers in WHSF, NPM, NARA, contains background information on Liddy, the former "wild man" and "superklutz" of the FBI who was encouraged to leave the agency in the mid-1960s out of fear over his gun-craziness. Yet Ehrlichman and other top Republicans in

Washington, D.C., kept recommending him to one another (and to others) because of his "highest sense of integrity" and because of his usefulness on "gun control, bombing, narcotics and IRS enforcement . . . [his] special competence in law enforcement." After all, Maurice Stans fired Liddy from the CRP finance committee only when he refused to answer questions about the Watergate break-in. In addition to Box 21, see Powers, *Secrecy and Power*, pp. 111–12; and J. Anthony Lukas, *Nightmare: The Underside of the Nixon Years* (New York: Viking Press, 1976), pp. 86–87, 237, passim.

5. Kutler, *Wars of Watergate*, pp. 200–201. See also Donald Freed, "Gemstone—The Bottom Line," in *Big Brother and the Holding Company*, ed. Steve Weissman (Palo Alto, Calif.: Ramparts Press, 1974), pp. 91–105.

6. Kutler, *Wars of Watergate*, p. 201; Colodny and Gettlin, *Silent Coup*, 134, 147–49, 157, 214.

7. Nixon to Kissinger, November 20, 1970, Box 229, presidential memoranda, Haldeman Papers, SMOF, NPM, NARA; Ehrlichman Notes, January 10, 1970, no. 31, Ehrlichman Materials.

8. G. Goldman to Files, McCord interview, August 6, 1973, and Gordon to Files, McCord interview, September 19, 1973, McCord Witness File, RG 460, WSPF. McCord insisted that all the Cuban burglars referred to the DNC break-in using Mitchell's name, but this was never proved. He also used Mitchell's name in a December letter to the CIA.

9. McCord statement, May 4, 1973, McCord Witness File, WSPF, RG 460, NARA.

10. H. R. Haldeman, *The Ends of Power* (New York: Times Books, 1978), pp. 133–64, 203–6, 317–23; Garry Wills, *Lead Time: A Journalist's Education* (Garden City, N.Y.: Doubleday, 1983), p. 109; Colson, exit interview conducted by Jack Nesbitt and Susan Yowell, January 12, 1973, pp. 2, 5 (first quotation), 8, NPM, NARA.

11. Charles W. Colson, Oral History Interview, September 21, 1988, conducted by Fredrick H. Groboske and Paul A. Schmidt, NPM, NARA. Stephen Haberfeld to James F. Neal and Richard Ben-Veniste, July 31, 1973; Henry Hecht and Nick Akerman interviews with Colson, August 7, 1973 (in Akerman to Files, August 10 [first quotation]); Hecht to Merrill, August 14, 1973 (other quotations, with attached Colson to Senator Ervin et al., June 28, 1973); Phil Bakes to Files, August 15, 1973; Martin to Files, August 16, 1973 (analyzing interviews with Colson)—all in Colson Defendant File, WSPF, RG 460, NARA.

12. Jim Hougan, *Secret Agenda: Watergate, Deep Throat and the CIA* (New York: Random House, 1984), pp. 139–57, 176–213, 243–260 (esp. 211–12); Kutler, *Wars of Watergate*, pp. 202–3. Unfortunately, Kutler does not clearly evaluate this theory about the break-in. Instead, he buries in the footnotes two contradictory comments, saying first that Hougan offered the "best account of the break-in and certainly the most careful reading of the FBI record" (p. 646n1) and then referring readers to a very critical 1983 book

review by J. Anthony Lukas that "dissected . . . Hougan's assumptions and hypotheses" (p. 648n27). Since Kutler admits that Hougan's book constituted the "most revisionist account of the origins of Watergate" (p. 203), one is left wondering why he did not attempt to prove or disprove it. Fortunately, Colodny and Gettlin take up where Hougan left off.

13. Kutler, *Wars of Watergate*, pp. 205–8.

14. FBI reports for September 1972, R. Spencer Oliver Files, WSPF, RG 460, NARA.

15. Colodny and Gettlin, *Silent Coup*, pp. 126–33, 145–46, 229–31; Hougan, *Secret Agenda*, pp. 111–14, 172–74. These two books disagree on which women, who also worked out of the nearby Columbia Plaza Apartments, were involved with Bailley. They agree, however, that Bailley's trial and sentencing were handled in a bizarre and suspicious way that ensured his documents would be "sealed" from future scrutiny.

16. Hougan, *Secret Agenda*, pp. 123–38; 243–60; Colodny and Gettlin, *Silent Coup*, pp. 142–60.

17. Hougan, *Secret Agenda*, pp. 139–57, 173–213; Colodny and Gettlin, *Silent Coup*, pp. 161–204 (Liddy quoted on p. 166).

18. Hougan, *Secret Agenda*, pp. 206–13; Colody and Gettlin, *Silent Coup*, pp. 126, 134–40, 187–93.

19. Nixon, *Memoirs*, pp. 500–501 (quotation); WSPF interview of Raymond Zumwalt, October 31, 1973, Buzhardt Papers; Colodny and Gettlin, *Silent Coup*, pp. 322–36; Hougan, *Secret Agenda*, pp. 58–59.

20. Maaja Krusten, former archivist with the Nixon Presidential Materials Project, to author, November 26, 1993. In this letter Krusten discusses in general terms the inaccuracies in and disputes over the transcripts and cautions researchers about their questionable reliability.

21. Haldeman Notes, April 26, 1973, Box 47, Haldeman Papers, SMOF, WHSF, NPM; White House Tapes, April 26, 1973, conversation no. 431-009, pp. 71, 78–79. For particular reference to some of the inaccuracies in the transcripts, see Woodward and Bernstein, *Final Days*, pp. 134–36, 171–73; John Ehrlichman, *Witness to Power: The Nixon Years* (New York: Simon & Schuster, 1982), p. 345.

22. *Stanley Kutler and Public Citizen v. Don W. Wilson*, Complaint for Declaratory and Injunctive Relief, Civil Action 92-0662, U.S. District Court, D.C. March 19, 1992; deposition by Maarja Krusten in Civ. A. 92-0662-NHJ, September 29, 1992.

23. White House Tapes, June 23, 1972, conversation nos. 741-002, 741-010, and 343-036.

24. *Bozeman Daily Chronicle* (Mont.), February 17, 1993, p. 19.

25. White House Tapes, May 5, 1971, conversation no. 491-014, pp. 9–10; March 30, 1972, conversation no. 697-015, pp. 11, 20; April 14, 1973, conversation no. 428-019, p. 87; April 14, 1973, conversation no. 896-004, 005, p. 49; March 25, 1973, conversation no. 430-004, p. 56—all in WSPFFS, NPM, NARA. Sentenced to one to two years, Colson served only seven months.

26. White House Tapes, April 14, 1973, conversation no. 428-019, p. 27, WSPFFS, NPM, NARA.

27. White House Tapes, April 16, 1973, conversation no. 897-004, p. 43; April 16, 1973, conversation no. 427-005, 006, p. 1; March 20, 1973, conversation no. 903-019, p. 10—all in WSPFFS, NPM, NARA.

28. AP press release, May 17, 1993 (byline Mike Feinsilber), NPM, NARA. On p. 635 of his *Memoirs*, Nixon paraphrased much of this June 21 conversation, but in doing so he indicated that Ehrlichman, not Haldeman, had come up with the idea of using Liddy and that he agreed with it.

29. AP press release, May 17, 1993.

30. Ibid.

31. White House Tapes, April 14, 1973 transcript of conversation no. 428-019 (quotations), WSPFFS, NARA.

32. White House Tapes, transcript of a dictabelt recording of a conversation between Howard Hunt and Charles Colson, November 1972 (n.d.), p. 7, conversation no. 000-000 [*sic*], p. 7, WHPFFS, NPM, NARA.

33. *Washington Star-News*, May 9, 1974.

34. *New York Times*, May 12, 1974, p. 40; *Washington Post*, May 12, 1974, p. A10, and May 13, 1974, pp. A1, A5.

35. White House Tapes, June 4, 1973, conversation nos. 442-001 through 069, pp. 18–19.

36. White House Tapes, June 23, 1972, conversation no. 741-002; April 14, 1973, conversation nos. 896-004, 005; April 19, 1973, conversation no. 000-000 [*sic*]—all in WSPFFS, NPM, NARA.

37. White House Tapes, May 5, 1971, conversation no. 491-014, p. 13; October 25, 1971, conversation no. 601-033, p. 9; June 23, 1972, conversation no. 741-002, p. 2—all in WSPFFS, NPM, NARA.

38. White House Tapes, June 4, 1973, conversation nos. 442-001 through 069, pp. 20–23, 68–73, WSPFFS, NPM, NARA

39. *New York Times*, May 12, 1974, pp. 1, 40; *The New Yorker*, December 14, 1992, pp. 76–95; Woodward and Bernstein, *Final Days*, p. 171; *Washington Post*, May 13, 1974, pp. A1, A5. Of the two other negative references to Jews purportedly made on March 20, 1973, one was in reference to the Securities and Exchange Commission: "Those Jew-boys are all over everybody. You can't stop them" and the other to "those Jews in the U.S. Attorney's office." See Fred Buzhardt Papers. Neither can be found on either the tape or the transcription for that day.

40. Author's interview with Ehrlichman, April 9, 1984; author's interview with Nixon, June 6, 1984. See also White House Tapes, June 23, 1972, conversation no. 741-002, p. 6; March 14, 1973, conversation no. 855-010, p. 11; April 14, 1973, conversation no. 428-019, pp. 36, 94; April 19, 1973, conversation no. 902-001, pp. 7–9—all in WHPFFS, NPM, NARA.

41. Author's interview with Ehrlichman, April 9, 1984; author's interview with Nixon, June 6, 1984; Colodny and Gettlin, *Silent Coup*, pp. 390–403.

42. Colodny and Gettlin, *Silent Coup*, pp. 199–200.

43. Ibid., pp. 373–425. The Nixon-Sampson agreement can be found in Box 24, John Marsh Files, esp. Philip Areeda to Ford, December 2, 1974; Buchen to Ford, December 13, 1974; Sampson to Marsh, January 14, 1975; Casselman to March, January 24, 1975. See also Boxes 30 and 32, esp. Buchen Files, Buchen to Ford, August 25, 1975 (reviewing the controversy over Nixon's papers), Box 30.

44. Ford to Saxbe, August 22, 1974 (proposed draft for information about legal status of Nixon papers), Ford to Buchen to Ford, October 18, 1974, and November 6, 1974; Sampson to Buchen, November 5, 1974, Box 31; Buchen to Ford, August 25, 1975 (administratively confidential), Box 30—all in Buchen Files. Buchen to Frank Church and John Tower, August 1, 1975, Box 75, Marsh Files; transcript of press conference, September 8, 1974, p. 29 (quoting Buchen), Nixon Files, Box 4, Ford Papers. Buchen's 1989 comments were made at a Hofstra University Conference on the Presidency, April 8.

45. Seymour M. Hersh, "The Pardon," *Atlantic* 252 (August 1983): 55–78; Colodny and Gettlin, *Silent Coup*, pp. 436–38.

46. Joseph Kraft to Thomas Powers, September 27, 1974, Box 32, Buchen Files, Ford Papers. In this letter Kraft regretted the use of the word *small-time* to describe Buchen but continued to insist that he lacked the experience necessary to go "deeply into profound questions of public policy." For Buchens's lingering uncertainty about the legal issues involved in indicting an "officeholder covered by the impeachment provision," see Mayer W. Leib to Ford, July 6, 1976, Buchen to Ken Lazarus, July 13, 1976, Buchen to Leib, August 9, 1976—all in Box 32, Buchen Files, Ford Papers.

47. Garment to Buchen, August 28, 1974, and Buchen to William Greener, December 19, 1975—both in Box 32, Buchen Files; Ron Nessen to Cheney and Marsh, January 30, 1976 (quotation), Marsh Files, Ford Papers; Colodny and Gettlin, *Silent Coup*, pp. 426–29; Kutler, *Wars of Watergate*, pp. 556–63.

48. Henry S. Ruth, Jr., to Leon Jaworski, September 3, 1974 (listing matters other than Watergate that might have "personally involved" Nixon), and Jaworski to Buchen, September 4 and 10, 1974, Box 32, Buchen Files; Jaworski to Saxbe, October 12, 1974, Box 25, Marsh Files, Ford Papers; Colodny and Gettlin, *Silent Coup*, pp. 430–32.

49. Jaworski to Buchen, September 4, 1974, Box 32, Buchen Files, Ford Papers. Robert T. Hartmann's recollection both in his book, *Palace Politics: An Inside Account of the Ford Years* (New York: McGraw-Hill 1980), pp. 240–71, and on April 8, 1989, was that as late as September 5, 1974 (the day Becker flew to California), Ford told him, Haig, Marsh, and Becker confidentially *for the first time* that it was his "intention," his "inclination," to pardon Nixon, but that he had still not made up his mind with "absolute finality"; Colodny and Gettlin, *Silent Coup*, pp. 429–32; Kutler, *Wars of Watergate*, pp. 561–63.

50. Kutler, *Wars of Watergate*, pp. 553–60; Clark R. Mollendorff, *The Man Who Pardoned Nixon* (New York: St. Martin's Press, 1976), p. 91.

51. Presidential *amnesty* refers to the formal proclamation or executive order given to a group of individuals, while *pardons* are usually granted on an individual basis. For data on modern presidential pardon rates, see Charles S. Clark, "Reagan's Parsimonious Use of Pardon Power," *Congressional Quarterly Weekly Report,* November 3, 1984, pp. 2878–80; Peter Earley, *Washington Post,* March 19, 1984, p. A17; Irving Molotsky, *New York Times,* August 16, 1985, p. A12. For Ford's attitude and actions on pardons, see George Lankevich, *Gerald R. Ford* (Dobbs Ferry, N.Y.: Oceana, 1977), pp. 21, 46, 105.

52. September 8, 1974, Pardon Proclamation, Ford's *Public Papers, 1975* (Washington, D.C.: Government Printing Office, 1976), pp. 103–4; Gerald R. Ford, *A Time to Heal: The Autobiography of Gerald R. Ford* (New York: Harper & Row, 1979), p. 164.

53. Nixon's Response to Pardon Statement, September 8, 1974, Box 25, Marsh Files, Ford Papers.

54. William Casselman to Buchen (with routing slip from William Skidmore), September 30, 1974, F. Lynn May to Buchen, October 30, 1974, Roy Ash to Representative Jack Brooks, November 18, 1974, Representative John E. Moses to Buchen, February 18; 1975, Buchen to John Fender, May 9, 1975, Buchen to Max Friedersdorf, November 23, 1976, Friedersdorf to Representative Donald M. Frazer, November 23, 1976, Box 28; Dick Cheney to Buchen, January 27, 1975, David C. Hoopes to Buchen, January 29, 1975, Buchen to Cheney, February 4, 1975, Box 31—all in Buchen Files. David C. Hoopes to Stanley Enber, October 4, 1974, Marsh to Senator Joseph Montoya, October 8, 1974, Hoopes to Howard Kerr, October 9, 1974—all in Box 25, March Files. Russ Rourke to Marsh, January 20, 1975, and Casselman to Rourke—both in Box 24, Marsh Files, Ford Papers. Nixon had formalized the informal briefings of ex-presidents on February 14, 1969, with Executive Order No. 11456, and by the beginning of 1975 members of his San Clemente staff had requested that such briefings be sent to him by government courier aircraft.

55. Quote from Elizabeth Holtzman at the Hofstra University Conference on the Ford Presidency, April 8, 1989.

CONCLUSION. WATERGATE IS MORE THAN NIXON

1. Suzanne Garment, *Scandal: The Crisis of Mistrust in American Politics* (New York: Times Books, 1991), pp. 38–42.

2. Congress made attempts at the end of 1993 to rectify some of the worst excesses of campaign financing, but without significantly curbing PAC spending. In 1994, it also renewed legislation authorizing independent prosecutors to investigate administration officials outside the direction of the Justice Department. The original Watergate legislation expired in December 1992, with Republicans blocking renewal until 1994 because of the cost and embarrassment associated with the Iran-contra investigation. See *New York*

Times, November 18, 1993, p. A17; November 23, 1993, pp. A1, A14; and February 11, 1994, p. A10.

3. Paul D. Wolfowitz to Robert T. Hartman, September 13, 1974, Box 32, Buchen Files, Ford Papers.

4. Garry Wills, *Newsday*, June 13, 1982, p. 11.

5. John L. McKenzie, S.J., ed., *Dictionary of the Bible* (New York: Macmillan, 1965), p. 298. I want to thank Dee Scriven for this reference.

6. Len Colodny and Robert Gettlin, *Silent Coup: The Removal of a President* (New York: St. Martin's Press, 1991).

7. Wills, *Newsday*, p. 11; Michael Schudson, *Watergate in American Memory: How We Remember, Forget, and Reconstruct the Past* (New York: Basic Books, 1992), pp. 9–66.

8. Walter Karp, "The Hour of the Founders," *American Heritage* (June/July 1984): 26, 28; Wills, *Newsday*, p. 11 (quotation).

9. Wills, *Newsday*, p. 12; James A. Reichley, *Conservatives in an Age of Change: The Nixon and Ford Administrations* (Washington, D.C.: Brookings Institution, 1981), p. 256.

10. Wills, *Newsday*, p. 11; Nicholas von Hoffman, "How Nixon Got Strung Up," *The New Republic*, June 23, 1982, pp. 24–27.

11. Wills, *Newsday*, p. 11; Stanley I. Kutler, *The Wars of Watergate: The Last Crisis of Richard Nixon* (New York: Knopf, 1990), p. 618.

12. Karp, "Hour of the Founders," pp. 25–26 (emphasis added).

13. Ibid., p. 29; Kutler, *Wars of Watergate*, pp. 480–81.

14. Kutler, *Wars of Watergate*, pp. 461–64.

15. Colody and Gettlin, *Silent Coup*, pp. 379, 415; Kutler, *Wars of Watergate*, p. 431.

16. Colodny and Gettlin, *Silent Coup*, pp. 161–72 (quotation on p. 167); see also pp. 177, 325.

17. Oliver L. North and William Novak, *Under Fire* (New York: HarperCollins, 1991); *New York Times*, January 28, 1994, pp. A1, A11. For a review of how the administration successfully stonewalled on Iran-contra, see *Time*, October 28, 1991, pp. 36–69.

18. Kutler, *Wars of Watergate*, pp. 608–11.

19. *Newsweek*, May 30, 1987, p. 61 (quoting historian Stanley L. Kutler).

20. Robert Sherrill, "There Was a Crooked Man," *The Nation*, July 7–14, 1984, pp. 22–24; R. J. Lambrose, "The Abusable Past," *Radical History Review* (August 1987): 135–36. For uniformly critical reviews of the TV production "Final Days," see the *Journal of American History* 74 (December 1990): 1127–28; and *New York Times*, October 30, 1989 (op/ed), p. A19, November 12, 1989, p. E22, and November 26, 1989, pp. H1–H18. With *Silent Coup*, Len Colodny and Robert Gettlin have destroyed what little plausibility Woodward and Bernstein had. For earlier criticisms, see John Osborne, "The Woodstein Flap," *The New Republic*, April 24, 1976, pp. 8–9; Nicholas von Hoffman, "Unasked Questions," *New York Review of Books*, June 10, 1976, pp. 3–8; James Boylan, "Newspeople," in *American Media: The Wilson*

Quarterly Reader, ed. Philip S. Cook et al. (Washington, D.C.: Wilson Center Press, 1989), pp. 67–68; and Schudson, *Watergate in American Memory*, pp. 114–15.

21. *USA Today*, June 15, 1992, p. 1A; *Los Angeles Times*, June 16, 1992, p. A1; Paul Johnson, *Modern Times: The World from the Twenties to the Eighties* (New York: Harper & Row, 1983), pp. 697–734, passim; Garment, *Scandal*, pp. 3–4, and *New York Times*, April 26, 1994, p. 2.

22. Segments of this staff farewell can be found in Richard Nixon, *RN: The Memoirs of Richard Nixon* (New York: Grosset & Dunlap, 1978), pp. 1088–89. Significantly, in his memoirs Nixon left out the phrase "sometimes wrong, sometimes right," in reference to Roosevelt, although he included it in the preface to the 1979 edition of *Six Crises*. The fact that his 1990 book takes its title, *In the Arena*, from this reference to Roosevelt in the farewell address to his staff shows how important it remained to Nixon.

23. Richard Nixon, *Six Crises* (New York: Warner Books, 1979; Doubleday, 1962), p. xii. The new introduction to the 1990 Touchstone Book edition of *Six Crises* contains no reference to Watergate.

24. Richard Nixon, *In the Arena: A Memoir of Victory, Defeat, and Renewal* (New York: Simon & Schuster, 1990), pp. 34–42.

25. Nixon quoted in David Frost TV interview, March 1977, and on CBS "Morning News," June 10, 1982.

26. See, for example, the transcript of the two-hour interview of Nixon by Brian Lamb (a former minor appointee in the Nixon administration) on C-Span, February 23 and March 1, 1992, p. 31.

27. James Reston, *New York Times*, August 9, 1974, p. 33 (op/ed); author's interview with Nixon, June 6, 1984.

28. Robert K. Murray and Tim H. Blessing, "The Presidential Performance Study: A Progress Report," *Journal of American History* 70, no. 3 (December 1983): 535–55; Tim H. Blessing, "The Ronald Reagan Presidency: An Evaluation of Presidential Performance," unpublished 1991 article.

29. See Herbert S. Parmet, *Richard Nixon and His America* (Boston: Little, Brown, 1990), and Tom Wicker, *One of Us: Richard Nixon and the American Dream* (New York: Random House, 1991). Both books attempt to place Nixon's entire life into a comprehensive American cultural and political context.

30. Eric Alterman, *Sound and Fury: The Washington Punditocracy and the Collapse of American Politics* (New York: HarperCollins, 1992), pp. 72–75.

31. Stephen E. Ambrose, "Comparing Ike and Dick," in *Richard M. Nixon: Politician, President, Administrator*, ed. Leon Friedman and William F. Levantrosser (Westport, Conn.: Greenwood Press, 1991), p. 21; Jodie T. Allen, "Last of the Big Spenders," *Washington Post*, February 24, 1983, p. A15; Sam Smith, *Shadows of Hope: A Freethinker's Guide to Politics in the Time of Clinton* (Bloomington: Indiana University Press, 1994).

32. Humphrey had personally requested that Nixon attend his funeral in the last days of his life as "a farewell" gift because of his concern for the former's

president's continued depression four years after resigning. See Paul Rexford Thatcher, Sr., "Comity: A Hubert Humphrey Story," *International Herald Tribune,* January 22, 1993, p. 4.

33. For comments on the umpire's strike and other aspects of Nixon's "rehabilitation," see *New York Times,* June 13, 1985, p. 14, October 16, 1985, p. 24N, and March 2, 1990, p. B2; *Christian Science Monitor,* October 8, 1985, p. 16; *Wall Street Journal,* October 8, 1985, p. 30E; *Washington Post,* February 24, 1983, p. A15, October 14, 1985, p. A2, and May 21, 1987, p. D2; *USA Today,* January 31, 1984, pp. 1–2; Los Angeles *Times,* March 8, 1984, pp. 1 and 14, May 21, 1987, p. 10, and July 26, 1988, p. 20; *Newsweek,* April 16, 1984, pp. 34–37, and May 19, 1986, pp. 26–34. This May 19, 1986, issue of *Newsweek* proclaimed Nixon had "rehabilitated himself," but all the scholars quoted denied that this was possible because of Watergate (p. 27).

34. *New York Times,* November 19, 1992, p. A27, and March 9, 1993, pp. 1 and A4; *International Herald Tribune,* March 26, 1993, p. 7.

35. Ambrose, *Nixon,* vol. 3, p. 575. Ambrose believed in 1991 that Nixon's comeback was already complete and that it had little to do with any of his achievements as president but was simply the product of a "carefully crafted campaign featuring hard work, willpower, luck, brass, and political skill" (p. 555). This interpretation exaggerates the degree of his current rehabilitation while it downgrades his contributions when president.

36. Neil Howe and William Strauss, "The New Generation Gap," *Atlantic Monthly,* December 1992, pp. 74–78.

37. Tom Wicker, "One of Us," in *Richard M. Nixon: Politician, President, Administrator,* pp. 33–34 (emphasis added).

38. *New York Times,* September 13, 1981, p. 22.

39. Leo Rangell, "Lesson from Watergate: A Derivative for Psychoanalysis," *Psychoanalytic Quarterly* 45, no. 1 (1976): 45; Steven R. Brown, "Richard Nixon and the Public Conscience: The Struggle for Authenticity," *Journal of Psychohistory* 6 (Spring 1978): 94–95, 101–2.

40. Author's interview with Nixon, June 6, 1984.

BIBLIOGRAPHY

AUTOBIOGRAPHIES, BIOGRAPHIES, AND MEMOIRS

Agnew, Spiro T. *Go Quietly Or Else*. New York: Morrow, 1980.

Allen, Gary. *Richard Nixon: The Man Behind the Mask*. Boston: Western Islands, 1971.

Alsop, Stewart. *Nixon and Rockefeller*. Garden City, N.Y.: Doubleday, 1960.

Ambrose, Stephen E. *Nixon: The Education of a Politician 1913–1962*. New York: Simon & Schuster, 1987.

———. *Nixon: The Triumph of a Politician 1962–1972*. New York: Simon & Schuster, 1989.

———. *Nixon: Ruin and Recovery*. New York: Simon & Schuster, 1991.

Anson, Robert Sam. *Exile: The Unique Oblivion of Richard M. Nixon*. New York: Simon & Schuster, 1984.

Barber, James David. *The Presidential Character: Predicting Performance in the White House*, 3rd ed. Englewood Cliffs, N.J.: Prentice-Hall, 1985.

Brodie, Fawn M. *Richard Nixon: The Shaping of His Character*. New York: Norton, 1981.

Chesen, Eli S. *President Nixon's Psychiatric Profile: A Psycho-dynamic-Genetic Interpretation*. New York: Peter H. Wyden, 1973.

Clifford, Clark. *Counsel to the President: A Memoir*. New York: Random House, 1991.

Colson, Charles W. *Born Again*. Old Tappan, N.J.: F.H. Revell, 1977.

Costello, William. *The Facts About Nixon: An Unauthorized Biography*. New York: Viking Press, 1960.

de Toledano, Ralph. *One Man Alone: Richard Nixon*. New York: Funk & Wagnalls, 1969.

Edgar, David. *Dick Deterred: A Play in Two Acts*. New York: Monthly Review Press, 1974.

Ehrlichman, John. *Witness to Power: The Nixon Years.* New York: Simon & Schuster, 1982.

Eisenhower, Julie Nixon. *Pat Nixon: The Untold Story.* New York: Simon & Schuster, 1986.

Evans, Rowland, Jr., and Robert D. Novak. *Nixon in the White House: The Frustration of Power.* New York: Random House, 1971.

Ford, Gerald R. *A Time to Heal: The Autobiography of Gerald R. Ford.* New York: Harper & Row, 1979.

Gardener, Gerald. *Everything You Always Wanted to Know About Nixon.* Greenwich, Conn.: Fawcett, 1971.

Goldwater, Barry. *With No Apologies: The Personal Politics of Barry Goldwater.* New York: Morrow, 1979.

Haldeman, H. R. *The Ends of Power.* New York: Times Books, 1978.

———. *The Secret Diaries of H. R. Haldeman* (forthcoming).

Hoyt, Edwin P. *The Nixons: An American Family.* New York: Random House, 1972.

Hunebelle, Danielle. *Dear Henry: A Confession.* New York: Berkeley Medallion Books, 1972.

Isaacson, Walter. *Kissinger: A Biography.* New York: Simon & Schuster, 1992.

Klein, Herbert G. *Making It Perfectly Clear.* Garden City, N.Y.: Doubleday, 1980.

Koreff, Baruch. *The Personal Nixon: Staying on the Summit.* Washington, D.C.: Fairness Publishers, 1974.

Kornitzer, Belinda. *The Real Nixon: An Intimate Biography.* New York: Rand McNally, 1960.

Lippman, Theo, Jr. *Spiro Agnew's America: The Vice President and the Politics of Suburbia.* New York: Norton, 1972.

Mankiewicz, Frank. *Perfectly Clear: Nixon from Whittier to Watergate.* New York: Quadrangle, 1973.

Marsh, Robert. *Agnew, the Unexamined Man: A Political Profile.* New York: Evans, 1971.

Mazlish, Bruce. *In Search of Nixon: A Psychohistorical Inquiry.* New York: Basic Books, 1972.

Mazo, Earl, and Stephen Hess. *Nixon: A Political Portrait.* New York: Harper & Row, 1968.

Mollenhoff, Clark R. *Game Plan for Disaster: An Ombudsman's Report on the Nixon Years.* New York: Norton, 1976.

———. *The Man Who Pardoned Nixon.* New York: St. Martin's Press, 1976.

Morris, Roger. *Richard Milhous Nixon: The Rise of an American Politician.* New York: Holt, 1990.

Myers, Robert J. *The Tragedy of Richard II.* Washington, D.C.: Acropolis Books, 1973.

Nixon, Richard M. *Six Crises.* New York: Doubleday, 1962.

———. *RN: The Memoirs of Richard Nixon.* New York: Grosset & Dunlap, 1978.

———. *Leaders: Profiles and Reminiscences of Men Who Have Shaped the Modern World.* New York: Warner Books, 1982.

———. *In the Arena: A Memoir of Victory, Defeat, and Renewal.* New York: Simon & Schuster, 1990.

Parmet, Herbert S. *Richard Nixon and His America.* Boston: Little, Brown, 1990.

Price, Raymond. *With Nixon.* New York: Viking Press, 1977.

Reston, James, Jr. *The Lone Star: The Life of John Connally.* New York: Harper & Row, 1989.

Safire, William. *Before the Fall: An Inside View of the Pre-Watergate White House.* New York: Ballantine Books, 1977.

Schoenebaum, Eleanora W., ed. *Political Profiles: The Nixon/Ford Years.* New York: Facts on File, 1979.

Scobie, Ingrid Winther. *Center Stage: Helen Gahagan Douglas: A Life.* New York: Oxford University Press, 1992.

Stans, Maurice H. *The Terrors of Justice.* New York: Everest House, 1978.

Voorhis, Jerry. *The Strange Case of Richard Milhous Nixon.* New York: Popular Library, 1973.

Ward, Dana. "Kissinger: A Psychohistory." *History of Childhood Quarterly: The Journal of Psychohistory* 2, no. 3 (Winter 1975): 287–348.

Whitfield, Stephen J. "Richard Nixon as a Comic Figure." *American Quarterly* (Spring 1985): 114–132.

Wills, Garry. *Nixon Agonistes: The Crisis of the Self-Made Man.* Boston: Houghton Mifflin, 1970.

Woodstone, Arthur. *Nixon's Head.* New York: St. Martin's Press, 1972.

CARTOONS, NOVELS, PLAYS; ALSO PORNOGRAPHIC, OPERATIC, AND TELEVISION REPRESENTATIONS

American Experience, "The Life and Career of Richard Nixon." PBS-TV documentary, 1990.

Block, Herbert. *Herblock's State of the Union* (cartoons). New York: Simon & Schuster, 1972.

DeHart, Frank. *Traumatic Nixon.* Privately published, 1979.

Edgar, David. "Dick Deterred: A Play in Two Acts." New York: Monthly Review Press, 1974.

Ehrlichman, John. *The Company.* New York: Simon & Schuster, 1976.

———. *The China Card.* New York: Simon & Schuster, 1986.

"The Final Days." ABC-TV movie, based on the book by Woodward and Bernstein. Aired October 29, 1989.

Guthman, Les, ed. *The King and Us* (cartoons). Los Angeles: Clymer Publications, 1974.

Hunt, John, with the collaboration of Martin Kaplan. "Knights Errant," in *Best Plays of 1982–1983*, ed. Otis L. Guernsey, Jr. (New York: Dodd, Mead, 1983).

Korff, Baruch. *The Personal Nixon: Staying on the Summit.* Washington, D.C.: Fairness Publishers, 1974.

431

Lurie, Ranan R. *Nixon X-Rated Cartoons.* New York: Quadrangle/Times Books, 1973.

Margolis, Jack S., comp. *The Poetry of Richard Milhous Nixon.* Los Angeles: Cliff House Books, 1974.

Myers, Robert J. *The Tragedy of Richard II.* Washington, D.C.: Acropolis Books, 1973.

"Nixon in China: An Opera in Two Acts." Music by John Adams, libretto by Alice Goodman. 1987.

Ross, Frank. *The 65th Tape.* New York: Bantam, 1980.

Roth, Philip. *Our Gang.* New York: Random House, 1971.

"Secret Honor: A Political Myth." One-man play, written by Donald Freed and Arnold M. Stone; and movie, directed by Robert Altman and starring Philip Baker Hall. 1984.

Spark, Muriel. *The Abbess of Crewe.* New York: Viking Press, 1974.

DOCUMENTS

Congressional Quarterly. *Nixon: The First Year of His Presidency.* Washington, D.C.: Congressional Quarterly, 1970.

————. *Nixon: The Second Year of His Presidency.* Washington, D.C.: Congressional Quarterly, 1971.

————. *Nixon: The Third Year of His Presidency.* Washington, D.C.: Congressional Quarterly, 1972.

————. *Nixon: The Fourth Year of His Presidency.* Washington, D.C.: Congressional Quarterly, 1973.

————. *Nixon: The Fifth Year of His Presidency.* Washington, D.C.: Congressional Quarterly, 1974.

————. *Watergate: Chronology of a Crisis.* Washington, D.C.: Congressional Quarterly, 1975.

Ford, Gerald. *Presidential Papers.* Ford Presidential Library, Ann Arbor, Mich.

Johnson, George W., ed. *The Nixon Presidential Press Conferences.* New York: Earl M. Coleman Enterprises, 1978.

New York Times. *The Watergate Hearings: Break-in and Cover-up.* New York: Bantam Books, 1973.

Nixon, Richard M. *Nixon Presidential Materials Project.* National Archives, Alexandria, Va.

————. *Nixon Speaks on the Issues.* New York: Nixon-Agnew Campaign Committee, 1968.

————. *Nixon Speaks Out: Major Speeches and Statements by Richard M. Nixon in the Presidential Campaign of 1968.* New York: Nixon-Agnew Campaign Committee, 1968.

————. *U.S. Foreign Policy for the 1970's: A New Strategy for Peace.* A Report to the Congress, February 18, 1970.

————. *U.S. Foreign Policy for the 1970's: Building for Peace.* A Report to the Congress, February 25, 1971.

————. *Public Papers of the President, 1969–1974.* Washington, D.C.: Government Printing Office, 1970–75.

North Atlantic Assembly Reports. *The State of the Alliance, 1986–1987.* Boulder, Colo.: Westview Press, 1987.

Oliphant, Pat. *Four More Years.* New York: Simon & Schuster, 1973.

Oudes, Bruce, ed. *From: The President: Richard Nixon's Secret Files.* New York: Harper & Row, 1989.

Presidents's Advisory Council on Executive Organization. *Memoranda for the President of the United States.* April 1969–November 1970. Privately bound White House volume given to author by John Whitaker.

U.S. Congress. House. Committee on Foreign Affairs. *The Foreign Military Sales Act.* 90th Cong., 2d sess., June 26, 27, 1968.

U.S. Congress. House. Committee on Foreign Affairs. Subcommittee on the Near East and South Asia. *The Persian Gulf, 1974: Money, Politics, Arms, and Power.* 93d Cong., 2d sess., July 30, August 5, 7, and 12, 1974.

U.S. Congress. House. Committee on U.S. International Relations. Special Subcommittee on Investigations. *The Vietnam-Cambodia Emergency, 1975 Part 1—Vietnam Evacuation and Humanitarian Assistance.* 94th Cong., 1st sess., April 9, 15, 16, 18, May 7, 8, 1975.

U.S. Congress. House. Subcommittee on Europe of the Committee on Foreign Affairs. *Hearings on Détente.* 93rd Cong., 2d sess., May 8, 15, 22, June 10, 12, 26, July 17, 25, 31, 1974.

U.S. Congress. *Inaugural Addresses of the Presidents of the United States from George Washington 1789 to Richard Milhous Nixon 1969.* 91st Cong., 1st sess. Washington, D.C.: Government Printing Office, 1969.

U.S. Congress. Senate. Committee on Commerce. Subcommittee of the Subcommittee on Communications. *Freedom of Communications.* 87th Cong., 1st sess., August–November 1960.

U.S. Congress. Senate. Committee on Foreign Relations. *Foreign Military Sales Act Amendment: 1970, 1971.* 91st Cong., 2d sess., March 24, May 11, 1970.

U.S. Congress. Senate. Committee on Foreign Relations. *Foreign Military Sales and Assistance Act.* 93d Cong., 1st sess., May 2, 3, 4, 8, 1973.

U.S. Congress. Senate. Committee on Foreign Relations. *Hearings on Détente.* 93rd Cong, 2d sess., August–September 1974.

U.S. Congress. Senate. Committee on Government Operations. Subcommittee on Intergovernmental Relations. *Confidence and Concern: Citizens View American Government.* 93d Cong., 1st sess., December 3, 1973.

U.S. Congress. Senate. *Presidential Vetoes, 1789–1976.* Washington, D.C.: U.S. Government Printing Office, 1978.

U.S. Congress. Senate. Select Committee on Presidential Campaign Activities. *Presidential Campaign Activities of 1972: Phase 1—Watergate and Related Activities.* 93d Cong., 1st sess., May 17, 18, 22, 23, and 24, 1973.

U.S. Department of State. *United States Foreign Policy, 1969–1970.* General Policy Series, no. 254, March 1971.

Washington Post. *The Presidential Transcripts.* New York: Delacorte Press, 1974.

Watergate Special Prosecution Force. *Report*. Washington, D.C.: Government Printing Office, October 1975.

Wilson, Richard, ed. *Setting the Course The First Year: Major Policy Statements by President Richard Nixon*. New York: Funk & Wagnalls, 1970.

DOMESTIC POLICY

Alonso, William. "The Mirage on New Towns." *The Public Interest* 19 (Spring 1970): 3–17.

Berman, Larry. *The Office of Management and Budget and the Presidency, 1921–1979*. Princeton, N.J.: Princeton University Press, 1979.

Bork, Robert. *Constitutionality of the President's Busing Proposals*. Washington, D.C.: American Enterprise Institute for Policy Research, 1972.

Bowler, M. Kenneth. *The Nixon Guaranteed Income Proposal: Substance and Process in Policy Change*. Cambridge, Mass.: Ballinger, 1974.

Bowles, Samuel, David M. Gordon, and Thomas E. Weisskopf. *Beyond the Waste Land: A Democratic Alternative to Economic Decline*. Garden City, N.Y.: Anchor Press, 1983.

Burke, Vincent J., and Vee Burke. *Nixon's Good Deed: Welfare Reform*. New York: Columbia University Press, 1974.

Calder, James D. "Presidents and Crime Control: Kennedy, Johnson, Nixon and the Influences of Ideology." *Presidential Studies Quarterly* 12, no. 4 (1982): 574–89.

Carleson, Robert B. "Objectivity Must Underlie Welfare Reform." *Journal of the Institute for Socioeconomic Studies* 7, no. 4 (Winter 1983–84): 70–78.

Cavala, Bill, and Aaron Wildavsky. "The Political Feasibility of Income by Right." *Public Policy* 18, no. 3 (Spring 1970): 321–54.

Conlan, Timothy. "The Politics of Federal Block Grants: From Nixon to Reagan." *Political Science Quarterly* 99, no. 2 (1984): 247–70.

———. *New Federalism: Intergovernmental Reform from Nixon to Reagan*. Washington, D.C.: Brookings Institution, 1988.

De Marchi, Neil. "The First Nixon Administration: Prelude to Controls." In *Exhortation and Controls: The Search for a Wage-Price Policy*, edited by Crawford D. Goodwin. Washington: Brookings Institution, 1975), pp. 295–352.

Dent, Harry S. *The Prodigal South Returns to Power*. New York: Wiley, 1978.

Derthick, Martha. "Defeat at Fort Lincoln." *The Public Interest* 20 (Summer 1970): 3–39.

———. *Uncontrollable Spending for Social Service Guarantees*. Washington, D.C.: Brookings Institution, 1975.

———. *Policy Making for Social Security*. Washington D.C.: Brookings Institution, 1979.

———. *An Agency Under Stress: The Social Security Administration in American Government*. Washington D.C.: Brookings Institution, 1990.

Donner, Frank J. *The Age of Surveillance: The Aims and Methods of America's Political Intelligence System*. New York: Knopf, 1980.

Doolittle, Frederick, Frank Levy, and Michael Wiseman. "The Mirage of Welfare Reform." *The Public Interest* 47 (Spring 1977): 62–87.

Duignan, Peter, and Alvin Rabushka, eds. *The United States in the 1980s*. Stanford, Calif.: Hoover Institution, Stanford University, 1980.

Dunn, Charles W., ed. *The Future of the American Presidency*. Morristown, N.J.: General Learning Press, 1976.

Edelman, Marian Wright. "Southern School Desegregation, 1954–1973: A Judicial-Political Overview." *Annals of the American Academy of Political and Social Science* 417 (May 1973): 34–35.

Epstein, Edward Jay. *Agency of Fear: Opiates and Political Power in America*. New York: Putnam, 1977.

Feldstein, Martin. "Facing the Social Security Crisis." *The Public Interest* 47 (Spring 1977): 88–100.

Forbes, Jack D. *Native Americans and Nixon: Presidential Politics and Minority Self-Determination, 1969–1970*. Los Angeles: University of California Press, 1981.

Freeman, Jo. "Women and Public Policy: An Overview." In *Women, Power and Policy*, edited by Ellen Boneparth. Elmsford, N.Y.: Pergamon Press, 1982.

Fried, Richard M. *Nightmare in Red: The McCarthy Era in Perspective*. New York: Oxford University Press, 1990.

Frieden, Bernard, and Marshall Frieden. *The Politics of Neglect: Urban Aid from Model Cities to Revenue Sharing*. Cambridge, Mass.: MIT Press, 1977.

Fry, Jon, and Robert J. Gordon. "Government Intervention in the Inflation Process: The Econometrics of 'Self-Inflicted Wounds.'" *American Economic Review* 71, no. 2 (1986): 288–94.

Ginsberg, Ruth Bader. "The Burger Court's Grapplings with Sex Discrimination." In *The Burger Court: The Counter Revolution That Wasn't*, edited by Vincent Blasi. New Haven, Conn.: Yale University Press, 1983.

Graham, Hugh Davis. *The Civil Rights Era: Origins and Development of National Policy, 1960–1972*. New York: Oxford University Press, 1990.

Graham, Otis L. *Toward a Planned Society: From Roosevelt to Nixon*. New York: Oxford University Press, 1976.

Green, Mark, and Peter Petkas. "Nixon's Industrial State." *The New Republic*, September 16, 1972, pp. 18–21.

Hays, Samuel P. *Beauty, Health, and Permanence: Environmental Politics in the United States, 1955–1985*. New York: Cambridge University Press, 1987.

Herschensohn, Bruce. *The Gods of Antenna*. New Rochelle, N.Y.: Arlington House, 1976.

Hoff-Wilson, Joan. "Outflanking the Liberals on Welfare." In *Richard M. Nixon: Politician, President, Administrator*, edited by Leon Friedman and William F. Levantrosser. Westport, Conn.: Greenwood Press, 1991.

Hopkins, Kevin R. "Welfare: Aid for Those in Need." *Journal of the Institute for Socioeconomic Studies* 7, no. 4 (Winter 1983–84): 64–69.

Hudson, William E. "The New Federalism Paradox." *Policy Studies Journal* 8, no. 6 (1980): 900–906.

Jensen, Ralph. *Let Me Say This About That.* New York: Holt, Rinehart & Winston, 1972.

Johnson, Haynes. *In the Absence of Power: Governing America.* New York: Viking Press, 1980.

Keller, Robert R, and Ann Mari May. "The Presidential Political Business Cycle of 1972." *Journal of Economic History* 44, no. 2 (1984): 256–71.

Klein, Herbert G. *Making It Perfectly Clear.* Garden City, N.Y.: Doubleday, 1980.

Kotz, Nick, and Mary Lynn Kotz. *A Passion for Equality: George Wiley and the Movement.* New York: Norton, 1977.

Lowery, David. "The Keynesian and Political Determinants of Unbalanced Budgets: U.S. Fiscal Policy from Eisenhower to Reagan." *American Journal of Political Science* 29 (1985): 428–60.

McBreen, Maureen. *Federal Revenue Sharing: Background Information and Comparison of the Various Proposals Introduced During the 91st Congress, 1st Session.* Washington, D.C.: Congressional Research Service, 1970.

————. *Federal Revenue Sharing: A Review of Major Proposals and Contending Positions in the 92nd Congress.* Washington, D.C.: Congressional Research Service, 1971.

McQuaid, Kim. *Big Business and Presidential Power: From FDR to Reagan.* New York: Morrow, 1982.

Metcalf, George R. *From Little Rock to Boston: The History of School Desegregation.* Westport, Conn.: Greenwood Press, 1983.

Miller, Roger Leroy, and Raburn M. Williams. *The New Economics of Richard Nixon: Freezes, Floats, and Fiscal Policy.* New York: Harper & Row, 1972.

Morris, Charles R. *A Time of Passion: America 1960–1980.* New York: Harper & Row, 1984.

Morrison, Rodney J. *Expectations and Inflation.* Lexington, Mass.: Lexington Books, 1973.

Moynihan, Daniel P. "Policy vs. Program in the '70's." *The Public Interest* 20 (Summer 1970): 90–100.

————. *The Politics of Guaranteed Income: The Nixon Administration and the Family Assistance Plan.* New York: Random House, 1973.

Panetta, Leon E., and Peter Gall. *"Bring Us Together": The Nixon Team and the Civil Rights Retreat.* Philadelphia: Lippincott, 1971.

Patterson, James T. *America's Struggle Against Poverty, 1900–1985.* Cambridge, Mass.: Harvard University Press, 1986.

Phillips, Kevin. *The Emerging Republican Majority.* New York: Arlington House, 1969.

Porter, William E. *Assault on the Media: The Nixon Years.* Ann Arbor: University of Michigan Press, 1976.

Randall, Ronald. "Presidential Power versus Bureaucratic Intransigence: The Influence of the Nixon Administration on Welfare Policy." *American Political Science Review* 73, no. 3 (1979): 795–810.

Reagan, Michael D., and John G Sanzone. *The New Federalism.* New York: Oxford University Press, 1981.

Richardson, Elliot. *The Creative Balance: Government, Politics, and the Individual in America's Third Century*. New York: Holt, Rinehart & Winston, 1976.

Robins, Leonard. "The Plot That Succeeded." *Presidential Studies Quarterly* 10, no. 1 (1980): 99–106.

Rowland, C. K., Robert A. Carp, and Ronald A. Stidham. "Judges' Policy Choices and the Value Basis of Judicial Appointments: A Comparison of Support for Criminal Defendants Among Nixon, Johnson, and Kennedy Appointees to the Federal District Courts." *Journal of Politics* 46, no. 3 (1984): 886–902.

Schoenbrun, D. *America Inside Out: At Home and Abroad from Roosevelt to Reagan*. New York: McGraw-Hill, 1984.

Schultze, Charles L., and Arthur M Okun. *President Nixon's New Economic Policy*. Washington, D.C.: Brookings Institution, 1971 (reprint 212).

Schwarz, John E. *America's Hidden Success: A Reassessment of Twenty Years of Public Policy*. New York: Norton, 1983.

Senter, Richard, Jr., Larry T. Reynolds, and David Gruenenfeld. "The Presidency and the Print Media: Who Controls the News?" *Sociological Quarterly* 27, no. 1 (1986): 91–105.

Shachtman, Tom. *Decade of Shocks: Dallas to Watergate, 1963–1974*. New York: Poseidon Press, 1983.

Siegel, Frederick F. *Troubled Journey: From Pearl Harbor to Ronald Reagan*. New York: Hill and Wang, 1984.

Silk, Leonard. *Nixonomics: How the Dismal Science of Free Enterprise Became the Black Art of Controls*. New York: Praeger Publishers, 1972.

Spear, Joseph C. *Presidents and the Press: The Nixon Legacy*. Cambridge, Mass.: MIT Press, 1984.

Stein, Herbert. *Presidential Economics: The Making of Economic Policy from Roosevelt to Reagan and Beyond*. Washington, D.C.: American Enterprise Institute for Public Policy Research, 1988.

Stone, David M. *Nixon and the Politics of Public Television*. New York: Garland, 1985.

Storey, James R. "Systems Analysis and Welfare Reform: A Case Study of the Family Assistance Plan." *Policy Sciences* 4 (1973): 1–12.

Theoharis, Athan. *Spying on Americans: Political Surveillance from Hoover to the Huston Plan*. Philadelphia: Temple University Press, 1978.

Tufte, Edward. *Political Control of the Economy*. Princeton, N.J.: Princeton University Press, 1978.

Ungar, Sanford J. *The Papers and the Papers: An Account of the Legal and Political Battle over the Pentagon Papers*. New York: Dutton, 1972.

Vernon, Raymond, ed. *The Oil Crisis*. New York: Norton, 1976.

Vietor, Richard H. K. *Energy Policy in America Since 1945: A Study in Business-Government Relations*. New York: Cambridge University Press, 1984.

Weber, Arnold R. *In Pursuit of Price Stability: The Wage-Price Freeze of 1971*. Washington, D.C.: Brookings Institution, 1973.

Whitaker, John C. *Striking a Balance: Environment and Natural Resources Policy in the Nixon-Ford Years.* Washington, D.C.: American Enterprise Institute for Public Policy Research, 1976.

Wilkinson, J. Harvey, III. *From Brown to Bakke: The Supreme Court and School Integration, 1954–1978.* New York: Oxford University Press, 1979.

Wills, Garry. *Explaining America: The Federalist.* Garden City, N.Y.: Doubleday, 1981.

Wilson, David E. *The National Planning Idea in U.S. Public Policy: Five Alternative Approaches.* Boulder, Colo.: Westview Press, 1980.

FOREIGN POLICY

Allison, Graham, and Peter Szanton. *Remaking Foreign Policy: The Organizational Connection.* New York: Basic Books, 1976.

Amter, Joseph A. *Vietnam Verdict: A Citizen's History.* New York: Continuum, 1982.

Anderson, Jack. *Fiasco.* New York: Times Books, 1983.

Ball, Desmond. *Déjà Vu: The Return to Counterforce in the Nixon Administration.* Santa Monica: California Seminar on Arms Control and Foreign Policy, 1975.

Ball, George W. *Diplomacy for a Crowded World: An American Foreign Policy.* Boston: Little, Brown, 1976.

Barnet, Richard J. *The Giants: Russia and America.* New York: Simon & Schuster, 1977.

Barnett, A. Doak. *China Policy: Old Problems and New Challenges.* Washington, D.C.: Brookings Institution, 1977.

Belknap, Michael R. "Vietnam and the Constitution: The War Power under Lyndon Johnson and Richard Nixon." *This Constitution* 10 (Spring 1986): 19.

Bell, Coral. *The Diplomacy of Détente: The Kissinger Era.* New York: St. Martin's Press, 1977.

Bernstein, Barton J. "SALT: The Dangerous Illusion." *Inquiry* 1 (July 24, 1978): 16–19.

Bill, James A. *The Eagle and the Lion: The Tragedy of American-Iranian Relations.* New Haven, Conn.: Yale University Press, 1988.

Binning, William C. "The Nixon Foreign Aid Policy for Latin America." *Inter-American Economic Affairs* 15, no. 1 (1971): 31–45.

Bowman, William, Roger Little, and Thomas Sicilia. *The All-Volunteer Force After a Decade: Retrospect and Prospect.* Washington, D.C.: Pergamon-Brassey's, 1986.

Brandon, Henry. *The Retreat of American Power.* Garden City, N.Y.: Doubleday, 1973.

Brodine, Virginia, and Mark Selden, eds. *Open Secret: The Kissinger-Nixon Doctrine in Asia.* New York: Harper & Row, 1972.

Brown, Seyom. *The Crises of Power: An Interpretation of United States Foreign Policy During the Kissinger Years.* New York: Columbia University Press, 1979.

Bryson, Thomas A. "American Diplomacy in the Middle East." In *American Diplo-*

macy in the Twentieth Century, edited by Warren F. Kimball. St. Louis, Mo.: Forum Press, 1980, pp. 1–16.

Brzezinski, Zbigniew. "U.S. Foreign Policy: The Search for Focus." *Forum Affairs* 51, no. 4 (July 1973): 708–27.

Bundy, McGeorge. *Danger and Survival.* New York: Random House, 1988.

Calleo, David. *The Imperious Economy.* Cambridge, Mass.: Harvard University Press, 1982.

Cohen, Samuel I. "Whatever Happened to the Nixon Doctrine?" *Policy Review* 26 (Fall 1983): 88–92.

Cohen, Steven. *Vietnam: Anthology and Guide to a Television History.* New York: Knopf, 1983.

Cohen, Warren I. *America's Response to China.* New York: Columbia University Press, 1990.

Coker, Christopher. *The United States and South Africa, 1968–1985: Constructive Engagement and Its Critics.* Durham, N.C.: Duke University Press, 1986.

Colby, William (with James McCarger). *Lost Victory: A Firsthand Account of America's Sixteen-Year Involvement in Vietnam.* New York: Contemporary Books, 1989.

Committee for Economic Development Report. *Soviet Progress vs. American Enterprise.* Garden City, N.Y.: Doubleday, 1958.

Congressional Quarterly. *U.S. Foreign Policy: Future Directions.* Washington, D.C.: Congressional Quarterly, 1979.

Cook, Blanche Wiesen. *The Classified Eisenhower: A Divided Legacy.* New York: Doubleday, 1981.

Dallek, Robert. *The American Style of Foreign Policy: Cultural Politics and Foreign Affairs.* New York: New American Library, 1983.

Destler, I. M. *Making Foreign Economic Policy.* Washington, D.C.: Brookings Institution, 1980.

Divine, Robert A. *Foreign Policy and U.S. Presidential Elections, 1952–1960.* New York: New Viewpoints, 1974.

———. "Vietnam Remembered." *Diplomatic History* 12, no. 1 (1988): 79–93.

Draper, Theodore. "Appeasement and Détente." *Commentary* 61, no. 2 (1976): 27–38.

El-Khawas, Mohamed S., and Barry Cohen, eds. *The Kissinger Study of Southern Africa: National Security Study Memorandum 39.* Westport, Conn.: Lawrence Hill, 1976.

Evans, Rowland, Jr., and Robert Novak. *Nixon in the White House: The Frustration of Power.* New York: Random House, 1971.

Fanning, Louis A. *Betrayal in Vietnam.* New Rochelle, N.Y.: Arlington House, 1976.

Fedder, Edwin. *NATO and Détente.* St. Louis, Mo.: Center for International Studies, 1979.

———, ed. *NATO in the Seventies.* St. Louis, Mo.: Center for International Studies, 1970.

Gaddis, John Lewis. *Russia, the Soviet Union, and the United States: An Interpretive History.* New York: Wiley, 1978.

————. *Strategies of Containment: A Critical Appraisal of Postwar American National Security Policy.* New York: Oxford University Press, 1982.

————. "The Rise, Fall, and Future of Détente." *Foreign Affairs* 62, no. 2 (Winter 1983–84): 354–77.

Gallucci, Robert. L. *Neither Peace nor Honor: The Politics of U.S. Military Policy in Vietnam.* Baltimore: John Hopkins University Press, 1975.

Gardner, Lloyd, comp. *The Great Nixon Turnaround: America's New Foreign Policy in the Post-Liberal Era (How a Cold Warrior Climbed Clean Out of His Skin).* New York: New Viewpoints, 1973.

————. *The American Age: U.S. Foreign Policy at Home and Abroad,* vol. 2, 2nd ed. New York: Norton, 1994.

Garthoff, Raymond L. *Perspectives on the Strategic Balance: A Staff Paper.* Washington D.C.: Brookings Institution, 1983.

————. *Détente and Confrontation: American-Soviet Relations from Nixon to Reagan.* Washington, D.C.: Brookings Institution, 1985.

————. *Policy versus the Law: The Reinterpretation of the ABM Treaty.* Washington, D.C.: Brookings Institution, 1987.

George, Alexander L. *Presidential Decisionmaking in Foreign Policy: The Effective Use of Information and Advice.* Boulder, Colo.: Westview Press, 1980.

Gibson, James Williams. *The Perfect War: The War We Couldn't Lose and How We Did.* New York: Vintage Books, 1986.

Gilpin, Robert. *The Political Economy of International Relations.* Princeton, N.J.: Princeton University Press, 1987.

Goodman, Allan E. *The Lost Peace: America's Search for a Negotiated Settlement of the Vietnam War.* Stanford, Calif.: Hoover Institution, 1978.

Gowa, Joanne. "State Power, State Policy: Explaining the Decision to Close the Gold Window." *Politics and Society* 13, no. 1 (1984): 91–117.

Graubard, Stephen R. *Kissinger: Portrait of a Mind.* New York: Norton, 1974.

Haley, P. Edward. *Congress and the Fall of South Vietnam and Cambodia.* Rutherford, N.J.: Fairleigh Dickinson Press, 1982.

Hall, David K. "The Indo-Pakistani War of 1971." In *Force Without War: U.S. Armed Forces as a Political Instrument,* edited by Barry M. Blechman and Stephen S. Kaplan. Washington, D.C.: Brookings Institution, 1978, pp. 175–217.

Halperin, Morton H. *Bureaucratic Politics and Foreign Policy.* Washington, D.C.: Brookings Institution, 1974.

Hartley, Anthony. *American Foreign Policy in the Nixon Era.* London: International Institute for Strategic Studies, 1975.

Herr, Donald Furse. "Presidential Influence and Bureaucratic Politics: Nixon's Policy Toward Cuba." Ph.D. diss., Yale University, 1978.

Herring, George C. "Vietnam: An American Ordeal." In *American Diplomacy in the Twentieth Century,* edited by Warren F. Kimball. St. Louis, Mo.: Forum Press, 1980, pp. 1–16.

————. *America's Longest War: The United States and Vietnam, 1950–1975.* Philadelphia: Temple University Press, 1986.

Hersh, Seymour M. *The Price of Power: Kissinger in the Nixon White House.* New York: Summit Books, 1983.

————. *The Samson Option: Israel's Nuclear Arsenal and American Foreign Policy.* New York: Random House, 1991.

Herz, Martin F. *The Prestige Press and the Christmas Bombing, 1972.* Washington, D.C.: Ethics and Public Policy Center, 1980.

Hoff, Joan. "Richard Nixon, Vietnam, and the American Home Front." In *An American Dilemma: Vietnam, 1964–1973,* edited by Dennis E. Showalter and John G. Albert. Chicago: Imprint, 1993, pp. 187–97.

Hoffmann, Stanley. *Primacy or World Order: American Foreign Policy Since the Cold War.* New York: McGraw-Hill, 1978.

Hoff-Wilson, Joan. "Economic Issues and Foreign Policy." In *Guide to American Foreign Relations Since 1700,* edited by Richard Dean Burns. Santa Barbara, Calif.: ABC-Clio, 1983.

————. "Richard M. Nixon: The Corporate Presidency." In *Leadership in the Modern Presidency,* edited by Fred I. Greenstein. Cambridge, Mass.: Harvard University Press, 1988, pp. 164–98.

————. "Nixingerism, NATO, and Détente." *Diplomatic History* 13, no. 4 (Fall 1989): 501–25.

————. "The Foreign Policy of Nixon and Ford." In *American Foreign Policy Since 1945,* edited by John Brewer. Baton Rouge: Louisiana State University Press, forthcoming.

Hoopes, Townsend. *The Limits of Intervention.* New York: David McKay, 1969.

Hung, Nguyen Tien, and Jerold L. Scheter. *The Palace File.* New York: Harper & Row, 1986.

Hunt, Michael H. *Ideology and U.S. Foreign Policy.* New Haven, Conn.: Yale University Press, 1987.

Irish, Marian D. "The President's Foreign Policy Machine." In *The Future of the Presidency,* edited by Charles W. Dunn. Morristown, N.J.: General Learning Press, 1976.

Isaacs, Arnold. *Without Honor: Defeat in Vietnam and Cambodia.* Baltimore: Johns Hopkins University Press, 1983.

Jackson, Henry F. *From the Congo to Soweto: U.S. Foreign Policy Toward Africa Since 1960.* New York: Morrow, 1982.

Johnson, Robert. "Vietnamization: Will It Work?" *Foreign Affairs* 48, no. 2 (July 1970): 629–47.

Johnson, U. Alexis. *The Right Hand of Power: The Memoirs of an American Diplomat.* Englewood Cliffs, N.J.: Prentice-Hall, 1984.

Kalb, Marvin, and Bernard Kalb. *Kissinger.* Boston: Little, Brown, 1974.

Kaltefleiter, Werner. "Europe and the Nixon Doctrine: A German Point of View." *Orbis* 17, no. 1 (1973): 74–94.

Kaplan, Lawrence S. "NATO and the Nixon Doctrine Ten Years Later." *Orbis* 24, no. 1 (1980): 149–64.

Karnow, Stanley. *Vietnam: A History.* New York: Viking Press, 1983.

Kegley, Charles W., Jr., and Eugene R. Wittkopf. *American Foreign Policy: Pattern and Process.* New York: St. Martin's Press, 1979.

Keohane, Robert, and Joseph Nye. *Power and Interdependence.* Boston: Little, Brown, 1977.

Kissinger, Henry A. *Nuclear Weapons and Foreign Policy.* New York: Harper & Row, 1957.

———. *The Necessity for Choice: Prospects for American Foreign Policy.* New York: Harper & Row, 1961.

———, ed. *Problems of National Strategy.* New York: Praeger Publishers, 1965.

———. *American Foreign Policy.* New York: Norton, 1969.

———. *White House Years.* Boston: Little, Brown, 1979.

———. *Years of Upheaval.* Boston: Little, Brown, 1982.

———. *Diplomacy.* New York: Simon & Schuster, 1994.

———, et al. "NATO: The Next Thirty Years." *Washington Quarterly* 2, no. 4 (Autumn 1979): 3–53.

Kohl, Wilfrid. "The Nixon-Kissinger Foreign Policy System and U.S.-European Relations: Patterns of Policy Making." *World Politics* 28 (1975): 1–43.

Kolko, Gabriel. *Anatomy of a War: Vietnam, the United States, and the Modern Historical Experience.* New York: Pantheon Books, 1985.

———. *Confronting the Third World: United States Foreign Policy, 1945–1980.* New York: Pantheon Books, 1988.

Korbel, Josef. *Détente in Europe: Real or Imaginary?* Princeton, N.J.: Princeton University Press, 1972.

Krawlow, David, and Stuart H Loory. *In Secret Search for Peace in Vietnam.* New York: Random House, 1968.

Krishnan, Kunhi. *The Unfriendly Friends, India and America.* New Delhi: Indian Book Company, 1974.

Kusano, Atsushi. "The Two Nixon Shocks and Japan-U.S. Relations." Research Monograph no. 50, Center for International Studies, Woodrow Wilson School of Public and International Affairs. Princeton University, March 1987.

Lafeber, Walter. "Kissinger and Acheson: The Secretary of State and the Cold War." *Political Science Quarterly* 92, no. 2 (1977): 189–97.

———. *Inevitable Revolutions: The United States in Central America.* New York: Norton, 1984.

Laird, Melvin R. "A Strong Start in a Difficult Decade: Defense Policy in the Nixon-Ford Years." *International Security* 10, no. 2 (Fall 1985): 5–26.

Lake, Anthony. *The "Tar Baby" Option: American Policy Toward Southern Rhodesia.* New York: Columbia University Press, 1976.

Landau, David. *Kissinger: The Uses of Power.* Boston: Houghton Mifflin, 1972.

Lenczowski, George. *American Presidents and the Middle East.* Durham, N.C.: Duke University Press, 1990.

Lewy, Guenter. *America in Vietnam.* New York: Oxford University Press, 1978.

Lippmann, Walter. *U.S. Foreign Policy: Shield of the Republic.* Boston: Little, Brown, 1943.

Litwak, Robert S. *Détente and the Nixon Doctrine: Foreign Policy and the Pursuit of Stability.* Cambridge, U.K.: Cambridge University Press, 1984.

McQuaid, Kim. *Big Business and Presidential Power: From FDR to Reagan.* New York: Morrow, 1982.

Maresca, John J. *To Helsinki: The Conference on Security and Cooperation in Europe, 1973–1975.* Durham, N.C.: Duke University Press, 1985.

May, Ernest R. *Lessons of the Past: The Use and Misuse of History in American Foreign Policy.* New York: Oxford University Press, 1973.

Mazlish, Bruce. *Kissinger: The European Mind in American Policy.* New York: Basic Books, 1976.

Medick, Monika. "The Nixon New Economic Policy: Economic Security Interests in U.S.-European Relations." *Amerikastudien* 23, no. 1 (1978): 78–89.

Metz, Steven. "Congress, the Anti-apartheid Movement, and Nixon." *Diplomatic History* 12, no. 2 (1988): 165–85.

Morris, Roger. *Uncertain Greatness: Henry Kissinger and American Foreign Policy.* New York: Harper & Row, 1977.

———. *Haig: The General's Progress.* New York: Playboy Books, 1982.

Moulton, Harland B. *From Superiority to Parity: The United States and the Strategic Arms Race, 1961–1971.* Westport, Conn.: Greenwood Press, 1973.

Murdock, Clark A. *Defense Policy Formation: A Comparative Analysis of the McNamara Era.* Albany: State University of New York Press, 1974.

Nachmias, Nitza. *Transfer of Arms, Leverage, and Peace in the Middle East.* Westport, Conn.: Greenwood Press, 1988.

Newhouse, John. *Cold Dawn: The Story of SALT.* New York: Holt, Rinehart & Winston, 1973.

Nixon, Richard M. *U.S. Foreign Policy for the 1970's: A New Strategy for Peace.* A Report to the Congress, February 18, 1970.

———. *U.S. Foreign Policy for the 1970's: Building for Peace.* A Report to the Congress, February 25, 1971.

———. *The Real War.* New York: Warner Books, 1980.

———. *Real Peace.* Boston: Little, Brown, 1984.

———. *No More Vietnams.* New York: Arbor House, 1985.

———. *1999: Victory Without War.* New York: Simon & Schuster, 1988.

———. *In the Arena: A Memoir of Victory, Defeat, and Renewal.* New York: Simon & Schuster, 1990.

———. *Seize the Moment.* New York: Simon & Schuster, 1992.

———. *Beyond Peace.* New York: Random House, 1994.

Nutter, G. Warren. *Kissinger's Grand Design.* Washington, D.C.: American Enterprise Institute for Public Policy Research, 1975.

Odell, John S. *U.S. International Monetary Policy: Markets, Power and Ideas as Sources of Change.* Princeton, N.J.: Princeton University Press, 1982.

Oglesby, Carl, and Richard Shaull. *Containment and Change.* Toronto, Canada: Macmillan, 1969.

Osgood, Robert, et al., ed. *Retreat from Empire: The First Nixon Administration.* Baltimore: Johns Hopkins University Press, 1973.

Palmer, Bruce, Jr. *The 25-Year War: America's Military Role in Vietnam.* New York: Simon & Schuster, 1985.

Pastor, Robert. *Congress and the Politics of U.S. Foreign Economic Policy.* Berkeley: University of California Press, 1980.

Pelz, Stephen. "Alibi Alley: Vietnam as History." *Reviews in American History* 8, no. 1 (March 1980): 139–43.

Peterson, Peter G. *A Foreign Economic Perspective.* Washington, D.C.: Government Printing Office, 1972.

Petras, James, and Morris Morley. *The United States and Chile: Imperialism and the Overthrow of the Allende Government.* New York: Monthly Review Press, 1975.

Pipes, Richard. *U.S.-Soviet Relations in the Era of Détente.* Boulder, Colo.: Westview Press, 1981.

Porter, Gareth. *A Peace Denied: The United States, Vietnam, and the Paris Agreement.* Bloomington: Indiana University Press, 1975.

Prados, John. *Keepers of the Keys: A History of the National Security Council from Truman to Bush.* New York: Morrow, 1991.

Pranger, Robert J. *Détente and Defense: A Reader.* Washington, D.C.: American Enterprise Institute for Public Policy Research, 1976.

Quandt, William B. *Decade of Decisions: American Policy Toward the Arab-Israeli Conflict.* Berkeley: University of California Press, 1977.

Ranelagh, John. *The Agency: The Rise and Decline of the CIA.* New York: Simon & Schuster, 1986.

Schaller, Michael. *The United States and China in the Twentieth Century.* New York: Oxford University Press, 1979.

Scheer, Robert. *America After Nixon: The Age of the Multinationals.* New York: McGraw-Hill, 1974.

Schlafly, Phyllis, and Chester Ward. *Kissinger on the Couch.* New Rochelle, N.Y.: Arlington House, 1975.

Schulzinger, Robert D. *Henry Kissinger: Doctor of Diplomacy.* New York: Columbia University Press, 1989.

Schurmann, Franz. *The Foreign Politics of Richard Nixon: The Grand Design.* Berkeley, Calif.: Institute of International Studies, 1987.

Schwartz, David N. *NATO's Nuclear Dilemmas.* Washington, D.C.: Brookings Institution, 1983.

Secretary of State. *United States Foreign Policy, 1969–1970.* Washington, D.C.: Government Printing Office, 1970.

Shawcross, William. *Sideshow: Kissinger, Nixon, and the Destruction of Cambodia.* New York: Simon & Schuster, 1979.

———. *The Quality of Mercy: Cambodia, Holocaust and Modern Conscience.* New York: Simon & Schuster, 1984.

Small, Melvin. *Johnson, Nixon, and the Doves.* New Brunswick, N.J.: Rutgers University Press, 1988.

Smith, Gerard C. *Doubletalk: The Story of the First Strategic Arms Limitation Talks.* Garden City, N.Y.: Doubleday, 1980.

Snepp, Frank. *A Peace Denied: An Insider's Account of Saigon's Indecent End Told by the CIA's Chief Strategy Analyst in Vietnam.* New York: Random House, 1977.

Sobel, Lester A. *Kissinger and Détente.* New York: Facts on File, 1975.

Sorley, Lewis. *Arms Transfers Under Nixon: A Policy Analysis.* Lexington: University Press of Kentucky, 1983.

Spanier, John, and Eric M. Uslaner. *How American Foreign Policy Is Made*. New York: Praeger Publishers, 1974.

Spiegel, Steven L. *The Other Arab-Israeli Conflict: Making America's Middle East Policy, from Truman to Reagan*. Chicago: University of Chicago Press, 1985.

Starr, Harvey. *Henry Kissinger: Perceptions of International Politics*. Lexington: University Press of Kentucky, 1984.

Stevenson, Richard W. *The Rise and Fall of Détente: Relaxations of Tension in U.S.-Soviet Relations, 1953–84*. Urbana: University of Illinois Press, 1985.

Stoessinger, John G. *Henry Kissinger: The Anguish of Power*. New York: Norton, 1976.

Stookey, Robert W. *America and the Arab States*. New York: Wiley, 1975.

Sulzberger, C. L. *The World and Richard Nixon*. New York: Prentice Hall, 1987.

Sutter, Robert G. *China Watch: Toward Sino-American Reconciliation*. Baltimore: Johns Hopkins University Press, 1978.

Szulc, Tad. *The Illusion of Peace: Foreign Policy in the Nixon Years*. New York: Viking Press, 1978.

Thornton, Richard C. *The Nixon-Kissinger Years: Reshaping America's Foreign Policy*. New York: Paragon House, 1989.

Tuchman, Barbara W. *The March of Folly: From Troy to Vietnam*. New York: Knopf, 1984.

Van der Linden, Frank. *Nixon's Quest for Peace*. Washington, D.C.: Robert B. Luce, 1972.

Van Hollen, Christopher. "The Tilt Policy Revisited: Nixon-Kissinger Geopolitics and South Asia." *Asian Survey* 20, no. 4 (1980): 339–61.

von Geusau, Frans A.M. Alting, ed. *NATO and Security in the Seventies*. Lexington, Mass.: Heath, 1971.

Weihmiller, Gordon R. *U.S.-Soviet Summits: An Account of East-West Diplomacy at the Top, 1955–1985*. Lanham, Md.: University Press of America, 1986.

Wicker, Tom. *One of Us: Richard Nixon and the American Dream*. New York: Random House, 1991.

Willrich, Mason, and John B. Rhinelander, eds. *SALT: The Moscow Agreements and Beyond*. New York: Free Press, 1974.

POLICY FORMATION, POLITICS, AND THE PRESIDENCY

Alterman, Eric. *Sound and Fury: Thu Washington Punditocracy and the Collapse of American Politics*. New York: HarperCollins, 1992.

American Institute for Political Communication. *The Credibility Problem*. Washington, D.C.: American Institute for Political Communication, 1972.

Anderson, Patrick. *The President's Men*. Garden City, N.Y.: Doubleday, 1969.

Arnold, Peri E. *Making the Managerial Presidency: Comprehensive Reorganization Planning, 1905–1980*. Princeton, N.J.: Princeton University Press, 1986.

Beer, Samuel H. "In Search of a New Public Philosophy." In *The New American Political System*, edited by Anthony King. Washington D.C.: American Enterprise Institute for Public Policy Research, 1978.

Bekaert, Jacques. *Nixon's the One or Trente ans d'Amérique.* Brussels: Pierre de Méyere, n.d.

Berman, Larry. "The Office of Management and Budget That Almost Wasn't." *Political Science Quarterly* (Summer 1977): 281–303.

———. *The Office of Management and Budget and the Presidency, 1921–1979.* Princeton, N.J.: Princeton University Press, 1979.

Berry, Mary Frances. *The Politics of Parenthood: Child Care, Women's Rights, and the Myth of the Good Mother.* New York: Viking Press, 1993.

Blumenthal, Sidney. "Marketing the President." *New York Times Magazine,* September 13, 1981, p. 43.

Bochin, Hal W. R. *National Scapegoat.* Westport, Conn.: Greenwood Press, 1990.

———. *Richard Nixon: Rhetorical Strategist.* Westport, Conn.: Greenwood Press, 1990.

Bromwich, David. "Reagan's Contempt for History." *Dissent* (Summer 1985): 266, 268.

Chester, Lewis, Godfrey Hodgson, and Bruce Page. *An American Melodrama: The Presidential Campaign of 1968.* New York: Viking Press, 1969.

Cole, Richard L., and David A. Caputo. "Presidential Control of the Senior Civil Service: Assessing the Strategies of the Nixon Years." *American Political Science Review* 73, no. 2 (June 1979): 399–413.

Collins, Robert M. "Richard M. Nixon: The Psychic, Political, and Moral Uses of Sport." *Journal of Sport History* 10, no. 2 (1983): 77–84.

Committee on Environmental Decision Making, Commission on Natural Resources, National Research Council. *Decision Making in the Environmental Protection Agency.* Washington, D.C.: National Academy of Sciences, 1977.

Crass, Philip. *The Wallace Factor.* New York: Mason Carter, 1976.

Cronin, Thomas E., ed. *Inventing the American Presidency.* Lawrence: University Press of Kansas, 1989.

Demac, Donna A. *Keeping America Uninformed: Government Secrecy in the 1980's.* New York: Pilgrim Press, 1984.

Dent, Harry S. *The Prodigal South Returns to Power.* New York: Wiley, 1978.

Donovan, Hedley. *Roosevelt to Reagan: Nine Encounters with Nine Presidents.* New York: Harper & Row, 1985.

Drew, Elizabeth, *Portrait of an Election: The 1980 Presidential Campaign.* New York: Simon & Schuster, 1981.

Eells, Richard. *The Political Crisis of the Enterprise System.* New York: Macmillan, 1980.

Ehrenhalt, Alan. *The United States of Ambition: Politicians, Power, and the Pursuit of Office.* New York: Times Books, 1991.

Erskine, Hazel. "The Polls: Pollution and Its Cost." *Public Opinion Quarterly* 36, no. 1 (Spring 1972): 120–35.

Flynn, James J. *Winning the Presidency: The Difficulty of Election.* Brooklyn, N.Y.: Theo. Gaus, 1976.

Fraser, Steve, and Gary Gerstle, eds. *The Rise and Fall of the New Deal Order, 1930–1980.* Princeton, N.J.: Princeton University Press, 1989.

Friedman, Leon, and William F. Levantrosser, eds. *Richard M. Nixon: Politician, President, Administrator.* Westport, Conn.: Greenwood Press, 1991.

Fulbright, James William. *Old Myths and New Realities, and Other Commentaries.* New York: Random House, 1964.

Garment, Suzanne. *Scandal: The Crisis of Mistrust in American Politics.* New York: Times Books, 1991.

Garrow, David J. *The FBI and Martin Luther King, Jr.* New York: Penguin Books, 1981.

Genovese, Michael A. *The Nixon Presidency: Power and Politics in Turbulent Times.* Westport, Conn.: Greenwood Press, 1990.

George, Alexander L. *Presidential Decisionmaking in Foreign Policy: The Effective Use of Information and Advice.* Boulder, Colo.: Westview Press, 1980.

Graham, Otis L., Jr. *Toward a Planned Society: From Roosevelt to Nixon.* New York: Oxford University Press, 1976.

Greene, John Robert. *The Limits of Power: The Nixon and Ford Administrations.* Bloomington: Indiana University Press, 1992.

Greenfield, Meg. "Our No-Good Presidents." *Newsweek,* November 28, 1983, p. 120.

Halberstam, David. *The Best and the Brightest.* New York: Random House, 1972.

Harrington, Mona. *The Dream of Deliverance in American Politics.* New York: Knopf, 1986.

Hart, John. "Executive Reorganization in the U.S.A. and the Growth of Presidential Power." *Public Administration* 52 (Summer 1974): 179–208.

Heale, M. J. *The Presidential Quest.* New York: Longman, 1982.

Heclo, Hugh. "OMB and the Presidency—The Problem of 'Neutral Competence.'" *The Public Interest* 38 (Winter 1975): 80–98.

———. *A Government of Strangers: Executive Politics in Washington.* Washington, D.C.: Brookings Institution, 1977.

———. *Studying the Presidency: A Report to the Ford Foundation.* New York: Ford Foundation, 1977.

———. "Issue Networks and the Executive Establishment." In *The New American Political System,* edited by Anthony King. Washington, D.C.: American Enterprise Institute, 1978.

———, and Lester M. Salamon, eds. *The Illusion of Presidential Government.* Boulder, Colo.: Westview Press, 1981.

Hess, Stephen. *Organizing the Presidency.* Washington, D.C.: Brookings Institution, 1988.

———, and David S. Broder. *The Republican Establishment: The President and Future of the G.O.P.* New York: Harper & Row, 1967.

Hoff-Wilson, Joan. "Richard M. Nixon: The Corporate Presidency." In *Leadership in the Modern Presidency,* edited by Fred I. Greenstein. Cambridge, Mass.: Harvard University Press, 1988, pp. 164–98.

———. "'Nixingerism,' NATO, and Détente," *Diplomatic History* 13, no. 4 (Fall 1989): 501–25; reprinted in *American Historians and the Atlantic Alliance,* edited by Lawrence S. Kaplan. Kent, Ohio: Kent State University Press, 1991, pp. 95–115.

————. "Outflanking the Liberals on Welfare." In *Richard M. Nixon: Politician, President, Administrator,* edited by Leon Friedman and William F. Levantrosser. Westport, Conn.: Greenwood Press, 1991, pp. 85–106.

Hoxie, R. Gordon. *The White House: Organization and Operations.* New York: Center for the Study of the Presidency, 1971.

————. *Command Decision and the Presidency: A Study of National Security and Policy and Organization.* New York: Reader's Digest Press, 1977.

————, ed. *The Presidency and National Security Policy.* New York: Center for the Study of the Presidency, 1984.

James, Dorothy Buckton. "The Future of the Institutionalized Presidency." In *The Future of the American Presidency,* edited by Charles W. Dunn. Morristown, N.J.: General Learning Press, 1975.

Johnson, Haynes. *In the Absence of Power: Governing America.* New York: Viking Press, 1980.

Johnson, Paul. *Modern Times: The World from the Twenties to the Eighties.* New York: Harper & Row, 1983.

Johnson, Richard Tanner. *Managing the White House: An Intimate Study of the Presidency.* New York: Harper & Row, 1974.

Keogh, James. *President Nixon and the Press.* New York: Funk & Wagnalls, 1972.

Kessel, John H. *The Domestic Presidency: Decision-Making in the White House.* North Scituate, Mass.: Duxbury Press, 1975.

Kraft, Joseph. "The Post-Imperial Presidency," *New York Times Magazine,* November 2, 1980, p. 31.

Kuklick, Bruce. *The Good Ruler: From Herbert Hoover to Richard Nixon.* New Brunswick, N.J.: Rutgers University Press, 1988.

Ladd, Everett C., and Charles D. Hadley. *Transformations of the American Party System.* New York: Norton, 1975.

Lengle, James I., and Byron E. Shafer, eds. *Presidential Politics: Readings on Nominations and Elections.* New York: St. Martin's Press, 1983.

Leuchtenburg, William E. *In the Shadow of FDR: From Harry Truman to Ronald Reagan.* Ithaca, N.Y.: Cornell University Press, 1983.

Livingston, James. "Pitfalls of Presidential Politics." *Democracy* 3, no. 3 (Summer 1983): 50–57.

Lurie, Leonard. *The Running of Richard Nixon.* New York: Coward, McCann & Geoghegan, 1972.

McConnell, Grant. *The Modern Presidency.* New York: St. Martin's Press, 1967.

McGinnis, Joe. *The Selling of the President 1968.* New York: Trident Books, 1969.

Massaro, John. *Supremely Political: The Role of Ideology and Presidential Management in Unsuccessful Supreme Court Nominations.* Albany: State University of New York Press, 1990.

Matusow, Allen J. *The Unraveling of America: A History of Liberalism in the 1960's.* New York: Harper & Row, 1984.

Michalos, Alex C. "Rationality Between the Maximizers and the Satisficers." *Policy Sciences* 4, no. 2 (June 1973): 229–44.

Milkis, Sidney M., and Michael Nelson. *The American Presidency: Origins and Development, 1776–1990.* Washington, D.C.: CQ Press, 1990.

Mollenhoff, Clark R. *Game Plan for Disaster: An Ombudsman's Report on the Nixon Years.* New York: Norton, 1976.

Morris, Charles R. *A Time of Passion: America 1960–1980.* New York: Harper & Row, 1984.

Murphy, Arthur B. "Evaluating the Presidents of the United States." *Presidential Studies Quarterly* 14, no. 1 (Winter 1984): 117.

Murphy, Reg, and Hal Gulliver. *The Southern Strategy.* New York: Scribner, 1971.

Murray, Robert K., and Tim H. Blessing. "The Presidential Performance Study: A Progress Report." *Journal of American History* 70, no. 3 (December 1983): 535–55.

Nathan, Richard P. *The Plot That Failed: Nixon and the Administrative Presidency.* New York: Wiley, 1975.

———. "The 'Administrative Presidency.'" *The Public Interest* 44 (Summer 1976): 40–54.

———. *The Administrative Presidency.* New York: Wiley, 1983.

Neustadt, Richard E. *Presidential Power: The Politics of Leadership.* New York: New American Library, 1960.

Osborne, John. *The First Two Years of the Nixon Watch.* New York: Liveright, 1971.

———. *The Third Year of the Nixon Watch.* New York: Liveright, 1972.

———. *The Fourth Year of the Nixon Watch.* New York: Liveright, 1973.

———. *The Fifth Year of the Nixon Watch.* New York: Liveright, 1974.

Patterson, Bradley H., Jr. *The Ring of Power: The White House Staff and Its Expanding Role in Government.* New York: Basic Books, 1988.

Pearl, Arthur. *Landslide: The How and Why of Nixon's Victory.* Secaucus, N.J.: Citadel Press, 1973.

Pfiffner, James J., and R. Gordon Hoxie, eds. Proceedings of the Center for the Study of the Presidency. *The Presidency in Transition* 6, no. 1 (1989).

Phillips, Kevin P. *The Emerging Republican Majority.* New Rochelle, N.Y.: Arlington House, 1969.

———. *Post-Conservative America: People, Politics, and Ideology in a Time of Crisis.* New York: Random House, 1982.

Polsby, Nelson W. *The Citizen's Choice: Humphrey or Nixon?* Washington, D.C.: Public Affairs Press, 1968.

Porter, Roger B. *Presidential Decision Making: The Economic Policy Board.* Cambridge, U.K.: Cambridge University Press, 1980.

Pranger, Robert J. *The Decline of the American National Government.* Washington, D.C.: American Enterprise Institute, 1976.

Reichley, James A. *Conservatives in an Age of Change: The Nixon and Ford Administrations.* Washington, D.C.: Brookings Institution, 1981.

Relyea, Harold C., ed. Proceedings of the Center for the Study of the Presidency. *The Presidency and Information Policy* 4, no. 1 (1981).

Reuben, William A. *The Honorable Mr. Nixon.* New York: Action Books, 1960.

Richover, Hyman G. "Thoughts on the Presidency," *New York Times,* February 21, 1988, p. E19.

Rose, Richard. *Managing Presidential Objectives.* New York: Free Press, 1976.

———. *The Postmodern President: George Bush Meeting the World,* 2nd ed. Chatham, N.J.: Chatham House, 1991.

Rossiter, Clinton. *The American Presidency.* New York: New American Library, 1956.

Saffell, David C. *American Government: Reform in the Post-Watergate Era.* Cambridge, Mass.: Winthrop Publishers, 1976.

Safire, William. *Safire's Washington.* New York: Times Books, 1980.

Scammon, Richard M., and Ben J. Wattenberg. *The Real Majority: An Extraordinary Examination of the American Electorate.* New York: Coward-McCann, 1970.

Schell, Jonathan. *The Time of Illusion.* New York: Knopf, 1976.

Schlesinger, Arthur M., Jr. *Kennedy or Nixon: Does It Make Any Difference?* New York: Macmillan, 1960.

———. *Imperial Presidency.* Boston: Houghton Mifflin, 1973.

———. *The Cycles of American History.* Boston: Houghton Mifflin, 1986.

Schoenebaum, Eleanora W. *Political Profiles: The Nixon-Ford Years.* New York: Facts on File, 1979.

Shactman, Tom. *Decade of Shocks: Dallas to Watergate, 1968–1974.* New York: Poseidon Press, 1983.

Shani, Moshe. "U.S. Federal Government Reorganization: Executive Branch Structure and Central Domestic Policy-making." *Public Administration* 52 (Summer 1974): 193–208.

Small, Melvin. *Johnson, Nixon, and the Doves.* New Brunswick, N.J.: Rutgers University Press, 1988.

Stein, Herbert. *Presidential Economics: The Making of Economic Policy from Roosevelt to Reagan and Beyond.* New York: Simon & Schuster, 1984.

Stone, I. F. *Polemics and Prophecies, 1967–1970.* New York: Random House, 1970.

Thompson, Hunter S. *Fear and Loathing: On the Campaign Trail in '72.* New York: Popular Library, 1973.

Tugwell, Rexford G. *Off Course: From Truman to Nixon.* New York: Praeger Publishers, 1971.

Unger, Irwin, and Debi Unger. *Turning Point: 1968.* New York: Scribner, 1988.

Vale, Vivian. "The Obligation to Spend: Presidential Impoundment of Congressional Appropriations." *Political Studies* 15, no. 4 (1977): 508–22.

Waterman, Richard W. *Presidential Influence and the Administrative State.* Knoxville: University of Tennessee Press, 1989.

Whalen, Richard J. *Catch the Falling Flag: A Republican's Challenge to His Party.* Boston: Houghton Mifflin, 1972

———. *Taking Sides: A Personal View of America from Kennedy to Nixon to Kennedy.* Boston: Houghton Mifflin, 1974.

Whitcover, Jules. *The Resurrection of Richard Nixon*. New York: Putnam, 1970.

White, Theodore H. *The Making of the President 1968*. New York: Atheneum, 1969.

———. *The Making of the President, 1972*. New York: Atheneum, 1973.

———. *Breach of Faith: The Fall of Richard Nixon*. New York: Atheneum and Reader's Digest Press, 1975.

Williams, Walter. *Mismanaging America: The Rise of the Anti-Analytical Presidency*. Lawrence: University Press of Kansas, 1990.

Wills, Garry. *The Kennedy Imprisonment: A Meditation on Power*. Boston: Little, Brown, 1981.

———. *Lead Time: A Journalist's Education*. Garden City, N.Y.: Doubleday, 1983.

Wilson, David E. *The National Planning Idea in U.S. Public Policy: Five Alternative Approaches*. Boulder, Colo.: Westview Press, 1980.

Wise, David. *The Politics of Lying*. New York: Random House, 1973.

Wolin, Sheldon S. *The Presence of the Past: Essays on the State and the Constitution*. Baltimore: Johns Hopkins University Press, 1989.

Woodward, Augustus B. *The Presidency of the United States*. New York: Derick Van Veghten, 1825.

Young, James Y., ed. *Problems and Prospects of Presidential Leadership in the Nineteen-Eighties*. New York: Lanaham, 1982.

WATERGATE

Abrahamsen, David. *Nixon vs. Nixon: An Emotional Tragedy*. New York: Farrar, Straus & Giroux, 1977.

American Enterprise Institute Round Table. *Watergate, Politics, and the Legal Process*. Washington, D.C.: American Enterprise Institute for Public Policy Research, 1974.

Ball, Howard. *"We Have a Duty": The Supreme Court and the Watergate Tapes Litigation*. Westport, Conn.: Greenwood Press, 1990.

Ben-Veniste, Richard, and George Frampton, Jr. *Stonewall: The Real Story of the Watergate Prosecution*. New York: Simon & Schuster, 1977.

Bernstein, Carl, and Bob Woodward. *All the President's Men*. New York: Simon & Schuster, 1974.

Breslin, Jimmy. *How the Good Guys Finally Won: Notes from an Impeachment Summer*. New York: Viking Press, 1975.

Buchwald, Art. *I Am Not a Crook*. New York: Putnam, 1973.

Colodny, Len, and Robert Gettlin. *Silent Coup: The Removal of a President*. New York: St. Martin's Press, 1991.

Dean, John W. *Blind Ambition*. New York: Simon & Schuster, 1976.

———. *Lost Honor*. Los Angeles: Stratford Press, 1982.

Dean, Maureen. *"Mo": A Woman's View of Watergate*. New York: Simon & Schuster, 1975.

Dent, Harry, S. *Cover Up: The Watergate in All of Us*. San Bernardino, Calif.: Here's Life Publishers, 1986.

BIBLIOGRAPHY

Dobrovir, William A., Joseph D. Gebhardt, Samuel J. Buffone, and Andra N. Oakes, *The Offenses of Richard M. Nixon: A Guide for the People of the United States.* New York: Quadrangle/Times Books, 1974.

Donner, Frank J. *The Age of Surveillance: The Aims and Methods of America's Political Intelligence System.* New York: Vintage Books, 1981.

Ehrlichman, John. *Presidential Impeachment: An American Dilemma.* Saint Charles, Mo.: Forum Press, 1974.

———. *Witness to Power: The Nixon Years.* New York: Simon & Schuster, 1982.

Ervin, Sam J., Jr. *The Whole Truth: The Watergate Conspiracy.* New York: Random House, 1980.

Fernandez, Julio. *White House Enemies or How We Made the Dean's List.* New York: New American Library, 1973.

Gulley, Bill. *Breaking Cover.* New York: Simon & Schuster, 1980.

Haldeman, H. R. *The Ends of Power.* New York: Times Books, 1978.

Halpern, Paul J. ed. *Why Watergate?* Pacific Palisades, Calif.: Palisades Publishers, 1975.

Hoff-Wilson, Joan. "Researching the Nixon Presidency." In *Watergate and Afterward: The Legacy of Richard M. Nixon,* edited by Leon Friedman and William F. Levantrosser. Westport, Conn.: Greenwood Press, 1991, pp. 263–67.

Hougan, Jim. *Secret Agenda: Watergate, Deep Throat and the CIA.* New York: Ballantine Books, 1984.

Jaworski, Leon. *The Right and the Power: The Prosecution of Watergate.* New York: Reader's Digest Press, 1976.

Kutler, Stanley I. *The Wars of Watergate: The Last Crisis of Richard Nixon.* New York: Knopf, 1990.

Lukas, J. Anthony. *Nightmare: The Underside of the Nixon Years.* New York: Viking Press, 1976.

Lurie, Leonard. *The Impeachment of Richard Nixon.* New York: Berkeley Medallion Books, 1973.

McCarthy, Mary. *The Mask of State: Watergate Portraits.* New York: Harcourt Brace Jovanovich, 1974.

Magruder, Jeb Stuart. *An American Life: One Man's Road to Watergate.* New York: Atheneum, 1974.

Mankiewicz, Frank. *U.S. v. Richard M. Nixon: The Final Crisis.* New York: Quadrangle, 1975.

Mosher, Frederick C. *Watergate: Implications for Responsible Government.* New York: Basic Books, 1974.

Muzzio, Douglas. *Watergate Games: Strategies, Choices, Outcomes.* New York: New York University Press, 1982.

Myers, Michael. *Watergate: Crime in the Suites.* New York: International Publishers, 1973.

Powers, Richard Gid. *Secrecy and Power: The Life of J. Edgar Hoover.* New York: Free Press, 1987.

Powers, Thomas. *The Man Who Kept the Secrets: Richard Helms and the CIA.* New York: Pocket Books, 1979.

452

Rangell, Leo. *The Mind of Watergate: An Exploration on the Compromise of Integrity.* New York: Norton, 1980.

Rather, Dan, and Gary Paul Gates. *The Palace Gates.* New York: Harper & Row, 1974.

Ross, Frank. *The 65th Tape.* Toronto, Canada: Bantam Books, 1979.

Saffell, David D. *Watergate: Its Effects on the American Political System.* Cambridge, Mass.: Winthrop Publishers, 1974.

Schell, Jonathan. *The Time of Illusion.* New York: Knopf, 1976.

———. *Observing the Nixon Years.* New York: Pantheon Books, 1989.

Schudson, Michael. *Watergate in American Memory: How We Remember, Forget, and Reconstruct the Past.* New York: Basic Books, 1992.

Sirica, John J. *To Set the Record Straight: The Break-in, the Tapes, the Conspirators, the Pardon.* New York: Norton, 1979.

Stans, Maurice H. *The Terrors of Justice.* New York: Everest House, 1978.

Sussman, Barry. *The Great Cover-up: Nixon and the Scandal of Watergate.* New York: Crowell, 1974.

von Hoffman, Nicholas. "Watergate Under the Bridge." *The New Republic,* July 16 and 23, 1984, pp. 29–32.

von Hoffman, Nicholas, and Gary Trudeau. *The Fireside Watergate.* New York: Sheed & Ward, 1973.

Watergate Special Prosecutor's Force Report. Washington, D.C. October 1975.

White, Theodore H. *Breach of Faith: The Fall of Richard Nixon.* New York: Atheneum, 1975.

Wise, David, and Thomas B. Ross. *The Invisible Government.* New York: Vintage Books, 1964.

Woodward, Bob, and Scott Armstrong. *The Brethren: Inside the Supreme Court.* New York: Simon & Schuster, 1979.

Woodward, Bob, and Carl Bernstein. *The Final Days.* New York: Simon & Schuster, 1976.

INDEX

CPSIA information can be obtained
at www.ICGtesting.com
Printed in the USA
BVHW071432030922
645899BV00003B/107